A History of Women

IN THE WEST

Georges Duby and Michelle Perrot, General Editors

II. Silences of the Middle Ages

A HISTORY
OF WOMEN

IN THE WEST

II. Silences of
the Middle Ages

Christiane Klapisch-Zuber, Editor

The Belknap Press of
Harvard University Press
Cambridge, Massachusetts
London, England
1992

Originally published as *Storia delle Donne in Occidente,* vol. II,
Il Medioevo, © Gius. Laterza & Figli Spa, Roma-Bari, 1990.
Portions of the text have been adapted for the English-language
edition.

This book is printed on acid-free paper, and its binding materials
have been chosen for strength and durability.

Text design by Lisa Diercks

Library of Congress Cataloging-in-Publication Data

Storia delle donne in Occidente. English
    A history of women in the West / Georges Duby and
Michelle Perrot, general editors.
        p. cm.
    Translation of: Storia delle donne in Occidente.
    Includes bibliographical references and index.
    Contents: 1. From ancient goddesses to Christian saints /
Pauline Schmitt Pantel, editor — 2. Silences of the Middle Ages /
Christiane Klapisch-Zuber, editor.
        ISBN 0-674-40370-3 (v. 1 : acid-free paper). —
    ISBN 0-674-40371-1 (v. 2 : acid-free paper)
        1. Women—History. 2. Women—Europe—History.
    I. Duby, Georges. II. Perrot, Michelle. III. Title.
    HQ1121.S79513 1992
    305.4'094—dc20

91-34134
    CIP

Contents

Writing the History of Women ix
  Georges Duby and Michelle Perrot

Including Women 1
  Christiane Klapisch-Zuber
  Translated by Arthur Goldhammer

ONE. NORMS OF CONTROL 11

1. The Clerical Gaze 15
  Jacques Dalarun
  Translated by Arthur Goldhammer

2. The Nature of Woman 43
  Claude Thomasset
  Translated by Arthur Goldhammer

3. The Protected Woman 70
  Carla Casagrande
  Translated by Clarissa Botsford

4. The Good Wife   105
   Silvana Vecchio
   Translated by Clarissa Botsford

5. Regulating Women's Fashion   136
   Diane Owen Hughes

TWO. FAMILY AND SOCIAL STRATEGIES   159

6. Women from the Fifth to the Tenth Century   169
   Suzanne Fonay Wemple

7. The Feudal Order   202
   Paulette L'Hermite-Leclercq
   Translated and adapted by Arthur Goldhammer

8. The Courtly Model   250
   Georges Duby
   Translated by Arthur Goldhammer

9. Life in the Late Middle Ages   267
   Claudia Opitz
   Translated by Deborah Lucas Schneider

THREE. VESTIGES AND IMAGES OF
        WOMEN   319

10. The World of Women   323
    Françoise Piponnier
    Translated by Arthur Goldhammer

11. The Imagined Woman   336

    Chiara Frugoni

    Translated by Clarissa Botsford

FOUR. WOMEN'S WORDS   423

12. Literary and Mystical Voices   427

    Danielle Régnier-Bohler

    Translated and adapted by Arthur Goldhammer

Affidavits and Confessions   483

    Georges Duby

    Translated by Arthur Goldhammer

Notes   495

Bibliography   541

Contributors   555

Illustration Credits   557

Index   559

Writing the History of Women

Georges Duby and Michelle Perrot

WOMEN WERE LONG RELEGATED to the shadows of history. The development of anthropology and the new emphasis on the family, on a history of *mentalités* interested in everyday life, in what was private and individual, have helped to dispel those shadows. The women's movement and the questions it has raised have done even more. "Where have we come from? Where are we going?" These are questions women have begun asking themselves. Both inside and outside the university they have set out in search of their forebears and attempted to understand the roots of their domination and the evolution of male-female relations.

"The History of Women" is a convenient and attractive title, but the idea that women in themselves are an object of history must be rejected firmly. What we want to understand is the place of women, the "condition" of women, women's roles and powers. We want to investigate how women acted. We want to examine their words and their silences. We want to look at their many images: goddess, madonna, witch. Our history is fundamentally relational; we look at society as a whole, and our history of women is just as much a history of men.

It is a history of the *longue durée*: five volumes cover the history of the West from antiquity to the present. And our history covers only the West, from the Mediterranean to the Atlantic. Histories of the women of the Orient, Latin America, and Africa are sorely needed, and we hope that one day the women and men of those regions will write them.

Our history is "feminist" in that its outlook is egalitarian; its intention is to be open to the variety of interpretations. We want to raise questions, but we have no formulaic answers. Ours is a plural history: a history of *women* as seen from many different points of view.

It is also the work of a team. Georges Duby and Michelle Perrot are responsible for the overall coordination. Each volume has one or two editors: Pauline Schmitt Pantel (antiquity), Christiane Klapisch-Zuber (Middle Ages), Natalie Zemon Davis and Arlette Farge (early modern), Geneviève Fraisse and Michelle Perrot (nineteenth century), and Françoise Thébaud (twentieth century) have chosen their own collaborators—some sixty-eight scholars in all, a representative sample of those working in this field in Europe and the United States.

We hope that this series will provide a handy summary of the results achieved to date as well as serve as a guide to further research. We also hope it will bring the pleasures of history to new readers and act as a stimulus to memory.

A History of Women

IN THE WEST

Silences of the Middle Ages

Including Women

Christiane Klapisch-Zuber

IN THE FIRST CHAPTER of *The City of Ladies,* Christine de Pisan discusses the misfortune of having been born a woman. "In my folly," she writes, "I despaired that God caused me to be born in a female body." Her disgust with herself at one time encompassed all her sex, "as if Nature had given birth to monsters," and she blamed God. But when she dissected the roots of her misery, she came to blame her misfortune on a "series of authorities."[1]

This is an astonishing text. Here was a woman unwilling to accept the usual commonplaces about feminine "imbecility," the alleged failing to which other women all too readily resigned themselves. Christine understood that most women wrapped themselves in robes tailored by others: men had singled them out as "fundamentally wicked and given to vice." Nevertheless, she bravely launched a counterattack, brandishing her sword where men for centuries had dueled among themselves. At long last the "women's issue" had come to be: a woman had raised her voice. It happened just as the Middle Ages were giving way to the Renaissance—around 1400.

Who was this polemicist who dared to defend her sisters? She was a widow who worked for her family's daily bread, an educated woman conscious of her true worth. She was, unusually for the time, literate; still more unusual, she recorded her thoughts in writing. Most of the issues of medieval women's history come together in her. Historians discuss such matters as demographics, economics, juridical autonomy, productive labor, and intellectual activity without any clear idea of where women fit in. A Christine de Pisan is not easily incorporated into any of the standard historical narratives. Was she more than just an extraordinary woman? Was she perhaps a beacon for others? Did armies of women rally to her banner? Was she a harbinger of women's emancipation or merely an example of neglected potential, a lone spark in an age of darkness? Does it make sense to look for followers, to ascribe to her a "feminist" consciousness and an ambition to unite her sisters in common cause? How, in other words, are we to adjust our sights to take in the other half of humanity, the half that so many historians (and not just historians) are so quick to forget?

It is tempting to place a woman like Christine on a pedestal and leave her there. Many have sung the praises of exceptional women the better to disparage the rest, who contributed nothing to "history." Many have defended women by writing biographies of the most remarkable of the sex. Christine de Pisan herself defended her sisters in this way. For many of the portraits in her *City of Ladies,* she found models in Boccaccio, who himself raided ancient authors and familiar folktales for his portraits of "illustrious women," portraits that displayed the desirable virtues and undesirable excesses of the female character. In fact, the history of women began by recounting the fate of exemplary heroines, as if each new generation of women had to reconstitute the memory of the sex by knitting together a repeatedly severed thread. Many who have explored the territory of women since the end of the nineteenth century have focused primarily on the most notable of its landmarks. Much of the history of the sex has thus been cast in the form of biography. These explorations certainly achieved worthy results. They demonstrated the capabilities of women and thereby restored a forgotten part of the past, creating what Joan Kelly has called a "compensatory" historiography.[2] Such a long, valuable, and fruitful tradition is not to be dismissed out of hand. The biographical approach can be useful at certain stages of feminist historiographical research.[3] By itself, however, it is incapable of revealing the full complexity of past societies. The figures on whom biographers lavish attention may be fascinating, but for that very reason we need to be wary of their hold on us.

The story of Christine de Pisan focuses our attention on an important question: Should remarkable women be regarded as exceptions, or do they typify their time and social group? Precisely because they are not run-of-the-mill, we are tempted to see exceptional women as somehow typical of turning points in the historical process. But which events are significant for the kind of history we are trying to write? What periodization is relevant?

The general editors of this series explain their concept of the project in the introduction to Volume I: the *History of Women* is a collaborative effort. It champions no particular thesis. We are not attempting to prove that women either did or did not make progress in any of the periods into which we have divided our work. We do not claim to offer a new formulation of the great historical issues of the day. Nor do we aim to present either an exhaustive summary or synthetic overview of recent work in the field.[4] Much of our knowledge of medieval women is new and fragmentary, and any attempt at summary would be premature. It seems more important to offer a new point of view, to encourage a new reading of the historical "facts" according to which gender difference and gender relations are both cause and effect of social forces.

To be born a man or a woman in any society is more than a simple biological fact. It is a biological fact with social implications. Women constitute a distinct social group, and the character of that group, long neglected by historians, has nothing to do with feminine "nature."[5] "Gender" is the term now widely used to refer to those ways in which a culture reformulates what begins as a fact of nature. The biological sexes are redefined, represented, valued, and channeled into different roles in various culturally dependent ways.[6] An American anthropologist has put it well: a "sex/gender system [is] a set of arrangements by which a society transforms biological sexuality into products of human activity, and in which these transformed sexual needs are met."[7]

The roles assigned to women are assigned not by virtue of women's innate characteristics (ability to bear children, relative physical weakness compared to men) but by virtue of a series of arguments that, taken together, constitute an ideological system. Women are characterized not so much by "nature" as by their alleged inability to enter into "culture."[8] This view can be traced back to Aristotle, who, as Carla Casagrande and Silvana Vecchio point out, exerted enormous influence on late medieval social and political thought and teaching. As a result of Aristotle's influence, men and women were segregated and obliged to carry on distinct activities in their respective domains. So thoroughly was public space separated from the domestic sphere that this division too came to seem natural, and for some it soon came to coincide with the division between masculine and feminine. Historians today who adopt the public-private dichotomy are in some ways repeating the error of social thinkers of the thirteenth to fifteenth centuries, themselves under the spell of ancient philosophers.

Anthropology was the first discipline to react against this way of formulating the issue. In consequence, medieval historians were obliged to rethink their theory and practice. Since 1975 there has been an outpouring of historical work on these topics.[9] Misrepresentations of women in the time of the courtly poets, of Marian devotion, and of the "age of cathedrals" have drawn vigorous critiques. Many recent works of women of all conditions—nuns and holy women, betrothed maidens, needy wives—have demonstrated the central importance of marriage. Other works have deciphered value systems, images, and representations as reflected in everyday behavior. Still others have investigated the role of women in intellectual and religious life—ordinary women, as opposed to those exceptional figures occasionally rescued from obscurity by some action of the authorities. Last but not least, some historians have followed the legal historical tradition of the late nineteenth century to uncover the juridical aspects of woman's condition. Some of the earliest new work in women's history concerned woman's place in society; the work of Eileen Power before World War II comes to mind.[10] Despite this, economic and social history are perhaps the areas least affected by the outpouring of recent research. Yet, as the remainder of this volume will demonstrate, history has much to gain by expanding its view of the past to include women.

In this volume of the *History of Women* we concentrate exclusively on men and women who lived in areas dominated by the culture of Catholicism between the sixth and the fifteenth centuries. We thus deliberately avoid the issue of assimilation and exchange between people of different religious and cultural traditions. What contemporaries have to say about such differences can be illuminating, but we have chosen to exclude these sources from our study, even though the surprise of a Palestinian Saracen at the sight of men and women newly arrived from France or of a Frankish knight upon discovering the vast city of Constantinople can sometimes tell us more about relations between the sexes in

Normandy than many a regional synod, moral treatise, or confessor's manual.

To some readers our decision to include a millennium of medieval history in a single volume may seem absurd, as may our decision to end with the fifteenth century, consistent with the most banal of textbook periodizations. On the one hand we challenge conventional wisdom by claiming that "gender" is a crucial component of social relations and that women deserve to be counted as full-fledged historical actors, while on the other hand we seem to concede that the conventional periodizations, based more on institutional than on scientific criteria, remain valid.

Does the history of women require a new periodization? Does it have a chronology of its own?[11] The question is not peculiar to medieval history, but the medieval period does bring certain matters into sharp relief. A number of recent developments in medieval historiography have been based on the idea that certain long-term developments culminated in profound changes in medieval society. Growth and decline, progress and regression, flourishing and decadence, are key terms in medieval social and economic history. In assessing such developments, historians generally have focused on the most prominent figures in the economic, political, and cultural arenas. These figures are of course male, because men enjoyed the legal autonomy and right to speak publicly that were either denied to women or granted only grudgingly. Men wielded power, hence our sources speak mainly of them. It is especially difficult to peer beneath the surface of the Middle Ages to find out what life was like for humbler members of society.

This being the case, is the usual periodization valid for women? Historians are in the habit of dividing the period in which we are interested into a number of segments: the Carolingian renaissance (political and cultural); the eleventh and twelfth centuries, a period of demographic growth and consequent economic progress; the thirteenth century, high point of medieval civilization; and the crisis of the late Middle Ages. Is there any reason to think that this periodization, based on economic progress, changes in the power structure, and class relations, can easily be applied to the history of women? Our task here should be to ask, for example, whether historians have paid sufficient attention to the way in which women experienced economic and demographic growth and recession in different countries and situations. The role of women often is assumed, almost by reflex, to have been limited to reproduction and family life. But do we really know whether demographic growth and decline affected men and women in the same way? What chance did women have of escaping or even of protesting against what is sometimes mindlessly referred to as "the feminine condition?"

In a 1977 article rightly considered a model of feminist criticism, Joan Kelly asked whether or not women had had a Renaissance.[12] Her answer was no. Although her exclusively cultural approach to the problem drew some criticism, the force of her argument and thoroughness of her documentation proved that the question was a useful one.[13] By challenging the dogma that legal advances, economic progress, and cultural change between the fifteenth and seventeenth centuries had improved the condition of women, Kelly demonstrated a certain blindness on the part of historians in their treatment of women and of relations between the sexes. Of course a view of social relations that challenged decades of historical research was bound to raise many new problems.

It is tempting to say that, for medievalists, the difficulty in working out the proper chronology of the history of women has to do with the nature of the sources. The medieval archives lack not only biographical works and private writing (letters, diaries, and the like) but also the kinds of consistent, serial information that bureaucracies are good at compiling. The data are abundant but incomplete, complicating the task of quantitative historians. To be sure, there is far more information available about the fourteenth and fifteenth centuries than about earlier periods. The process of state construction was under way, and written records had begun to be kept in many different walks of life. Officials were more concerned than ever before about maintaining control over subjects or citizens and about gathering information concerning local communities and conditions. Yet although the sources for this period are relatively abundant, their quality varies widely, and gaps in the record make it difficult to assemble a coherent picture of social change. Erler and Kowaleski point out how difficult it is to draw conclusions about the "power" of women from such diverse information as the distribution of seals, the proportion of female saints, changes in the laws governing matrimonial property, and the shifting ratio of male to female births.[14] How are we to make sense of apparently contradictory information concerning, on the one hand, courtly love and the cult of the Virgin and, on the other hand, an apparent decline in the political power of women? Can we even identify what events were significant in the history of women?

The compilation of homogeneous series (and hence of a chronology based on comparison of such series) is a hazardous business, based on judgments that are open to criticism. What does it mean to say that demographic conditions created a situation "favorable" to women on the "marriage market," or that there was an "excess" of women, or that a woman's chance of marriage or remarriage was high or low? By what criteria do we measure progress or regression in the status of women or improvements in their condition? The very terminology is problematic. The vocabulary itself is value-laden, and the periodization of women's history inevitably is affected by implicit value judgments.

The primary task of the history of women is therefore not to stand the old history on its head but to look at the past from new angles. Rather than search for new sources, we hope to reevaluate traditional ones in order to grasp male-female relations in all their complexity.

The object of our investigation is women, not "woman." "Woman" is a creation of the masculine gaze. Before we can see how women thought of themselves and of their relations with men, we must find out how they were seen by men. The masculine conception of woman gave rise to idealizations and norms that strongly influenced the behavior of women, who lacked the power to challenge the male view of their sex. We begin by discussing these norms and models, which in the Middle Ages more than in any other period largely determined women's place in society. By analyzing these constraints, we can gain a better understanding of the social relations from which they derived.

The only voices we hear are those of men. Not all men; the vast majority were condemned to silence. The written word was controlled by the clergy, men of the cloth and of the Church, who controlled the flow of knowledge and determined how people conceived of women or, rather, Woman. Much of our evidence about medieval women derives from the fantasies, certainties, and doubts of the clergy. The Middle Ages differ from other periods in that what was said about women was said by men who rejected their society, men whose position obliged them to embrace celibacy and chastity. Lacking daily commerce with women, these men were harsh in their criticism of female vices and imperfections. Since much of their knowledge came from books, their portraits were caricatures more than true likenesses. Ancient views were piled one upon another like archaeological relics, devoid of any scientific or ethical basis. Bizarre images took on a life of their own. For example, as Claude Thomasset shows, medical views of female physiology were a palimpsest of contradictory opinions.

Our goal is not to explicate these systems of belief but to reveal their inner structure and to show how negative traits could suddenly turn into positive ones. Jacques Dalarun shows how theological views of femininity were restructured through a reinterpretation of the sacred triad: Eve, Mary, and Mary Magdalene. Carla Casagrande and Silvana Vecchio show how, in the thirteenth, fourteenth, and fifteenth centuries, preachers, moralists, teachers, and writers on household economy challenged traditional views of the relations between the sexes. They reveal how a new ethics of marriage slowly emerged from incessant warnings about the need for obedience, temperance, chastity, steadiness, and silence—requirements scarcely less demanding than those imposed on nuns.

Sumptuary laws increasingly regulated female dress and adornment from the thirteenth century on. Laymen joined clerics in thus attempting to control the lives of women. Diane Owen Hughes shows how these laws reflected the potent influence of representations of the female body as an instrument of perdition and indelible sign of original sin.

We then turn to the question of marriage. At certain critical moments in a woman's life a choice of strategies was possible; through this choice women were sometimes able to express their wishes and even their vocations. Marriage or religion, motherhood or solitude—these were decisions in which family and individual ambitions played a large and often contradictory role.

To understand these strategies we cannot rely on either male "authorities" or isolated female voices. Here the nature of the sources dictates our approach. Suzanne Wemple examines the sixth to the tenth centuries, using a combination of narrative and normative documents. Paulette L'Hermite-Leclercq draws on similar sources in treating the feudal period, but she is also able to introduce evidence of a more pragmatic kind by exploiting the archives of religious institutions, seigneuries, clerical correspondence, and the letters of lay men and even women. Nowadays "microhistorical" inquiries are also in fashion: individual stories are gleaned from judicial archives, private correspondence, and personal diaries. When available, such materials enable us to answer questions about how women resisted oppression and created countervailing institutions. L'Hermite-Leclercq is able to exploit these kinds of sources to explore family strategies and women's tactics from the eleventh to the thirteenth century. As a counterpoint to her chapter, Georges Duby examines strategies inspired by, and making use of, the civilizing model of courtly love, strategies primarily masculine in conception and execution.

The sources become more abundant toward the close of our period, so abundant that quantitative analysis becomes possible. By themselves, however, numbers tell nothing about the changing condition of women. Claudia Opitz's chapter shows how fragmentary demographic data led some historians to make hasty, unsound generalizations. Comparative demography is still a fledgling discipline. We know little about the economic role of women, about their share in the production of goods and the distribution of surpluses at a time when new sources of wealth were being exploited and trade was on the rise.

In this, as in the other volumes in this series, a chapter is devoted to representations of women in the plastic arts. Chiara Frugoni explores the iconography and production of female images and shows that women, more often than one might think, played a part in creating them. But female artists rarely signed their works, and much of what we think we know about women's art is still conjectural. The archaeologist Françoise Piponnier shows how seemingly insignificant items and traces—the pattern of wear on a hearthstone, footsteps on an earthen floor, fingerprints on a terracotta pot, needles, combs, scissors—can be used to reconstruct the daily lives of women of the past both inside and outside the home.

Paradoxically, although husbands, masters, and censors steadfastly denied medieval women the right to self-expression, we know more about what they wrote and said than we do about many material aspects of their lives. Up to the twelfth century, as Suzanne Wemple and Paulette L'Hermite-Leclercq show, certain women did make themselves heard. Was this only because they were important, abbesses of well-known convents and wives or widows of the ruling dynasties of the feudal period? In the thirteenth, fourteenth, and fifteenth centuries women of all ranks were bold enough to speak out. Although their voices are all but drowned out by the chorus of men, Danielle Régnier-Bohler is able to reconstruct their part in literary and mystical pursuits. If the voices of women sometimes inspired awe or admiration, they also aroused suspicion that led to redoubled attempts to control by those officially entitled to a monopoly of the means of knowledge and expression.

It may strike some readers as odd that we choose to begin this "history of women" with the words of men, indeed of clergymen, those most removed from the sensibility and experience of women, and physicians, the possessors of a scientific knowledge that was almost exclusively masculine. Are we not conceding too much to masculine authority and domination and favoring representations over material and social factors? In the current state of research we have no alternative. We hope to give readers the means with which to judge for themselves just how important these centuries-old religious representations of women were.

We end by allowing women to speak for themselves. This is not to suggest that by the end of the Middle Ages women had somehow acquired the right to speak. The texts commented on by Danielle Régnier-Bohler and Georges Duby allow us to see, rather, how women developed the models imposed on them by their male teachers and confessors, how they treated the distorted images of themselves that men held up for them to see. Occasionally they rejected those images, but inevitably the imposed images inscribed themselves in women's very flesh and shaped their lives.

TRANSLATED FROM THE FRENCH BY ARTHUR GOLDHAMMER

one

Norms
of Control

"A horse, whether good or bad, needs a spur; a woman, whether good or bad, needs a lord and master, and sometimes a stick."[1] The sententious Florentine who recorded this proverb in the fourteenth century captured sentiments that were no doubt repeated countless times throughout Christendom, particularly by the best educated, whose views we are about to examine.

Women, through whom death, suffering, and toil came into the world, were creatures dominated by their sex. So taught the Bible and patristic tradition. To control and punish women, particularly their bodies and their dangerous, disruptive sexuality, was therefore man's work. Masculine philosophy and science showed little reluctance to shoulder the task. Proverbs, maxims, medical treatises, works of theology, textbooks, and manuals of ethics had been honing an arsenal for the purpose ever since antiquity. Scientific, ethical, and political thought converged in the notion that woman must either remain chaste or devote herself solely to procreation. All her functions were directed toward one end: reproduction. Those physicians who dared dissect the female body found the evidence they were looking for. In due course we shall discover the limits of empirical observation, which could only confirm the vision of woman as a creature dominated by her womb and made for childbearing and nurturing. Galenic physicians and the theologians who absorbed their teachings granted women a right to pleasure only because it accorded with their erroneous theory that conception required the participation of female "sperm."

In the final centuries of the Middle Ages this school of theorists at last found opposition in the Aristotelians, schooled in the art of intellectual combat by their leader, Thomas Aquinas. It was during this period that efforts were made to limit women's legal capacity and ability to exercise power, efforts that seem to have found their theoretical justification in Aristotle, whose works provided the necessary philosophical armature. The reinterpretation of Aristotle's philosophy in the medieval West provided what was perhaps the most coherent and systematic statement of the essential weakness of woman and of her necessary subjection to man. The high clergy of the twelfth and thirteenth centuries had considered the mediating role of the redeemed sinner, modeled on Mary Magdalene, and the casuists of the late Middle Ages would devote considerable attention to the needs of ordinary women. By contrast, neo-Aristotelian images and principles established a firm connection between male anxieties and fantasies and female bodies, thereby giving Aristotelian doctrine its cutting edge. Spearheading the drive toward a new ethics of sexual relations were Aristotelians such as Giles of Rome and the Mendicant Orders, who exhorted princes and governments to purge their cities of sumptuous female fashions. Aristotle provided just the right concepts to justify the hierarchy of the sexes, the "protection" of women within the home or convent, women's exclusion from public activities, the superiority of masculine authority over the will of the couple, the limitation of female spirituality within marriage, and the weakening of the mother's role in the education of her children.[2]

Since women's emotions were alleged to stem ultimately from physiology, they could be explained in terms of a reductionist psychology. Women by themselves were deemed incapable of controlling their desires or regulating their relations with others. They needed men to tame and channel the intrinsic excesses of their "nature." Wives, it was alleged, were slaves to their love of husbands and children, whereas husbands were temperate and wise. Sexual morality and marital fidelity were subject to a double standard. For women, fidelity was required as a guarantee of legitimacy and family honor, hence less virtuous than the fidelity that a man might freely choose.

Medieval thinkers referred constantly to woman's nature. Thus they accredited the western notion that female is to male as nature is to culture.[3]

C. K.-Z.

1

The Clerical Gaze

Jacques Dalarun

ONCE AGAIN we must begin with men, with
those men who held a monopoly on learning and
on the ability to write in the feudal age: the clergy,
and especially the most literate, influential, and
prolific among them. Regular monks and secular
prelates felt it incumbent on themselves to think
about the nature of humankind, human society,
and the Church, to point the way to salvation, and
to assign women to their proper place in the divine
scheme. Going one step further, some even spelled
out the ways in which members of their flock
might achieve, or at any rate aim for, perfection.

Yet these men, especially before the thirteenth
century, were completely cut off from women.
They lived and worked in an exclusively male universe, shut up in cloisters and *scriptoria,* in schools
and faculties of theology, and in those communities of canons where, from the eleventh century
on, clerics charged with overseeing worldly society
attempted to live as immaculately as monks. Consider Guibert of Nogent, who died in 1124. Guibert was an *oblate,* that is, a monk who entered a
Benedictine monastery while still a child. His
knowledge of women was limited to memories of
a mother who had married at the age of twelve,
painful memories that he embellished so as to eliminate any hint that his mother might have been

"defiled" by marriage. Everything else about the other sex he condemned. Clerics, who from the eleventh century on were strictly enjoined to remain celibate, knew nothing about women, or, rather, about Woman, other than what they imagined. They represented her as a distant, strange, and frightening figure of profoundly contradictory nature.

It should come as no surprise that clerical thought in this period was misogynist. It would be a simple but unrewarding task to amass textual evidence for this assertion, from the most learned treatises to the most frivolous of Latin poems, from commentaries on Scripture to common proverbs whose facile irony unmasked the abyss hidden in the unknown Other. Secular literature from the princely courts to the unbuttoned poetry of the Goliards, from the literature of courtly love to the bawdiest of ribaldry, leads to the same conclusion. But why describe a society as more or less misogynist when no culture that could reasonably be described as nonmisogynist had yet emerged? And what is the point of taking an apologetic line, of describing the great sanctuaries at Le Puy, Rocamadour, Walsingham, and Lorette to which large numbers of people went to pay homage to the Virgin, or the great cathedrals at Chartres, Laon, Paris, Coutances, and Amiens, where columns, towers, and steeples soared heavenward as if in praise of the one who was and remained "blessed among women?" What good did this exceptional benediction do for the others, for all the women who were not so blessed? Better to avoid anachronism, to listen instead to what the representative figures of high clerical culture had to say. The idea of woman interested them, and it is the nature of this interest that I want to explore here.

Interest usually leads to change, but clerical literature gives the impression of standing still. Medieval commentaries, drawing on Scripture and tradition, ruminated endlessly on the thoughts of the Church Fathers who lived and wrote in the first few centuries after Christ's birth. Marie-Thérèse d'Alverny remarks that we must not look to these texts "for original ideas."[1] Did Ambrose, Jerome, and Augustine say everything there was to say for and against women? Admittedly, any attempt to identify a positive or negative trend in either the image or condition of women in the Middle Ages is doomed to contradiction. But we must not allow ourselves to become discouraged by the apparent immobility of the abundant literature on women. The danger of such discouragement is that we may be tempted to explain the contradictory images of women as a product of immutable hieratic archetypes, ahistorical figures of the eternal feminine.

Our medieval authors detested the very idea of novelty. When they introduced innovations they were especially apt to hide behind tradition, to pretend to be going back to the original source. They created the new out of the old. Just as there is no point in branding the Middle Ages misogynist, there is no reason to go to the opposite extreme, to single out certain isolated phenomena as harbingers of feminist sympathies. Ahistorical interpretation is also to be avoided: Mary was no avatar of Isis or the Great Mother. To refute these simplistic notions, it is enough to remember that the same men, the same clerics, who praised woman to the skies also condemned her out of hand and yet believed wholeheartedly that all human beings, male and female alike, had a place in the scheme of salvation. Every one of them suffered from this contradiction, which, as René Metz points out, was also embedded in canon law.[2] And each one tried to resolve it in his own way. As a group, however, the clergy attempted to respond to the world in which they lived, to move that world in the direction in which they wished to see it go. Theology had a pastoral purpose. A product of history, in turn it shaped history.

Reforming the World

To make things concrete, let us look at a particular region, western France, at a particular point in time: the eleventh and twelfth centuries. And let us concentrate on men whom Raoul Manselli describes as typical of the "crudest misogyny": Marbode of Rennes (died 1123), Hildebert of Lavardin (died 1133), and Geoffroy of Vendôme (died 1132).[3] The first two were men of modest background, products of the cathedral schools that were just beginning to spread learning beyond the monasteries. One was named bishop of Rennes in 1106, the other bishop of Le Mans in the same year. In 1125 Hildebert became archbishop of Tours. Geoffroy, scion of a line of barons allied with the counts of Anjou, came from more illustrious stock. He entered the Benedictine monastery of Vendôme as a child and in 1093 became abbot, a post he held until his death. The three prelates—two secular and one regular—are little known today except to specialists. Their reputation has stood up less well than that of their contemporaries Anselm of Canterbury (died 1109) and Yves of Chartres (died 1116), with whom they were in frequent contact. For our purposes, however, they are ideal witnesses.

The three men represent the culmination of one of the fundamental movements of medieval Christianity, a reform movement that began in the tenth century. At first it took the form of a flourishing of new monasteries: Cluny in 910, Camaldoli and Vallombreuse at the beginning of the next century. In the second half of the tenth century the principal thrust of the movement passed from the monasteries to the popes, so that historians tend to refer to the movement as the "Gregorian reform" in homage to the decisive role played by Pope Gregory VII (1073–1085). It was called a "reform" because in the minds of its promoters it represented a return to evangelical purity, to the ideals of the Apostles. But in reality it was an innovation, an attempt to regulate the lives of clerics as well as laymen and to shape relations between the Church and the secular world. What were the reformers' aims? Above all they wanted to free ecclesiastical institutions from the control of the secular authorities. By ecclesiastical institutions I mean things ranging from the tithe, oversight of parish churches, and appointment of priests, all things over which local lords claimed authority, to the appointment of bishops and popes, over which princes and emperor held sway. The reformers also sought to improve the morals of the clergy by extending to secular priests the rule of celibacy incumbent on monks. Chapters of canons were established to regulate the daily lives of secular priests. Finally, laymen were encouraged to participate in the reform movement. Lay brothers were invited to enter the Carthusian monastery at Cîteaux, for example. Other laymen were urged to join the Crusade and set out on the road to Jerusalem. And around the turn of the twelfth century marriage took on new meaning: henceforth it was to be monogamous, indissoluble, and a sacrament of the Church.

Our three prelates were active a quarter of a century after the pontificate of Gregory VII. They were named to their posts in the aftermath of Urban II's epic journey of 1095, during which he preached the Crusade in France. All three belonged to the generation whose task it was to consolidate the reform and implement its changes in practical ways, step by step and in the face of considerable complexity, tension, and resistance. Their writings offer a remarkable account of the progress of reform at the grass roots. As writers the three men were at home in many genres:

theological treatises, biblical commentary, hagiography, Latin poetry, sermons, official correspondence. They moved constantly
from theory to practice and then attempted to use the lessons of
reality to improve the theoretical concepts with which they began.
Their knowledge of the essence of femininity came from the
Church Fathers, and they attempted to apply it to the female
members of their flock, from the most illustrious to the most
obscure.

The Enemy

At first sight they would appear to deserve Manselli's allegation
that they were the crudest of misogynists: "The [female] sex poisoned our first ancestor, who was also husband and father [to the
first woman]; it strangled John the Baptist and delivered brave
Samson to his death. In a manner of speaking it also killed Our
Savior: for had [woman's] sin not required it, Our Savior would
not have had to die. Woe unto this sex, which knows nothing of
awe, goodness, or friendship, and which is more to be feared when
loved than when hated!"[4] The first woman to appear, around
1095, in the writings of Geoffroy of Vendôme was Eve, the first
of her sex and epitome of all who came after her. The story of the
Creation and Fall, which Monique Alexandre analyzed in Volume
I of this series, continued to weigh on the medieval view of woman.
The story of Genesis is of course complex in both its composition
and its content, but its most salient features, reinforced by incorporation into the Epistles of Paul, were highly unfavorable to the
second sex. To begin with, the Yahwist asserts man's primacy over
woman, who is created after man and from one of his ribs, in
order to give him "an help meet for him."[5] Eleventh-century artists
hit upon a remarkable iconographic shorthand for the creation of
Eve, who began to be portrayed as springing directly from Adam's
flank.[6] Perhaps the most important element in the story of Genesis
is that Eve, after being seduced by the serpent, persuades Adam
to join her in disobedience to God's will. For this she bears the
brunt of Yahweh's curse: "I will greatly multiply thy sorrow and
thy conception; in sorrow thou shalt bring forth children; and thy
desire shall be to thy husband, and he shall rule over thee." On
being banished from Eden woman receives her name from man
(another sign of domination). She is called Eve, "mother of all

living things."[7] Traditionally she was seen as bearing a greater share than Adam of the blame for the Fall. Thus Ambrose of Milan (died 397): "Woman was the author of man's fall, not man of woman's."[8] The serpent was identified with the Devil, Eve with the temptress. Tertullian (died circa 223) addressed himself to all women: "Dost thou not know that thou, too, art Eve? Even today God's judgment applies to all thy sex, hence thy sin must also subsist. Thou art the Devil's portal; thou hast consented to eat of his tree, and thou wast the first to renounce the law of God."[9]

Geoffroy's letter was addressed to monks. Its purpose was to convince the companions of the Immaculate Lamb that they had been right to renounce the flesh and cut themselves off from woman, that morally hideous creature whose superficial beauty was in fact the deadliest of traps. In the tenth century Odo of Cluny (died 942) repeated for the benefit of his monks John Chrysostom's warnings against the daughters of Eve: "Physical beauty is only skin deep. If *men* could see beneath the skin, the sight of *women* would make them nauseous . . . Since we are loath to touch spittle or dung even with our fingertips, how can we desire to embrace such a sack of dung?"[10] It seems never to have occurred to the abbot of Cluny that the same noxious substances might also lurk beneath the rougher exteriors of male bodies.

In 1105 Geoffroy expressed similar sentiments in a letter warning Bishop Hildebert of Lavardin against the machinations of his inveterate enemy, the Countess Euphrosine of Vendôme. The Countess, widow of a slain crusader, had inherited her late husband's property and contested certain of Geoffroy's claims in the region. What would otherwise be a commonplace feudal conflict thus takes on added interest: the misogynist abbot finds himself confronted with a female adversary. He issues a warning to Hildebert: "Take heed, venerable prelate, lest the woman take advantage of your guileless nature and compel you to act against your mother, the Roman Church. The female sex is in the habit of deception." Perfidious Geoffroy is afraid that the bishop of Le Mans might take up Euphrosine's cause. According to Yves of Chartres, before becoming bishop Hildebert allegedly had fathered quite a number of children through his shameless affairs with *mulierculae*, impoverished women.[11] Geoffroy points out that "the [female] sex deceived the first man and misled the apostle Peter. It drove the first to sin and the second to renunciation. The sex thus discharges its office in the manner of a guardian of the gate: those whom it seduces, it either excludes from life, like Christ's Peter, or admits unto death, like Adam of Eden."[12]

The "guardian of the gate" is from the Gospel of John.[13] Because she induced Peter to renounce Christ, as Eve had induced Adam to taste of the forbidden fruit, this biblical figure became a favorite stand-in for Eve in the patristic literature. "Eve misled Adam; the guardian of the gate misled Peter," explained Maximus of Turin in the fourth or fifth century.[14] In most traditional cultures women are more closely associated than men with the mysterious forces of life and death. Not only is woman the portal through whom children enter the world, she is also the guardian of the exit from this life, who keeps vigil at the bedside of the dying. Yet neither Maximus of Turin nor Geoffroy of Vendôme, though separated by seven centuries, had much use for this traditional symmetry. For them the guardian of the gate showed men the way to one destination only: perdition. But just as the Romans built Christian churches out of the ruins of pagan temples, the authors of the eleventh and twelfth centuries imposed new meanings on the traditional phrases they borrowed from their predecessors. Geoffroy repeats Maximus' sermon almost word for word, except that he never mentions Eve. Figuratively she is present, but unnamed and unnameable.

Wicked but Weak

The reason for Geoffroy's omission is that a monumental battle was under way, and no tactic was forbidden in a war whose aim was to bring about one of the most sweeping moral reforms history has ever known. Hildebert had lived with many women and fathered many children. Robert d'Abrissel (died 1116) was the son of a priest. Upon replacing his father in his Breton parish he too had sampled the sins of the flesh. He then took to the roads as a hermit and preacher and soon attracted a following of men and women who lived together, promiscuously, in the woods. Around 1098 Marbode of Rennes denounced this behavior as scandalous, making clear his contempt for women and the flesh. Woman, he said, was a temptress, a sorceress, a serpent, a plague, a vermin, a rash, a poison, a searing flame, an intoxicating spirit. What could come of such scandal, of such senseless mingling, other than female bellies swollen like "old wineskins" full of "new wine"?[15] Were the women who were the principal targets of Marbode's attack as disgusted by pregnancy as the men for whom Marbode spoke? Although the medieval sources do not tell us, aversion to childbirth seems to have been a male characteristic. Augustine (who died in 430) lamented: "We are born between urine and feces."[16]

Guy Devailly points out that the name Eve, though everywhere implicit in Marbode's long letter to Robert d'Abrissel, is never explicitly mentioned.[17] In his poem "On the Wicked Woman," which forms the third part of the *Book of Ten Chapters,* the bishop of Rennes charged his muse with the task of gathering together misogynistic images gleaned from his vast knowledge of classical and patristic literature. Rosario Leotta has analyzed the language of the poem, one of the most misogynistic works in the history of literature.[18] It far surpassed Juvenal's *Sixth Satire,* on which Marbode drew freely, and easily rivaled the "Ode on Contempt for the World" of Roger of Caen (died circa 1095). Marbode, again avoiding explicit mention of "the mother of all living things," attacked *femina* as "the deadliest of the Enemy's traps," the "root of all evil," the "child of all vice." It was a short step from *femina* to *meretrix* (prostitute): "A lion's head, a dragon's tail, and in between nothing but ardent fire."[19] The warning to the clerical scholars who pored over Marbode's book was clear: do not expose yourself to the heat of that searing furnace.

Hildebert of Lavardin also wrote poems filled with fire and ash. Man's three worst enemies were woman, money, and honors: "Woman is a fragile thing, steadfast in nothing but crime and always harmful. Woman is a voracious flame, the utmost folly, man's intimate enemy, who learns and teaches every possible way of doing harm. Woman is a vile *forum,* a public thing, born to deceive, for whom success is the ability to commit crime. All-consuming in vice, she is consumed by all. A predator of men, she becomes in turn their prey."[20] As Marbode hinted in his discussion of the pain of childbirth, woman ends up the victim of her own crimes: a "voracious flame," she is also a "weak vessel." That last epithet comes from 1 Peter 3:7: "Likewise, ye husbands, dwell with them according to knowledge, giving honor unto the wife, as unto the weaker vessel, and as being heirs together of the grace of life."[21] Later we shall see that Hildebert, when speaking of marriage, could take this rather less aggressive tone, though he is always careful to indicate the superiority of man. As for woman's weakness or, as Isidore of Seville (died 636) would call it, her "softness," if it was not a fact of nature, it was, in feudal society, more than a mere figment of the imagination.[22]

She-Wolves in the Sheepfold

Our prelates were unabashed misogynists. To bolster their prejudices they drew on both Christian and classical Latin traditions. "On the Wicked Women" was a veritable anthology of antifemale sentiments. The prelates agreed with the teachings of the Church Fathers, particularly the most widely read authors of the fourth and fifth centuries. This deep sympathy was based on a similarity of situation. In the fourth century, as martyrdom gave way to asceticism, some men, anxious to protect their virginity, withdrew from communal life to confront temptation in the desert: these were the first monks. Increasingly evil was identified with the flesh (and this identification was not without dualist overtones). Later, in the late eleventh and early twelfth centuries, with dualism once again on the rise, monks still sought protection in sanctifying isolation: "Pastors, drive the rapacious she-wolves from your flocks," Roger of Caen commanded.[23] But in the meantime a new need had arisen. Temptresses now threatened much of the secular clergy as well: Nicolaitan bishops; irrepressibly curious scholars; itinerant priests avid for new experience. A generation earlier the great reformer Peter Damian (died 1072) had lashed out with unprecedented violence against those he branded "clerical concubines," "sties for fat hogs," "impious she-tigers," and "furious vipers."[24] Yet none of his pamphlets were addressed to women or even laymen; they were purely a matter of ecclesiastical discipline.

What was new was not the substance of the attacks on women but the violence and the unwillingness to name the enemy. For these later writers "woman" no longer meant Eve but "the Unnameable," in the strongest possible sense. What accounts for this strange reserve? According to Isidore of Seville, whose *Etymologies* were a key element of the medieval cleric's world view, *Eva* was *vae*, misfortune, but also *vita*, life.[25] And according to the famous hymn *Ave Maris Stella*, attested as early as the ninth century, *Eva* was an anagram for *Ave*, the honorific with which Gabriel had greeted the "new Eve." In other words, to evoke Eve was to invoke Mary. Jerome (died 419) put it in a succinct formula: "Death through Eve, life through Mary."[26] And Augustine: "through woman, death; through woman, life."[27] Anselm of Canterbury maintained the symmetry: "So that women need not despair of attaining the state of the blessed, given that a woman was the cause of so great an evil, it was necessary, in order to restore their hope, that a woman be the cause of so great a good."[28] But the authors in whom I am interested here were more radical: they severed the tie between Eve and Mary. For them, the unnamed Eve was the antithesis of the inaccessible Mary.

The Virgin Mother

The twelfth century, it has often been said, marked the high point of Marian devotion as well as the flourishing of cathedral-building: it was the age of "Notre Dame." In fact, as Jean Leclercq has pointed out, it was a time when seeds planted in the eleventh century began to bear visible fruit. Make no mistake: men like Marbode and Geoffroy prayed fervently to Mary, to whom they confessed their worst sins and dedicated their poems. But Mary was not like other women. She was an exception, and Geoffroy and Hildebert contemplated the mystery of that exception. In several Carolingian anthologies we find these words: "Alone, without parallel, Mary virgin and mother."[29] Thus, as Jules Michelet rightly divined, praise for the Virgin Mother in no way extended to her less illustrious sisters.

The Sinner's Refuge

Henri Barre has assembled a fine collection of prayers to Mary (*Prières anciennes de l'Occident à la Mère du Sauveur*) in which it is all but impossible to find, prior to the twelfth century, a woman's prayer or even request for intercession addressed to Mary, most "blessed of all women." When the German nun Hrotswitha composed a prayer to the Virgin in the tenth century, she put the words in the mouth of Theophilus, a bishop's assistant whom Mary had released from a pact with the Devil. In the late eleventh century another nun collected a book of prayers to Mary, but there was nothing specifically feminine about their content. The *Book of Gertrude,* composed at around the same time for use by a noblewoman of high rank, contained prayers to the Virgin of a more personal character and written in a first-person female voice. Yet most of Gertrude's requests to the Virgin are in behalf of her only son, Peter, of royal blood. If we hope to find large numbers of women looking to the Mother of Christ for salvation, we must turn to less prestigious genres such as the literature of alleged miracles attributed to the Virgin.

Marbode of Rennes, like Geoffroy of Vendôme and Fulbert of Chartres (died 1029) before him, prayed fervently to the Virgin. Their homage to Mary was less passionate, perhaps, than that of their friend Anselm of Canterbury or of Bernard of Clairvaux and his many disciples and imitators (many of whose writings are wrongly attributed to him). Still, they were firmly within the tradition explored by Henri Barre, one of poetic exaltation of the "always precious virgin," of *stella maris* (the star of the sea, according to the well-known play on words), of filial piety for the Mother of Christ, of confidence in the intercessory powers of Mary, "the sinner's refuge" and "man's hope."[30] Marbode considered himself to be among the most culpable of men, hence one of those most in need of the Virgin's assistance. Mary was the mother par excellence, in whose bosom the unworthy son could bury his shame.

Ever More Virginal Mary

"Alone, without parallel, Mary, virgin and mother." Not only was Mary an object of prayer, she was also a subject of meditation and speculation as to her nature, identity, and specific virtues. Of the four major dogmas concerning her—Mother of God, Virgin Birth, Immaculate Conception, and Assumption—the last two did not become official Church doctrine until 1854 and 1950, respectively. Yet both had been objects of impassioned debate much earlier, as early as the eleventh century in the case of the Immaculate Conception and the eighth century in the case of the Assumption. The idea that Christ was both fully human and fully divine and that he was the son of God, engendered in the flesh of a woman who thus deserved the appellation "mother of God," achieved currency quite early in the course of debates on the "nature of the Son," debates that, by pitting Catholics against Arians, Gnostics, and others, poisoned the atmosphere of Christianity from the second to the fifth century. By the medieval period no one doubted these truths of the faith, proclaimed as such by the Council of Ephesus in 431 and reaffirmed by the Council of Chalcedonia in 451.

Mary's virginity too had ceased to be a matter of controversy, though the precise significance of her state still exercised some thinkers. Only two of the gospels affirm her virginity, which ends with the conception of Christ: Joseph "knew her not till she had brought forth her firstborn son," according to Matthew,[31] while Luke reports that "Mary said unto the angel, How shall this be, seeing I know not a man?"[32] The Protogospel of James, probably composed in the second century, was the first to state unambiguously that Mary's virginity remained intact after the birth of Jesus. Early in the fifth century Jerome insisted on the point in his *Anti-Helvidius,* and doubt became impossible. Some authors went even further: Clement of Alexandria (died circa 215), Zeno of Verona (died circa 372), Ambrose, Augustine, Peter Chrysologus (died circa 450), Leo the Great (died 461), Gregory the Great (died 604), and Paschasius Radbertus (died 863) all insisted that Mary remained a virgin through the delivery of her son, which was effected "without opening the uterus," according to Gregory the Great,[33] who took his information from Saint Ephraem (died 373); Hincmar of Rheims (died 882) noted that both "vulva and uterus remained closed,"[34] and Peter Damian repeated this assertion.

With God anything is possible, even the most incredible things, but virgin birth was a particularly difficult point to get across. At the time Geoffroy of Vendôme drafted his sermon "On the Nativity of the Lord," doubts must have persisted, because he states that his purpose is to refute the error of those who claim that Mary was a virgin both before and after delivery but that the portal [of her womb] opened during the event. He commented on Ezekiel 44:2: "This gate shall be shut, it shall not be opened, and no man shall enter in by it."[35] Gregory of Nyssa (died 392), Ambrose, and Jerome had already identified this verse as a precursor of Mary's virginity along with other Old Testament symbols: the burning bush not consumed by the flames; the Ark of the Covenant, whose wood could not rot; the dew on Gideon's fleece; and the locked garden and sealed fountain in the Song of Songs. Rupert of Deutz (died 1129), commenting on Ezekiel in the twelfth century, placed even greater emphasis on anagogical interpretation, that is, on the presumed parallel between the Old and the New Testaments: "She was closed when she conceived and no less closed in giving birth."[36] Geoffroy of Vendôme argued that Mary's virginity existed "before, during, and after delivery."[37] Hildebert of Lavardin used the same formula in his sermon

"Against the Jews" and in commenting on the same verse of
Ezekiel.[38] Was this phrase, which sounds so familiar, relatively new
at the time? Was it in common use before the eleventh century?
Its logical rigor anticipates the scholastic spirit, and the scholastics
did in fact take a keen interest in the matter. Although there is
nothing new in the substance of the proposition, its form focuses
attention on the exact moment of birth; before and after are played
down. The texts of Hildebert and Geoffroy, the priest who knew
women and the priest who did not, make for astonishing reading.
The two men bent their extraordinary curiosity to the task of
exploring the entrails of the Virgin. Their conception of Mary's
virginity seems even narrower than that of preceding centuries. Its
effect is not to hold Mary up as a model for other women but
rather to banish her to an inaccessible heaven where virgins can
give birth yet remain inviolate.

Listen once again to Geoffroy: "Virtuous Mary gave birth to
Christ, and in Christ she gave birth to Christians. Hence the
mother of Christ is the mother of all Christians. If the mother of
Christ is the mother of Christians, then clearly Christ and Christians are brothers. Not only is Christ the brother of all Christians,
he is also the father of all men and primarily of Christians. From
which it follows that Christ is the Virgin's father and husband as
well as her son."[39] Much earlier Ephraem and Peter Chrysologus
had developed the notion that Mary was the "sister, wife, and
servant of the Lord"[40] and the "mother of all living things by
grace"—as opposed to Eve, the "mother of all dying things by
nature."[41] Yet it is striking to see Geoffroy of Vendôme, the scion
of a feudal lineage, express his piety in terms of what Marc Bloch
would have called "invented kinship." The vertical lineage of
Christ as father, husband, and son is contrasted with the horizontal
kinship of his brother Christians, much as the verticality of the
donjon contrasted with the horizontality of the feudal court. The
whole drama is played out within a mother's womb, closed to all
yet mysteriously open to one. And recall that it was at about this
same time that Guibert of Nogent had his well-known dream
about his mother.

Virgins and Others

Our three prelates were not just theorists; they were also pastors.
What did they have to offer the women of this world? There were

still, thank God, a few women on this earth who had not yet fallen. Among them were Eva, the English nun who wrote to Geoffroy; Atalise, an unknown recluse who wrote to Hildebert; and Muriel, Agnes, and Constance, who were exhorted to preserve their virginity in letters, written by their friend Baudri of Bourgueil (died 1130), reminiscent of the great epistolary tradition of Saint Jerome. These women, like those for whom the *Mirror of Virgins* was written at about the same time in Germany, had nothing to fear so long as they persevered. Hildebert congratulated Atalise for having "chosen an eternal posterity over the bonds of mortal marriage." While mindful of the reward that awaited these Companions of the Lamb in the hereafter, Hildebert, echoing Ambrose and Jerome, extolled even more the freedom that these virgins enjoyed here below. Man had no power over their bodies, and they need not fear for their progeny: "One pays a great price for children whose conception is a threat to chastity and whose birth is a threat to life."[42] Yet in a sermon "On Mutual Consent" the same Hildebert tried to show that marriage is an indissoluble sacrament based on *dilectio* (love).[43] Despite this prodigious optimism, Hildebert was very aware of the terrible realities of feudal marriage, realities made manifest by the legend of Saint Godelive of Ghistelles (who, in 1070, was allegedly strangled and then drowned by assassins acting on orders of her husband).[44]

The really difficult pastoral issue was what to say to married women, to those who had renounced virginal serenity yet still wished to be saved. Marbode therefore composed a fourth chapter to his *Book of Ten Chapters,* a pendant to "On the Wicked Woman" entitled "On the Virtuous Woman." In it he holds up the matron as a shining example, the enemy of the whore. His argument makes us smile. "A good wife is the best thing in the world." A good woman is better than any material possession, since she is like man in all things "except sex." Would humanity exist without woman? "Without a field to plant in, what good is your seed?" Women are helpful and knowledgeable. They excel primarily in "the little things of everyday life."[45] No one is worse than Judas, but no man is as good as Mary. Unfortunately the only examples of good women that Marbode can cite in support of his argument are virgins. At best his argument justifies the social function of women without making much of a case for their salvation.

Hagiography by its very nature spoke to this second need.

Hildebert of Lavardin proposed a new version of the life of Saint Radegund (died 587), combining information gleaned from her two sixth-century hagiographers, Venantius Fortunatus and Baudonivia.[46] The saintly queen, unwilling wife of Clovis' son Chlotar (died 562), retired to a monastery near Poitiers that later came to be known as Sainte-Croix. Five centuries later Hildebert held her up as a model to the high-ranking aristocratic matrons with whom he was in correspondence. Such reworkings of old hagiographies were never merely cosmetic, as Jean-Yves Tilliette points out.[47] Fortunatus' account says nothing about marital difficulties between Radegund and her husband, but Hildebert stresses her virginity prior to marriage and her disgust at being obliged to give in to her husband's demands. Subsequently various mediocre hagiographers pretended that Radegund and Chlotar had never consummated their marriage. Hildebert had led the way by suggesting that all the saint's virtues were as nothing compared with the virtue she had forever sacrificed. In a rare expression of doubt as to God's omnipotence, Peter Damian, following Jerome, asked if God could restore a fallen virgin.[48]

The class of women was divided, according to a widely held belief, into three orders of merit: virgins would be rewarded a hundred times their deserts; widows, sixty times; and wives, thirty times. This scheme, first proposed by Jerome, had been taken up by Paschasius Radbertus and Bruno the Schoolman (died 1101). It remained in common use until the time of Thomas Aquinas (died 1274), and Geneviève Hasenohr notes that in some quarters it persisted until the fifteenth century.[49] Pierre Toubert has shown that in the ninth century Carolingian moralists inspired by Augustine composed "Mirrors of Married Couples" as models of princely marriage. Great ladies presumably had all the time they needed to discharge the duties of office, motherhood, and religion. From this literature "a positive image of woman, and even of femininity," emerged. The image of Eve was not banished but counterbalanced by that of the Virgin Mary and, even more, of Mary Magdalene.[50] In the tenth and eleventh centuries the Ottonian dynasty, heir to Carolingian tradition, made models of its queens: Edith (died 946), Mathilde (died 968), and Adelaide (died 999) were portrayed as ideal wives as well as saintly women.[51]

Already, however, the supremacy of virginity was being proclaimed, and even in the "Epitaph of Adelaide," under the impetus first of Cluny and later of the Gregorian reform. Chastity was praiseworthy primarily for clerics of course, but by extension for laymen as well, and especially for women. Around the middle of the eleventh century the hagiographer of Saint Ame told consecrated virgins that their state would enable them to overcome the curse of Eve.[52] By contrast, the hagiographer of Ide, countess of Boulogne (died 1113), tried, like our three prelates, to prove that a woman, even a married woman, could live a holy life. He praised Ide as a chaste wife and above all as the mother of praiseworthy sons, Godefroy of Bouillon and Baldwin of Jerusalem. After becoming a widow, moreover, she had had the good taste to enter a monastery under the jurisdiction of Cluny.[53] The communion of saints was never so reluctant to accept women as between 1050 and 1100.[54] Women therefore found outlets for their inchoate yet powerful religious impulses in deviance, mysticism, and even heresy.[55]

Through the Back Door

Pastoral concerns were expressed even more explicitly in letters of guidance than in hagiography. Hildebert of Lavardin sent seven such letters to Adele of Blois (died 1137), daughter of William the Conqueror. (In this period we should not expect to find letters addressed to people of humble origin.) The first three letters, written before Adele withdrew from the world, are nothing more than the flattery of a courtier. The last four were written after 1122, when the countess went into retreat at the Cluniac priory of Marcigny, one of the few convents open to women at the time. The last of these is the most important, for in it Hildebert celebrated the marriage between the religious widow and her new husband, Christ. The prelate referred to Adele as his "lady": "The wife of my Lord is my lady."[56] It was not a new idea for a woman to become the bride of Christ; Jerome had addressed the virgin Eustochium in similar terms. But here the conceit resonated with other conceits of the courtly poets then busily polishing their first verses in the courts of southern France. Hildebert, who was much subtler than Anselm of Canterbury in his letters to Gunhild, the daughter of King Harold of England, attempted to reassure his correspondent but only after cleverly raising her anxieties. Did she risk repudiation by her new husband because she had previously chosen a man over God, a knight over the King? No, Hildebert insists, and in support of his contention he cites a number of examples of redeemed women from the Bible: the prostitute married by Hosea, the Egyptian woman married by Moses—these were not particularly flattering examples—but above all the famous sinner of the Gospels, the sister of Martha and Lazarus.

Peter the Venerable, abbot of Cluny (died 1156), told the story of his own mother. Seeking to flee a marriage she abhorred, she had flung herself at the feet of any holy man who passed by, begging forgiveness and protection as Mary Magdalene had done at the feet of the Savior.[57] For the ecclesiastical writers of this period, the salvation of married women (of the highest rank) depended on redemption. Loss of the seal of virginity was irreparable, morally as well as physically. Penitence was the only way. The woman of sin, the *meretrix*—in plain language, the prostitute—was the only available model for women who had chosen not to emulate Mary's feat of transforming a sealed womb into a portal unto eternal life. These other women—women who had known sin and needed to repent—were daughters of the guardian of the gate, of the gateway unto death. For them the only way to salvation was through the back door.

Mary Magdalene

Theophilus was the intendant of the church of Adana in Cilicia (Asia Minor). Upon the death of the bishop an attempt was made to promote him to the episcopal throne, but he declined. Another man was chosen, and Theophilus was disgraced, whereupon he fell victim to rancor and envy. Abetted by a Jew, he signed a pact with the Devil. Soon, however, he realized his error and called on the Virgin for help. So ran the sixth-century Greek legend, which made its way to the West and was translated into Latin during the Carolingian period. This precursor of Faust enjoyed considerable popularity in the eleventh and twelfth centuries. It was repeated in countless texts and even embodied in sculpture on the tympanum of the abbey church in Souillac. The reason for the story's popularity was that it illustrated the omnipotence of the Virgin, more powerful even than the Devil. Fulbert of Chartres made use of the tale. Geoffroy of Vendôme alluded to it in one of his sermons. An Angevin man of letters, possibly Marbode of Rennes, composed a *Life of Theophilus* in verse. Unaware of the nun Hrotswitha's tenth-century prayer, which was based on the same legend, the author closely followed the Latin translation of the Greek original. Theophilus appears before Mary to plead his case at considerable length. He mentions numerous celebrated instances of repentance: Rahab, David, Peter, Zacchaeus, Paul, Cyprian. The poet is faithful to his model, with one exception. An additional name is inserted between Peter and Zacchaeus: that of Mary Magdalene, "she whose tears wiped away the stain of her sins and who thereafter became precious to the Lord and celebrated through the centuries."[58] Thus Mary Magdalene was wrapped in the mantle of tradition and, probably under the influence of a homily of Gregory the Great, included in the list of repentant sinners. Because her inclusion was of interest primarily to women, it is worth asking just how long she had been "celebrated through the centuries."

The Mary Magdalene venerated in western Christendom does not exist as such in the Bible. She is a composite of three distinct biblical figures: Mary of Magdala, whom Christ healed of seven devils and who then followed him to Calvary and became the first witness of his resurrection; Mary of Bethany, the sister of Martha and Lazarus; and the anonymous woman sinner who, at the home of Simon the Pharisee, moistens Christ's feet with her tears, wipes them with her hair, covers them with her kisses, and anoints them with perfume.[59] Although certain features of their stories made it possible to combine the three women into one, this was never done in the East. In the West, Gregory the Great was responsible for merging the trio into the single figure of Mary Magdalene. Victor Saxer has magisterially retraced the stages of her ascension, beginning with her appearance in eighth-century martyrologies and liturgy and, at around the same time, the first mention of her relics at the abbey Notre-Dame de Chelles.

But the real flourishing of her cult, which appears to have originated in the Eastern Empire, was connected with the success of the church at Vézelay. In 1059 the Burgundian abbey there, originally dedicated to the Virgin, was placed under the patronage of Mary Magdalene. At a time when piety needed tangible support, the monks of Vézelay suddenly discovered that they had been in possession of the saint's relics since time immemorial. A rather convoluted tale had to be invented to explain how the holy remains had come to Burgundy from the East, and, since other churches were vying for the same honor, the story had to be made consistent with the legend according to which Martha, Mary, and Lazarus had traveled by boat from the Holy Land to Provence. The results proved worth the effort. Vézelay flourished as a pilgrimage site in the eleventh and twelfth centuries before being partially eclipsed in the thirteenth by Sainte-Baume and Saint-Maximin of Provence, which also laid claim to Magdalenean relics.

Salvation in Penitence

Western France was no stranger to what Saxer calls the great "Magdalenic fermentation of the eleventh century."[60] In 1084 and 1093 girls born in Tours and Le Mans were the first in France to be named Madeleine. In 1105 Geoffroy of Vendôme wrote a sermon "In Honor of the Blessed Mary Magdalene" in which he gathered together most of what was known about her. His text gives evidence of what Dominique Iogna-Prat calls Magdalene's "blessed polysemy."[61] Geoffroy began his sermon with the woman anointing the feet of Christ at the home of Simon the Pharisee. Magdalene is described as a "sinner in the city," and in the Middle Ages everyone understood that her sins were of the flesh, that she was a prostitute. Peter of Cella (died 1183) referred to her as *meretrix* and insisted on her insatiable lust.[62] She had, according to Luke, hurled herself at Christ's feet, and according to Geoffroy the woman in Luke was obviously "the famous woman sinner." Following Augustine, he compared her with the proud Pharisee: "This creature of the weaker sex feared the Pharisee, a hard, merciless man who despised the woman and disdained her touch." But Christ gladly accepts her homage. Caught between hope and fear, she "confesses her sins" and in so doing saves herself. She even becomes an agent of redemption, a woman who "has healed not only her own wounds but those of many other sinners and who every day heals still more."[63] Had Mary Magdalene the *meretrix* thus become a redemptress? Such a title had been difficult for even the Virgin to obtain. Geoffroy contrasts her not only with the Pharisee but with Peter; the sinner is more fervent in her love of Christ than the Apostle himself. Was she not the first to see the resurrected Christ, who ordered her to spread the good news of his triumph over death? Unwilling to end his story here, Geoffroy carries on where the gospels end. Taking his inspiration from *The Eremitic Life,* a legend current in the ninth-century West, he portrayed Mary Magdalene far from home, mortifying her flesh, subjecting herself to harsh penance, submitting to the punishment of the young, and wearing herself out with prayer and vigils.

Geoffroy's account drew on the work of many earlier writers, including Ambrose, Augustine, Gregory the Great, and a sermon attributed to Odo of Cluny. That sermon, apparently written around the year 1000, described the Magdalene's role in the economy of salvation: "This was done so that woman, who brought death into the world, need not remain in disgrace. Death came into the world through the hand of woman, but news of the Resurrection came through her mouth. Just as Mary, always a virgin, opens for us the gates of Heaven from which we were excluded by the curse of Eve, so, too, is the female sex saved from disgrace by Magdalene."[64] Geoffroy of Vendôme was thus following a movement, but in his writings he gave the saint an even more powerful role: her "pious tongue" became the "gateway to Heaven." She, and not Mary, opened the gates of Paradise to all who were ready to repent.[65]

Sinners: Male or Female?

Does Mary Magdalene represent a rehabilitation of woman and of femininity? Before celebrating an ambiguous triumph, we should take a closer look. Geoffroy was not writing for a female audience. He was speaking to his monks, exhorting them to honor "this glorious woman" and entrust "their souls and bodies" to her.[66] In Odo's sermon Mary Magdalene was above all a metaphor for the militant church. For the abbot of Vendôme she was essentially a symbol not of woman but of the feminine element in man: the soul (as opposed to the spirit), that is, the part of the inner man which drags him down into the world, toward the body and the senses. When Geoffroy speaks of the frailty of woman, he means the frailty of humankind.

Origen (died circa 252) borrowed a distinction first introduced by Philo (died 50): "The inner man consists of a spirit and a soul. The spirit is said to be male, and the soul can be called female."[67] Ambrose added: "The spirit is therefore like Adam, the sensibility like Eve."[68] Augustine later elaborated on this idea. Medieval authors from the ninth century to the time of Peter Lombard (died 1159) preferred a cruder formulation: Adam was the spirit and Eve the flesh. But this was still a metaphor and did not imply any denial of woman's humanity. Misinterpretation of a remark made by Gregory of Tours (died circa 594) at the Council of Mâcon in

585 has lent credence to the idea that clerical thinkers seriously doubted that women have souls. Geoffroy of Vendôme imagined a dialogue between a male sinner (himself) and his "sinful soul," the "bride of Christ" fallen because of sin to the status of "daughter of the Devil" and "concubine of the vilest of fornicators." It is to this soul—his own soul—that he recommends confession of sin and the model of "penitent Mary Magdalene."[69] Marbode of Rennes and Anselm of Canterbury also looked to Magdalene to redeem their *anima peccatrix*. Their thundering confessions, like those of Peter Damian before them, were larded with rhetoric, modeled on Augustine's *Confessions* and on the lamentations of Jerome, who moistened Christ's feet with his tears and wiped them with his hair and who tried to tame "his rebellious flesh by fasting for weeks on end."[70] But these confessions were not all rhetoric; they were also constrained by grammar, and since *anima,* soul, was feminine in gender, it was naturally a feminine *peccatrix* who offered herself as guide for the repentant sinner.

Hagiography, however, teaches us that this rhetorical movement captured a part of reality: the reality of women. Marbode of Rennes was reputedly the author of a verse life of Thais, and Hildebert was the author of a life of Mary the Egyptian. Although both men lived in an age not noted for "creating" female saints, it was also a time when ancient legends were frequently rewritten, and there was particular interest in the stories of women who had gone into the desert to repent of their sins. Thais was a celebrated courtesan who was saved by the abbot Paphnutius. Mary the Egyptian, who once had offered the charms of her body to all comers, later crossed the Jordan to live in solitude on its far shore. Her legend was the inspiration for *The Eremitic Life* of Mary Magdalene. The choice of these two themes was significant. Woman was sinful, and by nature her sins were of the flesh. Her only salvation was through repentance and penance, mortification of her guilty flesh. Early Latin translations had cast Paphnutius as a harsh disciplinarian, but his image softened when the story was rewritten in the eleventh century. In the new version he refers to Thais as "my friend." He apostrophizes her: "O, beloved of God, image of the heavenly King!"[71] In these new phrases woven into the texture of an old story we may read something more than the contamination of hagiography by the vocabulary of *fin' amor.* Indeed, it may be that the court poets borrowed their vocabulary of love from the clerical lexicon. Genesis had stated that both man and woman had been created in God's image,[72] but the First Epistle to the Corinthians reserved that honor for man alone; woman became the "reflection" not of the Creator but of man.[73] Augustine labored over this contradiction, as did many who came after him: Isidore of Seville, Arnaud of Bonneval (died 1156), Gratian (died circa 1159), Thomas Aquinas. Now, suddenly, the unworthiest of women, the courtesan, was unambiguously declared to be an "image of the heavenly King."

The change, reflected in words and deeds, was not limited to hagiography. Robert d'Arbrissel and Vital de Savigny (died 1122), both of whom founded new orders, concerned themselves with the fate of genuine *meretrices,* not only professional prostitutes but also wives rejected by their husbands on the advice of reformist clerics; priests' concubines now condemned by the Church; and other women on whom Peter Damian had vented his fury half a century before. Vital gave them dowries and married them off. The heretic known as Henry of Lausanne, known to have been present in the diocese of Le Mans in 1116, was a new Hosea who forced the male members of his errant flock to marry these scorned women. Robert d'Arbrissel welcomed them into his order and consecrated a priory for them: it was known as La Madeleine (Magdalene) of Fontevraud.[74]

Twice Redeemed

To some the Middle Ages were infuriatingly misogynistic; others are amazed by the extraordinary role ascribed to women. Such judgments, I think, are largely beside the point. We began our inquiry with the writings of a small number of thinkers, a minuscule sampling of the vast literature produced by western Christendom over a period of more than a millennium. These thinkers and their contemporaries drew heavily on the work of the Church Fathers. What we found was that the representation of women in high clerical culture was extraordinarily complex. It would have been easy to select quotations from the abundant sources to support any number of different theses. I chose not to do this. It made more sense, I felt, to examine in some depth the at times contradictory views of a small number of individuals whom I consider to have been representative of their time.

The Bible shaped these men's ideas. What they perceived of reality was filtered through the prism of Scripture. Or, rather, they were convinced that what we call reality is merely the shadow of an idea, the idea of Woman, which can be most fully grasped through study of those texts in which the Revelation of all that is true was vouchsafed unto man. Their thinking about women began with an antithesis: Eve versus Mary. One stood as a symbol of women as they are; the other represented the ideal. As the eleventh century gave way to the twelfth, Eve became the object of ever harsher criticism, partly for strategic reasons having to do with ecclesiastical politics, partly as a matter of clerical discipline, and partly in support of a movement of moral reform. She was portrayed as a peril to the clergy, as the woman whom princes must not marry, as the daughter of the Devil. Meanwhile, the Virgin Mother was cast as a woman utterly unlike the women of this world. The figure of Mary Magdalene emerged from the widening gap between these two diametrically opposed symbols. Veneration of her memory was never more fervent than in the eleventh and twelfth centuries. Although the history of the Magdalene figure can be traced back to the gospels, the need for her suddenly became more acute. She took on a new, more vivid reality—more vivid because men, clergymen, clothed her in garments spun from the fabric of their own minds, which is to say, from their feelings of guilt. But who really needed this new Mary Magdalene? Women, for whom the road to salvation was steep indeed, if not unending. This sinful woman pointed the way to possible redemption. She held out a slim but real hope, which depended on confession, repentance, and penance to open a third pathway between the existing portals of life everlasting and eternal damnation.

This third path to eternity was not unrelated to the birth of purgatory as a third locus of the afterlife (in addition to heaven and hell), a birth that Jacques Le Goff tells us took place in the second half of the twelfth century. For Purgatory too was a place of hope, fear, and repentance where sinners could free themselves from the sins that had been part of their condition since birth.[75] Yet it often seems as though the women who took Mary Magdalene for their patroness had to redeem themselves not once but twice: once for being sinners, and again for being women.

The New Age

So far the picture I have presented is largely one of unanimity. But we need not search far afield to find disagreement. Anselm of

Canterbury's ideas about women reflect his characteristic optimism, an optimism he owed to confidence in the Incarnation. Abelard, a more innovative thinker, combined "speculative antifeminism with practical feminism."[76] Authors such as Hugh and Richard of Saint-Victor (died 1141 and 1173, respectively) considered how masculine and feminine might be transcended through a conception of marriage that emphasized love while minimizing sexuality.

Over the next few centuries there were interesting changes in the three images of women that dominated clerical culture: woman as temptress; woman as redeemed sinner; and woman as Queen of Heaven (an iconographic motif inaugurated perhaps by abbot Suger of Saint-Denis, who died in 1151). Individual writers combined these three images in characteristic ways. Around the middle of the twelfth century the circumstances of clerical culture also began to change. Roles within the church became more specialized: priests became theologians (the term was new), canonists, preachers, pastors, hagiographers, encylopedists, and mystics. These specialists henceforth divided responsibility for a range of knowledge over which earlier clerical scholars had roamed freely. It became rare for any single author to exhibit interests as wide-ranging as those of our Angevin writers. Furthermore, the variety of local customs and practices complicated the task of those clerics whose mission was to proclaim the unity of the faith. Among these disruptive influences women's voices were particularly troublesome. For women were at last beginning to make themselves heard, to express their religious anxieties, desires, and hopes. Once pastors had disclosed to their flocks the divine order of things. Now more and more of them were forced to respond to initiatives launched by the faithful, initiatives with which the clergy was ill prepared to deal.

In the Name of the Mother and the Son

From Chartres to Amiens, Mary enjoyed her moment in the sun. The most spellbound of her admirers were the monks, especially the Cistercian followers of that mellifluous man of learning, Bernard of Clairvaux. Bernard, as Jean Leclercq points out, contributed little that was new to the theory of "Mariology," and the astonishing success of his writings was a consequence of one thing:

"their beauty."[77] In the thirteenth century the Mendicant Orders, especially the Franciscans, carried on the tradition. Medieval mysticism reached new heights in contemplation of the Virgin—a form of filial piety, the piety of sons. Virginity ceased to be the focus of attention; Mary triumphed as mother.

The faculties of theology were hotbeds of speculation in the dogmas of the faith. The question of the Virgin's conception led five mendicant friars to embark on lengthy theological investigations: Alexander of Hales (died 1245), Bonaventure (died 1274), and Duns Scotus (died 1308) were Franciscans, and Albertus Magnus (died 1280) and Thomas Aquinas (died 1274) were Dominicans. Within half a century these men laid the theoretical groundwork for two last important articles of faith concerning the Virgin. The first was the doctrine of Mary's sanctification: alone among humans, the Mother of Christ had been healed of original sin. But Duns Scotus went further, arguing that Mary from the beginning had remained free of the taint of original sin, an idea that led directly to the doctrines of the Immaculate Conception and the Assumption (implying bodily ascent to heaven, hence freedom from putrescence of the flesh, though not from death). Thus, Mary more than ever escaped the human condition in regard to both conception and death.

In spite of this, she moved closer to humanity, as can be seen most clearly perhaps in iconography, in the caresses the humble peasant Mother bestows upon her adored Son and even more in the depth of the grief she feels for his loss. The thirteenth, fourteenth, and fifteenth centuries resounded with the laments of mystics such as the Franciscan Conrad of Saxony (died 1279), the Spirituals Jacopone of Todi (died 1306) and Ubertino of Casale (died circa 1328), and the Observantine Bernardino of Siena (died 1444) contemplating the Mater Dolorosa who takes her son from the Cross and lays him to rest. Renaissance painting and sculpture gave dazzling representation to these Marian motifs. The religion of the new age was exemplified by the theme of the Pietà, which first appeared in Germany, made its way to Italy at the beginning of the fourteenth century, and spread from there to the rest of Europe. The Pietà symbolized a late-emerging alliance of women and priests in a religion of the Mother and the Son, who, brought to grief by the Passion, suffer in isolation from the rest of the world, cut off from the absent Father.

Scripture versus the Spoken Word

Meanwhile various writers made Eve their subject, among them Peter the Painter, Bernard of Morlaix (died circa 1140), Hugh of Fouilloy (died circa 1172), Walter Map (died circa 1210), Alvaro Pelayo (died 1352), Gilles Bellemère (died 1407), Jean Nider (died circa 1438, author of the *Formicarius*), and the redoubtable Henry Institoris and John Sprenger (authors of the *Hammer of Witches,* first printed in 1486). These men merely rehearsed themes that Marbode of Rennes had so assiduously collected. By the thirteenth century, however, scholars had begun to play down Eve's role as the source of the world's evil. Here, medical thinking, which Claude Thomasset will examine in the next chapter of this volume, played an important part. Thomas Aquinas, in attempting to reconcile Genesis with Aristotle's physiology, according to which the male seed is the crucial element in procreation, came to the conclusion, similar to that of Augustine, that original sin was passed from Adam through the male line to the entire human race. All initiative was masculine; woman, for Aristotle a truncated male, was doomed to occupy a subordinate position.[78]

Toward the end of the Middle Ages the portrayal of woman changed in two ways. Previously, women had been cast as allies of the serpent in propaganda aimed primarily at monks and priests, to warn them against the snares of the flesh. From the middle of the twelfth century on, however, such warnings appeared in literature intended for a broader audience, including texts on canon law, ethics, and, from the fourteenth century on, inquisitors' manuals. The second change was thematic: the classical topos of woman as gossip gained new currency. Its roots can be traced back to the Old Testament, classical antiquity, and early patristic texts such as the writings of John Chrysostom. During the early Middle Ages it went into relative eclipse. Now, however, Gratian, Gilbert of Tournai (died 1284), Thomas Aquinas, Alvaro Pelayo, and the *Hammer of Witches* repeatedly denounced female chatter as the scourge of the new age and called for its suppression. Women, an outraged Gilbert observed, actually dared to speak out in public and, worse yet, on matters of dogma and Scripture.[79] Thomas Aquinas sternly reminded women that they were permitted to speak only in private. Prophecy of course was permissible, since it was the expression of a charismatic gift.[80] He followed Gratian closely: "A woman, even if she is learned and holy, must not presume to teach men [*viros*] in the congregation."[81] Why was the apostle's ancient lesson reiterated now?[82] Because the danger was present and real: women—nuns, Beguines, mystics, and other inspired souls—were speaking out on sacred matters in Liège, Brabant, Umbria, and Tuscany, thus threatening the monopoly of the guardians of Holy Writ. This was intolerable, and the impetuous torrent of women's words somehow would have to be brought under strict control.

New Voices

A composite of several biblical characters, Mary Magdalene constantly assumed new guises. Victor Saxer has traced the history of her veneration, from the decline of her cult at Vézelay to its triumph at Saint-Maximin and its extension not only throughout France but also to England, Germany, and Italy.[83] Franciscans and Dominicans worked zealously in her behalf, as Daniel Russo has shown.[84] In Italian iconography there is even some tendency to confuse the figures of Saint Francis and Mary Magdalene, one of the few instances in the history of iconography in which gender differences break down. In fifteenth-century painting and sculpture the woman sinner's abundant hair became a familiar symbol. Homes for repentant prostitutes proliferated under Mary Magdalene's patronage.

New saints appeared in large numbers. The proportion of new saints who were female rose to 25 percent between 1250 and 1300 and to almost 30 percent in the first half of the fifteenth century.[85] In Italy the proportion of female saints who had knowledge of the flesh attained its maximum between the thirteenth and fifteenth centuries, a period during which one-third of all new female saints had been married (and perhaps widowed), compared with two-thirds who had remained virgins.[86] Although this figure may seem low, it would not be approached again until recent times. The hagiographer of Margaret of Cortona (died 1297) tells us that Christ himself revealed to his beloved daughter the story of an incredible redemption: Mary Magdalene, an emblem for Margaret, herself a repentant sinner, is received into a heavenly choir of virgins just behind the Virgin Mary and Catherine of Alexandria.[87] What Jerome could not even imagine and what Peter Damian could admit only with difficulty was here accomplished: God, omnipotent, had restored a fallen woman's virginity.

41

Can this story be interpreted as a sign of women's progress? A mountain of contradictory evidence could easily be set against this atypical tale. The Gregorian reform had aimed to impose discipline first on the clergy, second on princes, and third on all others. In later centuries the clergy became increasingly concerned with the discipline of women. In this campaign female models proved useful. Women such as Bridget of Sweden (died 1373) and Catherine of Siena (died 1380) lectured the high and mighty of this world, including even the pope. The same reformist zeal found expression in suspicion of Beguines, tertiaries, and mystics of every stripe. Ultimately it led to persecution of witches. Can it really be said that Henry Institoris and John Sprenger were more generous to women than Augustine?

Yet things did change. By the thirteenth century the key developments were taking place outside the church. Voices other than those of priests began to be heard, not only in the parallel, and strictly secular, culture of the princely courts but also among those who began to seek God outside the Church. Dante (died 1321), though a layman, was nevertheless steeped in the most advanced theology of his day, a student of Bernard of Clairvaux, Thomas Aquinas, and Bonaventure. The mystical poet created Beatrice, who transcended and resolved the previously contradictory image of woman. Other women dispensed with mediation and raised their own voices in search of the Consort of the *Song of Songs*.

Let us therefore turn our attention away from the clergy. We have more to learn from the loud murmurs that were beginning to make themselves heard elsewhere and that on occasion intensified to the level of screams—more to learn, even if on occasion these voices too became caught up in the thickets of the old learning.

TRANSLATED FROM THE FRENCH BY ARTHUR GOLDHAMMER

2

The Nature of Woman

Claude Thomasset

IF WE MUST SEEK a source for how women were represented in the Middle Ages, Isidore of Seville's *Etymologies* is as good a place as any to start. Isidore, a bishop who lived in the most Romanized of the Spanish provinces in the first third of the seventh century, compiled *Etymologies,* a twenty-volume compendium of ancient knowledge. It was a work that combined wide learning with persistent questioning of language, of the words God had chosen to be the repositories of knowledge. Isidore's expository method, search for immanent guarantees of validity, and concern with proof were characteristic of medieval thought. Anatomy, like other scientific disciplines, reflected these principles. In Book XI of *Etymologies* we find a description of man *de capite ad calcem:* each member, each organ of the body is discussed in a sentence or two, described in terms of its function. From Isidore on, anatomical description in the Middle Ages was strictly teleological. The description of woman's anatomy therefore focused on her primary function: everything about her—even the weakness that made her subservient to man—was directed toward one end, procreation. Consequently, woman's theological detractors could dispense with any consideration of her psychology. She was seen as a body undisciplined by mind, as a creature ruled by her internal, and particularly her sexual, organs—a disturbing force of nature. Because she was the instrument of human continuity, woman was to the core a creature of Nature, of that active force that brought the universe into being and preserved its order. In medieval French the word *nature* sometimes referred to the genitals, especially, in certain dialects, the female genitals. Woman's affinity with matter, inscribed as it was in language itself, could hardly fail to incur the disapproval of clergymen whose vocation it was to sever the ties that bound them to the material world.

A Chronological Overview

Medieval representations of women and sexuality originated with the ancients and were passed on by Arab scholars—men who did not share the Christian conception of morality. Yet the Church, determined to regulate sexuality and marriage, drew on these alien sources. In Leviticus sexual impurity was associated with various skin diseases; medieval readers naturally interpreted these as forms of leprosy, a scourge epidemic in the West from the sixth century on.[1] The prevalence of leprosy exacerbated fears of sexual sin and bolstered the theological doctrine that man is guilty in his very flesh. Even the most liberal of medieval scholars shared these fears and consequently misinterpreted the ancient texts, which were by no means easy to fathom because they often incorporated contradictory ideas from two and even three different cultures.

Etymological interpretation of the sort practiced by Isidore of Seville suited the temper of the medieval mind, which preferred fragmentary, moralizing interpretations to grand theoretical systems. Hence from the time of Isidore of Seville to that of Rabanus Maurus (ninth century) there was little innovation in medieval thinking, which if anything became more misogynist than ever. For new ideas it was necessary to turn to sources other than the etymological tradition.

Few texts were available to physicians other than the *Gynaecia* of Soranus of Ephesus (first century A.D., translated by Moschion in the sixth century). The situation began to change in the second half of the ninth century, when Alfanus of Salerno translated *De natura hominis* by Nemesius of Emesa (fourth century A.D.), a text that brought not Galen but a systematic corpus of Galenist teachings within reach of medieval scholars. The Salerno School of physicians was one of the most active centers of scientific research in the period. In the second half of the eleventh century Constantine the African's translations made Arabic medical knowledge available in the West: works translated included Ali ibn al-Abbas' *Pantegni;* Ibn al-Jazzar's *Viaticum; De coitu,* possibly by the same author; and the pseudo-Galenic *De spermate,* which was destined to exert considerable influence on medieval thought. The Salerno School also produced a celebrated series of *Anatomies,* which were presented as practical textbooks on dissection. Gerard of Cremona, a product of the intellectual ferment in twelfth-century Toledo, further enhanced the authority of Arab medicine by translating the two great compendia of medical knowledge from the Arabic: Avicenna's *Canon,* and, from the previous century, Rhazes' *Liber ad Almansorem.*

The last important development in the history of medieval medicine was the rediscovery of Aristotle. *De animalibus* was translated by Michael Scotus and William of Moerbeke in the second half of the thirteenth century. Aristotle's ideas subsequently exerted considerable influence on anatomy and physiology. Albertus Magnus' commentary on *De animalibus* may be our most important source for learning about a thirteenth-century ecclesiastic's views on women. In the second half of the thirteenth century the conjunction of Aristotle's philosophy with Averroes' not only inspired new work in theology but also encouraged a naturalistic outlook and a more liberal attitude toward sexual behavior. Reacting against this, Etienne Tempier in 1270 and again in 1277 condemned extravagant philosophical and scientific ideas that he claimed struck at the very foundations of religion.

Finally, the thought of Galen was also influential throughout the Middle Ages, but filtered through the work of other thinkers. His own *De usu partium* did not become available in the West until the first half of the fourteenth century.

This rapid summary gives a broad overview of medieval developments in anatomy and physiology. Medieval science was of course based on authority; when authorities conflicted, scholars inevitably weighed in with mounds of quotations from the canonical texts. Although these texts were accessible only to trained physicians, medical knowledge was communicated to a wide audience through encyclopedias, which, rather than aim at synthesis, at times merely juxtaposed the contradictory opinions of the authorities; in some cases, however, an encyclopedist might favor one theory over another. The earliest of the medieval encyclopedias was the *Dragmaticon* of William of Conches (died 1150), which incorporated many of the teachings made available by Constantine the African. The second half of the thirteenth century witnessed the appearance of several encyclopedic surveys, including Vincent of Beauvais's *Speculum Naturale,* Bartholomew the Englishman's *De proprietatibus rerum,* and Alexander Neckham's *De naturis rerum.* All three works treated the processes of reproduction and pregnancy with particular attention to female anatomy and physiology. Around the same time theologians began to reflect on the question of Christ's conception. In the *Commentary on the Sententiae* and *Summa Theologica,* for example, Thomas Aquinas proposed a rather fanciful theory in order to deny that the divine seed had ever come into contact with impure menstrual blood (believed to be the nutrient of normal human embryos). At no other time was female physiology a subject of more intense controversy and research.

Galen's Analogy and Its Consequences

The history of the representation of women cannot be separated from the history of collective consciousness. Theologians, following Genesis, held that woman, created after man, was therefore inferior, and in various ways the anatomical evidence was made to support this view. Aristotle and, even more important for medieval thought, Galen believed that the male and female sexual organs were mirror images of each other. Avicenna put it this way in the *Canon:* "I say that the instrument of generation in woman is the womb *(matrix)* and that it was created to resemble the instrument of generation in man, namely, the penis and its accompanying parts."[2] The only difference was that the male organ was complete and turned outward, whereas the female organ was incomplete and turned inward—the opposite of the virile member. Extending this analogy even further, the ovaries were said to be homologous to the testicles, but smaller. Medieval physicians found female anatomy hard to interpret. One reason for this was that on principle they chose the male as their model. They were committed to teleological interpretation, moreover, and preferred to defer to authority rather than attempt unbiased observation.

The clitoris, for example, was simply omitted from medieval

anatomy. To be sure, Moschion had noticed the structure and given it a name, but no one followed his lead. In Constantine's translations the Arabic word for clitoris was simply transliterated, not translated. The word therefore had no meaning, and apparently no one asked what anatomical structure it named. The leading Arab physicians had commented on the organ only in cases of hypertrophy. The idea of a strict male-female symmetry was so appealing, it seems, that no male physician, Arabic or Christian, was willing to risk compromising it by raising empirical objections to the theory, particularly when to have done so would have meant recognizing that women have the ability to experience sexual pleasure on their own as well as undermining the teleological principle on which all anatomical interpretation was based. In the early fourteenth century even so remarkable a surgeon as Henri de Mondeville mistook the clitoris for the extremity of the urethra; he accordingly preserved the teleological principle by drawing an analogy between clitoris and uvula. More astute observers, such as Albertus Magnus, noted that the clitoris was a region of extreme sensitivity, and the physician Peter of Abano reported that stimulation of the organ produced an intense sensation of pleasure. Various preconceptions nevertheless prevented anyone from drawing the obvious conclusion, so that Gabriel Fallope later would be able to claim that he had been the discoverer of the clitoris.

The teleological principle also made it difficult to interpret the significance of the female breasts. The breasts are of course the organ that supplies the newborn with milk, which was believed to be nothing other than blanched menstrual blood. As such they attracted little attention from writers who commented on erotic foreplay. Only Avicenna in the *Canon* alludes to caressing the breasts as a preliminary to lovemaking. Avicenna's commentators showed little interest in this passage. In literary texts prior to the fourteenth century the breasts were conventionally described as "small and hard," terms that bespeak little in the way of sensual response. By contrast, descriptions of elderly women cruelly emphasized their shriveled mammaries. Medical accounts of the female bosom were often astonishingly unperceptive.

Women and Vapors

Medieval observers believed that the womb could move up and down within the body and that the consequences of this motion were of great medical significance. Yet the medical literature had little to say on the subject. The belief apparently stemmed from ancient notions of female physiology. In Plato's *Timaeus,* for example, we read that "in females what is called the womb or uterus is like a living thing, possessed of the desire to make children" (91c). The Hippocratic corpus also described movements of the uterus, based perhaps on observations of uterine prolapse, perhaps on *globus hystericus,* the choking sensation sometimes experienced by hysterics, which is known to have been observed in the early Middle Ages. In any case, people believed that the uterus had a life of its own inside the body. In order to end the choking sensation associated with hysteria, the womb had to be forced back down to its proper place. The technique for accomplishing this involved exposure to various fumes. Noxious vapors were administered to the upper part of the body, while the lower part was exposed to aromatic fumes intended to entice the uterus downward. A fifteenth-century commentator on Avicenna claims that the women of Navarre resorted to similar practices before sleeping with their husbands in order to increase the likelihood of conception. It was also believed that a woman's breath reproduced the odors to which her genitals were exposed. This belief in woman's permeability to odors appears to have been related to her alleged ability to respond to the exhalations of the earth, as in the case of the ancient Sibyl.

Men were troubled by woman's sensitivity to vaporous emanations. Henri de Mondeville's astonishing comparison of the clitoris to the uvula reflects an obsession with protecting women from such effusions. Albertus Magnus reports the case of a woman who claimed to derive sexual pleasure from the wind. He also mentions the frequent comparison of women to mares, which were supposedly capable of conceiving from exposure to the wind in the absence of actual copulation. A manuscript, composed around 1200 and reflecting the influence of the Salerno School, repeats this story. Much additional evidence attests to men's obsession with the possibility that women might give birth without their participation.

Galenic Theory

The alleged inverse symmetry of male and female sex organs was only one element of Galen's comprehensive medical theory. Fol-

	South	
DRY	Fire Summer Yellow Bile Choleric	HOT

| West | Earth
Autumn
Black Bile
Melancholic | Element
Season
Humor
Temperament | Air
Spring
Blood
Sanguine | East |

	North	
COLD	Water Winter Phlegm Phlegmatic	MOIST

Based on W. D. Sharpe, "Isidore of Seville: The Medical Writings," *Transactions of the American Philosophical Society*, 44(2)1964:24.

lowing Aristotle, Galen claimed that all matter was a combination of four fundamental elements: earth, air, fire, and water.[3] In addition to these four elements, there were two pairs of opposing attributes: hot and cold, dry and moist. Galen's physiology of the human body was subordinated to this representational scheme (see the accompanying diagram). Each of the four fundamental elements was said to correspond to one of the humors identified by the Hippocratic physicians. Food and drink, like everything else, contained the four elements in varying combinations, and the body transformed what it ingested into blood, phlegm, yellow bile, and black bile. The four humors determine the body's *temperamentum*, or equilibrium, which was equated with good health.

This system proved to be an effective analytical tool. It stressed the identical composition of the macrocosm (the world) and the microcosm (man). It defined the four principal temperaments (Galen actually defined nine) and associated each with a season and a time of life. Medieval physicians welcomed the adaptation of the Hippocratic doctrine of temperaments to the Galenic system. Many authors copied or revised the four distichs of the Salerno School, which defined physical appearance and character. These were sometimes elaborated to include individual sexual capacities. Foods could be classified in the same way, and from this schematic structure grew a whole dietetic science whose purpose was to correct excess quantities of various humors so as to restore the body to equilibrium. Medications were classified even more minutely according to a scheme that allowed for different degrees of dryness and warmth. Thus remedies could be precisely calibrated to the nature of the malady they were intended to treat. Early in the fourteenth century Arnaud de Villeneuve attempted to give a mathematical treatment of quality (as opposed to quantity).

Galenic theory, transmitted to the West through Arab thinkers, was extensively revised by medieval physicians. The most complicated aspect of Galen's physiology was his theory of *pneuma,* or spirits. The vital pneuma, carried by the arteries to all the organs of the body, was the active agent in respiration and all the combustive processes. The psychic pneuma filled the brain and was produced from the vital pneuma by the choroid plexus at its base. The transformation process involved purification by means of circulation through a network of capillaries, a key concept in medieval physiology. Arab physicians had introduced a third pneuma into Galenic theory: the natural pneuma *(spiritus naturalis),* which was located in the liver and responsible for the vegetative functions. For various reasons Christianity accepted Galenism without hostility, and Galen's theories remained the fundamental dogma of official medicine until the seventeenth century.

The foregoing is a brief summary of a highly sophisticated theory, whose terminology will occur frequently in the texts we shall be examining. Words such as "spirit" and "ventosity," originally derived from Galenic medicine, entered common parlance. Medieval writers frequently repeated that, in order for a sexual act to result in conception, three things had to be present: heat, spirit, and humor. These terms apparently circumscribed the limits of scientific explanation of the mystery of procreation. Even so shrewd a physician as Avicenna ends his explanation of reproduction with the invocation of a "spirit." Erection, he said in the *Canon,* was the result of a powerful "ventosity" resulting from the *spiritus desiderativus,* which transformed the affected body part into a pneumatic machine. Verbal analogies introduced a certain conceptual confusion. Since ventosity also meant flatulence, the ingestion of foods likely to produce flatulence was said to stimulate sexual desire; physicians therefore recommended that religious communities avoid consuming such items.

The most rigorous of physiologists, such as Albertus Magnus, argued that ejaculation was the result of a spasm triggered by a "ventosity" in the male member. Some writers held that a similar process at work in woman resulted in the emission of a female seed necessary for conception to take place. One thirteenth-century text claimed that the purpose of the physical movement of the partners in coitus was to introduce these spirits into their respective bodies so that, at the moment of orgasm, male and female seeds would be simultaneously emitted, thus maximizing the likelihood of conception.[4] Here the pneuma is referred to in the vulgar tongue as "wind" or "spirit." This wind was both present inside the body and, at the same time, inhaled through respiration, in keeping with Galen's doctrine. Not all the texts are this precise, but in interpreting any medieval document one must be attentive to the explanatory power of individual words, which signal acceptance of certain medical theories and doctrines. In medieval science it was the system that counted, not critical judgment.

The Female's Internal Organs

Medieval anatomical description of the female body was shaped by this amalgam of philosophical and medical ideas. It is naive to think that anatomy is based on objective observation of self-evident structures. The example of the clitoris shows that what is accepted as fact is determined by cultural authority and intentions. This is particularly true when it comes to the abdominal anatomy of the female.

Isidore of Seville claimed that the vulva owed its name to an analogy, *valva* being the Latin word for gate and the vulva being the gateway to the womb. The twelfth-century *Anatomia Magistri Nicolai Physici* states that vulva was derived from the verb *volvere*, which means "to turn, to form by turning."[5] An analogy with the whirlpool Charybdis was also mentioned, the idea being that the female organ mixed the male and female seeds in a kind of whirling motion that transformed liquid into solid, resulting in the formation of an embryo. Motion led to coagulation: for the medieval mind, this explanation by metaphor was enough. Another image, borrowed from Aristotle and repeated in Job 10:10, involved the curdling of milk. The formation of the embryo nevertheless remained so mysterious, so far beyond rational explanation, that the Church decreed that forty days must pass before the nascent embryo could be considered a living thing.

In the West the uterus was at first depicted as bicornate. Arabic medical texts gave a more accurate description: the womb was said to resemble the bladder, but attached to it were two lateral tubes that supplied blood and pneuma. The womb itself was composed of fibrous muscle that allowed it to expand as the fetus developed. According to the *Pantegni* (translated by Constantine), the inner wall of the uterus was lined with hairs whose purpose was to retain both sperm and fetus. In the original these hairs were probably folds, but Constantine's rough translation turned folds into villosities. Nevertheless, this description gained widespread acceptance. In the *Dragmaticon* William of Conches (died circa 1150) explained the sterility of prostitutes as a consequence of the clogging of the matricial hair by various kinds of filth, which he said interfered with the retention of sperm.[6]

Dissections carried out by physicians of the Salerno School provided interesting new information. The "Anatomy of a Sow," which was probably published between 1100 and 1150, was significant because the reproductive anatomy of the sow was believed to be identical to that of the human female. Not surprisingly, the application of the Salerno physicians' findings to human females had certain unfortunate consequences. Medical theory and medical practice were inextricably intertwined: "Next, cut through the center of the womb [that is, the cervix]. Above it you will find two testicles [the ovaries], which send female sperm into the womb, where it joins with the male sperm to form the fetus." The womb was said to comprise seven "cells." It is not easy to say where the figure seven came from. It was not part of the Arabic medical tradition. Was it perhaps taken from *De spermate,* a text attributed to Galen that does not appear to have been available in the West until fairly late?[7] Or was there some mystical significance to the number seven? In any case, the figure is repeated in nearly all the major anatomical texts. The remarkable thing is that this hypothetical figure was invariably confirmed empirically by dissection. The seven cells were arranged symmetrically with respect to the central axis of the womb: three on the right side, three on the left, one in the center. If male and female seeds joined to form the embryo in one of the cells on the right, the offspring's sex was male; if the seeds joined on the left, the sex was female; if they joined in the central cell, the result was a hermaphrodite. There were further complications to the theory, about which I shall have more to say later on. For the time being suffice it to say that the various possible combinations and permutations accounted for the diversity of human types. Physiognomy, a way of classifying those types on the basis of external appearance, was an important medieval discipline. Classification was a constant concern of both the secular and the religious authorities, and physiognomy provided a way of understanding individual human beings that filled some of the same needs as our psychology.

Another text from the Salerno School is one of the few from this period to describe the womb as consisting of two rather than seven cavities. According to this document, the womb contained two orifices: the *collum matricis* was the external orifice through which coitus was accomplished, whereas the *os matrici* was an internal orifice which, in the seventh hour after conception, closed so tightly that, according to Hippocrates, not even a needle could penetrate it. The female testicles (ovaries) were said to be smaller and harder than the male. They were located at the ends of the hornlike protuberances of the uterus and connected through veins to the kidneys.

Still another text, the *Anatomia magistri Nicolai physici,* of which three different versions were in circulation, rejected the model derived from dissection of the sow. It emphasized the importance of a so-called female vein *(kiveris vena),* the purpose of which was to funnel a portion of the menstrual blood into the womb and another portion into the mammary glands, there to be transformed into milk for the nourishment of the newborn.

Many of the texts that incorporated the anatomical descriptions of the Salerno School also included Arab medical doctrine made available to western readers by the translators of Toledo. These texts reinforced the notion that male and female sex organs were mirror images of each other. The female organs thus came to be seen as inferior copies of the male.

The first human dissections were carried out in Bologna at the end of the thirteenth century. The findings were incorporated in Mondino de' Luzzi's *Anatomia,* which was completed in 1316. Traditional ways of thinking were so firmly ingrained, however, that when Mondino dissected female cadavers he found their wombs to contain the expected seven cells. He felt it necessary, however, to elaborate on earlier descriptions: "These cells are nothing but empty spaces in the womb where the sperm may coagulate with the menstrual blood." Thus the benefits of experiment were minimal, an object lesson in the "theory-ladenness" of scientific observation.

It was not until the Renaissance that anatomists like Gabriel

Fallope began to chip away at the conventional wisdom. But their work resulted more in a return to the letter of Galen's text than in a fundamental challenge to medieval theories. Although the theory of the seven cells was soon abandoned and real progress was made in anatomical observation, the medieval approach to physiology would survive for several more centuries.

Feminine Emissions

Menstrual blood, which was thought to nourish the embryo in the womb, was believed to have harmful effects on people forced to live in proximity to a menstruating woman. Menstruation was etymologically linked to the lunar cycle (via the Greek *mene*, moon). Trotula, a well-known Salerno midwife, referred to the menses as "flowers" because, "just as trees do not bear fruit without flowers, so women without flowers are frustrated in their purpose of conception." This was just one of many comparisons between human reproduction and the reproduction of plants. The texts unanimously affirm that the purpose of menstrual blood is to nourish the embryo after conception. To that end the circulation of the blood had to undergo a modification. The most careful writers, such as Ali ibn al-Abbas, associated menstrual blood with the "subtle blood" and the animal pneuma. Thomas Aquinas drew on these kinds of distinctions in elaborating his theory of how the divine embryo formed in Mary's breast. The blood that went to make up that embryo was not impure menstrual blood but an intermediate by-product.

Blood circulated through the membrane surrounding the fetus. The liver was believed to be the source of blood in the human body. When the embryo's liver formed, a vein connecting it to the mother's body delivered menstrual blood and hence nutriment until the moment of delivery. Once the child was born, it began to feed on its mother's milk, which was nothing other than cooked menstrual blood, thereby ensuring a smooth transition from one form of nourishment to another.

Throughout the Middle Ages it was repeatedly asserted that women possess little natural heat. The warmest of women had less heat in their bodies than the coldest of men. When a woman was not pregnant, this insufficiency of natural heat precluded adequate cooking of the blood, and the uncooked residue was expelled from the body through the menstrual flow. Aristotle, and the medieval writers who followed him, invoked similar arguments to explain why women did not bleed from the nose, lacked hemorrhoids, and possessed soft, smooth skin. In males uncooked bodily residues were purged by way of body and facial hair and, in animals, by the growth of horns. Propositions such as these were frequently extracted from their theoretical context and popularized in the form of question-and-answer texts, which often seem naive and haphazard. In context, however, it is easy to appreciate, if not the accuracy of such statements, at least the logic behind them.

Hunger interfered with menstruation. Albertus Magnus observed that poor women, who worked hard to eke out a living, often did not menstruate. The little they had to eat was barely enough for their own survival. The theory of expurgation provided a ready explanation for this phenomenon. It is curious, however, that medieval theorists, for all the keenness of their attention to the menstrual cycle, never suspected that fertility too follows a regular monthly pattern.

Menstrual blood could be seen clearly. By contrast, the existence of female sperm could neither be confirmed nor denied by direct observation. The question therefore became an important issue of scientific and theological controversy. Belief in the existence of a "feminine principle" having an essential role in conception had a long and prestigious pedigree that could be traced all the way back to India and to most of the Greek philosophers. It was widely believed, for example, that the sex of the embryo was determined in the encounter between a male and a female component. But this tradition found a resolute adversary in Aristotle, who held that the menstrual blood was the counterpart of the male semen and that no individual could produce two spermatic secretions. Hence the secretion produced by the female during coitus was not comparable to the male semen. The nature of this female secretion varied from woman to woman and depended on diet.

After Aristotle's works were translated in the middle thirteenth century, the female-sperm theory began to be challenged. Its defenders invoked the authority of Hippocrates and Galen. Even earlier, in the eleventh century, some writers were familiar with the work of Nemesius of Emesa, who had called attention to the difference of opinion between Aristotle and Galen. Opinions as to the precise purpose of the "female seed" varied widely. According to strict Galenic tradition, one of its functions might be to nourish the male seed prior to the advent of menstrual blood for that purpose. It might also be a diluting agent intended to thin the sperm so as to facilitate its entry into the womb. Or it might be the source of the second membrane that develops around the fetus.

The sources are not always clear about these complex matters. Hildegard of Bingen (died 1179) not only recorded her mystical visions but also elaborated a scientific interpretation of the natural world. Among other things, she reflected with remarkable candor on questions of sexuality. Yet she appears to have been unsure what to think about female sperm.[8] Sometimes she denies that any such thing exists, at other times she seems to say that women produce small quantities of very weak sperm. Conception, she says, results from the mixing of two frothy liquids *(spuma)* produced by stirring the blood. In this account the male seed seems to do its work without the need for any female counterpart.

The most ardent champion of female sperm was the encyclopedist William of Conches, whose *Dragmaticon* incorporated ideas gleaned from Constantine's translations. This authoritative work was widely copied by later encyclopedists and therefore highly influential. William was the first to argue that prostitutes do not conceive because they experience no pleasure during intercourse, hence emit no seed. But the flesh is weak, so much so that rape victims, he insisted, may in some cases experience pleasure at the conclusion of the act and consequently become pregnant. These assertions stirred up a fairly lively controversy. The thirteenth-century encyclopedist Thomas of Cantimpré berated those who doubted the existence of the female seed in no uncertain terms: "Whoever makes such statements is telling lies."[9] Note in passing that one document from the Salerno School claimed that in adultery the male sperm was the decisive factor because the male will overpowered the female at the moment the two seeds came together.

Defenders of the Aristotelian doctrine took a more philosophical line, as exemplified by Giles of Rome's "On the Formation of the Human Body in the Uterus" (1267).[10] Although they conceded the possibility that a female sperm might exist, they denied that it played any part in conception; if it existed, it possessed no "formative virtue" and contributed nothing to the constitution of the embryo. Here we see the influence of Aristotle's distinction between substance and form: the substance of the embryo came from the menstrual blood, whereas the form was imposed by the male sperm. If there were a female sperm with an active, formative capacity, then women, whose bodies also produced menstrual blood, could conceive on their own, without men. This ancient male obsession thus reared its head once again in the guise of philosophical argument. One way out of the dilemma was the suggestion that the female sperm, if it exists, might resemble the "prostatic liquor" in having no function.

Averroës was the first to cite the notorious example of the woman who allegedly became pregnant after bathing in water into which a man had discharged his semen. Even though the woman experienced no pleasure and emitted no sperm of her own, conception took place.

The problem with denying the existence of female sperm was that the female "testicles" (ovaries) were then left without a function, which posed a problem for an anatomy based on teleological interpretation. Most authorities therefore opted for a compromise solution. The preeminence of the male seed was virtually unquestioned. Vincent of Beauvais, the most important of the thirteenth-century encyclopedists, stated that the male sperm incorporated both animal heat and the heat of the sun. Saint Thomas believed that semen was subject to the influence of the stars, through which God worked his will in the world. The male seed, he argued, contained three kinds of heat: the semen's own fundamental heat, the heat of the father's soul, and the heat of the sun. In terms of the traditional Aristotelian simile, the semen was the carpenter and the woman's menstrual blood was the wood.

The philosophers showed little concern for the observations of physicians. Nature's telos was embodied in the perfect being: the male. Substance—female substance, the menstrual blood—constituted an obstacle to the realization of this perfection by the force embodied in the male sperm. The female was merely a *mas occasionatus,* a potential male prevented from achieving full development, a defective, incomplete, mutilated creature.[11] The consequences of this severe judgment were not immediately clear. In the final quarter of the thirteenth century philosophers gleefully seized upon Aristotle's account of the forces of nature (as modified by Averroës). But this was not enough to overcome the influence of the earlier, lapidary formulation: a female is an incomplete male. Aristotle's preeminent authority made it that much easier for antifeminist clerics to trumpet this judgment for all to hear.

Albertus Magnus, a Dominican, sought to clarify a number of

ambiguous points in the controversy. He inquired into the nature of certain bodily emissions, drawing on information gathered from female "experts" and from nuns' confessions. Erotic dreams, he discovered, were not the cause but the "sign" of nocturnal emissions and could occur even in women who experienced no sexual desire—nuns innocent of guilty thoughts who nevertheless sometimes polluted themselves. This finding conflicted with contemporary medical thinking, according to which the hypothetical female sperm had three functions: to transmit maternal characteristics to the embryo, to serve as host to the male seed, and to demonstrate the woman's pleasure in sex. Thus one term, female sperm, covered such distinct functions as ovulation, cervical secretions, and vaginal lubrication. Aristotle, who denied even the existence of female sperm, had no explanation for these phenomena, nor did Galen, who took the opposite position.

Paradoxically, the theory that least resembles the modern scientific view was the one that made room for female physiology and psychology. Proponents of the Galenist view were much more inclined to acknowledge a woman's role in conception. Casuists attached considerable importance to the idea of a female seed, controversial as it was. For them, the emission of the female seed coincided with orgasm. Sexual practices intended to cause "ejaculation" in the female were therefore to be prohibited on the grounds that they occasioned a needless spilling of seed. The favor that Galen enjoyed among theologians ensured the survival of this view until well into the eighteenth century. Even Descartes, when he described the formation of the embryo, waxed lyrical about the "seeds of both sexes mingling together, each serving as leaven for the other."[12]

The Unpredictable Being

The Sex of the Embryo

According to Galen and his followers, the womb was the battleground on which the child's sex and other external characteristics were determined. The crucial factors were heat and cold and location of the embryo (on the right or left side of the uterus). Because the right side of the uterus and the right female testicle (ovary) were connected directly to the liver, they were warmer than their counterparts on the left side, hence more likely to produce a male offspring. The sex of the embryo was also determined by a battle between the male and female seeds. The theory of the seven cells further complicated matters. Males formed in the three right-hand cells, females in the three left-hand ones, hermaphrodites in the center. Before this spatial theory was developed, however, Hildegard of Bingen had proposed a theory of her own that emphasized psychic factors. The sex of the embryo, she argued, was determined by the potency of the male seed, but the parents' love for each other determined the child's moral qualities. A large quantity of sperm together with a virtuous love between parents yielded a male child blessed with every possible virtue. A small quantity of sperm produced a daughter, virtuous if her mother and father felt true affection for each other. A small amount of sperm and loveless parents resulted in the worst possible outcome: a wicked daughter. Hildegard went on to argue that a strong, healthy woman possessed sufficient heat to produce a child apt to resemble its mother; the child of a vigorous man and a delicate woman was more likely to resemble its father. Hildegard, being a woman, carefully allowed for the possibility that a child might resemble its female parent, a possibility curiously lacking in most medieval theories, which held that nothing could affect the stamp a man left on his offspring.

Hildegard also commented on that part of the body in which (sexual) pleasure manifested itself: in men that pleasure tended to be sudden and violent, whereas in women it was more like the sun, which gently and steadily sheds its heat upon the earth, that it may bear fruit. She conceded that women are cooler and moister than men but argued that these characteristics encouraged moderation and fertility. Few other medieval texts were as subtle in their description or as favorable in their attitude toward women. Albertus Magnus held that childbirth with its attendant risks tended to dampen young women's plethoric humors and excessive ardor. Most writers relied on simple mechanical schemes. William of Conches produced a more subtle variant of the left-right spatialization: an embryo located on the right side of the uterus, but not the extreme right, was likely to develop into an effeminate male; one on the left, but not the extreme left, was likely to become a mannish woman, one with more heat than other women and therefore more body hair. Medieval authors also toyed with various classificatory schemes borrowed from ancient writers, primarily Hippocrates. Generating wild combinations of types was a popular pastime, much in evidence in works of vulgarization in the vernacular. The *Dialogue of Placides and Timeo* invokes such factors as spatial location, relative quantity of male and female seed, and disposition of body heat. If the female seed was ejaculated on the right side and the uterine heat flowed inward, the result was likely to be a female of pale complexion and pleasant disposition but proud in manner and bearing. Possessed of masculine heat within their bodies, such women could produce children even with relatively cold men; their sexual appetite was apt to be rapacious. When the uterine heat flowed outward, however, the result was likely to be a dark-complexioned female with facial hair. If such a woman mated with a good male, she was apt to produce a strong, tall, handsome male offspring. Such were the means with which medieval writers attempted to classify human beings, males yes but especially females, because it was of the utmost importance to understand the different types of women, not only in order to anticipate their sexual desires but also to ensure that they would produce children. Physicians may have been called upon to give advice in the choice of mates. The Middle Ages have been called a "masculine" epoch, and in their obliviousness to the fact that children sometimes resemble their mothers, they certainly deserved the epithet. Even the bastards of the well-born were thought to reflect the qualities of their prestigious fathers.

Pleasure

At one time sexual pleasure was for men only, and in the twelfth and thirteenth centuries, before the translation of Arabic medical texts changed men's ideas about the importance of female pleasure, a wife's duty was clear: "A man never has more than one wife. He must take her as she is, cold in her discharge of her *debitum*, and must not do anything to warm her."[13] Prostitutes were sterile—science proved it—and with them young men could experience sex before marriage. Theologians conceded that, to ensure the perpetuation of the human race, the abominable act of intercourse must be accompanied by pleasure. Galen even provided scientific justification. Nature, he said, had made the sexual organs more sensitive than the skin, hence these parts became a locus of extreme pleasure preceded by intense desire. The Church, anxious to regulate sexuality and make marriage a sacrament, turned its attention to the question of sexual pleasure. Aristotelians could neglect female pleasure, but most theologians were Galenists and therefore obliged not only to consider the woman's role but also to define the limits of proper female behavior. All discussion of sexuality hinged, however, on the question of procreation. More poetic than most medieval writers on the subject, Hildegard of Bingen had compared a woman's pleasure to the radiance of the sun. Other authors put it less eloquently. They compared the sexual desire of women to moist wood, slow to take flame but apt to burn for a long time. Men were intrigued by the secret ardor of women.

Sexual Knowledge

Hera condemned Tiresias to blindness for revealing that women experienced greater pleasure in sex than men. The medieval mind thirsted after what Tiresias already knew. Clerical writers in search of readers often hid discussions of sexuality behind such esoteric titles as "women's secrets." In the *Dialogue of Placides and Timeo*, which claimed to have been inspired by Ovid, Hermaphrodite is portrayed as the mythical embodiment of this thirst for sexual knowledge. He plucks out his beard, dons women's clothing, and lives among women and girls in various parts of the world, many of whom, trusting in his discretion, grant him their favors. At the same time he asks for and receives their confidence and is therefore able to penetrate the mystery of the feminine. When he grows old and tires of this life, he once again dresses as a man and reveals what he has learned. As an initiator into the mysteries of womanhood, Hermaphrodite's only rival is the Salerno midwife Trotula. Of course the clerical author of this tale is emulating both Hermaphrodite and Trotula in attempting to claim exclusive possession of secret knowledge about sexuality. Not even medical writing was exempt from this kind of voyeurism and male fantasizing. Physicians described female masturbation with such a wealth of detail as to betray the authors' pleasure in the telling.

As marriage was deferred, young men found themselves excluded from the world of women. To gain access they required the services of an *entremetteuse* prepared to reveal the secrets of the female sex. The Old Woman, a character in the portion of the *Roman de la Rose* written by Jean de Meung, cynically discloses the ways of venal love and explains the art of fleecing the gullible. In the *Tree of Knowledge* Raymond Lull describes an even more cynical mother, who delights in, and on occasion even witnesses, her daughter's debauch and who "shamelessly spoke to the girl of lust and recounted the pleasures she had known with men, pleasures she would have blushed to describe to her son."[14] This is an extreme case, to be sure, yet one that reveals male anxieties in the face of coveted but unobtainable information about women's ways. The procuress was a staple of western literature, with Fernando de Rojas' *Celestina* (1499) the crowning example of the genre. In the Middle Ages the only nonparticipating observers of the sexual act were women, whether procuresses or midwives charged by the courts with providing expert testimony in cases of alleged impotence. Men felt threatened by this kind of power, and literature, both scientific and fictional, reflected their fears. Trotula owed her renown not so much to her treatise on midwifery as to her capacity to fill such a threatening role. Adept in the arts of concocting potions and restoring virginity, she knew how to deceive men, and they, afraid of falling victim to such occult arts, reacted hostilely. The old woman became the witch.

Various beliefs reinforced these fears of women. The womb, cold and moist, was likened to the serpent that seeks to warm itself by entering a sleeping person's mouth. The sexual capacity of women was particularly troubling. In sexual relations, according to a tradition stemming from the *Pantegni,* women enjoyed pleasure of two kinds: that of receiving the male seed, drawn by the "attractive virtue" of the vulva; and that of ejaculating her own female seed. Aristotelian doctrine contributed further worrisome details: the excess humidity of the female body enabled women to indulge in unlimited sex. The female was impossible to satisfy; she could be *lassata sed non satiata* (worn out but not satiated), Juvenal had said in an oft-repeated phrase. The human female, it was claimed, is the only animal that desires sexual relations after fertilization. Ribald literature, particularly the *fabliaux,* made the most of this troubling female power. The fear that first found expression as ridicule later metamorphosed into contempt. In the Christian West the conditions for a true dialogue, an erotic art, did not exist.

In Search of an Erotic Art

Marriage and childbearing—to the medieval way of thinking complementary duties—undoubtedly influenced attitudes toward sexual pleasure. Did the literature and philosophy of courtly love have a similar effect? In literature it was not unthinkable for lovers to have sexual intercourse, but the texts leave a great deal to the imagination. Did courtly love explore the clitoridean pleasures? It is all but certain that the Middle Ages did have a concept of extramarital eroticism that required the male to exercise perfect self-control. The sources are difficult to interpret, because the metaphors and symbols used might apply to homosexual as well as heterosexual relations. Like other, similar works, Constantine the African's *On Coitus* does not live up to the promise of its title. There is little advice on sexual technique beyond recommendations concerning when, in relation to mealtimes, to engage in intercourse; the rest is all physiology and pathology.

New thinking about eroticism came once again from Arab medical sources. Arab civilization being polygamous, men needed to understand their bodies, and women were encouraged to explore pleasure for themselves. Avicenna's *Canon* asserted a right to pleasure. Frustrated wives, it was commonly believed, would inevitably seek satisfaction with men other than their husbands or with other women. The West was a long way from such understanding, but within reason sexual pleasure in marriage was tolerated. Albertus Magnus recognized the usefulness of foreplay, and other medieval writers were willing to tolerate female masturbation prior to marriage. Erotic art flourished in the late thirteenth and early fourteenth centuries. Physicians such as Magninus and John of Gaddesden offered advice that would not seem out of place in a modern marriage manual. They explained in detail how a woman should be touched to prepare her for intercourse. The aim was to achieve simultaneous emission of male and female seeds, that is, simultaneous orgasm. Peter of Abano recommended stimulation of the clitoris (which of course he did not name) as a means of bringing a woman to a state resembling a swoon. This technical advice was coupled with recommendations to women about perfuming the breath. Ideally intercourse was to be performed in such a way as to prevent air from entering and corrupting the seed.

It is impossible to know how many people read these texts. But there was another obstacle to accepting the notion that sexual technique could be refined. If a marriage turned out to be barren and no female pathology was involved, then the husband might be thought to bear a share of the responsibility for failing to prepare his wife properly for conception. This was a burden that even the most open-minded of medieval males was unlikely to shoulder willingly.

Nevertheless, positive value was attached to sexual experience. Intercourse was considered necessary to maintain the body's equilibrium. Trotula insisted that sexual abstinence led to serious problems in women, such as suffocation of the womb, a condition known to afflict widows. By the end of the thirteenth century the body had asserted its rights. A treatise was even published on the art of love, or, more precisely, on sexual positions. It was included, along with Trotula's treatise, in a Catalan manuscript with the revealing title *Speculum al foderi* (Mirror of Making Love).[15] Twenty-four positions are described in a dry, technical manner. In the West sexual techniques were not, as in the East, a means of achieving harmony with the cosmos. Still, the *Speculum* was a far cry from the single position recommended by the Church and advocated by the doctors. While the avowed purpose of the work is to enhance sexual pleasure, its method is clinical: the woman is exposed and manipulated. There is nothing especially audacious about the text's exploration of either the erogenous zones (the clitoris is ignored) or "unnatural" couplings. But clearly eroticism could be separated from medical discourse and its constant preoccupation with procreation. The *Speculum,* in advance of its time, would find its continuation in the work of Aretino, yet it hardly advanced the erotic art. The woman in the text is entirely passive, and the man is free to do with her as he pleases. John of Gaddesden, who told women how to arouse masculine desire, may have provided a more practical if less systematic introduction to the subject.

Complicity thus replaced secrecy and hostility. Men and women discovered reciprocity in the sexual act. These texts certainly did not constitute the dominant discourse on the subject, but they do show that, despite religious taboos, sexual pleasure, particularly the pleasure of women, was a central concern in the thirteenth and fourteenth centuries. The forces of nature were both recognized and celebrated. Despite medicine's still feeble capacity to treat disease, people began to see the body in a positive light.

Women's Diseases

Sterility was a medieval obsession. Physicians called in to examine women could not touch or examine the patient directly. If a pessary or other treatment was called for, the services of a midwife were needed. But surgeons were allowed to operate to remove membranes or other growths that prevented normal sexual relations. After the operation, a cannula was inserted to prevent the formation of scar tissue from closing the orifice and to allow the woman to urinate. But surgery was reserved for cases of manifest malformation. Treatment of less serious conditions relied on salves, powders, drugs, and special diets to correct the excess of heat or cold responsible for the patient's sterility. The abundance of ancient folk remedies and of saints believed to have the power to make women fertile is a sign of just how important the issue was. The reproductive demands on women were a source of guilt feelings as well as of sisterly solidarity.

The scientific and medical literature on the subject contains some astonishing insights, but it was also full of superstitious lore. *Exempla,* brief texts intended to illustrate some piece of scientific knowledge, conveyed the ideas of the learned to large numbers of people. Nearly all the encyclopedists repeated the litany, taken by Isidore of Seville from Pliny and transmitted to the Middle Ages, about the nefarious effects of menstrual blood. That foul substance was blamed for preventing seeds from germinating, for turning grape mash bitter, for killing herbs, for causing trees to shed their fruit, for rusting iron and blackening brass, for giving dogs rabies. It could even dissolve pitch too hard to be scraped away with iron. More disturbing was the belief that a child conceived during menstruation would be born with red hair, with all the connotations that the medieval mind attached to that condition. Any child could contract measles or smallpox, diseases caused by the young body's effort to purge itself of menstrual blood absorbed by its "porous" members.

Medieval authorities followed Aristotle in his belief that the gaze of a menstruating woman could darken a mirror. Albertus Magnus gave a scientific explanation of the phenomenon: the eye, a passive organ, received part of the menstrual flow and, in keeping with Aristotelian and Galenic theories of vision, caused an alteration in the air, through which a harmful vapor flowed to the mirror. After menopause women became extremely dangerous because various excess humors no longer eliminated by menstruation now exited through the eyes. The *Admirable Magical Secrets of Albert the Great and the Small* asserted that old women could poison infants by staring at them in their cradles. Poor women, who ate only coarse, hard-to-digest foods, were the most poisonous. This pseudoscientific argument justified the exclusion of a whole segment of society: women who had lost not only their allure but also their social function (the ability to reproduce). These elderly women were so accustomed to their own poison that they were immune to its effects. In this they resembled Mithridates, king of Pontus, who enjoyed immunity from poison. Avicenna lent scientific authority to this belief when he noticed that starlings can eat hemlock without ill effect.

In the Middle Ages such Mithridatic powers were ascribed to a young woman of legend. The fullest version of the tale occurs in the *Dialogue of Placides and Timeo*. A king fearful of Alexander's growing power ordered that a girl at his court be fed poison for many years. After surviving this upbringing, she is bedecked with seductive fabrics and jewels and sent as a gift to Alexander. The great general is about to succumb to her charms when his court scholars, Aristotle and his teacher Socrates, notice the presence of poison in her body. But Alexander is not convinced, so an experiment is attempted: the girl kisses two serfs. They die immediately, as do the animals she touches subsequently. The girl is burned at the stake. In other versions of the tale the poison is transmitted by a kiss, a breath, or sexual intercourse.

This story, which enjoyed a great vogue in the second half of the thirteenth century, left a lasting mark on literature. It reflected not only fears of menstruation but also the terror of leprosy, whose transmission posed a dilemma for medical science. Some physicians held that leprosy could be contracted through sexual relations with a menstruating woman; others argued that a child conceived under such conditions could become leprous. Although historians have been obliged to reduce their estimates of the prevalence of leprosy in the medieval population, the disease exerted enough of a hold on the imagination to encourage countless myths. Physicians knew a great deal about the malady, but the length of its incubation period defied their conception of causality. Unfortunately for women, this gap in medical understanding was filled by the old theory that diseases could be transmitted through sexual intercourse. William of Conches explained that if a man with leprosy slept with a woman, not she but the next man who slept with her would come down with the disease. The reason was that the woman, being cold, could resist the masculine corruption. But putrid matter from the leper could be transmitted to her through intercourse and subsequently passed on to the genital organs of the second man. In other words, leprosy was thought to be a venereal disease. Symptomatic similarities made it easy to confuse the affliction with infection by *Chlamydia trachomatis,* a true venereal disease. Women seemed to enjoy a certain immunity, perhaps because men were more mobile and therefore more at risk. Women, in constant contact with infected husbands, may have developed resistance to the disease. Hence the number of female lepers was probably less than the number of male lepers. Accordingly, women were seen as carriers but not victims of this devastating malady, and the myth of lethal lovemaking took root.

In Béroul's *Tristan* the connection between Iseut and the lepers is clear. King Mark devises for his allegedly adulterous wife a punishment as extravagant as his misogynist fears: he plans to hand her over to a band of sex-starved lepers. The queen escapes. In one particularly important episode Iseut proves her innocence to the knights of King Arthur's court and then crosses a swamp mounted on the shoulders of Tristan, who is disguised as a leper. The details of the text prove that this escape is to be read as a monstrous copulation. The author refers to Iseut as a *givre,* or viper, a venomous animal that changes its skin as lepers do. To the assembled king and barons Iseut declares that she has no fear of the disease, that she is immune; her radiant beauty rises above the decay of the swamp. Already woman is a two-faced creature, beauty and putrefaction combined—an image that can be traced through many subsequent centuries of literary history. The men are transformed into spectators of the woman's triumph. In other contexts men are reduced to spying on women: the desire to see links the mythical figure of Hermaphrodite to Melusina's husband and all the other brave heroes and courageous knights who, for better or worse, happen upon nude women or fairies exposing the mysteries of femininity while bathing in fountains.

In *Tristan* the leper stands for unbridled sexuality, which in fact corresponds to woman's true nature. In the chanson de geste *Ami et d'Amile,* written just before or just after the year 1200, we find a different but related attitude toward disease.[16] The very title of the work suggests that the story's two heroes are somehow alike. Indeed, they are as similar as twins, and when Ami, standing in for his friend Amile, gives a promise of marriage even though he is already married, he is punished by being stricken with leprosy. The sacraments are not to be trifled with, not even with the best of intentions. Ami's physical appearance is so horrible, so repulsive, that his wife is able to convince the barons, the people, and even the bishop that a separation is warranted. The general view is that there is no way so buxom a lass can be made to lie with so decrepit a man. A sacrifice followed by a miracle saves the day, but the hero, cured of his affliction, is angry because his wife had accused him, more than once we may assume, of impotence.

The text is a realistic account of the devastating effects of leprosy. Contrary to a widely held medieval belief, the disease in this case actually diminishes the man's sexual drive, and his healthy wife triumphs by virtue of her overwhelming vitality. The disease drains the man's strength, so that he becomes his wife's impotent victim. But she is also an accomplice of lepers, who are represented as they appear in male fantasy: a sexually threatening community, the only place where the insatiable woman can find sexual gratification. The medieval attitude toward leprosy was divided. Victims of the disease were the objects of everyday acts of charity, yet in the imagination they symbolized decay. Many physicians uncritically incorporated images from folklore into their thinking. Leprosy definitely is not transmitted through sexual intercourse. Yet the idea that it was somehow reinforced feelings of fear and guilt associated with the sexual act (as syphilis did in a later period). Medieval women were seen both as the instruments of sin, hence deserving of divine punishment, and as agents in the transmission of a disease that made sin a public fact.

The medieval representation of woman's nature, diverse and contradictory as it was, was destined to enjoy a long life. The theories and vocabulary developed at this time would shape the imagination for centuries to come. The medieval concept of women's physiology, with its false but alluring notion of a female seed, would influence ethical thinkers long after science had adopted new theories. The Church in this period was rather moderate in its prohibitions and condemnations, and the bold pronouncements of certain physicians and even theologians are rather striking. They forthrightly explored issues of sexuality and reproduction, and their conception of erotic art recognized the woman's right to pleasure, provided it was in the service of procreation. Unfortunately, medieval thinking was also shaped by fear: fear of women inherent in the male psychology, fear born of insufficient understanding of disease, and fear inherited from the past and inscribed in the texts. Male fantasies enshrined in myth and accepted uncritically acquired deep roots. Some medieval ideas would prove favorable to women, but others would be used to justify the persecution of witches. Medicine, whose goal was to make humankind aware of the forces of nature, played an important part in the change that took place in the second half of the thirteenth century. But in the last two centuries of the Middle Ages, as fanatical preachers pronounced the imminent end of the world, medicine was forced on the defensive. Fear was always lurking in the wings, and ultimately it was fear that determined how medieval thinkers combined the various possibilities implicit in their view of women and the world. Subsequent centuries did not always do better.

TRANSLATED FROM THE FRENCH BY ARTHUR GOLDHAMMER

3

The Protected Woman

Carla Casagrande

WE DO NOT KNOW how many Western women in the Middle Ages lived quietly within home, church, or convent walls, obediently listening to learned, loquacious men who imposed all sorts of rules and regulations on them. The sermons of preachers, the advice of fathers, the warnings of spiritual supervisors, the prohibitions of confessors, the orders of husbands, may well have been effective, but what do they tell us about a woman's life? All we know is that women had to deal daily with these men, entrusted by society (and supported by a precise ideology) with the delicate task of controlling their bodies and souls. Part of the history of women lies, therefore, in the history of these words, spoken arrogantly, affectionately, and sometimes anxiously.

Speaking to Women

From the end of the twelfth to the end of the fifteenth century these words multiplied; secular and sacred texts by clerics and laymen testified to the urgent need to formulate new values and models of behavior for women. It is hard to define precisely what women were doing that was so strange and so different from that of their counterparts in previous centuries to produce such an outburst from the self-proclaimed moral trustees of society. It is true that their religious involvement had increased in quality and quantity. Some women participated in heretical movements; many joined recognized orders; still others chose a religious life devoted to God and to the poor outside ecclesiastical institutions. Many of them began to write about their desire for a more intense and direct relationship with God. At the same time women continued to contribute to society in various ways—at an economic, political, or family level. Many worked in the fields or participated in the production and sale of goods; some found themselves at the center of politics and power struggles; all played the role of wife, mother, or daughter. The new wave of pastoral letters and pedagogical literature set out to define these roles.

The background against which we must imagine these women was complex. A number of cities had grown up in what had once been countryside and forests. In addition to the hierarchy of feudal relations, a new network based on mercantile and monetary exchange had appeared. New forms of power and culture grew alongside the traditional models of lords and monks. Society, from the eleventh throughout the thirteenth century, never stopped changing, and this constant evolution made women's lives more complicated.

It was no coincidence that the main protagonists of the new educational program for women were mendicant friars: the official church turned to members of new religious orders in the hope that they would know how to respond to the religious and ideological mood of a changing society. These friars traveled through the cities, universities, courts, and countryside; they talked to heretics, kings, peasants, merchants, laborers, and intellectuals; they were committed to bringing the word of God back to those who had lost, challenged, or forgotten it. Franciscans and Dominicans, believing that women were an important piece in the mosaic of their ambitious pastoral project, often preached to them directly.

Among the many texts which for three centuries spoke to women about women, those composed between the end of the twelfth and the beginning of the fifteenth century were the most influential. In those years a serious attempt was made to set up a flexible ethical model suitable for women in an increasingly involved and differentiated society; a lasting pedagogical and pastoral foundation was laid.

Texts written in this crucial period became a frame of reference for later didactic and pastoral literature aimed at women. But they also harked back to the past, often a very distant past. Concerned with pointing out the path to virtue and salvation, monks, clerics, and laymen analyzed tradition, speaking to women in the words of their forefathers. Whether it was Holy Scripture or pagan works filled with ancient wisdom; exegetical, moral, theological, or hagiographic works written by the Church Fathers, or by monks and teachers from more recent times—nothing was left out of the new behavioral model for women, in the hope that authority handed down from the past would help it function in the present and continue to do so in the future.

Which Women?

Some Men, Many Women

Both men and women make history. We almost always know the man's name, his cultural background, his friendships, travels, date and place of birth. If he was in the Church, we know to what order he belonged and his role in it; if he was a layman, we can determine his social condition and cultural prestige. We deal here with intellectuals such as Alan of Lille (died 1202) and Giles of Rome (died 1316); preachers and pastors such as James of Vitry (died 1240); Dominicans such as Vincent of Beauvais (died 1264), William Peraldo (died 1261), Humbertus de Romanis (died 1277), and Jacob of Voragine (died 1298), and Franciscans such as Gilbert of Tournai (died 1284), John of Wales (died 1285), and Durandus of Champagne (died 1340?). We are also concerned with cultured laymen such as Philip of Novara (died 1261–1264) and Francesco of Barberino (died 1348); and with a saintly king, Louis IX of France (died 1270). Their words to women were privileged in being written down—in Latin by the clergy, in the vulgar tongue by laymen. They have come down through the centuries in the traditional form for normative discourse: the sermon, or the moral or pedagogical tract. Like their authors, these works can be identified and recognized one by one. We know their titles and we can trace their sources, reconstruct their contexts, follow their fortunes.

But the names and biographies on the other side of our history are for the most part unknown. In pastoral and instructional literature women appear in a series of female categories constituting the whole range of their situations. They were present in great numbers; all of them. The education of women was particularly ambitious. Preachers were not satisfied to speak to just some of them—either because they were high up on the social scale or dedicated themselves to a holy and virtuous life. The challenge was to develop a model applicable to all women, at all times.

A woman's position and function in social and religious life was studied in detail in order to arrive at a precise range of activities. The curiosity and enthusiasm with which female life was examined produced an unprecedented effort of classification: those who preached to women for moral or didactic purposes tried to elaborate a typology of the audience. To describe and classify women was by no means simple, however. Traditionally women were rarely considered an intrinsic part of society, but placed in the basic category of "woman." This category lent itself conveniently—following purely moral criteria—to comparisons of the well-worn images of Lustful Woman (subject and object of sin), and Chaste Woman (symbol of virtue and instrument of salvation). The shift from "woman" to "women" produced uncertainty and perplexity against which preachers and intellectuals struggled to find effective solutions. In this experimental phase, which lasted throughout the thirteenth century, the issue of women dominated pastoral letters and didactic pamphlets. Their authors never quite agreed on the criteria for classifying their female audience.

Classifying Women

Alan of Lille's female audience was composed of virgins, widows, and married women. The same categories, with the addition of nuns and maidens, listened to the preachers James of Vitry and Gilbert of Tournai.[1] Vincent of Beauvais and William Peraldo, in treatises on the education of young princes, addressed girls of the court who were preparing for their future as wives, widows, or consecrated virgins.[2] The Franciscan John of Wales, in his moral compendium, dealt with married women, widows, and virgins; the Dominican Jacob of Voragine, in his sermons as well as his history of Genoa, turned his attention above all to wives and mothers.[3] The lay writer Philip of Novara, in a tract on the four ages of man, proposed a set of rules for girls and young, middle-aged, and old women.[4] A king, Louis IX, addressed queens in a short collection of prescriptions for his daughter, a future ruler. Similarly, a Franciscan, Durandus of Champagne, composed a *speculum* for the wife of the king of France.[5]

Giles of Rome, his arguments rooted in Aristotelian political theory, distinguished women according to their place in the natural political community of the family; he spoke of wives, mothers, and daughters.[6] The Dominican Humbertus de Romanis thought sermons should be different for different categories of women. His manual for preachers produced an extraordinary multiplication of examples: religious women were divided into Benedictine, Cistercian, Dominican, Franciscan, Humiliatae, Augustines, Beguines, and convent-educated girls; laywomen were grouped into various classes—nobles, wealthy bourgeois, servant girls in rich families, poor women in small country villages, and prostitutes.[7]

An explosion of female categories came about with the jurist Francesco of Barberino. Starting with young girls and adolescents ready to marry, he went on to discuss married women, those who had passed the age for marriage, and those who married late in life. Each of these categories was further subdivided depending on whether the woman came from an aristocratic, imperial, or royal family, or whether she was the daughter of a knight, judge, doctor, merchant, artisan, peasant, or laborer. Not satisfied, he then addressed widows, women who led a religious life at home, nuns, solitary recluses, ladies-in-waiting, maidservants, and wet nurses, concluding with a list of more humble women—barbers, bakers, grocers, weavers, millers, chicken dealers, beggars, hawkers, and hostel-keepers. Prostitutes, Francesco of Barberino specified, "I do not intend to write about, nor even mention, since they are not worthy of note."[8]

This last remark is important because his classification of women, by far the richest and most complete, is probably the closest description we have of the real social situation. Francesco of Barberino, however, did not set out to write a neutral description; there were some women he refused to discuss. His *Reggimento e costumi di donna,* and even more so the other texts listed, presented a much-debated compromise between what a woman actually was and what she ought to be. The preacher, the moralist, and the teacher selected from reality, and even constructed from reality, those categories of women which embodied, or had the potential to embody, the values he was proposing. Only women belonging to predetermined categories had the potential to be virtuous; the others were doubly doomed to social marginalization and a sinful life. In short, women were the subjects of a sociology that was for the most part ideology; of a description that nearly always served a moral purpose; of a classification that was already a model.

Young Women and Old Women

The criteria of classification are a significant clue to the value-systems and models of behavior for women. There were many different criteria in the texts, and often an author applied more than one to his classification. The simplest, and apparently the most neutral (it applied to both men and women), is that of age. Preachers divided the female universe into young girls and old women.

Old women, often included in the category of widows, occupied an important position. If they were wise and virtuous, they could be models to be imitated and could teach and correct younger women. Many older women, however, led sinful lives. They talked too much; they attempted to disguise their aging bodies with fancy clothing and ornaments; they sought pleasures of the flesh no longer suitable for their age. Sermons and treatises often ridiculed them, combining classical images of the interfering procuress wiling her way into people's houses, of the go-between bearing lovers' messages, and of the old sorceress cheating simple women with her magic and witchcraft. According to preachers and moralists, these old crones were particularly skilled in leading other women into sin. William Peraldo wrote with great concern that, "where neither man nor the devil succeed in working their vice, the old woman will."[9] And yet, in contrast to these pernicious women—whom James of Vitry did not hesitate to define as "ministers of the devil," and against whom Peraldo claimed the devil should send infernal tongues of fire in a blasphemous parody of Pentecost[10]—sermons and moral tracts continued to call up images of the sober and modest old woman who cared for her family and indulged in intense devotions, prayers, and fasts.

For the first time young girls became the object of specific indoctrination. Noble girls were addressed by Vincent of Beauvais and Peraldo, while Humbertus prepared two sermons, one for schoolgirls and one for convent-girls. Francesco of Barberino and Philip of Novara dedicated chapters specifically to young girls;

Giles of Rome spoke to burghers' young daughters. This group represented a sensitive and important challenge. Girls were the testing ground for values and models to be proposed to other women. They were considered difficult to teach, however, because of their natural lack of discipline and undeveloped moral sensibility. Francesco of Barberino spoke to girls who were just beginning, after their first unanticipated blush, to be able to distinguish between good and evil.[11] Giles of Rome suggested that young girls needed stricter discipline than their older counterparts because, as Aristotle had pointed out, of the lack of rationality associated with their femininity, compounded by their youth.[12]

Throughout what might be called their adolescence (there is almost no information available about their childhood), girls were never just "young girls." They were also either rich, poor, or noble; from secular or religious families. Even Philip of Novara, who adopted the criterion of age as his primary distinction, was obliged to resort to more detailed categories when discussing subjects such as work and literacy, adapting his approach for girls destined for marriage or the convent, of noble or humble origin.[13]

Social Levels and Family Roles

The criterion of age alone was not adequate to define a woman. Other factors, such as the position she occupied, or was destined to occupy, in society also had to be taken into account. The Dominican Humbertus de Romanis, and the layman Francesco of Barberino, were the first to tread this path. In their works women were grouped according to the organization of society as a whole, that is, according to ecclesiastical institution, power, wealth, lineage, occupation. Apparently the feminine society described by the French Dominican differed from that described by the Florentine jurist. Humbertus categorized religious women according to the order to which they belonged and stressed the institutional (or semi-institutional in the case of the Beguines) nature of women's religiosity. Francesco diffidently addressed the question of religious activity in the home and that of the solitary recluse and spoke of nuns and their unworldly community life in general terms. The princesses, noblewomen, wives and daughters of professionals, merchants, artisans, peasants, and female laborers in the secular society depicted by Francesco lived under a wider range of conditions than the noble and bourgeois women, house-servants, countrywomen, and prostitutes considered by Humbertus.

For both writers, however complex a society they portrayed, the female half was identified according to a value-system and a hierarchy set up by the male half. There were, on the one hand, religious women playing roles defined by their ecclesiastical affiliation, and, on the other, laywomen who were part of society as wives, daughters, or mothers of men who were either influential or subject to the influence of others, who fought or labored, owned property and enjoyed wealth or were poor. The relation of laywomen to society was mediated by the family; their social criteria were based primarily on their roles in the family. Francesco of Barberino's categories divided women according to their role as daughter, future wife, present wife, or widow. Similarly, Humbertus, when he addressed noble, bourgeois, or poor women, was really speaking to wives of noblemen, burghers, or peasants. His prescriptions concerned relations with the husband and the rest of the family.

Not even a woman's work altered this almost total identification between social level and a woman's family role. Humbertus, like the other preachers, distinguished domestic servants from the rest, but their work was done within the private realm of the family of which they were a part. The only female workers recognized as independent of the family were of course prostitutes. Humbertus assigns them a separate place, but recommends that they follow the comforting example of Mary Magdalene, abandon their shameful activity, and dedicate themselves to a new, penitent life.[14]

For the Dominican Humbertus, women who worked outside the house either did not exist or were, by definition, sinful. The lay Francesco of Barberino, by contrast, provides many examples of working women, though their work did little to enhance their status. Relegated to one of the last chapters of his *Reggimento* so as not to dishonor all the noble and important women to whom the rest of the work is dedicated,[15] they are listed "con brevitate" only to note their most common faults. "It's not my task to talk about their virtues," wrote Francesco, "may those who do good live well, / for on their great habits / this book does not care to dwell." He would have preferred not to discuss these chicken-vendors, barbers, and weavers; everything he felt he needed to say had already been said to the wives and daughters of more or less important men. Almost as an afterthought, it was decided to "make the book more universal"[16]—an ambiguous, and certainly reluctant, recognition that the condition of women was much more involved and varied than the classifications of preachers and moralists acknowledged.

Giles of Rome, who always worked at a theoretical level in attempting to define general principles, had no need to compromise with reality. A woman's social position, as far as he was concerned, could be defined only within that primary, natural, and necessary political community—the family. He made no references to women who entered monasteries or to those who engaged in strange or humble activities outside the realm of the family. Women were exclusively wives, mothers, or daughters; their function was exclusively to produce and rear children; their work exclusively domestic. Preachers found confirmation of what they were saying in the clear, unequivocal language of Aristotelian politics, which also provided the foundation of their moral vision: in order to be a part of society, women had to be part of a family—forever.

Queens, Princesses, and Ladies

Some families were more important than others. Accordingly, some wives, mothers, and daughters were more important, and attracted more attention, than others. Queens, princesses, court ladies, and aristocrats often were the main interlocuters of the pastoral and pedagogical works examined here. Some of them even emerged from the anonymity in which most women were held. Humberto de Romanis wrote a sermon for noblewomen; Francesco of Barberino dedicated many pages of his treatise to the daughters of emperors, kings, marquises, counts, and barons; Vincent of Beauvais and William Peraldo dealt with the education of noble girls; King Louis IX gave lessons to his daughter Isabel, Queen of Navarre; Durandus of Champagne did the same in his *Speculum dominarum,* dedicated to Joan of Navarre, wife of Philip the Fair.

This did not mean that the personal lives of Joan or Isabel were of any particular interest to the authors; nor did it mean that the model of behavior proposed was suited only to the aristocracy. On the contrary, the more universally effective the values and models proposed, the more noblewomen were called up as examples. In the view of preachers and moralists, queens, princesses, and ladies could become concrete, living models for all women precisely because of their God-given superior social status, which obliged them, Humberto de Romanis wrote, to observe moral rules all the more strictly.[17]

At the center of everyone's attention, Louis IX's queen-daughter was told to "be perfect in every way, so that whoever hears about you or sees you can follow your example."[18] In Durandus of Champagne's account, a queen was an object of curiosity for the whole country. Since people came from all corners of the nation to set eyes on her, she was no longer simply "a woman, but an example of holiness, an embodiment of good manners, a mirror of honesty."[19] Francesco of Barberino thought that queens and princesses, obliged by their social status to adopt "noble habits,"[20] were a perfect model for noble, middle-class, and peasant women to emulate, each in proportion to her own inferiority. As one went down the social scale, rules could be restricted, discipline slackened, and values eroded, but all women were urged to look up to the woman with perfect habits that only a queen could fully personify.

Virgins, Widows, and Married Women

Three categories of women attracted like magnets this numerous female audience of girls, mothers, old women, queens, peasants, abbesses, novices, maidservants, ladies, and so on, redistributing them into three groups. These ancient categories, consistently found in the works of wise and holy men, starting with the Church Fathers, are virgins, widows, and married women.

When Alan of Lille, James of Vitry, Vincent of Beauvais, William Peraldo, Gilbert of Tournai, and John of Wales decided to address women, the models they considered (as had many others before them) were women who used their sexuality in different ways. Some, virgins, gave it up forever as a voluntary and conscious act of renunciation; others, widows, were able to give it up when a fortuitous event deprived them of a husband; still others, married women, limited themselves to frugal sex within and for the good of the family.

All these women were chaste; the thirteenth-century classification of virtues in theological and pastoral works did not hesitate to define them as virtuous. They knew how to use that form of temperance known as chastity, or continence, that created order out of the perilous chaos of sexual pleasure. Considered the only remedy for the lust to which the whole of humanity was condemned after the Original Sin, chastity was often recommended for men and women, but more often for women. When theological and pastoral texts dealt with chastity, it was nearly always exemplified by the three forms of chastity practiced by virgins, widows, and married women. It was as if once the victory of chastity over concupiscence was guaranteed by women—naturally more lustful and less able to restrain their physical desires—it would be easier for everyone else. In short, women were the theoretical and practical testing ground on which the whole of society created and experienced a particular concept of sexuality.

The chastity of virgins, widows, and married women placed sexuality in a gray area between denial and control in order to procreate. Both extremes show how spiritual and rational considerations were supposed to vanquish corporeal and sensual ones. Like all virtues, chastity—a virtue of the body, but above all of the soul—was highly demanding. Repression and exterior discipline were not enough; intention, rationality, and assent also were required. "Chastity," wrote Thomas Aquinas, "finds its home in the soul, though its nature lies in the body."[21] A woman was considered a virgin not only through the integrity of her body but also because of the purity of her thoughts, which were unsullied by lust, thanks to the difficult choice she had made and maintained. If she were violated without her consent and without experiencing pleasure, she would still be a virgin. Similarly, a widow was virtuous not only because of a chance event that freed her of sexual obligations but also because she could free her mind of carnal desire. A married woman was virtuous in her marriage as long as her intentions were pure, chaste, and geared toward paying her conjugal debt and procreating.

Although this insistence on the spiritual and intentional nature of chastity allowed women who had once surrendered the integrity of their bodies (widows), or who continued to do so (wives), to be defined as chaste and therefore virtuous, the purity of their intentions could not be considered equal to that of a virgin who could still, except in exceptional circumstances, count on an uncontaminated body. A body's integrity was less important when defining chastity as a virtue than it was when it came to establishing a hierarchy of the forms charity could take. The spiritual chastity of virgins, widows, and wives was different because the chasteness of their bodies varied. An uncontaminated body allowed virgins to embrace a spiritual life wholeheartedly. This was more difficult for widows and married women whose tainted bodies inevitably dragged the spirit back down to earth.

Virgins, widows, and married women represented not only three possible kinds of chastity but also three rungs on the ladder of its perfection. The virginal state is the highest and safest step, the married state the lowest and most dangerous. Widowhood is halfway, dragged downward by the gravity of past contamination yet, at the same time, attracted upward by the possibility of future purity. Just as "some seeds . . . fell into good ground, and brought forth fruit, some an hundredfold, some sixtyfold, some thirtyfold" (Matt. 13:8), so a virgin's chastity was worth more than double a widow's and more than triple a wife's.

A Spiritual Path and Sociology

The virgins, widows, and wives addressed by preachers and moralists were both very similar and very dissimilar. United by the fact that their life was determined by sexuality (actually by a denial of sexuality), they were separated by the different degrees to which that denial was put into practice. Common values and shared ideals produced virtuous behavior by all: the three groups agreed on the necessity for prayer, on the evils of ornamentation, and on the advantages of controlled gestures, words, and diet. Virgins reached such high levels of perfection and excellence, however, that they became necessary but unattainable models for widows and married women.

On the moral scale based on chastity, virgins were the equivalent of queens on the social scale. Both represented unattainable superiority. (Widows and married women could no more regain their once virginal bodies than middle-class or peasant women could upturn the social hierarchy ordered by men and ratified by God.) At the same time, both figures perfectly embodied the moral values all women were urged to pursue within the limits of their condition.

With the threefold division of women into virgins, widows, and wives, preachers and moralists were able to speak to "women" without abandoning the essential "woman." A woman's virtue and saving grace was her chastity; women embodied the three possible levels of its perfection. This tripartition on the basis of chastity was more than a criterion for classifying the female population; it indicated a spiritual path for women that led either to immediate attainment of the highest level or to an approximation of perfection at an intermediate level.

The advantage of this division of the female universe was that the three stages of perfection could be made to correspond to real situations in the real world. It was possible to fuse moral judgments harmoniously with real-life values, to blend ideal figures of women with the variety of their true conditions, to close the gap between what women were and what they should be. Thus an idealized figure of a married woman became a model of behavior for women who played the roles of mothers or wives within the family. Similarly, a virtuous image of a widow responded to the needs of a clearly defined, potentially destabilizing social group of unprotected, often old, single women. The figure of a virgin was suspended ambiguously between the ideal and the real. At times, she was represented as a nun, at others, as a young girl. Often, though, she was so sublimely perfect that she could only exist on an ideal level—represented, not surprisingly, by the Virgin Mary. Alan of Lille, James of Vitry, and Gilbert of Tournai's sermons for virgins, and Vincent of Beauvais and Peraldo's descriptions of the virginal state were, more often than not, eulogies on virginity aimed at demonstrating the superiority of the religious condition. But they were also an example of virtuous perfection to be proposed to young girls and women in general.

Pastoral letters and educational works addressed to women were able to apply an eminently moral system of classification to many of the personal, social, and institutional conditions experienced by women. The classification was severely rigid insofar as the values and models proposed were concerned; at the same time it was flexible enough to adapt itself to the variegated, constantly mobile world of its subjects and to lend itself to other kinds of classification when needed.

A Successful Mold

Virgins, widows, and married women were the main interlocutors for preachers and moralists from the end of the twelfth century to the beginning of the fourteenth. At times they were treated alongside other female categories; at others, they were subsumed under or included other groups; often they stood alone. The astonishing success of the threefold division lasted for centuries. Nearly all the sermons and moral tracts addressed to women, which proliferated in the centuries that followed, classified women on the basis of the spiritual criterion of chastity, leaving social categories apart or ignoring them altogether. Work, power, wealth, culture, residence, social or geographic origins, were not considered important criteria—if they were considered at all—for comprehending the world of women. Christine de Pisan was the only one to underscore the burden on women's lives of the hierarchical organization of a society of men. But she had personally experienced the advantages of a wealthy existence, the uncertainty and hardship of poverty, and the toils of labor outside the home. While *La cité des dames* (*The City of Ladies,* 1404–1405) ended with an appeal to the traditional triad of wives, virgins, and widows, the *Livre des trois vertus* (Book of Three Virtues, 1405) spoke to women of all social levels: women who lived with kings, noblemen, merchants, artisans, and laborers; who worked inside or outside the home, were educated or illiterate, humble or powerful, rich or poor.[22]

Throughout the fourteenth and fifteenth centuries the vast majority of pedagogical and pastoral literature for women—nearly all written in the vernacular, even by churchmen—continued to address wives, widows, virgins, young girls, and nuns. The author of *Ménagier de Paris* (1393) was a husband speaking to his young wife; wives and mothers were addressed in the Dominican Giovanni Dominici's *Regola del governo di cura famigliare* (1403); Chevalier de La Tour Landry wrote for his young daughters (1371), while the Augustinian Simone Fidati (died 1348) addressed his spiritual pupil, a virgin.[23] Similarly, the voluminous *Libre de les dones* (1388), by the Franciscan Francisco Ximenes, reviewed the conditions of young girls, adolescent girls, married women, widows, and nuns.[24] Another Augustinian, Jerome of Siena (died 1420), also dealt with virgins, widows, and married women in his *Soccorso dei poveri.*[25] In the repertory of sermons of Bernardino of Siena (died 1444) many homilies were addressed to married women, widows, and virgins.[26] Antonino of Florence (died 1459) dedicated *L'Opera a ben vivere* to a married woman and the *Regola di vita cristiana* to a widow.[27] Similarly, married women and adolescent girls were addressed in two of the tracts of Giovanni Certosino (died 1483), the *Decor puellarum* and *Gloria mulierum.*[28] Dionysius the Carthusian (died 1471) wrote three separate treatises for virgins, widows, and married women.[29]

Women were first and foremost bodies to be committed either to the Church or the family: uncontaminated virgins totally dedicated to a spiritual life; fertile matrons ready to guarantee family continuity; or widows ready to embrace the spirit and forget the flesh. It was to this apparently well-ordered and reassuring public, which seemed stationary and indifferent to historical transformations, that sermons, suggestions, instructions, and warnings were directed by preachers, clerics, monks, husbands, and fathers.

Women's Virtues and Vices

Wanderers

One day a girl named Dinah stepped out of her house to see the "daughters of the land" in the foreign country to which her family had brought her. She was curious, she wanted to see everything, find out, learn. But she was immediately seen: the king's son fell in love with her, "lay with her, and defiled her." He wanted to marry her, but Dinah's family would not forgive the insult. Her brothers took arms, sacked the town and slayed all its men, including the king and his rash son.

Dinah, the daughter of Jacob and Leah, was a biblical character. Her story, told in Genesis, chapter 34, harks back to faraway times and places. Yet Dinah became a familiar figure for western women in the Middle Ages, present in their everyday life; a young, unwary, unlucky friend one had better not be friendly with and certainly not imitate. Her presence was almost obligatory in sermons and moral tracts for women to remind them how dangerous it was to leave the home or the convent. In the streets and squares or on the way to church a woman might be seen and might, preachers warned, arouse men's ill-advised lust, especially if they were young men. Violence, treachery, and adultery provoking disorder and discord in the family and community were the inevitable consequences. A woman who wandered away from the home was dangerous for others—"loud and stubborn; her feet abide not in her house: Now she is without, now in the streets, and lieth in wait at every corner," was a frequently quoted biblical verse (Prov. 7:11–12)—but she was above all a danger to herself. She risked compromising or sacrificing altogether the very chastity that fathers, husbands, and spiritual tutors agreed was her supreme virtue. Giles of Rome declared that a girl used to walking about and engaging in social relations could no longer count on her natural modesty to protect her chastity from men. Once she lost her shyness and social embarrassment, she was no better than "one of those wild animals which grow accustomed to the company of men and become tame, letting themselves be petted and stroked."[30]

Going out of the house was dangerous, whether it was to stroll in the streets, dance at a party, have fun at theatrical events, attend mass in the church, or listen to the word of God in a sermon on the square. In the last two cases the dangers of *vagatio* could well be mitigated and compensated for by the spiritual advantages of these religious practices; nevertheless, the game of glances to which a woman was inevitably subjected during religious ceremonies was a risk, since the brashness of lust could be combined with the foolhardiness of sacrilege. Thus, women who wandered out of the house were not only guilty of restlessness and indecency, they were also considered, as Peraldo put it, "arsonists of sacred places."[31]

Women who went out to participate in activities such as parties, dances, meetings, or performances in which whole families or social communities participated, were even more worrisome. Women flaunted themselves on such occasions, flashing the wealth, prestige, and honor of their families. All that was necessary was a furtive glance or an uncontrolled gesture, and that wealth, prestige, and honor were seriously jeopardized. A party by definition favored encounters and released hidden desires: the circular movement of the dances made even pallid, uninteresting women appear flushed and febrile;[32] lascivious songs seduced the heart and inflamed the senses. Of all women who unwarily set forth into the world, those who frequented parties and public affairs were by far the most imprudent and inconsiderate.

In an attempt to allow women to continue playing their role as family representative, lay writers such as Philip of Novara and Francesco of Barberino went to great lengths to indicate acceptably modest, composed behavior in public: women were not to enjoy themselves too much, but affect superiority, eat little, dance with composure, and move measuredly.[33] Preachers were more severe, condemning all parties, dances, and shows, considered the perilous result of women's roving. The most disturbing image was conjured up by James of Vitry when he compared women's songs and dances to diabolical rituals mimicking religious ceremonies: "the woman who leads the chorus is the chaplain of the devil; those who respond are her priests."[34]

Women did not have to wander very far, nor join particularly suspicious gatherings, to commit a sin; it was enough to go to the door or window. Standing in the doorway or leaning out of the window was "going out"—a limited, but still dangerous, attempt to establish a rapport with the outside world and to abandon oneself to the desire to go out and join the world of men. In pastoral and pedagogical literature for women, the window was a recurring image, a backdrop against which maliciously curious, unwary women moved. Francesco of Barberino ridiculed women who sewed at the window: "those who sit at the window to sew, often end up sewing their hands instead of their clothes."[35] Conrad of Megenberg (died 1374), author of an Aristotelian treatise on home economics, described how girls in the silence of the night hung girdles out of their windows and waited for their lovers to pin letters or gifts onto them, or dropped a thread to the ground so lovers could determine the height of their bedroom windows and construct rope ladders to reach them.[36]

Restless and Curious

Behind these vigils at the window, at the root of this criticized desire to leave the house and experience the world, there was a kind of intellectual and moral restlessness in women that deeply disturbed preachers and moralists. Their constant unquietness, insatiable curiosity, and profound instability of temperament and affection led them always to seek something new, to want to know the strangest things, to change their minds continually, to desire what they could not have, and to allow themselves to be influenced by impulse and passion. Durandus of Champagne thought there was a connection between Eve's audacious curiosity in seeking to know more about good and evil, Dinah's desire to see wonderful, hidden things outside the home, and the frivolous desire of those women who sought more refined and precious clothes and jewels.[37]

The only reassuringly stable element in this vortex of feminine instability was its paradoxical permanence: nothing seems to have been more constant than the reckless restlessness and inconstancy of women. A long-standing tradition, often a commonplace, survived the transformations of centuries to be incorporated into pastoral and pedagogical literature: the obsessively uniform image of women as restless, capricious, and inconstant as "melted wax, which is ever ready to change its shape according to the seal pressed into it,"[38] or "instable and mobile as a leaf on a tree shaken by the wind."[39]

About the middle of the thirteenth century preachers and moralists received "scientific" comfort from philosophers who found in Aristotle's texts systematic treatment and authoritative confirmation of themes that had circulated throughout the Middle Ages. In these Aristotelian commentaries women were defined as imperfect men, men with something missing. Endowed with a form well suited to the weakness and imperfection of their sentimental nature, lacking the rationality needed to govern their passions, women were considered fragile, malleable, irrational, and emotional. Their bodies, contrasted to male bodies by an excess of humidity, meant they were able to receive but not to conserve. Damp, limp, and yielding, women wandered around searching for novelty because they were incapable of holding opinions and standing their ground. If women's instability and restlessness was despised by religious writers, for an Aristotelian philosopher such as Giles of Rome it was the scientifically proven consequence of a rigorously pursued syllogism: "The soul matches the constitution of the body; women's bodies are limp and unstable, and so women are unstable and unsteady in desire and will."[40]

Custody

Wayward in body and restless in spirit, women had to be in somebody's custody. Obsessively repeated in titles, headings, and conclusions of treatises and sermons, "custody" became a key word in the entire corpus of pastoral and pedagogical literature for women. "Custody" stood for everything that could and should be done to educate women in good manners and save their souls. It meant, on the one hand, to repress, watch over, and shut in; on the other, to protect, preserve, and care for. A woman in custody was loved and protected like a jewel of inestimable value, hidden like a fragile and precious treasure, guarded as a source of imminent danger, imprisoned as a well of inevitable evil. This complex series of operations, ranging from the strictest repression to the most loving care, had to be begun in her earliest infancy and continued—whether she was sworn to the Church or not—throughout the various phases of her life.

Many texts in pastoral and pedagogical literature spoke directly to women, considering them their own best guardians. Women were created by God; through the Virgin Mary they took part in the mystery of the Incarnation; they contributed numerous holy and pious women to the spiritual development of Christianity. They possessed a soul capable of relating to divinity; they had the capacity to save and be saved, practice virtue and shun vice, and become examples of moral perfection. They were therefore perfectly able to be their own custodians. Moreover, women were gifted with instinctive fear and shyness, congenital bashfulness or coyness, which made them naturally timid and antisocial and helped them stay clear of evil and corruption. Whether this coyness was God's gift after Original Sin to help women defend themselves against the turpitude of the flesh, or whether it was a consequence of women's natural imperfection, what mattered was that coyness was a providential instrument women could use to protect themselves.

Preachers and moralists insisted that women should practice the reserve that so often paralyzed them, continue to be bashful and insecure in social relations, shy away from encountering any man, blush, and behave like untamed animals. Modesty was a form of custody because it kept women apart from the community, relegated them to enclosed, protected areas such as the home or convent, preserved their chastity, and kept them on an instinctive, animal level. Even a highlight in a woman's social life—her wedding—when the whole community witnessed her passage from one family group to another, the ideal woman depicted by Francesco of Barberino (who even as a girl was always shy and reserved when she went out in public) was advised to reassert her social insecurity during the ceremony. Embarrassed, fearful, and immobile, she should not hold out her hand but wait until it was almost taken from her forcefully. Once installed in her new home, she should be timid with everyone, speaking only if spoken to, and even then, "briefly, in a low tone, fearful," revealing herself to her husband as "an untamed novice . . . in the work of love."[41]

Though potentially capable of being their own custodians, women never succeeded in completely assuming their own custody. The spiritual dignity of their souls, created by God and saved by Christ, made them capable of virtue, but they still bore the stain of sin thanks to generations of women before them, starting with Eve herself. Women could receive the word of God only through the mediation of the most masculine of institutions, depositary of the word of God: the Church. This ambiguous position in the order of salvation was no less problematic than the constant recourse to women's nature that supposedly protected them from evil. Women's coy, reserved instincts resulted from the very same nature that made them excessive, restless, and vagrant. Thus women were judged by an ambiguous process that swung constantly between two extremes: they were at once saved by a timid, animal nature that made them recoil from evil, and condemned for behaving as impulsively and irrationally as an animal.

Submissive Custody

So women cannot be their own guardians. The *infermitas* of their condition, which makes them weak and inconstant, requires them to accept other forms of custody, aside from their own coyness. Jacob of Voragine—like Saint Augustine nine hundred years earlier—confidently listed these forms of custody in order: submission to men, terror of the law, fear of God.[42] Men (fathers, husbands, brothers, preachers, spiritual tutors) shared with God and with the law of the land the difficult but necessary task of guarding women. Fortunately, thanks to their nature, wisely molded by providential divine intervention, women were accustomed to being subject to the authority of their mates and were therefore ready, if not willing, to submit themselves to the custody of men.

Aristotle's commentators found in the *Ethica,* and even more in the *Politica,* examples of women naturally acquiescent to men who naturally took command and made decisions, confident of the superiority of their bodies and minds. Both men and women, according to Aristotle's scheme, were potentially virtuous, but they expressed their virtues in different ways, according to the role they played in the political organism. Men were virtuous when they exerted their power efficiently and successfully; women revealed their virtue when they executed orders efficiently and correctly.

Biblical commentators, often the same men who read and commented on Aristotelian texts, recognized the natural submissiveness of women in a line of Saint Paul: "But I would have you know, that the head of every man is Christ; and the head of the woman is the man; and the head of Christ is God" (1 Cor. 11:3). Women's submission to men was thus part of the hierarchy that ruled relations between God, Christ, and the rest of humanity whose origins and divine foundation lie in the creation of Adam and Eve and their adventures after the Fall. The biblical story provided commentators with the firm belief that women were created inferior to men. The male body, created first, was considered superior to the female's, created subsequently from the male body; woman was God's gift to man, a providential instrument to help him reproduce.

In contrast to this interpretation, which reduced the difference between the sexes to a question of superiority and inferiority, subordination and supremacy, there is the revolutionary force of the evangelical principle that all human beings are equal in God's eyes. The idea that a woman could have been endowed by God with a soul equal in nature and dignity to that of her male counterpart recurred in different forms throughout medieval thought. In the Augustinian tradition (founded on a clear dualism between body and soul) a woman's soul was considered equal in every way to a man's. Thomas Aquinas (who embraced the Aristotelian definition of the soul as a form of the body) considered them equal only in part, in essence but not in reality.[43] In any case, the problem of the equality of male and female souls, whether directly or only halfheartedly advocated, was a purely spiritual matter; the natural superiority of the male body chosen by God at the Creation was never questioned. Women were potentially able to enjoy an intensely satisfying spiritual life, as much as or at times even more than men, but their bodies were different and inferior and therefore necessarily subordinate to men. Moreover, this subordination, to which Eve willingly submitted as a peaceful fulfillment of her nature before Original Sin, was transformed after the Fall into a truly servile relationship women had to suffer in silence as a punishment for Eve's sin. "Thy desire shall be to thy husband, and he shall rule over thee" (Gen. 3:16): the divine curse that accompanied Eve as she fell from Paradise on Earth was echoed in the life of every woman to follow, condemning her irrevocably to the domination of men.

Men were justified in keeping women in custody, whether they were obeying a law of nature or an imperious divine command. Women were required to appreciate this custody by practicing the whole range of submissive virtues (humility, gentleness, obedience) propagated through sermons and prescriptive treatises. The adventurous alternative of independence—experienced, for example, by Mary Magdalene who, according to Jacob of Voragine, was sinful and exerted a bad influence over other women because she was free and her own mistress *(sui domina et libera)*[44]—was eyed with disapproval and suspicion.

Widows, especially young widows, were most exposed to the dangers of freedom because they were no longer under their parents' protection and were free of their late husbands' custody. Hostility toward second marriages, a topos of didactic and juridical literature, whose foundations were the spiritual superiority of the state of widowhood over that of matrimony, as well as fear that a new family would jeopardize the patrimonial rights of children born of the first marriage, underscored a widow's freedom and the peril she was in. It was no chance that widows—more than any other group of women—were obliged to observe strict religious practices, ranging from fasts and prayer to acts of charity. When the custody of husbands or fathers was missing, spiritual tutors were called in: Christ himself claimed the newly liberated woman, body and soul.

Outside and Inside

The complex anatomy of custody, though developed in different periods, in different places, and by different men, offers a few central, seemingly connected, themes. Whatever recommendations were made to women—to be temperate in eating, controlled in gesture, soft-spoken, abjure ornamentation and makeup, restrict their movements, and keep their contact with the outside world to a minimum—the intent was to diminish the exterior aspect of their lives and strengthen the interior. A woman was encouraged to detach herself from public life in the community and remain within the private realm of home or convent. Corollary to this was the recommendation that she detach herself from the external aspects of her body and concentrate on the internal aspects of her spirit. A woman vowed to a convent followed this advice to its logical conclusion: her detachment from the outside world was as final as relinquishing her property or renouncing the pleasures of the flesh. For a woman who stayed at home, it was a matter of making a series of compromises in order to reconcile her way of life—inextricably linked to the "external" needs of society and of her body—with the ideal of domestic seclusion and spiritual supremacy over the body. One form of custody or another presided over each of these delicate passages between inside and outside. In a nun's case it was to annul any relation between the convent and the outside world and to make sure that the needs of the body were denied in favor of those of the spirit. In a laywoman's it was to reduce and regulate the inevitable contact between domestic and social worlds and to restrain the disordered impulses of the flesh through the rules of chastity.

Educational and pastoral literature used all its cultural authority and rhetorical force to underscore the good of custody. Holy Scripture was combed to find worthy examples of women who voluntarily detached themselves from the outside world, inflicting upon their bodies the strictest disciplinary regimes. There was Judith who took refuge in a safe corner of the house to fast; the old prophetess Anna who never left the temple where she prayed and fasted day and night; and above all, the Virgin Mary who sat in silence awaiting the Annunciation. Alongside these models, women were given instruction and advice, often taken from the ancient and authoritative texts of monks or Church Fathers. Women who were wise enough to listen and put these precepts into practice gradually learned to immunize themselves against flattery and desire and slowly succumbed to the quiet rhythm of withdrawal within the four walls of home or convent.

Clothes, Jewelry, Cosmetics

Precepts and advice concerning clothing, jewelry, and cosmetics were countless. The controversy about overdressed and artificially made-up women—an age-old question the Church Fathers had already addressed—filled pedagogical and pastoral literature from the end of the twelfth to the end of the fifteenth century, gaining breadth and intensity throughout the period. The outraged insistence and minute attention with which this theme was treated resulted from the fact that clothes and makeup were a way for women to externalize their bodies in society that went against the path indicated by the rules of custody. A sumptuously dressed and ornamented woman subverted God's will by privileging the cheap exterior of her body over and above her precious inner spirit. The enjoyment of an item of clothing, a color, or a hairstyle betrayed too much interest in external features and too little for the loving cultivation of her virtue. Cosmetics above all revealed boundless conceit. A woman who painted her cheeks red, dyed her hair, or attempted to conceal her age with wigs and unguents was considered no better than Lucifer. To contest the looks endowed by God—worse, to try to improve them—was sheer pride, an unforgivable attempt to defy the God-given laws of the world.

Love of clothes and ornamentation revealed not only an idolatrous consideration of the body but also an irrepressible desire to put that body on show for others. In an emblematic scene portrayed by James of Vitry, later reworked by Gilbert of Tournai, a virgin looked in the mirror, set her expression, rehearsed her public appearance: "she smiles to see if this makes her more beautiful . . . She lowers her eyes; is she more pleasing with her eyes wide open? She pulls her dress to one side to reveal bare skin, loosens her sash to reveal her cleavage. Her body is still home, but in God's eyes she is already in a brothel, trussed up like a whore preparing to ensnare the souls of men."[45]

Women dressed elaborately to go out, then. They wore jewelry and makeup to appear in public and be admired, desired, envied. Women used the language of their artificially adorned bodies in order to interact with society. But this language more often than not challenged established social regulations, creating chaos and corruption at the heart of the community. Countless examples were given: women who dressed gaudily, with showy ornaments in order to appear richer and nobler than they actually were; others who would rather drag their families into financial ruin than do without their vain trinkets; still others who with their painted faces kindled lust in men's loins, lost their virginity, wrought domestic havoc, and provoked family feuds. There were those, moreover, who "made up and adorned others, or taught them to do it themselves, seeking out and imitating all sorts of frivolities, usually between sisters, cousins, friends, neighbors, and other women."[46] Thus a woman's natural propensity for ornamentation produced a perverse and unpredictable female solidarity that went beyond the confines of home and family, laying the foundation within the community for a society of women whose bonds were envy, emulation, complicity, and exchange.

The damage brought about by a woman's overzealous attention to her body had to be kept to a minimum by assiduous control and repression. The undertaking was not simple. As Giles of Rome pointed out, women naturally inclined toward appearances because they were known to be lamentably lacking in substance.

Their traditional irrationality and insecurity led them to prefer the imperfect, transient benefits of external appearance, being incapable of aiming on their own for the perfect, eternal gifts of virtue.[47] Only a drastic reduction in women's attention to and exhibition of their bodies, which was demonstrated by the immoderate use of clothing and jewelry, can end a ruinous process for women and society as a whole.

For a woman pledged to the Church the solution was simple and final: seclusion in a cloister and the imposition of a nun's habit repressed the urge to appear at its very source. To compensate she could anoint herself with the unguent of temperance; color her face with good reputation; decorate herself with a necklace of doctrine, earrings of obedience, a ring of faith; she could wear the linen of chastity and gird herself with the sash of discipline. Some of the sermons of James of Vitry and Gilbert of Tournai offered the woman who gave up worldly clothes, decorations, and jewels a vast wardrobe of symbolic ornaments that promised to make her more beautiful and more adorned than any woman ever was.[48]

For a laywoman, however, the question was more complex. Alongside the more rigid points of view on vanity and the dangers of ornamentation, others were expressed that permitted laywomen more leeway in the care and display of their bodies. Francesco of Barberino recommended that when they went out, women, noblewomen especially, should dress suitably for the power and wealth of the family they represented.[49] Giles of Rome, and many other writers inspired by Aristotle, objected to makeup but did not criticize women who attempted to improve their appearance either to please their husbands or to emphasize their social condition.[50] Everything had to be in moderation, however, and without scandal. If not, that cherished and idolized body might be corrupted, losing not only the chastity that made it precious but also the well-being that made it efficient. Gilbert of Tournai referred to several doctors who believed that women's frequent headaches resulted from immoderate use of hair lotions.[51]

Just as a nun detached herself from her body to commit it to monastic seclusion and discipline, so a laywoman, though she dressed and made up with care, was no longer mistress of her own body. Her body belonged to her family, for whom it was displayed as a status symbol, and above all to her husband, for whom it had to remain inviolate, attractive, and healthy.

Modest and Sober

The essence of another set of restrictions regarding women's gestural communication sought to repress extravagant or theatrical body language. A particular brand of moderation was called for to regulate corporeal expression: modesty. A series of rules, mostly from the monastic tradition, recommended that a woman's gestures should be neither agitated nor lively; her ultimate aim should be expressionless immobility. She should not laugh, but smile without showing her teeth; she should not look straight ahead, wide-eyed, but look down, with eyelids half-closed; she should not sob, wring her hands, or shake her head, but weep in silence.

The rules became more rigid and detailed when external gestures were to take place outside the home in a social context. Francesco of Barberino dealt in great detail with the problem of women going out for walks. When strolling, a woman had to be accompanied at all times by a member of the family or by a servant; she had to walk through the crowd without looking around, "taking little steps, of equal size."[52] Jerome of Siena and Antonino of Florence advised women to go from home to church as quickly and furtively as possible, "your eyes so low, that nothing but where you put your feet matters to you."[53] Once in church, they were to remain still, in silence, "not like those vain females who discover the whole market, all their neighbors, friends, and relations in God's church."[54] With every limb, every action, every expression under control, these women revealed true modesty and reverence. In the reserved atmosphere imposed by these controlled gestures, contact with the male world was difficult and the temptations of the world were far away. Together with moderation in ornaments, modesty was prescribed to women as yet another means of defending the supreme virtue of her chastity—decidedly at risk in the public display of her body.

Another virtue—sobriety—like modesty, the daughter of temperance, was also recommended to women to defend their chastity. Modesty took charge of women's gestural communication; sobriety was to preside over her consumption of food and drink. Explicitly defined as an instrument of control and custody of female chastity, sobriety was supposed to inhibit a woman from drinking and eating to the point where an uncontrollable lust might overcome her. The result was a long list of alimentary rules, in religious and lay works alike, such as avoiding wine, overeating, and overheated or too spicy meals. These regulations, though applicable to all women, were aimed in particular at widows and nuns. A married woman, after all, had to strike a nutritional balance to keep her out of trouble without endangering the efficiency of her body for procreation; a nun or a widow, however, could push herself a little further, mortify the flesh and practice strict sobriety with occasional fasting.

As time went by, from the end of the fourteenth throughout the fifteenth century, insistence on the value of sobriety and fasting became more radical and far-reaching, and sometimes included married women. Regulations regarding when and how much to eat and when to fast became more detailed. Combined with a series of proscriptions concerning corporeal discipline, they took on an increasingly ascetic value. In texts from an earlier period the emphasis was always on guarding chastity: virgins, married women, and widows needed sobriety to keep their bodies intact for the home or the convent. A body fatigued by overeating, enfeebled by drink, enervated by overstimulation, and exhausted by lust was no good to a husband and displeasing to God.

Industrious and Merciful

These daughters of temperance, carefully controlling dress, gestures, and food, are powerless against idleness, another insidious enemy of chastity. Idleness threatened the whole of humanity because it was considered to be at the root of many other sins; but women were in particular danger. In idle moments their "natural" inconstancy and infirmity, compounded by the repetitive rhythms of a retired and restrained life, gave rise to evil, illicit thoughts and desires. The willingness with which women seemed to abandon themselves to the pleasure of inertia, their availability to anyone or anything that would feed their strange fantasy world, left little choice for their custodians. The only solution was work: honest activities such as spinning, weaving, sewing, embroidering, and mending kept a woman's hands and, more important, her thoughts, busy.

The ideal figure of an active and industrious woman, attacking moments of indolence with needle and thread, spindle, wool, and linen, was commonplace in pastoral and pedagogical literature, in preachers' sermons, in the moral tracts of the Aristotelian school, and in lay pedagogical works. In praising women's manual activity and industriousness it was also common to find, especially in lay literature, remarks on the economic value of female labor. Philip of Novara believed that poor women should learn to sew and spin at a young age, in order to have a trade.[55] Francesco of Barberino commented that it would do no harm if even daughters of knights, judges, and doctors learned to spin and sew in order to be prepared for any change in their destiny. Even though their status did not force them to work to earn their keep, he added, the incessant activity of needle and spindle would help distract them in their more melancholy moments and keep them out of sloth's way.[56] The productivity and economic value of female labor, however, was a secondary consideration for Francesco, as it was for the majority of preachers and moralists. Foremost in their minds was that women should never be left idle long enough to harbor potentially dangerous desires and fantasies—dangerous for the stability of their minds and the integrity of their bodies. In short, women's work was yet another form of custody.

Apart from the work that kept them busy at home, women were allowed to dedicate their energies to another activity: charity. It would be hard to find a text in pastoral and pedagogical literature that did not exhort women to be pious and merciful. Women, after all, had a natural tendency to suffer for others and help them whenever possible. Giles of Rome remarked that the same softheartedness that made women inconstant and irrational caused their inability to tolerate other people's suffering and their desire to alleviate it instantly.[57]

A concrete way to satisfy this natural mercy was to give alms—a practice highly recommended as a specific duty for all women, rich or poor. Durandus of Champagne's ideal image of a queen was that of a benefactress who extended her bounty to the poor and needy, taking care of lepers, visiting convents, making sure her alms reached the most hidden corners of her kingdom.[58] This ideal was a perfect example of female charity for every woman—be she married, nubile, or widowed, noble or bourgeois—to imitate. To engage in acts of charity, moreover, was a means for women to come into contact with the outside world beyond the domestic or convent walls. It was a desolate world of beggars and paupers, cripples, invalids, and vagrants; nevertheless, it provided a taste of social contacts outside the family and allowed women the flavor, if only for a few seconds, of the real world.

Preachers and moralists soon understood that women's charity could be a potential source of danger, a possible loophole in the custody of women; so they transformed it into a further means of control. Charity was a necessary instrument for restraining female passion, channeling it into something that was right and just, rather than dispersing it in illicit affections and vain desires. Charity had to be subject to strict regulations and cautionary measures. Before giving vent to their charitable passion, it was important for women to determine whether clients were really poor invalids, not impostors. It was also important for women to avoid causing their own families financial trouble through excessive generosity; the task of judging the real need for alms often could be left in the reasonable and reassuring hands of husbands or spiritual tutors. To sum up, charity offered women contact with the outside world, but it was only partial, cautious, often mediated, and ultimately controlled by men.

Taciturn

Women's gestures, dress, eating habits, manual activities, and acts of mercy were guarded, but women also had the gift of speech. As far as preachers and moralists were concerned, women talked too much and badly: they were expert liars, malicious gossipers, constant arguers, persistent whiners, and chatterboxes. Clichés from centuries of misogynous literature were deposited throughout sermons and moral treatises for women, giving contemporary readers a disturbing image of petulant and loquacious women who perversely abused the supreme human gift of words. In Christine de Pisan's passionate defense of women's words, the *City of Ladies,* she was forced to contest stupid and blasphemous preachers who claimed that Christ chose to come to Mary Magdalene after his resurrection because he knew that, being a woman, she would soon spread his word far and wide.[59] Texts inspired by Aristotle provided further evidence of this attitude. Giles of Rome wrote that the deplorable, unfortunately natural, tendency of women to speak before thinking resulted from their defective rationality. Constitutionally unable to check their flow of words, women inevitably said stupid and frivolous things; once they started an argument, an uncontrollable passion took over and they were unable to stop.[60]

This intemperate and perverse loquacity was seen not only as a potential source of disorder within family or community but also as a threat to women's chastity, which could never be guarded enough. A woman who talked too much revealed too much interest in the outside world, an unhealthy desire to weave a social network with her words. A woman who was too friendly and available was all the easier to corrupt. Nourished by this negative view, preachers and moralists constructed an impregnable wall of rules and prohibitions around women's words. The unconcealed and resigned scorn with which garrulous women were treated in pastoral and pedagogical texts, the proliferation of irritated anecdotes and vexed invectives against the evils of the tongue, turned into real concern when it came to the problem of when, where, and how women should speak. After all, to control women's words was to maintain custody of the authority and privileges of men's words.

As far as women's words and silence was concerned, the authority was Saint Paul, who considered women inferior to men and prohibited them from teaching (1 Tim. 2:12) and addressing assemblies, allowing them, if they wanted to obtain specific information, to question their husbands at home (1 Cor. 14:34–35). These two biblical passages, commented on for centuries by many prestigious exegetes, were the cornerstones of the custody recommended by preachers and moralists. The first act was to banish women's words from the public forum into the private. The fact that a public dimension was denied to women was not a matter of place but of function. Whenever words go beyond the function of communicating between two individuals to take on the political role of founding and governing the city, then women should hold their tongues and let men speak. Women were not allowed in the courts; they could not govern, teach, or preach. The vocabulary of justice, power, culture, and salvation was masculine. Political and juridical laws had already effectively excluded women from exercising justice or power, in different ways for different social and historical contexts. Sometimes regulations were less strictly applied, and women were allowed into the courts to indict or to act as witnesses, or to take on administrative positions: abbesses presided over the monastic community, and noblewomen occasionally were allowed to command, either in the absence or after the death of their husbands.

The laws denying women's words an educational function in both cultural and religious fields were upheld strictly. Canon law, exegesis, and theology all conspired to prove that women were unsuitable for teaching and preaching. Secluded within domestic or convent walls, subordinated to men, burdened with naturally defective intellects, endowed with fragile bodies the mere view of which kindled lust in men, and incapable of dominating rhetorical techniques, women were excluded from the universities where great sages, experts in the arts of lecturing and debating, worked on and transmitted their knowledge to other men.

The same arguments were used to deny women the possibility of preaching the Word of God. The rigidity with which theologians and preachers upheld this stricture resulted from the fact that women had begun and continued to cast doubt on the absolute privilege of clerics as the only legitimate depositaries of the words of salvation. Women in several heretical movements did in fact preach the Word of God. Starting in the thirteenth century, an increasing number of women expressed—either within or on the edge of ecclesiastical institutions—mystical tendencies that gave them the power to speak to God, about God, and for God. Clerics categorically denied that it was possible for women to preach, since the office required a condition of superiority and intellect that the female sex simply did not possess. They were obliged to admit, however, that women could become imbued with the Word of God, often linked to the gift of prophecy—but the task of verifying whether the prophecy was real or influenced by an evil spirit was left strictly to the men of the Church.

These reflections and proscriptions were included in didactic and pastoral texts which took the fact that women could not air their thoughts in public as given, then turned to an analysis of the forms women's words might take in the private sphere. In this area extra attention and caution were needed. Banned from public functions and social situations, women's words threatened to invade homes and convents, eluding all control and establishing a powerful and protected realm of female discourse. Whenever they were allowed or obliged to speak, it was very important for women to follow the rules of *taciturnitas,* that is, to speak moderately, quietly, and only when necessary. Just as avowed nuns broke their silence only in precisely proscribed moments, so women who lived at home were advised to speak only if they had to, wait reverently until they were spoken to, and address their husbands or parents with humility.

If they followed these rules, they gained the right to give advice and admonish others. Some authors recognized the persuasive force of admonishment in women's words—a praiseworthy way for women to comfort and instruct their husbands and children, especially their daughters. Often, however, serious doubts about the validity of women's advice were cast, first of all by a section of Aristotle's *Politics*. Giles of Rome, together with all the other Aristotelian commentators, considered women's advice passionate and changeable, incoherent and irrational. It was prompt and effective if the problem was unimportant; but when serious decisions were to be made, it should be taken with extreme caution. Furthermore, women's incapacity to keep a secret should induce members of the family to keep the number of confidential exchanges down to a minimum, in proportion to the intimacy of the house.[61] In most cases the contradiction between women's recognized role as moral instructress and the difficulty of entrusting this role to women's words, considered fragile and disordered, was resolved by delegating admonishment to actions and behavior rather than to words, so that women could become models of perfect moral conduct.

Women's relation to the written word was viewed with suspicion. "A woman should learn neither to read nor write, unless she is interested in taking vows, because women's reading and writing has brought about many evils."[62] Philip of Novara's drastic view, shared by the Florentine merchant Paolo of Certaldo among others,[63] was only partially attenuated by the opinions of Vincent of Beauvais, William Peraldo, Francesco of Barberino, and Giles of Rome, all of whom extended the privilege of reading and writing to women of noble lineage as well as nuns.[64] It was only later that a wider range of women living at home were given the possibility of learning to read, sometimes even to write.[65] However, the written words women were encouraged to read, memorize, and recite among themselves in the hushed atmosphere of their homes belonged exclusively to edifying religious literature, certainly not to the licentious books of poets and romance writers, and, least of all, to furtive lovers' letters. Preachers and moralists turned the activity of reading into another powerful form of custody, one able to increase women's religiosity, conquer idleness, and keep temptation at bay. "It is a good thing to instruct women in the art of letters," wrote Vincent of Beauvais, "so that, assiduously intent on this honest occupation, they may drive out all evil, lascivious, or vain thoughts."[66]

Only isolated and measured words should disturb the halo of

silence surrounding the ideal woman sketched by preachers and moralists: a meek pitter-patter of humble questions and obsequious answers with husbands or fathers; well-meditated advice and peaceful admonishment in the family or with the servants; repetitive and edifying readings of Holy Scripture; and the occasional sincere and complete confession—respecting the time and place established by the Church, checking first on the confessor's integrity, and taking care not to talk about sins as though they were fairy tales.

Although in thirteenth-century pastoral literature women were occasionally reminded of their duty to confess their sins (more obsessively in fifteenth-century texts), it was never considered as important as prayer, which should at all times fill the hearts and mouths of pious women. It was only in later texts that a detailed set of rules was developed about the number and nature of the prayers to be recited at particular times of day and in particular places. In these earlier texts the importance of prayer was a central, recurring theme; women of all ages and conditions were encouraged to adopt this devotional practice. A woman who prayed was a woman who kept worldly temptations away, who preferred peace and quiet, and who knew how to be her own custodian by virtue of her privileged relation with God. Recited out loud or in a whisper, words of prayer filled the silence created by *taciturnitas*, and followed women wherever they went—in churches, monasteries, or at home—contributing at all times, during a religious ceremony or while working at home or in moments of calm or leisure, to the custody of their virtue.

Chastity, humility, modesty, sobriety, silence, industriousness, mercy, custody: these words rang in women's ears for centuries, whether pronounced by preachers in church, reiterated by family members, or deposited in texts written expressly for them. As time went by the women who listened to these words—queens, nuns, wealthy bourgeoises, poor peasants, servants, mothers, young girls—changed. The men who pronounced these words—preachers, philosophers, theologians, court functionaries, learned laymen—also changed. Even the ways in which they addressed women changed. At times they used the spoken, at others the written word; at times they used an imperious and generically assertive tone, at others, they offered persuasive, more personal advice. But the words were always more or less the same.

The staying power of the vocabulary of pastoral and pedagogical literature addressed to women from the end of the twelfth to the end of the fifteenth century demonstrates the staying power of the feminine model invoked by these words. The model was strongly rooted to begin with. It was founded on the authority of tradition, justified by exegesis of Holy Scripture, and confirmed by the providential rediscovery of Aristotle's theories. It was malleable and easily molded to the needs of those who first developed it (clerics) and of those who did not hesitate to take it over (laymen). A woman in custody, at home or in the convent, whose movements, gestures, words, clothes, fertility, and religious spirit were constantly under control, was more easily guided toward eternal salvation, while the honor and continuity of her family was better guaranteed. In short, she was a woman whom preachers and spiritual tutors could approve of and fathers and husbands appreciate.

Clerics and laymen were convinced that all women could practice the virtues of a life in custody if they applied themselves. There were those who were obliged to be more virtuous than others, or to be so in a different way from others. There were those who were advised to give up ornamentation altogether, and those who used it with moderation; those who were urged to spend the rest of their days inside the convent, and those who were allowed to make occasional cautious appearances outside the home; those who chose to be chaste by avoiding physical contact, and those who were chaste within marriage. The model, though inspired by the ideal figure of the nun, was easily adapted to the needs of the varied, many-sided female audience. The capacity of this model to absorb so many transformations without losing its essential nature undoubtedly was one of the main reasons for its duration.

There was one kind of woman, however, as we shall see in the pages that follow, for whom the model was made to adapt to such drastic variations that it risked becoming ineffective and impractical: the wife and mother. It was not always easy to propose the tranquil image of a woman immune to worldly worries and corporeal concerns, intent on prayer and charity, to a wife and mother who had to take care of the family, please her husband, produce and rear children. Faced with this dilemma, preachers and moralists had to push themselves to their limits of rhetoric and theory to include the married woman in the inventory of women in custody, pushing the adaptability of the model to its extreme and trying to make a wife into a "good wife."

Translated from the Italian by Clarissa Botsford

4

The Good Wife

Silvana Vecchio

Sarah

"Her parents, after hugging and kissing her, let her go, recommending that she honor her mother- and father-in-law, love her husband, look after the family, run the house, and behave irreproachably at all times" (Tob. 10:12–13).

Of all the heroines in Holy Scripture, Sarah—a minor figure, almost entirely disregarded until that time—was a particular favorite in thirteenth-century pastoral literature. Although the devil conspired seven times to kill her husband on the eve of their wedding, she was married to Tobias, after three nights of prayer and armed with the holiest of intentions. Obedience, chastity, and devotion: in the view of the clergy, Sarah incarnated all the virtues of a good wife. The list of duties her parents rattled off before the wedding provided an opportunity to catalog a wife's multiple roles in the family and draw up precise behavioral rules for each.

The Parisian Robert of Sorbonne (died 1274) used Sarah and Tobias as an example of the sanctity of the marriage contract.[1] Gilbert of Tournai, Jacob of Voragine, William Peraldo, Vincent of Beauvais, and Paolinus the Minorite constructed a complete educational theory for married women based on the figure of Sarah.[2] Durandus of Champagne presented her as the ideal chaste wife and perfect mistress of the house.[3] She was a model of what every woman should aspire to become: a respectful daughter-in-law, a faithful wife, a thoughtful mother, a thrifty housekeeper—in short, unexceptionable in every way. Sarah represented and incarnated the web of duties within which the clergy imagined and described a married woman's life.

Wives were in the forefront of the renewed attention paid to women by ecclesiastical intellectuals at the height of the thirteenth century. Though at the bottom of the scale of perfection, a married woman nonetheless played an essential role in the social model the clergy was in the process of drafting. They were in fact the most dynamic element in the whole system. To present new pastorals for wives meant reshaping traditional molds in the light of the new requirements of a society in which the control of family strategies through a newly devised marriage ideology was the prize clerics and laymen had been fighting over for two centuries.[4]

The definition of the sacramental nature of marriage marked the end of a long theological debate as well as the triumph of the ecclesiastical model. It was the task of pastoral literature to disseminate and popularize the new marriage doctrine, stripping it of theological subtleties while creating an educational theory and a set of family morals which took the value of marriage into account.

Only isolated fragments of the antimarriage debate, which in the course of the twelfth century drew heavily on Saint Jerome's *Adversus Jovianum* in order to describe the snares of married life, survived in thirteenth-century texts.[5] The explicit premise for all attempts to devise new moral rules for couples was a eulogy of marriage. Directly instituted by God in the Garden of Eden, preserved thanks to divine intervention after the Universal Flood, the sanctity of marriage was confirmed by the presence of Christ, the Virgin, and the Apostles at the wedding at Cana and by the operation in that context of Christ's first miracle. Marriage was the condition ordained by God for the mother of Christ; it had the triple function of generating offspring, avoiding fornication, and conferring sacramental grace.

In the search for behavioral models to propose to couples, theological and pastoral literature ran through its entire scriptural and patristic repertoire. Pages of Genesis describing the creation of Adam and Eve and their subsequent doom were continuously called forth as evidence that the diverse destinies of men and women lay in God's Word. Those admonitions of Saint Paul that made woman's subjugation to man an essential element of matrimonial morality were resurrected. Figures of holy and faithful wives were called back from the Old Testament—Rebecca, Leah, Rachel—to join the ranks of early Christian saintly spouses—Cecilia, Agnes—and, above all, the inimitable model, the Virgin Mary, perfect wife and mother.

Increasingly frequent translations of Aristotelian texts from the mid-thirteenth century onward confirmed scriptural references. Aristotle's *Nicomachean Ethics* provided the premise for a definition of the marriage tie which went beyond pure naturalism into the sphere of a specific ethicality. Similarly, his *Politics* placed the family in the context of a state community, analyzing the various relationships that rotate around the head of the family, while the pseudo-Aristotelian *Economics* (translated near the end of the century) focused more directly on the home as a woman's place, defining her tasks there.

Glossed repeatedly throughout the thirteenth and fourteenth centuries, Aristotle's works undeniably were the basis for this interest in things domestic and for every attempt at defining a possible morality. The *Economics* in particular laid the foundations for a doctrine of home administration that often followed the path of the biblical model. For many decades husband, children, servants, and the home were the ideal chapters of a married woman's education, the topoi around which every attempt at speaking to or about women was constructed.

At the end of the Middle Ages, Sarah still represented an ideal female figure in the works of Francisco Ximenes, Dionysius the Carthusian, and Cherubino of Spoleto.[6] This proves the vitality and persistence of a tradition that not even humanistic literature was able to counter with a comparably influential model.

Honor Your Mother- and Father-in-Law

The first duty Sarah was reminded of was to honor her mother- and father-in-law. As Gilbert of Tournai explained, this meant treating them with reverence, using respectful words and gestures; paying homage and providing concrete help when needed; avoiding being aggressive, even verbally, and appeasing any conflicts with sweetness and light.[7] Respect, kindness, support: the same forms of respect the fourth commandment—honor your father and your mother—demanded for parents.

To honor your mother- and father-in-law, then, meant to extend to a husband's parents the same attention due one's own; to place new links instituted by a marriage contract on the same level as blood ties. It is not by chance, Jacob of Voragine reminds us, retracing Isidore of Seville's etymology, that the term *socer* (father-in-law) comes from the verb "to associate" *(socer a sociando),* because it indicates the particular form of affiliation that introduces a son's wife into new family relations.[8]

The theme of respect for parents-in-law also was present in the *Economics* and allowed commentators grounds to reflect on family relations created by marriage. Nicolas Oresme noted that the love of husband and wife bound both to revere and support their in-laws according to formulas modeled—at least outwardly if not by real affection—on obligations due to parents.[9]

The commitment to each other's parents, expected of both but more often the specific duty of a wife who went to live in her husband's family, allows us to consider the marriage bond from an external point of view (the links that marriage created in the social body) before looking into internal relations. Marriage was a bond not only between two people but between two families. The creation of a new family nucleus implied the constitution of a whole network of kinships and alliances that modified the social and political situation in the community.

At an ideological level the consciousness of the political function of marriage was always there. Peraldo, Vincent of Beauvais, and Giles of Rome all reiterated the concept that marriage helped preserve peace, quell discord, and confirm alliances. The wedding that often united discordant family groups could easily become the linchpin of a strategy for increasing the scope of friendships and for extending a network of alliances within the city, with beneficial effects in terms of social harmony.

In this dimension the wedding ceremony itself was imbued with both social and religious significance. The recurrent stigmatization of clandestine marriages in canonical literature aimed at social control—with the publicity of the ceremony—over marriage politics. Similarly, the wedding feast, in the view of an acute preacher like Humbertus de Romanis, had an important function: the united families offered the community a visible version of the new strategy of alliances.[10]

The theme of harmony was reworked incessantly in treatises and pastorals on matrimony from the thirteenth to the fifteenth century. Social harmony, generated and perpetuated through marriages, was both the cause and effect of wider peace; domestic harmony was indispensable for a family's formation and survival. Albert of Saxony in his comment on the *Economics* lucidly observed that concord or discord within a couple were immediately mirrored in the behavior of friends, while benevolent attention toward a spouse's friends and relatives invariably increased love and unity all around.[11]

A wife was the fulcrum of this delicate balancing act, with a twofold responsibility for peacemaking. Her task was, above all, to ensure conjugal unanimity, through submission to her husband; it was almost equally important to manage and maintain good relations with her husband's parents and family. By definition malleable, a woman was expected to soften people's spirits, smooth over contrasts, suppress conflicts both inside and outside the marriage. The key to her role as peacemaker appears to lie in her docility and capacity for submission rather than in specific positive qualities or a particular talent in diplomacy. Only in Christine de Pisan's works does a woman's pacifying role assume a less passive connotation and actively extend outside the home. The duty of a prince's wife—a noble model but to some extent applicable to all women—was not only to stay on good terms with her in-laws, to love, honor, and defend them in her husband's eyes but also to absolve the political function of guaranteeing and preserving peace within the court and in the state.[12]

Love Your Husband

A husband was by definition the center of a married woman's universe. He was not only the user and receiver of his wife's attitudes and conduct, but the hub around which the system of values proposed to married women revolved. Talking to or about wives inevitably meant talking to or about husbands. It also implied focusing on a series of mutual obligations and specific tasks in order better to define each component of the couple.

A wife's first and foremost duty was to love her husband. The exhortation to love *(dilectio)* was a constant recommendation; in some cases it summarized a woman's many obligations toward her spouse. Before talking about conjugal love, however, important specifications and distinctions had to be made. The preacher Gilbert of Tournai, who was most sensitive to the psychological implications of marriage pastorals, distinguished two types of love.[13] The first was carnal, fed by lust and characterized by excess. It was comparable to adultery in that it produced the same disastrous consequences—lasciviousness, jealousy, madness. In contrast, Gilbert described true conjugal love, essentially social since it established an equal relationship between husband and wife. The roots of this relationship go back to the primordial setting of woman's creation from man's rib in order to become his mate (socia) rather than his servant. Thus the rib cliché, often used in pastoral literature to demonstrate woman's inferiority, was by the same token a solid claim to building equality and reciprocity in a married couple.

It was Gilbert again who depicted an idyllic picture of married life where the reciprocity of love guaranteed serenity, honesty, and peace in the home, which in turn brought about mutual fidelity and support and, ultimately, salvation. Similarly, William Peraldo listed sixteen good reasons for choosing conjugal love, mixing the more traditional biblical arguments with forcefully evocative images.[14] Marriage was like a graft that fused a cut branch and the sterile growth into which it was planted into a single, fertile tree; the wedding band, threaded onto the finger through which the vein to the heart passes, was a perfect symbol for the love that must flow between husband and wife.

Equality or Submission?

All this emphasis on conjugal love, stressed even by theologians, cannot remove the impression of a clear imbalance between the two sexes one gets from a global reading of the literature on the subject. Jacob of Voragine, perhaps better than any other, succeeded in defining the precise terms of this imbalance. There is no doubt, he said, that husband and wife must love one another intensely and help one another to achieve salvation. The husband, however, is required only to reciprocate his wife's perfect love with moderate love (discretus). A wife's love is perfect, he continued, when she is blinded by her feelings and loses all sense of proportion and truth, sincerely believing that "nobody is wiser, stronger, or handsomer than her husband," when she is pleased by everything about him, when she finds everything he does or says right and just.[15]

This blindness and lack of moderation was forbidden to the husband. His love must never be too ardent; it should be well-tempered and measured. Reelaborating a passage from Saint Jerome that placed excessive love on a par with adultery, Jacob joined ranks with a vast choir of disparate voices—from William Peraldo to Giles of Rome, from Philip of Novara to Vincent of Beauvais—in condemning the man who loved injudiciously with too much affection, lost control of his rationality, or let himself be ruled by sentiment. Jealousy, passion, and, in the extreme, madness are the consequences of intemperate love for one's wife, emblematically represented by Herod who was led to murder his beloved wife Marianna, and by Adam who disobeyed God in order not to sadden Eve and ended up thrusting the whole of humanity into a state of sin.[16]

The Aristotelian doctrine of marriage as a friendly relation between unequal partners was a useful springboard for later attempts to rationalize a couple's affective imbalance. Conjugal friendship, claimed Albertus Magnus and Thomas Aquinas, is based on justice; it cannot but adapt to the different levels of virtue present in husband and wife. A husband receives more love because he is endowed with greater rationality and is capable of greater virtue. A wife is naturally inferior, so she receives a lesser portion of friendship, though enough to suit her nature.[17] John Buridanus went as far as to claim that "a husband loves more than a wife and with a nobler love, since a husband is to his wife as a superior being is to an inferior, as perfect is to imperfect, as giver is to receiver, as benefactor is to beneficiary. The husband gives his wife the child, and she receives it from him."[18]

A wife was ensnared in the net of such reasoning, which was both descriptive and normative. A woman teetered on the edge of an unbridgeable contradiction: the obligation to love her husband, essential to her wifely function, turned out to be inexhaustible, the very mark of her inferiority. Since a woman was dominated by senses and incapable of attaining the self-control expected of the male sex, she was condemned to an all-consuming but mistaken love in the attempt to achieve the unachievable: the limited but perfect love her husband gave in return. What is more, his wife—the usually passive object of this love—was held responsible. She had to make herself lovable so that her husband would not fall prey to the lust the Church had instituted marriage to avoid. If she was too desirable, on the other hand, she herself would sin by inspiring that same lust in her husband. In short, she was expected to love without measure but to impose on her husband's love the moderation she could not or was not allowed to exercise on her own affectivity.

If we ask ourselves what a wife's love really meant, we realize that it was impossible for a woman to take rational control over her affectivity; she had to find external criteria to give meaning to her all-consuming love for her husband. The criteria and meaning were to be found in the husband's whims, to which the wife was not expected to do anything but pander in respectful, reverent silence. In the exegesis of William Peraldo and Vincent of Beauvais, to love your husband meant to bow to voluntary submission. The potential equality alluded to in the Bible was exorcised by referring to original sin, which dragged women down from a position of equality to one of almost servile submission.

The exhortation to obedience that dominated prescriptions for wives turned up in many different sources. Texts inspired by Aristotle stated clearly that unanimity in the couple should not be considered the result of common aims and desires but rather of a well-ordered regime in which a husband's decisions were reinforced by a wife's obedience. Even Christine de Pisan considered humility and obedience to be vital requisites of a wife's love for her husband.[19] A treatise written for a wife by her husband, the so-called *Ménagier de Paris,* provides us, not by chance, with a resounding example of insistence on obedience.[20] In this work the identification between love and obedience led to a wife's absolute submission to her husband's will, to the point where she no longer had any moral responsibility. This long plea for conjugal obedience was enriched with countless examples ranging from Scripture to the animal world, culminating in the terrible story of Griselda from Boccaccio's *Decameron.*

Conjugal Rights and Fidelity

Within the context of a wife's absolute subordination to her husband, the last bastion of the equality and reciprocity that moralists and theologians had stressed was sexual activity, although it was never recognized as being vital to marriage. Justified by the need to avoid fornication, marriage had to guarantee legitimate sexual activity to both spouses. Conjugal rights was the only area of reciprocal and equal exchange, the only one where both husband and wife could initiate requests (in order to avoid sin) or refuse them (when legitimate conditions were not satisfied).

The far-reaching debate on conjugal rights that developed at a theological level during the thirteenth century, and was reflected in pastoral texts particularly in the fifteenth century, tried to define the nature and limits of sexuality. The attempt was to go beyond the penitentials, which severely limited sexual activity by dictating prohibitions on where and when it could be practiced, in order to focus on the problem as it related to the doctrine of matrimony, which tolerated sexuality only as a means to produce offspring to be educated in the Church or to avoid fornication.

Control over sexual activity was exercised by a specific virtue: conjugal chastity. Since a married couple could not be expected to forgo sex entirely, chastity meant keeping sexual activity within the limits of the marriage doctrine. During the marriage sacrament, James of Vitry asserted, the miracle at Cana—in which the vile water of sin was transformed into the precious wine of virtue—is continuously reenacted. In fact "the very virtue that before marriage was called virginity is never lost; in marriage it goes by the name of conjugal chastity."[21] The reciprocity of conjugal rights suggested, at least in principle, harmony in all decisions regarding a couple's sexual life. Nothing, not even the desire to achieve greater holiness, could justify the withdrawal of either partner from his or her sexual duty.

The reciprocal possession of bodies implied above all an exclusive relationship, protected by absolute mutual fidelity. Considered an indispensable ingredient of marriage, together with sacramental grace and the blessing of progeny, the reciprocal obligation of fidelity was one of its main gifts, pressed unanimously by pastoral and theological literature. Sermons, however, pointed out some discordance in this unanimous choir. Gilbert of Tournai underscored the reciprocity of the obligation, while reminding his audience that many husbands erroneously believed they were less bound by it than their wives were.[22] Similarly, Jacob of Voragine stressed that both spouses should be faithful but recognized that a wife "keeps faith better than her husband," guarded as she was by four elements of custody, only one of which affected him: "the fear of God, her husband's control, public shame, and fear of the law."[23]

The impression that fidelity, imposed on both husband and wife, was more binding for the woman is confirmed by Aristotelian texts and by theological-moral treatises on the theme of adultery. Giles of Rome dealt with the problem in general terms: a woman should be bound to one man not only because it was a widely accepted practice but also because a series of practical concerns had to be taken into account. To have a relationship with more than one man subverted the natural subordination of a wife to her husband and created an obstacle to domestic harmony; most of all, it harmed the offspring. On the one hand, frequent and diverse sexual relations "blocked the generation of children, as prostitutes who are more sterile than other women prove." On the other, sexual promiscuity and anything else that "clouds the certainty of paternity, impedes fathers from taking diligent care of their children in terms of heredity and nurturing."[24]

The welfare of children occupied a central position in the discourse that regulated relations between husband and wife. Procreation, once simply the legitimation of a couple's sexual activity, was transformed into the keystone holding the entire system of family ethics. In these terms, moral discourse on couples could be modeled only on the natural differences between a husband's and a wife's role in reproduction. For Giles of Rome, modesty, chastity, and fidelity in a wife were important for a husband because nothing else could guarantee his legitimate paternity. All other feminine virtues were in some way related to this need for assurance. Abstinence and sobriety moderated natural female lasciviousness; silence and stability made a wife pleasant company for her husband and reassured him of her good behavior. Together with Giles, all the commentators of Aristotle, from Thomas Aquinas to Albert of Saxony, from Oresme to Buridanus, recognized that female fidelity was the only way to ensure the legitimacy of progeny and that a husband's control over his wife's body was the only means of ensuring his paternity.[25] Fidelity thus became a uniquely female virtue. Male fidelity became little more than just compensation for his wife's sexual behavior. A woman's "physiologically" obliged fidelity to ensure legitimate reproduction was countered by a man's less binding but more virtuous faithfulness.

Only this premise can justify apparently contradictory attitudes toward adultery. A man's greater moral responsibility implied a greater obligation to virtue and a greater portion of blame. On the other hand, the consequences of a woman's adultery were direr and included a vast range of sins, from lust to betrayal, sacrilege to robbery. The woman was blamed for the profound repercussions on her children: legitimate children robbed of their inheritance by the birth of bastards; illegitimate children exposed to the risk of incest because of uncertainty surrounding their birth. The debate that raged in penitential and canonic literature from the twelfth century onward concerning what to do with an adulteress (pardon, punish, repudiate, or put to death?) confirms the disparity with which male and female adultery was treated. It underscores the fact that the obligation of fidelity was considered binding only for the wife.

Confined to a purely physical level, the question of fidelity was applied almost exclusively to the female body, an object of repression since time immemorial. Since the new ideology of marriage had placed the procreation of legitimate children at the top of its list of priorities, a woman's body had to be guarded even more than before. Chastity and fidelity replaced virginity as the grand ideal. As with virginity, though, as soon as the virtue became exclusively female, it was defined strictly in physiological terms, translated into repressive practice. Custody of a woman's body was no longer for God's benefit—but for her husband's. Custody over a female body remained, even in married women, a value par excellence.

Help for Salvation

An interesting form of penitence made its appearance in Thomas of Chobham's *Summa Confessorum* (1215). A confessor could turn married women into "preachers to their husbands." Every wife should "speak softly to her husband in the bedroom while she embraces him: if he is cruel, unforgiving, or oppresses the poor, she must urge him to have pity; if he is a bandit, she must deprecate his banditry; if he is mean, she must coax him to be generous and secretly offer alms, using common money."[26] This idea, particularly recommended for usurers' wives, noted a woman's capacity for effective persuasion superior to that of any priest. Her words were implicitly compared to the holiest and most effective words of all, the preacher's. This allowed women an opportunity to intercede actively, their specific mission being the salvation of the couple. Exceptional in the emphasis placed on women's words—more often connoted negatively as overabundant, unruly, and guilt-laden—Thomas of Chobham's proposal was echoed nearly a century later by an equally surprising project. Pierre Dubois (died 1321) had the idea of using Christian women as missionaries, helping them, after suitable indoctrination, to find non-Christian husbands, in the hope that a wife's persuasive force would convert them.[27]

The proposals of Thomas of Chobham and Pierre Dubois were the literal application of the verse of Saint Paul which states that an unbelieving husband is sanctified by a wife with faith (1 Cor. 7:14). Preachers and moralists throughout the century repeated, with less emphasis no doubt, that wives could contribute to the salvation of their husbands. They proposed Saint Cecilia—a wife who through prayer, persuasion, and example, succeeded in converting her perverse and unbelieving husband—as a role model. The typical "softness" of the female sex, considered a sign of her weakness, in this context became her strength to be used to soften her unyielding husband.

Within an ideological framework of a wife's total subordination to her husband's rules and ideas, however, the possibility of entrusting wives with moral responsibility for their husbands' behavior was not explored fully. Saint Cecilia was briefly mentioned in surveys of saintly spouses and immediately forgotten. The obligation to admonish a husband, at least until the end of the fourteenth century, was never included in the list of wifely duties.

The assertion that a wife should help her husband, confirmed by the biblical story of woman's creation, was solemnly repeated in the widest range of contexts, though her help was rarely interpreted as being an active collaboration for salvation. Alongside the most obvious and widespread interpretation of a woman's function as reproductive collaborator, there were other ways a woman could help a man. First, as James of Vitry, Robert of Sorbonne, and William Peraldo commented, a wife was a bulwark against sinful lust in that her sexual availability helped a husband avoid the temptations of the flesh.[28] Second, she was a companion and gave spiritual support, as Saint Bonaventure and Conrad of Megenberg claimed.[29] Above all, as Jacob of Voragine noted, along the same lines as the Aristotelians, she helped manage the family.[30] Lay literature considered in more detail the question of how a wife could help her husband; it allowed for the possibility of a woman's becoming her husband's spiritual guide and adviser. Francesco of Barberino stated that a queen should not only assist her husband in his everyday needs but also counsel him in his moral attitudes and political ventures, encourage his clemency, and guard him against court intrigues.[31] The *Ménagier de Paris,* insisting that a wife should submit totally to her husband's directives and desires, nevertheless allowed her the opportunity of criticizing him sweetly and discreetly if he did anything "foolish" or unfair to her.[32] Christine de Pisan's *Livres des trois vertus* goes even further: here a wife is considered her husband's soundest adviser and spiritual guide toward salvation. The marriage tie is presented as being, for women of all ranks, first and foremost a commitment to help a husband in every aspect of his life, in public and in private, in his material and spiritual needs. Christine advised princesses to take good care of their husbands' spirits and bodies, to admonish them kindly and correct their ways, if necessary through a confessor. Middle-class women were advised to keep a smile on their faces and help their husbands forget their cares. The wives of artisans and peasants were told to check up on their husbands' moral probity at work and to help them by learning the rudiments of their trade. Wives of the poor had little option but to comfort their husbands and help them keep hoping.[33] Christine de Pisan seems to have turned Thomas of Chobham's idea into concrete instructions: women's words became instruments of domestic pastorals, and wives were empowered to help their husbands achieve salvation.

The Choice of a Wife

An analysis of the criteria used for choosing a spouse often precedes the discussion of family obligations. There were a very few vague indications for a woman to follow (do not look for wealth in your husband but good manners and wisdom); in contrast the male point of view is well represented. Knowing how to choose the right woman was in fact the first step toward setting up a successful marriage.

It was not easy. Peraldo declared it almost impossible without direct divine intervention through prayer and almsgiving.[34] The English Dominican John Bromyard (died 1352), adopting Saint Jerome's antimatrimonial ideas, thought it doomed to fail; be she ugly or beautiful, fertile or sterile, a wife spelled trouble.[35] Philip of Novara, Giles of Rome, and Jacob of Voragine were less pessimistic, indicating factors to take into consideration when choosing a wife. The size of a woman's dowry, in everyday practice a vital consideration, should be irrelevant; even in a worldly lay context, other exterior blessings such as family status, a good reputation, and an abundance of friends are more important. The woman's honest conduct was essential and could be guaranteed, according to Jacob of Voragine, by observing the behavior of the mother—or even of the grandmother, thought Paolo of Certaldo.[36]

Nor should the importance of a woman's appearance be underestimated. William Peraldo felt that a wife should be more or less the same age as her husband in order to guarantee homogeneity in the couple, vital for harmony and stability. Jacob of Voragine's ideal was a mediocre-looking woman, a good compromise between a beauty that is hard to guard and an ugliness intolerable to live with.[37] Giles of Rome, on the other hand, advocated a decidedly beautiful, tall woman so that she could hand down these qualities to her children, who receive most of their physical characteristics from their mother.[38]

There was agreement on one point only: that the woman should be young, or at least, following Aristotle's indication, a virgin rather than a widow. Ingenuousness and inexperience, far from being defects in a future wife, were the husband's guarantee that she could be molded into shape. A widow, by contrast, transferred to the new house—if not children from a previous marriage—at least previously consolidated habits and traditions which potentially threatened domestic harmony. A virgin came to her spouse with only the rudiments of her family education, which had taught her above all to preserve her body. She was ready and willing to learn from her husband everything there is to know about her new status as a married woman.

A Husband's Duties

The debate over the reciprocal obligations of love, sexuality, and fidelity in a married couple was at the heart of marriage pastorals. It allows us to put into focus the contradictory dynamics of equality and subordination within the couple. These dynamics are even more evident when the picture is completed by the specifically male duties—the almost omnipresent triad: support, instruction, correction. These three prerogatives were strictly interconnected; not only were they based on a woman's "natural" inferiority, they corroborated her position.

A husband was obliged first and foremost to maintain his wife who received everything she needed for survival, since she was cut off from any form of production and her domestic role was limited to conserving what was already there. In pastoral literature, however, the obvious affirmation that a wife should receive everything she needed from her husband took on moral overtones. To look after a wife's needs was no mere economic function. It was a husband's duty to make sure that a wife's requests were based on real necessity rather than on vain desire for the superfluous. A husband's obligation to maintain his wife evoked the phantom of *ornatus* with all its accompanying moral emphasis. The requirement that a woman dress and adorn herself according to her station in life was translated into an obligation for a husband to see to the needs of his wife's decorum, which obviously varied according to the couple's social status.

Thus, even in an area as specifically feminine as this, moral responsibility was shifted from the wife to the husband. A husband who did not repress his wife's taste for excessive, vain, or superfluous ornaments would be held responsible for encouraging typical female frivolity. It was even worse when a husband was indirectly responsible for his wife's behavior. Often, preachers observed, wives claim that they dress and make up for their husbands' benefit. The truth is that they go around the house dressed carelessly and make themselves beautiful only when they go out in order to be noticed in public, thus feeding their own vanity and the lust of those observing them.[39]

The educational function implicit in this control over clothes, jewelry, and cosmetics became an explicit educational practice in what was one of the most important prerogatives for the husband: instruction. A wife had everything to learn from her husband. His function, according to Saint Paul, was to be her religious guide, an intermediary between the assembly of the faithful and his wife, condemned to silence. Aristotle's *Economics* also considered teaching a specific conjugal task for a husband in order to prepare for the generation and education of children. Thirteenth- to fifteenth-century pastoral literature is full of husband-cum-teacher figures.

The first thing to teach was home economics. A wife had to be able to administer the family house and property, solicitously multiplying, cautiously conserving, and prudently distributing family goods. A husband's most important task, however, was to take care of his wife's moral and religious education and to check up on her behavior. The premise on which *Ménagier de Paris* was based was that a wife had to learn everything from her husband. The tract was no more than a detailed and exhaustive manual for the young wife, starting with a chapter on religious duties (prayer, mass, confession) and moving onto a moral plane. The work deals with the whole system of vices and virtues, the problem of choosing good company, and rules for how to behave. It discusses in great detail conjugal duties, the tasks of a perfect mistress of the house, caring for the house and family, cooking, and gardening.

A husband's instruction was more a matter of exercising control over his wife than acculturation. John of Wales, Jacob of Voragine, Giles of Rome, and Albert of Saxony all insisted on the need for moral instruction, which continuously oscillated between the educational emphasis of doctrine and the repressive practice of custody. To be the custodian of one's wife meant to guard her manners and behavior, besiege her with repressive attention (to make up for her constitutional weakness and moral lightheadedness), keep her out of temptation's way, and correct any fatuous or reprehensible attitudes.

Correcting one's wife was considered a sign of real love and had to be accepted gracefully. Again the discussion of correction covered the familiar topoi of a woman's weakness and indicated places where a wife is likely to sin: marketplaces and public squares where women tended to indulge in idle chatter; dances or performances where feminine curiosity went hand in hand with the desire to show off. An obsession with ornamentation characterized many of the sermons: without a husband's skillful control, a woman's lust for adornment might drag the whole family down into economic ruin and bring the wife close to prostitution.

Husbands, Jacob of Voragine advised, should not be too strict with their wives, however. Extreme severity is one of the main defects of the male sex, the cause of many family disagreements. To correct a wife with "bad habits," a man should follow John Chrysostom's suggestions: first, insist on her learning divine law; then move on to criticism in the hope that her typical female bashfulness will prevail. Use the stick only as a last resort, "beating as a handservant, she who does not feel shame like a free woman."[40]

The entirely male prerogative of resorting to physical punishment represented the final, most tangible result of the imbalance of the couple that had been defined gradually. Any statement of principle about equality, unanimity, and reciprocity had to come to grips with the real subordination established between women, whose primary duty was obedience, and men, whose principle function was to control, support, instruct, and correct. The restricted scope allowed to admonishment, a wife's meager counterpart to her husband's correction, together with the limitation of the debate on equality to the purely sexual sphere, indicate a process which, while exalting and creating an ideology for the couple, sealed the terms of its inequality.

Looking After the Family

Sarah's third duty was to look after the family and take care of her children and servants. The potentially vast scope this obligation appeared to offer women was cut down to size by an increasingly Aristotelian view of the family in which the male was firmly entrenched at the center. The problem was to define tasks and functions for a wife so as to create a small area of specifically female intervention, without encroaching on the husband's indisputable dominance over children and servants.

Insofar as servants were concerned, things were relatively straightforward. Preachers as well as laymen tended to reduce the role of the mistress of the house to a generic obligation to love, instruct, and exert moral control. A woman's daily task was not so much to organize the servants' work but to prevent promiscuity between maidservants and manservants, to keep an eye on everyday behavior, and to suppress the first signs of lust or irregularity, thus preserving the family's morality and eliminating any potential danger for the conduct of the masters of the house.

A mother's relationship with her children was a more complex and demanding matter. Procreation and education were, as we have seen, among the rewards of marriage, vital elements in maintaining the dignity and stability of the tie. Giving birth to children was simultaneously atoning for Eve's sin (Gen. 3:16), an instrument for redeeming that sin and achieving eternal salvation (1 Tim. 2:15), and the most natural way, preordained by God (Gen. 2:18), to help men. A mother's primary obligation was to bring offspring into this world. To "generate children continually until her death," in the words of the Dominican Nicholas of Gorran (died 1295),[41] was the only real alternative to achieving salvation through virginity. It is not coincidental, Saint Bonaventure observed, that the word "matrimony" indicates a set of maternal functions, while "patrimony" alludes to the specifically male domain of material goods.[42]

Considering the mentality that envisaged procreation as a continuing commitment rather than a sporadic episode, it is not surprising that moral discourse was dominated by the physiological aspects of maternity. Procreation, gestation, childbirth, breast-feeding—these were the keys to the debate on mothers and children which rarely went beyond its purely natural aspects. Clerics such as Gilbert of Tournai and John Bromyard and secular writers such as Francesco of Barberino were preoccupied with sterility, which spelled doom for a woman and disaster for a couple's union.[43] Fear of bringing sick or deformed children into the world sustained and reinforced sexual prohibitions. And the obsession with legitimacy was the basis of the entire structure of family relations and values.

As if to confirm the biblical condemnation, pregnancy and childbirth were the most tragic moments of what was considered a miserable life for everyone, but particularly for women. Durandus of Champagne, elaborating on themes found in Pope Innocent III's *De Contemptu Mundi,* described in gloomy terms the journey from conception (the result of an "itch of flesh and the ardor of lust"), to gestation (disturbed by anxiety and fears for the lives of both woman and child), and on to delivery (dominated by pain and the specter of death).[44] Francesco of Barberino's view was less tragic. With a layman's eye he saw pregnancy as a time to be on guard, in a medical rather than a moral sense. At the beginning of gestation a woman should avoid "jumping and running and any brisk movement." When she first feels the fetus moving she should "eat and drink with moderation and live happily as God's friend so that the new spirit within her takes on a gentle aspect." She should avoid intercourse after conception and after delivery and breast-feed if she wants to "please God and her child."[45] Similar suggestions appeared in Conrad of Megenberg's *Yconomica,* whose emphasis on the attention and precautions owed children before their birth make him a precursor of the humanistic point of view.[46] A mother's duty to give life and ensure her offspring's good health made women almost entirely responsible for offenses—frequently mentioned in penitentials and confessionals—aimed at limiting births, including contraception, abortion, and infanticide. Women risked sinning if they tried to cure their infertility or their children's poor health through witch-craft or sorcery.

Where were the mother's feelings in this purely physical rela-tionship and what was her role in educating her children? In pastoral literature maternal love was not considered a duty; it was taken for granted. Everyone could see that mothers loved their children. Considering the close physical relationship they shared, it was entirely natural. A mother, Jacob of Voragine observed, sees part of herself in her child; she suffers for the child much more than the father does, and she recognizes it as her own with absolute certainty.[47] Saint Thomas confirmed this view. A mother, he wrote, "loves her child more than the father does, and she is gratified by loving more than by being loved."[48]

But it was precisely this intense physical love that the Church condemned. It could never enter the sphere of virtuous love be-cause intensity weakened it. It was carnal, passionate love, which privileged the body (the health and well-being of the child) with the risk of losing the spirit. A mother's love was compassionate and given to sacrifice; a mother suffered more than a father through her child's adversities and exulted less in her child's suc-cess. Scholars such as Albertus Magnus, Thomas Aquinas, and John Buridanus stressed that maternal love was stronger, more manifest, and more constant than paternal love.[49] They also noted that, because it was less rational, it was less noble.

The debate over maternal love highlights the contradiction, already evident in the realm of conjugal love, within which a woman's affectivity was forced to move. A mother by definition could love only passionately and naturally, but this natural love was blameworthy. A father loved less, but his love was intrinsically virtuous, aimed at perfecting the spirit rather than at maintaining the body. Children's affections confirmed this theory, according to Jacob of Voragine. They love their father more than their mother because they recognize that he is the active generating principle and the source of wealth and honor they will inherit.[50] Saint Thomas too concluded that, despite the fact that mothers loved their children more, from an ethical viewpoint children should love their fathers more because they gave them more by begetting them. Buridanus contended that once the period of early infancy, when needs are more physical, was over, children themselves tended to move from physical to rational love, shifting progres-sively from their mothers to their fathers.

Given this exclusively physiological view of maternity, it is not surprising that the mother was not given an important pedagogical role. William Peraldo, Humbertus de Romanis, and John of Wales spoke vaguely of an educational role for mothers, but the issue was outlined more clearly in the sermons of Jacob of Voragine and Gilbert of Tournai.[51] Moral and religious instruction could be undertaken by a mother if and only if she managed to moderate her carnal love for her children and develop an attitude of spiritual awe. Since a mother was constantly concerned with her children's salvation, her role was to watch over their moral behavior and religious practice rather than specifically to teach them.

Above all, it was a mother's task to safeguard her daughters, to keep them out of bad company and away from parties or dances. Mothers, themselves in their husbands' custody, replicated the same repressive practices on their daughters, with the same goal: to preserve the female body from any contact that might damage its fundamental virtue, its chastity. The control of her daughters' sexuality seems to have been a mother's exclusive privilege, one of the only areas where she was responsible, independent of her own morality. Bad women, Philip of Novara observed, can become even better mothers than virtuous ones, because they can recognize in their daughters the signs of "madness" they themselves experienced.[52]

But when education went beyond mere upbringing or custody and required real schooling, then the responsibility shifted from the mother to the father. Two fathers in particular—the Chevalier de la Tour Landry and the King of France, Louis IX—educated their daughters, but in general fathers were responsible for the instruction of their sons once they were no longer young boys. Gilbert of Tournai stated clearly that adolescent sons had to be educated by their fathers.[53] Francesco of Barberino advised widows to entrust the education of their sons to a knight from the deceased husband's circle of family and friends, who would serve as a surrogate father.[54]

The extreme limitations to which a mother's pedagogical role was subjected in thirteenth-century pastoral literature were further endorsed by Aristotelian texts. The *Politics,* which dealt with children only in relation to their father, and even more so the *Economics,* which established a clear division of roles (the father must educate, the mother nourish), contributed to a more radical exclusion of mothers from their children's education. Saint Thomas went as far as to say that the basic reason for getting married was to ensure a male figurehead for the education of the offspring.[55] Commentators on the *Economics* stressed that the father should oversee all aspects of education, including moral instruction, leaving the purely natural function of nurturing to the mother.

Even Christine de Pisan appeared to share the view that a woman was naturally inclined to take care of her children and must therefore relegate their education to the father. Nevertheless, Christine managed to restore several educational functions to a mother, recognizing her specific pedagogical role.[56] Thus a princess was required to supervise her children's tutors and teachers, originally selected by her husband. This supervision included not just checking on the tutors' moral attitude, but overseeing the contents of the doctrine taught. A mother had the right to make sure her children learned, first to serve God, then to study letters, Latin, and the sciences. She also would want her children to learn morals and the ways of the world, and to be sure that even her daughters learned to read and write, overseeing their reading herself. This supervision was not to be limited to noblewomen; mothers had a specific educational role according to their place on the social scale. Middle-class women should educate their children personally; artisans' wives should make sure their children are able to read and can learn the basics of a trade; working-class mothers should guard children's morals, carefully controlling their behavior.

Administering the House

If there is one point on which there is unanimous agreement where the model of a good wife is concerned, it is that the house is the woman's domain. A good wife stays at home and takes care of the house. Founded on scriptural and patristic authority and universally accepted since the beginning of time, this position was amply reinforced by Aristotelian texts whose focus on the house as a political and economic nucleus produced a precise definition of a woman's role in the domestic realm. Aristotle's distinction between a closed, guarded space containing women and an open space where men could circulate freely was rooted in the distinction between two basic economic modes: production (a male activity) and conservation (typically a female activity). Also the unification of husband and wife was economically complementary;

in it each exerted his or her natural function for the common good. To conserve and administer whatever a man produced, earned, or accumulated was a wife's contribution to the household, one more way for her to help her husband.

The home was, therefore, the center of a woman's activities. These included administering material goods and regulating the work of domestic servants—as well as her own labor. The keeper of the house might weave or spin, clean and take care of the house, look after domestic animals, and perform the duties of a hostess for her husband's friends—as well as managing the children and servants. Her labor, Gilbert claimed, equaled that which her husband performed outside the house to earn the family's daily bread.[57] The description of the strong woman in Proverbs 31 and the image of prudent Abigail were often cited to demonstrate how the hard, often hidden, work that women had to perform required specific and important virtues: wisdom, diligence, foresight, and the kind of strength that revealed itself in the humility of daily occupations rather than in the glory of war escapades.[58]

The home may have been the center of her activities but, even there, a woman was not totally independent. The same Aristotelian texts that founded the specificity of female labor declared that the master of the house, owner of its property and patron of its dependents, was in any case the man. Commentators dwelt on the fact that the administrative role assigned to women was simply part and parcel of the nurturing process; ultimately women were unable to make independent decisions concerning the estate. Since a woman could neither stipulate contracts nor handle her husband's money, her activity was limited to administering the family's physical subsistence: clothes and food. Nicolas Oresme argued in fact that the essential virtue for home economics was parsimony, toward which women naturally were inclined; they were therefore perfectly suited to the specific task of conservation.[59] For the woman home represented more than an economic domain; it was, first and foremost, a moral one. The house was a physical representation of a woman's state of custody, its walls and doorways surrounding and isolating the interiors, preserving them from external contagion. Home was a symbol of stability, exorcising the phantom of *vagatio* with all its dangers. The home was so highly charged symbolically that Durandus of Champagne turned it into a metaphor for conscience. It has also been used to represent the Church, heaven, and hell. Its more immediate connotations, however, were security and feminine virtue. To stay at home—for the married woman as much as for the virgin—meant to keep out of trouble's way. It also provided an opportunity to exercise those virtues intended to reassure a husband: fidelity, control, modesty, and coyness.

Ironically, the house became a place for the woman to guard. Incapable of managing by herself, needful of the custody and moral guidance of her husband, she became responsible for the entire family's behavior. Protected by the domestic walls, she had to guard family morality, temper her husband's moods, and control the behavior of her children and servants. Only a woman's supervision kept her house, home of legitimate matrimonial sexuality, from becoming a temple of sexual aberration, of fornication, or, worse still, of incest. In the guarded domain of the home a woman could find time to attend to her religious duties. Gilbert of Tournai used Saint Jerome's pleas and the model of Judith to remind women that their home commitments should not absorb them completely. They should take the trouble to provide a quiet area for prayer in the place where they live and work, transforming domestic space into religious space.[60]

Irreproachability

Last but not least of Sarah's duties was to be irreproachable at all times. After such a long list of obligations toward parents-in-law, husband, children, servants, and the home, the addition of a specific injunction of irreproachability might appear superfluous, a rhetorical expedient for summarizing in one word the whole range of behavior expected of a woman. This was Gilbert of Tournai's exact viewpoint: a woman who had performed all her motherly, wifely, and housekeeperly duties was definitely blameless in the eyes of the supreme judge, God.[61] If a woman achieved her mission in life fully, by caring for her children and her home, her domestic tasks not only did not conflict with religious duties but actually could enhance them. A good wife was by definition a good Christian, irreproachable in the eyes of God.

Gilbert's view seems very radical, yet it is in many ways conciliatory: the final judgment on a woman's behavior was left to God; thus any conflict between religious and family life was eliminated. Other writers, such as William Peraldo and Vincent of Beauvais, distinguished between the religious aspect (sanctity) and moral aspect (modesty) of women's behavior. It was the latter, however, that dominated their sermons: modesty in dress and gesture, silence, simplicity, humility, shyness, and sobriety—qualities which made a wife irreproachable to her husband—were ultimately the same qualities that made her saintly in God's eyes.[62]

Jacob of Voragine considered a wife beyond reproach if "she bears no stain, in her life, in her reputation, in her conscience."[63] A wife's daily behavior was judged by a double standard. On one level there was a religious standard: following her conscience and mirroring herself in the teachings of the scriptures and the lives of the saints, a woman could rid herself of her sins. On the other level there was a profane standard: gossip and street talk, whether called for or not, was vital for a woman's reputation, a sounding board of her vices and virtues. A good reputation, secular literature often stressed, was the only ornament a woman could proudly show off in public. It was her most precious "dowry" with the power to alter even her social status, a "perfume" which wafted around her at all times. To be irreproachable a wife had not only to behave well but to avoid any insinuations or gossip which, whether true or false, might ruin her image and the family's reputation.

Jacob of Voragine was not unaware that the only possible judge of a woman's behavior was her own conscience, seat of her most intimate religious sentiments. His sermons played with the mirror images of conscience and reputation, analyzing the problem of the spouse's blamelessness both from the point of view of her innermost spirit and from that of her external, public image. Jacob's model, based on the premise that in the final analysis God's judgment corresponds with man's judgment, represented a highly refined attempt (shared by most thirteenth-century marriage doctrines) to strike a balance between religious requirements and family duties.

This delicate equilibrium was soon to be devastated as women were faced with divergent and potentially conflicting responsibilities and expectations. This situation was brought about by a new wave of interest for the family and, at the same time, a new demand for profound religious experience.

Women and the Family in the Fifteenth Century

In 1403 the Dominican Giovanni Dominici wrote *La regola del governo di cura familiare,* commissioned by Bartolomea degli Alberti. Bartolomea, twice married but forced to live away from her husband, who was banished from Florence, was directly responsible for her family. She asked the Dominican for spiritual advice and suggestions, which he promptly produced in his *Regola,* providing a potentially universal model for family life. Dominici's tract started a new fashion by placing the family, in a more modern sense, at the center of a woman's life. Throughout the fifteenth century in Italy, particularly in Tuscany, problems related to the family remained the center of attention.

Following Dominici's example, men of the Church started to write manuals on family life, with women readers in mind, offering handy rules and regulations for everyday domestic and spiritual life. Saint Antoninus, Archbishop of Florence and disciple of Dominici, wrote his *Opera a ben vivere* for Dianora Tornabuoni in 1450; his mighty *Summa theologica* dedicated a long chapter, which later circulated independently, to problems related to couples and families. A Franciscan named Cherubino of Spoleto produced his *Regola della vita matrimoniale* in 1450. Giovanni Certosino composed *Gloria mulierum,* a long treatise for married women, around 1470. His brother monk Dionysius dwelt extensively on the problems of matrimony, dedicating a specific treatise, *De laudabili vita coniugatorum,* to the question. This literature, not by chance written in vulgar Italian rather than Latin whenever women were specifically addressed, can be read alongside the sermons dedicated to marriage and families of one of the most important fifteenth-century preachers, Bernardino of Siena.

Interest in the family was not merely a phenomenon confined to religious literature. There was also an enormous production of memoirs and family volumes in which merchants, mainly Tuscans, annotated every detail of events affecting the family—births, marriages, and deaths, but also business deals, credits and debits, and so on. This demonstrates that even laymen placed great emphasis on the family nucleus.[64] Such emphasis was echoed loudly at a theoretical level in humanistic writings. As part of the renewed debate on the compatibility of marriage and intellectual activity, Francesco Barbaro wrote in 1416, *De re uxoria.* Giovanni Campano turned his mind to the problem in *De dignitate matrimonii* (1460). Matteo Palmieri wrote his *Vita civile* between 1431 and 1438. In these same years Leon Battista Alberti composed the most famous and fortunate treatise on the subject: *I libri della famiglia.* Finally in 1468 Antonio Ivani wrote a short pamphlet for his wife: *Del governo della famiglia civile.*[65] This concentration on the family was reinforced by a more specifically educational series of works by Vergerio, Bruni, and Vegio.

Humanistic literature, produced by men and almost always aimed at other men, appears to have been directly influenced by the Aristotelian tradition on which a secular conception of the family was based. The praise of marriage, definition of roles for wife and husband, and concentration on home and children in humanistic works shifted away from a religious point of view. References and examples taken from classical literature were substituted for scriptural and patristic authorities; faithful and modest wives of the Greek and Roman world (Penelope, Alceste, Andromache, Lucretia) took the place of the saintly wives of Jewish and Christian traditions.

In this period religious literature clung more faithfully than humanist writings to the model promulgated in the thirteenth century regarding women. Marriage doctrine adopted and developed the motifs formulated in another ideological context. A woman's role in the family was essentially the same as in the traditional topoi; Sarah, if not directly evoked, remained an easily identifiable reference for preachers such as Antonino, Bernardino, Dionysius, and Cherubino. What remains to be seen is to what extent (apart from the different language used and leaving aside the simplistic comparison of secular and religious models) the extraordinary attention paid to the family and its problems in the fifteenth century actually modified the general perception of women.

Husband: Master or Spiritual Guide?

The husband stood firmly at the hub of a woman's universe throughout the literature of the period. The obligations of reverence, affection, and, above all, obedience of a wife toward her husband were neither contested nor modified by religious and lay writers. On the contrary, humanists accentuated the husband's central position within the family network, basing their theories on a faithful reproduction of the Aristotelian model, with the master of the house at the center of the family's relations. Involved in and committed to the administration of both home and outside business, a husband expected his wife to be a useful assistant in achieving material well-being. He also required her to perpetuate the family lineage by producing a great number of healthy, strong, handsome, legitimate, male heirs. In return, a husband would hand over to the wife, after careful instruction, the administration of the house. Moreover, the honor of the family was entrusted to a wife's irreproachable behavior and good reputation. A husband, however, kept the most important business transactions for himself, keeping a careful written account which his wife would not have been allowed to see. Children's education was a man's exclusive domain. His wife's guide, lord, and master, the "humanist" husband was obsessively present and domineering. A marriage contract required the same shrewdness as a good business deal, a wife being his most precious commodity.

Not that religious literature placed less emphasis on the husband. Fifteenth-century writers insisted less on the couple's unanimity and more on the wife's subordination to her husband. Bernardino, Cherubino, and Dionysius spoke of female duties in terms of fear and service, stressing the need for absolute obedience.[66] This was not to be questioned even if a husband forbade his wife to practice her religion.[67] The only universally recognized exception was refusal of sexual intercourse that was "against nature."

Despite this obsessive presence, one senses that for some of these writers something had changed. Husbands might have been physically more apparent, but they might have become less important. Dominici's *Regola,* divided into four parts (spirit, body, property, children), did not dedicate a chapter specifically to husbands. The second part of the treatise, however, gave him an important role. The husband was master of his wife's body and, despite the reciprocity of conjugal rights, he could claim greater rights over her body than she could claim over his. Giovanni Certosino's *Gloria mulierum* concluded with the same clear distinction: a woman's spirit belonged to God, her body to her husband.

For the first time we can see the female spirit freed from her husband's control. Whatever was written about the reciprocal love and support of a married couple, a crack could be seen in the utopia of conjugal harmony so often exalted in the thirteenth century. Genevieve Hasenohr's studies have shown that the development of a more deeply seated religious sentiment in women, together with the establishment of the figure of spiritual director, helped to deprive the husband of his long-standing role as religious intermediary.[68] Naturally many of these writers insisted it was the husband's duty to give his wife religious instruction, but the problem of compatibility between family and spiritual life, which marriage doctrine in the thirteenth century presumably had solved, was again brought to the fore. A need to provide more time and space for religious practice, even as part of married life, and a search for spiritual interlocutors other than a husband to satisfy this purpose gave the problem new urgency. Bernardino, Antonino, and Giovanni Dominici all swung between the necessity for considering care of home and family a top female priority and the temptation of opening up new religious vistas, perhaps even of entrusting a woman with the role of religious intermediary—once a uniquely male prerogative. Admonishment and alms, it was suggested, might be the vehicles. Thanks to the former, a woman could discreetly and prudently control her husband's morality. With the help of the latter she could make up for his lack of charity and religious sentiment, indirectly helping him attain salvation.

Domestic duties in contrast were considered an obstacle to achieving saintliness. Of course a woman could not avoid these obligations, but since she would never be able to achieve real religious heights through them, she was not required to spend too much time over them. Antonino of Florence suggested that Dianora rush through her household tasks, dedicating to manual labor only brief interludes in a life of prayer.[69] Giovanni Certosino put a woman's dealings with husband, home, and children on a par with tolerance, patience, and fatigue.[70] Dominici reminded his readers that a woman's body belonged not only to her husband and children, for whom nonetheless she was required to provide tender, loving care, but also to God and to her spirit, whose needs should take precedence even over family duties.[71]

This conflict, which not only posed the practical problem of reconciling female duties but also touched on the very essence of marriage, could not avoid bringing to the forefront the issue of sexuality. Humanistic works never really tackled the problem directly or never went beyond a vague negative prejudice and an equally vague appeal for moderation. On the other hand, religious writers such as Antonino, Cherubino, and Bernardino produced reams of analyses, distinctions, and counterdistinctions on the subject. The only way to solve the daily war a woman waged between the duty of absolute obedience to her husband, who owned her body, and the duty of following the path of purification and perfection the Church proposed for her soul was to produce a detailed, case by case analysis of possible situations.

Usually envisaged as passive, just about capable of holding back their husband's sexual appetite but not much more, women were presented for the first time with a new form of matrimonial chastity. This model suggested the use of persuasion, even subterfuge, in order to reduce the frequency of—or abolish altogether—sexual activity. Paragons of virtue in this respect were the Virgin Mary and Saint Elizabeth of Hungary.[72] With this radical solution the everlasting conflict between virginity and marriage had come full circle: the way to holiness was open only to those women willing to forgo sex.

Mothers and Children

Removing the spiritual component of a woman's life from the direct control of her husband also should allow, at least in principle, more independence for a mother's pedagogical leanings. However, fifteenth-century writers seemed to disagree violently about the question of mother-child relations. Very often the discriminating factor was religious. Without jeopardizing the premise that a father was the principal educator, a few religious authors regarded a mother's role in a better light. The traditional sphere of moral education and the control of her daughters' behavior was steadily broadened to include more concrete tasks.

Giovanni Certosino committed mothers to correcting their children on a daily basis.[73] Bernardino suggested that mothers pay constant attention not only to the conduct of their daughters, keeping them busy at all times and punishing them if they were restless or frivolous, but also to their offspring's early religious education, teaching them their first prayers and punishing them for sins committed in the house, such as swearing and lying.[74] The general educational rules that Dominici traced for Bartolomea to follow were based on Saint Jerome; they gave mothers sole responsibility for the religious education of their children. Without leaving the domestic arena, but "making the house a temple," the mother should mold her children's souls and introduce them to religious practices as if they were a game, chiding them sweetly but strictly for their failings and turning them gradually into little ministers of the domestic cult.[75]

Some humanist pedagogues shared the opinion that religion and morality were particularly suitable areas for women to work within. Leonardo Bruni, who wrote *De studiis et litteris* for an exceptionally cultured woman, Battista Malatesta, is an example.

His educational course included all the classical writers, but it ultimately aimed at providing a moral and religious education.

The fact remained that an ideal humanistic education in civil life and *studia humanitatis* excluded women. Even within the family she had little to teach. The central position occupied by the question of children in treatises on the family stressed the father's role in the formation of his children; it drastically relegated the mother to purely natural functions. It was the father who cared for his children, be it before conception by choosing a strong, healthy, well-mannered wife suitable for bearing children, or during pregnancy by watching over his wife's diet and state of mind, taking care to avoid any turbulence that might endanger the child-to-be. The first years of life were the only ones in which the mother was allowed to intervene, to surround the child with love and attention, and to fulfill her specific mission of breast-feeding.

The question of breast-feeding created widespread discussion among religious and lay writers and rewarded mothers with their only truly "educational" role: nutrition. A mother who chose not to breast-feed was considered unnatural, selfish, insensitive, even cruel. A mother unable to breast-feed transferred the responsibility of deciding a child's destiny—that is, hiring a wet nurse—to the father. The choice of the right wet nurse, according to medical, hygienic, and also moral criteria, was the first step on a long educational course the father would complete with no further assistance from his wife.

Only a humanist such as Maffeo Vegio, filled with religious spirit, demanded a more important position for mothers in the education of their children: in both the traditionally exclusive area of daughters, usually completely ignored in humanistic treatises, and the possibility of playing a role in educating sons.[76] Mothers were taught to try to develop modesty in their daughters, a crucial virtue, especially in view of the fact that girls were destined to marry. Other virtues to work toward, useful in their future as wives, were malleability, prudence, wit, constance, sobriety, diligence, and coyness. As far as sons were concerned, mothers should oversee their moral and religious conduct, using the only instrument at their disposal: admonishment, either directly or via an entrusted mediator. A model for this double pedagogical role was Monica, Augustine's holy mother, who was an incarnation of maternal virtue and an example of behavior for both parents. Monica's commitment to converting her son was held up as a symbol of hope for the most desperate cases. Her tools, however—prayers and tears—were both an indication and an accusation of the structural weakness of female interference in family affairs.

While the family played an increasingly important part in fifteenth-century culture and ideology, women, who had always been seen within the context of the family, increasingly were afforded little consideration. Religion was the only area in which, at least at a theoretical level, new ground was being broken for them. The debate over the existence of a female renaissance, engendered by Joan Kelly's seminal article, has shown how women throughout the Middle Ages gradually lost out in terms of status, power, and "visibility."[77] David Herlihy's hypothesis[78] that one can talk about a female renaissance only in terms of the spiritual charisma accorded figures such as Catherine of Siena, Margery Kempe, Julian of Norwich, and Catherine of Genoa is confirmed by fifteenth-century treatises on the family which reveal only one real novelty: the discovery that women had souls.

TRANSLATED FROM THE ITALIAN BY CLARISSA BOTSFORD

5

Regulating Women's Fashion

Diane Owen Hughes

BY THE RENAISSANCE most social critics had come to agree that fashion rose on the backs of women, confirming an association between clothes and the female sex that would endure for centuries. "Dame mode et dame élégance / sont deux soeurs" (Dame fashion and dame elegance / are two sisters), goddesses rather than gods, explained a fascinated and generally sympathetic analyst of their progress in the France of Louis XIII, "because Fashion is a Disease of women, whereas it is merely a passion of men. We esteem ways that are in vogue, but they idolize them."[1] The association had been noticed in imperial Rome, where satirists and moralists developed a style of mockery and derision of women's attachment to luxurious dress that would be borrowed and developed by early Christian critics like Clement of Alexandria and Tertullian.

Their arguments, however, lost both force and an audience in the long centuries of Germanic settlement that produced a new and less urban Europe. If Germans took to the luxuries of empire with greater gusto than Tacitus had cared to admit, moralists within the Germanic world tended to portray them as a male vice. It is true that Saint Aldhelm criticized Anglo-Saxon nuns for wearing satin underclothes, scarlet tunics, silk-striped sleeves, and fur-trimmed shoes, but it was the nuns' vocation rather than their gender that rendered the clothes inappropriate. When his countryman Alcuin blamed Danish raids on English worldliness, he directed his remarks to men—clerics and courtiers. So too, across the Channel, the first medieval sumptuary controls, issued by Charlemagne and his pious son, drew no special attention to the costume or ostentation of women.

An Extravagant Fondness for Appearance

Nor was the fashion revolution of the high Middle Ages perceived initially as a female conspiracy. As economic revival made luxury goods more readily available and as better communication stimulated the spread of fashion, the new shimmer and shape of women's clothes began to attract attention. What attracted criticism was their adoption by men. Twelfth-century monastic chroniclers found signs of moral decline not in the close-fitting, elongated costumes of women, but in the tight lacing and exaggerated trains of men, whose flowing locks and mincing gait completed a transvestite assault on the styles of a martial past. They also traced the invention of some particularly odious fashions directly to male vanity. Orderic Vitalis, for example, lambasted the new fashion of long, pointed shoes, which he attributed to Fulk of Anjou, who had designed them as a way of hiding the shape of his malformed feet and to conceal "protuberances, which are commonly called bunions."[2]

Within a century, however, the moralists' gaze had turned toward women and their increasingly insatiable appetite for fashion. The characterization of Marguerite of Provence as a fashion-hungry queen who tried to persuade a reluctant Louis IX to adopt an ostentatious dress more suitable to their royal station is a case in point. If Robert of Sorbon's story exemplified the king's renowned asceticism, it also relied on a new perception of women as unnatural peacocks. Apparently Marguerite desisted only when her husband demanded in return that she assume more humble robes—an act of renunciation of which women were becoming increasingly incapable. In playing on the fashion hunger of women and developing it into a misogynic theme, the *Roman de la Rose* allegorized and promoted an appetite that was already on the way to gaining a wide European audience, as it threatened to devour the world of men. Not content with fur-lined gowns, fine woolen hose, shoes with pointed toes, rich mantles, and elaborate head-dresses, voracious fashionmongers of the thirteenth century hungered for a piece of their lover's flesh *(un tronson de vo pel)* to attach to the borders of their dresses—or so claimed the author of a contemporary rondeau. The new prominence of women in the world of fashion required an adjustment of old arguments. As once men had been charged with adopting the fashions of women, now women would be chastised for their masculine attire—for prancing through the streets of fourteenth-century Milan like Amazons, in gold girdles and beaked shoes symbolic of their martial, masculine hearts; or, in England, for riding horseback at tournaments dressed in bicolored tunics with daggers at the belt, looking more like participants than spectators.

Responsibility for the translation and transmission of fashion gradually shifted to women. English chroniclers would point out that the Flemish, French, and central European styles that seemed to exert a corrupting influence on the fourteenth- and fifteenth-century court had been introduced by the foreign consorts of their kings. By the sixteenth century it seemed easy everywhere to find a source of a newly dominant Spanish style in the flock of princesses sent from Castile to marry abroad. Englishmen were quick to note, as she rode to her marriage in London, that the costume of Catherine of Aragon conveyed "the straunge dyversitie of rayement of the contreth of Hispayne."[3] Frenchmen, more critically, upbraided Leonor of Castile not only for wearing Spanish fashions in France but also for tempting the king himself to adopt them. By that time women had become the visual embodiment of a *varietas vestium* symbolic of political fragmentation and moral confusion, as their costume seemed to blur proper boundaries of nation, gender, and even species.[4]

Yet it can hardly be argued that women had come to monopolize the wares of Europe's important luxury fashion industry. A French princess might require for her 1351 wedding a costume of the reddest velvet, "richly embroidered and covered with large and small pearls,"[5] but her brother the dauphin more than rivaled her in a striped cape made of cloth woven of gold and silver thread and embroidered with at least two thousand large pearls. Nor is it clear that only women ran the race of fashion. If they responded with relish to temptations from abroad, they were not very different from the young Genoese gentleman who appeared at the court of Milan in German hat and boots, Catalanese belt, Italian doublet, and Burgundian-styled gown cut from English cloth. Indeed clothing inventories suggest that in Renaissance Rome it was men who were more consistently à la mode. Why, then, did the burden of fashion come to weigh so heavily on women's shoulders?

Costume, Consumption, and Female Status

The economic and social transformations of the eleventh and twelfth centuries had been spun out of cloth, which was not only a primary commodity of trade in Europe's widening markets and a basic industrial product of its fledgling towns but also a chief means of marking the distinctions of a new society. Rich cloth, often woven in the East, which had earlier served as a static icon of exceptional status or power, was now domestically available to costume the myriad social changes wrought by the political and economic reorganization of the high Middle Ages. Cloth, along with the costumes produced from it, quickly became a preeminent mark of social status and a signal of social mobility, as well as a means of fashioning social and political distinction.

As new wealth allowed investment in clothes, clothes were invested with new meaning. At court cloth flowed through the hands of kings and princes not only to mark patronage and hierarchy but also to blur old boundaries and assert new ones. It has been argued that the sumptuary law issued by Philip the Fair in 1294, which denied the bourgeoisie the vestimentary marks of aristocracy, was actually a concession to the nobility, which resented royal patronage of that valuable and chameleon class. At the fifteenth-century court of René of Anjou, where the giving and wearing of cloth had long been a mark of royal patronage and esteem, a shift apparent around 1470 distinguished the royal line from others by making exclusive to it certain fabrics and costumes. In cities mercantile governments outlawed crowns, trains, cloth of samite and precious metals, ermine trims, and other pretensions of aristocratic fashion as they sought to establish a visual record of their new political order. There, however, the absence of fixed social boundaries combined with an availability of cloth to create a stylistic riot so threatening to social stability that many cities began to regulate, through endless sumptuary laws, the costume of their citizens from birth to the grave.

Society's Impress

Women were especially vulnerable to the social fashioning that costume allowed, for its visible marks helped to fix and solidify a social identity necessarily more fluid than that of the men who shaped it. A change that occurred almost simultaneously with the rise of cloth production in the twelfth and thirteenth centuries accentuated the ambiguity of their social position and contributed to their dependence on costume's distinctions and definitions: the development of a patrilineal ideology of descent through the male line. Designed to conserve the wealth and social position of families by limiting claims on their resources, patrilineal organization made the wife an outsider, lineally distinct not only from her husband but even, in a sense, from the children she bore him and his line. Her visual incorporation thus became more necessary as a way of blurring that distinction for the duration of the marriage in order to create an illusion of complete marital union. An unusual list of dresses, registered in Florence in 1343 so that they might continue to be worn in contravention of a recently promulgated sumptuary law, gives us a rare glimpse of such a process, as the matching costumes of wives of the Albizzi family form a clear patrilineal design in a riot of urban color. Shimmering white mantles embroidered with ivy and red grapes cloaked their natal identity and made wives from various parts of the city visual representatives of the Albizzi clan.

Less heraldically, gifts of clothes and jewels that husbands gave their wives at marriage should be seen not as mere sumptuary counters to trousseaux but as the means by which a husband might pretend to clothe his naked Griselda, placing on her an unmistakable sign of his claims. Looked at this way, queens who insisted on flaunting the fashions of their native lands seemed to reject both a marital and a national stamp. Similarly, bourgeois women who changed their clothes according to the whims of fashion threatened to develop individual personae that defied a husband's authority and weakened the collective identity of a line.

The Trousseau and the Dowry

At the same time, marriage became an ever more central social rite, a fundamental tool of social and political reconstruction. Within it more forceful ecclesiastical insistence on monogamy surely enhanced the bride's position, as it also added religious meaning to civil union. The trousseau worn and displayed at this visible ceremony was a sign of the honor the bride bore from her natal home, the clothes she received from her husband a token of the honor she would receive in her new one. Only the funeral could rival the wedding as a focus of community attention and sumptuary exhibition; and weddings, as any reader of Mauss will understand, invited a competition of giving, as each side struggled to dominate and to derive broader social benefit from the match.

The bride, ultimate award in this tournament of value, was also the beneficiary of an exchange made ever more exhausting by the inventions of an expanding fashion industry. It is not surprising that marriages were therefore among the first sumptuary events to be controlled by urban law. If in some German cities gifts to the groom were valuable enough to deserve equal sumptuary notice and regulation, south of the Alps everything focused on the bride. Few could hope to rival the extraordinary trousseau, filled with gowns of glimmering splendor—one embroidered with 8,966 pearls and 70 ounces of silver—that Ippolita Sforza brought to her marriage with Alfonso of Aragon in 1465. Yet even bourgeois women arrived at their husband's threshold with several changes of gowns, sleeves, and overcoats, numerous hats and veils, pairs of slippers and shoes, an array of jewelry, as well as purses and a host of smaller accessories. As the importance of marriage increased the social significance of trousseaux, they grew in size and complexity. Their rising value began to displace the hard cash given as dowry, inviting criticism and, then, legislative limits. Ippolita Sforza's jewel-encrusted trousseau had represented one-third of her enormous 200,000-florin dowry, a ratio that became the goal of many urban legislators.

Perishable Cloth and Corruptible Flesh

While the coin of dowry would underwrite the marriage and support its offspring, the cloth of trousseau might crumble into dust—a contrast intensified in the reign of fashion. The slashed sleeves and striped or bicolored gowns of the late fourteenth century were of a different nature from the long trains and sleeves criticized in the earliest sumptuary law. They more clearly consumed the cloth from which they were made. Such clothes, spattered with holes or pieced from strips of cloth, could not be easily unstitched and refashioned for future generations. This consumption was accelerated by a Renaissance fashion boom. One of its chief chroniclers, the fashion writer Cesare Vecellio, despaired at ever writing a fully complete account of women's costumes, because "they are highly susceptible to change and vary more than the shape of the moon . . . So it is to be feared that, while I am writing about one fashion, they may change to another, making it impossible for me to cover everything."[6]

The extreme variability of fashion dated trousseaux and made dress a less durable good, not passed on gradually to daughters but traded off quickly to servants, whose rich costume consequently introduced confusions of hierarchy and occasioned bitter satire. If the need to keep up with the constantly more fickle demands of fashion encouraged women to include bolts of uncut cloth among the fashionable dresses of their trousseaux, it also drove husbands into the legislature to outlaw the new fashions in ruffs, bodices, and sleeves which, if they were to bow to social pressure and keep their wives à la mode, threatened to consume lineal wealth for the duration of the marriage.

As fashion became so important a determinant of their social definition, its characteristics clung to women's flesh. Vecellio's description of a fashion as changeable as the moon accompanies his observation of "the instability and love of variety that are common among women."[7] As fashion's scissors transformed cloth from a commodity of production and exchange into a sumptuary good, they also seemed to cut women out of a reproductive exchange system. Like the costumes they wore, women became static sumptuary icons, consumed in their social value and thus destructive of a system of demographic and social reproduction. Florence's call for new sumptuary controls in 1433, after almost a century of plague had heightened demographic awareness, uses almost these terms to attack the city's fashionable women, who,

> heedless of the fact that the sons they are carrying have been propagated by men, whose sacks of semen, perfect by nature, make them men. Women are unmindful that nature deems it inappropriate for them to adorn themselves with such sumptuous ornamentation that men refrain from marital coitus on account of these inappropriate garments, which cause manly vigor to fail. Women should remember that their role is to replenish the polity with children, to preserve their chastity

within the confines of marriage, and to forswear the wearing
of gold and silver garments and jewelry.[8]

In attributing the need for such legislation to the "barbarous
and untamed bestiality of women," Florentines called attention to
a carnal sexuality which costume flaunted rather than covered. If,
as some anthropologists have proposed, a socially dangerous sexuality—usually associated with flesh, decomposition, and
women—can be opposed to an ancestral fertility celebrated
through the male line, fashion's consumptive force made Renaissance women particularly susceptible to that analysis.

The decaying cloth of fashion also strengthened a relation
between women and the corruptibility of the flesh. Almost from
its inception fashion had served to accentuate a religious contrast
between pure, eternal, spirit and corrupt, mortal flesh. In one of
their earliest literary encounters, three living men who are guided
to spiritual understanding on meeting a corpse whose outward
dignities are evaporating with his flesh ask, "Where are the beautiful robes / With golden girdles / The finger rings / With precious
stones?"[9] To this vestimentary enumeration, later confraternal
lauds added gowns, hats, and fashionable trimmings, which lay
rotting, along with eyes, flesh, and pieces of hair, in the disarray
of the grave. Fashion fed a macabre imagination, which saw
through its consumptive fripperies to the corruptible flesh beneath,
and which denied its apparent power of restoration and renewal
by locating in every new design a potential for decay.

By the fifteenth century, in step with fashion's inflations,
women had moved to assume a central place in popular representations of the macabre, as they do in a Triumph of Death from
Palermo. There the rich jewels, dresses, and remarkable headdresses of a group of idle fashionplates form the most static and
poignant contrast to death's sudden, ugly fury. In more intimate
encounters costume often contributed to the eroticism of the macabre. Nicholas Manuel Deutsch's arresting 1517 image portrays
a common theme: the embracing of a young woman by death,
who is represented as a decomposing corpse. Deutsch intensifies
the erotic element by dressing the woman in a fashionable and
inviting gown, under whose raised skirts death inserts his bony
fingers. Her costume suggests a sexuality that not only invites the
kiss of death but also excites a male desire which will produce no
issue. Fashionably dressed women—"painted coffins with rotten

bones," an English critic described them[10]—thus become the ulti-mate symbol of a too transitory material world, corrupted initially by Eve's sin.

Fashion for Eve's Daughters

As daughters of Eve, the women of medieval Europe further suf-fered from a Christian reading of clothes as evidence for the evolution of sin rather than as a reflection of the civilizing process. An invention of sin's necessity, clothing pushed man backward to reverse the process of creation. The skins in which Adam and Eve had clothed their nakedness were an outward sign of a new bes-tiality that diminished their resemblance to the God who had created them in his image. "Next it led to wool; next to dung of worms, that is, to silk; next to gilded pieces of cloth; finally to precious stones," as countless sermons outlined the devolution.[11] Rich clothing was thus an inverse token of man's shrinking stature in creation, recording his descent from the gods to the beasts that live above the earth, to those which crawl beneath it, and finally to the immobile and infertile world of metal and stone. Its evo-lution, an English preacher explained to his flock, was accom-plished in response to a developing complex of sin:

> At first a tunic of skins was fashioned for the naked body, in token that through his sin man was become like the beasts which by nature are clad in raiment of skins alone. But later, as their pride grew, men used garments made of wool. Third, through much more ample nourishing of carnal delight, they used garments made from plants of the earth, namely of linen, and fourth, silken garments, which are fashioned from the entrails of worms—all of which kinds of raiment are now rather for vainglory and worldly pomp than for the necessity of nature . . . and assuredly most of all to excite lust.[12]

Costume, Symbol of Sin

If costume was the result and sign of sin for all mankind, how much more potent a symbol could it be for those made in the likeness of Eve, whose original temptation and fall had initiated the vestimentary process. The voice of Tertullian echoed through the Christian centuries, reminding women of their particular relation, through that first mother, to the clothing he castigated in his influential *De Habitu Muliebri:*

> If from the beginning of time the Milesians had been shearers of sheep, the Chinese spinners of silk, the Tyrians dyers, the Phrygians embroiderers, and the Babylonians weavers of tapestry; if pearls had gleamed and brilliants sparkled, if gold itself had already emerged from the earth, bringing greed with it, if furthermore mirrors had already existed to reflect lying images, Eve would have coveted all these things, once she was banished from paradise and, in my view, already dead. A woman therefore, if she hopes for rebirth [in heaven], should not long for them now, or even know of them, since she did not possess them or know of them when she was truly alive [before banishment from Eden]. For all these things are the trappings of a woman who is damned and dead, arranged as if to lend splendor to her funeral.[13]

The funeral was not only her own, for the finery symbolizing her pride and lust could also assume an active role in destroying civilization itself. Moralists stressed its peculiar bestiality, paying special attention to two bits of frippery: trains, whose Latin name *(cauda)* invited comparison with an animal's tail, and fantastic headdresses, whose feathers and form suggested the barnyard. A French satire described women who donned two-pointed headdresses, *cornettes*, as fuming like devils, pricking and striking the men in their path—as if to suggest that through such frivolous fashions women might perpetually reenact the original temptation and defeat of Adam by Eve.

If, in the authoritative opinion of Thomas Aquinas, women's love of clothing might be treated as a venial sin when it was fostered by vanity rather than lust, later mendicant preachers regarded it as a mortal sin. In their creative hands fashion became a key to understanding the social and moral crisis of the age. Bernardino of Siena and his Observant followers, preaching amid local dislocations of plague and under a global threat of fifteenth-century Turkish advance, found a primary source of Christendom's decline in the costume of its women. First, they argued, women so increased the fashion ante that marriages were delayed until the pieces of an ever-expanding trousseau could be bought and paid for, thus depriving society of the births needed to overcome demo-

145

graphic decline. Even worse, the lack of marriage opportunity encouraged the perversion of sexuality into a sodomitic sterility: "Who can make so many species?" asked Bernardino. "And because of this the population is down and sodomy is on the rise."[14] The devolution of costume downward through the creative process to the gold, silver, and precious stones that were woven into fifteenth-century gowns, thus quite literally signaled and reproduced the sterility of that geological past.

As Christian society was diminished by fashion, the friars' argument ran, so were the Jews enriched, for men resorted to Jewish usurers to feed the fashion hunger of their wives and daughters. This silent partnership between the female fashionmonger and the Jewish moneylender represented the final perversion of the natural order—not only because Jews became rich at Christian expense, but because the course of natural fertility was thereby reversed. As women's costly fashions impeded human reproduction, they also allowed the usurer to breed money in ways that any Aristotelian found unnatural. That world of gold and stone, which represented at once the height of fashion and the abyss of mankind, thus achieved its final supremacy.

It is tempting to dismiss such a serious social and moral reading of fashion just as Chaucer's irrepressible Wife of Bath brushed off ecclesiastical admonitions:

> Thou seyst also, that if we make us gay
> With clothying, and with precious array,
> That it is peril of oure chastitee;
> And yet, with sorwe! thou most enforce thee,
> And seye this wordes in the Apostles name:
> "In habit maad with chastitee and shame
> Ye women shul appaille yow," quod he,
> "And noght in tressed heer and gay perree,
> As perles, ne with gold ne clothes riche."
> After they texts, ne after they rubriche,
> I wol nat wirche as muchel as a gnat.[15]

That seems to have been the response of the women of Flanders and Artois who had been forced to renounce their steeple headdresses in the wake of a 1428 preaching tour by the friar Thomas Couette. Once the fire of his rhetoric had cooled, they discarded the simple peasant caps he recommended and built steeples even higher than before. To privilege such individual responses, however, is to ignore the cumulative weight of the mendicant challenge, issued over the course of several generations in missions that ranged from Sicily into Flanders, from Spain into Hungary and Dalmatia—in settings that were often lit by great bonfires of the vanities, which consumed in rites of public purification the follies of fashion against which the friars railed.

The Mendicant Challenge

Monarchal governments were probably the least receptive to the changes demanded by the friars. In Aragon the queen herself may have been so moved by their sermons that she trimmed the trains from her gowns as an example to her subjects, but such example at court seldom led to transforming legislation for a kingdom. Hierarchical considerations made costume too valuable a mark of social boundaries to allow its redefinition according to sexual categories. When her Franciscan confessor complained of the luxury and license at the Spanish court, Isabella felt obliged to respond by comparing the plainness of her dress and that of her ladies with the rich costume of the men. However, when she and Ferdinand soon after began to issue a long series of sumptuary edicts, their categories continued to be determined by status, not gender—as they also were in northern kingdoms.

It is within the cities, many of which secured their wealth from the clothing industry, that sumptuary law, issued with new urgency by bishops and municipal councils, encoded the friars' message. The codes influenced by their sermons betray a single-minded focus on the fashions of women, who are treated as a single group, undifferentiated by social hierarchy. Some places went so far as to abolish exemptions that had earlier allowed the wives and daughters of nobles, doctors, and men of law to escape the full rigor of vestimentary control. The fact that their costume confirmed social hierarchy now seemed less important than the sexual message it conveyed. Sumptuary distinction throughout the urban world became more clearly defined by a thundering mendicant question. After describing the ornate and extravagant footwear and clothing worn by women, one challenged, "what more can harlots add?"[16] Those whose rich dress flouted the sumptuary law would now risk passing for prostitutes rather than for noblewomen. Trains, whose extravagant use of cloth had once been enough to condemn them, now became a hiding place for devils rather than a sign of aristocratic pretension. Some attributed their invention not to the court but to the brothel, which may be why the bishop of Ferrara spared only prostitutes from the excommunication threatening women who wore them in his city. Urban councils often responded by permitting changes in the dress of prostitutes, who might now cast off the signs and degrading costumes of the past to assume the sumptuous fashions denied other women. If, by increasing their allure, some cities hoped to attract men away from the graver offense of homosexuality, more were simply anticipating Montaigne's suggestion that assigning luxury to prostitutes would be the most effective way of degrading it. Such a program nevertheless reflects a progressive sexualization and demonization of women's fashion.

Special Forms of Sin

The castigation of two Renaissance fashions shows some of the ways in which ecclesiastical and secular approaches could join in a sexual reading of women's clothes. Both fashions enormously increased—and probably had been designed to increase—the amount of cloth a woman's gown could display. But their critics mounted a moral rather than an economic attack.

Chopines

Chopines—shoes set on platforms of leather, wood, or cork—had become popular by the fifteenth century in some Italian cities, as well as in Spain, where Queen Isabella's confessor complained that the elbow-length-high shoes of his day were depleting the nation's cork supply. More to the domestic point, and as Italian legislators noticed, by raising women high above the ground, they made a mockery of laws regulating the amount of cloth in a dress through the limitation of trains that trailed on the ground. It was the moral rather than economic extravagance threatened by chopines that really condemned them, however. Everyone noticed the extraordinary immobility they produced in women who hobbled about on them, as if on stilts. Here were shoes that prevented walking—which prompted a comparison in fifteenth-century Venice with the Chinese custom of binding feet. Legislators in that city went further, condemning the fashion because "pregnant women, going about the streets on chopines so high that they cannot keep their balance, have fallen and in some cases were hurt so badly that they miscarried or gave birth to premature children, destroyed in mind and body."[17] The contribution to sterility and spiritual loss of such shoes made them more appropriate for prostitutes, to whom some governments consigned them. What a sixteenth-century English critic called their prisoner's gait condemned them for citizen wives because it transformed women into hobbled figures of display, keeping them from serving as vessels of social reproduction.

Farthingales

The farthingale, one of the most condemned yet enticing of Renaissance fashions, at first might seem to belie such an interpretation. A frame that held dresses away from the hips, it eventually became a hoop or series of hoops whose shieldlike rigidity suggested in Italy and Spain the name *guardinfante*. As hip-extenders, these *verdugos* conquered the fifteenth-century Castilian court, whence that court's extensive diplomatic wooing sent them abroad. English observers immediately noted that Catherine of Aragon and her ladies wore "benethe their wast certayn round hopys, berying owte the gowns form their bodies aftr their country manr."[18] But by the reign of Queen Elizabeth, who fancied it, the farthingale had become fully Anglicized, as the identical *vertugalles* had become a French fashion at the court of Francis I. Hoops became a mark and support of late Renaissance style, holding dresses far from the natural contours of the body and requiring, like chopines, yards of extra fabric to cover them. Yet critics of the fashion preferred moral to economic arguments, citing the secrets the farthingale hid rather than the cloth it displayed. It is true that some, like two Genoese women who disapprove of the style in a *Ragionamento di sei nobili fanciulle genovesi* (Discussion of Six Noble Genoese Maidens, 1583), noticed that beyond the difficulty in getting through doors, it "is not very comfortable for sitting, since you first must take a great deal of trouble in arranging it if you do not wish to make a spectacle of yourself."[19] But what generally troubled moralists was not only the constriction it placed on a woman's natural function and its concealment of prostitute pleasures. Like chopines, it was criticized for bending the female body to serve fashion, forcing a perversion of its natural use, the bearing of children, whose fetal development its rigid hoops and stays threatened to harm. Moreover, in keeping pregnancies hidden under the voluminous gowns it supported, the farthingale allowed women unacceptable sexual license.

The Puritan parson Stephen Gosson went further than most in attributing the invention to prostitutes as a means of holding the fine fabric of their skirts away from their pox-soiled underclothes. Many, however, would have agreed with the anonymous author of *Le blason des basquines de vertugalles* that hoops served to hide the consequences of sexual liberty: "What good are these Gallic virtues / But to engender scandals?"[20] This question brings us back to the earliest Spanish explanation of their origin, in 1468, at the court of Juana de Portugal, notorious consort of Henry IV, the Impotent. According to a courtier-historian who seems to have been in the know, the queen had found in the farthingale a means of keeping secret the consequences of an indiscretion. Her example encouraged its use among the ladies of the court, who consequently took on the appearance of pregnant matrons. If the so-called guardinfante protected the unborn child, it was, therefore, a child whose legitimacy might be called into question. Far from implanting a mark of patrilineality, the fashion allowed wives to hide the most noticeable sign of its claims.

The threatening sterility of both fashions is implied in a contemporary drawing of a fashionably attired Venetian courtesan. Lifting with both hands the great skirt that covers her farthingale, she exposes not only giant chopines but also the elegant male trousers that seem to have formed a part of the extensive wardrobe of most Italian courtesans. Whether or not the trousers suggest the sale of sodomitic pleasures, they certainly reveal a transvestite freedom that let her control her body as if she were a man. At first glance her chopines and farthingale seem to provide a feminine contrast to their mannish style, but actually they are of a piece. For by subverting costume's assigned role as an instrument of patrilineal design, the hoops and stays and platform shoes offer transgressive freedoms of their own.

A sexual reading of costume might also produce fashion. Thirteenth-century ecclesiastics had tried to create a visual category of female honor by insisting on the veil as a sign of the properly married woman—a fashion specifically denied by many urban governments to public prostitutes, who had to walk the streets with bare faces. That initiative had faltered with the invention of veils of transparent silk, which hid nothing, and more elaborate face coverings, which hid too much, dangerously masking a woman's identity and status. Although civic authorities were less inclined to create special vestimentary styles, preferring merely to react to fashions as they arose, the black pall cast over many women in the seventeenth and eighteenth centuries suggests a pressing need, even at that date, to mark women by sexual category rather than rank or status.

The Color Black

A Florentine ducal statute of 1638 abandoned earlier hierarchical codes cloaking women progressively in the black of sexual abstention, once a mark of widows and ecclesiastics. After six years of marriage—years during which fashion might legitimately serve as a sexual enticement to strengthen the marriage bond—the wives of Florentine citizens were required to pack away their colorful gowns and instead don robes of black, which might, however, have colored bodices, sleeves, and collars. These splashes of color had to be discarded in their turn after twelve years of marriage, when presumably the productive sexuality of the childbearing years was drawing to a close. Siena's deprival of color to all married women after the second year of their first marriage was accompanied—in an implicit nod to the old mendicant categories—by its award to whores. Florence and Venice's permitting of color only to non-nobles in the countryside and non-citizens within the town suggests how sexual distinction came not only to control the signs of female honor but also to mark the propriety of the urban space from a garish cacophony of rural and lower-class license. This contrast was strengthened by the early association of black with noble virtue in the courts of Burgundy and Spain. The move into black may also have served mercantilist ends by withholding from Mediterranean women the colorful textiles of a new Atlantic manufacture. If so, ideas of sexual and economic extravagance had once more merged to define female sumptuary categories.

Women's Response

The forced attachment to fashions of the flesh charged women's dressing and undressing with particular symbolic meaning. Those who sought to subdue the flesh as a means of freeing the spirit

151

had difficulty in escaping costume's categories and definitions. While male saints like Francis of Assisi might dramatically strip off their clothes as a sign of spiritual detachment from worldly entanglement, women found it more difficult to undress in public. Mary Magdalene's penitential nudity, covered only by her flowing hair, may have been a mark of her sanctity, but it also stood as a sign of the sexual nature of her sin. Even in rejecting rich clothes for a costume of penitential rags, women raised questions about the social identity and sexual honor not only of themselves but of their families—questions that apparently only the habit and cloister could put to rest.

Renunciation

Secular women of a spiritual persuasion found clothing dangerously confining, its collective social and sumptuary value a threat to the integrity of their individual souls. A thirteenth-century sermon, cast in the form of a mother's instructions to her young daughter, describes the peril posed to every married woman by the clothing demanded by the marriage game: "Hate, my beautiful daughter, and despise with all your heart worldly dress and finery, and never wear them even once."[21] Her model should be Esther, who disdained the honors she could not reject. Such a sermon might have served as a model for women like the beautiful wife of Jacopone da Todi, who dutifully wore the finery that served as a mark of family rank and status. Only after her sudden death at a young age did her husband discover that her fashionably elegant attire had always concealed a hair shirt, which protected her spirit. Like the courtesan's trousers, the spiritual women's hair shirt offered a secret freedom from costume's authorized definitions. If Jacopone celebrated the discovery of his wife's spiritual undergarment as a step in his own conversion and a source of the religious lyric on which his fame would rest, for other women the hair shirt was a secret way of keeping the public and collective marks of clothing from searing through the flesh to contaminate the soul.

It is not surprising that renunciation of fashion is a more frequent theme in the hagiography of female than of male saints. When Umiliana dei Cerchi tried to develop a spiritual life within the confines of a marriage that forced on her the dress suited to her rich husband's station, for example, she trimmed the hems short and saved the excess, along with all her headdresses (except one of linen and a portion of another made of silk), to distribute to the poor of Florence. The gesture goes back to Saint Martin, but in Umiliana's case it moves beyond charity to become a sign of stubborn resistance to patriarchal control. More surprising is the apparent reluctance of women like Umiliana to step beyond private renunciation and denounce publicly the attachment to fashion of members of their sex. The ornaments of female vanity that Francesca Romana had removed from Roman women were offered in evidence of her sanctity in her canonization investigation. Yet neither she nor others like her found a voice to criticize rich costume if it was worn soberly and legitimately, that is, as a means of confirming familial status and social hierarchy.

Feminine Cunning and the Law

Women were more critical of restraints placed on their vestimentary freedom when they kept them from heeding fashion's call. Although sumptuary law regulated the costume of both sexes, women rightly felt particularly threatened by its controls, and it was usually they who petitioned for release from its constraints. In Italy, where most controls emanated from local legislatures or episcopal palaces, individual exemption might be sought from a higher authority. One noble Venetian woman secured from the pope the right to the clothes and jewels she had worn "for the sake of her parents' honor and her own advanced years" before a local sumptuary statute ruled them dishonorable. And the rhetorically skilled Battista Petrucci requested as a reward for her eloquent recitation before the emperor Frederick III release from Sienese sumptuary restriction.

Women more often used their skills, eloquence, and what Florentine legislators described as their "proliferating subtleties" to evade the law. Sacchetti's story of a harried enforcement officer, who tried to arrest a woman for wearing illegal buttons only to be told, "[these] are not buttons, they're couplings," records an inventive struggle preserved in the legal and administrative records of many Italian cities. They show that women kept an eye cocked for roving enforcers of the law, rushing into churches to avoid citation, and, if caught, defending their forbidden finery with a legal and linguistic virtuosity which the novelist's characters might have admired.

By the fifteenth century women were going beyond mere ex-

153

emption or evasion and mounting a spirited assault on the premises of control itself. The poet Christine de Pisan opened it obliquely in *Le Trésor de la Cité des Dames,* composed in 1405 as an allegory specifically directed against the misogyny of the *Roman de la Rose.* In her city, which Reason, Justice, and Rectitude built to protect women from the arrows of male attack, fashionable dress becomes a legitimate desire, worn not to seduce others but for the pleasure of the wearer alone. Within less ideal Italian cities, signs of a more extensive campaign, based on ethical and social rather than aesthetic arguments, can be detected.

Nicolosa Sanuti, the beautiful and aristocratic Bolognese whom Sabadino degli Arienti remembered clothed in a gown of purple silk with a rose-colored cloak lined with the finest ermine, issued an elaborate response to a sumptuary code imposed on the women of her city in 1453 by Cardinal Bessarion. Although he continued, through an intricate system of fabric, color, and style, to mark the boundaries of urban hierarchy through the dress of women, he nevertheless denied to all women, even aristocrats like Sanuti, cloth of gold and silver, which thus became a prerogative of men. This Nicolosa found hard to accept. Drawing on examples of noble women from antiquity to her own day, she challenged the law's right to treat women as a single, less virtuous category of humankind. Far from accepting the identification of women with the ephemeral goods of a transitory, material world, she argued that her sex alone offered a means of escaping the inevitable ravages of time—whose personification as the voracious male god Saturn, who devoured his sons, she took some pains to explicate. Only the fertility of women can mitigate his destructiveness, for "women are the ones who rebuild families, republics, indeed the whole human race, and restore what is high and immortal."

This is not the sterile sexuality of Eve, which leads but to the grave, but the socially creative power of the Sabines, whose collective womb produced an empire. In Sanuti's creative argument female clothes and finery do not prepare for a funeral and ensuing decay, as they had for Tertullian and the moralists who followed him, but for a wedding and its promise of rebirth. They should also serve, she claimed, as a unique means of rewarding women of distinction, who in her day were denied the offices expected by noble and virtuous men. For such women clothes must stand as a single, defining mark of status and value: "Adornment as well as refinement, for we must not allow, if we can prevent it, the signs of our virtue to be stripped from us."[22] If fashion is a woman, it is because women have been left only their clothing as a means of tailoring a social persona.

Not all agreed. From Venice came the more conventional voice of Laura Cereta, who was by her own admission drab of face and dress, a lover of letters not flashy clothes. In such finery she read the history of Venetian decline, with women its chief perpetrators—Delilahlike sappers of imperial strength. Seduced from republican virtue by a female appetite for luxury, Venice had become a lazy imitator and plunderer of the East, which, in the form of the Turk, would rise to smite her if women were not reduced to wearing "costumes that are not those of whores." The latter is the costume of women whose sexuality is uncontrolled by men. Predictably she called on the opposite sex to control the frailties of her own, warning in a voice of Hebraic prophecy that "the stricter the prohibition, the greater the guilt."[23]

In Defense of Fashion

Venetian councils were certainly doing this by the beginning of the seventeenth century, when Lucrezia Marinelli composed *La Nobiltà e l'Eccellenza delle Donne*. Regulatory legislation every other year (in contrast to a law every decade or so in the previous century) showed the new sumptuary fears of a city where consumption had replaced production as a major preoccupation of the governing class. Unlike kingdoms abroad and despotisms within Italy, republican Venice did not use the law to mark the social boundaries of hierarchy. Its sumptuary control touched everyone, but within its restriction limits butchers might dress like nobles. It may have been this social and legal situation that let Marinelli go beyond Sanuti's social defense of costume as a legitimate mark of status to allow the legitimacy of fashion itself—so long as it appeared on the back of a woman. Fashion allowed women a kind of self-definition that served as proof of the superiority of their sex. Men were too publicly defined by marks of trade and hierarchy to benefit from its transformations and thus were made ridiculous by its demands. Like the artisan husband, "all soiled with oxblood," whom she pictured waiting at home while his fashionable wife strolled through the streets in her silks, jewels, and chopines, men were indelibly marked by social position. Women, on the other hand, could take advantage of fashion's chameleon possibilities to become as noble as they looked. And this was just. For costume allowed them to display an inner dignity whose deficiency in men deprived their fashion of the power of social transformation.

Although the case for superiority was made on behalf of all women, the argument for fashion applied most perfectly to those of Italy. In contrast to French and Spanish women, who might exercise feudal power, or German and Flemish ones, who were free to take up a trade, Italian women, according to Marinelli, were especially susceptible to the self-definition that fashion allowed. Undefined, and thus unfettered, by the political and economic marks suffered by men everywhere and by women elsewhere, they were freer to express themselves through dress. Marinelli may have exaggerated the political and economic power of other women, but she was not alone in assigning to Italians a peculiar ability to exploit the creative and transgressive qualities of fashion.

By means of their clothes, women visibly participated in the self-fashioning that Burckhardt saw as a defining feature of Renaissance culture. As despots used arms and diplomacy to forge individual political identities, free of the constraints of older feudal and hierarchical ideals, so their wives and daughters used scissors and fabric to fashion individual social personalities, which might take precedence over a collective identity. Their position as in-marrying wives made such courtly women the natural conduits of foreign fashion, but they went further to blur the vestimentary marks of both their natal and marital home by seeking abroad for new inventions. Bona of Savoy wrote from Milan to Ginevra Bentivoglio to secure silk *fazzoletti* popular in Bologna. Beatrice d'Este, "innovator of new fashions in clothing," as Muralto described her, secured drawings of the queen of France's costume in order to introduce her style of headdress into Lombardy. Her sister Isabella became so renowned for the emissaries she sent abroad from Mantua to secure the fabrics and fashions necessary to create an international style that Francis I requested that she send to Paris a doll dressed in her latest fashions as a model for the ladies of his court.

In women's creative hands, costume's collective mark became less important than the individual statement it made. Thus color lost symbolic value as it was used to flatter eyes, hair, and skin. *Berettino,* a gray of mourning, would become a favorite color of

Isabella d'Este because she thought it suited her. And if the Venetian government put its women in black as a sign of their humility, contemporaries attributed the color's rapid adoption to its flattery of their fair complexions and bleached hair. Aesthetic appeal would likewise triumph over social prohibition as courtly women rejected clothing's symbolic meanings. Even earrings, with which, under mendicant pressure, many Italian cities had marked Jewish women in the fifteenth century, by the mid-sixteenth century had found a place in Christian ears.

What fashion signified became as changeable as fashion itself, always in need not just of recognition but also of interpretation. As its most perfect embodiment, women themselves demanded attention not as stable symbols of social value but as players in an endless game of social negotiation. If the individualism of the Renaissance turned such self-fashioning into an art, fashion threatened to make women the period's ultimate paradigm.

A Modern Assessment

Modern social critics have not been so quick to see in fashion a means of women's empowerment. Far from granting it the kind of fashioning possibilities that Marinelli celebrated, they have portrayed fashion's costumes as cloaks that hide the chains of a new female enslavement, an enslavement bound up in the cloth and clothing revolution of the later Middle Ages. Whereas hierarchical governments may have failed in their attempts to use costume to indicate inherited social boundaries, a nascent merchant capitalism did succeed in making it a principal social signifier, a mark of the conspicuous consumption on which its economy depended and which became a measure of economic growth and social success.

Although men managed and profited from the consumer economy, women bore the brunt of its demands. As Veblen argued, the progenitors of rising capitalism were able to escape some of the most troubling manifestations of the world they created by encouraging households to consume vicariously through the fashions of women. The restless invention and planned obsolescence inherent in a consumer society thus became clearly associated with the female character, as men competitively clothed their women while themselves retreating from fashion's game. Of course men too could be peacocks. Yet apparently there was no sumptuary law directed at women equivalent to the directive Venice issued to its male ruling class in the fifteenth century: that it dress more colorfully and splendidly. If their sober garb was deemed threatening to the prestige of a city that had profited enormously from a trade in flashier wares, it also signified a character of conservation and stability that was becoming increasingly appropriate to a governing class that was beginning to distance itself from its trading origins.

The male patriciate could dress like monks, however, only because its wives and daughters asserted family status by rising to fashion's challenge and changing costume with the season—visual proof of consumer success. According to this scenario, women dressed in the service of men, losing in the process the attributes of constancy, prudence, and stability deemed necessary to good governance and spiritual seriousness. They had been fashioned into the most temporal of creatures in an increasingly time-conscious world.

This argument must be modified by acknowledging the enthusiasm with which women played the fashion game and by recognizing that, as the qualities of fashion bound themselves to women's flesh and defined the character of the wearer, its costumes also offered women a means of reordering social distinction and of reenacting the social process. Women not only played the game, they sometimes made, or at least altered, the rules. A collaboration between fashion-hungry women and profit-hungry manufacturers in the thirteenth century, for example, could transform an ecclesiastical requirement that forced married women to veil their faces from a marking device to a transgressive opportunity, as silken veils obscured and elaborate headcoverings masked patrilineal identities. Fashion might also attach male styles to female dress, not to turn women into men but to suggest to its wearer (and her critics) a new virile empowerment.

That such transformations were more imaginary than real is a sign of fashion's limitation. It is also a sign of its power. From the ubiquitous chopines and farthingale, to the eight hundred peacock feathers a Florentine silk merchant bought to make a hat for his young bride, or the Turkish garb that Beatrice d'Este stitched for the ladies of her court, fashion was fantasy. A fantasy of dreams but also of utopian possibility. That may be why women worshiped it.

two

Family
and Social Strategies

The Hidden Power of Women

If we were to take at their word the men who wielded legal power over women and heard their confessions, who assailed them with endless treatises and sermons, we would have no choice but to conclude that women were ensnared in webs of rules so constraining that they could not utter a word or move a muscle. Were women in fact passive in the face of these exhortations to obedience? Were they objects of exchange among men, their fate sealed by the dictates of matrimonial strategy and family ambition? Part Two of this book examines the extent to which the representation of gender affected the destinies of individual women. In so doing we occasionally discover ways in which women were able to capitalize on the handicaps and advantages afforded by the system of relations between the sexes. Within the family and in certain social contexts women exercised real power. They also wielded what may be called compensatory or supplementary powers. And of course vast occult powers were ascribed to them out of fear and ignorance.

Law exists at the intersection of social representations and social practices. It imposes rules and prohibitions. It extends certain protections to women but in return enforces certain limitations on their actions. The law is molded by ideas and images. The Germanic tribes that settled in what had been the Roman Empire brought with them a variety of legal systems. Although these "barbarian" codes conflicted in some ways with the principles of Roman law as embodied in the Code of Justinian, the clash proved invigorating. Tribal laws varied as to women's rights and obligations. Suzanne Fonay Wemple examines the diversity of the law from late antiquity to the Carolingian period. Yet despite this diversity one concern loomed above all others: how to regulate marriage and therefore women.

Marriage, which determined how the fundamental cells of society related to one another, was the theater in which the destinies of women were played out, and understanding it is the key to understanding relations between the sexes, between individuals and groups, and between the domestic and public spheres. In medieval Europe marriage was a rite of passage between childhood and adult life. Its preliminaries and forms were a mirror of social aspirations. Theologians and canonists reflected endlessly on its meaning, and both Church and state hoped to shape the new institution of matrimony as it passed from theory into practice. The eleventh and twelfth centuries were a period during which marriage became a sacrament of the Church. The process was a difficult one, marred by missteps and regression.

In discussing historical change it is often easier for historians to agree about obstacles and impediments than about meaning. The facts are clear, but their implications are not. The facts about the status of women in the Middle Ages can be read in different ways, depending on whether one chooses to emphasize legal, economic, or demographic factors.

The subject of marriage, for example, has interested demographic and legal historians as well as historians of women. Demographic history, austere as it is, has been a fruitful source of insights in recent years. Among other things, it has focused attention on the place of women in preindustrial societies. To one degree or another all four of the chapters in this section draw on demographic findings.

The implications of demographic research for the history of women are problematic, as indeed the demographic history of the whole Middle Ages is problematic. Demographers interested in the period lack the data necessary to match the rigor of demographic research on more recent periods, after governments and the Church began compiling vital records. The findings of medieval demographers, although dubious and hard to generalize, have profoundly influenced historians' thinking about the place of women in medieval society.

Consider the concept of a "marriage market," the rather incongruous term used to cover the phenomenon of matrimonial supply and demand. The state of this market usually is described in terms of demographics, particularly the ratio of men to women or the age at which marriage is considered possible. Other nondemographic factors may also play a part: laws of inheritance, customs bearing on property exchange in connection with marriage, and the desire for economic independence may encourage or discourage individuals considering marriage. Thus marriage statistics can tell us a great deal about a society. Demographers such as Hajnal use these statistics to generate what they consider a fundamental indicator of historical change.[1] But can medieval marriage statistics be used in this way? The available data are scarce, widely scattered, heterogeneous, and often pertinent only to the upper echelons of society. The danger is that, relying as we must on such scattered impressions, we may be tempted to build an elaborate theory on a few scant items of information.

Little work has been done to compare matrimonial practices in different parts of medieval Europe or to classify variant behaviors and statistical sources.[2] In one recent project, David Herlihy attempted to examine the constitution of the western European "household" from antiquity to the fifteenth century.[3] Herlihy treats marriage in terms of an innovative set of data connected with marital age. The figures were gleaned from such disparate sources as chronicles, hagiographies, Carolingian census counts, and late-medieval tax rolls. The result is a sweeping overview of European development. Of course the early figures reflect mainly the upper strata of society, for even the saints sprang mainly from the privileged classes. Not until the end of the Middle Ages does it become possible to catch a glimpse of humbler, more representative groups. Comparison with earlier periods rests on a narrow, hence tenuous, base. The results of the survey must be treated as a working hypothesis.

With that caveat in mind, what did Herlihy find? From antiquity to the Middle Ages, Europe witnessed a succession of different matrimonial models. In ancient times girls in early adolescence married much older men. From the very early Middle Ages until roughly the twelfth century, husband and wife were of approximately the same age, in keeping with customs of the Germanic tribes as described by Tacitus. Late in the Middle Ages the "ancient" model reemerged, and the ages of husband and wife once again diverged.

The age difference between husband and wife at first marriage is undoubtedly correlated with customs of property exchange between the spouses' families. The change that occurred in the late Middle Ages was surely related to the revival of the dowry system, which in turn was related to the twelfth-century rediscovery of Roman law. Under this system the bride and her family bore the brunt of the burden of constituting the dowry. The parallel development of the new marital and the new legal system involved a series of complex interactions, but in the final analysis historians explain the change as the result of a shortage of prospective husbands—an excellent *deus ex machina*. This explanation is generally bolstered by certain propositions concerning domestic structure and internal household hierarchies as well as the quality (affective or authoritarian) of male-female relations.

Numerical disparity between the two sexes is clearly the crucial factor, however. This factor has also been invoked in various debates concerning the place of women in medieval society. The common thread in all these arguments is the assumption that many women had no prospect of marriage (or, in the case of widows, of remarriage), and that this in turn was a natural consequence of a shortage of men.

Since the work of Karl Bücher at the end of the nineteenth century, the so-called *Frauenfrage,* or Woman Question—that is, the problem of women without prospect of marriage—which is discussed in Chapter 7 by Paulette L'Hermite-Leclerq and in Chapter 9 by Claudia Opitz, has been dealt with up to now primarily by demographic methods. Early in this century the only available figures were derived from late-medieval urban census data. At best the sources shed light on relations between age groups or in some cases between the sexes, but there was no way of getting at individual behavior through statistical methods similar to those used in the study of more recent periods. Of the whole arsenal of techniques developed by historical demographers, medievalists have tended to focus on only one: the ratio of males to females. This became a key element in a number of different arguments. It was invoked to explain variations in the legal status of women, and marriage regulations in particular. It was used to account for the willingness of families to keep daughters at home and to explain the level of misogyny in society. And it has been cited to account for the participation of women in the economy and for the level of their religious involvement.

When these arguments are examined closely, however, it becomes clear that their documentary underpinning is weak. Given the dubiousness of most medieval statistics, all numbers are best taken with a grain of salt, yet overzealous researchers have at times taken them literally. As historians have begun to ask new questions, moreover, the narrow base of some of the statistical reconstructions has to be called into question.

The male-female ratio in the Middle Ages is notable for its variations. One reason for this is that the figures used to calculate it have been based on different types of communities. If we focus exclusively on a particular village or town, however, it seems plausible to assume that social relations between men and women are strongly influenced by the ratio of their numbers. The numbers are rarely equal in any particular locality, but the question is how to interpret the imbalance. Take, for example, the territory dominated by the abbey of Saint-Germain-des-Prés in the ninth century. Males far outnumbered females in the population, particularly among the children. The same was true in the regions of Farfa (Italy) and Rheims (France) around the year 800.[4] Yet women slightly outnumbered men and girls greatly outnumbered boys on the estates of Saint-Victor of Marseilles in

813–814.[5] These isolated figures from scattered localities are contradictory and difficult to interpret.

Matters do not become any clearer if we look at more recent times. Few accurate figures have survived from the central Middle Ages, but from the end of the thirteenth century on the sources are more abundant. Poll-tax records for thirty-six English villages in 1377 record the sex of residents above the age of fourteen; men outnumbered women 112 to 100.[6] The Tuscan *catasto* of 1427–1430 is a source of detailed information; here there was a shortage of women in both urban and rural communities. Overall the number of men was about 20 percent higher than the number of women.[7] But figures from elsewhere in Europe contradict these findings. At the end of the Middle Ages in cities of northern France (Rheims) and of Germany and the Netherlands (Freiburg, Basel, Nuremberg, Ypres) women outnumbered men.[8] Thus before 1500 we notice a contrast between northwestern Europe and the Mediterranean region; the northern pattern became general throughout Europe in urban areas in the sixteenth century.

From such contradictory results can we conclude, as many scholars have done, that when men outnumber women the reason is that the figures often underestimate the number of girls?[9] Daughters allegedly were easier to hide than boys from seigneurial, communal, and royal agents. In any case, we are told, both the authorities and the populace were less scrupulous in their accounting of women, who were of no interest militarily and who yielded little in the way of income or taxes. Such arguments are often used to cut short further inquiry, even though they raise an important issue: How were the standard sources of quantitative data compiled? Did the sex of those who furnished and assembled the data distort the results? But another issue needs to be raised first: the question of a difference in male and female mortality rates or, on a more pessimistic view, of the possibility that females were deliberately put to death. The American scholar Emily Coleman asked precisely these questions in a study of villages south of Paris based on the polyptych of Irminon, abbot of Saint-Germain-des-Prés. She argued that the imbalance of the male and female populations could not be the result of faulty statistics or underrepresentation of females alone; rather, it was the outcome of deliberate discrimination against females from the moment of birth.[10] The Carolingians, she concluded, must have put female infants to death. This, as we can well imagine, was a controversial proposition, and most scholars have rejected it or at any rate qualified it substantially on the basis of a detailed reexamination of the sources and comparison with polyptychs from other regions.[11]

This episode points up some of the obstacles facing anyone who would do research on the history of women. Findings with a whiff of scandal about them are particularly vulnerable to attack, no matter how scientific the method claimed. In dealing with relations between the sexes it is unwise to limit oneself to a single set of explanatory factors. What makes the arguments against female infanticide on the estates of Saint-Germain-des-Prés convincing is that they invoke such a wide range of factors. Men and women were affected differently, for example, by the leading causes of mortality—chiefly, in the late Middle Ages, the bubonic plague.[12] But we know very little about the physical and mental effects of poverty, hard labor, disease, and childbearing. Ignorance is one reason why the male-female ratio, which is easier to determine than certain other demographic indicators, has been so eagerly seized upon as the key parameter for explaining certain features of social evolution.

An alleged excess of the female population has been cited to explain the increasingly important role of women in the economy, in the artisanal sector in the late Middle Ages and in the industrial sector during the Renaissance. Feminist historians have vigorously challenged this interpretation. A number of recent works, which Claudia Opitz discusses in Chapter 9, have distinguished between the availability of work and the quality of that work, quality being defined in terms of social prestige and access to public responsibilities. Since at least the fifteenth century the discredit attaching to female labor has meant that female workers were generally employed in the production of low-status goods. The nature of employment mattered more than the access to jobs. Conversely, the concentration of female labor in relatively unsatisfying jobs further reduced the esteem in which women workers were held. Karl Bücher's single-factor argument thus fails to capture the complexity of the situation. Other important factors besides the male-female ratio include family structure, economic activity of family members, relative strength of guilds in the community, political organization, and underlying ideology of gender. In short, the relative economic status of men and women cannot be explained solely in terms of the male-female ratio—or of any combination of demographic indicators.

What was the source of women's power if it was not simply strength of numbers? Where and on whom was that power exerted? In Chapter 7 Georges Duby challenges the notion that courtly love led directly to an empowerment of women in the feudal era. Although learning the art of "sophisticated love" changed the way men at the top of the social hierarchy looked at women and understood their hearts and minds, it also reinforced the traditional structure of domestic power according to which men dominated women. But the ritual of courtly love did tame certain aspects of courtship that had proved disruptive to family matrimonial strategies. It helped to reconcile the often conflicting but sometimes convergent aims of families and the Church and thus strengthened the matrimonial system, and it did allow women more room to be treated, for a time, as individuals.

Male voices of necessity filled much of the first part of this volume. In the next few chapters we look not only at marriage and childbearing, whose consequences weighed so heavily on all women, but also at those fleeting moments in which women managed to achieve some measure of autonomy.

C. K.-Z.

6

Women from the Fifth to the Tenth Century

Suzanne Fonay Wemple

THE DECLINE of the Roman Empire may be traced to the second century, when social and economic institutions began to break down. Third-century civil wars and attacks from the outside accelerated the process, with growing economic disasters besetting countryside and cities. The Empire gradually ceased to be a community of city-states and became a pure dictatorship. This process was further complicated in the late third century, when the Empire was divided in half, the military and civil command separated, and the army staffed primarily with men of Germanic extraction. In the fourth century Constantine adopted Christianity as the honored religion of the Empire and rescinded Augustus' marriage laws, which had allowed unmarried females of twenty-five or more years unlimited freedom to control their persons and property.

Roman Law and Germanic Customs

When the Germanic tribes began to settle in the Western Empire in the fifth century, they were fascinated by the Roman Empire—except for the

Vandals in North Africa. They wanted to adopt the Roman system, but they ignored the basic principles upon which the Western Empire was based. They lacked its laws, discipline, religion, and economic system, and they ruled the land as the king's absolute property. They did not impose a uniform system of administration. Instead of the territoriality of law, the Germanic tribes followed the principle of the personality of law, which meant that each individual had to live under the law of his or her father or, in the case of a married woman, the law of her husband. In areas where the Roman world had penetrated, especially Italy, Spain, and France south of the Loire, a simplified form of Roman law continued to be observed; elsewhere, Germanic customs prevailed. As people intermarried and moved from their birthplaces, the intermingling of customs gradually brought about new assumptions in law, especially in matrimonial arrangements and property claims. These new concepts, incorporated into feudal customs, defined the rights of women as daughters, wives, and widows for centuries to come.

In the Frankish kingdom Christianity did not begin to influence family law until the middle of the eighth century. Elsewhere, particularly in Italy and Spain, Christianity was felt earlier in the law of the household. The position and influence of women in the early Church also were important. Women were the staunchest supporters of the new religion, converting their husbands, baptizing their children, building churches, and nourishing the faith with monastic foundations. Their role in the monastery in Italy, however, was curtailed in the era that followed the papacy of Gregory the Great, and this control spread to France in the Carolingian epoch.

Records for women's history in secular and religious life are more limited for the earlier period, the sixth and seventh centuries, than for the Carolingian epoch, when writing came into more general use. For the earlier centuries I have relied extensively on secular and ecclesiastical legal sources. To judge the extent to which the laws were obeyed, I have supplemented them with information derived from narratives—letters, poems, and histories. The more numerous legal sources for the Carolingian period cover a broader range and the literary sources are richer; in addition to these, I have used monastic cartularies. For the tenth century I have employed literature, chronicles, and hagiographies.

Secular Women

Earliest Centuries

The best description of the early Germanic tribes is found in Tacitus' *Germania*.[1] Kinship was the most cohesive bond, and by the end of the first century it included both the agnates of male descent and the matrilateral kin of female descent. The rules of inheritance favored the males. Women were valued greatly because they provided a network of kinship ties as wives and mothers and gave inspiration as nurturers and supporters. They tended the men on the battlefield, bringing food and encouragement and caring for the wounded. Some women were honored as priestesses and prophetesses. The main tasks of women included the cultivation of the fields, housework, and nursing children. They were also responsible for making the textiles. We can tell from the early graves that they spun a variety of patterns on simple looms and sewed them into clothing and household items. Those Germanic women who lived near the source of the Rhine prepared an especially very fine wool.

Chastity was required of them; those caught in adultery were punished severely—flogged and buried alive. According to the majority of historians, the matrimonial arrangements of the Germans followed three patterns of wedlock: marriage by purchase *(Kaufehe)*; marriage by capture *(Raubehe),* in which it did not matter whether the girl cooperated or not with her abductor; and marriage by mutual consent *(Friedelehe).* In referring to the bride-price, it is not clear whether Tacitus meant the *morgengabe,* given to the bride after consummation in both the marriage by purchase and the marriage by mutual consent, or to the *dos,* a bride-price agreed upon at the betrothal, which later was given, in part or totally, to the bride. Tacitus also spoke of the gift the bridegroom received before the wedding. If the bridegroom was a well-placed man, a king or a chieftain, he did not have to pay; wives were offered to him without compensation. We may thus conclude that two directly opposed notions governed relations between the sexes: the wife was a helpmate, but the daughter was a chattel whose fate depended upon her nearest male relative.

Women's position improved considerably in the Roman Empire. The *Digest* published by Justinian communicated the growing custom of the *sine manu* marriages, in which power over the woman was not transferred to her husband.[2] This represented a step toward female emancipation, as may be seen from the Theodosian Code.[3] When women attained majority, they could control their own property and marry whomever they wished, but their freedom of action continued to be restricted by double standards governing divorce and sexual behavior as well as by society's rigid stratification. Lower-class women had little choice when they attracted the master; they were forced to become his concubines.

Although Christianity did not end sexual discrimination in the late Roman Empire, it did offer women the opportunity to regard themselves as independent personalities rather than somebody's daughter, wife, or mother. According to the Acts of the Apostles, it enabled women to develop self-esteem as spiritual beings who possessed the same potential for moral perfection as men.[4] Moreover, Christianity upheld the sanctity of monogamous marriages—with the exception of Matthew (19:9), who allowed divorce for unchastity. But the Apostles were not free from prejudice regarding the female sex. Women were barred from speaking, teaching, and exercising any authority in congregations.[5] Early Christian women, however, were not denied the opportunity to act as equal partners in facing wild animals and executioners in the arena. The Church Fathers tended to see women as a creature of extremes: either a daughter of Eve or a pure virgin emulating Mary. (See Figure 1 in Chapter 11, "The Imagined Woman," by Chiara Frugoni.) Only Ambrosiaster, in his *Commentary on the First Corinthians,* went so far as to question whether women were made in the image of men and gave the opportunity to husbands to divorce their adulterous wives.[6]

There were two exceptions among the Christian Fathers: Caesarius of Arles and Gregory the Great. Caesarius in southern Gaul, who wrote around the time Clovis was setting up his kingdom in the north, spoke up in defense of women.[7] In his sermons he unmasked the hypocrisy of men who demanded sexual purity on the part of their family members while they themselves sought sexual exploits, even boasting about them to their friends. Toward the end of the century, after the Ostrogothic, Byzantine, and Lombard invasions, Pope Gregory the Great spoke out in favor of female monasteries and argued against prohibiting women from receiving communion when they had the menses or were pregnant—with the proviso that if they chose not to do so, it would greatly benefit their souls.[8] This latter precept was included in a letter cited by the Venerable Bede in his *History of the English Church and People.*[9]

Merovingian Times

By the sixth century Germanic women no longer exhibited the martial spirit ascribed to them by Tacitus. Many converted their husbands to Christianity. Clotilda, the Burgundian princess who married Clovis, persuaded her husband to recognize the true God and give up the worship of idols. When Clovis' troops were almost annihilated by the Alemanni, he turned to God and emerged from battle victorious. Ethelberga of Northumbria influenced her husband's conversion. Queens often founded monasteries and churches on their own lands. They extended their power by having some of their favorites appointed bishops. Archaeological evidence attests that it was usual for women to be buried with their jewelry,[10] their status symbol, and the Alemannic Code prescribed a double fine for the robbery of a woman's grave.[11]

The high value placed on the lives of women by the law codes indicates that their ability to bear children, rather than their worth as helpmates or prophetesses, was prized.[12] Any man who harassed women could receive heavy punishments. According to the Pact of the Salic Code, if a man pressed the hand of a woman, he was fined 16 solidi; if he touched her above the elbow, 35 solidi. The Code of the Alemanni went so far as to punish a man who falsely accused a woman of witchcraft or poisoning; he paid a fine of 80 solidi if she was a freewoman, 15 solidi if she was a maidservant. In 546, when the Ostrogoths captured Rome, their king, Totila, had forbidden the rape of the Roman women, much to the surprise of the city's inhabitants.[13] Under Burgundian law rape and seizure were among the most serious breaches of law that could be committed against a woman.[14] Generally speaking, churchmen upheld the position that men were more rational than women.[15] Although the Germanic women were equally capable of founding churches— the *History of the Lombards* tells us that Theuderata established just as many churches as her husband[16]—good women were characterized by their biographers as obeying their spouses.[17]

Roman and Germanic customs were rapidly assimilated in marriage law. As a result, under Roman law the authority of the husband over his wife was strengthened. The Roman marriage of *sine manu,* which enabled a woman to remain under the control of her family, was not recognized by the Visigothic and Burgundian codifications of Roman law. In the sixth and seventh centuries, unmarried women were under the authority of their fathers. If married, that is, if they went to live with their husbands of their own volition, they were under the authority of their husbands. This meant that a husband had to represent his wife in court and manage her property, even though he could not transfer it without her consent. Visigothic law, however, provided that a woman could administer her own property. The right to have protection over a woman, both a legal and a property right, was expressed with the word *mundium* that was acquired by the husband in the other Germanic codes. Visigothic women, in short, possessed the most rights among the Germanic females. They not only could dispose of their own property and leave it to whomever they wished if they were childless, but they could represent themselves in court, appear as witnesses if they were fourteen years of age, and, most important, arrange their own marriages if they were over twenty. But under any other Germanic code the man who held a woman's *mundium* settled her suits and was responsible for handling and selling her property.[18]

Whether she lived under Roman or Germanic law, a widow became the head of the household, gained control of the property, and was the guardian of her minor children. The unmarried woman, on the other hand, remained under the tutelage of her family until she reached the age of maturity, which was twenty-five under Roman law issued for the Burgundians,[19] and twenty under Visigothic law.[20] But girls usually married much younger; generally they were engaged by the age of twelve, and married by fifteen. The legitimate age for males was also very young, fifteen under Salic and twelve under Ripuarian law.[21]

A marriage involved three steps, the suite *(petitio);* the betrothal *(desponsatio);* and the wedding *(nuptiae).* The suitor generally sealed his agreement by giving a pledge *(arrha).* Once the pledge was accepted, the engagement could not be broken unilaterally. The law codes generally specify how much could be asked. For example, under Burgundian law a jilted groom could ask only 300 solidi, but if the engaged girl married another, she could be killed.[22] But a groom had to pay merely the *dos,* bride-gift agreed to at the time of the betrothal.[23] He could also wait several years before honoring the betrothal according to Gregory of Tours, *The*

History of the Franks.[24] The Lombard law stated that two years could elapse between the betrothal and the wedding.[25]

This was not the only form of marriage known to the Germanic people. The woman still could be captured, and Saint Radegund was taken on the battlefield by her husband's family. Fortunatus, in *De vita sanctae Radegundis*, tells the formidable details of her capture.[26] She was the daughter of the vanquished king of the Thuringians, and her hand was contested in a judicial battle by the sons of Clovis. This kind of marriage within the kingdoms was resisted, as can be seen from the story of Chuppa, who tried to carry off as his bride the daughter of Badegisel, the late Bishop of Le Mans. The mother of the young girl with her men resisted and Chuppa lost several of his men.[27] There was also the *Friede- lehe*, by which means the Merovingian kings married women who were their inferiors. The women had little economic protection in such wedlock. For example, Ingund implored her husband, Clo- thar, not to abandon her when he married her sister, Aregund.[28] The Lombard marriage, where the bridegroom did not pay the bride's *meta* and her protection, like that of her children, remained with her family, was this kind of union.

The blood feuds recorded attest that in marriage the bride's family's wish sometimes was disregarded. Hucbald reported that Rictaud's brothers killed her husband of several years, even though the union had already produced a number of children.[29] Unions between a free woman and an unfree man were condemned as illegitimate *contubernia*. The woman stood to lose her life, free- dom, and property, and her children were reduced to servitude and could not inherit. But no law prevented a man from having sexual unions with his slaves, and he could recognize the children as heirs.[30] Marriages between close blood relations and in-laws were dissolved. This prevented the creation of closed aristocracy and encouraged exogamous unions, facilitating the social ascent through marriage of women of lower birth.[31] In other words, if the woman was pretty and clever, she could rise through marriage in the Merovingian hierarchy.

In the Merovingian royal family four kings are known to have indulged in polygyny. As Gregory of Tours, Fredegar, and the anonymous author of the *Liber historiae Francorum*, tell us, these were Clothar I, Charibert I, Chilperic I, and Dagobert I.[32] Two of Clothar's wives, Ingund and Aregund, were married to him at the same time. Charibert divided his attention between two sisters,

Merofled and Marcoveifa, and an additional wife, Theudegild. Chilperic practiced polygamy, before he married Galswintha. Dagobert married the desirable Nanthild and two other women. Most of their marriages of course were *Friedelehe*. Polygyny was forbidden only by the Visigothic Code, and keeping a concubine while married was prohibited only by the Roman Code issued for the Visigoths.[33]

Divorce laws enshrined sexual double standards. In addition to dissolution by mutual consent, allowed by both the Roman and Germanic laws,[34] the Germanic codes made it easy for a man to divorce his wife. Under Roman law a man could dissolve his marriage only if his wife committed adultery or sorcery, or was a procuress.[35] Under Germanic law a man could repudiate a woman for her inability to bear children as well as for any serious crime. If she was beyond reproach, he still could divorce her if he was willing to relinquish control over her property and pay her a compensation equal to that of bride-gift.[36] A wife had to remain faithful and obedient to her husband, even if he were a drunkard, a gambler, mistreated her, or was adulterous.[37] Under the simplest Germanic laws—the Burgundian Code—she was to be smothered in mire if she attempted to divorce him. Under Roman law she was allowed to divorce her husband if she could prove him guilty of homicide, necromancy, or violation of graves, in other words, of very heavy crimes indeed.[38] The Visigothic law permitted her to sue for divorce if he were found guilty of pederasty or having forced her to fornicate with another.[39] The way for a woman to escape from an unhappy union was to have her husband murdered. This was what Fredegund did, according to the *Liber historiae Francorum*.[40] There is no evidence that the Frankish church— except for the Council of Orléans in 533, which forbade divorce on account of illness—legislated on divorce until Carolingian times.[41] But that does not mean that conscientious churchmen did not excommunicate the guilty party. The Lombard laws moreover stated that the penalty for fornication was less harsh than for adultery.[42] If a free woman was discovered to have fornicated, her relatives could either take vengeance or arrange her marriage with the man. Fidelity in marriage was required of the wife only, not of the husband, unless he sinned with another man's spouse.

The most important development in the history of women from the time Tacitus wrote to the codification of Germanic laws was economic improvement. Germanic women initially did not inherit and could not hold property. But by the end of the fifth century the bride-price had evolved into the bride-gift that the bride received in part or in whole. This was called *wittemon, meta, nuptiale pretium,* or *uxoris pretium,* which came to be designated in time as the *dos.*[43] Thus the codes brought the situation of the Germanic bride in line with the more favorable lot of the Roman woman. Nevertheless Saint Leander described it in unflattering terms as the price paid for the loss of modesty.[44] The difference between the *dos* and the *morgengabe* was that the latter was given after the wedding and was generally smaller than was the former.[45] The *morgengabe* was also given to the *Friedelfrau.*

Under the influence of Roman laws, Germanic inheritance laws became less restrictive. The Visigothic law ruled that in the case of intestates all the children, boys and girls, inherited equally. On the opposite end were the Saxon and Thuringian codes. The Salic Code in later redactions as well as the other codes allowed a woman to inherit the land that was purchased but not the land that was her parents' patrimony.[46] Women could inherit the personal belongings of female relatives, and they received a trousseau when they married. The trousseau consisted of household and personal goods, as can be seen from the description of the fine and costly robes, gold and silver, and many precious objects given to Rigunth, daughter of King Chilperic and Fredegund.[47] Admittedly such wealth was appropriate for a king's daughter, but lesser people gave as much as they could.

Women of the lower classes presumably had greater freedom to marry men of their own choosing.[48] The chastity of lower-class women, like that of noblewomen, was protected from violation by outsiders, albeit not from the attentions of their masters. The least value was attached to the life and virtue of the ordinary *ancilla,* followed by the semifree *lita,* and the freed *liberta;* at the very top were church and crown slaves, according to Burgundian law.[49] A further distinction was made between skilled and unskilled workers. Those who worked as domestics or artisans in a gynaeceum had a higher *weregeld* than did ordinary female slaves, according to the *Pactus legis Salicae.*[50] As can be seen in the Ripuarian Frankish Code, the children of an upper-class woman who married a lower-class man were denied the higher rank she held.[51] The rank among the lower classes apparently was insignificant. By the late sixth century, despite the laws, freewomen married slaves. In fact the lords encouraged such unions.[52] We can see from the *Formulae* that masters, undoubtedly prompted by the desire to have a sufficient labor force, acknowledged the wife's free status and guaranteed that the children would be free.

After Reccared converted from Arianism to Catholicism in 587, he began to persecute the Jews in his kingdom. He approved of the decision by the Third Council of Toledo that the children of mixed Jewish and Christian marriages had to be baptized.[53] Disagreeing with Isidore of Seville, who was an opponent of the Jews in other matters, Reccared's successor demanded that Jews who would not convert leave his country. Jewish men, women, and children were treated alike, and thousands departed for North Africa or Merovingian Gaul.[54] Worse was to come. Before the Muslim occupation, in 711, children of former Jews not only were turned over by the state to Christian families, but they had to marry practicing Catholics. Small wonder that these children and their parents treated the invading Muslims as the liberators of mankind.[55]

The Carolingian Period

The historical importance of the Carolingian period lies in the fact that for the first time the term European culture can be used. While the Merovingian kingdom was secular, theocratic unity was the predominant feature of the Carolingian dynasty. In 752, when Saint Boniface crowned Pepin the King of Franks, he did so with papal permission. Henceforth, the Carolingians protected the Holy See. But their effort to be the representatives of Christianity was short-lived, and after Louis the Pious' death in 840, the empire gradually fell apart.

Marriages in the Merovingian period remained free from the influence of Christianity. In early Carolingian times, however, the very weak position of the new dynasty allowed the indissolubility of marriages to become a central issue. Pepin the Younger found Saint Boniface to be a valuable ally. According to Boniface's observations, continental marital customs were very troublesome. He sought advice from popes, who answered him with prescriptions on incest and on impediments to marriage. Pepin's pronouncements in the capitularies were inspired by these very precise precepts,[56] which extended consanguinity to the seventh degree and kinship to affinity and spiritual relations that included the godfather and godmother, the sister- and brother-in-law, the father-

and mother-in-law, and so on. In short, Pepin prevented aristocratic families from forming extended alliances. Boniface extended these concepts to extramarital fornication, which under Charlemagne was punished by not only lifelong penances but also loss of property.

Pepin proceeded more cautiously on the question of the indissolubility of marriage, probably remembering only too well his attempt to repudiate Bertrada in order to marry Angla, the former wife of a certain Theodrad.[57] Unlike his relatives, he did not intend to practice polygyny. (His grandfather Pepin the Middle had two wives, and his father was married to two women, Chrodtrud and Swanahild, at the same time; in addition, each had a concubine.[58]) Pepin compromised between the position of the Church Fathers and local customs, whose predilections were reflected in the formulas of the period which indicate that divorce by mutual consent remained very popular.[59] Also, at the synod of Verneuil, he issued an edict that all marriages of the realm had to be public.[60]

Charlemagne's image of a Christian emperor was more demanding. In 789 he prohibited the remarriage of any divorced man or woman. In 796, to the bishops assembled at Friuli, he declared that adultery could not be considered a cause for dissolving the marriage bond. In 802 he incorporated this order in his *Capitulary to the Missi*.[61] He enunciated this rule after his two marriages ended in divorce. Nevertheless, he allowed his own daughters to marry in *Friedelehe*,[62] and kept several concubines between and after his own marriages. Only Liutgard was honored by being raised from the status of a concubine to that of a queen.

Judith of Bavaria, second wife of Louis the Pious, was charged by her enemies with immorality. This beautiful daughter of Count Welf and his wife, Heilwig, a Saxon lady, was twenty years younger than the emperor. The worst allegations were levied by Paschasius Radbertus and Agobard of Lyon, who accused her of fornication with the emperor's trusted adviser, Bernard of Septimania.[63] The actual cause underlying the charges was that Judith wanted her son Charles the Bald to have territory that had previously been partitioned among the sons of Louis' first marriage. Her enemies called Judith names such as Jezabel and Justina, but they could do no more than imprison her in a convent, from which Louis the Pious subsequently freed her.

In attempting to define lawful marriage, the Frankish church moved closer to the secular model during the second half of the ninth century. Notwithstanding some churchmen's insistence on religious ceremony, the traditional Germanic procedures of parental consent and property settlement were recognized as necessary steps for the legitimization of unions. To these definitions Archbishop Hincmar of Rheims added the stipulation that a marriage was not valid until consummated.[64]

Hincmar participated in the great controversy surrounding the divorce of Lothar II, King of Lotharingia, from Theutberga. She was a politically desirable wife, whom Lothar had failed to impregnate. Thus, after two years he decided to dissolve the union and marry his concubine Waldrada, who had rewarded his affection with a child. But he failed to perceive the difficulties his plan would cause him. First, he tried to get rid of his queen by accusing her of incest with her own brother, but she purged herself by ordeal. Next, he imprisoned her until she declared that she wanted to join a convent. But the bishops, unwilling to dissolve the marriage, merely suspended relations between the couple. Eventually Theutberga, probably threatened with torture, confessed to an assembly of Lotharingian magnates and bishops. She confessed not only to incest but to one involving abnormal intercourse that had resulted in the conception of a child that she had aborted. She was sentenced to do public penance, but the king's request for divorce was postponed until more experts on canon law could be consulted. Hincmar of Rheims, one of these experts, replied in a long treatise, *De divortio Lotharii et Tetbergae,* in which he upheld incest as the only cause leading to dissolution of the union.[65] In the meantime Theutberga appealed to the pope, who directed two of his legates to intervene. But Lothar managed to bribe the legates, dissolved his marriage on grounds of incest, and married and crowned Waldrada. Pope Nicholas, furious with this outcome, called a synod to the Lateran where he annulled the proceedings and asked Lothar to restore Theutberga to his bed. In 865, under pressure from his two uncles, Lothar complied. The following year he again sought dissolution by coercing Theutberga to request a divorce on the grounds that she was barren and wished to enter a monastery. Nicholas' answer was the same: Lothar could not remarry even if Theutberga took the veil. The sordid affair was ended by the death of Lothar II as he was returning home from Rome, where, in 869, he had obtained absolution from Hadrian II, Nicholas' successor.[66]

Lothar's case was famous enough to have elicited interest

throughout western Europe. None of the reasons—not adultery, not barrenness, not even entrance into a monastery by one of the partners—had produced an ecclesiastical divorce. Following the death of Lothar II, things in Frankland changed substantially. The Church continued legislating on the indissolubility of marriage, but the laity paid little attention. Desertions and abductions, even on the highest level of society, proceeded unabated. Injunctions against endogamous unions were also defined, as the attempts of late ninth-century councils to dissolve these unions prove. The Church stood adamant on no divorce, and in the tenth century we find few cases to the contrary.[67]

Marriages between equal partners in Carolingian times allowed wives some security but also increased their duties. Wives, especially those of the Carolingian royal family, were chosen by the husband's father. The Carolingian queen supervised the palace and the royal estates and was her husband's representative in his absence. She acquired this position when she was anointed and crowned, and her name was incorporated in the *laudes* sung in honor of her husband. In his capitulary *De Villis* Charlemagne declared that whatever the queen ordered the judges, ministers, seneschals, and cupbearers to do must be carried out to the letter.[68] This was a tremendous authority at a time when no distinction was drawn between a ruler's private and public power. When, two generations later, Hincmar of Rheims explained that the queen with the help of the chamberlain was also in charge of the royal treasury, he added that the king could not be concerned with such domestic trifles.[69] Merovingian queens also had access to the palace and treasury, but they were not entrusted with such administrative functions.

In the ranks of the aristocracy, royal service and warfare absorbed the energies of men, and the supervision of the family estates was left in the hands of women. Dhuoda, the wife of Bernard of Septimania, remained at home in Uzès and ran the domains, while he spent his time at court as imperial chamberlain.[70] Gisla, daughter of the Saxon Count Hessi and widow of Unwan, did not choose her son to help run the estates but a girl of lesser social stature, Liutberga, who was removed from a convent and trained for the task.[71]

Childbearing and child-rearing also kept women well occupied. They had to make sure that their children received proper religious training. Monasteries usually would not take them before six or seven years of age. Boys intended for life in the world would be taken from their mothers' sides and sent to the court of a lord at the age of seven. Girls remained at home until they got married, at the age of twelve to fifteen. Thus we can conclude that Carolingian women spent fewer years raising children than modern women do, but they married earlier and had more children. They also had much shorter lives.

On the basis of life spans of four generations of Charlemagne's descendants, compiled by K. F. Werner, we can conclude that a woman's average age at death was thirty-six.[72] Only 39 percent of the women lived to be forty or more, compared to 57 percent of the men. The highest proportion of male deaths occurred between the ages forty and fifty-four, and female between twenty-five and thirty-nine. Clearly the disparities between the two mortality rates had some connection with the biological function of women. Since women in the royal family were not more prone to be victims of violence than men, we must attribute their low survival rate to inadequate health care and an iron deficiency in the Carolingian diet, aggravated by menstruation, gynecological problems, and childbearing.

Prostitution was an accepted profession in the Roman Empire. The Church Fathers frowned upon it but had to accept it as a social phenomenon of a worldly society. Those who profited from its money-making possibility felt the wrath of the Council of Elvira (circa 300), whose fulmination was often repeated in the Middle Ages.[73] But in the early Middle Ages very little was written about prostitution, probably because it was a marginal side phenomenon in the villages. Saint Boniface described the whorehouses that lined the roads to Rome—probably in an attempt to scare the nuns from going on pilgrimages.[74] A capitulary, probably of Louis the Pious, entitled *De disciplina palatii Aquisgranensis,* used the word *meretrix* (harlot), intending to warn the men in the palace not to associate with women of questionable conduct.[75] Jonas of Orléans also relied on the term to indicate such women.[76] A century later Liudprand of Cremona employed the word in connection with Marozia, who was possibly the illegitimate wife of Markgrave Alberich, and certainly the legitimate spouse of Wido of Tuscany and of King Hugh of Italy.[77] Hroswitha used whorehouses in two of her dramas: *The Fall and Conversion of Mary* and *The Conversion of the Harlot Thais.*[78] Thus we cannot deny that houses of ill repute existed before the eleventh or twelfth century. They were in existence, but they were not particularly important. More interesting are the regulations about lesbian love and masturbation that appear in Frankish penitential books. Lesbian couples and masturbating women are placed on the same level as wives who make magical love potions for their husbands; they were substitutes for women who did not receive enough love from men.[79]

Charlemagne paid attention to the importance of peasant women in the same capitulary *De Villis* that laid out also the authority of the queen.[80] Women of the royal domain owed certain services to the lord. On the Carolingian estate, as in manufacturing establishments of the later Middle Ages, women's exclusive province was the making of cloth. To supply the emperor and his retainers with household items and the cloth they needed, the women of his estates worked at set periods in the great hall of a manor, providing linen, wool, vermilion and other herbs related to dying, wool combs, teasels, soap, grease, and other objects. In addition they performed duties related to the provision of food—lard, smoked and salted meat, wine, butter, malt, beef, mead, honey, wax, flour. In short, the clothing and feeding of the upper classes was the duty of the peasantry. We learn with pleasure that Charlemagne commanded that the places where women worked had to be surrounded by hedges, have strong doors, be kept warm by stoves, and have cellars where goods could be stored. Thanks to Eileen Power, who has described the practices of peasant women, we know that Ermentrud, Bodo's wife, was in charge of the household and helped her husband whenever he needed it; in addition she raised the chickens and saw to it that they laid eggs; sheared the sheep; made the cloth, thread, and garments and washed them when they were dirty.[81]

The Tenth Century

With the disappearance of the Carolingian Empire, power shifted to the noble families. Charlemagne's institutions proved incapable of sustaining themselves under the dual assault of invasions and claims of blood that caused the emperors to divide their dominions among their sons. Land, power, and title passed from one to another of the warring successors. Out of the ruin of the Carolingian state, the family emerged as the most stable unit in the world, and, profiting from the power of their families, for two centuries women were able to play an economic, social, and political role.

In the sources we find a great deal about girls, brides, wives, concubines, mothers, widows, and spiritual women. We know practically nothing about the childhood of women, except that they had to be seven when they were received into a religious community. In the tenth century women theoretically could choose their life-style; they could select marriage or the cloister. Actually, however, quite a few were already engaged as children and married early. Thietmar, Bishop of Merseburg, in his Chronicle states that the wife of his uncle Liuthar was barely thirteen years old when she married.[82] We learn from Hrotswitha that Edith, half-sister of King Athelstan, was asked in marriage by the messengers of Otto's father, Henry I. Athelstan agreed, and Edith was dispatched to Saxony with many presents and a large following. In case Otto did not like her, her sister accompanied Edith as an alternative bride. Otto preferred Edith.[83] The brides not only had to come from a similar background but had to be well mannered, noble, and of healthy body. If a suitable marriage partner could not be found for a girl, she had to enter a monastery. The two elder daughters of Otto II and Theophano were made abbesses, and a third sister married an inferior count palatine.[84]

On the subject of concubines, we hear from Liudprand of Cremona that King Hugh of Italy had several mistresses. Hugh detested his second wife, Berta, widow of King Rudolf, and loved three of his concubines especially. These were Pezola of servile origin who was called Venus; Roza who was called Juno although her father was beheaded; and Stephania who was called Semele. They were jealous of each other and kept bickering but all bore him children whom the king placed in influential positions.[85] But concubines had no legal pretensions; their future depended upon the will of their master and their children.

Married women, on the other hand, had many claims and ambitions. A growing number of tenth-century wives became castellans, mistresses of landed property, proprietors of churches, participants of secular and ecclesiastical assemblies, and exercisers of military command and attendant right of justice. Land was the only source of power, and women could inherit land from their husbands or family; they could exercise the power if their husbands were away at war or feuds at the royal or imperial court, or had died. Mathilda, mother of Otto I, gave up all the property that her husband, King Henry, had left her, because her sons accused her of wasting it on the poor. But she was able to remain in her own domain, which she had inherited from her parents.[86] Liudprand of Cremona, who had a venomous tongue when describing certain ladies of Italy, said only bad things about Marozia, daughter of the disgraceful family of Theodora.[87] Marozia, the mother of Pope John XII by Pope Sergius, after the death of her second husband, Wido, who was King Hugh's half-brother, sent envoys to Hugh, who also was widowed, inviting him to come, marry her, and take the city of Rome. Naturally Hugh complied, and the nuptials were celebrated in Rome in the Castel San Angelo. But Alberic, Marozia's son by her first husband, the dead Marquess Alberic, prevented a happy ending. Alberic revolted against Hugh, who had to escape in the middle of the night, slipping ignominiously down the castle wall and leaving Marozia in her son's clutches, unable to reap the benefits of the marriage.[88]

Another bishop, Rather of Verona, was more favorably inclined toward women. But like all men of the time, he derived *mulier* from *mollitia*, weakness, and associated the male with the mind and the female with the flesh. Furthermore he distinguished between the single woman and the wife who must be subject to her husband. The wedding must be publicly celebrated and the married woman must be faithful in both mind and body. The real virtue of a wife was her modesty. Rather posited the duty of disciplining the children to fathers and mothers. He counseled widows not to enjoy worldly pleasures, because a widow given to self-indulgence was as good as dead.[89]

More pleasurable were Liudprand's nasty comments concerning the delights of the couch. He hated Berta, King Hugh's mother, charging that her cunning and exercises in bed were the cause of much strife. He disliked Ermengard, who after the death of her husband, Adalbert of Ivrea, was willing to sleep with prince and commoner alike. He disapproved also of the two Willas—the wife of King Hugh's brother, Boso, and her daughter, the wife of Berengar of Ivrea. Boso's wife hid her husband's jewelled belt within her buttocks, and her daughter had her priestly lover castrated by her husband after he was caught by a dog on his way to his mistress' bed. These were not timid women. They wanted power and did whatever was necessary to get it.[90]

A woman's position was determined by her wealth, the status of her relatives, and the might of her sons. Childbearing was subordinated to being her husband's helpmate. She was in charge of the household, the poor, and the Church. Her political power was to acquire enough property to make donations to the Church and establish religious houses to which she might retire in case of widowhood, though such gifts usually were made in the names of both spouses. When her husband was absent, a wife had to pray that he would be successful, at his death that his memory would be kept alive.

A widow could exercise power as long as her children were minors. Although she came under the special tutelage of the emperors and kings, her position was not at all secure. The best opportunity a widow had to retain political power was through her sons. But not every mother was fortunate enough to have sons who loved her. Emma, widowed queen of France, sent a pleading letter to her mother, the Empress Adelaide of Germany, asking for help against the son who had become her enemy and accused her of having fornicated with the bishop Adalbero of Laon.[91] A bishop, Bernward of Hildesheim, teacher of Otto III, accused Theophano of having been too lenient with her son simply to gain his good will.[92] Political enemies also could threaten a woman's position. As a result, some widows went to live in their fathers' houses, or with a clerical brother, or entered a convent.

Women and Religion

The Monastery

Only women who escaped to a monastery, abiding there in virginity and widowhood, or those who remained at home as God's holy women were free from the cares of marriage. The widows of the Merovingian, Lombard, and Anglo-Saxon kings preferred to retire to a religious institution. Queen Clothilda, after the death of King Clovis, passed the rest of her days in the Basilica of Saint Martin.[93] The Lombard Queen Ansa joined her daughter in the monastery of Saint Salvatore at Brescia after her husband was dethroned by Charlemagne.[94] Queen Etheldreda, who had long wanted to retire from the world, finally obtained the reluctant consent of King Egfried to enter the monastery of Coldingham.[95] The very nature of the wifely role in the aristocratic family, replete with its movable wealth of jewels, food, and articles of clothing, allowed women an opportunity to cement alliances with bishops and abbots.

The Merovingian chronicles and hagiographies are replete with stories about the perceptions of virginity and sexual continence. The sexual double standards to which they were subjected, fear of childbearing, and in certain cases the brutality of husbands probably prompted women to avoid marriage and remarriage. Fortunatus, in *De vita sanctae Radegundis,* tells that Radegund ended her marriage when she discovered that her husband had murdered her own brother. Gregory the Great recounts how Saint Monegund took a religious vow after the death of her children.[96] And the anonymous life of Saint Sigolena of Albi describes how she offered her husband all her goods in exchange for her freedom. But she was able to build a monastery with her father's help only after her husband's death.[97]

In the eighth century the tension between parents and daughters was frequently resolved by a friend or relative who was a churchman. In this manner Saint Bertila of Chelles had the good fortune of gaining as her champion Audoen, frequently called Dado, one of the most influential churchmen in the Merovingian kingdom.[98]

Finally, in the ninth and tenth centuries, a third type of consecrated woman appeared: the obedient daughter of very devout parents who took a vow of chastity at her parents' request. This seems to be the case of Herlinda and Renilda, as well as of Saint Hathumoda,[99] which illustrates the tendency of parents to encourage daughters to remain celibate. Another group of religious women married and raised children, postponing their religious vocations until after the children were grown. An example of this is Saint Salaberga.[100]

These three patterns of behavior—rebellion against parents or husbands; tension and accommodation through the intercession of an influential man; and dutiful obedience—correspond roughly to three different phases in the history of female monasticism. In the sixth century, when nunneries were few in number, it took heroic steadfastness to serve God in religious life. During the seventh and eighth centuries female institutions were built everywhere, and women could find religious men to intercede for them. In the ninth and tenth centuries, when the strict cloistering of the nuns was urged, parents pushed their daughters to join monasteries. One can observe this pattern not only in Gaul but also, in a diluted form, in Italy. After the invasion of the Ostrogoths, Byzantines, and Lombards, the efforts of Pope Gregory and the Lombard nobility stand out. In Rome, Pope Gregory gave several buildings, designated by their donors as male institutions, to abbesses. He called upon the clergy to protect the female institutions, reminding the churchmen to tell the nuns to remain chaste, stationary, and not squander the community's property.[101] The most unpleasant communication from Gregory, to Ianuarius, Bishop of Sardinia, charged that the bishop did not guard sufficiently the female communities. As for men found in the monasteries, if laymen, they were to be excommunicated, if clerks, they were to be deprived of office and locked up in a male monastery. The guilty nuns were to be subjected to prayers and fasting to atone for their sin.[102] Fewer female monasteries were founded in the Carolingian era and its aftermath. Only in the second half of the tenth century do we see in Italy the frequent building of nunneries. This resulted from the Ottonians' influence, which showed itself also in Germany.

In the heroic age of monasticism only a few monasteries existed in southern Gaul. The most famous was Saint Jean of Arles, which Saint Caesarius, Bishop of Arles, built, organized, and endowed with a Rule for his sister Caesaria.[103] In central and northern Gaul female monasticism exhibited greater vigor. We know from Gregory of Tours that institutes for women were built in the cities, where women were safe from attack.[104] By the end of the sixth century female monasteries were located in all the urban centers of Gaul. The same situation prevailed in Italy, where the hazards of the countryside did not encourage people to construct female communities outside of the cities. Gregory the Great's efforts were all located within the towns. In addition to Rome, he wrote letters for female monasteries located in Naples,[105] Pisa,[106] Lilybitano,[107] Luna,[108] Nola,[109] and the towns of Sicily[110] and Sardinia.[111]

At a council in Paris held in 614 Chlothar II heralded a new epoch by passing a law providing capital punishment for abductors of women. After this women in the Frankish kingdom who wanted to eschew marriage and lead an ascetic life needed less courage to prevail.[112] The Church allowed entrance into monastic houses to widows seeking equal status with virgins and as a form of penance to lapsed women.[113] The Lombard laws were somewhat more lenient, although they punished women who gave up their religious status. They lost their property and became chattels of the king, who could do with them as he pleased.[114] There were also professed virgins and widows who lived in their own homes, outside the walls of monasteries.[115] This form of religious life suited women who did not wish to marry; others undertook a true religious vocation.

In the seventh century the efforts of Saint Columban, an Irish monk, bore fruit. He arrived in Frankland in the last decade of the sixth century, and was as friendly toward women as toward men. His disciples in the monastery of Luxeuil, which he founded, exhibited toward religious women a different spirit than had existed in the previous century. They worked in partnership with women and discovered a practical solution of setting up nunneries outside the cities. To protect the female religious, to help run their establishment, and to provide sacerdotal services, these enterprising men attached a contingent of monks to each newly founded female community. They created a new institution, the double monastery, which had some precedents in the East and possibly also in Ireland. In these monasteries the nuns did not live like parasites on the monks. They were required to perform manual labor. Cooking, cleaning, serving, sewing, fishing, brewing, and fire-building were among their daily assignments.[116] We also know from Mary Bateson's *Origin and Early History of Double Monasteries* that the nuns performed multiple functions and that their superior was usually an abbess.[117] Even personal matters were subject to rules. For example, sleeping in the dormitory was arranged according to certain principles; younger sisters were assigned places alternating with older ones to avoid levity or carnal temptation. Hair was washed only on Sundays, in clear view of everyone.

Irish penitential rites were introduced on the Continent, and the abbesses, especially in the double communities, had to hear members' confessions three times a day. They also performed the quasi-sacerdotal function of giving benediction to members of their community. The abbesses' normal duties included administration, discipline, and caring for spiritual welfare.

The tremendous popularity of the double institutions was of great inspiration throughout the West. Earcongota, daughter of the King of Kent, served God in Frankland, in a monastery founded by Abbess Fara in Brie. Many others who had the same purpose also went to live in Gaul.[118] Several double houses were also founded in England. Hilda, abbess of Whitby, ruled over both women and men, after spending thirty-three years in secular occupations. The great-niece of King Edwin of Northumbria, she had planned to enter Chelles, near Paris, where her mother was.

But Aidan, bishop of Lindisfarland, called her back home, where she founded several monasteries, including Whitby. Her great fame resides in her religious life; she urged all to maintain the peace of the gospel. One of her monks was Caedmon, the first poet of the English tongue.[119] A few double monasteries were founded in Italy, but these did not have the abbess as their head. Saint Maria and Saint Petrus in Alife, for instance, were under Saint Vincenzo al Volturno, a male community. Saint Stefano and Saint Cesario in Rome were governed by an abbess and an abbot, but they were under the Basilica of Saint Paolo.[120]

In their effort to restore the monastic system to its pristine purity, churchmen in Charlemagne's entourage reintroduced the principle that women were the weaker sex and had unstable minds. In 742, when Boniface initiated reforms in the Frankish church, he called for the observation of the Benedictine Rule by monks and nuns alike.[121] Thirteen years later the Council of Verneuil offered the choice between Benedictine life and canonical order to men and women who wanted to serve God. Since 766 the Rule for canonical life of men stood ready, thanks to the efforts of Chrodegand of Metz. What constituted the office of a canoness had to wait until 813, when the Council of Chalon formulated the principle, and 816, when the *Institutio Sanctimonialium* was published.[122] Because it was claimed that they were weak and had unstable minds, canonesses led more austere lives than canons did. They were strictly cloistered and management of their private property was relegated to an outsider. Moreover, they had to veil their faces in church and be carefully guarded from any contact with men. Even their communication with priests was limited: they could make a confession only within sight of the sisters.[123]

Tenth-century churchmen instructed women to behave humbly in church. If virgins, they should imitate Mary, "the mirror of chastity, the inscription of virginity, the token of humility, the honor of innocence," wrote Rather of Verona.[124] Similar precepts were included in the *Capitulary* of Atto of Vercelli. Women could not approach the altar, but had to remain in their places where the priest would accept their offerings. Indeed females, including nuns, should not touch the sacred vessels or holy vestments, or carry incense to the altar. Atto went further than the rest of the bishops. He included in his *Capitulary* the rule that even learned and intelligent women should not presume to teach men.[125] In short, while the bishops could do nothing to prevent women from exercising power in the world, they did reduce their activity in the Church.

The cloistering of nuns was an issue that had weighed on the minds of earlier Carolingian churchmen. The Council of Verneuil in 755 allowed abbesses and other members to leave the community only if the king summoned them. The reiteration of similar and even greater restrictions indicated that cloistering was not easy to enforce.[126] Like their Anglo-Saxon sisters, the Frankish nuns apparently were accustomed to go on pilgrimages, until the Council of Friuli, held in 796 or 797, ordered them not to go.[127] Similar considerations prompted council after council to inveigh against nuns wearing male attire, and to caution against unnecessary visits by bishops, canons, and monks.[128] Charlemagne not only approved these rules, but ordered abbesses to build cloisters into their monasteries.[129]

An extension of the attempt to avoid the danger of close association of the sexes within female monasteries prohibited nuns and canonesses from educating boys.[130] Even hospices for the poor and pilgrims had to be located outside the monastery, adjacent to the church where the clergy could look after them. Nuns and canonesses were permitted to tend only poor and sick women.[131] Abbesses could not give benediction to the opposite sex, nor could they consecrate members of their own community, a religious rite reserved for bishops.[132] Nuns and canonesses could participate in the work of the Church only by ringing church bells, lighting candles, praying, singing, reciting psalms, celebrating canonical hours, and educating girls.[133]

Religious women living in the world had to join communities, and very small monasteries were combined into larger ones. Increasingly nunneries were used in the ninth century to segregate women considered undesirable, socially dangerous, or unproductive.[134] The most important criterion for admittance was wealth rather than sanctity. The *Miracles of Austroberta* report that the saint took pity on the young daughter of a poor family who was denied admission. After being refused, the girl set up her abode in the cemetery, near the tomb of Austroberta. The saint then intervened: the abbess was struck by illness, she duly repented, was healed, sent for the girl, and accepted her as a postulant.[135]

The outstanding quality of ninth-century Frankish abbesses was not their sanctity but their ingenuity. Ermentrud, abbess of Jouarre, exemplifies this. She obtained important relics for Jouarre and, once the monastery had become a place of pilgrimage, she received from Charles the Bold, through the empress, grants of immunity with attendant rights of marketplace and coinage.[136] Moreover, local families whose daughters administered monasteries as lay abbesses took over the fiscal management of monastic revenues. They transformed the monasteries into institutes of canonesses where strict cloistering was no longer required.

This relaxation of ecclesiastical controls also took place in Germany. Among early female monasteries east of the Rhine were some founded by nuns from Anglo-Saxon England, the friends of Saint Boniface. The most famous was Tauberbischofsheim, whose abbess was Lioba. She was generous enough to instruct young girls in her monastery, which met with Boniface's approval. Other nunneries were established at Kitzingen and Ochsenfurt by the abbess Tecla. In Thuringia, Cynechilde and her daughter Berhtgyth were the teachers.

Around 800 the Saxon noble Waltger founded a monastery on his property at Herford. He enriched it and procured relics from England. Royal protection was obtained from Louis the Pious. Adalhad and Wala, Charlemagne's cousins, made significant alterations in the monastery life. As a model they used the Benedictine Notre Dame of Soissons, whose abbess, Theodrada, was their sister. Herford's abbess and nuns came from Soissons. Its conversion to an institute of canonesses did not occur until the next century. There is an ongoing debate whether the communities founded in ninth-century Germany followed Herford's Benedictine Rule, or were institutes of canonesses.[137] At any rate, by the tenth century many of the female monasteries, especially those located in Saxony, were canonical. To the sixty-one female monasteries listed by Albert Hauck, only one can be added; and thirty-five of these were located in Saxony.[138] Thus Saxony was indeed an important monastic center in the tenth century.

Why did the Saxon nobility favor houses for women in the tenth century? There are many reasons. Saxony was newly conquered and converted to Christianity. Infanticide was known to take place, and the victims frequently were baby girls.[139] Marriages were expensive, as we can see from the presence of many unmarried girls among the nobility. There was a danger of promiscuity, either with family members or with those of lower social status. The threat of war against Slavic neighbors enhanced the vulnerability of worldly life. Nevertheless, the foremost reason for the proliferation of monasteries—both male and female—was the Ottonian preference for monastic life.

Female communities in Germany usually were founded by women, alone or with their husbands and clerical relatives. Some noblemen, whose sons had died prematurely in battle, built female houses and lavished their attention on their daughters. K. J. Leyser has written in great detail about female monasteries in the ninth and tenth centuries.[140] Among the ninth-century monasteries of the Liudolfing clan, the most important was Gandersheim, founded by Count Liudolf and his wife, Oda, the great-grandparents of Otto I. Its abbesses came from the reigning family. When, in 947, Otto I invested the seventh abbess with her authority, Gerberga became the head of a small kingdom with an army, courts of her own, a mint, and representation to the imperial assembly. Not only at Gandersheim, but also at Quedlinberg, Essen, and a little later at Elten and Gernrode, abbesses were appointed *Reichsfürstinnen*. As such they had the privilege of participating with the prelates in the imperial diet, where they could approve the advocate selected for them by the lord of the monastery, who was generally a bishop or the emperor. Nonetheless, in the Saxon houses where they were addressed as *Reichsfürstinnen,* they were also known as *metropolitana*. At least Mathilda of Quedlinburg, the sister of Otto II, held this title in the tenth century.[141]

All the houses for women sought royal protection and immunity in tenth-century Germany. But once the king provided this, it meant that the monastery's endowment was consecrated to permanent religious use and could not be touched by relatives of the founder. The endowment of a community to which the emperor made a protective commitment was royal property. The emperor could not alienate it or put it to secular use, but he had the right to convey it to bishops. Thus the nobility gradually became aware that when noble widows and virgins turned their property over to a monastery, the land was irretrievably lost to them. Therefore, beginning with the reign of Henry II in the eleventh century, they required, frequently by force, noble widows and daughters to marry.

In Italy the Carolingian emperor and empresses, as well as the nobility, favored the establishment of female monasteries. More men participated in initiating female communities than in the

Lombard period. Perhaps we could say that the husbands, whose names precede those of their wives, were convinced by their spouses to establish such benefits for religious women. Although in the tenth century Italian kings favored some of the women's communities, the real benefactors were the German emperors and their wives. Abbesses were elected by the community only when the king, emperor, pope, or founder so provided. In a dependent house, the leader of the community from which it was ruled selected the abbess. The ruler could also order a layperson to administer the property. At times, the founder of two monasteries, a male and a female, specified that the abbot should choose the abbess. Quite a few convents became subjugated when the choice of the abbess was left to the bishop or the founder's family.

Deaconesses and Priests' Wives

Opposition to female ministers began in the Frankish church in 511, when the bishops learned that two Breton priests were celebrating the Eucharist with *conhospitae*, cohostesses. These priests and their female assistants traveled through the countryside saying mass and distributing communion in the hut of the peasants. The bishops were disturbed by the fact that the *conhospitae* were polluting the sacrament by offering the chalice to communicants and sleeping under the same roof with priests. We do not know whether the women disparaged as *mulierculae* were the priests' wives or deaconesses. During the first quarter of the sixth century some Frankish bishops could still be persuaded to impart consecration to the feminine deaconate. The deaconesses were Helaria, the daughter of Remy, saintly bishop of Rheims, and Saint Radegund. Fortunatus' words leave no doubt that she was identified with a professed widow, who has dedicated her life to abstinence, charity, and prayer.[142] The absorption of the diaconate into the order of widows was accomplished by the Councils of Epaon and Orléans, in 517 and 533.[143] By this time it was accepted that a deaconess was a widow, and the legislation of Epaon stated that the consecration of widows, called deaconesses, be given henceforth only benediction as penitents. The sum of this legislation was to assure that deaconesses could not claim clerical status. The Council of Orléans went further. It disqualified women from the office and degraded the status of widows in the Frankish church.

The synod held at Auxerre around the late sixth century subsequently declared that women by nature were impure, hence they had to be veiled and could not touch anything that was consecrated.[144]

We cannot exclude the possibility that consecration of female deacons resumed in the seventh century. The anonymous life of Blessed Sigolena of Albi, including her consecration as a deaconess, was probably based on the life of Saint Radegund.[145] A charter from the Rhineland, dated 636, and two inscriptions—one found at Pavia to "Theodora diaconissa" and one from Dalmatia to "Ausonia diac."—establishes this. In Rome deaconesses existed in 799, for when Pope Leo III entered Rome after his terrible ordeal, they received him there. We also know of deaconesses living around the same time in southern Italy.[146] But in Carolingian France the title deaconess reappears only in the third quarter of the ninth century. The Council of Worms reissued canon fifteen of Chalcedon, which stipulated that women over forty could be ordained to the deaconate.[147] This legislation may have been suggested by the wish to find some suitable title for a queen or princess who withdrew to a monastery that already had an abbess.[148] The title may also have served lay abbesses who, like lay abbots, held communities from the king. We have also a gloss that claims that the title deaconess was identified with the abbess. Around 940 Atto of Vercelli explained that a deaconess was an abbess, although he admitted that in earlier times deaconesses held church office. At the time of the conversions, Atto added, the deaconesses baptized women.[149]

Legislation against priests' wives was more extensive. Frankish councils tried to prevent clerks from resuming sexual relations with their wives by threatening deposition.[150] The churchmen charged that clerical incontinence was either a form of incest or a form of heresy; in either case the punishment was removal from office. Clerks, beginning with the grade of subdeacon, were called upon to transform their matrimonial ties into a brother and sister relationship. They were not to sleep in the same room with their wives. Wives had to be constantly accompanied by a slave girl. Finally the councils ordered that they had to live apart from their husbands. This removed the temptation from the priests, but it also decreased the influence of women in parish life. No one bothered about the subsequent fate of these women, who had the dubious honor of being called *diaconissae, presbyteriae,* or *episcopiae,* a designation that reflected their husbands' positions.

Ecclesiastical sanctions were defied both by clerks and their wives. The Burgundian Penitential, which included special provisions for infanticide committed by married clerks, corroborated this defiance.[151] Moreover, the councils treated the incontinence of a clerk with his own wife as a more serious offense than fornication with a woman to whom he was not married. A priest was not deposed from office for having a child with a concubine or living with a concubine after the death of his wife. In the seventh and eighth centuries a woman living with a clerk in the higher grades was treated like an adulteress. Saint Boniface comments that it was not uncommon to find clerks with several concubines each night.[152] A capitulary issued by Charlemagne suggests that some priests had several wives, shed the blood of Christians and pagans, and refused to obey the canons.[153]

Synod after synod in Carolingian times forbade clerks to live with women other than close blood relatives.[154] The goal was to transform the clergy into a celibate body; there no longer was a question of asceticism. It was ritual purity that counted. Recidivists were incarcerated and subjected to two years of penance. Their female companions were punished by confinement in monasteries. The warning of the Carolingian churchmen that some nunneries were like whorehouses suggests that the cloistering of women did not solve the problem of clerical incontinence.

Around 940 Atto of Vercelli angrily charged that above the grade of subdeacon clerical sexuality be considered adultery.[155] Some priests had even gone so far as installing prostitutes in their homes, eating and living with them publicly. The clerics robbed their churches and oppressed the poor to adorn these whores; the women were made beneficiaries of the priests' estates. Because these unfortunate women and their children were under secular jurisdiction, unscrupulous secular authorities accepted bribes from the clerics concerned and used the situation to keep them subservient. Priests abandoned their sacerdotal objectivity in disputes with neighbors, becoming partisan in favor of their own women and children. As punishment, Atto merely reprimanded married priests and ministers and ruled that clerks guilty of adultery be spurned by fellow priests. This measure was ineffective, for in Atto's second letter on the same subject he hinted at a deposition.

Scholarly and Artistic Activity

In the early Middle Ages, in addition to clerks and monks, some noble or religious women were well educated. One of the first such Germanic women was Amalasuntha, daughter of Theodoric the Great, the Ostrogothic king of Italy. Her mother, Audofleda, was a sister to King Clovis. Amalasuntha's reign of nine years ended with her murder; she was strangled in her bath while being held prisoner. Like her father, she had a tremendous respect for Roman culture, literature, and law. Three of her letters written to Theodora and Justinian have been preserved, as has another, to the Senate of the City of Rome. Another renowned secular woman was Eucheria, who was married to the governor of Marseilles and whose epigram was preserved by Fortunatus.[156] Her short poem about a lowborn suitor is full of subtle and complex methods of metaphor. The third educated woman whose work has survived was Dhuoda, wife of Bernard of Septimania, who instructed her elder son, William, in the spiritual, moral, and feudal duties of her day. Her book, the *Liber Manualis,* tells of her love for her husband and two sons, her trouble with moneylenders, and her illness.[157]

The opportunities for education, administration, and literature available to women who wished to embrace celibate life were greater. Many monasteries developed in the same town, some large, others smaller. Religious communities provided a supportive environment and an atmosphere of peace where women could live, work, and pray. By serving God and each other in humility, they could participate in liturgy and find an outlet for their administrative and intellectual talents. Some women served as deacons, wardrobe mistresses, cellarers, and portresses. Others acted as librarians, scribes, and teachers. Caesarius of Arles's *Regula sanctarum virginum* included the requirement that the sisters should be old enough to read and write.[158] All extant Rules attest to a similar prescription for religious women. Nuns who were slow learners were subjected to the rod, the standard punishment for lazy monks. Beyond the elementary skills of reading and writing, the education of both sexes was limited, at least until the ninth century, to a thorough knowledge of the Bible, the works of the Church Fathers, and some elementary acquaintance with civil and canon law. Fortunatus testifies that the Greek fathers were read at Holy

Cross in Poitiers.[159] Gertrud of Nivelles was familiar with divine laws and capable of lecturing on scriptural allegories.[160]

Saint Boniface's companions were equally well versed in Christian literature, and some knew how to write poetry. This was one of the strong points of Lioba, who came from an aristocratic family and was related to Boniface. She was educated at the nunnery at Thanet, and later at the abbey Wimborne where she was sent to study the sacred sciences; there too she became a nun. She wrote Boniface from her monastery. Prompted by her letters and perhaps by her relation to him, Boniface asked the abbess of Wimborne to send her, along with some companions, so he could set up a monastery in Germany. Soon Lioba was the abbess of Tauberbischofsheim, a monastery well known for its help to the poor and advice to the great. She not only served in the monastery's scriptorium and school but also participated in work in the kitchen, bakery, brewery; she also was a good gardener. She committed to memory everything she read and asked the nuns to read to her while she was napping. Boniface also obtained manuscripts from Eadburga, abbess of Thanet, who transcribed for him in gold letters Saint Peter's Epistle.[161]

Books and teachers were needed to educate the nuns and children. Originally the Frankish monasteries sent to Ireland for books and monks; later, in the seventh century, they obtained them from Rome. Until the Carolingian period some of the monasteries accepted as pupils in their schools boys as well as girls.[162]

Books sometimes were left as legacies. Eckhard, Count of Autun and Macon, left five books to three members of the monastery of Faremoutiers.[163] He left two religious books to the abbess Bertrada, a psalter and a volume of prayers to his sister Adana, and a book on gynecology to his sister-in-law Tetrada. At the death of these women, the books probably became part of the community's collection. The fact that Eckhard left Tetrada a book on female medicine seems to indicate that the monasteries took care of women's health. These religious houses, with their books and their large herb gardens, served the population around them.

In Italy the libraries of the female institutions were quite rich. The library of Saint Salvatore in Brescia contained an elegant *Breviarium,* written in gold and silver and dedicated to abbess Angilberta's mother, Queen Ansa. From the same era there is Saint Eusebius of Caesaria's *Concordance to Scriptural Authors,* with profuse illustrations from the life of Jesus and Mary, obviously intended to be read by the nuns. A ninth-century necrological index is especially valuable for the list of nuns' names it contains.[164] The priest John in 990 left the monastery of Saint Maria da Fontanella his private property, to be accompanied when he died by his private goods, which consisted of books and religious articles.[165] An inventory taken at Saint Lucia in Ravello showed among the books the Epistles of Paul, two books by Saint Jerome and Saint Vitus, Saint Isidore's collection, a book of homilies, a book of liturgy and sacraments, a small book containing benedictions for Palm Sunday, and a book of canons, antiphonies, and psalter.[166]

Ever since Bernhard Bischoff identified the female scribes of the monastery of Chelles who copied for Bishop Hildebald of Cologne,[167] articles on manuscripts copied by women who had withdrawn to monasteries have appeared. In addition, the nuns themselves were authors. Baudonivia wrote the second biography of Saint Radegund.[168] Radegund was the author of two poems that have come down to us; Caesaria of Arles wrote a long letter to Radegund and Richild.[169] Aldegund of Maubeuge dictated her visions to Subinus, abbot of the neighboring Nivelles.[170] The life of Queen Balthild probably was composed by a nun at Chelles.[171] About 760 Hugeburc, a religious woman of the convent of Heidenheim, produced a travelogue of Saint Wunibald's trip to the Holy Land.[172] The library at Chelles, where both Charlemagne's sister Gisla and his daughter Rotrud retired and corresponded with Alcuin, attests to the interest of nuns in books. Alcuin asked them for criticism of his unfinished gospel of Saint John, and sent them the writings of Bede. In return, they asked him to explain some obscure part of Saint Augustine, requested a letter of Saint Jerome, and urged him to finish the commentary.[173]

In the tenth century a German canoness achieved fame by producing enduring classics of devotional and secular literature. She was Hrotswitha of Gandersheim, a prolific author equally talented in prose and poetry, who composed plays, legends, and epic poems.[174] Her works apparently were not very popular in the Middle Ages, although some of her plays were copied anonymously. It has been suggested that her flirtatious charm influenced the poems written by the nuns at Regensburg a hundred years later. Only a few manuscript copies of Hrotswitha's works remain in existence. But she was rediscovered in the sixteenth century, and her works were translated into many languages and continue to be read today. She was of noble birth and must have spent some time at court, probably as a young girl. Among her epic poems, *Gesta Ottonis* celebrated the life of Emperor Otto I, and *Primordia Coenobii Gandeshemensis* recorded the foundation of her monastery and subsequent history to 919. Two women appear in *Gesta Ottonis:* Edith of England and Adelheid of Italy, the two wives of Otto I. Otto's female relatives who established and directed Gandersheim are introduced in the *Primordia.* Hrotswitha was familiar with many authors, but her favorites were Virgil and Terence. She used Virgil as a model in her epic works. Her plays were written with a mischievous Terentian sense of humor, though their plots are not Terentian but based on legends of saints. The most famous of Hrotswitha's prose works is *Gongolf,* which is quite similar in theme to the Faust legend.

Monasteries were also repositories for artistic works. For example, we know from Brescia that in the eighth century frescoes were painted and jeweled crosses were used at Saint Salvatore.[175] Moreover, women were not supplanted as the representatives of the liberal arts. In an early example of the *quadrivium* from the State Library in Bamberg four subjects—music, arithmetic, geometry, and astronomy—are represented as tenth-century ladies. Women also embroidered tapestries and smaller objects. The accomplishments of two eighth-century nuns, Herlinda and Renilda of Eyck, may have been exaggerated by their ninth-century biographer.[176] It is even possible that the nunnery, in Valenciennes, where the biographer says they were educated, did not even exist at the time. What is fascinating, though, is the skills the author attributes to them because of their learning. They knew not only the divine office and ceremonies, reading and singing, and copying and illuminating, but they were instructed in every art usually produced by the hands of women: spinning and weaving, making and interlacing gold designs, and silk flower embroidery.

The Carolingian effort to introduce indissolubility into marriage worked quite well. In Thietmar of Merseburg we read of divorce only in Polish lands. The attempt to restrict women to cloisters proved premature. In the tenth century abbesses again assumed positions of leadership, wielding political, economic, and religious power. In the very early Middle Ages, in the fifth, sixth, and seventh centuries, society was loosely organized and the role of women proved open-ended, their contributions to life extensive.

In Carolingian times, when kings triumphed over the aristocracy and bishops over the monasteries, the scope of women's activities was delineated narrowly and their involvement outside the home or monastery was curtailed. But the oppression of women in the Middle Ages did not continue unabated. Decentralization of church and state in the tenth century allowed them to make dynamic and creative contributions, as their position became more privileged, their rights and prerogatives more protected by the preceding century's imperial decretals.

7

The Feudal Order

Paulette L'Hermite-Leclercq

IN THE ELEVENTH and twelfth centuries the West achieved a unity and vitality previously unknown. Safe at last from invasions, which had tended to obscure long-term trends, Europe entered an expansionary phase. Ideologically it was held together by its adherence to Christian values. Long-rebellious regions such as Scandinavia, the lands beyond the Elba, and Hungary were firmly lashed to old Europe. The border with Islam was pushed back in Spain. The Church was not content, however, merely to gain territory and win souls. With invincible ardor it purified itself and set out to strengthen the roots of the faith. Parishes and monasteries multiplied. Meanwhile, the population increased, the area under cultivation grew, cities and commerce revived, and new political authorities asserted their power.

Decades of historical research have resulted in broad consensus concerning the new relations established among men. But what about women? In the context of the Middle Ages as a whole, were these two centuries favorable to the female half of humanity? Opinions differ. The intrepid Robert Fossier entitled a chapter in one of his books "The Reign of Women."[1] His argument is easily summarized. Despite the misogyny of the clergy, Fossier contends, all signs point to a major advance for the female sex. Europe entered "a matriarchal phase." Why? Because the demographic situation was favorable: there were fewer women than men. Economic, legal, and social factors also favored women, particularly peasant women—the vast majority. Women enjoyed exceptional, and hard to explain, sexual freedom. The twelfth century, like the nineteenth, was a golden age of adultery. The Church was helpless to do anything about it. Fossier does not rely, as so many works of popular history do, on the testimony of a few princesses. He has, he believes, plumbed society's depths and taken the pulse of the masses.

Not everyone agrees with this optimistic view. The most widely accepted assessment, based on the work of Georges Duby, Jacques Le Goff, and David Herlihy, is the exact opposite. Women lost ground not only in their theological representation but in their actual social role. There were too many of them for the number of men, hence their value diminished. Clearly the difference of opinion is radical.

The main reason for the difference is the scarcity of sources bearing on the history of women in this period. Women almost never speak for themselves. Scholars still are not sure whether Héloïse wrote the letters traditionally attributed to her. Later the documentation becomes less scarce, but the feudal period is difficult, and historians still are in the initial stages of research. Archaeology may be of some help. It has already been suggested that women in these two centuries were healthier than before, although this finding needs to be confirmed by further research. Skeletal remains excavated at Saint-Jean-le-Froid in the Aveyron show that improvements in diet benefited women more than men.[2] After 1050 people grew taller and were less likely to suffer from rickets. Poverty appears to have loosened its grip for a while, although disease would again make serious inroads after 1300.

The inadequacy of the sources is not the only reason for the differences of opinion. The philosophical, political, and religious views of historians have influenced their judgment, especially in two areas. The Church's influence was at its height in the twelfth century. How did that influence affect the condition of women? Some authors hold that it resulted in a decisive advance, thanks chiefly to the flourishing veneration of the Virgin. But Jacques Le Goff contends that "Christianity did little to improve the material or moral position of women."[3] He argues that the cults of the Virgin and of Mary Magdalene were effects, not causes, of an improvement in the condition of women that began in the eleventh century and ended either before or during the twelfth.

The role of women in the Waldensian and Catharist heresies, the period's most serious challenges to the authority of the Church, is even more controversial. Marxist historians see economic, social, and legal causes for the prominent role played by female heretics: gender struggle is one aspect of class struggle. Why did their protest take a religious form? First, because the Church helped to maintain the society of orders by providing it with an ideology, and second, because in a world where everyone was steeped in religious ideas, the only way to express rebellion was to found a counter-Church. Obviously not all historians share this view, particularly those of traditionalist bent. For them it is axiomatic that only religious factors can explain religious phenomena. The bitterness of women toward the Church had little to do, they argue, with woman's place in the larger society.[4] History is never neutral, and women's history less so.

A Conspiracy of Women

Hugh of Lincoln, who ultimately became a saint, was born in Avalon in Burgundy, a descendant of knights. A Carthusian monk who later became bishop of Lincoln, he died in 1200 and soon was canonized. Adam of Eynsham, a monk who was his confessor and friend for three years, wrote a life in which he portrayed his master meting out episcopal justice.[5] One case grew out of a notorious scandal involving Thomas of Saleby, a knight of Lincoln County. Thomas, an elderly man, had a wife, Agnes, who was sterile. His very large estate would therefore revert to his brother on his death. But Agnes disliked her brother-in-law and detested the prospect of becoming his ward. "With the cunning of a viper," she conceived a plot. She pretended to be pregnant by hiding a cushion under her robes. Her brother-in-law suspected a ruse, but how could he prove it? Eventually, moaning as if in the throes of labor, Agnes took to her bed and feigned giving birth to a daughter, Grace. Agnes had obtained the baby girl from a poor woman in a nearby village, whom she now hired as a wet nurse. Sir Thomas' brother filed a complaint with the royal courts, but the bishop asserted jurisdiction in the case and summoned the husband. The word in the county was that Thomas was incapable of fathering a child, but, being more afraid of offending his wife than of offending God, he was reluctant to testify. Eventually, however, he admitted that he was old and sick and for some time had scarcely touched his wife, though he protested that he had no idea what she was up to. The bishop warned that if he did not return the following day, he would be excommunicated. When Thomas went home and told his wife, she forbade him to speak to the bishop again. The next day was Easter. In his sermon Hugh denounced Thomas' crime against his own brother and excommunicated the guilty couple. Thomas died in his sleep the next night. The hagiographer's comment on this story is from Ecclesiasticus: "An evil wife is an ox yoke which chafes." It would take more than excommunication to intimidate the young widow. But at this point the story takes a new twist.

It was incumbent on the king of England to see to it that his vassals' heirs were protected. Little Grace was not yet four years old when the king gave her, along with her inheritance, to Adam of Neville, the brother of England's chief forester. However, until the marriage could be completed, Adam was the girl's guardian only. Afraid of losing the estate, he therefore pressed for an early marriage. The bishop intervened, partly because he opposed marriage of girls under the age of seven but even more because the mystery of the child's birth had yet to be cleared up. Taking the bull by the horns, he ordered the priests of his diocese to refuse to perform the wedding. But when duties of office called the bishop to Normandy, Adam's friends and relatives took advantage of his absence to persuade a thick-witted but greedy priest in an out-of-the-way parish to celebrate the marriage. "And so a serf married a nobleman." Upon his return Hugh suspended the priest, confiscated his benefice, and excommunicated anyone who had had anything to do with the affair, which had already cost one life. In a panic Agnes' servant went to confession, and the confessor sent her to the bishop, to whom she told all. Agnes too gave in and confessed her terrible sin; shortly thereafter she died a miserable death. The next order of business was to force Adam of Neville to renounce his claim to the inheritance, which Thomas' brother was suing to recover in the royal courts. Hugh alerted the archbishop of Canterbury, who was also the lord chief justice. Adam argued in court that under English law a child recognized by the mother's husband is considered to be legitimate. Hugh issued a threat: if Adam continued his efforts to marry the little peasant, he would not enjoy the fruits of his victory for long. Through his kin Adam exerted pressure on the London judges assigned to hear the case. Everything was going smoothly when Adam, drunk and happy, lay down to sleep; he never woke. Whereupon the king gave the little girl in marriage to one of his chamberlains, who thus gained control of her inheritance; but he too died. Grace, now eleven, was married to yet another husband, even more wicked than the first two. From various sources we know that she was childless and that when she died her inheritance reverted to Thomas' brother, the legitimate heir.

This story epitomizes many of the questions and difficulties of women's history. It shows, first of all, that social and economic differences must be carefully delineated. Four women are bound together by secret knowledge: a noblewoman, her servant, a serf, and an unborn baby girl. The child is caught up in a conspiracy hatched before her birth, the purpose of which is to make her a traitor to her caste by snatching her from her mother's womb and placing her in the noblewoman's bed. The timing must have been carefully worked out. Another aspect of the story that catches the historian's eye is the conflict between rival authorities: the common law, royal authority, feudal law, and ecclesiastical justice (competent in matrimonial matters) were all involved. The ecclesiastical courts may have been armed only with spiritual weapons, but in the right hands they were lethal.

The story is told by a churchman. This was not unusual for the period, but it does have significant consequences: Hugh's hagiographer sees women with a man's, indeed with a monk's, eyes, so his judgment is biased against them. We must check to make sure that his information is accurate and that he is not lying. Adam of Eynsham, it turns out, is intelligent and generally trustworthy, though on occasion he embellishes the truth: he is, after all, writing a panegyric and is apt to exaggerate the bishop's supernatural powers. The record shows that Adam of Neville did not immediately succumb to the bishop's malediction. In fact he outlived Hugh by several months.

In this tale hangs a method for approaching women's history. Nothing is more fatal to history than the idea that human nature is constant and universal. In other times Thomas and Agnes, being childless, might simply have adopted Grace—and too bad for the brother-in-law. Had there been no serfdom, Grace's origins might not have been an impediment to her marrying a nobleman. The circumstances of the case might have been different. "One is not born a woman," Simone de Beauvoir wrote, "One becomes a woman." The formulation is striking, but was it true in the eleventh and twelfth centuries? One way to answer the question is to do what Agnes did: to seize upon Grace's birth as a lever of fate. A woman's destiny was not strictly determined. As the story illustrates, there was always room for maneuver. Agnes, though young enough to make a credible mother, is saddled with an elderly and obviously senile husband. Had she done nothing, she would have been left a widow and subjected to the will of her brother-in-law, who could have forced her to remarry. Given the state of Thomas' health, time was of the essence; Agnes' options were limited. She no doubt considered them all. What alternatives were available? Could she have thwarted her brother-in-law's designs by entering a convent? Not without her husband's permission. Perhaps she did ask and he refused, or maybe she did not relish the idea of convent life. Was she convinced that she was sterile? In the Middle Ages sterility was always blamed on the woman. Could she have tried to have a child with a man other than her husband? In the end she took another couple's child and passed it off as her own. At the very least she must have counted on her husband's tacit consent. Was he still capable of fathering a child? Might he have believed the child was his own? We cannot answer these questions because they were of no interest to Hugh's hagiographer. We cannot scratch below the surface of the affair: Agnes plotted to escape an unpalatable fate. A poor woman conspired with her for the same reason.

It's a Girl!

Did men outnumber women in the eleventh and twelfth centuries, and were women more highly valued as a result?[6] To apply the law of supply and demand in any straightforward way is a risky business. More than that, the demographic statistics themselves are based on unreliable sources. Can local findings be generalized to the West as a whole? Male births slightly outnumber females in all human societies, but there is no proof that in the period that interests us girls were any more vulnerable than boys to exposure, infanticide, or neglect. In many cultures women took steps designed to ensure the birth of male offspring, but there is no evidence that such measures were employed by the women of the eleventh and twelfth centuries.

Girls probably were less welcome than boys, but the evidence for this assertion is indirect. A principle of masculinity prevailed in the aristocracy of the time, hence progenitors very likely hoped for a male heir to whom land and title could be passed on. The disparity between the sexes seems to have been less pronounced among commoners. Women were excluded from warfare, the vocation of the nobility, but not necessarily from other forms of economic activity. Cultivating the land placed a premium on strength, however, as did other varieties of manual labor. In all probability the sexual division of labor, reflecting a male-oriented hierarchy of values, tended to devalue female specialties. One has the impression, which may or may not be well founded, that daughters were a burden: they had to be watched, provided with dowries, and married off. The Middle Ages had yet to shed the ancient prejudice that women, immature and dependent creatures—created, as Bossuet remarked, out of a man's superfluous rib—are inferior to men.

We have no evidence at all by which to gauge the psychology of prospective parents or their emotional response to the birth of a child. How important was sex in determining a child's future? Suppose that Suger, who was born a serf, had had a twin sister. She would have had the same legal and social status, the same family background, and the same genetic heritage as the future abbot. Would she have become as illustrious as he? She could never have served as an adviser to kings or as regent of France; therefore she could never have come close enough to great men to have written their history. But might she have married a prince and become an abbess, prophetess, and writer like Hildegard of Bingen? One feels instinctively that it was easier for boys to break the mold than it was for girls, but such a contention is hard to prove. The question deserves to be raised at every stage of our inquiry. A story like that of Grace of Saleby provides an opportunity for *in vitro* observation.

Agnes, when she hatched her plot, could not know what sex the child would be. The case is interesting because it allows us, as in mathematics, to isolate an unknown. Did it make any difference that Grace turned out to be a girl rather than a boy? At first sight, no. The sequence of events would have been the same. Agnes passing herself off as the real mother, the real mother passing herself off as a wet nurse, the putative father, the suspicious brother-in-law who sues to recover his lost inheritance, the bishop who assumes jurisdiction in the case—all these would have been the same regardless of the child's sex. Terrorized by both wife and bishop, Thomas would have died in any case. So far, so good. But suppose the child had been a boy. It would have been brought up to become a knight, probably under the mother's tutelage. To be sure, Thomas' brother would have pursued his lawsuit against Agnes at Westminster, but the royal courts were slow, corrupt, and in this case powerless: the father was the husband of the mother, the child had been duly recognized, and Thomas had died without making a public disavowal. Nor could the bishop have done much, because Thomas never returned to denounce his wife's machinations. The case had first come to light in 1194, and Hugh had died in 1200. A boy very likely would have given Agnes what she wanted: a peaceful end to her life in the company of the Saleby heir. Her plan went awry, it seems fair to say, because the child was a girl.

A daughter of the aristocracy was fair game from the moment of birth. As the heir to a major fief, Grace under English custom enjoyed the protection of the law. A husband had to be found for her. Heiresses were in such demand that the king succumbed to temptation and awarded the prize prematurely. Kings had always been apt to take advantage of such windfalls, but King John had gained a reputation for driving a particularly hard bargain when it came to young girls with fiefs. The royal archives are blunt about the enormous sums he extracted from the child's three successive husbands "for the girl and her inheritance." At the age of four, when a son would have been playing knight on his rocking horse, Grace was taken from her mother and entrusted to old Adam of Neville, who immediately married the child. Until that point Agnes' gamble might have succeeded, but the very early marriage allowed the ecclesiastical court to assert jurisdiction in the case. Hugh did all he could to thwart Adam's plans. When the marriage took place anyway, the bishop excommunicated the conspirators. First the servant, then the counterfeit mother succumbed to the pressure. Of course the servant, the child's actual mother, soon drops out of sight. Her only role was to provide the baby and her milk; beyond that she was nothing but a mercenary, a woman of bad blood.

At this point we come up against a crucial gap in the record.

What we need to bring these women to life is the sound of their own voices: a diary, perhaps. Earlier we asked about Agnes' motives. All we know is that she died in humiliation and defeat, perhaps also in remorse and fear of damnation. What about Grace, who in this account is nothing but a pawn? What might she have thought about herself and about life? She knew that, because of her, her counterfeit father was dead and probably in hell and her counterfeit mother had become, in Hugh's words, a "criminal." Still a child, she already had been married three times. Even a legitimate heiress might have found reason for despair in the discovery that she herself counted for nothing. The men who burned to marry her coveted not the child but her property. But she might have internalized the aristocratic system of values to the point of taking pride in her role as inheritor of the past and mother of a noble line. She was a prize of considerable social and symbolic significance. Yet Grace was a fraud and everyone knew it. She was an impostor and a curse. Her husbands died, one after another. She must have been scorned. Did she suffer from a guilty conscience? If she was a child of normal intelligence, how could she not have despised her three husbands? Nobles who knew full well that she was not one of them, they nevertheless pretended to believe that she was. They had bought her to lay hands on her fortune and then bought the king and his courts to protect their asset.

The Church, whose mission is eternity, is keenly sensitive to time and therefore to women. For time is in women's genes. They stand at the intersection of cyclic and linear time. Reconciling the irreconcilable takes work: wait until the time is ripe, wait some more while time does its work, then make haste because time is running out.

Childhood

Childhood in the Middle Ages was short for both boys and girls. Death ended many lives prematurely, and circumstances compelled those who survived to grow up quickly. There is little evidence concerning when or how the parents of little girls broached the question of sexuality. No primers on the subject have survived, and the sources are mostly silent on the subject. Girls and boys appear for the most part to have been educated separately, particularly in the upper echelons of society. From very early on parents made it clear to girls that they were different from boys in capability and even in nature. Daughters of the aristocracy grew up in the women's quarters, the gynaeceum, where they spent their time doing women's work; some were sent to convents to await marriage or to remain permanently as nuns. A girl who married prior to puberty usually went to live with her husband's family until the marriage could be consummated. What was the psychological effect of being taken from one's mother at such an early age? What kind of emotional relationship could a daughter expect with her parents, nurse, brothers, and sisters? What did little girls dream about?

Girls born into families of humbler station seem at first sight to have had it better than the daughters of the aristocracy. For one thing they were unlikely to marry quite so soon. The daughters of peasants and artisans began to help out with the chores at an early age. The segregation of the sexes required by apprenticeship in the trades was less strict than that entailed by the military training of young noblemen. Humble families may have remained together longer, and daughters may have enjoyed closer relations with their fathers and brothers.

Were children loved? There is evidence that when children fell ill, parents cried and prayed for their recovery or, failing that, for their souls. Yet it is striking to see how easily parents, and particularly female saints, abandoned their very young children. Juette of Huy left two children behind when she went to do penance among the lepers.[7] The elder of the two was eight years old. Circumstances, most notably poverty, often interfered with parental love. It takes strength and hope to sing lullabies. Could the maternal instinct survive in women worn out by hard labor and repeated pregnancies and obliged to live in mean peasant huts? Why did Grace's mother, a Lincolnshire serf, bargain her child away even before it was born, much as starving, debt-ridden peasants sold their crops even before the harvest? We do not know if she was married, unmarried, or a widow. Was she too poor to raise the child, or too greedy? We may assume that Agnes paid for the infant and agreed to assume the cost of the girl's upkeep. Perhaps the poor mother dreamed of avenging herself on an unjust world. She would have the pleasure of seeing her daughter raised as a noble, and from time to time the girl might even bestow a kiss on her humble nurse. And what about Agnes? We are told that she was a "barren woman, unable to hatch anything other than a plot," but that she brought Grace up "as her own daughter." Was this simply an act? As the two women, aristocrat and serf, bent over the baby's cradle, perhaps there was something nobler in their action than the narrator wants us to believe—something like love mingled with the joy of thumbing one's nose at fate. To these women fate came in the shape of a man: the husband, the brother-in-law, the king, the gold-digging suitors, and above all the bishop. The saint was there to thwart the perfidious females who in duping one man and robbing another were circumventing every law known to man, the most sacred of which, for Saint Hugh, was the law of marriage, that guarantee of a social order the conspirators were bent on subverting. In the end morality was preserved: the inheritance was returned to Thomas' kin. And both the counterfeit mother and the counterfeit daughter were punished with sterility.

Daughters were taught proper behavior, but we have no idea how. When young Christina of Markyate runs away from her husband, she feels shame because she is forced to dress like a man and ride a horse like a man.[8] A girl's first lesson probably was what to do with her eyes: boys gazed forthrightly into the distance; girls either lowered their eyes or raised them unto heaven. Modesty, gentleness, and reserve defined the feminine ideal. Women sat at their sewing or spinning; they took care of the house and the children; and they prayed. These timeless images embodied the essence of womanhood.

How did girls learn the rudiments of religion? Christina, who was born around 1100, was told while still very young that Jesus is "handsome, good, and everywhere." Lying awake in bed, she spoke to him out loud. She knew how to read and had her own psalter—the young noblewoman's primer, according to Hildegard of Bingen.

Virginity was inculcated as the supreme value in girls of all stations. Many societies value virginity above marriage, and Christianity not only placed virginity at the pinnacle of its scale of values but justified that choice on the basis of Scripture. Virgins could expect greater rewards in heaven than women who married. The gospels provided women with an archetype in the shape of Mary. There was nothing new about the exaltation of virginity, but it never had been carried to such extremes as in the eleventh and twelfth centuries. There were many reasons for this: fear of the end of time; the spiritual influence of the monasteries and of clerical reform; and the flourishing of the cult of Mary.

In bringing up a daughter, virginity was as much a social value as a religious one. Not only the fate of the child's soul but the honor of the family depended on it. Girls were continually exhorted to guard their treasure with their lives. Even today the words purity, virtue, and honor bespeak virginity. The abstract qualities signify the intact seal, just as in the medieval texts. But this metonymy could easily turn to metaphor: the intact seal became the signifier of a woman's essence. Society treated the virgin as an angel whose innocence was to be cultivated and protected. That innocence could be put at risk in only one way: if a girl's parents decided to hand her over to a male as though she were "a filly" (the simile is George Sand's). In view of the widespread acceptance of the virginal ideal, it must have been difficult for a maiden to marry, to endure what the clergy portrayed as a state of corruption and defilement. There is in fact considerable evidence that marriage was traumatic for young women because the female experience in this respect exemplified church teachings.

A girl's purity usually was protected only long enough to be sacrificed in marriage. The vessel was kept tightly sealed for some years, then opened. Boys were increasingly free to roam in body and mind. Warriors, peasants, merchants, clerics—men in all walks of life saw the world changing around them and were encouraged to take a chance, to try their luck. Urban schools and universities proliferated in the twelfth century. The number of students hungry for knowledge and for the advancement that knowledge promised increased dramatically. It would be centuries before girls would be sent to schools or universities. Those few young women to receive instruction, like Héloïse, were educated at home. In this respect the divorce between the sexes may have been consummated in the twelfth century; it was destined to last for nearly a millennium. Women remained confined to traditional roles, serving humanity or God, while men enthusiastically discovered the world and all that it held in the way of instruction, adventure, and experience.

Marriage and the Church

Marriage is central to our story. Some of the reasons for this are general: marriage perpetuates the race and marks a major change in a woman's life. But some of the reasons are peculiar to the period that interests us here: in the eleventh and twelfth centuries the Church gave marriage its modern form. The considerable attention devoted to this problem in recent years has made the importance of these two centuries abundantly clear.[9]

Church thinkers had never been able to give a clear statement of the nature and purpose of Christian marriage. And the Church had had even less influence on the practice of marriage than on the theory. But the reform movement had given churchmen the prestige necessary to elaborate a new matrimonial theory and to enforce its principles. To do so, however, they first had to overcome a number of ingrained traditions. Since priests were now forbidden to marry, the resistance to the Church's efforts came from laymen.

Marriage is a sacrament, but until the twelfth century the precise content of that sacrament had been quite vague. Clarification was necessary before marriage could be included in the official list of sacraments promulgated by the Church in 1215. Marriage differed from the other six sacraments in troubling ways. It was the only one mentioned in Jewish law: the first man and the first woman had been joined in matrimony. But marriage was logically as well as chronologically prior: it was the foundation of all human society, a necessary condition if human beings were to reproduce and multiply without concupiscence. Unlike the other sacraments, it remained to some degree tainted even though it enjoyed God's blessing. Sexual reproduction was a consequence of original sin. Marriage therefore had to be indissoluble and subject to strict conditions. Incest was to be avoided at all cost. The new regulations in this regard were more stringent than ever before: no one was allowed to marry a godparent, and marriage to affine or cognate kin was forbidden down to the seventh degree.

Marriage was also unusual in that it transformed the binary relation between man (or woman) and God into a ternary relation: God, man, woman. Who or what tied the knot? The Church puzzled over this question for a long time before finally reaching a consensus in the second half of the twelfth century. Was marriage cohabitation or a merging of wills? Pragmatists and idealists differed. Much of the high clergy in this period would have preferred that everyone lead lives of at least continence if not abstinence; hence it is not surprising that the Church (following the Romans) chose to make the free consent of the parties the basis of indissoluble wedlock. Among other benefits, this position made it possible to portray the unconsummated marriage of Mary and Joseph as perfect. But few laypeople accepted the idea of marriage without sex, so some compromise was necessary. The sexual act thus became the final consummation of the marriage. The emphasis on consent meant that marriage did not require the participation of a priest. A union based on mutual consent was valid even without a priest's blessing, although the Church disapproved of the practice. The participation of a priest did not become a necessary component of Catholic marriage until 1563.

So much for theory. What actually happened in practice? We have little information except as regards the upper strata of society, where marriage was a strategic maneuver. It may also have been so among peasants and the urban poor. At this humble level marriage may have served to round out a plot of land or to take over a neighboring shop, but we have little hard information.[10] The children, especially the daughters, of nobles were pawns in strategies designed to increase the family's power and wealth. Endogamic marriage, divorce (especially when the wife was sterile), and remarriage had created a situation of "serial polygamy" whose purpose was to maximize power and wealth. The Church had to fight for more than a century to impose its monogamous model, designed to protect the weaker half of the couple: the woman. But nobles found loopholes in the new laws. The incest taboo had been extended so broadly that, when a man wished to get rid of his wife, it was tempting to claim that a hitherto unsuspected kinship with her rendered the marriage invalid. To close this loophole the taboo was pared back in 1215 from the seventh to the fourth degree.

In sum, the Church succeeded in establishing indissoluble marriage as a sacrament of the faith. Fickleness, misjudgment, and change of heart were no longer tolerated as reasons for ending marriage, now based on mutual consent, that is, on the liberty and equality of husband and wife. To our ears the words "liberty" and "equality" have such resonance that they warrant a brief digression.

Liberty and Marriage

Twelfth-century canonists and theologians agreed that marriage should be based on mutual consent, and by the end of the century this idea was widely accepted. Papal legates, backed by church councils, enforced the new regulations. Hence it might seem that the case of little Grace, who was married before she was four and who had been married to three men by the time she was eleven, was a grotesque exception. But nagging questions remain. Why did the primate of England, a bishop, and a king intervene in the case? And why did Hugh's hagiographer choose to underscore the bishop's sense of duty by noting that he refused to allow children to marry before the age of discretion: seven years? The case not only points up the disparity between theory and practice but reveals how in practice the Church limited free marital choice.

Customs, always stubborn, dull the cutting edge of even the keenest principles. After some hesitation the principle that serfs could marry without their masters' consent was accepted in canon law. Hugh of Lincoln, however, could not accept the idea that a nobleman might marry a woman of unfree birth. Caste prejudices outweighed the Gospel. Significantly, the new theory of marriage implied certain restrictions on marital choice. It is often claimed that Christianity, a universalist religion, was open-minded in such matters. But the Church never championed liberty in the legal sense. It accommodated itself to slavery by citing 1 Peter 2:18–19: "Servants, be subject to your masters . . . For this is thankworthy, if a man for conscience toward God endure grief, suffering wrongfully." Because slaves were the property of their masters, slave marriage was meaningless. The Church also prohibited marriage with infidels. Sexual contact of any kind between Jews and Christians was treated more harshly than fornication and adultery between Christians. Indeed, copulation with a Jew was considered bestiality and could be punished by burning at the stake.[11] The theological argument against incestuous marriage was that the elect are joined together by a stream of love and this stream must encompass ever-widening circles of humankind. Here below, however, the wall between the great religions remained unbreachable. These restrictions make perfect sense in view of the Church's goal: not freedom as a fundamental individual right but salvation even of resisting souls.

It is a fundamental principle of law that a person must possess certain capacities in order to enter into a binding contract. Legal aptitude, determined in part by age, is thus a precondition of commitment. The minimum age of engagement, which at the time carried with it a strong obligation to complete the marriage, was a major concern of canon law; here too there was much hesitation before a choice was finally made. Yves of Chartres, who made a crucial contribution to the debate in the late eleventh century, believed that marriage should be permitted at age seven. Hugh, who lived a century after Yves, agreed with him. But most canonists agreed that seven was an appropriate age for engagement; for marriage, the approved age, as determined by puberty, was twelve for girls, fourteen for boys. Thirteenth-century decretals were more accommodating: if a marriage could restore peace between two families, it could be celebrated before the officially sanctioned age. Clearly these rules show that the Church fully accepted the idea that parents should determine when and whom their children could marry. What did this imply for the principle of mutual consent? On their wedding day the bride and groom were free to renounce the contract that had been made on their behalf. But this hardly amounts to freedom of choice as we understand the concept. Did a girl affianced at seven and slated to marry at twelve know what she was doing? Did she have any options? Dom Leclercq thinks she did.[12] Saint Ode, he argues, did not wish to marry but was forced into an engagement by her parents. On her wedding day she refused to give her consent. Everyone was aghast. The wedding procession fell into disarray. Ode returned home and, to prevent any further attempt to force her to marry, cut off her nose. This story, Leclercq would have us believe, proves that she was a free woman. How many women were willing to pay such a price for freedom?

The very early age of consent may well have seemed reasonable because youth was so brief in the Middle Ages. The experts in canon law might have been acting in good faith when they held that children so young were capable of making binding promises. The first half of the twelfth century was of course a crucial turning point in the history of western thought.[13] Ancient philosophy, transmitted to the West by way of Arab thinkers, stimulated new thinking about the questions of conscience and responsibility. Meanwhile, new monastic orders such as the Carthusians and Cistercians repudiated the practice of oblation, under which children had been sent into the cloister at a very early age. Many oblates proved to be bad monks. The new orders wanted only mature adults capable of free choice. It was inconsistent to argue that children were incapable of committing themselves to the service of God yet capable of committing themselves to married life. How could such glaring inconsistency be justified? Two possibilities come to mind. The Church was pragmatic. Knowing that it could not dictate a complete revolution in marriage customs at one stroke, it chose to deal first with the most serious problem: by making marriage indissoluble, it put an end to the repeated exploitation of matrimonial advantage, but it could not prevent families from seeking to secure their children's future as soon as possible. If this argument were correct, however, we would expect to see an increase in the age of consent within a very short period of time. This did not happen.

The explanation must lie elsewhere. The solution of the riddle, I contend, lies in the clergy's image of women. For who in fact married young? In the vast majority of cases it was little girls, not little boys. It is impossible to give quantitative proof of this assertion in general, although persuasive evidence has survived from the late Middle Ages.[14] Nevertheless, all indications point in the same direction. In aristocratic marriages the age difference between husband and wife was often ten to twenty years or more, and the younger partner was always the wife. Among commoners we observe a similar, though less marked, disparity in age. Thus the question of consent in marriage primarily concerned women. A young girl was free in one sense only: to consent to her parents' choice of a mate. Any number of arguments were cited in support of this restriction of female choice: women were sensual, weak-minded creatures, hence their purity was always in danger. Yves of Chartres warned that it was the husband's task to tame his wife's sensuality as the soul tames the body and as man tames the beast. The sooner a woman (or girl) was subjected to the will of her lord and master, the better off she was. On this all the authorities agreed, from Plutarch to Paul. Women thus suffered a major setback in the twelfth century, just as men were being encouraged to explore the world a little, to learn to know themselves before marrying and to reap dividends on their intellectual and moral capital as urban merchants were doing on their mercantile capital. But girls continued to marry young and to enter convents young. The most lucid and rigorous thinkers, those who had reflected on the Socratic injunction "know thyself," did not think about or even speak to women.

Georges Duby has argued that the life of Saint Arnulf can be read as indicative of a new spirit in the Church, of a reluctance to permit parents to force their children to marry.[15] A girl, the story goes, refuses the husband chosen for her by her parents because she loves another man. She threatens to commit suicide if forced to marry against her will. Beside themselves, the parents turn to the saint for advice. Arnulf recommends that the girl's choice be respected. If that were the end of the story, Duby's case would be convincing. But the remainder of the tale shrewdly resurrects time-honored principles. The saint, who can see into the future, reassures the parents that their daughter, soon to become a widow, will then gladly marry the man they have chosen for her. If the parents can just be patient, family harmony can be maintained and their authority will soon be restored. If allowed to indulge her romantic escapade, the girl will soon recognize the error of her ways and the correctness of her parents' choice. Arnulf, like Hugh of Lincoln, can tell the future. Some saints have that gift, which is why they understand women so well.

As the only authority with jurisdiction over marriage, the Church zealously enforced its conception of free consent. It set up courts and judicial procedures for hearing the complaints of wives who claimed that they were coerced into marriage. If the allegations were proved, the marriage theoretically could be annulled. But what was the reality? Sources for the twelfth century are scarce, but it is possible to make inferences based on documents from later periods.[16] Certain facts must be kept in mind, however. Nearly all young women were dependents in both the legal and the economic sense. Precious few had the means to choose freely how they would like to live. Dowries were bestowed on them by parents or, if the parents were dead, by brothers. If a girl wished to marry a man other than the one chosen by her parents, her dowry might be withdrawn or her allowance withheld. In many areas, particularly in the south of France, customary law allowed fathers to disinherit disobedient daughters; lords could seize the person and property of undesirable suitors.[17] The dissuasive power of such threats cannot be overestimated. Fear of scandal and impoverishment must have dissuaded many.

Suppose that a woman forced to marry against her will chose to avail herself of her right to protest to an ecclesiastical tribunal. She would have to overcome her modesty and risk the wrath of her own kin as well as of her husband and his family. If she did so, what sort of reception might she expect from the Church? The great thirteenth-century jurist Hostiensis is quite clear on this point: any woman who opposed her family's will was a priori suspected of the "vice of ingratitude." But let us assume that the woman's innocence softens the hearts of her judges—all of them celibate males. The first question asked would be why, if the marriage was coerced, she did not flee on her wedding night, before the union was consummated. But if she had fled, where would she have gone? If she lived with her husband after the wedding, the judges would presume that she had consented to the marriage, notwithstanding any pressure to which she might have been subjected on her wedding day. The only way to avoid this verdict was to prove that she had been raped. Only the most exceptional women were capable of fleeing their husbands to avoid legal rape. Under the circumstances it seems naive to point to the small number of complaints actually filed with the courts as evidence that most marriages were not coerced. It is remarkable that there were any complaints at all.

The Marriage of Christina of Markyate

Christina was truly fortunate in her birth.[18] Her parents, of old Anglo-Saxon stock, lived in Huntingdon on England's east coast. Her father, a wealthy merchant, was the leading member of the local guild. She had kin throughout the county. In her immediate family there were five children, including herself, plus the two parents. Christina's maternal aunt was for a long time the wife or concubine (it is hard to say which—all the terminology was in flux) of the most important man in the kingdom after the king himself: Ranulph Flambard, who in 1099 became bishop of Durham. She bore him several children, one of whom grew up to become bishop of Lisieux. Protected by the king, Ranulph thumbed his nose at the pope's warnings and continued to live a very dissolute life. Eventually, however, he separated from Christina's aunt, for whom he found a most respectable husband, a burgher of Durham. Afterward he maintained close relations with Christina's family, and when he traveled from London to his bishopric he often stayed with his ex-wife.

An intelligent, serious child, Christina was her parents' favorite. Her father, Autti, entrusted her with the keys to the family coffers, filled with gold and silver. The family lived quite lavishly and counted a chaplain among its staff. Little Christina was very happy, and her parents were very proud of her. Her piety augured well for the future. The family hoped to find her a husband who would make them even more prosperous and give them the grandchildren they desired. Christina's uncle the bishop hit upon the perfect husband: a wealthy young nobleman from the city. The engagement was made without consulting Christina. But the fiancé was in a hurry. When Christina's parents broke the news to her, she told them that she had vowed to remain a virgin. At first they laughed, then they fell silent. Silence soon turned to anger, cajolery, and threats. Love potions failed, and so did beatings. But Christina finally gave in just outside the church on the day of the wedding, which was celebrated immediately.

Because the couple's new home was not yet finished, Christina remained at home with her parents. Everything possible was done to compel her to submit to her husband. The girl was plied with drink. Her husband was admitted to her room while she slept. When he proved too willing to accede to Christina's wishes, her relatives egged him on with prods. But he refused to take the girl by force, and for that he was accused of being cowardly, unmanly, and weak. Christina's disobedience was taken as a challenge to the honor of both her husband and her father, who became the laughingstock of the town. The most charitable of the townsfolk took pity on the father; a delegation of prominent citizens finally persuaded him to consult the authorities. But who had jurisdiction in such a case? Certainly not the civil authorities. Under the recently drafted legal code of Henry I, marriage was a private affair. In order to pressure Christina into complying, her father therefore turned to the Church. No one doubted that the ecclesiastical authorities would be able to talk sense into the girl and remind her of her duties. First the local canons were consulted, then the bishop of Durham, and finally, on two occasions, the bishop of Lincoln. Meanwhile, Christina's friends, the pious hermits and monks of the county, came to her aid in the hope of saving her virginity. One of them went to Canterbury to consult the archbishop.

The year was 1114, shortly before the death of Yves of Chartres, the canon-law expert whose works were well known in England, and a generation before the drafting of the Decretum of Gratian, which in 1141 laid the groundwork for a new marital code. Thus the reactions of the various prelates consulted in this case are of particular interest. It should come as no surprise that the Church was powerless: the law was still evolving, its implements had yet to be forged, its tribunals had yet to be created. In the absence of law there was room for common sense. In the eyes of the churchmen the first thing to consider was Christina's motives. Was she a virgin? Was she refusing to submit to her husband because she loved another man? An affirmative answer to the second question (for us the very meaning of freedom of choice) would have ended all discussion. It was perfectly normal for a father to choose his daughter's husband. Autti conceded that he had coerced his daughter on her wedding day, but that was a mere peccadillo, a clumsy move. But the girl, by stubbornly persisting in her refusal, dishonored her family. On that point everyone agreed, until Christina raised the issue of her vow of virginity. There the men of the cloth divided, because the issue now was no longer whether she was free to love a man but whether she was free to love Christ. This was the only choice that not only absolved a woman of disobedience to her father or husband but required it. Such a choice the celibate men of the Church could understand, and they were prepared to allow a woman to join them so long as she remained a virgin. While Christina, threatened with rape, was held in protective custody, one of her defenders, a hermit, went to see the archbishop of Canterbury. The archbishop stated that "if he had Christina's mother, whose persecution of her daughter was even worse than her father's, in custody, he would impose on her a penance as harsh as that for homicide." But he had no way of influencing either the girl's parents or the bishop of Lincoln, who supported them. The intrepid hermit asked what Christina ought to do, and the primate answered that she ought to flee. Canon law had no teeth and could recommend nothing more satisfactory than a flight into the wilderness. Christina, a girl of astonishing mettle, did flee, to a convent, where she received the Church's blessing only because the freedom she claimed for herself was to accomplish the sacrament of virginity. A woman was free to seek grace but not fulfillment.

In laying down the principle of free consent, the Church was not defending freedom per se, nor was it championing a woman's right to happiness. The assertion of such a right, which came late in the history of the West, owed nothing to Christianity. Preoccupied with the salvation of souls, the Church feared that happiness might be a reason to forget God, to let up in the battle against evil. The purpose of the principle of free consent was to prevent laymen from destroying the stability of the conjugal cell on which the perpetuation of the species depended. Yet theologians also spoke of *dilectio,* love between husband and wife. What did they mean?

Love and Marriage

In western societies today marriage implies love, meaning a relationship between a man and a woman that engages them totally, body, mind, and soul. How was it in the eleventh and twelfth centuries? Consider the following case, on which Hugh of Lincoln consulted Pope Celestine III (1191–1198).[19] John, the husband of Alice, commits adultery with Maxilla. He repents, and the ecclesiastical court (which by this time had gained real power) sentences him to resume his married life. But John reneges on his promise and begins seeing his concubine again. Alice dies, and for ten years John lives with Maxilla. After producing ten children, they decide to marry. Their case is brought to the attention of the pope, who rules that they must do public penance, then separate. The children only make matters worse. "Steps must be taken," the pope wrote, "to make sure that they share the burden of bringing them up."

This decision strikes us as odd. To our modern way of thinking, John and Maxilla have demonstrated their love by remaining together for so long, and, since there is no impediment to their marriage, that love ought to be rewarded. The twelfth-century Church did not see it that way. In its eyes the sin of adultery had forever defiled Maxilla. Nothing could be done about that. In this we sense the clergy's revulsion from the flesh. For them the goal was not to encourage the couple to seek fulfillment in marriage, much less in carnal pleasure. The Church Fathers, particularly Jerome, whose influence was considerable, had warned that excessive ardor in marriage was adulterous. Augustine had summed up the purpose of marriage in three words: procreation, fidelity, sacrament. To these men of the Church, *dilectio* meant something quite different from what we understand by love. J. T. Noonan has called attention to the ambiguity in the notion of affection, itself borrowed from Roman law.[20] The concept, which was used by the courts to mean something like consent, figured in discussions of the difference between legitimate marriage and concubinage. The term sometimes had a moral and affective component, but it was applied not only to married couples but also to filial and fraternal sentiments. It was even used as a synonym for charity in the broadest sense, as when Christ exhorts humankind to "love one another." Eleventh- and twelfth-century theologians considered love not a psychological prerequisite of marriage but a moral precept, a duty incumbent on married couples. Marriage, being indissoluble, endured even if love vanished or turned to hatred.

Late in the twelfth century a woman fled her husband's home and sought refuge with the man she loved.[21] She said she would rather die than return home. Her mother, a "latter-day Herodias," supported her. The abandoned husband took his case to the bishop, who summoned the couple to his church and admonished the wife, "mingling affectionate words with threats." He then led the woman to the altar and urged her to bestow the kiss of peace on her husband, but she outraged all present by spitting in his face. Thereafter she persisted in her sinful ways, and when she died a short while later, her soul was carried off by demons. If a couple could not bear to live together, the Church countenanced only two possibilities: separation without possibility of remarriage or withdrawal of both husband and wife from the world.

The Curse of Beauty

Beauty was a subject of great concern to the clergy. The ancients had exalted it, and the burgeoning vernacular literature of the twelfth century saw it as the irresistible source of love. Isolde continues to fascinate us even today. It is difficult, however, to gauge the impact of beauty in real life. Of course no shepherdess, no matter how pretty, ever had a ghost of a chance of winning the love of a prince. But all other things—rank, fortune, age— being equal, beauty may have been the deciding factor in the choice between two women. The clergy complained bitterly that fathers lavished dowries on their prettiest daughters and turned the ugly ones—whom Bernardino of Siena ungraciously called "the earth's vomit"—over to the Lord. Contemporary chroniclers claimed that marriages often came about from love at first sight rather than calculated self-interest, but we need not take them at their word. Nevertheless, a wife who was beautiful as well as wealthy and who could therefore add distinction to a household was that much more desirable. We have no idea what the situation was in the humbler classes of society.

The Church, straddling the divide between the worldly and the cloistered life, was forced to develop its own theory of beauty. Peter Lombard, the bishop of Paris and one of the leading thinkers of the twelfth century, cited beauty as one of the principal factors in the choice of a mate. Yet beauty was always dangerous and sometimes downright harmful.

Even men of the cloth, though bound by oaths of chastity, were all too likely to become beauty's victims. They reminded themselves that beauty is only skin deep and that below the skin lay a "sack of filth," yet they could not always stifle the desire it stirred within them. Hugh had been lucky: as a young Carthusian, he had burned with desire, but one night a saint came down from heaven and castrated him. From that moment on he had known only calm. The Desert Fathers had warned that the devil liked to disguise himself as a beautiful woman. Gilbert of Sempringham, who in the twelfth century founded an order of women, found this out for himself.[22] He was living in the home of a man with several luscious daughters. One night he dreamed that his hand had somehow found its way to the breast of one of the girls and that he could not remove it. When he awoke, the memory of his hand welded to that shapely bosom made a convert of him. He moved out of the house, mortified his flesh, and preached warnings against lustful women. As an old man he surprised a glint of guilty desire in the eyes of one of his nuns.[23] The next day he delivered a fiery sermon against lust, at the conclusion of which he unfastened his tunic. Underneath he was totally naked, "fleshless, hairy, wild." As he passed back and forth among the nuns, he spoke to the Cross: "Cursed be the body that kindled desire in a wretched woman!"

Beauty could cause problems. A beautiful woman, attractive to other men, might arouse jealousy in her husband. Or she might choose to marry Christ and hide her charms in a nun's habit. Even behind convent walls she still might burn with desire or inflame men's hearts, as one nun's horrifying story suggests. She lived in Watton, a monastery of the Order of Saint Gilbert, during the lifetime of the order's founder. But she disliked the cloistered life, which was all she had known since the age of four. After falling in love with the young canon who served as the nun's spiritual adviser, she found herself pregnant.[24] The other sisters, aghast at the disgrace to the order, laid a trap for the lover, who had fled. He was caught and brought back to Watton, where, in the presence of the other nuns, the guilty woman was forced to castrate her lover and then returned to her cell. But a miracle took place. Her legs in irons, the pregnant nun was about to deliver when two angels came and snatched away the fruit of her sin!

Most dangerous of all was the woman aware of her own beauty. If she merely passed her time in narcissistic contemplation, the only danger was to her soul. But if she used her beauty to seduce men, she became evil incarnate. A corrupt soul in a beautiful body threatened the metaphysical order. Beauty was an attribute of the divine, and if a man succumbed to the beauty of a woman of pure soul, only he was to blame, not God. But a sublime physiognomy that hid a perverted soul was a misleading sign, a reminder of the insoluble problem of the existence of evil in a world the Creator had wanted to be beautiful and good. When churchmen thought about marriage, they reflected over and over again on the primordial couple, on Eve's seduction by Satan and her subsequent seduction of hapless Adam. Why had Adam listened to her? "Because he loved her," Abelard affirmed more than once.[25] Eve had been in league with the Devil. At times the serpent coiled around the Tree of Life had even assumed Eve's ravishing features. Beauty could thus be a lethal trap, "all the more deceptive because it is not always so." Beauty is never harmless or innocent, except in the case of the Virgin.

Equality and Marriage

The new definition of marriage raised the question of equality between husband and wife in the expression of consent. Miniatures illustrating the Decretum of Gratian sought to demonstrate the perfect symmetry of the two spouses.[26] From the time of Saint Paul, equality in sexual relations had been prescribed. Husband and wife had rights over each other's body. Fidelity too was required of both parties. But these prescriptions do not give an adequate sense of the reality of marital relations.

The requirement of mutual consent did not imply equality in decisionmaking after marriage. The wife was subject to the power of her husband, "woman's sovereign." The metaphor of Christ married to the Church is eloquent in this regard, as is that of God wedded to the soul. Why, given this duly sanctioned inequality in marriage, was the consent of both parties required in accepting the sacrament? In order to prevent families from making and breaking couples at will, the initiative in contracting a marriage was shifted from the father to the daughter. The bride had to become a full party to a bilateral contract binding on both partners. Actually there were three parties to the contract. The model was God, Adam, and Eve. God made Eve subject to Adam. Perhaps the best comparison is with the contract of vassalage. The lord entered the relationship as his future vassal's superior, and he remained so. That superiority was expressed in two phases of the vassalage ritual: the homage and the oath of fealty. But between those two phases came the kiss on the mouth, which established for an instant the equality necessary for a contract for reciprocal exchange of services to be sealed. Inequality then reasserted itself.

Once again I turn to the life of Hugh of Lincoln for an illuminating anecdote.[27] Hugh, as we know, was freed of temptation by castration, and his biographer is struck by how easy this enables the future saint's relations with women to be. He invites women to dine with him and kisses them; they show him their babies and tell him their secrets. One day a woman confesses to Hugh that her husband is not fulfilling his conjugal duty—not paying his debt, as Paul would have it. "Do you want to rekindle your husband's ardor?" Hugh asks. "I shall make him a priest! . . . The moment a man becomes a priest, he begins to burn with desire." Only a man as irreproachable as Hugh would have risked so lascivious a gibe. Shrewdly, the bishop adopts his lay interlocutor's point of view. She is perfectly entitled to insist that her husband do his conjugal duty by her. Hugh can also allow himself to criticize the clergy, because he is one of them, and because he is chaste. But in so doing he demeans conjugal sexuality by associating it with sinful clerical dreams. Guilt is subtly shifted from the husband to the wife: she is lucky enough to be married to a continent male, so how can she be so nasty, or so lustful, as to complain of her good fortune? The theologians were unanimous: it was no sin to do one's duty if one's partner required it, but it was a sin, though not a very serious one, to insist on one's due.

This story shows how difficult it was to achieve equality in marriage. Paul had treated the problem of sexual exchange in terms of the law of debt. But in ancient law debts were legal obligations only until repaid, and they could be paid off in advance. Popular wisdom held that the man who paid his debts prospered as a result. The clergy took a very different view of marital debt. The debtor was praised for refraining from payment as long as possible, and the creditor for not demanding payment. Since husband and wife were at once debtors and creditors, the worthiest couple was the one in which each spouse attempted to outdo the other in abstinence. The ideal, as always, remained the unconsummated marriage or, at worst, the marriage that became chaste after bringing a certain number of children into the world. Yet even in hagiography we read of the discomfiture of husbands whose wives withhold their sexual favors. The reverse seems to have been rare. As for the requirement of mutual fidelity, the Church seems to have ignored the reality of the situation: because of the need to ensure the legitimacy of offspring, adultery was necessarily a far more serious matter for women than for men. The insistence on mutual fidelity, noble though it was, remained a pious wish.

Marriage defined the place of women in society, and their position was far less favorable in the eleventh and twelfth centuries than in the Carolingian period.[28] The fascination with virginity and monasticism tended to diminish the value of secular life, maternity, and the wife's role in the household.

Family Life

So much for marriage. What came next? How did married couples live? They rarely lived together for very long, because the average life expectancy was little more than thirty years. Because of the usual age difference between husband and wife and the frequency of death in childbirth, marriage often ended in the death of one of the partners, and remarriage was common. Children often were brought up by foster parents. Few knew their grandparents.

The study of domestic life raises many difficult methodological issues. Customs varied from region to region. In some places couples formed nuclear families, while elsewhere they joined extended families. Legal status, social rank, and economic wherewithal all influenced life at home. The nature of a woman's dowry or settlement was also important. What proportion of the husband's wealth was settled on the wife? Did she stand to inherit from her father, or was she excluded because she had received a dowry? Did the local laws grant women any legal capacity? Could they testify in court, make wills, sign contracts? Was the wife entitled to scrutinize the management of communal property? What was the status of the widow? Did widows normally assume guardianship over their children? If we could answer these questions, we would still be faced with the problem of determining how far the reality differed from what was prescribed by law. Given all the uncertainties, the best we can hope to do is provide some glimpses of domestic life. Women were for the most part invisible companions of men. When Gilbert, bishop of Limerick, described early-twelfth-century society, he borrowed the by then familiar theme of the three orders: those who pray, those who fight, and those who work.[29] "I do not say," he added, "that the function of women is to pray, to toil, or to do combat, but they are married to those who do, and serve them."[30]

The Women of Iceland

By comparison, Iceland, located at the northernmost extremity of Christendom, was a country with a homogeneous if primitive population, rather small for a land its size. What we know about Icelandic society comes by way of its laws and sagas, and these tell us far more about the tribal chieftains than about the rest of the population.[31] Late to embrace Christianity, the country by this time had developed a standard ecclesiastical structure, with a hierarchy ranging from bishopric to parish. A number of salient points about the society emerge from eleventh- and twelfth-century sources. It was highly masculine and very violent. Sexuality was neither disparaged nor disciplined; virginity and the monastic model had not yet made inroads. Women were not only inferior to men, they were treated "almost as livestock." Christianity had only further degraded woman's image. Volcanoes bore female names, and women often were labeled with unflattering epithets, such as "dead man's mare." They were forbidden to inherit any of their father's property and had no political rights. In civil law a man's word was to be taken over a woman's. Although a woman was her husband's property, her progeny were protected. Unmarried mothers were asked to name the father of their children.

Sexual mores in Icelandic society were surprisingly free. Concubines were common, as was polygamy, and many children were illegitimate. Celibacy was held in low esteem. All the priests and bishops about whom we know anything were married. The first Benedictine monastery in Iceland was not built until 1186. Few nuns were virgins: they had husbands, concubines, and children. Marriage existed as a legal institution, but it could be dissolved. Choice of partners depended on social status, and it was considered best that bride and groom not see each other prior to the wedding. The bride's consent was not required. An episcopal order requiring such consent was issued in 1269, but it failed to take hold. At the time of marriage the husband settled a portion of his property on his wife and also gave her the traditional *morgengabe* (morning gift). Divorce could be sought by either party, but people disapproved if a woman took the initiative.

The Icelandic aristocracy differed markedly from its continental counterpart. As on the Continent the lord and his wife lived among their children, both legitimate and illegitimate, servants, and clients. A change that had long been under way elsewhere was only just beginning in Iceland at the end of the twelfth century: the evolution from a clan structure with multiple nuclei toward a lineage structure defined by primogeniture, exclusion of bastards from inheritance, and indivisible patrimony. During the two centuries that interest us, fathers were free to choose their principal heir, who did not have to be a legitimate child. It is surprising to see how long the martial Icelanders preserved their ancient pagan traditions in the face of the Church's efforts. The religious authorities failed to persuade people that sex outside marriage was a mortal sin or that virginity was a virtue. Even worse, native-born bishops were not persuaded either.

The Three Orders

Nine-tenths of the people in western Christendom were peasants. Geographical location, social rank, and economic class profoundly influenced the way people lived.

In the Countryside

The wife of a landless peasant (assuming he married at all) had little in common with the wife of one of those well-to-do peasants who later came to be called *coqs de village* and who were wealthy enough to employ domestic servants. The rural world was by no means unchanging, certainly not in the eleventh and twelfth centuries. Living conditions were in flux everywhere. In Italy and Provence peasants moved into fortified villages *(incastellamento)*. Elsewhere they formed village communities. In Spain and eastern Europe new colonies advanced into previously virgin territory. New land was opened to cultivation around the *bastides* (ranch-houses) of southwestern France. All of these developments affected the history of women.

In rural areas women assumed broad responsibilities and contributed significantly to the family's productivity. Robert Fossier points out that women were in charge of storing the harvest, of growing vegetables, and of maintaining the hearth (now located inside the home rather than outside). They also helped out with the major farm work. So women were ubiquitous and indispensable, but they still were not considered to be men's equals; after all, slaves too were indispensable. We know next to nothing about life in peasant households. The villein and his wife appear in literature as bestial savages, subhumans as far beneath the notice of the well-born as the serf woman in the story of Agnes of Saleby. Nothing is known about the role of women in village life, in collective labor, or in festivals. Did women gather, as they would in later periods, at washhouses, bread ovens, and grain mills? We know that village assemblies were held in Lombardy.[32] Did women attend, and, if so, were they allowed to speak? There is some evidence for later centuries but almost none for the eleventh and twelfth.

It is discouraging to go on at length about all that we do not know, so let us turn for a moment to Catalonia, a region for which the work of Pierre Bonnassie has begun to fill in some of the gaps in our knowledge.[33] In the eleventh century Catalonia was not far from the border with the infidel: Muslim territory. Its substantial peasant population was freeborn and supported the count. Catalonian peasants were less oppressed than their counterparts in some other parts of Europe. The Visigothic institutions that had shaped their traditions had been relatively favorable to women. Although bastards were excluded from inheritance, all legitimate children, including daughters, shared in their father's patrimony. Nearly all peasants lived in nuclear families. Women owned their dowries and marriage portions, the latter constituted out of one-tenth of the husband's property. For that reason women participated in all of their husband's real estate transactions. Half of any property acquired after the marriage belonged to the wife. Adult women enjoyed full civil rights. They could bring suit, swear oaths, and testify in court. When a man died, he generally left his wife the income on his property and appointed her guardian of his children.

In the City

We have very little information about the lives of urban women in the eleventh and twelfth centuries. There was a revival of urban life almost everywhere in Europe, largely because of peasant immigration. It would be interesting to learn more about how people moved. Did they migrate as couples, or did single men move to the city and marry later? As the cities changed, social relations were also in flux. Urban populations were relatively large and anonymous. People from many walks of life mingled: monks and nuns, merchants, prostitutes, students, usurers, pickpockets. In the cities there was great variety in housing, diet, manners, and mobility. But there is little specific information about women prior to the thirteenth century except in a few parts of Europe, particularly Italy.[34] There is, for example, no information concerning what lines of work women were permitted to engage in independently or with their husbands prior to Etienne Boileau's *Livre des métiers* and the *taille* (tallage) registers from the end of the century.[35] Hence we cannot answer the crucial question of whether or not economic autonomy was a possibility for women. Early in the twelfth century Christina's father hired her to serve at the Huntingdon guild festival. Juette of Huy, a widow, lent money at interest. Women earned less than men for the same work, in Paris at any rate. Guibert of Nogent reports that at the beginning of the twelfth century eighty women took part in an insurrection at Amiens. But we know nothing about changes in the relations between men and women or, for that matter, among women. Nor do we know anything about the feminine confraternities of the period or about women's religious or other organizations. The Peace of God and Truce of God movements of the eleventh century and the construction of hospitals for poor women in the twelfth century show that the authorities were aware of the precarious conditions in which some women lived, but we do not begin to get a clear picture before the thirteenth century.

We do, however, have information about three aspects of urban history that affected women: slavery, prostitution, and anti-Semitism. In the period that interests us there were far fewer slaves, particularly in the far north (Scandinavia and Iceland) and south (Italy and Spain), than there had been during the Roman Empire and in the first millennium after Christ. Female slaves usually became prostitutes or domestic servants, and the latter were frequently required to service their masters' sexual as well as other needs. Large numbers of Welshwomen were sent off to the harems of Turkey, and the bishop of Uppsala recommended that they not be overfed.[36] In countries bordering the Mediterranean urban slaves were common throughout the Middle Ages.

Large-scale urban prostitution was a more recent development. The biblical image of the city was generally negative: after all, the first city was built by Cain. As cities began to flourish once again, urban issues became one of the Church's central concerns. The city symbolized two great evils: sex and money. Indeed money, always suspect, could be used to purchase sex, which was evil outside marriage. Although the evidence is scanty compared with later periods, we know that many cities, including Paris, Angers, and Toulouse, had brothels. Prostitution was subject to regulation in Toulouse prior to 1201.[37] There is little information about the social background of prostitutes. Psychological, economic, and social factors no doubt played a part in determining which women became whores. Many of them reportedly became disciples of the itinerant, and in some cases heretical, preachers who constitute one of the novel features of this period and who preached equality between the sexes and participation of women in the sacraments. They may have been joined by women once married to priests but cast out by their husbands after 1139, some of whom joined Robert of Arbrissel at the convent he founded in Fontevraud. Before long local authorities elsewhere were building shelters for such female penitents.

A word must be said about the rise of anti-Semitism, which had important implications for women. In 1215 a Church council ordered Jews to wear distinctive clothing, in part to prevent Christians from unwittingly having sex with Jewish women. This harsh new legislation gave official sanction to growing hostility toward Jews. Christina's persecutors in 1110 sought the help of an elderly Jewess, whose magic they hoped would persuade the girl to consent to marriage. By the end of the twelfth century hostility toward Jews had manifested itself throughout Europe, and rulers attempted to exploit it for their own ends.

A striking instance of anti-Semitism occurs in a story told by the Cistercian monk Caesarius, who entered the monastery of Heisterbach in the final years of the twelfth century.[38] A poor young priest in Worms falls in love with his neighbor, a very pretty Jewess, whom he seduces and makes pregnant. She confides in him that she is pregnant and afraid that her father will kill her. The priest advises her that if her parents question her, she should tell them that she is a virgin and has no idea how she became pregnant. Late one night, he climbs up to her parents' window, slips a tube through a narrow opening, and whispers these words: "Blessed are you both. Your daughter has conceived a child who will be the savior of your people!" The proud couple believes the story, and the news spreads through the Jewish communities of nearby towns. As the pregnancy approaches its term, people gather in anticipation of a miraculous birth. But the Messiah proves to be a girl. An outraged Jew grabs the infant and dashes it against a wall.

Regardless of whether or not this story has a basis in fact, it is fraught with meaning. It raises numerous issues concerning the hostile relations between the Christian and Jewish communities. Here, however, I am concerned with the response to the young priest's sin: it is not only absolved (as male escapades generally were) but blessed. He becomes a Christian hero, an instrument of vengeance against the "deicide race." Significantly, the shame of the affair is borne first by a young woman, then by her family. Having lost her virginity, the girl is pitilessly cast out in disgrace. This sacrilegious parody of the Annunciation points up all that was ambiguous in the exaltation of the Virgin Mary. Caesarius' story implies that only Christians are entitled to such a paragon of womanhood: a virgin mother who gives birth to a savior. The Jews, he suggests, have only false prophets and counterfeit virgins. Their savior turns out to be a female, and the child therefore deserves its horrible fate.

In the Castle

We come now to the most privileged of women, fewest in number yet magnified by myth: those of noble birth. The most famous of these aristocratic ladies have achieved something like star status: eliminate the fantasies and only a specter remains. Historians disagree vigorously about their status, role, influence, and authority, as the vagueness of the terms in which power is discussed suggests.[39] Two problems dominate all others. Can we know these women as women? Can we discover how they felt as daughters, lovers, mothers, friends, and worshipers of God? And did they have an official public role? Public office was the source of the cultural models that shaped social behavior.

We know nothing at all about the vast majority of noblewomen, whether aristocrats of Europe or princesses of the Latin East. Occasionally we come upon a name or a signature at the bottom of a parchment, but we have no idea whether the woman who signed the document participated in drafting it. We therefore have no choice but to turn to those few women about whom something is known, and who have already been widely discussed. They are very different from one another.

The male discourses to which these women gave rise can be interpreted in different ways, depending on whether we consider the women discussed to have been prototypes or exceptions. During the two centuries in which we are interested, no French queen wrote anything that has survived, and none was the subject of a biography. The empress Adelaide died in 999. Daughter of the king of Burgundy, she married the king of Italy and later became the second wife of Otto I, who was crowned emperor of the Holy Roman Empire in 962.[40] She, like many German princesses before her, conformed to a certain ideal: she built churches and monasteries and was a highly cultivated woman. When her son Otto II succeeded his father, her influence waned, however, and she retired to Burgundy. After regaining her son's good graces she became the ruler of Italy. When her son died in 983, the heir apparent was only three years old. Adelaide returned to Germany as regent. The eastern portion of what had been Charlemagne's empire had its own traditions. Married women were viewed much more favorably there than in the West because even after the reform marriage was still understood in terms of eighth-century theology. A few illustrious noblewomen exercised power alongside men, but only when the situation required it and at the pleasure of the prince. These women enjoyed privileges in private life, public life, and religion. The Church canonized several queens to honor their performance of queenly duties.

Strong women could thus govern "virilely," as contemporaries said. Sometimes this happened at more modest levels of society. Ermengarde, viscountess of Narbonne, was lord of a fief for fifty years. Although she had a series of husbands, she was the one who wielded the real power.[41] When her father died in 1134, she managed to free herself from the menacing tutelage of the count of Toulouse and placed her property under the protection of the king of France, who had the advantage of being a great distance away. As the ruler of her fiefdom, she decided when to make war and when to make peace. She lavishly endowed abbeys on her land and assembled a brilliant court. Her case, like Adelaide's, is often cited to reassure us that, despite all the handicaps, women of strong personality could assert themselves if they wished. But there is reason to doubt that the examples prove what they are said to prove. Claudie Amado points out that Ermengarde, who inherited her fief in the absence of male heirs and who did indeed possess special personal qualities, probably still would not have been able to govern without the support of her powerful family.[42]

The Trials of a Princess

Marie of Montpellier, another woman whose life has been studied by Claudie Amado, was the daughter of Guillaume VIII, lord of Montpellier.[43] Guillaume had married Eudoxia, the daughter of the Byzantine emperor, but divorced her when their daughter Marie was six years old. Guillaume then married Agnes of Castille, who bore him eight children, including several much-wanted sons, in quick succession. Guillaume's intention was to pass his lands on to one of his sons, not to Marie, who had to contend with two major obstacles. Her mother, a princess from a far-off land, could offer no support. And Marie herself was an impediment to her father's plans, so that he sought to marry her off as soon as possible, not to further his own ambitions but to destroy whatever chances his daughter had. Thus Marie, aged eleven, married the viscount of Marseilles, who died soon thereafter. She returned to her father's home in Montpellier as a widow. In 1197, when she was sixteen, her father married her off a second time to Bernard IV, count of Comminges, who had divorced his two previous wives. Marie was still too young to defend herself. Her father had made sure that her two marriage contracts contained clauses indicating that she renounced all claims on his estate. He also took steps to make sure that Marie would never become the *dame* of Montpellier. Marie bore Bernard two daughters, but after four years of marriage he divorced her too. The sources tell us that he no longer felt "marital affection" for her. When Guillaume died in 1202, the question was who would inherit his fief: Marie or the eldest son (also named Guillaume).

Innocent III was then pope. The Church's long struggle to redefine marriage was beginning to bear fruit. Hugh was busy keeping a close eye on marriages in his diocese. But the case of Guillaume of Montpellier confronted the pope with a painful dilemma. Innocent had every reason to want the seigneury to pass to the son, because Guillaume had served the pope as a loyal vassal in the ongoing struggle with the Catharist heretics. But since Eudoxia was still alive, Guillaume was strictly speaking a bigamist.

The pope had refused to authorize his marriage to Agnes. Would he also refuse to authorize the son's inheritance? The issue was whether to condemn the man's private vice or to reward the vassal's public loyalty.

Marie's fate hung in the balance as preparations were made for battle with the count of Toulouse, who supported the heretics. But now the burghers of Montpellier intervened. The difficulties over the inheritance offered them an opportunity to extract from their lord a charter guaranteeing certain liberties. They threw their support behind Marie, drove Agnes and her children from their midst, and became a party to negotiations then under way in preparation for their lady's third marriage, to Pedro, king of Aragon. Marie soon gave birth to a daughter, and Pedro immediately gave the child in marriage to the count of Toulouse; he also forced Marie to bestow her seigneury, Montpellier, on her daughter as dowry. Marie, who declared herself "crucified," filed a formal protest denouncing the pressure to which she had been subjected: "He [Pedro] wanted no land, no seigneury, no woman, nothing at all that he could not dispose of as he saw fit." Pedro wanted to divorce his wife, with whom relations were by now obviously strained, but he needed a pretext. In view of her tangled past, it was not difficult to find one. In 1206 Pedro notified the pope that he was charging his wife with adultery: Bernard of Comminges was still alive!

To whom could the young woman turn for help? Her father's family, though very powerful, did nothing, nor did her mother's kinsmen come to her rescue. But the city of Montpellier did: in 1206 it rose in rebellion against Pedro of Aragon. At this point, however, friends attempted to effect a reconciliation. Pedro and Marie met. She became pregnant and in 1208 gave birth to a boy, Jacme. The divorce proceedings were still under way, in theory at least. But in fact the pope was otherwise occupied. That same year he launched a crusade against heresy, led by Simon of Montfort and a group of northern barons. The massacre of Béziers took place in 1209. Montpellier, true to its tradition, remained neutral. Meanwhile, Pedro had several irons in the fire. He gave his four-year-old son Jacme in marriage to the daughter of Simon of Montfort, snatched the boy from his mother, and sent him to the crusaders as a hostage.

The year 1213 began well for Marie. In January the pope finally made a ruling on the inheritance: Guillaume's only legitimate marriage had been to Eudoxia, and Agnes' eight children were bastards. Montpellier therefore belonged to Marie. In April the pope rejected Pedro's petition for an annulment of his marriage. But it was too late: Marie died the same month at the age of thirty-two. Pedro did not enjoy his victory for long, however. He had joined the count of Toulouse in the struggle against Simon of Montfort and was killed in the battle of Muret. What would become of little Jacme? Marie, worried on his behalf, had had time before she died to make a will and to entrust her son to the pope. Innocent III sent the boy to be brought up in a monastery run by the Templars—an austere childhood. He inherited Aragon from his father and Montpellier from his mother. Feelings—filial, conjugal, maternal, paternal—clearly counted for little in these affairs of state. A woman could inherit a fief and she could fight, but she rarely fought with equal arms. In between battles she had time to give birth. To the suggestion that noblewomen of less exalted station might have led more tranquil lives it is tempting to respond that the case of Agnes of Saleby is hardly reassuring.

As usual, happiness has no history. Life in the lap of luxury was sometimes all it was reputed to be. The vast majority of marriages were arranged, but nature may have kindled affectionate feelings later on. About Cupid in the Middle Ages we know nothing. Christina of Stommeln had the same vision for six months running: a man and woman playing tenderly with their child and repeating over and over that there is no greater happiness than that which binds a man to his wife or than a child gives to its mother.[44] Admittedly this vision of familial bliss was a demonic ruse to tempt the saint, but the demon must have taken the idea from life. Hatred, fear, boredom, and indifference were not the only emotions available to the wellborn. The medieval idea of love may not have coincided with that of modern romance, but noble ladies undoubtedly had their compensations when their husbands were off fighting wars, jousting in tournaments, or covering themselves with glory in the Crusades: they kept the house, managed the estate, and amused themselves. Did they, as Robert Fossier suspects, indulge in extramarital affairs? There is reason to doubt it. In any case these noble ladies were not alone in their castles. There were plenty of illegitimate daughters, spinsters, and servants, "lonely" women already "confined to history's backwater," as Georges Duby has observed.[45]

When women did play a role in political life, it was almost

always temporary and circumstantial. A woman could be called upon to take the place of a man, but the fact that she was a woman was never without consequence. Women did not fight in battles and were not trained in the schools of law and administration that began to develop in the twelfth century. By nature and vocation they were destined to return to the one role for which they were truly fitted: to make sons who would in turn make history.

Women and the Love of God

We do not know how many women withdrew from the world at some point during their lives. The ones about whom we know most—and it is very little—were those who entered convents. Convents for women were fewer in number and less well endowed than monasteries for men, and their histories were more turbulent. Nuns were transferred from one place to another. Many convents, along with their archives, disappeared at the end of the Middle Ages. But there is another reason why we know so little about them. Most monastic histories were written by clergymen who were uncomfortable talking about women.

Nuns were not the only women to choose lives of continence or virginity, and others may have outnumbered them. Certain women, such as the mother of Guibert of Nogent, chose to live by the gates of monasteries and lead pious lives. Female hermits became followers of such "God-crazed" pastors as Robert of Arbrissel and Gilbert of Sempringham, who later founded orders. Some turned to heresy, the best known being the Catharist "perfects."

Other women lived as recluses. The Church in the twelfth century began to concern itself with their physical and spiritual well-being. The great Cistercian Aelred of Rievaulx, a friend of Saints Bernard and Gilbert, wrote an admirable treatise for his sister, who was a recluse. Hildegard of Bingen received her religious training from a recluse, and Juette of Huy spent most of her life in a hermitage. Christina spent several years in one before becoming the abbess of a convent, and many other women followed a similar path. Women who shunned marriage and the world lived many different kinds of lives—too many for the Church.

The Mirror of Virgins

This variety creates problems. To bring some semblance of order to a very complex story, let us turn once again to a contemporary document, an anonymous confessor's manual composed around 1100 in the region of Cologne. It evidently enjoyed some success, because fifty-four copies have survived. The document reflects the period's fascination with virginity.[46] It has two main themes: the organization and the spiritual life of a community of nuns. One of the topics discussed is recruitment. Many nuns had been placed in convents by their parents as young girls. The manual notes that while it would have been better if they had chosen the religious life of their own volition, they nevertheless must resign themselves to it: their parents' wishes are as binding as their own vows. Better to be saved even against one's wishes than to be damned. The author invokes the name of Yves of Chartres. Stray virgins are to be brought back into the fold. He condemns, and in 1139 a Church council would forbid, anarchic forms of the religious life. There is only one choice: the world or the cloister. And the cloistered life was to be strictly segregated. Within the community women were exhorted to root out the remnants of pride in their noble origins or wealth. Members are to respect their elders, to call them Madame and to allow themselves to be addressed as Sister. The only true distinction is that of the spirit.

The text examines the religious life at some length. Excesses in the quest for an ascetic existence are to be avoided. Women, we are told, are more fragile than men. Their primary concern must be the preservation of their virginity: loss of virginity would mean the end of a woman's marriage to Christ, a sign of the gravest possible disrespect. The fallen virgin remained forever corrupt, a stain on the entire Church. But true virginity demanded more than an intact hymen. It also required purity of heart. A woman did not choose the virginal life once and for all; she had to work at it constantly. A woman who entered the convent with a vocation chose to spend her life listening to Christ, in which case the cloister became a garden of earthly delights. The work in question has little to say about spiritual exercises: nothing about personal prayer or the Eucharist, nothing about participating in Christ's suffering, nothing about the need to know oneself.

This manual is striking for its conservatism. Free yourself from the constraints of the world, it recommends to its female audience, and you will find fulfillment in the service of your husband, Christ. Little is said about developments in spirituality new to this period: enthusiasm, mysticism, suffering in love, meditation on the Bible. In general the recommendation is that women adopt an honorable if not particularly fervent form of piety; as always they are asked to preserve their virginity in an atmosphere of contemplative calm. Research has shown that, as with marriage, fathers decided which of their daughters would spend their lives in this way.

Not all monks in this period were Saint Brunos or Saint Bernards. Oblation, the practice of sending very young children to monasteries or convents, still existed. Hugh of Lincoln was sent at age eight to be brought up by a chapter of canons, and Thomas Aquinas was sent to Monte Cassino at age seven.

Monasteries and convents were not only repositories of religious vocations, they were also important social institutions. They took in girls from families with so many sisters that there simply was not enough property to give each a dowry appropriate to her rank; they sheltered daughters who suffered from physical or mental handicaps that made marriage impossible. Convents fulfilled many other functions: they were educational institutions, orphanages, homes for widows, shelters for abandoned wives. Their number grew at a spectacular rate, especially in the twelfth century. The ninth and tenth centuries had been a time of turmoil, and the religious institutions that had survived that period were far too few to meet society's growing needs. New convents sprang up everywhere, particularly in England after the conquest and in France. But building and endowing these institutions was a complex and costly business that required favorable circumstances and concerted wills. The nobles, who not only wielded political power but also furnished the indispensable novices, and the clergy—pope, bishops, monks—had to agree to provide the necessary lands, rights, privileges, and benedictions.

The number of convents continued to fall far short of society's needs. In the twelfth century the aristocracy, which had previously been much more generous, became concerned about unduly weakening its economic base. Nuns were drawn primarily from the elite. A dowry was required of most novices, and this reinforced the worldly temptations denounced in the *Mirror of Virgins*. The reality was thus a long way from the theory. The clergy believed that nuns should be truly cloistered, as Caesarius of Arles had insisted as long ago as the sixth century. But convent gates in fact remained open, particularly to the founders' families: relatives went in, nuns went out. Partly because of this, monks, particularly the purest of them, were reluctant to serve as nuns' confessors and spiritual guides. Against this background the interest that a few religious leaders of the new generation took in the spiritual life of women stands out in even sharper relief. Robert of Arbrissel founded Fontevraud. Gilbert of Sempringham founded an order that eventually extended its influence to some fifteen convents. Four communities coexisted in each of these: a community of Benedictine nuns; a community of canons who heard the nuns' confessions; and, to do the heavy work, communities of lay brothers and sisters recruited from the lower social strata. Men like Robert and Gilbert appear to have been keenly aware of the problems and aspirations of women and of their exclusion from important institutions. But there were few like them.

Most of the leaders of the monastic movement and the canonic reform movement refused to take charge of female religious communities. The capacity of monasteries to accept male vocations began greatly to outstrip that of convents to accept female vocations, particularly since monks could also advance in the secular hierarchy of the Church. It took a century and a half for the Cluniac order to found Marcigny, its first convent for women, in 1055. The Premonstratensians, Cistercians, and Carthusians were just as reluctant and just as slow to act. In 1147 Gilbert applied to the chapter general of the Order of Cîteaux, presided over by the former Cistercian Eugene III, to allow the convents he had founded to affiliate with the order. The order was well established in England, and it would have been a simple matter to assign a few of its hundreds of affiliated monks to work with Gilbert's nuns. But Gilbert's application was denied, and he was forced to turn to the canonic chapters for help. The Great Carthusian monastery was founded in 1084, but two generations would pass before the first convent was admitted to the order in 1140. The extraordinary success of the Mendicant Orders in the thirteenth century only made matters worse.[47] The reasons given are familiar: women, we are told, often resist discipline and are therefore a burden and a menace. Even in Germany, where female spirituality had flourished in the tenth century under Otto, there was a noticeable decline in the next century. The monastic reform movement, which had originated in Cluny and Gorze, had placed great emphasis on prayers for the dead. Laymen contributed to the support of monks who specialized in saying prayers for the souls of the departed. But nuns were not priests; their prayers were not as valuable as those of monks. And the religious supervision available to nuns was often of poor quality. There was of course no specifically feminine order. In religious matters women in this period seem to have been treated like poor relations.

Were nuns more cultivated than other women of the time? Hildegard of Bingen and Herrad of Landsberg, author of the beautiful manuscript *Hortus deliciarum,* are often cited as proof that they were. But if the general cultural level of convents in this period is compared with that of convents in the seventh and eighth centuries, the impression is one of overall decline. If women made progress, we must look elsewhere to find it. Great abbesses such as Hildegard and Héloïse (the reluctant nun who became abbess of Le Paraclet) assumed the inferiority of their sex as a basic principle. Somewhat later the great mystic Gertrude of Helfta remarked that women suffered from the defects of the sex's virtues, an observation that could only have confirmed men in their complacency. Women were still denied access to religious orders and participation in other sacraments. Indeed, their disabilities were reinforced. Nuns were not permitted to confess to the mother superior, and Innocent III eliminated the few sacerdotal and liturgical privileges that had been granted to certain abbesses. Male tutelage—the power of bishops and abbots—was strengthened everywhere. In the vast majority of cases women were obliged to submit silently to male authority.[48]

How nuns lived is a fascinating but as yet little studied subject. Glimpses of convent life reveal some of the same tensions one would expect to find in any community: between nuns of different ages, different social and ethnic backgrounds, and different rank. Convents were extremely hierarchical, from the mother superior on down to the various officials, choir nuns, novices, and lay sisters. Communities of nuns occupied a seigneurial position in the larger society and therefore enjoyed certain powers over the peasants who worked their estates and managed their temporal property. Nuns also maintained relations with lawyers and merchants. And of course they were in constant contact with the order's prior, abbot, or other officials. It would be interesting to know what strategies they adopted in the face of male oppression, indifference, or contempt.

Convents met only a small portion of the social and spiritual needs of the time. The first beguinages did not come into being, however, until the very end of the twelfth century. Women were not offered any real alternatives, such as the possibility of joining tertiary orders or doing charity work in hospitals, until the thirteenth century. But from the twelfth century to the end of the Middle Ages many women did choose to live as hermits or recluses. Eremitism, like monasticism, dates back to the Desert Fathers, but in the eleventh and twelfth centuries it took on new guises and developed to a greater extent than ever before. Although this period strikes us in many ways as a time when people lived in the grip of a kind of spring fever, they also suffered from anxious anticipation of the imminent end of the world and therefore felt an urgent need to do penance. Many who chose reclusion agreed to devote themselves to prayer in exchange for their upkeep. They lived in rudimentary cells symbolically stationed in bustling town centers, adjoining city walls, next to bridges, or outside churches, cemeteries, or leprosariums, and they relied for their food on the charity of passersby. The Church in this period generally approved of these activities but felt a need to keep an eye on them. It therefore discouraged women who claimed the right to preach and prophesy on city streets or in nearby forests. But women willing to shut themselves up in the cells of a hermitage, where they could not be seen, chose a vocation the Church could tolerate: they sat still and prayed. Hence new rituals of induction were worked out in the twelfth century. The bishop generally celebrated a solemn mass, usually the mass for the dead. He then administered extreme unction to the new recluse, locked her in her cell, and sealed the door. From that moment on her only communication with the outside world was through the tiny window of her cell.[49]

Recluses were recruited from many segments of society. Some nuns chose reclusion. Following the Rule of Saint Benedict to the end, they rated solitary existence above the cenobitic life. But the vast majority of recluses were laywomen without any particular religious training. Some lacked the dowry needed to enter a convent. Others numbered among life's unfortunates: unmarried women, orphans, wives of priests, abandoned wives, widows, converted heretics, repentant prostitutes. Around this time a new biography was written of Thais, who had entered a hermitage to expiate the sins she had committed as a courtesan. Recluses were primarily poor women and repentant sinners whose vocation, in anticipation of the coming apocalypse, was to pray for their own salvation and for that of their families and humankind.

Women led many different kinds of religious life. What did they want of their faith? Above all, salvation, which was difficult to come by anywhere else. And virginity was the way; marriage was at best a lesser evil than fornication. Virgins were three times as likely to be saved as married women. During the Carolingian period and in Ottonian Germany it had been possible for married mothers to live sanctified lives. The eleventh and twelfth centuries were far more pessimistic. The religious life was the only way to achieve what the Church described as freedom, namely, a state in which the soul is available for contrition and adoration. Living on intimate terms with Christ and his saints could open the mystical way to eternal life. Traveling that road was a specialty of women, but we will not follow them down it, because mysticism belongs more properly to a later period.

I do, however, want to return to the case of Christina of Markyate in order to shed light on one little-studied aspect of female mysticism. Although she discovered her love of Christ in early childhood, she had been forced to hide her devotion. By the time she came under the spiritual guidance of the holy hermit who gave her shelter, she had already prayed a great deal, read the psalms countless times, and absorbed all that her parish priests had to teach. Although her judgment is good, she is a young girl with all the usual female weaknesses, hence she still has a great deal to learn. The hermit, Roger, is wary of women and promises himself never to look at Christina. But Providence dictates otherwise. One day he finds her lying face down in front of the altar. He averts his eyes and steps over her. Then he changes his mind. He is responsible for her. He must check to make sure she has assumed the proper position for prayer, because the body's attitude is important. Christina, meanwhile, is keen to see how a holy man prays. Both turn, their eyes meet, and a spiritual thunderclap strikes the soul of each. Roger trains his disciple, whom he calls "Sunday's little girl."

Some years later Roger dies. Christina is still living in retreat, a short distance from the prestigious monastery of Saint Albans, but Geoffrey, the abbot of the monastery, is unaware of her presence. One day she receives a message from on high: she is to warn the abbot that God is most displeased because Geoffrey, swollen with pride, is making decisions without consulting his monks. When she conveys this warning to Geoffrey, however, he scoffs at the messenger, a mere woman. The next night demons come and give him a sound thrashing for his failure to heed the admonition.

Geoffrey then pays a call on Christina and is won over. He becomes her pupil, and from then on he does not make a move without consulting her. She can read his soul like an open book. Here we have a reversal in the usual male-female relation. Christina, having sacrificed her life and chosen reclusion in what might appear to be a quasi-suicidal gesture, gains more power than she otherwise would have had.

The sanctification of sexual purity could give rise to an astonishing desire for power, and through it women could achieve a status otherwise granted only to a few holy men. Through the window of her cell a woman could perform miracles and exorcise demons—things that in other circumstances the Church prohibited her from attempting. Christina's personal psalter, preserved at Hildesheim, has survived.[50] Of particular interest are three of the miniatures in this early-twelfth-century relic. One depicts the Virgin on Ascension Day: she is portrayed as a huge figure dwarfing the Apostles among whom she stands. The second shows Mary Magdalene facing the Apostles, about to tell them what only she knows, because Christ chose her to receive the message of the Resurrection. Here there is a fundamental transfer of power from one sex to the other: a woman was able to hold her tongue, to keep the secret that had been vouchsafed unto her alone. This holy woman thus gains mastery over time. She escapes from the physiological cycle in which women are normally imprisoned and accedes to the linear time of salvation. She is granted knowledge of the future and therefore can prophesy. She can even step back in time in order to raise the dead.

The Church, as one might expect, was wary of such powers. Hugh of Lincoln heard about a woman who could see into people's hearts and detect thieves and criminals. He had her brought before him.[51] His biographer tells us that he was very angry, not at her but at the demon within her. She was obliged to prostrate herself at the bishop's feet and answer his questions. Where had she learned the art of divination? Naturally she was unable to answer. Hugh ordered her locked up in a priory and forbade her ever again to disclose another person's sins. Being a saint, he worked a miracle: he made her humble and silent. Thus the Church once again placed its stamp on women's history: God is male, and men interpret his Word.

But with God's blessing women were permitted to establish certain countervailing powers. In the third miniature in Christina's psalter we see her facing Christ, their hands touching. Behind her stand the monks she has helped to find the Lord.

Women do not exist, any more than monads do. What does exist is systems of representation, which vary from one society to another. Each element in such a system is related to all the other elements. All the systems of representation in use in the Christian West in the eleventh and twelfth centuries insisted that woman is constitutionally inferior to man. Since essence in this ideology precedes existence, it followed that woman needed man's guidance. Those areas in which the Germanic heritage survived longest, including Germania, England prior to the Norman conquest, and Visigothic Spain, maintained, up to the eleventh century, a view of the world much more favorable to women, and particularly to those women who remained in the world. But that older view was on the wane everywhere, primarily among the aristocracy, where the principles of masculinity and primogeniture were diminishing the role of women.[52] As the Church asserted its exclusive jurisdiction over marriage, it simultaneously hardened its view of women. The female body was declared to be mature at twelve, but the female mind, though fully developed, was still weak. Past the age of twelve a girl had nothing more to learn, but she still could lose what was most precious. The only solution was to marry her off. Marriage was made indissoluble to limit, but not preclude, paternal interference. After marriage the code of conduct was now clearly fixed, but there was still plenty of room for maneuver before the wedding, particularly since women enjoyed little freedom (in today's sense).

The vast majority of women probably saw nothing unusual in this state of affairs. They were taught to obey, and in turn they taught their children to obey. And they gave their instruction in the mellifluously persuasive mother tongue. The hierarchy was thus perpetuated in the first instance by women themselves, and rebellion must have been infrequent.

Medieval society was one in which men had the initiative and women were passive. In contemporary texts women usually figure as direct objects. A father "marries off" or "gives away" or "conventizes" his daughter. The time factor was important in the "utilization" of women, but it worked in different ways at different levels of society. The aristocrat was a man of large views. The world was his, he traveled a great deal, and he was at ease everywhere. His view of time was as broad as his view of space. It extended far into the past: the great families carefully reconstructed their memories to reveal the illustriousness of their origins. But it was also bold and far-seeing when looking ahead. Planning was necessary to safeguard the future of the lineage. A nobleman who married need not have immediate use for a wife. When Adam of Neville returned from the church after celebrating his marriage to Grace of Saleby, he probably dandled the child on his knee and then sent her off to play. What mattered was not the girl, but what she brought with her: her heritage, her possessions. The rest could wait. Adam had no need of a companion or of a mother for his children. Those capacities remained in reserve.

Such a casual attitude was not always possible, however. The dynastic principle exacted a price: it required an heir, and that heir was sometimes slow to arrive. Time, as importunate as a creditor, could teach a cruel lesson in humility, reducing the world's greatest knight or the most powerful of kings to the level of the humblest of creatures, anxious slaves to a nature that could so easily squander the noblest of seed. The destiny of a dynasty, the future of a kingdom, might well turn on a fleeting nocturnal embrace.

Plebeians knew neither such heights nor such depths. Without prestigious past or radiant future, memory was myopic. The humble man needed not a budding rose but a full-grown helper, someone to heat the soup, keep him company, and share what little he owned. He also needed someone to share his work, his table, and his bed and to take care of the children when they came. These were vital needs, not luxuries like the dreams and stratagems of the high and mighty.

When the Church finally settled on its new standard of behavior for laywomen, it proved to be much less generous than in the past. The clergy never really accepted the loss of so many virgins and never elaborated an ethics of marriage and motherhood. The most scrupulous women were inevitably torn between what they owed to God and what they owed to Caesar. The ideal wife was expected to give as little as possible: in fact, she was not to give at all but only to lend.

Conjugal duty was unlike any other: the act was to be performed as infrequently and as unenthusiastically as possible. Even maternity, which earlier texts had presented as one of the primary sources of charity, was now disparaged. The woman of the world was deprived of her last refuge. Power and knowledge both became masculine preserves. Women, long excluded from warfare and the priesthood, were excluded from literacy as well. The Bible could not be translated, and women did not know Latin. In this respect too they were second-class children of God. They had no alternative but to occupy themselves with oral tradition, with old wives' tales, with occult potions and powders. Of course the Church could, if it wished, give in to the dangerous temptation to use women's seductive powers to bring recalcitrant husbands back into the fold, as Georges Duby's study of confessors' letters makes clear. The Church would rely even more heavily on this pillow-proselytism in the thirteenth century. In that sense the future of God lay in women's hands. And some frustrated women took matters into their own hands by withdrawing from the world altogether.

This period gave us few female saints.[53] The feminization of sainthood did not begin until the thirteenth century, but the groundwork was already laid. Women adopted the religious life, and the exaltation of their mystical marriage to Christ tended to give new immediacy to their relations with God, which became "perceptible in the heart." Christ knelt at the feet of his lady, like an obedient knight in the sublimest of romances. To one Carthusian nun Jesus is supposed to have sighed: "Tell me what you want. I cannot refuse you anything!" Caught in that most ingenious of traps, metaphor, men looked on in awestruck silence. They had encouraged women to imitate Mary, the most perfect of their kind, and to surrender to God's will. The flight into the supernatural meant silencing the demands of the body and repudiating much of human experience. But even such drastic amputation brought soothing consolation. For women the only possible journey was within. Unable to learn, she could only burn with spiritual desire, and the singular, ineffable experience this brought her pointed up the inadequacy of the universal language of reason.

TRANSLATED AND ADAPTED FROM THE FRENCH BY
ARTHUR GOLDHAMMER

8

The Courtly Model

Georges Duby

DID THE CONDITION of women improve in the feudal era? Those who answer this difficult question in the affirmative rely primarily on one fact: the emergence in twelfth-century France of a model of male-female relations that contemporaries referred to as *fine amour* (refined love). For the past hundred years or so, since historians of medieval literature began paying close attention to this model of emotional and physical relations between the sexes, it has been known as "courtly love."

The Model

The model is simple. A female figure stands at the center: a "lady" *(dame)*. The term, derived from the Latin *domina*, signifies that this lady is in a dominant position. It also defines her status: she is married. A young man, a *jeune* (at the time the word referred to an unmarried youth), notices her. What he sees of her face and what he divines of her hair (hidden by a wimple) and of her body (concealed by clothing) makes him uneasy. Everything begins with a glance. Metaphorically, this glance is an arrow that pierces the eye and goes straight to the heart, where it kindles flames of desire. Wounded by love (and bear in mind that in the vocabulary of the time, "love" in the proper sense referred to carnal appetite), the youth thinks of nothing but possessing his beloved. He lays siege to his prize and to breach the walls of the fortress uses a strategy of deception: he pretends to bow down before her, to abase himself. The "lady" is the wife of a lord, often his own lord. She is in any case the mistress of a house he visits often. According to the social hierarchy of the time, she ranks above him. He calls attention to this fact through various gestures of allegiance. He kneels down, assuming the posture of a vassal. He speaks, pledging his faith, promising, like a liege man, not to offer his services to anyone else. He goes even further: in the manner of a serf, he makes a gift of his person.

He is no longer a free man. The woman, for her part, is still free to accept or reject his offer. At this point female power manifests itself. The man is put to the test by a woman, by this chosen woman, who summons him to prove his mettle. But if, at the end of this examination, the lady accepts, if she lends an ear and allows a web of words to be woven around her, she in turn becomes a prisoner, because in this society it is understood that every gift calls for a countergift. Modeled on the provisions of the vassalage contract, which obliged the lord to reward the loyal vassal with value equal to what he received, the rules of courtly love obliged the chosen lady to reward loyal service, ultimately by full surrender. In intention courtly love was not, contrary to what many people believe, platonic. It was a game, and as in all games the player was motivated by the hope of winning. To win meant, as in hunting, to capture one's prey. Let it not be forgotten that this was a game controlled by men.

Although the lady, like the queen in chess, was an important piece in the game, she could not, because she was a woman, use her body in any way she wished—that was where her power ended. That prized body, which had once belonged to her father, now belonged to her husband. It was the repository of his honor and, conjointly, of the honor of all the adult males of his household. Hence was kept under close surveillance. In noble residences, where there were no interior walls or truly private places, where people lived at close quarters day and night, the body of *la dame* could never escape for very long from the scrutiny of prying eyes, of men only too ready to believe that this woman, like all women, was deceitful and weak. At the slightest indication of misbehavior she would be declared guilty. And if caught she became subject, along with the man believed to be her accomplice, to the cruelest of punishments. What made this game interesting was the danger to which the partners exposed themselves. To love *de fine amour* was to run a risk. The knight who decided to attempt it knew the odds. Obliged to be prudent and above all discreet, he had to express himself by means of signs; in a crowded household he somehow had to build a secret garden, a space of intimacy in which he and his lady could hide.

There he confidently awaited his reward, the favors that his chosen lady was obliged to grant him. The code of love required that those favors be parceled out in small doses, however, and the woman thereby regained the advantage. She gave herself, but not all at once. According to the prescribed ritual, she first allowed herself to be kissed, then offered her lips, then submitted to more ardent caresses whose effect was to spur her partner's desire even more. Courtly lyric described the ultimate trial—*assaig* (essai), the troubadours called it—the final ordeal to which the lover dreamed of being subjected. It was an obsession, a breathtaking fantasy. The lover imagined himself lying beside his lady and allowed to take advantage of the proximity of her naked flesh, but only up to a certain point. At the last possible moment the rules of the game required him to hold back, to desist, in order to prove his worth by demonstrating total physical self-control. The final surrender of the beloved, the moment when her servant might take his pleasure in her, was thus postponed indefinitely. The locus of the male's pleasure was thus shifted from the satisfaction of desire to anticipation of that satisfaction. Pleasure climaxed in desire itself. Thus courtly love was a fantasy. It gave women a definite power, but it kept that power confined within a well-defined sphere, that of fantasy and play.

Literature and Society

The model of behavior I have just outlined is known from poems written for the amusement of people at court. The oldest of these poems are presumably the eleven chansons that later manuscripts attribute to a certain William (Guillaume) of Poitiers, traditionally thought to be the ninth duke of the Aquitains, who was active in the early twelfth century and famous in his time for spicing his conversation with bawdy stories. If the author of the eleven chansons is indeed this prince, a man keen to defend the province entrusted to him from his direct rivals, the "Franks" of the Loire Valley, and from the encroachments of the Capetian monarch, his lord, and therefore eager to emphasize the distinctive culture of the region, it is not surprising that he should have chosen to express himself in the Limousin dialect, which was different from that spoken in Tours or Paris or for that matter in Poitiers. His political heirs adopted the same policy, particularly Henry Plantagenet, the husband of Eleanor, William's granddaughter, who protected the troubadours for the same reason. The only surviving traces from prior to about 1160 of what we now call courtly love are to be found in the work of these troubadours, poets who wrote in the so-called *langue d'oc.*

Does the courtly poets' preference for the *langue d'oc* indicate that *fine amour* was an Occitanian invention? This claim has been made by certain adepts of Occitanian history, of whom René Nelli was the most reasonable. But there is absolutely no evidence for another of Nelli's assertions, that courtly love was an invention of women, a claim he based on the unsubstantiated assumption that the situation of women in the south was not as bad as it was in the north. That the opposite was in fact the case has been shown by research on the area around Toulouse.[1] Furthermore, during the lifetime of William of Aquitaine, Abelard, according to the account of his life that purports to be his autobiography, also sang tenderly of love to the applause of a Parisian public. Perhaps he sang in a different key, but we do not know for sure; these chansons are lost. At any rate, it is certain that Abelard was not alone, at least among intellectuals passionate about Ovid and inspired by the *Song of Songs.* The Goliard poets followed the same order as the Occitanian chansons in recounting the preparatory stages of the attack on the proud "castle of Venus": exchange of glances, exchange of words, caresses. True, the Goliards used the language of the schools, Latin, which is why some of their poems have survived. In the north, where the *langue d'oïl* was spoken, it was not yet customary to record the vulgar tongue on parchment, whereas in the south, where ecclesiastical culture was less arrogant, so daring an exploit was already possible. In any case, the literature of the vulgar tongue escaped oblivion in the south sooner than in the north. It began to be preserved earlier, that is, but can we conclude that it was also created earlier? However that may be, the groundwork had clearly been laid north of the Loire for acceptance of the troubadours' themes. In the final third of the twelfth century those themes spread to the great princely courts of Normandy, Touraine, Champagne, and Flanders and mingled with another literary form: romance. The model matured and took on new substance, then spread very quickly in both Provençal and French. It gained influence. In the early fourteenth century Dante felt its fascination. Lyrical poetry and romantic narrative were an intoxicating brew. All over Europe well-born gentlemen and the parvenus who emulated them were urged by the poets to treat women as Peire Vidal said he treated them, as Lancelot supposedly had done.

Poets did the urging, then—those poets on whom courtly society depended to feed its dreams and divert it from the vexations and difficulties of daily life. The historian interested in what life was actually like for women in this period must not forget that *fine amour,* as we know it, is a literary creation, a cultural object that evolved according to laws of its own. The forms and values associated with that object became increasingly complex and diverse in response to changes in taste and the absorption of a variety of influences. Most of the writings in question were sophisticated enough that their meaning is not easy to unravel. Susceptible of a variety of interpretations, these texts work with a highly complex symbolism to which we no longer possess the keys. Over the past century a cluster of commentaries has gathered around these texts, commentaries that confuse rather than clarify the picture. Bear in mind, moreover, that this was a literature of escape.

Faced with sources that require extremely delicate handling, social historians must guard against giving the impression that the texts offer a straightforward picture of everyday experience. They must not mistake what the troubadours and romantic heroes *said* they thought or did for an accurate reflection of what the people who liked to listen to chansons and narratives actually thought and did. In particular they must not assume that the wives of lords regularly behaved like Genièvre or Enide or the fanciful countess of Die. The risk is particularly serious when it comes to assessing the condition of women, for in the sources that tell us everything we know the man, not the woman, occupies the foreground. All these texts were written to entertain men, more precisely, men of war, knights—young knights. All the romantic heroes were young knights, and the female figures served simply as a pretext for the demonstration of youthful mettle, of virile qualities. Only young knights speak in the first-person singular in the chansons. When on occasion a woman was permitted to speak, her words were calculated to please the audience by expressing the feelings and attitudes conventionally attributed to her sex. These poems show not women but men's image of women.

That said, it is nevertheless clear that what the poets invented was not unrelated to the way in which the people whose attention they hoped to attract led their lives. These works met with success—immense and lasting success, as evidenced by the fact that not all of them were lost at a time when only the most essential words were written down. In order to be so well received, the gist of the story they told could not have been too far from the audience's concrete experience. More important, these works beguiled their audience and therefore exerted some influence on the way people lived. Hagiographic literature was also intended to influence behavior. The chansons and romances, like the lives of saints, dramatized exemplary lives so that they might be imitated. Although their heroes embodied to perfection certain virtues, they were not supposed to seem utterly inimitable. Owing to this obvious accord of poetry with truth, we must try to identify those aspects of the feudal social structure in twelfth-century France that may have contributed to the development and rapid spread of what has been called the "courtly neurosis."

Why Was the Model Accepted?

Men in this society were divided into two classes. One consisted of workers, mostly peasants living in villages, the so-called villeins. The other consisted of masters, who lived on the fruits of other people's labor and gathered in courts. Gaston Paris made an inspired choice when he hit on the word "courtly" to define the type of amorous relations with which we are concerned, for it was at court that the game of *fine amour* took shape. The courts of feudal French princes were festive gatherings. Every lord was obliged to organize such gatherings periodically in order to demonstrate his generosity. His men, all who did him homage, were obliged to put in an appearance or else be suspected of betraying their commitment. For a few days the lord's household swelled to grand proportions as the patron gathered his allies around him for lavish banquets. The preservation of order and peace within the aristocracy depended on these gatherings. The guest at court, whether a noble or merely a common companion of the prince, entered into the game of love; he tried to treat women in a more refined way, to demonstrate his skill at captivating them not by force but by verbal or manual caresses, in order to show that he was one of the privileged few who shared in the profits of seigneurial exploitation and who was exempt from the oppression that weighed on common folk. In this way he clearly demonstrated the distance that separated him from the villein, who was summarily dismissed as living a life of ignorance and bestiality. The practice of courtly love was first and foremost a criterion of distinction within masculine society. That is why the model proposed by the poets proved so powerful and why it was able to influence certain men's attitude toward women.

It was able, at any rate, to influence the attitude of certain men toward *certain* women, for the same class division that existed among men carried over to women. Thus "ladies" *(dames)* and "maidens" *(pucelles)* were sharply distinguished from peasant women *(vilaines),* whom the men of the court could treat as brutally as they pleased. But the ladies and maidens invited to join the game of courtly love were entitled to certain marks of respect and, while the game lasted, enjoyed some power over their male partners.

Note, however, that William of Poitiers spoke not of courtly love but of "knightly love" *(amour de chevalier)*. Of all the males at court, it was the knights who were invited to wait on the ladies. Society was divided not into two but into three parts. Within the dominant class were two distinct groups: those whose function was to pray, the clerics; and those whose function was to fight, the knights. The two groups vied for the favors of the prince and the benefits of power. Owing to this rivalry, and at a time of vigorous economic growth, a culture specific to the men of war and fiercely independent of the culture of the clergy established itself quite rapidly. Poetry in the vulgar tongue was one of the principal forms of expression of this knightly culture. More than anything else literature revealed the distinctive features of this culture, which was based on the exaltation of profane love, masculine desire, and the pleasure afforded by women. After all, the fundamental distinction between clerics and knights was sexual. In principle at least, clergymen were forbidden to have commerce with women, whereas knights prided themselves on assailing the fair sex. Banished from the cloister, women filled the court.

At court, however, custom raised a barrier that kept men and women apart. To be sure, that barrier was less impermeable than in some other civilizations, particularly the Islamic. The Syrian prince Uzama professed astonishment at what he took to be the scandalous way "Frankish" crusaders exhibited their female companions, conversed with them in public places, and even visited the Turkish bath in their company.[2] Nevertheless, the wall was high enough to thwart communication between the masculine world and the feminine and to sow incomprehension and mistrust on both sides. It was customary to remove boys from the gynaeceum at age seven, to disentangle them from the skirts of their mothers, sisters, and nurses in order to form regiments of young males, who from then on lived together, whether in the "schools" that trained future clerics or in the rather more tumultuous squadrons in which young men learned to tame horses and handle weapons. This separation, which encouraged homosexual tendencies, also fostered nostalgia for the inaccessible but consoling female world among the young knights who would be called upon to participate in the game of love. It left these men forever fascinated and frightened by what women, if left to themselves, might contrive, and it led them to attribute to women a mysterious and awesome power that was seductive but also inhibiting. The segregation of the sexes implanted in male minds an anxiety that knights tried to overcome by bold talk, affectation of contempt, and loud assertion of their natural superiority. In the voluminous literature that has grown up around courtly literature, the comments of Dragonetti, Rey-Flaud, and Huchet, critics influenced by the psychoanalyst Jacques Lacan, are of particular interest.[3] They suggest that the fantasies around which *fine amour* was constructed should be interpreted as one of the artifices that men used at a certain point in history to overcome their fear of being unable to satisfy women, strange creatures thought by all males to be insatiable and fundamentally perverse. To defend themselves men ostensibly developed the misogynist ribaldry and obscene braggadocio that do indeed furnish a counterpoint to the courtly ethic in the work of William of Poitiers. In any case, to idealize desire, learning ultimately to take pleasure in desire itself, to sublimate desire into an ineffable "joy" that the troubadours' poems attempted to approximate, was a more subtle, more "refined" way of overcoming the malaise that stemmed from the "sexual impasse" and of confronting the "unfathomable mystery of the female orgasm."

In order to understand why the rules of courtly love were adopted in the twelfth century by the feudal aristocracy, we must consider the matrimonial practices then current in this social milieu. Because the aristocracy passed its privileges from generation to generation through the blood, marriage was the very foundation of its structure. During the lifetime of William IX of Aquitaine the Church succeeded in forcing princes and knights to accept its principles in regard to matrimony, so that on this crucial point the morality of the priests was in harmony with the morality of the aristocracy. Because the reproduction of society depended on the solidity of the matrimonial institution, marriage was a serious business, serious enough to warrant strict controls. Wedlock, it was felt, should rest on emotional accord between husband and wife. But when clerics referred to this emotional bond they spoke of affection, or *dilectio* in Latin, not of *amor,* the passionate quest for pleasure that naturally leads to disorder. The strictest ecclesiastics declared that the only justification for sex, the only thing that mitigated its sinful nature, was procreation, and that, because marriage was sacred, a husband who demanded too much of his wife was guiltier than one who went elsewhere to fornicate. The clergy thus encouraged the virility on which chivalrous knights prided themselves to find an outlet outside the marriage bed, in the realm of gratuitous play.

Every marriage, moreover, was a dynastic marriage, the culmination of lengthy negotiations conducted by the heads of both families. Preoccupied with family interests, these men had no interest in the feelings of the betrothed. For the young men themselves, the girls that others conspired to bring to their beds, in some cases girls whom they had never seen and who were often quite young, represented nothing more than an opportunity to escape their dependent status by way of marriage. They desired not the woman but the chance to establish a household of their own. Thus what went by the name "love," namely, male sexual appetite, scarcely counted in the negotiations leading up to the conjugal pact. This too helped direct amorous desire elsewhere.

Finally, the policy of aristocratic families was to keep the family patrimony intact by limiting the number of sons permitted to marry. The strategy generally was to marry one son well, usually the eldest; the others were left to their own devices. The fortunate few might hope to obtain, most likely from a patron they had served well, the hand of a maiden of good family and without any brothers, hence in line to inherit a seigneury on which they could establish dynasties of their own. But most remained celibate. In the twelfth century the vast majority of knights—the men the writers of chansons and romances most wanted to please—were *jeunes,* unmarried adult males, frustrated and jealous of men with wives. Not that their sexual activity was the least bit bridled; they had no problem at all finding outlets for their lust among the many prostitutes, servants, and bastards associated with any great household or among the peasantry, whose daughters they could force to submit whenever they pleased. But such prey was too easy. Glory belonged to the ingenious knight who managed to seduce and possess a woman of quality. What adolescent did not dream of defying his kinsmen and abducting a maiden of good prospect? What a challenge, to take the wife of a brother or an uncle or of one's own lord! What a daring, symbolic exploit! To brave extreme danger was to give proof of rare courage. The lady of quality was protected by the sternest of taboos because the lawfulness of inheritance depended on her behavior; she had to be not only fertile but also faithful: no seed other than her husband's must be allowed to enter her womb.

The troubadours probably did not celebrate adultery as often as has been said, but when they did they touched on a sore spot in the masculine conscience. They also revealed the principal danger that male-female relations resulting from aristocratic matrimonial strategies posed to the social order. That danger stemmed from a contradiction. The court was an organ of regulation and control. Those in power hoped to restrain the restless energy of the unmarried males who constituted the bulk of the knightly order. But the court was also the prime ground for hunting noblewomen. Because such pursuit could not be prevented, it had to be regulated. Courtly literature, responsive to the needs of its primary audience, therefore kindled the ardor of unmarried knights, but shrewdly inculcated a code of behavior whose function was to limit the damage that the irrepressible sexual exuberance of young knights might cause to the military aristocracy.

· · ·

The court was a school, or *scola* (as Carolingian moralists called the royal household, the model for the households of feudal princes), to which boys came to learn from the lord of their father or maternal uncle. Those who did not marry and start households of their own continued their training beyond this early apprenticeship. The patron's wife, the "lady" of the household, naturally played a part in educating these young men. Although a woman was subordinate to her husband in the social hierarchy, the lord and lady ruled the household together. Their mission was to discipline and counsel the young, to offer guidance.

Enthroned at the center of the court, the lady was not without power. The keys to the house hung from her belt. She supervised the wardrobe, the cellar, and the stores of provisions. All the women of the household were under her authority. She judged them, disciplined them, and offered her opinion when the master decided to marry one of them off. Moreover, the ecclesiastics who supervised the spiritual life of these matrons assigned them a role similar to that of the Virgin vis-à-vis Christ. They were supposed to favor their husbands with good advice, incline them toward leniency, and champion the cause of those who came seeking favors. They were the official protectresses of the youths brought up at court, most of whom were close relatives of the lord and therefore to be coddled and cajoled. To them the lady of the house was like a surrogate for the mother from whom they had been snatched away as young boys. They were apt to confide in her, and she, in return, disciplined and instructed them. Was the initiatory role that the author of *Lancelot in Prose* ascribes to the Lady of the Lake purely imaginary? She is portrayed as revealing the myths of knighthood's origins to one who is about to be dubbed a knight. This image captures the unquestionable influence that the lord's wife exerted on boys younger and less experienced than herself. She derived her power from the fact that she shared not only the master's bed but also his secrets, as well as from her physical attractions, which were so great that, according to the hagiographers, future saints could resist them only by immersing themselves by night in the icy water of the cisterns. Along with the lord, the lady gauged the mettle of each contestant in the endless competition among the men at court not blessed with either property or wives. These men vied with one another in the hope of winning the master's "love," which could lead to the lavishing of valuable gifts. And just as Christians naturally venerated a female mediator, Mary, the "love" of these "youths" quite naturally was given to a woman, who it was hoped would deflect it toward its final destination, the lord, source of all power and beneficence.[4] It should come as no surprise that a woman figured at the heart of an instructional system designed to discipline male sexual activity, prevent excesses of masculine brutality, and pacify—civilize—the most violent segment of a society undergoing widespread and rapid change.

The Influence of the Model

Courtly love contributed to the establishment of order by inculcating a morality based on two virtues, self-restraint and friendship. The knight was encouraged to display "continence," to take himself in hand and restrain his passions, particularly those stemming from the instincts of the flesh. Brutal abduction was outlawed; rape and kidnapping gave way to the courtship ritual, the "decent" (honnête) way of conquering women of good society. The powers of reason extended their influence over the vast range of misbehavior subsumed under the head of la folie (folly, madness, unreason). The courtly ritual helped suppress the disturbances usually caused by women and to which the court, which was full of women, was particularly vulnerable. All males, clerics and laymen alike, came to see the provocative presence of women at court gatherings as the most virulent source of disorder.

First self-restraint, then friendship: in the vocabulary of the troubadour Marcabru the word amistat (friendship) is always used in counterpoint to the word amor, and knights who strove to imitate Sir Gawaine called the lady they had chosen to serve their mie, short for amie, friend. To win her love they swore to forget themselves, to serve her faithfully, to sacrifice themselves in her service. These were the very same virtues that lords expected of their vassals. Poems developed around the theme of courtly love emphasized the self-denial implicit in serving the lady, which meant serving not one's equal, another man, but one's inferior, a woman. They thus reinforced the ethics of vassalage on which the whole political structure of the time rested. Courtly poetry thereby helped to firm up the foundation of the feudal state. All evidence suggests that these poems were consciously made an integral part of the upbringing of knights. The great princely patrons—such as William, duke of Aquitaine, and, a half-century later, Henry Plantagenet, duke of Normandy, count of Anjou, and husband of Eleanor—whose luxurious courts set the tone, launched new fashions, and offered protection to poets, countered the austerity of the Capetians and the claims of the Church by encouraging the development of a profane culture. But these princes also worked to rebuild the state and, in their concern for peace, promoted what might be called a civic ethic. There is no doubt that they encouraged, if not initiated, the ritual of courtly love and contributed greatly to its diffusion. It served their policy.

The practice of *fine amour* clearly was intended to showcase the values of virility. Men were exhorted to screw up their courage and develop specific virtues. In contests of chivalry knights were put to the test, as in tournaments. Their partners had to resist if these tests were to prove anything. Hence at the beginning the woman was in the dominant position. She temporarily abandoned her normal condition of passivity and docility in order to play her assigned role: that of bait, of a lure. Like the quintains that new knights were required to knock down on the day of their dubbing to demonstrate their expertise with the lance, women were "set up" as a test. What power they had was granted for one reason only: to complicate the assault and make victory that much more glorious. The outcome was not in doubt. The game was as carefully regulated as a bullfight. It was up to the man to mount the attack, distract his adversary with passes and whirls, and finally subdue her. The lady could no more escape her fate than the bull in the ring—to have done so would have been to disrupt the established order. Nevertheless, the game required her to be "brave" and to succumb "decently," with honor. The code therefore insisted that she demonstrate courage, prudence, self-restraint, self-control. She had to repress her impulses and correct her womanly faults such as frivolity, duplicity, and unbridled lust. From the moment she joined the game she could no longer violate its laws, whether by withholding herself too stubbornly or surrendering too quickly, without incurring penalties: loss of "courtly" status and exclusion from the court by the judgment of other women, her rivals.

In high society, therefore, courtly love was also a device for disciplining women, for restraining those traits that provoked anxiety in men, for confining the female sex within a web of carefully orchestrated rituals, for drawing woman's sting by diverting her combativeness to the harmless realm of sport. The game of love did not disturb and in fact strengthened the social hierarchy, in which women were subordinate to men. Once the game was over and everyone returned to serious business, the *amie* returned to the place God intended for her kind, her "gender," under the strict authority of the man on whom she depended as wife, daughter, or sister. But in the course of play she had improved herself. *Fine amour* contributed decisively to the education of ladies and damsels, and it is in this sense only that one can speak of an "advance" for women.

The social utility of courtly love proved so great that the scope of the practice soon grew. Conceived to please unmarried knights, the earliest forms of the model (at least the earliest forms known to us) featured an unmarried male and a married female. As courtly literature gained acceptance and its themes began to influence behavior, the game quickly expanded to include maidens and married men. In Capetian France in the final third of the twelfth century courtly rituals gained a place among the preliminaries to marriage. After an engagement was concluded, it was deemed proper for the young lady to receive the amorous attention of her betrothed, who, before taking possession of her body on the wedding night, little by little won her heart: in the first *Roman de la rose* the flower that the lover wants to pick is still a bud. As for men with wives, custom allowed them to choose an *amie* (friend) and serve her as a young man would have served his beloved. Thus all of court society went courting. Courtly love became a general amusement that distinguished people of "quality" from the common horde, from the peasants who supposedly made love in the manner of beasts. As a result, what the poets had once described as an exploit so dangerous as to be beyond the reach of most men now became a necessary skill of the cultivated man or woman. The crucial thing was to maintain one's self-restraint, which meant reinforcing the sovereignty of the will over the body: this was what the rules of courtly love taught the men and women of high society.

Let us turn to Andreas Capellanus' *Treatise on Love,* a work not of fiction but of etiquette written in Paris shortly before 1200 and in Latin, the language of the schools. The book is not easy to interpret. One must be sensitive to the subtleties of its rhetoric, careful not to be misled by the turns of a dialectic pro and con, and above all prepared to give the irony of the style its full due. This complexity accounts for the fact that the book has been the object of an amazing variety of contradictory commentaries. In fact Alfred Karnein showed that it was not a primer on courtly love but a critique.[5]

Andreas was a cleric, a studious man, with a prodigious knowledge of subjects ranging from canon law and Roman law to medicine and the natural sciences. He also knew all the latest poetry of the court and of the streets, in both the *langue d'oc* and the *langue d'oïl*. He claims he wrote his moralizing treatise for men, and more precisely for those highly cultivated young men pursuing their apprenticeship in the royal household, youths still in that period of life when it was considered proper for them to be concerned with matters of love. The author explains in detail what *fine amour* is and how the game is played. But he also reminds his readers that one day they must learn to control that passion, that tendency rooted in the flesh, that inclines human beings to sin. For Andreas, love is a disease; it is the fever of growing up. It is an ordeal that toughens the man who survives it. But the obstacle must be surmounted valiantly; if not one risks becoming what Chrétien de Troyes calls a *recréant* (recidivist) and succumbing once more to the power of women. Clearly this text is not addressed to women. Toward the end of the book in fact Andreas becomes quite vituperative, denouncing their innumerable failings and suggesting, in a series of sarcastic remarks, remedies for restoring the absolute rule of virility, as God intended.

Laughing up his sleeve, the chaplain was providing answers to the numerous difficult questions that the practice of courtly love had raised when it was borrowed from the courts of the feudal princes and brought to the court of the Capetians. Mocking, in the name of reason, the troubadours' extravagant idea of *fine amour,* Andreas laid down rules for the healthy indulgence of masculine pleasure. His treatise met with quick and lasting success, and the fact that it was the only profane work of the time to be preserved in the registers of the royal chancellery suggests that the state found it useful. And so it was. It counseled respect for the hierarchy of the court. It recommended distinguishing carefully between what was appropriate for clerics and what was appropriate for laymen, between what was suitable for parvenus and what was becoming for the minor and higher nobility. It thus helped the sovereign to control the heterogeneous and rambunctious group of men who shared his table. Above all, the book proposed limiting extramarital sex, and Rüdiger Schnell has shown that this was in perfect harmony with the evolution of matrimonial law.[6] Finally, if Danièle Jacquart and Claude Thomasset are correct, the book bristles with hidden allusions, more evident in subsequent translations into the vulgar tongue than in the original Latin, to various methods of ensuring that the practice of courtly love would not disturb society's peace.[7] To those not yet prepared to give up sexual pleasure Andreas recommended that "pure" love be replaced by what he called "mixed" love: during intercourse the use of certain positions and techniques permitted sexual enjoyment with reduced risk of illegitimate offspring.

For our purposes the most important point about the *Treatise* is that it gives a clearer idea of how courtly love affected the condition of women. Despite the abundance of misogynist statements, whose very extravagance casts doubt on their sincerity, Andreas was one of the first writers to allow women to speak in their own voice, and in some of his dialogues women clearly have the better of the argument. The treatise also reveals how women benefited from the adoption of customs and practices that made male sexual aggressiveness less brutal and dangerous. Because of the discipline that the literature of courtly love encouraged, surveillance of women by husbands and fathers gradually diminished. The rules of the game required this relaxation of scrutiny, and it seems reasonable to assume that when lovers met in the privacy that thus became available to them, however limited, ephemeral, and carefully controlled it may have been, female power began for the first time to extend beyond the limits of the gynaeceum. What is more, the overall progress that reached its peak in France at the turn of the thirteenth century freed individuals from some of the collective restraints that had previously held them in check.

I fully agree with Daniel Rocher that the practice of courtly love soon made male behavior and matrimonial strategies much less crude than they had been.[8] In listening to chansons and romances, men who wanted to consider themselves properly behaved had to recognize that women were not simply bodies to be seized for a moment's pleasure and impregnated in order to propagate one's line. They learned that it was also important to win a woman's heart, that is, to ensure that she was willing, which meant taking account of her intelligence, sensibility, and unique feminine virtues. To be sure, *fine amour* enabled knightly culture to assert its autonomy vis-à-vis priestly culture. But the precepts of the amorous code accorded with the teachings of the Church concern-

265

ing the equality of male and female rights not only in the marriage bed but in the exchange of consent that sealed a lawful marriage. Was it accidental that these courtly fashions triumphed around the year 1200, at the same time that preachers were beginning to open their eyes to the spiritual needs and aspirations of women?

There can be no doubt that this game—this man's game—helped the women of feudal Europe to rise from their humble status. But there also can be no doubt that the condition of men improved similarly, so that the hierarchical distance between the sexes was not noticeably diminished. But to measure the precise influence of courtly love on social practices, we must not look to the model itself. We must not look at the illusory and precarious power that literature ascribed to the female partner in the amorous joust, much less to the emblematic princesses whom the poets, in search of patronage, flattered and honored with dedications and whom they portrayed as presiding over imaginary courts of love, seated among their vassals and handing down judgments just as their husbands did. Much more important than the model itself was the fact that society abided by it, that the society of this period was so quick to adopt the code for the treatment of women prescribed by this entertainment literature. New manners took hold. Other chansons and stories and proliferating images taught people through the ages what to say and do and thus spread new attitudes to ever-expanding circles of society (following the customary pattern, as aristocratic models gradually filtered down to the very lowest strata). Male-female relations thus took a singular turn in western society. Even today, despite the upheaval in relations between the sexes, traits derived from the practices of courtly love are among those that distinguish our civilization most markedly from others.

TRANSLATED FROM THE FRENCH BY ARTHUR GOLDHAMMER

9

Life in
the Late Middle Ages

Claudia Opitz

MEDIEVAL SOCIETY in Europe was primarily
masculine in character, with a culture reflecting
the dominance, power struggles, and prejudices of
men. Women appear in literature and documents
almost exclusively as reflections of male ideas
about them, as the idols or demons of men's fantasies. But we should not be misled into neglecting
women by "the many loud male voices who alone
proclaimed their deeds and dreams."[1] In recent
years a growing interest and awareness among
women themselves has led scholars to separate
women's history from "male fantasies" and study
the lives of the daughters, mothers, wives, saints,
and less virtuous females of the Middle Ages.
Gradually a picture is being reconstructed of their
own experiences and activities, their views, needs,
and wishes.

It remains no easy task, given the androcentric
nature of the sources, which contain varying
amounts of information about women in different
epochs, classes, or walks of life. In the early centuries firsthand accounts are extremely rare. The
situation improves markedly toward the end of the
Middle Ages, not only because women occasionally began to produce works of literature—such as
Christine de Pisan, who was particularly con-

cerned with women's issues. Many other sources become available from the thirteenth century on, reflecting a general increase in the production of written documents (and improved chances of their preservation). More and more people, particularly upper-class women, began to participate in the intellectual life of their age as listeners, readers, and patrons. Documents from this and other social classes show women participating in and shaping medieval life in roles such as legal guardian and testator.

This is not to say that women could escape male hegemony in the cultural field or any other area of social life. Their daily experience must be culled from accounts informed by male idealization and devaluation—as continues to be the case long after the Middle Ages. Women's opinions and wishes frequently remain a matter of speculation, hidden behind the veil of male authority and regimentation by fathers, husbands, and confessors, their sphere of action limited by social norms and pressures. Nevertheless, the late medieval period—despite its catastrophes and conflicts, economic and cultural upheavals, the prevalence of religious hysteria and expectations of the end of the world—was a period of awakening and positive change, not least for members of the female sex. While women shared in the ravages wrought by economic crises and epidemics, they also profited from increased possibilities for social mobility, technical innovations in agriculture and urban trades, and even from new cultural and religious movements, although their gains were particularly vulnerable to attack in this last quarter. (The great changes occurring in European society at the end of the period were accompanied by widespread belief in witchcraft and persecution of women as witches.)

Women's place in medieval society may be seen clearly in the evolution of their legal position toward the end of the epoch, although this is not always easy to follow. Enormous variations for different regions and social classes make it impossible to summarize women's legal status in a few words, but I hope to be able to demonstrate certain general trends. Medieval law codes, which, despite their basis in tradition and long-established practices, tended to be more prescriptive than descriptive, perhaps reflect not so much the realities of the era as the ideals and wishes of their authors. This may be most particularly true where the status of women is concerned, since in general women were neither actively involved nor consulted in the formulating of such codes. The law thus emerges as an element in women's daily lives that, more than any other, was male-dominated. Accordingly I have chosen to begin with a discussion of the laws that confined women to male tutelage and left them unable to act independently in many spheres, in order then to investigate how they dealt with such a disadvantageous framework and what strategies they developed for circumventing or altering it.

Women's Inferior Legal Status

The legal position of men and women in the Middle Ages was determined by a profusion of special regulations, rights, and privileges. Geography, social class, and ethnic origin played decisive roles, as did religion in the case of Jews. City-dwellers usually were governed by city statutes, which began to be codified in the twelfth and thirteenth centuries. The exceptions were members of religious orders, for whom canon law prevailed. At the beginning of the epoch the rural population of central Europe was governed by traditional ethnic laws, such as the *Sachsenspiegel,* which was codified in about 1260 and valid for the northern areas of the German empire, and the *Schwabenspiegel* in the south. In most Mediterranean regions Roman law continued to apply, while in northern France the *coûtumes* prevailed, a system of traditional rights and privileges later codified. The growing social mobility of the late Middle Ages created a virtually impenetrable thicket of conflicting regulations that continued in existence in many places for centuries. In France, for example, clarification was not achieved until the introduction of new codes during and after the revolution (1789–1795), and even then it was only partial.[2]

Nearly all of these legal codes contained special provisions for women, most of which limited their rights both within the family and in the public sphere. The most striking is the almost universal denial of legal competency to women, who were treated as wards of male family members. The traditional laws of Germany excluded all females, both free women and bond-servants, from all public affairs and transactions. They could not appear in court but had to be represented by their "guardian," usually a father or husband. In the case of orphans and widows, guardianship passed to the closest male relative in the male line. The holder of this office possessed not only the right to speak for his female ward in all legal dealings, but also to use and dispose of all her property, to punish her misdeeds with sanctions up to and including death in extreme cases, to arrange for her marriage as he saw fit, and even to sell her.[3]

Such subjugation of women, which greatly limited their economic independence and access to political power as feudal rulers or monarchs (although women are occasionally to be found in such roles throughout the later Middle Ages), was somewhat reduced in late medieval times, especially in western and central Europe. Unmarried women in particular acquired greater rights; the thirteenth-century law codes granted them considerably more freedom to make decisions and act on their own behalf than the old Germanic system had. In the private sphere, for example, they could dispose more freely over their own property and also serve as guardians of their underage children.[4]

Married women, however, remained under the legal guardianship of their husbands, with certain exceptions if they were active as traders or shopkeepers in their own right. A woman's status as spinster or wife became increasingly decisive for her freedom of action. While the extended family or clan never disappeared as a vital element in medieval economics and politics, the institutions of marriage and the nuclear family gained importance in the late Middle Ages, particularly in cities, where households were often smaller and limited to two generations. A woman's position both within and outside the family was determined more than ever by marital status and her relationship with her husband.

Demographic Data

A further set of conditions influenced day-to-day existence in the Middle Ages: the demographic framework. The very incomplete nature of sources and existence of few special studies make it virtually impossible to speak in general terms about women's life expectancy, health, fertility, or even their numbers in the total population. The available data do permit formulation of certain hypotheses, however; these shed light on legal, economic, and psychosocial developments as well as shifts in attitude.

Between 1250 and 1500 the population of Europe decreased by about one-third.[5] The available labor force and number of taxpayers shrank significantly, forcing alteration of the relationship between vassal and feudal lord. (It is significant that this period saw the great peasants' revolts and turmoil in the cities.) Marriage patterns were affected as well. More women remained unmarried, and the average age of women who did marry went up.[6] The traditional assumption that these observable changes in marriage patterns resulted from a surplus of women in the total population[7] has come under strong attack, since it is to be assumed that the birth ratio of boys to girls corresponded to the present figure (104:100) and the survival chances of females were somewhat lower than of male children. It is difficult to determine the proportion of adult males to females, since the younger, unmarried population showed a high degree of mobility in all social classes. Migration between country and city as well as between cities was common but followed varying patterns. Cities of patrician stamp tended to have more female household servants, while trade and craft centers reveal a high concentration of male servants, journeymen, and apprentices.[8] In general, cities seem to have had a particular attraction for unattached adult women, not only as places to find work or to retire in old age, but also as centers of religious and social reform.

Gender appears to have been less important in determining life expectancy than social class, profession, and geography. If famine or epidemics struck, the differences in their effect on particular regions or social groups were likely to be greater than between men and women of the same group. Even in such a widespread epidemic as the plague, certain professional groups faced the highest risk: the clergy and members of religious orders who cared for the sick; bakers whose work brought them into closest contact with the rats carrying the disease. Age may have been more of a determining factor than gender in this case; because older members of the population had often acquired immunity through previous exposure, it was children and the young above all who fell victim to the epidemic.[9]

An exception to this picture is the particular risk faced by women in pregnancy and childbirth. The mortality rate of females during their childbearing years was clearly higher than for males between the ages of twenty and forty, a circumstance that ought to have led to a surplus of males in the general population. The apparent surplus of females in many cities and communities of central Europe may result in part from incomplete records. Even more important, however, may be the fact that those women who had survived the dangers of childbirth had a substantially higher life expectancy than their male contemporaries—a finding that can be documented from the sixteenth century onward but also appears plausible for the late medieval period.[10] A further significant factor is represented by the limitation of this risk to married women for the most part. The large number of women in religious orders and female servants who traditionally remained unmarried for their whole lives in many parts of Europe also influenced the total population structure of the Middle Ages in a decisive manner.[11]

A Woman's Place: Marriage and the Family

Patterns of marriage, including the average ages of the contracting parties, were affected by economic and demographic fluctuations. From the fourteenth century on, for example, it became increasingly possible for laborers dependent on wage earnings to marry and start families. Different social classes developed their own specific strategies for advantageous marriages. Religious and philosophical values also played a role, as the medieval Church strove to influence marriage practices and the morals of its members.

Georges Duby has shown that the Church gradually succeeded in imposing its view of marriage as a sacrament and a monogamous, lifelong union on a population that had previously thought and acted quite differently. Thus from about the thirteenth century on it is possible to speak of a widely accepted "Christian model" of marriage, which was maintained well into the modern period: an indissoluble union based on mutual affection and the consensus of both partners.[12] This development brought about a shift not only in the relationship between feudal dependents and their masters—as the "marriage of consensus" stressed the right of vassals to make independent decisions—but also between parents and children and between the sexes. For men, the concept of monogamous marriage meant a limitation on the number of their legitimate children and heirs, while the older generation saw the marriage of consensus as a challenge to traditional hierarchical structures. In earlier centuries marriages had been largely a matter of negotiation between clans. Were young people now to be allowed to choose their future partners themselves? Would underage daughters be included or even autonomous in the difficult process of finding a suitable husband or determining whether to marry at all? And did consensus mean that wives were to be regarded as their husbands' equal partners in all matters?

Marriage from the Female Perspective

The theoretical freedom of decision granted to women in the ecclesiastical model had small chance of prevailing in the real world of the late Middle Ages, dominated by authoritarian, family-centered values and institutions. The enormous significance of marriage as a means of acquiring or maintaining power and property meant that young girls of the upper classes in particular would have little say in their elders' plans for them. Despite the Church's doctrine of consensus between spouses, the older generation continued to decide the future of their younger female relatives, and young men had not much more influence, especially if they were heirs to property.[13] Greater liberty in making such decisions was limited to the rural population and the lower classes in urban areas.[14]

The lack of freedom to choose a spouse cannot be regarded as a form of subjugation or oppression of women. It simply reflects an organizing principle of upper-class and propertied families in the high and late Middle Ages, which imposed similar limitations on the freedom of action of all "dependents"—young men and women alike, as well as children and servants.

The specific oppression of women in arranged marriages can be found in the reduction of their lives to an existence at a man's side in the service of his (family's) interests and needs, with strict control exercised over their bodies and sexuality and the psychological deformation inherent in being treated as an "alien" element. Nevertheless, young women attempted repeatedly to resist their families' plans, either by appealing to ecclesiastical courts for annulment of an already contracted marriage or by seeking the safety of convent walls, having taken a vow of chastity beforehand. The latter path was successfully followed by Agnes of Bohemia in the mid-thirteenth century and by Princess Isabelle, sister of King Louis IX of France (Saint Louis).[15]

The custom of "patrilocality"—the rule among the aristocracy and many urban patricians in the late Middle Ages—demanded that the girl be handed over to the care of her future in-laws as soon as a marriage was arranged. While men remained in their familiar surroundings, brides-to-be often were separated from their families while still children. Sometimes these precious pawns of political and/or economic interests were placed in convents; other times they were raised with their future husband under one roof, and treated like a child of the family.[16]

Some child brides may not have found the experience all that unpleasant; consequently, many women felt that since marriage was the best option available, they must find husbands for their daughters as soon as possible. This was the legitimation for the widespread practice of child marriage at the highest levels of society. But even among the lesser nobility and gentry girls between the ages of twelve and fifteen were considered marriageable.[17] At such an age, however, the chance of their own will being expressed or consulted was considerably reduced.

Contemporary sources show that delaying marriage until a girl had reached a more advanced age was the first prerequisite for improving her negotiating position, but still no guarantee that her own interests would be protected. Literary texts and legal documents suggest that only widows were granted relative autonomy in the question of remarriage; they could choose among several suitors.[18]

A girl resisting a marriage could expect little support from the clergy. In the case of Princess Isabelle of France (died 1270), who had raised religious objections, the pope himself urged her to marry, "for the sake of the good influence a virtuous lady could exercise upon her husband."[19] As we know from the biographies of several notable medieval women, girls wishing to escape the clan's iron grip were forced to resort to deceit and stratagems, hoping that God would indeed help those who helped themselves. Clare of Assisi, founder of the order of Poor Clares and abbess of San Damiano, and her younger sister Agnes stole away from home in the dead of night and found refuge with Francis and his unconventional band of friars. Without God's help, the hagiographer reports, they would never have been able to withstand the threats, curses, and beatings of their (male) relatives.[20]

That such tales are not merely pious fictions is shown by records of court cases dealing with unauthorized marriages from the later Middle Ages. Marriages entered into against the wishes of the spouses' parents continued to be regarded as invalid long after the Council of Trent (1546–1562)—in France until the revolution of 1789. Parties to such marriages could be disinherited by their parents or families. The records deal to a large extent with young men and support the assumption that authoritarian marriage practices could affect them harshly as well. At the same time they reveal that women were treated differently under the law and that their actions were measured by a different standard.

Evidence of young women's independence in selecting a husband is more likely to be found in cases treated as "abductions" and "forced marriages." Since the medieval perspective left no room for autonomous action on the part of women, such brides were regarded as victims of male aggression. The event was described as "kidnapping," that is, the result of purely male activity, although in most cases it could not have occurred without the young woman's participation.[21]

Early engagements, intimidation up to and including physical force, and legal prosecution in cases of disobedience—these were the means by which the older generation secured the compliance of the young, and their daughters in particular. How did these girls and young women experience daily married life at the side of men they often barely knew and for whom, in most cases, they could feel little or no affection?

The Power of Husbands

The Church doctrine of the "marriage of consensus" had little effect on social realities, nor did it truly strive to make equal partners of the participants: "Wives, submit yourselves unto your own husbands, as unto the lord. For the husband is the head of the wife, even as Christ is the head of the church" (Ephesians 5:22–23). This prescript from the New Testament had lost none of its validity in the late Middle Ages. In the eyes of the Church as well as the laity, the requirement for a good marriage was that the man "ruled" and the wife obeyed—unconditionally. Religious biographies of women in late medieval times frequently refer to the wife's subordinate position. The mother of Clare of Assisi is described as *maritali jugo subdita,* "under the yoke of her husband," and Duchess Hedwig of Silesia (died circa 1240) was "subject to the mighty Duke Henry under the law."[22] If the biographers are to be believed, these husbands, for their part, often displayed short tempers and violent behavior, supervising the smallest details of their wives' lives and (religious) activities. Many husbands repudiated their spouses on grounds of sterility or unconquerable antipathy.

Do such tales of marital life characterized by power on the one hand and subjection on the other reflect a general reality? Some light on this question is shed by records from fourteenth- and fifteenth-century Paris, where an episcopal court was constituted to deal above all with family matters. It is not surprising that most cases dealt with wives' complaints of violent treatment by their husbands, an indication that even in nonaristocratic circles husbands presumed an unlimited right of discipline, like that of a feudal lord over his retainers. However, the fact that as early as the thirteenth century such cases were brought to court by wives or their families, with requests for separation or even divorce, shows that women did not bow to the yoke of marriage as willingly as theologians and lay moralists could have wished.

Other cases, in which wives were cited for cursing and striking their husbands, confirm the suspicion that women did not always accept marital disharmony passively and were capable of defending their own interests, if necessary with physical action. Direct use of physical force in conflict was untypical for wives, however; they more frequently resorted to verbal opposition, ignoring or flouting their spouses' instructions, or disobeying them in secret. The court records contain several cases in which women were reminded of their theoretical duty to obey, one which they were clearly failing to practice.[23]

In actual fact the absolute power of husbands, stressed again and again by both ecclesiastical and secular authorities, was more the ideal of a male-dominated society than a reality—as was their view of marriage as a whole. Nonetheless, this ideology created the framework that shaped women's daily lives and conflicts both inside and outside the family. The extremely repressive nature of these patriarchal power structures for women is revealed not least by some of the criminal cases that came before late medieval courts. Female defendants were frequently accused of having tried to rid themselves of their husbands through sorcery or poison.[24] The unequal division of power between spouses often must have been an intolerable burden for women; yet virtually no path was open to them to escape the "marital yoke."

Society made husbands the first and primary instance of social control for their wives; this is proved not only by the secular law codes written from the thirteenth century on, but also by canon law, which emphasized the husband's responsibility for his wife. This doctrine found its clearest expression in the husband's right to discipline and punish his wife, upheld by both secular and ecclesiastical authorities, and the male privilege to commit adultery without sanctions.

Sexuality within and outside Marriage

"You often can't be with your lady, and it's hard for a young man like you to remain chaste. Why don't you try the maids?" The margrave Louis of Thuringia was teased in this fashion by his courtiers, we learn from his biography. Their remarks allude not only to their master's unlimited seigneurial rights over the female servants of his household, but also to his rights as a husband. Whereas law codes and public opinion at the time prescribed the death penalty for adulteresses, men who committed the same act went unpunished. Officially, the public brothels found in every city by the late fourteenth century were intended for the use of the young bachelor population of apprentices and journeymen, and no admittance was to be granted to the clergy, married men, and Jews. In practice, however, husbands caught *in flagrante delicto* were given very mild fines, while Jews were usually banished from the city for life.[25]

Although Church doctrines authorized sexual activity only within the bonds of marriage, conventual secular morality granted considerable freedom to men. Since a main purpose of marriage was to provide a man with *legitimate* heirs, however, women's sexuality had to be strictly controlled, and access to her body reserved for her husband. "Mes moult doit preudefeme soufrir et endurer avant qu'ele se met hors de la compagnie de son mari" (But a respectable woman must suffer and endure a great deal before she leaves her husband's company), wrote the author of the fourteenth-century *Coûtumes,* a compendium of legal traditions in the Beauvaisis; the obligations imposed by marriage applied above all to wives. To have no right over their own bodies was the norm for married women—and girls who intended to marry. The upper classes in particular zealously guarded the virtue of their young females; most daughters of aristocratic and patrician families spent the last few years before their—early—marriages behind convent walls. Even widows, if still of marriageable age, remained under strict family supervision. The canonization proceedings for Countess Delphine de Puimichel (died 1360) reveal that a sixteen-year-old widow in Provence could satisfy her erotic desires only by accepting a second marriage. As Duby's analyses have shown, widows who attempted to escape such coercion became the focus of family and neighborhood scandal.

Lower-class women were subject to fewer controls in fulfilling their sexual wishes, but in their case the danger of being forced into prostitution by economic necessity was great. Ecclesiastical courts in Normandy found guilty of "adulterous fornication" women who had become prostitutes, with their husbands' consent, in order to earn money. Premarital liaisons among young people in rural areas were considered "extramarital" only in the eyes of stern ecclesiastical judges; the peasantry regarded such couples as "promised" to each other and their sexual contact as licit. These forms of "free love" available to women—which always posed the risk of unwanted pregnancy—came under increasing attack toward the end of the Middle Ages, however, as a new, "bourgeois" morality spread. By the sixteenth century an unwed mother was likely to face death by drowning.

Yet despite these unfavorable conditions, women by no means ceased seeking affection and pleasure outside the marital bed. Monks and priests were especially popular partners; biographies of late medieval women are full of anecdotes about lascivious clerics who won first the trust and then the favors of their female parishioners under the pretext of concern for their spiritual welfare. The French village of Montaillou had its swashbuckling rake in the "incorrigible" priest Pierre Clergue, a "great carnivore" where women were concerned.[26] Medieval literature contains numerous examples of similar types. Often their "victims" were quite content with the arrangement, despite the risk of sanctions. Clearly it was difficult for both priests and women to draw a definite line between the proper "spiritual love" that should exist between confessor and congregation and more libidinous urges. The adoption of erotic imagery from courtly poetry into mystical religious texts and thinking—a widespread development in the thirteenth century—must have helped to blur the boundaries, until women's fear of the consequences of adultery paled beside their religious verve and sexual ardor.

As a rule women strove to keep their extramarital relations secret. Béatrice de Planissoles of Montaillou, "if she did not love her husbands . . . was very much afraid of them. She hid her escapades from them, though these adventures were minor enough during their lifetimes. She was afraid that if they found her out they would kill either her or her lover."[27] Naturally some of these women were caught and tried. Jean-Philippe Lévy has pointed out that a great number of cases heard before the bishop's court in

Paris involved unfaithful wives; out of a total of nineteen cases of adultery which he studied, six involved a husband and thirteen a wife.[28] This suggests not so much that women tended to be more unfaithful, as that women's transgressions were regarded as more serious by the law. Whereas traditional and civil codes provided for the death penalty for both an adulterous wife and her lover, a wronged wife had no legal recourse, at least in nonecclesiastical courts.

Marital Life among the Aristocracy

Biographies of women belonging to the high aristocracy tend to contradict this picture of powerless and submissive wives. The Duchess of Silesia, for example, was in charge of a huge staff of court servants of both sexes, which she ruled not only with a sharp tongue but also an iron hand. Even the pious Elisabeth of Thuringia (died 1231) was not above using force to ensure that her instructions were obeyed; on one occasion when a beggar woman resisted going to confession, saying she should be allowed to sleep instead, "the sainted Elisabeth thrashed her with switches until the recalcitrant woman finally went."[29]

The authoritarian and imperious behavior of women of the aristocracy, which is confirmed by other sources, seems at first to stand in stark contrast to the picture of the subordinate wife just developed. Yet it should be recalled that in such instances they are acting not in their capacity as wives, but as members of their class toward family retainers or the poor.

In addition to their social sphere of influence, upper-class women possessed considerable economic power, some of which was no doubt acquired through marriage. Wives had virtually unlimited control over the personal effects such as money, jewelry, clothing, and other "movable goods" that made up their dowries or marriage portions, as well as over the wares used in or produced by the household. Even the legal codes of the late Middle Ages granted the mistress of the house the "power of the keys" over such goods and a limited capacity to enter into business dealings. Many noblewomen oversaw the management of their estates and landed properties—although they were usually assisted by competent stewards. This furthered the practice, which had become common by the end of the era, of maintaining separate households for husband and wife at the great courts of Europe. Even though the household and treasury of the prince were usually far better equipped than those of his spouse, she still occupied the position of a formidable feudal ruler, with servants, serfs, and her own house or apartments. The freedom of movement she gained from all this brought to the life of a married woman in the highest circles of medieval society a unique and potentially tension-laden combination of independence and subjugation.[30]

It also contributed its share to the frequent lack of emotional ties between aristocratic spouses, who often spent little time together; marital "intimacy" consisted in large part of sharing a bedroom, and even that did not always occur on a regular basis. Biographies reveal that noble spouses frequently lived apart for years at a time, if business or the husband's duties to his feudal lord required it. Count Elzéar de Sabran, a vassal of Charles II of Anjou in the early fourteenth century, once spent five years at Charles' court in Sicily, while his wife, Delphine de Puimichel, a Provençal heiress, remained at home in southern France to supervise the family properties.[31]

Records of the travels of Margrave Louis of Thuringia (died 1227), the husband of Saint Elisabeth of Thuringia, provide further evidence that even a couple noted for their devotion to one another could not spent a great deal of time together. In August 1223, less than eighteen months after their marriage in 1221, Louis departed to lead a campaign against the Count of Orlamünde. In September he was away at court-day in Nordhausen, and at the beginning of 1224 he was preparing to set out after Epiphany, with a troop of knights, for assizes in Gross-Göschen in the Mark Brandenburg. From January 12 until the end of February he was away on a visit to his sister Jutta; after a short stay at home in Neuenburg, the family seat, he returned to the Mark on another military campaign. At Easter he was in Dresden and afterward attended assizes at Delitsch. He returned to Neuenburg in July, but in August he had to set out again for Poland on a month-long campaign. The end of September saw him at another court-day in Bardewik, north of Lüneburg, and in October he was encamped at nearby Blekede. Not until winter was he able to spend an extended amount of time at home in Neuenburg. Elisabeth accompanied her husband on some of these journeys, such as those to court-days or assizes; military expeditions were of course undertaken without wives, who also had duties of their own to see to at home. She gave birth to three children between 1221 and 1227, one of whom was born while Louis was away on diplomatic missions to Cremona and Prague. The marriage was thus characterized by long separations, amounting to between a third and a half of its total duration.[32]

A further obstacle to the development of a close relationship between husband and wife was the brevity of many marriages, owing to the high mortality rate. A chief cause was death in childbirth. Swift remarriages for practical reasons were common, especially if a young wife's death left small children to be cared for. Since widowers tended to take younger wives, the frequently large disparity in spouses' ages must also have contributed to a sense of distance. The picture then shifted if the older husband of a second (or third) wife died, and she took a younger husband; this happened out of necessity as much as preference, if an estate or workshop needed looking after. (Cases are common of widows of master craftsmen marrying one of his journeymen or assistants.)

The problems caused by large age differences between husbands and wives are a frequent topic of medieval art and literature. Although it is difficult to find reliable data for relative ages of spouses and the average length of marriages, an analysis of late medieval genealogical records of noble families shows that few marriages lasted longer than fifteen years. The assumption thus appears justified that few people in the Middle Ages regarded marriage as a "permanent" partnership; it was far more likely to be a temporary connection, and not the only one of one's life.[33]

Marital relationships tended to be correspondingly distant, not only for the aristocracy. In general marriage represented an institution designed to serve economic and social needs of the present and future rather than the emotional needs of individuals. Church doctrines continued to emphasize both the indissoluble nature of marriage ties and the foundation of Christian marriage in marital love (*dilectio* or *caritas*), but the search for a definition of this feeling shows how small a role affection was generally assumed to play.[34]

On a practical level, confessors and jurists among the clergy treated marital love as an extremely insignificant factor. Its absence was on no account reckoned as grounds for divorce, nor its presence regarded as establishing the validity of a marriage. In addition to parental consent, the sacrament of marriage was defined by the birth of children and mutual fidelity; for the rest it was left up to the individual participants to find a modus vivendi. That, nevertheless, not all medieval marriages were loveless and all wives unhappy contemporary sources reveal in numerous ways. Child marriage, which on the one hand could have a highly repressive effect on young brides, offered on the other the possibility for young people to develop a genuine understanding and affection for one another. Salomea and Coloman, for example, a child couple who lived at the Hungarian court in the late thirteenth century, received their education together, since they were of approximately the same age.[35] Louis and Elisabeth of Thuringia, whose married life has been discussed, had known each other since childhood.

Such examples help resolve, at least partially, the seemingly absurd contradiction between the injunction to make love the basis of conjugal life and the virtually universal custom of arranged marriages. Love between spouses was regarded as the result of a shared life rather than as grounds to enter into a marriage. Affection, which was not required for spouses to function as an effective social unit, was seen as a pleasant addition, if fortune so willed, or as the fruit of constant effort.

Married Life in Medieval Cities

Many of the same forces shaped married life among the urban middle class. In general, however, marriage customs appear to have been slightly less repressive for wives of the bourgeoisie. Their average age of marriage was higher, and saw a further rise toward the end of the epoch, a circumstance that probably increased women's ability to have some influence on the choice of a spouse. Furthermore their legal and economic position seems to have allowed them a significantly larger sphere of independence. Nonetheless here, too, a husband's will reigned supreme.[36]

A middle-class woman could acquire a considerable sphere of influence through marriage; a *materfamilias* was in charge of the household budget and, depending on the wealth and profession of her husband, a varying number of servants and retainers. As a rule of course middle-class city dwellers lived in far less spacious quarters than the aristocracy, with less room for indulgence in luxury. The separate households of great families were replaced by a smaller group, conscious of striving in a common interest. And whereas an important function of noblewomen was to oversee the family domains during their husbands' long absences, middle-class husbands and wives—with the exception of the great merchant and trading families, where of necessity the men often had to be away on long voyages—lived in far greater proximity to one another.[37] This was particularly true for artisans, whose workshops and living quarters were often under one roof. The significance of a husband's presence is expressed in many biographies of medieval women. While a noblewoman's actions were affected by the presence of other relatives, ladies-in-waiting, courtiers, and further members of a court or large household, in middle-class families the husband functioned as the sole enforcer of social norms and controls.

Rural women, and above all wives of urban craftsmen, enjoyed a certain recognized status because of the importance of their contribution to the total labor output of the family. They were far more than the mere breeders of heirs, which their aristocratic counterparts tended to be considered.[38] It is estimated that from one-third to one-half of all master craftsmen in central European cities plied their trade without journeymen, so that women and sometimes children had to perform a number of important tasks, including selling the wares produced and carrying out other necessary commissions. The notion that urban women of the late Middle Ages functioned exclusively or chiefly as "housewives" is a misconception, at least for regions north of the Alps.[39] The large numbers of urban artisans engaged in service trades—butchers, bakers, shoemakers, tailors, and so on—required their wives' active participation in the family business. In addition to caring for the household's daily needs for food and clothing, wives of artisans in particular often provided a necessary supplement to the family income through their own independent activities. They spun and wove cloth for the local market or for textile traders not subject to local guild regulations; they produced beer and foodstuffs to sell, or traded in other small commodities. Certain household tasks were delegated to paid servants if the mistress of the house could earn more with other work. Even pregnancy and motherhood limited these activities far less than might be assumed. Wet nurses, nursemaids, older siblings, and unmarried female relatives took over a great many maternal functions and responsibilities.

As wives' growing economic significance for the family—at least in the artisan class—ran up against the continuing legal and social hegemony of the husband, the ground was laid for tensions in relations between the sexes. The battle "to wear the pants" in the family that began toward the end of the Middle Ages provides the social background for the countless stage farces and comic tales—of cuckolded or henpecked husbands and shrewish wives—that so often reflect hostility toward women.

Motherhood and Maternal Behavior

Women's daily lives and position in society were affected as profoundly by motherhood as by marriage. Yet while bearing children was seen as one of women's chief tasks, the task of raising them seems to have been considered a "profession," in Mediterranean regions more than elsewhere. As we have seen, middle-class urban women in northern Europe often performed a variety of functions while their children were looked after by others, and the notable increase in the size of aristocratic families observable from the twelfth century onward suggests that infants and small children were handed over to the care of wet nurses instead of remaining with their mothers.[40]

Shulamith Shahar has pointed out how small a role mothers and motherhood play in medieval literature of all kinds—from religious lyrics to courtly epics, legal treatises, and works on education.[41] The reason for this is less likely to be a lack of medieval parents' interest in their children, however, as Philippe Ariès has claimed, than the fact that the authors of these works were men, who possessed little or no knowledge of the subject.[42] Motherhood was an expressly female domain, and clerical authors in particular remained aloof from its rites and secrets.

Although male authors showed little interest in the details of the maternal role, the identification of women with motherhood was fundamental to the medieval view of life. In a much-cited passage of his *Summa Theologica,* Saint Thomas Aquinas attributed the presence of females in the creation to this function alone: "It was absolutely necessary to make woman, for the reason Scripture mentions, as a help for man; not indeed to help him in any other work, as some have maintained, because where most work is concerned man can get help more conveniently from another man than from a woman; but to help him in the work of procreation."[43] Medieval society, and the aristocracy in particular, shared the opinion that God had created women in order to bring children—meaning heirs—into the world. The genealogies of noble families that appear with increasing frequency from the twelfth century on include women who had distinguished themselves by devoted motherhood, which is to say fertility. A good marriage meant many children, and a good wife, it went without saying, bore her husband heirs. Anything else was considered abnormal, although canon lawyers and moral theologians strove to have childless marriages recognized as a fully valid sacrament if the partners were devoted to one another in the fear of God. In the late Middle Ages the partners of unconsummated or childless marriages were even accorded special distinction, and a number of childless wives were canonized.[44]

Fertility and Sterility

The Church's efforts to have childless marriages recognized as equally valid met with little success among the lay population, however. It was still not unusual in the thirteenth century for wives to be repudiated if, after several years of marriage, they had not given birth. As we know from the canonization proceedings for Clare of Assisi (born 1253), a knight from Assisi had sent his wife back to her parents because she had not borne him children. They lived apart for twenty-two years, and he was persuaded to take her back only when Clare prophesied that, if he did, his wife would soon give birth to a son.[45] Occasionally, if the husband himself was unwilling to draw the consequences of continuing infertility—as in the case of the Provençal couple Elzéar and Delphine de Puimichel—his family would intervene and send the barren wife home.

Even outsiders could show great concern about the fertility of prominent families. A Franciscan monk in Kraków inquired of his patron saint Salomea, "whether her brother, Duke Boleslaus, and his wife, Kynga, Duchess of Cracow and Sandormin, would have children."[46] An abundance of children ensured the maintenance not only of family property, but also, if the family was important enough, of political constellations and the stability of whole regions. If an heir to the throne was lacking, then quarrels over the succession, internal and foreign conflicts, war, and suffering for the general population were sure to follow.

It is thus hardly surprising that women in the late Middle Ages, particularly among the upper classes, desperately sought advice and remedies when they failed to become pregnant. In one such case the following document has survived:

The bearer of this letter . . . is a noblewoman and wife of a beloved husband. She comes to you in profound and simple piety, although her station would allow her to travel on horseback with a large retinue. The reason for her coming is the following: she has remained infertile for a long time now, even though at the beginning of her marriage she gave birth to several sons.

As they all died, and she has borne no more children since then, she and her husband are deeply saddened. This is why she seeks refuge with you, the handmaiden and intimate of Christ. She earnestly hopes that through your merits and prayers God will be moved to make her more fertile and that she will be able to offer to Christ the blessed fruit of her womb for the preservation of her house and line. For this reason we ask your aid, as requested by this lady and her husband, that you may intervene on their behalf in your prayers and that they may be found worthy to receive the blessing for which they long.[47]

This letter, addressed to the renowned visionary and healer Hildegard of Bingen by five Cistercian abbots of Burgundy in the mid-twelfth century, was carried by no less a personage than Beatrice, heiress to the kingdom of Burgundy and consort of the Holy Roman Emperor Frederick Barbarossa. An alliance with spiritual authority was sought to end the potentially calamitous infertility of the imperial house. Hildegard responded with theologically impeccable advice, recommending humble prayer. But many other barren women were not content to leave it at that. They resorted not only to pilgrimages and vows, prayers and offerings to the Virgin and all other relevant saints, but also to magical practices not condoned by the Church. Unfortunately little is known about the latter. If we may assume, however, that certain fertility rites and practices of more recent times have older origins, then medieval women, like their eighteenth-century sisters in Burgundy, probably sought assistance from the fairies who brought children, by taking small gifts to the springs where they were said to dwell. Or did they secretly touch the phallic upright stones to be found in southern France, as a symbolic gesture of contact between male and female, as women were still doing a hundred years ago? Undoubtedly they also tried aromatic herbal baths, cures, and tinctures as remedies.

Infertility would rarely have met with passive acceptance, especially since for most women the tasks of raising and caring for children must not have made inordinate demands on their energies. Medieval women were not expected to be solely responsible for all their children's physical and intellectual needs. Among the upper classes wet nurses and servants were available to perform such daily tasks as bathing and changing, feeding and supervising; in combination with the young age of aristocratic brides this circumstance led to very large families. One study has put the average at eight to ten children.[48]

In artisan and peasant families maids, unmarried relatives, and older siblings assisted in the care and supervision of infants and small children, although the share of work falling to mothers was considerably greater than in aristocratic circles. Nursing, changing, and daily care were tasks more frequently performed by the mother herself, a fact reflected in the significantly lower birthrate among such groups. A mother's child-care duties frequently collided with performance of her other household and professional responsibilities; the fact that the latter took priority is indicated by the high mortality rate of small children in the artisan and peasant classes. In her study of child-rearing in late medieval England, Barbara A. Hanawalt has shown that children between the ages of two and four were particularly at risk of accidental death as a result of lack of adult supervision; as they became mobile and wandered through house, garden, or barnyard, they often fell into fires, wells, or streams and ponds. Infants were attacked by wild animals when their mothers left them at the edge of fields, in order to have them at hand to nurse. Other serious accidents occurred when unwatched babies were left too close to open fires or animals in stables.[49] The dilemma of conflicting demands for work and child care tended all too often to be solved at the child's expense.

On the other hand, older children—from about the age of four—could be assigned small tasks in the house or garden, areas for which women were chiefly responsible, and thus make their presence a useful asset. An important role for children was not as occasional assistants in household tasks, however, but as a form of old-age insurance. As clan ties ceded priority to nuclear families in the late Middle Ages, at least in western and central Europe, women must have relied increasingly on grown sons and daughters as a source of support in widowhood, and regarded raising them as a sound and prudent investment.

Such practical considerations by no means suggest that emotional ties between mothers and children were weak, as has been suggested. Among the lower classes in particular lack of space and the necessity of frequent nursing meant that infants and small children lived in extremely close contact with their mothers and often shared her bed. In 1270 a Hungarian peasant woman reported to the Inquisition her reactions on finding one of her children dead: "And when I found my second child dead in my bed, I took it by the feet, climbed out of bed and began to scream and weep over the child. I felt it all over, but it didn't move and lay as if dead. Then I grew very sad and mournful, because my son was dead like my other child (a daughter), and I prayed to Saint Margaret to make my son come back to life."[50] Many other cases of a mother's grief over the death of a child from accident or disease are reported. One mother of a young man who had died as the result of an accident was "so afflicted by grief that her loud groans and profound suffering moved all around her to tears and lamentation."[51] Prolonged separations could also cause mothers deep distress, as in the case of Jutta von Hoy of Flanders (died about 1230), whose biographer reports she could not bear to be separated from her two sons.[52] Her contemporary, Elisabeth of Thuringia, deemed it a sad necessity to live apart from her children after she had chosen the ascetic life of a Beguine and healer of the sick "in the service of Christ."[53]

From Contraception to Infanticide

Not all women were loving and devoted mothers or even wanted to have children. A number of biographies of late medieval female saints read almost like antimaternal tracts. The mystic Angela da Foligno (born 1309), for example, prefaced the account of her holy visions with an expression of thanks to God, who by causing her mother, husband, and children to be carried off by an epidemic had enabled her to devote herself entirely to His service.[54] Her contemporary, the visionary Rosanensis (born 1310), who took the veil and the name Umiltà, apparently left a husband and children behind with no regrets after deciding to enter a convent.[55] The converted sinner Margaret of Cortona (born 1297) is reported to have neglected her illegitimate son, "without a trace of maternal feeling," and served the poor as her Christian duty.[56]

While the separation of mothers and children in these accounts of saints' lives is intended to demonstrate their capacities for self-sacrifice and suffering, other contemporary sources suggest that less saintly women tried contraception and abortion as alternatives to motherhood. The evidence is too slight to permit conclusions about the extent of such practices or the methods used. The authors of the texts in question, usually clerics and theologians, assumed that at least the wish for birth control existed among their flock—and women in particular—in cases where the motive for sexual contact was pleasure or lust, as in extramarital affairs and brothels. Fleeting allusions are made to the means a woman might employ if she wished to carry on a clandestine relationship— or her profession—without consequences: abortive drugs and spermicidal tinctures, or a magical talisman such as the amulet of herbs placed around Béatrice de Planissoles' neck by her lover Pierre Clergue, the priest of Montaillou.[57]

To conclude from these scanty references and the clerics' polemics—as some historians have done—that medieval women possessed their own store of contraceptive lore and a corresponding autonomy in sexual matters seems unwarranted, however. It is certainly accurate to say that pregnancy, birth, and all associated knowledge and practices were a purely female domain in the Middle Ages. Men had neither experience nor a voice in such matters, and a sense of modesty forbade their presence at the birth of a baby—a major contributing factor, in combination with widespread illiteracy among women, to our lack of information today about medieval practices. Yet this much seems clear: the medieval matrons and midwives who concerned themselves with such matters knew far less about them, and the closely related questions of fertility and contraception, than is often assumed nowadays.[58]

Their relative helplessness is exposed by accounts of difficult births contained in the countless tales of miracles from the late Middle Ages, which also reveal how great the fear of childbirth was among women of all social classes. Ortulana, Saint Clare's mother, is said to have gone to the church of Assisi toward the very end of her pregnancy and prayed devoutly that Christ "might grant her a safe childbed."[59] The prayer was certainly appropriate in view of the limited means at midwives' disposal and the large number of possible complications. The practice of cesarean section did not begin until the thirteenth century; even then it was seldom employed, as it was permitted only after the mother was already dead. The number of women whose first pregnancy ended fatally was correspondingly high. Other and simpler means of intervention, such as episiotomies, drugs to increase contractions, and forceps, appear to have been largely unknown.

Let this one example stand for many. When the labor of Floriana, a mid-thirteenth-century Polish noblewoman, was complicated by the baby's position, the attending midwives gave her up for lost and "commended her to God's grace, for only half of the child's head emerged from the mother's body, and it could be neither pushed back in nor pulled out. Floriana lay in this extremity from nones (about three in the afternoon) until vespers (at six)."[60] The state of information available in Kraków at that time meant that even a woman from the highest class of society had to be left to her fate—in this case death.

A similar lack of information appears to have existed with regard to abortion. A particular problem was presented by the difficulty of establishing whether a woman was pregnant or not. This was usually left to the judgment of the woman herself, who could be certain only when she felt the fetus moving. Even specialists were able to confirm pregnancy only at a relatively late stage, on the basis of a swollen stomach and possibly an examination of the mouth of the cervix. These diagnostic methods, which are referred to more or less in passing in court records, usually involved the examination of women who had been condemned to death, to make sure that innocent life would not be destroyed along with the guilty.

Agace la Françoise and Jehane la Riquedonne, two fourteenth-century midwives, attested before a court in Paris that they had "seen and examined the above-named prisoner Marion de la Court with great diligence, by feeling and palpating her unclothed body." They determined that she could on no account be pregnant, since "she is flat in the stomach and was so agitated during the visit and examination of her stomach that we are convinced to the best of our knowledge and ability that she is not with child."[61]

The possibility of recognizing pregnancy at an early stage and effectively ending it thus appears to have been virtually nonexistent, and attempts at abortion grew increasingly dangerous to the expectant mother as the pregnancy progressed. Ergot, a fungus that attacks rye, was widely used as an abortifacient drug in the Middle Ages. But because it was highly toxic in the large doses required by an advanced pregnancy, mother and fetus frequently died together.

Infanticide or the abandonment of newborn babies was less

dangerous for mothers. The fact that the legal sources of the period treat them as purely female crimes may not result solely from an antifeminine bias of male authors, for illegitimate children of men and women were regarded in different lights. Whereas illegitimate offspring of the male line of a noble family were often recognized and could contribute as adults to the clan's wealth and power, women who gave birth to bastards risked severe punishment and sometimes death. (On the other hand it could be difficult to prove that a married woman had actually committed adultery.)

Infanticide remained a dangerous method of dealing with unwanted pregnancy, however, because it was viewed as an extremely serious offense under canon law, and later in secular law codes as well. A mother's poverty was the sole mitigating circumstance to be recognized; a woman who murdered her newborn child for reasons of selfish convenience or lust was treated with great severity by both ecclesiastical and lay court judges; secular law in fact required the death penalty.[62] Though the number of recorded convictions for infanticide in the period 1250–1500 is small, this should not be interpreted to mean that the crime was rare or the severe penalty necessarily an effective deterrent. It appears to reflect rather how difficult it must have been for legal and moral authorities to control the "private life" of the population, particularly since the borderline between infanticide and accidental death was fluid.

The frequency of such deaths explains the increasingly sharp warnings on better care of infants issued by Church authorities to mothers and wet nurses; the responsibility for fatalities of this sort was laid at their door. The secular law codes also changed to reflect what must have been seen as an alarmingly widespread practice. While the "Etablissements de Saint Louis," a set of thirteenth-century statutes for Paris and the Ile de France, recognized only repeated child death from negligence as a criminal offense, the laws of succeeding centuries were much stricter. Suspected child-murderers also were prosecuted more actively, so that more cases and convictions are reported in the fifteenth century.

Abandoning children appears to have been a last resort of the poor. It was practiced above all in cities (where the possibility of anonymity was greater). A fifteenth-century chronicle from Basel reports that women left infants they were unable or unwilling to raise "in front of the town hall or the hospital."[63] Even threat of the severest punishments—drowning in the Rhine River, being buried alive, or burned at the stake—could not put a stop to the practice. The poverty of the urban underclass was too great, and public opinion took a lenient view of those who were forced by extreme need to violate normal legal and ethical standards. At the end of the fifteenth century in Strasbourg between six and twenty foundlings a year were left in the cathedral "by poor people who have nothing to eat themselves and thus cannot bring up their children." Geiler von Kaysersberg, a lay folk preacher of Strasbourg, expressed his opinion that in extremity a father was even justified in selling his son; any method that offered such unwanted children a chance of survival was better than infanticide.[64] On this point the great preacher's view coincided with the secular law of the land, the *Schwabenspiegel*. Here too the parents' welfare and right to life were placed above those of the child. Midwives acted on the same principle: if a choice had to be made between the life of a woman in childbirth and the baby, the mother's life was given priority.

Toward the end of the fourteenth century the enormous drop in the population of Europe as a result of famine and plague led to the attaching of greater value to infants' lives and a reduction in infanticide and abandonment. Institutions for the care of foundlings and orphans were established, first in large cities such as London, Paris, and Strasbourg, and then in smaller communities as well.[65] Nevertheless, the degree of suspicion toward criminal or immoral behavior on the part of women increased with the coming of the Reformation and the development of a "new morality." The statutes of Paris, for example, contained the proviso that only orphans of "honest birth" would be received in the city's institutions, "so as not to encourage loose morals among adults."[66] As the Middle Ages drew to a close, the unchecked sexual license of the lower classes in particular was increasingly condemned, perhaps because economic circumstances now permitted more of them to marry and lead more regulated lives.

Daily Bread: Women and Work

Considerable attention has been devoted to the conditions of women's work during the Middle Ages in the last hundred years or so, particularly by German and American scholars.[67] They have pointed out again and again that the exclusion of women from crafts, production, and industry was a specific phenomenon of nineteenth-century (bourgeois) society, and that in previous centuries it was the norm for women to be gainfully employed in a number of areas.

Women played a significant role above all in the developing economy of medieval cities. While the economy of the early Middle Ages was unthinkable without female participation, the expansion of urban centers in Europe beginning in the early twelfth century created new working conditions that affected the range of tasks performed by women. The population was increasing significantly, and this growth and new density in cities and villages altered patterns of life and work. A larger number of men and women could begin to think of marrying and establishing their own household. Such a couple formed the nucleus of a new economic unit, the independent family operating its own small-scale craft workshop, trading business, or farm. More and more the group living under one roof shrank to the "nuclear" two-generation family. First the urban and soon after the rural population began to produce for local demand in a growing market economy, as the old feudal structures declined. Fewer people now lived as serfs or tenants on great estates, where conditions were determined by the small land-owning class and its need for large numbers of unmarried laborers. Emancipation from this kind of dependency could not be achieved by individuals, only by a married couple. Those who did not succeed in finding spouses had to seek protection from—and thus remain dependent on—another family. A state that guaranteed the protection of all its citizens did not yet exist.[68]

Simultaneously a population of specialized, independent craftsmen arose in the cities, and the creation of regular trade links between different regions and nations encouraged even further specialization and division of labor. Agricultural production intensified to meet population demands, and cultivation of grain crops increased. This intensification and specialization of agriculture, in turn, meant the rural population had only limited opportunity to produce even simple goods and implements for household use. Thus, as specialization was making for greater social and economic differences between town and country, their ties and dependence on one another were increasing.

The division of labor tended to apply to both sexes, with the female sphere generally considered to mean supervision of internal household affairs: house, garden, children, servants and retainers, small livestock, and possibly sale of goods produced on the premises.[69] Religious and secular literature of the period both make frequent reference to such traditional divisions. The Minorite preacher Andreas of Regensburg (died 1271), for example, proclaimed that a woman working outside the house is as much use as a hen that has flown the coop.[70] The husband who stays at home to mind the chickens while his wife goes out to see to business is a stock figure of old French and low German farces.[71]

Nevertheless, the stock figure of comedy did exist and must have reflected existing tensions concerning gender roles in medieval society. Men were active in certain traditionally "female" fields such as weaving and the production of textiles and foodstuffs, while women were not confined solely to reproductive functions and housework. The chief aim was to maximize the family income, which among the middle and lower classes was often at or near subsistence level. If women could earn more from other work, they hired servants to perform household tasks or bought food ready-prepared. The broad spectrum of food-preparing establishments that we know existed in medieval cities indicates how common the latter practice was.

Women's Work in Rural Areas

The majority of women worked in the agricultural sector, even though rural areas offered fewer opportunities than cities for paid labor. The tasks they performed were largely seasonal and related to the increasing demand for a flexible, migratory work force. Women were needed in the expanding grain cultivation, in vineyards, and in the harvest and preparation of crops that had become essential for the urban textile industry: flax and plants used in cloth dyeing, such as madder and woad. In some regions of Europe the care of livestock and dairy farming also required a labor force above and beyond the married couple who, in rural areas just as in the cities, formed the basic productive unit.[72]

Within the farming family a relatively clear division of labor between husband and wife can be observed: the female sphere encompassed chiefly house and garden, along with the supervision of livestock. Milking and producing dairy products also tended to be women's tasks, except in regions where it was undertaken on a large scale; in eastern Switzerland, for example, tending of cattle on the high Alpine pastures in summer and cheese-making remained traditionally male provinces. Women were responsible for basic household duties; they baked bread, brewed beer, and made and mended clothing and bedding. Such daily tasks as cooking meals, housecleaning, and child care tended to play a subordinate role, just as in the cities, since the specialization of agriculture required women's participation to an increasing degree, especially at harvest time. Plowing and sowing were essentially masculine activities, but the harvesting of grain and hay remained nonspecialized work and in some regions of Europe continued to be performed by both sexes until the beginning of the twentieth century. The same holds true for the grape harvest; here too men and women worked side by side and often received the same daily wages.

Sheep-shearing, tending gardens, picking hops, and mowing hay were other tasks for which female day laborers in particular were hired, as well as to help with doing laundry and baking bread. Many of these tasks were delegated to servant girls, who in the country tended to see their status as a temporary one that would end when they married. Country households saw far greater fluctuation among the servant population; the servant class in the cities was somewhat more permanent.[73]

The relatively large number of agricultural tasks requiring day laborers reflects the growing role of money in the rural as well as the urban economy. For this reason farm women often strove to contribute to the family income by selling for cash the products of their own labor, such as butter, milk, cheese, eggs, fruit, and occasionally linen, soap, prepared mustard, and the like.

Women Traders

Urban women too were active as traders, either of goods they had produced themselves or of wares they had bought or imported. It has already been mentioned that this circumstance led early on to certain limitations on a husband's legal rights to represent and speak for his wife in all matters; women traders were granted a limited capacity to transact business in their own name. The volume of trade varied enormously, and it was above all the women organized in guilds (primarily for long-distance trading) who acquired considerable wealth. Wills preserved in the archives of the Hansa city of Lübeck reflect this range. While one Mechthild of Bremen made a will in April 1353 leaving the sum of only 30 marks to her heirs, along with jewelry and other items, another trader named Alheyd of Bremen left her husband not only the impressive sum of 400 marks but also valuable jewelry, silver tableware, and a house.[74]

Importing goods from abroad was not without risk. Records of Basel from the early fifteenth century show that a number of traders suffered considerable losses when a goods train was set upon and robbed. Of the sixty-one merchants who had financed the shipment, thirty-seven were women. One of them, Cristina Oflaterin, had invested 501 florins, and another, an apothecary's widow, 270 florins. Most of the other women had invested only small sums, between 7 1/2 and 9 florins.[75]

The goods traded included virtually every kind of item needed in daily life as well as luxuries. While prices were determined to some extent by the market, both city and guild organizations supervised trade closely, inspecting the quality of imported goods and setting limits on the volume of trade and profits. These regulations by no means required specialization in one sort of merchandise, however. In 1420 a woman trader named Czachmannin in the German town of Görlitz is recorded as having dealt in crossbows, saddle bags, bridles, harnesses, halters, spurs, and stirrups, as well as sulphur, copperas, verdigris, arrow quivers, soap, parchment, wax, paper, and spices.[76]

In early medieval times, when the volume of trade was not yet regulated, one family might carry on both wholesale and retail trade in a particular item. In such cases the men would frequently travel to make the larger purchases, while the women of the family took care of the retail shop. Records show, however, that a large number of independent women merchants also engaged in long-distance trade. They appear in the records of the trading centers of northern Italy as early as the beginning of the thirteenth century. In Genoa a certain Mabilia appears to have entered with her son's assistance into a contract with one Rubaldus Galetta. Mabilia supplied him with canvas and linen, which she had imported from Swabia in southern Germany; Galetta undertook to sell it for her in Sicily in return for a quarter share in the profits.[77]

The heyday of women long-distance traders in Europe arrived in the fourteenth and fifteenth centuries, when records show increasing numbers of them in many regions beyond Italy. The 1353 will of Mechthild of Bremen mentions such a business arrangement. A woman of Cologne named Druitgen Koller is recorded as having formed a partnership with a producer of cloth, contracting to sell it for him in southern Germany. Four other women in Cologne were involved in business arrangements, usually with a single partner, between 1435 and 1505.[78] These cases involving large-scale trade with distant regions appear to be the exception, however,[79] since generally women's work in the late Middle Ages was conducted closer to home, enabling wives to combine it with their household functions.[80] Thus a typical sight in cities and smaller towns was the market woman or peddler, who hawked her wares as a sideline, usually home-grown fruit and vegetables or other small items of daily use.

Since this form of trade was not organized or officially supervised by any guild, competition was strong and prices determined by the local market. The opportunities for profit were correspondingly small. Although the field was open to virtually anyone, as a rule no fortunes were to be made. Thus the tax rolls of medieval cities usually list such market women in the category of those who were not required to pay any tax at all, since their assets were too meager.

Education, Healing, and Health Care

The women merchants organized in professional guilds could boast not only far greater profits than the local traders, but usually a superior education as well. Their complicated business dealings, which sometimes involved large sums of money, required at least rudimentary skills in reading, writing, and mathematics, knowledge a simple peddler or market woman could do without. In England a woman had to complete an apprenticeship of several years before she could be admitted to the guild of wholesale and international merchants. But this appears to have been the exception; in the rest of Europe the women acquired the necessary skills at home or in the schools for girls that existed as early as the thirteenth century in the great trading centers of Flanders. Beatrjis van Tienen, the daughter of a patrician family in the thirteenth century and later abbess of a Cistercian convent, is known to have attended Latin school from the age of seven; before that she had been instructed at home by her mother, herself a merchant. Another Cistercian nun, Ida of Nivelles, attended a municipal Latin school for boys and girls in the late thirteenth century and later became a mainstay of the famous scriptorium of her convent, La Ramée.[81]

Paris appears as a particularly progressive educational center in the late thirteenth century, with no fewer than twenty-one women listed as mistresses of approved elementary schools for girls. At the beginning of the fourteenth century coeducational schools were opened as well, but these were required to convert back to single-sex education by mid-century.[82] The great mercantile cities of northern Italy also had schools for girls from the thirteenth century on. In all these areas, however, children of wealthy parents usually were educated at home by private tutors.[83]

In the German-speaking countries public schools came into existence only in the course of the fourteenth century, as German gained acceptance as a written language. Here females were admitted both as pupils and teachers. The latter were occasionally "Beguines," as lay sisters were called, or nuns from the "new orders," but more often the women teachers employed in city schools were the wives of male teachers. Not infrequently a couple would open a school together, as in Bamberg, where city regulations specified that they had to be married to each other.

The economic situation of women teachers depended largely on the type of school where they were employed. Teachers in municipal institutions received a fixed salary (part of which was paid in goods), and sometimes free room and board.[84] Independent schoolmistresses lived more precariously from the fees paid by their pupils, frequently in the form of goods or produce. It is therefore not surprising to find them living in communities, as the Beguines did, or teaching as a sideline in addition to other responsibilities, usually in a household. This may be one reason why in many places municipal authorities would permit only married couples to run a school. Here again we encounter the married couple as the fundamental, socially acceptable economic unit, partners in a joint enterprise.[85]

Women played a significant role in the field of health care and obstetrics. Throughout Europe the latter remained the virtually exclusive province of midwives, but women were active as healers and in the care of the sick, including sometimes even the practice of surgery. As university medical schools were founded during the Middle Ages, academically educated (male) doctors began to guard their status jealously, making efforts to drive traditionally trained women healers out of the profession. Only very few women were admitted to university medical schools; Francesca Romano, who was licensed as a surgeon in 1321 by Duke Carl of Calabria, is the exception that proves the rule.[86] In Paris, the greatest center of learning in medieval Europe, the university faculty was extremely active in trying to suppress the practice of medicine by women. In 1322 a Jacqueline Felicie de Alemania was charged with practicing unlawfully, since she did not possess a university degree. The same prohibition was also applied to Johanna Belota and Margaret of Ypres, both well-known surgeons.[87]

In other regions of Europe, however, where the pressure from academic institutions was less intense, some female physicians enjoyed high prestige and flourishing practices. In Frankfurt the daughter of the city physician appears to have taken on his patients after his death; in 1394 she twice received payment from the city council for treating mercenary soldiers. In the next century city records show that Frankfurt had sixteen practicing women physicians, a number of whom were Jewish; they appear to have specialized largely in diseases of the eye and eye surgery. How many women physicians, healers, and barber-surgeons existed is impossible to estimate, since the great majority of unlicensed practitioners who were active until well into the nineteenth century were never officially registered. Records refer solely to physicians employed by municipal authorities or those who were expelled from a city or forbidden to practice, like the Jewish women in fifteenth-century Frankfurt. Nonetheless, official records do indicate the presence of women in all branches of medicine throughout the Middle Ages and beyond, even as army surgeons treating wounded soldiers—a small but ever-present minority.

One field of medicine that remained a female domain during the entire period, as has been mentioned, was gynecology and obstetrics. Tradition and prevailing morality forbid examination of women patients by men. When scholars and theologians did occupy themselves with the subject (chiefly in Italy, at the medical school in Salerno and elsewhere), it remained largely theoretical.[88] By contrast midwives (often referred to in contemporary documents as *matronae, obstetrices,* or *sages-femmes*) learned through practical experience, which they passed on to younger women who served a form of apprenticeship with them, just as in any other craft or trade. It appears that some exchange of information between these groups did take place toward the end of the period, as translations of Greek and Arabic texts became available. One indication is the appearance of references in thirteenth-century medical literature to cesarean operations, previously unknown in Europe. Another is the translation and growing use of the fundamental gynecological text known from the fifteenth century on as the *Liber Trotula*. Detailed information on these subjects is still lacking, however.[89]

The practice of midwifery grew increasingly professional and "scientific" as a result of cities' efforts to secure adequate obstetric care for their citizens. Many city records show that both physicians and midwives were employed by the community to provide health care for the inhabitants. They were freed from taxes and watch duty and supplied with free firewood—privileges that were sometimes extended to an entire family. In some large cities midwives employed by city councils received a regular salary quite early on; Nürnberg was paying 1 gulden quarterly in 1381, and Bruges reckoned their salary at 12 groschen per day for an estimated 270 working days in a year. In other cities, however, midwives were forced to charge for their services, a practice that led to inferior or nonexistent care for poor women. Abuses offered city councils the opportunity to regulate the profession with increasing severity, and written codes specified the conditions and qualifications for practicing midwifery. By the late Middle Ages virtually every city in Europe had such a set of regulations, not only prescribing training and qualifications but also making midwives agents of public morality by requiring them to report all illegitimate births and suspected cases of infanticide.[90]

Women in Crafts

The great majority of urban working women undoubtedly were employed in some branch of the craft industry, in a wide range of tasks and responsibilities. While many were participants in a family enterprise, others were independent producers, members of guilds, or wage-earning employees. Women dominated certain crafts, particularly those related to cloth and clothing production; they carded and spun wool, prepared flax, and worked as tailors, furriers, bag- and belt-makers, and gold spinners and embroiderers. Women in the last-named trade occasionally formed their own all-female guilds, as in Paris and Cologne.[91]

One of the oldest guild ordinances to grant men and women equal rights is that of the furriers of Basel, from the year 1226. Once accepted as members, women were permitted to work, buy, and sell under the same conditions as men. The same holds true for the later German furriers' guilds in Cologne, Frankfurt, Regensburg, Lübeck, and Quedlinburg.[92] With some few exceptions a similar situation prevailed in the clothing trades throughout central Europe in the late Middle Ages.

A further area in which women were especially active was food production: baking, the butcher's trade, fresh-water fishing, oil-making, and vegetable gardening. After the cloth and clothing trade, the craft most frequently practiced by women was beer-brewing, despite the physical demands involved. They are also to be found in other physically demanding trades; in addition to washing and bleaching, which has traditionally been considered women's work, women worked in fields that today are more likely to be considered "typically male," such as metalworking and the construction trade.[93]

In the years 1439 to 1477 there existed in the parish of Saint Sebaldus in Nürnberg nine female coppersmiths, seven brass workers, one cutler, one thimble-maker, one wiredrawer, three tin-smiths, a drawing-compass-maker, and six jug-makers. The situation was similar in other large cities like Cologne and Frankfurt. In the building trade women appear in Basel as members of the early guilds of masons, plasterers, and carpenters, although it seems likely that most of them were included as wives or relatives of male masters, rather than as masters in their own right. They assisted in mixing mortar, roofing, and installing glass, and were recruited as day laborers, because their wages were lower than men's. Toward the end of the fifteenth century women laborers at building sites in Würzburg earned an average of 7.7 pence per day, while men earned 11.6 pence. Their numbers were correspondingly higher: in the period between 1428 and 1524 statistics show 2,500 women workers as opposed to only 750 men.[94] Here, however, women were excluded from guilds and normal apprenticeships.

In many other crafts women could be admitted to guilds and open their own workshops; many were wives or widows of male craftsmen, but single women appear as well. Normally they were required to serve the usual apprenticeship of several years. As guild members they then worked under the same conditions as their male colleagues, with the same rights but also the same restrictions and communal obligations, such as night-watch and military duty. In the last case a woman with her own workshop was required to supply a journeyman or pay a fee in lieu of service.

A significant number of female masters are to be found in some crafts—above all the luxury field of silk and gold embroidery within the textile trade—but the majority of women held dependent positions, as female journeymen or wage earners. There were also a large number of maidservants, who either divided their time between household duties and workshop or, in some cases, could be hired directly by the master craftsman for certain tasks.

In addition many women worked outside the guild system in unregulated professions, such as the gold-spinners of Nürnberg, who do not appear in official records until 1526 and had previously worked without any system of regulation. In Strasbourg the large number of female wool-weavers operating outside the organized weavers' guild were the subject of repeated protests to the city council by the (male) guild members. The male weavers demanded that women either stop competing or buy into the guild and pay dues, something many of them could not afford to do. A later regulation kept the women's workshops small and uncompetitive by forbidding them to hire apprentices. These strategies were successful in driving women out of the city or into other trades; by 1500 women in the wool-weaving trade had virtually disappeared from Strasbourg records.

Women fought against exclusion from other trades as well, but it was often a losing battle. In the sixteenth century the women bag-makers of Nürnberg successfully protested an ordinance of 1530 that deprived them of the right to employ maids in their workshops, but their victory was only temporary. In 1540 a new ordinance allowed only those women to practice the trade who had undergone a regular apprenticeship, while at the same time forbidding all further training of women or the employment of untrained maids. With this stroke the female competition was condemned to extinction within a short time.

One major cause of such harsh competition probably was the amount of money at stake. Masters of a guild craft, both male and female, could earn a great deal. In Regensburg the unmarried daughter of a wool-weaver, Cecilie Wollerin, carried on her father's business and left a huge fortune in her will in 1341. The competition between various interest groups raged all the more fiercely, especially when times were hard. Journeymen played a key role in these battles; since female maids and apprentices earned a third less on average, the men fought successfully to have them excluded from virtually all guilds by the end of the Middle Ages.

Even female family members assisting in a family enterprise

came under increasing attack. In Strasbourg in 1566 journeymen protested that a belt-maker was employing his two daughters in his workshop. His employees cited the traditional right that said a journeyman could not be required to work alongside a woman. When the master continued to allow his daughters to work, all the journeymen belt-makers in the city laid down their work in protest. The matter finally came before the city diet held at Augsburg, and the master belt-maker lost: his daughters had to stop working.

No More Working Women?

"No female may lawfully practice a trade, even if she should understand it as well as a man." This sentence from Adrian Beier's 1688 book on craft laws appears to show that medieval developments ultimately led to the complete exclusion of women from crafts and trades.[95]

Much does indeed point to a growing hostility toward women and the suppression of independent female-led workshops near the end of the Middle Ages, particularly in guild ordinances. The trend can be observed in conflicts that began at different levels as early as the start of the fifteenth century: between journeymen and female apprentices, between trained artisans and untrained women day laborers and maids, and between master craftsmen in guilds and women competitors outside them. By the end of the sixteenth century men dominated the previously all-female guild of silk-workers in Cologne. In Rochlitz and Leipzig women were excluded from the weaving trade by the middle of the fifteenth century. From the sixteenth century on women disappear from the wool and linen cloth production of Strasbourg, and many other such examples could be cited.[96]

This observation has led many historians to conclude that the late Middle Ages saw the beginning of a process of "women's exclusion from professional life" that led more or less directly to female dependency and the confinement to the domestic sphere typical of the nineteenth and early twentieth centuries. This interpretation overlooks a number of factors, however, such as the fact that for women merchants engaged in both local and long-distance trade the decisive phase of exclusion occurred not in the fifteenth and sixteenth centuries, but—if it took place at all—in the thirteenth and early fourteenth centuries. For example, the ordinance for fish merchants in Nürnberg, passed in 1300, permitted a woman to run a stand only temporarily, in her husband's absence.[97]

The "exclusion theory" also overlooks the fact that guilds were not the only source of work for women, particularly at the beginning of the modern era. Many women had always worked as spinners, weavers, and seamstresses outside of organized guilds. The sixteenth-century economic developments merely increased a trend that had begun in the late Middle Ages.[98]

The discovery of the New World and the sea route to India opened up new markets and altered economic patterns in Europe, as trading centers shifted from central Europe to coastal nations. High costs promoted the development of cottage industries at the expense of the guilds, which reacted by closing ranks and forbidding the use of new production techniques. Increasingly women were forced into dependent positions as day laborers or cottage producers, a tendency demonstrated in classic form in the textile industry. Fewer and fewer women could maintain themselves as weavers in urban guilds, while more women in rural areas took up spinning at home as suppliers for large workshops.[99] The spinning of flax, cotton, and wool was transferred systematically to cottage production, since a weaver needed up to fifteen spinners to supply him, depending on the type of thread or yarn and the quality of the material. Since spinners in the cities could not meet the demand, this created new work opportunities for women, but only in the country. Urban women were the victims of this process of economic transformation, largely as a result of their weak social and political position.[100] While some opportunities for married women to pursue a profession and contribute to the family income continued to exist until the beginning of the modern era, single women now were often in a more advantageous position. The new conditions favoring larger manufacturers created a demand for a more flexible and mobile work force, and the family duties of wives and mothers came to stand as a larger hindrance to other kinds of work.[101]

The numbers of independent master craftswomen declined sharply, and in other fields where education or apprenticeships were required—such as the developing bureaucracies of cities or principalities, teaching, and health care—women were increasingly disadvantaged. Their education was limited more and more to domestic matters, and they were excluded from other types of training.

"A girl is destined to marry, and no one can say who her future husband will be," wrote Adrian Beier in the late seventeenth century. "But a girl trained to make shoes is of no use to a smith."[102] With this he summarized a trend that, by excluding women from guild crafts and the newer professions, darkened the prospects for women's work in the early modern era. The role of women was to become limited to "helpmeet" or assistant, if not for a husband then for another male employer. The limited opportunities for professional and social independence present in medieval cities were being choked off by new economic and political developments.

The Status of Single Women: Emancipation or Marginalization?

Although the importance of family ties and marriage was increasing by the end of the Middle Ages, the number of unmarried citizens in urban centers was considerable. In the early fourteenth century only 32.8 percent of the adult population of Basel was married; in Ypres the figure was 34.6 percent, in Freiburg 38.7, and in Dresden 50 percent at most. The figures tended to be higher in rural areas, up to 55 percent during the period of the Black Death.[103] Part of the discrepancy can be accounted for by the fact that convents and monasteries tended to be located in cities in the later Middle Ages.

Although more men than women remained unmarried, many women spent a part or all of their life alone, including the large numbers who lived in religious communities. In central Europe and England especially women could support themselves as day laborers and small traders in the work force, as long as they were strong and possessed of some skill. When, for example, Elisabeth of Thuringia left her court on the Marburg behind her and moved down to the town to lead a life of pious poverty, she took up wool spinning, a task that in the eyes of her maids was coarse and badly underpaid.[104]

Such preparatory or ancillary tasks in the production of textiles were performed chiefly by unmarried women—reflected in the modern meaning of the English word "spinster"—since they were rarely encompassed by guild ordinances and most girls learned the necessary skills at home. While such spinsters were legally and economically independent, they usually lived in poverty. Male journeymen could earn a decent living with their hands within the guild system, but women left to fend for themselves could rarely do more than keep body and soul together.[105] Many turned to more lucrative sidelines like theft and receiving stolen goods. Particularly those with young children to support were often prepared to break the law to put food on the table. Court records show that they were caught and tried on occasion, yet their poverty was so notorious that judges frequently turned a blind eye or imposed lenient sentences.[106]

More common than thievery or begging, however, was prostitution. Unmarried servant girls and young widows were objects of public suspicion—and sometimes persecution—if they were obviously poor and helpless. The thirteenth-century folk preacher Humbert de Romans warned the "poor women in the cities" against sorcery, gullibility, and contentiousness—all "sins" to which the desperately poor were liable—but above all against immorality, for poverty and unchastity often went hand in hand.[107] Such preaching against immorality did not spring from clerics' overheated imaginations or hostility to women, but was prompted by stark social realities. Prostitution in the late Middle Ages was not only a profitable line for brothel owners and city fathers, but a principal survival technique for the poorest women.

From Brothel to Convent?

There were distinctions between the "occasional" prostitution of needy women and the official houses that existed in many cities. The latter were maintained throughout the fourteenth and fifteenth centuries to "service" the large population of unmarried craft journeymen found in every urban center. Concerned city fathers strove to oversee and regulate the profession to prevent its falling entirely into the hands of criminals. They were as aware of the links between poverty, prostitution, and criminality as the women who tried to sell themselves in taverns and on the street.[108]

The "protection" supposedly accorded to professional prostitutes in Germany, at least (in France many brothels were organized almost like religious communities with an "abbess" at their head), was more than offset by the power and greed of the brothel proprietors, who obtained concessions from the city fathers. Low earnings, high expenses for food, lodging, and above all for the clothes and jewelry to make themselves attractive to customers meant that even the organized prostitutes remained poor. Many slipped so far into debt that they became virtual slaves or serfs of the brothel owners, a practice that though officially forbidden was nonetheless common. The occasional prostitutes, on the other hand, lacked even their minimal protection against violent or dishonest customers.

If a poor woman became unwilling or unable to continue earning a living as a prostitute—usually because she was too old—begging or procuring remained as last resorts. Earlier departure was usually impossible because of debts, and her position as social outcast made marriage extremely unlikely. Some convents were willing to take in repentant sinners, such as Adelheid of Thermannskirchen, who was so moved by a sermon of Berthold of Regensburg that she entered a religious community there in the mid-thirteenth century. In 1198 Pope Innocent III declared it a meritorious deed to marry a prostitute and help her give up a life of sin. In the knowledge that few women could escape prostitution except through marriage, charitable institutions such as the one in Halle were founded to encourage "pious journeymen" to "take a poor sinner to wife" out of love of God. In Vienna in 1384 three citizens founded a house to accept "poor freewomen who seek to renounce their public sinful life and mend their ways." The popular religious movements of the early thirteenth century had already prompted the founding of the Magdalene orders, in whose communities repentant sinners, prostitutes in particular, were to be aided in embarking on a better life. All late medieval popes encouraged such efforts, and even communities not associated with the order who took in former prostitutes received grants from the highest sources.[109]

The Magdalene house in Vienna, known as the House of Souls, was particularly well known; it was organized somewhat like a convent but did not require vows of its residents. Some of the women who sought protection from a life of prostitution here left it as the wives of respected citizens. Nonetheless, all these institutions could rescue only a small percentage of women from the "sin of unchastity"; in general, the halfhearted efforts of Church and city leaders made little headway against increasing prostitution in medieval cities. Even in rural areas secret prostitution was on the rise in regions experiencing social chaos and economic decline, such as France during the Hundred Years' War, when many young single and widowed women struggled to survive.

Among the specific dangers of life for women on their own there numbered not only dismal economic prospects but also the insecurity of their social status in a male world. The biography of Saint Odilia (died circa 1220) reveals typical perils. Widowed at a young age after a short marriage, she struggled to provide for herself and her young son in the town of Liège. She accepted the alms and counsel offered by a supposedly holy man, a priest, who remained well-disposed toward her, however, only as long as she accepted his advances. When she rebuffed him, he demanded repayment of his loans, "with compound interest," according to her biographer, and only with divine aid was the virtuous widow able to escape his clutches.[110] Women in other places might fare even worse, as is revealed by records of episcopal courts in northern France, which show that young widows in particular were considered "free game" by the young men of their villages. Gangs would set out at night to demonstrate how urgently such women needed a male protector, by breaking into their houses and raping and mistreating them. (It was the women who appear as defendants in these court cases, accused of immorality!)[111] Historians have labeled such group rapes and "charivaris" as "initiation rites," a cynical but accurate term, it would seem, since the aim was to show women living alone how much preferable even the worst marriage would be.

Freedom in Widowhood?

From the thirteenth century on, widows became increasingly freed from guardianship by either their own or their husband's family; upon the husband's death they lost their guardian, at least in formal legal terms. In reality they had gained little freedom, for they fell under newer legal norms or traditional rituals of censure and punishment. The decision to enter into a new marriage, in particular, was one their male relatives liked to control. Widows of the late medieval aristocracy had far more say in the matter than young girls, yet even this often amounted merely to a choice between two or three candidates proposed by the family. Remaining unmarried was extremely difficult for a widow of marriageable age, especially if she possessed land or a fortune.

The poverty of single urban women just described suggests that for most women spinsterhood or widowhood was not a particularly desirable state, and the fate of the widows convicted of immorality by the episcopal court in northern France shows the risks incurred by those who did not place themselves once again under the guardianship and protection of a husband as soon as possible. The "freedom of maiden and widow to serve their king" could be found only behind convent walls for the most part, and was accessible only to those with the means to buy entry into the rather exclusive communities of Benedictine, Cistercian, and later Dominican nuns. Poor women could hope to enter them only as lay sisters, that is to say, as servants. Such a step brought them no increase in personal freedom, for they lived at the beck and call of the religious sisters, noblewomen accustomed to giving orders.

While wealthy widows of high social standing had excellent chances for remarriage, many of them preferred the "chaste widowhood" propagated and favored by Church doctrines. This wish was frequently opposed by relatives who regarded the donations demanded by convents upon acceptance of a high-ranking widow as a "squandering" of the family fortune. Yet from the thirteenth century on widows were granted an increasing measure of independence by the law, which allowed them to dispose of the property from their dowries and husbands' wills as they themselves saw fit; they needed a male representative—who now tended to be a trained attorney—only for lawsuits and preparation of official documents. Thus widows now served as guardians of their children, rather than falling under their sons' guardianship as formerly. Even in regions where traditional customs prevailed, such as the area around Lyons, widows were more and more often made the beneficiaries of their husbands' wills with full powers.[112] Women's contribution to the family economy and the growing importance of wives for a family workshop or farm found recognition here and led to a noticeable decline in the older laws.[113]

These developments were finally included in the ordinances of urban guilds, many of which explicitly allowed widows to inherit and assume control of an enterprise, at least during the thirteenth and fourteenth centuries. Since such workshops could not continue to function in the same way after the husband's death, however, the ordinances also prescribed that a "masterless" household had to be supplemented by the best available journeyman as soon as possible. The male-oriented guild thus presumed the same rights as noblemen to press widows into remarriage, so that they would once again assume their proper sphere as "helpmeets."

Many widows of artisans may have been prompted to remarry

out of self-interest; the threatened loss of their economic and social position may have been more effective than any paragraph of a guild's official regulations. Nevertheless, we still find cases documented in late medieval sources of women who looked forward to widowhood and experienced it as a time of independence. One example is Humiliana, a central Italian middle-class woman married against her will around the year 1300 to an older man who kept her under extremely strict supervision. After a full day, Humiliana wove wool and linen cloth secretly at night, in order to sell it and give the proceeds to the poor. Her own possessions were too scanty and her husband's control of the family income too strict to allow her to pursue her religious and charitable inclinations. Her husband's early death thus appeared to her as a liberation, for now there was no one in the house to oppose her decisions and intimidate her with threats and beatings. Humiliana was free to invite as many paupers and beggars as she liked. But this period of freedom was short-lived; soon she was forced to give up her widows' rights—by deceitful means, as her biographer stresses—and return to her father's house. Had Humiliana been a "normal" woman, this dispossession might not have occurred. In the eyes of her relatives, however, her "senseless charity" required swift intervention.[114]

Elisabeth of Thuringia faced similar problems in her attempt to enjoy the freedom of widowhood. Only twenty years old and the mother of three children at the time of her husband's death, Elisabeth decided to leave court life and family behind and devote herself to a life of poverty, chastity, and good works. Her mother-in-law had taken a similar step only seven years before, asking that her inheritance be paid to her so she could retreat to a convent. Elisabeth had little interest in entering an already established institution and living a life of ease, however; she wanted to found a hospital in which she could play an active role in caring for the needy and sick, one that would continue to exist after her death. For this she needed land, so she treated her usufruct of certain properties as outright ownership and assigned them away: in her will she left to the hospital she had founded the land on which it stood. Her brothers-in-law appealed to ever higher instances, including the pope, but to no avail; Elisabeth had had the foresight to link her hospital to the powerful order of the Knights of Saint John of Jerusalem. The result was a protracted struggle between a family determined to retain its valuable property and the beneficiaries of her testament.[115]

Elisabeth's will was by no means an isolated instance; a considerable portion of all Church and monastic property stemmed from the donations of devout women. Small wonder, then, that codifiers of medieval laws sought to maintain the curtailment of widows' rights of inheritance or reintroduce guardianship by male relatives, in order to prevent dissipation of family wealth, legal conflicts, and the Church's acquisition of even more property.[116]

Even in nonaristocratic circles, where women tended to be given a larger share of responsibility for the family and its shop or farm, a certain mistrust remained that took the form of new restrictions in hard times. It is probably no coincidence that toward the end of the Middle Ages, just as considerable capital was coming to be concentrated in the hands of rich widows—especially in the prosperous trading centers of Italy—city governments began to concern themselves with the fate of widows and orphans, who previously had been left to the care of the Church. Now city fathers began to "protect" these more affluent citizens and restrict their freedom of action, as aristocrats had tended to do all along. In Strasbourg, for example, regulations that came into effect during the fifteenth century imposed limits on the amounts widows could donate or leave to charitable (ecclesiastical) institutions; as in the case of the widow Humiliana, the aim was to prevent families from losing their inheritance.[117]

Concern for the continuity of the existing social order and distribution of wealth gradually led to codification of laws restricting widows' rights. Male guardianship over them was reinstated in Italy during the fourteenth century, and the rest of Europe followed suit about a hundred and fifty years later. The image of women and relationship between the sexes acquired the stamp of a "bourgeois" ideology, according to which the virtuous wife and mother devoted herself to her family and lived in economic dependence on a "provider," taking no active share in his trade or profession.

Was There a Women's Movement in the Middle Ages?

Only one kind of institution existed where single and widowed women of the upper classes could be provided for in a manner befitting their rank: the convent. Missionaries in England and Ireland had founded the first communities that included men and women; on the Continent the first such foundations sprang up in the sixth century. During feudal times convents came into existence throughout Europe, as did some communities of canonesses, but they were few in number and largely limited to providing a home for unmarried and elderly members of the aristocracy. With the alteration of social and familial patterns from the twelfth century on, however, new needs arose, creating an enormously expanded population of potential nuns.

The Beguines

Beginning in the early thirteenth century, a large number of new religious orders and convents for women were founded, associated first with the Cistercians, and later the Franciscans and Dominicans (whose first convent of Prouille was located in southwestern France).[118] In addition a new, specifically female form of religious life was created, the Beguine communities, found chiefly in the textile and trading centers of Brabant, Flanders, and the German Rhineland. While the extent of all these new foundations and the number of women living in religious communities can only be estimated, some of the figures are extremely illuminating: around the year 1300 there were 74 Dominican convents in Germany alone (although the order had become active in Germany only fifty years earlier); they were overcrowded, as were the houses of the other new orders, the Franciscans (Poor Clares) and Cistercians. An even larger number of women lived in communities that did not require permanent vows. By the mid-fourteenth century there were 169 Beguine convents in Cologne alone, with approximately 1,170 residents. In Strasbourg there were 600 Beguines; it is estimated that up to 10 percent of the city's female population lived in some form of religious community.[119]

Earlier historians concluded that there must have been a large surplus of females in the population. The question of how they were to be provided for was, they thought, finally solved only by the foundation of a large number of religious communities, such as the Beguines, who supported themselves with needlework and care of the sick.[120] There is indeed much evidence for this theory, not least the difficult social and economic situation of unmarried women and widows I have described. During the thirteenth and fourteenth centuries it was the Beguines above all who provided housing and work for women from the poorer classes. Unlike the nuns who lived under the rules of their order, Beguine communities came under the supervision and jurisdiction of city authorities, just like hospitals, orphanages, and even brothels, and they were free to leave to marry. In Strasbourg only women and girls of good reputation were accepted; after a two-month trial period they adopted the simple gray dress of the order and took a limited vow of chastity and obedience. Those who possessed any personal fortune or property upon entrance retained full control over it, a further contrast to stricter orders and a source of some friction within the community.[121]

In addition to care of the sick for low wages, Beguines occasionally served as teachers in girls' and even boys' schools, as in Mainz, Cologne, and Lübeck. Toward the end of the medieval era some communities became more strictly organized and were assigned to hospitals as nurses; during outbreaks of the plague they could be required to perform hospital service by the city council, even against their will. Many Beguines also worked in the textile industry alongside their lay sisters. Particularly in the great textile centers of Flanders and the Rhineland their success was such that by the late Middle Ages they were frequently embroiled in quarrels with the guilds, which in most large cities attempted to stifle the unwelcome—and politically weaker—competition.

While all this evidence supports an economic theory for the rise of women's orders such as the Beguines—no doubt there was a surplus of women in the population that gave rise to social problems—it is not a complete explanation. Other historians such as Herbert Grundmann have noted the rise of a "religious women's movement" analogous to many other social and religious movements so characteristic of the intellectual life of the Middle Ages.[122]

Women Mystics: Heretics or Saints?

The twelfth and thirteenth centuries saw a profound and widespread religious unrest that drove many people to abandon traditional forms of piety in favor of new movements. Typically they banded together in small groups, which were frequently persecuted on suspicion of harboring heretical tendencies. North of the Alps these new practices were taken up above all by women, prompting the thirteenth-century German poet Ulrich von Lichtenstein to jest that suddenly all the ladies seemed possessed by a desire to dress like nuns, with rosary and veil, and take themselves off to church at all hours of the day and night, to the complete neglect of their knights and the cult of courtly love.[123]

The movement spread throughout the continent of Europe, flourishing particularly in the economically highly developed urban trading centers of Italy, France, Flanders, and the Rhineland. Its goals were manifold, but concentrated on a renewal of the ascetic and apostolic Christian values of poverty, humility, chastity, and an "active life" of work and service. Inspired by wandering preachers who assailed the materialism and social injustices of city life, groups of women gathered together to live from preaching and begging while practicing true Christian charity—a daring undertaking in a society that regarded unsupervised women in the streets more as whores than saints. Mounting pressure from both secular and religious authorities led to the condemnation and suppression of this kind of life, to which women such as Clara of Assisi, Elisabeth of Thuringia, and Mechthild of Magdeburg (circa 1250) had aspired.

As it became clear that the movement was gaining ground among the women of all social classes, the authorities devised a successful tactic of splitting and channeling it. They granted approval to those groups that had amassed enough property to found a permanent residence of their own. The others, which continued to live from begging in the streets and occasionally consisted of members of both sexes, were denounced as vagabonds and heretics. They were particularly suspect in the eyes of the authorities as they frequently preached outspokenly anticlerical doctrines. These "freethinking brothers and sisters" became the chief targets of the Inquisition in the fourteenth century. Many, like the fourteenth-century French mystic and freethinker Marguerite Porète, author of the treatise "Mirror of the Divine Soul," ended up being tried by the Inquisition and burned at the stake.[124]

Contemporaries were especially suspicious of the interest in theology displayed by many of these female communities; indeed the mystical texts produced and circulated among them—such as the verses of Hadewijch (around 1230), the autobiography of Beatrice of Nazareth, or the "Flowing Light of the Godhead" by Mechthild of Magdeburg (around 1250)—grew into a flowering of "women's culture" so unprecedented as to cause amazement even among the well-disposed.[125] The German Franciscan Lamprecht of Regensburg noted that "nowadays women express themselves on theological matters and appear to understand religious questions even better than competent men." He accounted for it as follows: "If a woman strives to lead a life pleasing to God, then her soft heart, inferior intellect, and weak will make her more swiftly inflamed, so that in her desire for God she grasps the wisdom of heaven better than a strong man ever could, whose hard character makes him less apt."[126]

Such an explanation does little justice to the intellectual gifts and theological education of women such as Marguerite von Porète, Hildegard of Bingen (died 1179), or Catherine of Siena, who declared their intention of presenting a new view of controversial theological issues. However, Saint Paul's dictum that women should be silent in the churches continued to prevail, forcing medieval women to follow the path of "mystical utterance." Hildegard of Bingen described herself as a "vessel of the Holy Spirit," an image that was taken up by later women mystics. It is not surprising that many of the faithful, confused by the schisms and political quarrels racking the Church before the Council of Constance (1414–1418), reacted favorably to their sincere fervor and claims to be the "instruments of God."

Throughout the later Middle Ages women wrote and spoke out on controversial issues, including political matters; Catherine of Siena and Birgitta of Sweden, who tried to end the Church schism, are the best known but by no means the only ones. Several women mystics in German-speaking regions not only published their visions and revelations but also were listened to when they addressed political and social conflicts; these included Margarethe Ebner of Switzerland and Christine Ebner of Nürnberg in the mid-fourteenth century. In Italy, in addition to Catherine of Siena, mystics such as Angela da Foligno and Clara a Cruce (died 1308) were active. Even in France, ravaged by the Hundred Years' War, women felt impelled to come to the defense of their country, the Church, and Christendom. Joan of Arc was only one of a number of women who achieved fame, or notoriety, in this respect. The Widow Rabastens in the southwest (circa 1350), and Jeanne-Marie de Maillé of Touraine (1331–1414) were nearly as unwelcome to the Inquisition as the Maid of Orleans.[127]

One indication of the significant role played by women in the religious and political life of the late Middle Ages is the number canonized, which reached a peak during this period. Nearly a quarter of all new saints were female, and a large percentage of these had been wives and mothers. Never before or since could women feel part of such a "feminized" faith, even though they naturally remained excluded from the priesthood and service at the altar.[128] Just as women clearly neglected to press for legal guaranties of their position in the work sphere, as Martha Howell has observed, so too did the women visionaries and mystics fail to use their newly acquired influence within the Church to secure institutional recognition.[129]

Although Birgitta of Sweden and Catherine of Siena achieved at least partial success for their political interests and theological ideas by pursuing a strategic policy of working behind the scenes under the protection of the papal curia and monastic orders, they were the exception. The majority of female "zealots" encountered increasing suspicion and mistrust as the fifteenth century wore on, and not only in theological circles. More and more of them were denounced as "false prophets," and many objects of general veneration, including Joan of Arc, were rejected as candidates for sainthood by Rome.[130] As the medieval period drew to a close, the first stirrings of the Reformation and its massive criticism of the Catholic Church's cult of sainthood reduced the influence women were able to have in the religious sphere. Scholarly knowledge of biblical texts and theological education began to outweigh piety and inspiration as qualifications, and the number of women revered or actually canonized dropped accordingly. By the seventeenth century women's spirituality, their "gentle hearts," "inferior intellect," and "weak will" had become targets of suspicion, as potentially influenced or even "penetrated" by the Devil. Acceptance of the mystics' ecstatic visions was replaced by the widespread persecution of witches.

Looking back at the manifold sources of information about women's daily lives in the late Middle Ages, we can see that it was a period of enormous change in many areas, including work, family life, and religion. It becomes clear that women were able to make gains against some of the patriarchal structures of their society, although these varied according to social class and region, and some were offset by new and negative developments toward the end of the period. Within the guild organizations of the cities and many legal codes, however, the relationship between the sexes appears less clearly discriminatory during this period than ever before.

The ongoing struggle is reflected in the polemics of Christine de Pisan, who defended her sex against an educational and religious tradition hostile to women in *The City of Ladies*,[131] but also in the increasing attacks aimed against the entire female sex by the male members of urban craft guilds, who gradually succeeded in excluding their unwelcome competitors. Gains and losses, acceptance and devaluation remain the two sides of the coin as the Middle Ages ended. The "querelle des femmes" remained the era's legacy to the modern period, which was never to die out even in the darkest days of witch-hunting.[132]

TRANSLATED FROM THE GERMAN BY
DEBORAH LUCAS SCHNEIDER

three

Vestiges
and Images of Women

New Appearances

When it comes to women, the presumptuous discourse of men cannot be taken as gospel. Nor can we correct the picture simply by examining how women reacted to men's ideas about them. The time has come to attempt a portrait of women in their own right, to round out our image by looking at objects representing women and at artifacts created or used by women. To do this we draw on techniques developed by archaeology and iconography.

Historians who approach the physical vestiges and artistic representations of women's lives with the methodological preconceptions of their own discipline are in danger of tripping themselves up. A new approach is needed. The plastic arts, for example, draw on folk traditions as well as high art, but artists frequently recast what they borrow from these sources in a formal language with its own vocabulary and syntax. The use of older models and formulas is as striking in art as the imitation and paraphrase of literary "authorities" in written texts, but the mode of transmission and transformation is unique. Anyone who studies images must face squarely the issue of innovation, the invention of novel iconographic motifs and formal structures. Aesthetic and iconographic choices do not immediately reflect, but in various ways do refer to, social and intellectual changes. The difficulty of interpretation lies in the delicate relation of figurative imagery to literary and intellectual representations and to reality, a difficulty that is compounded when the images are intended to be "realistic" or "naturalistic." What does it mean when women are portrayed in a new way, engaged in activities previously ignored by artists who suddenly depict them in attitudes never before represented? Are the artists or their audience seeing these things for the first time, or are they simply asserting that familiar things are now worthy of being illustrated? Why choose a flattering or unflattering color or an unusual composition that sets relations between people or things in a new light?

Medieval imagery covers a vast range. Choosing a limited and deliberately personal set of examples, Chiara Frugoni illustrates certain central questions of method and interpretation. One important issue is the role of women in the creation of particular objects and images. Until now the problem has aroused little interest among archaeologists, art historians, and iconographers. In fact, as Françoise Piponnier reminds us, archaeologists often neglect to note whether artifacts taken from a tomb accompanied the body of a male or female and show little interest in clues that might indicate the role of women in the production and use of familiar objects. Art historians and iconographers have said relatively little about works produced in the scriptoria of convents, about women's responses to representations of themselves, or about the significance of women's claiming authorship of their works.

Another important problem has to do with patronage and its influence on artistic choices. Earlier Paulette L'Hermite-Leclercq alluded to Christina of Markyate's personal psalter. It is interesting to think about the miniatures over which that holy woman meditated, especially the one in which she stands before Christ, apparently singled out as more important than the men who accompany her. It is plausible to assume that this image reflects and magnifies her womanly desires. Other evidence, rarely assembled convincingly in one place, might confirm this hypothesis if examined in the proper light (that of gender relations). That is what we shall attempt to do. Perhaps it will encourage others to delve deeper into this vast but as yet little explored territory.

C. K.-Z.

10

The World of Women

Françoise Piponnier

MEDIEVAL WRITINGS generally reflect men's image of women rather than the reality of women's activities, preoccupations, and aspirations. Painting and sculpture depicted two female stereotypes: the saint and the sinner. In the late Middle Ages, however, most profane images as well as many religious ones portrayed townswomen and even peasants in familiar settings and activities. Archaeological findings, uninfluenced by the prejudices of writers and artists, can shed light on many aspects of these realities: the nature and size of living quarters; the arrangement of the household; and the types of objects found in the home, objects that were all the more precious because they were rare and often costly. Whether used daily or reserved for special occasions, these objects were decorated in significant ways: some were symbolic, others precious, still others invested with preventive or therapeutic virtues. Traces of how these objects were used, found either on the objects themselves or in their vicinity, tell us a great deal about the repetitive, commonplace tasks that no one ever thought to record but that loomed large in the lives of women who went about their work quietly and attracted little notice from the men who produced most of the documentary and iconographic evidence.

Living Quarters and Work Areas

Physically weak and morally fragile, women in the Middle Ages were deemed to be in need of protection not only from others but also from themselves. Some belonged, by birth, to the "order" of warriors or to that of workers; others, by choice, joined the order of those who prayed. But all were subject to the scrutiny and guidance of the men of their order. The clerical order was the only one that cloistered its women away from the world.[1] Women of the warrior class were similarly subject to the surveillance and control of male clan members, but they were permitted to move about much more freely. In the third order, that of workers, which accounted for the vast majority of this strongly hierarchical society, the position of women varied widely and evolved as the Middle Ages progressed. There was little difference between the situations of peasants and artisans in the manorial economy. Serfs, men and women alike, were bound to their estates, within whose narrow confines they were obliged to live their lives and find their mates. With the emancipation of serfs and the growth of cities (which took place earlier in some regions than in others) greater mobility became possible, but this affected men more than women. The artisans who flocked to major construction sites, for example, were primarily male. Records of merchants participating in urban fairs and markets reveal that many were women, usually widows.[2] But men vastly outnumbered them and probably traveled greater distances. Emancipated female slaves, about whom a great deal of information can be found in Italian archives, remained close to where they had worked as slaves despite their lack of local roots.[3] Women at all levels of society enjoyed far less freedom of movement and action than men.

From the scanty and scattered sources available it is not easy to arrive at an accurate picture of what women did prior to the fourteenth century. If eleventh- and twelfth-century sculptures depicting the seasons of agricultural labor are accurate, farm work was a purely masculine activity.[4] But as the iconography of labor evolves and new art forms develop, we begin to see images of women engaged in various forms of field work, such as harvesting and haying. Although women were never shown with scythes, they were portrayed cutting wheat with sickles alongside men in works from northern Europe. In French and Italian art women were shown performing only the easier agricultural tasks: tossing hay with large wooden rakes and building haystacks with pitchforks; tying bundles of harvested crops; removing straw from the threshing ground with small pitchforks.[5] Through the study of skeletons archaeologists have been able to determine the relative stature of men and women in the same village: the women of Saint-Jean-Le-Froid in Rouergue were much thinner than their highly muscular male companions, who probably performed the more demanding physical chores.[6]

Women tended grapevines, which at the time grew in more northerly regions than they do now. The work included setting and staking vine shoots, thinning plants, and of course harvesting grapes. The number of pruning hooks and knives found in a single burned home in Burgundy tends to corroborate conclusions based on the iconographic evidence.[7] In Mediterranean regions women also harvested olives and fruits in the orchards planted around manor houses and villages. Whether picked by hand or gathered on large canvas sheets, the harvested fruit was collected in baskets, gathered skirts, or aprons and taken to a place where it could be pressed or put up as preserves. Manuscripts of relatively recent date contain images of women picking vegetables and various medicinal plants, occupations that surely predate the available evidence. One explanation for the delay in depicting women's activities probably is the influence of the clergy, which disliked any representation of women outside the usual moral stereotypes: saint or sinner.

At around the same time women began to be shown tending domestic animals: feeding pigs and chickens, tending and shearing sheep. They also did the milking, collecting milk in wooden pails or bowls. Skimming cream, churning butter, and making cheese were female duties. Like gardening, these activities were considered almost domestic chores because of their nature and proximity to the house. When the raising of livestock was carried on farther from home, it was considered man's work, as when hogs were taken to the woods to feed or when sheep were allowed to graze in the highlands. Men then took over the milking and the manufacture of cheese. If the testimony of the residents of Montaillou is accurate, women played only a marginal role in highland grazing.[8]

Images are useful for understanding the role of women, but taken out of context they can be misleading. The splendid miniatures that ornament the manuscripts of Christine de Pisan's utopian *City of Ladies* should not be taken as evidence that Parisian women engaged in iron work and masonry in the Middle Ages. Corroborating textual evidence is totally lacking for Paris or anywhere else in France. By contrast, as Claudia Opitz has pointed out, the documents do confirm that women in German cities engaged in a much wider variety of trades than did French women.

Guild regulations pertained chiefly to the most "noble" trades, those practiced by men, and to the work of "masters." Generally the only women allowed to engage in these trades were the widows of masters, and then only with the help of assistants well versed in the trade. Tax records (such as those for the Paris *taille,* or tallage) in which names are listed along with occupations enable us to identify a wide range of trades practiced by women. Only unmarried and widowed women are mentioned, however. What about married women? Were they excluded from independent occupations? Were they forbidden to help their husbands? It seems unlikely. The evidence suggests that artisans' wives played an important role in the sale of their products. Even if most women knew little about the tools and techniques of their husband's trade, they must have known something about the raw materials and finished products or guild regulations would not have allowed them to take over the business after their husbands died. In many trades women may have played at least an auxiliary role in the final phases of a job or when large or urgent orders had to be filled. The small fingerprints that archaeologists have found on certain vases do not prove that women and children actually turned pots, but they do show that women and children handled the pots prior to baking.

One craft remained the province of women, at least in part, throughout the Middle Ages: the production of textiles. The nature and location of this work varied with the period and the social class of the women involved. In the early Middle Ages women did the spinning, weaving, and preparation of raw materials in the women's quarters of the house under the supervision of the master's wife.[9] So much was known from documentary evidence. Archaeological research has shown that in the same period small buildings were erected to house vertical looms outside the family living quarters.[10] When the cloth industry later came to be concentrated in cities and horizontal looms came into wide use, the task of weaving wool apparently was taken out of the hands of women, who were assigned not the most unpleasant tasks, like degreasing and dyeing, but the easiest ones, like selection, carding, spinning, spooling, and threading.[11] In Italy, where silk work took on considerable importance in the twelfth and especially the thirteenth century, the growing of silkworms, preparation of cocoons, and spooling and milling of silk were entrusted to women and girls. This work was done outside the home, in workshops owned by entrepreneurs.[12]

Textiles were made of plant fibers as well as wool. Here too much of the work was done inside the home. The most common archaeological evidence includes not only terra-cotta spindle whorls but also spindles and distaffs.[13] Although not particularly valuable, these items sometimes figured in property inventories, along with fibers in various states of processing. The documents thus lend support to the countless images of women spinning at home or while tending sheep. Women of all classes of society were included, even the aristocracy, as is attested not only by miniatures but also by an inventory of one of the duke of Burgundy's castles, which mentions the duchess' distaff, no doubt an object of more symbolic than utilitarian importance.[14] Numerous images of decorated distaffs mounted on pedestals have survived, but distaffs usually were much simpler, little more than sticks to which the combed wool was attached and which peasant women often carried fastened to their belts. The spinning wheel, which was harder to transport than the distaff and spindle, came into use only much later, and then only in urban areas.

Sewing, according to some texts, was another female specialty. In the middle of the eleventh century the abbot of an important Alsatian abbey acknowledged that he could not do without the services of women, whose duties included "taking care of everyone's clothing."[15] By the fifteenth century, however, the tailor's trade in most cities had become a male province. The discovery of small scissors and thimbles, adapted to female hands, at various archaeological sites nevertheless proves that many women were skilled seamstresses, even in rural areas.[16] The romances portray noble ladies and damsels skilled in embroidery and in weaving girdles.[17] Archaeologists have found specimens of the frames used for this weaving, as well as their products. The technique, akin to braiding, was used to make girdles or sashes as well as to decorate clothing.

Images of knitting are much rarer, although thirteenth- and fourteenth-century portraits of Mary using five needles to knit the seamless tunic have survived from all parts of Europe, from northern Germany to the Iberian peninsula.[18] Mercers' inventories from fifteenth-century Dijon mention only small numbers of needles "for making socks," and the only knitted garments known from written documents and archaeological evidence are caps for adults and children, children's socks, and liturgical gloves.[19]

It is hard to say what proportion of the textile output was destined for the market rather than for domestic consumption. By the end of the Middle Ages domestic weaving had all but disappeared. Merchants offered wool and mixed fabrics in a range broad enough to meet the needs of all their customers. In rural as well as urban areas, however, people provided their own thread, made from plant fibers, to custom weavers, some of whom were women (a deduction based on evidence in certain Burgundian inventories).[20]

Woman's Work

Whatever a woman's status or fortune, her primary role was to take care of the family she belonged to or served. The care of family members involved a multitude of endlessly repeated tasks. Mothers, who gave birth at what was considered a "natural" rhythm, raised their children, either directly or, if they could afford it, with the aid of a nurse: feeding, bathing, and putting babies to sleep were constant chores. Certainly not all babies slept in cradles, found only in the homes of well-to-do townsfolk, or in the ornately painted and carved masterpieces reserved for the children of princes. Most of them probably shared a simple straw mattress on the floor with their parents, as in depictions of the Nativity.[21] Nevertheless, marks found in the excavation of an early medieval home in Brebières have been interpreted as traces left by the rocking of a cradle.[22]

The mother (or wet nurse) fed the newborn either from her breast or from a bottle made at first of horn and later of terracotta or glass. She also prepared meals for family members. To gain a better idea of what this entailed we must avail ourselves of the findings of archaeological research, which tell us how homes were arranged and furnished and what kinds of utensils (wood, terra-cotta, and metal) were used. Inventories sometimes mention stocks of fuel. From images and written documents (such as those stemming from the investigation of heresy in the Catharist village of Montaillou) we know that women and children too young to work in the fields were responsible for gathering fallen wood.[23]

Laying and maintaining the fire were jobs reserved for the women of the house.[24] At the end of the Middle Ages most rural houses and the poorest urban dwellings still had chimneyless open hearths of packed earth.[25] Fireplaces first appeared in monasteries and castles; from there they made their way into smaller aristocratic and bourgeois dwellings. Iron tripods were widely used, and pothooks, though found only in the homes of wealthier peasants, adorned all but the poorest urban dwellings. Iron and bronze frying pans and caldrons were found almost everywhere, but their number and size depended on the family's wealth. Ceramic cookware was in daily use in even the wealthiest homes; it was considered preferable to metal for the preparation of soup. In many kitchens there was a special bronze pot for making pap for the children. More specialized utensils for preparing pies, pâtés, and waffles and for grilling meat and fish are mentioned in inventories of well-to-do urban dwellings.[26]

Fetching the water needed for cooking vegetables as well as for drinking was woman's work. The type of vessel used depended on the region and on the proximity of the well or spring to the home. In Mediterranean regions ceramic pots of various sizes were used for collecting and storing water. Farther north, in Burgundy for example, smaller jugs were used, and inventories refer to iron-banded pails from which drinking water was ladled out.

Despite the growth of the baker's trade and, in cities such as Paris, the importation of bread baked elsewhere, bread-making was largely a woman's chore.[27] Although the development first of the watermill and later of the windmill made it unnecessary for women to mill flour by hand, they still had to run back and forth to the flour mill. Abelard did not think it unusual for an abbey of monks to employ "sisters" to knead dough and bake bread.[28] In the countryside peasants were obliged to pay the lord for the privilege of milling their flour. In the cities women took their bread to be baked in public ovens and bakeshops. The iconography amply demonstrates that women everywhere bore the responsibility of supplying the family with bread.

Meals usually were served by women. We have more images of aristocratic feasts than of family dining in urban and peasant homes. Did everyone eat at the same time? According to testimony taken by the Inquisition, heretics who visited Montaillou were offered meals at which only adult males sat at the table; the mistress of the house and her daughters served, and younger sons ate by the fire.[29] But there must have been regional variations in table manners and settings. Indeed, the table itself, which was in wide use in southern Europe (and not only in princely courts[30]), is rarely mentioned in accounts of common people's dining in fourteenth-century Burgundy. A smaller piece of furniture called a "buffet for eating," something like a bedside table, was enough to hold the few dishes that a poor home was likely to possess.

While table settings of decorated ceramics ranging in size from large platters to individual bowls were not uncommon in Mediterranean regions as early as the thirteenth century, only rare imported specimens were known in northern Europe at that time. Throughout the Middle Ages northerners continued to produce and use wooden vessels, plates, cutting boards, bowls of all sizes, turned goblets, and even, in Germanic and Slavic regions, drinking cups made of tiny staves.[31] In France the use of tin filtered down as far as the peasantry in the fourteenth century, and dozens of tin plates, pots, bowls, and sauce boats could be found in bourgeois homes. The use of silver was quite limited.[32] Glass began to be used in the Mediterranean region in the thirteenth century and later spread to the north, where it vied with stoneware vessels. Excavations at the site of the village of Dracy in Burgundy have shown that glass was virtually unknown there in the second half of the fourteenth century.

Cleaning all these items was of course a job for women, but we do not know how or where the job was done or what equipment was used. Nor do we have much knowledge of other cleaning chores such as bathing and washing clothes. To men these must have seemed so familiar and yet so strange that they rarely wrote about them. Even the fourteenth-century Parisian bourgeois who wrote a treatise on household maintenance for the edification of his young wife had little to say about cleaning, other than some advice about how to get rid of fleas and other troublesome insects.[33] Romances, court documents, estate inventories, and works of art contribute little to our understanding, even if the images they contain are sometimes quite vivid. Women in Montaillou and elsewhere picked lice from their husbands and children.[34] In one romance a nobleman enters the damsels' chamber and removes his shirt so that they may scratch him.[35] Out came brushes like small brooms and combs with two rows of teeth made of wood, bone, or ivory (items often found by archaeologists). In the cities public bathhouses and private baths helped the wealthy to keep clean, as did the wearing of good linen and the ministrations of the females of the household—wife, daughters, and servants. But among the urban poor, who had at best a bucket to bathe in and a basin for washing face and hands, and in peasant homes, where towels were a rarity, it is unlikely that women spent much time on grooming themselves or other family members.[36]

It was easy to care for linen, which came into wide use much earlier than scholars once believed. Although washtubs, often made of stone, are regularly mentioned in inventories of Dijon households from the fourteenth and fifteenth centuries, few images exist. The washing technique, which made use of ashes from the fireplace, was probably much like that used in rural France as late as this century. Inventories and miniatures attest to the existence of small brushes used for removing dust from woolen clothes, but we can only speculate as to procedures for the removal of stains and other cleansing techniques.

Cleaning was the only part of household maintenance that fell within the province of women. Structural repairs to walls, roofs, and doors were not the mistress' responsibility. Nor was she responsible for the upkeep of areas in which the men of the house worked: stables, barns, workshops. The nature of household cleaning of course varied greatly depending on the type of house and the availability of servants, but the basic tools were quite simple: brooms and rags.

The Domestic Setting

Even women who had to earn their living or help defray the family budget by working at home spent most of their time in what was widely agreed to be their natural role: taking care of the family to which they belonged by birth, marriage, or servitude. This involved mainly work at home or in the immediate vicinity. Of course different people lived in homes of different sizes and types, depending on the period, the region, and the social class. Archaeological research throughout Europe has extended our knowledge of medieval housing beyond the surviving castles and houses of the well-to-do, many of which were subject to later alterations. By excavating villages, poor urban districts, and the fortified houses of the minor nobility, archaeologists have taught us a great deal about the relatively modest homes in which most families lived.

For a long time the most common type of home, particularly in northern Europe, had cob walls and was built on pillars. Interior space was reasonably spacious and functionally differentiated. Gradually stone and brick replaced wood, first in southern regions, then through much of the Continent. Although it was still possible, as late as the thirteenth century, for nosy villagers in Montaillou to lift the corner of a neighbor's roof and spy on what was going on inside, medieval housing in general was not as wretched as has often been portrayed.[37] Archaeological research has demolished the caricature of the medieval home as a hovel in which animals and humans lived crowded together under one roof.

Although there are numerous studies of medieval housing, few scholars have ventured to cross the threshold and describe how people lived inside.[38] When dealing with complex structures such as castles, town houses, and multistory rural dwellings, the physical evidence is often difficult to interpret. Yet certain texts describe interiors in enough detail that we can say with confidence what the women's quarters were like. Consider, for example, Lambert of Ardres's celebrated description of the wooden castle built on a motte by the lord of Ardres, Arnulf II.[39] The main building contained storage rooms, bedrooms, attics, and cellars, in the center of which stood the bedroom of "the lord and his wife," flanked by two rooms whose character was strongly feminine: a room for female servants and a dormitory for children. A recess in the master bedroom in which the fire was laid was used for the care of the sick and the suckling of infants, which meant that it was under the jurisdiction of the lady and her attendants.

Even in dwellings where space was not so clearly differentiated, it is sometimes possible to determine how different parts of the structure were used by examining the location of artifacts in homes destroyed by fire (thus ensuring that everyday objects remained in the places where they were normally used or stored). In the fortified Sicilian village of Brucato,[40] as well as in the Burgundian wine-growing village of Dracy,[41] the typical house contained two rooms, one opening directly onto a street or courtyard, the other accessible only through the first.

In Sicily the first room appears to have been used as a kitchen and dining room. Often there were two hearths, the smaller one at floor level, the other higher up, either a bread oven or a brick hearth for baking biscuits. The utensils (or fragments) found nearby, including tripods, frying pans, sieves, metal carving knives, and earthenware pots and biscuit molds, allow us to imagine the cook at work, bending down to peer into the bread oven or to stir a pot boiling over the lower hearth. Discarded bones found in a corner of the room opposite the hearth suggest that this was where meals were eaten. The kitchen also contained various dishes, pots, and crockery. Since maintaining the fire, cooking meals, and fetching water were women's chores, this kitchen–dining room had a markedly feminine character, as is corroborated by the presence of spindle whorls and thimbles as well as buttons and other fasteners generally associated with women's clothing. Apparently there was no door into the second room, which was probably fairly dark. Not only humans but also pack animals slept in this room at night, and dogs and cats roamed about the house, gnawing at bones that fell from the table. Some homes contained stone benches or additional hearths near the doorway. The second room also served as a storage shed, as shown by the presence of large chests, earthenware crocks, stocks of grain, and tools.

The Burgundian wine-grower's house, which dates from about the same period, was quite similar. It had only one hearth, at floor level, but it was carefully constructed of beaten earth, sometimes edged with a row of stones stood on end. A simple bed (revealed by the presence of burnt cloth) stood in a corner opposite the fire. In the Burgundian house the second room was used primarily as a storeroom. Grains and nuts were kept in chests, while barrels, crocks, pitchers, and cups were obviously used for storing and drinking wine. The presence of an interior threshold, a lock, and iron hinges and fixtures indicates that there was a clear separation between the living room and storeroom. Vestiges of farm implements were also found in this room, along with property to which the family attached particular value: purses, wedding rings, sets of keys. Objects commonly used by the women of the house were kept near the door: thimbles, hemp combs, and a variety of cookware.

Furniture rarely turns up in archaeological excavations except where the ground is damp or under water. Fortunately we have inventories of the contents of both urban and rural dwellings for the later centuries of the Middle Ages. While the poor often had to settle for a straw mattress on the floor, beds with curtains were fairly common in wealthier homes. Bedspreads were dyed and sometimes lined with fur. Revolving benches, which allowed people to sit either facing the fireplace or with backs toward the heat, were still rare (as were fireplaces), but chairs, backless benches, and stools were in wide use. Tables, mostly of the two-piece trestle variety, were common in the cities but not yet found in most peasant homes, which made do with "buffets" just large enough to hold a bowl and tankard. One-piece tables seem to have been more prevalent in Mediterranean regions than in northern France. The most common storage container was the chest, often plain though sometimes painted or carved. It was used for storing grains and other foods, dishes, linen, clothing, tools, scales, and raw materials. Only the wealthiest townsfolk owned cabinets for displaying their tinware and silver.

Beyond the Walls

Women frequently were obliged to leave home in the course of their daily activities. Wood had to be fetched for the fire, water for domestic needs. Water was available inside the home only in urban dwellings that incorporated an internal well. Elsewhere repeated trips to springs or fountains were necessary. Women and children often made these trips together, carrying crocks, dishes, pots, or laundry. Tending the garden also meant spending a great deal of time outdoors. Besides planting, chores included staking shoots, fertilizing the soil with household waste and ash (as excavation has shown), and harvesting mature plants.

The residents of Montaillou spent part of their day in streets abandoned to women and children while the men went off to work in the fields.[42] Archaeological research in a number of French villages has shown that homes had yards, often shared by several dwellings, thus attesting to a need for an intermediate space between the "dark and smoky" interior of the home and the public street.[43] Here women could socialize while keeping an eye on the fire, the children, and the house. Things were much the same in the fortified Sicilian village of Brucato. Houses there opened directly onto the street, where, archaeologists tell us, nets were dried and mended. Men were naturally a more noticeable and constant presence in such settlements, as was generally true of urban areas.

Montaillou is a special case because part of its male population left during the summer months. But most of the peasant's work was done outside the home and even outside the village.[44] Hence the male dominion over the peasant household was only part-time. Many inhabitants of late medieval towns were farmers or wine growers whose lives were much the same as those of peasants. Where there were large numbers of merchants and other men who worked at home in their "studies," there was less contrast between the male and female parts of the home and less gender differentiation in urban life generally.

TRANSLATED FROM THE FRENCH BY ARTHUR GOLDHAMMER

11

The Imagined Woman

Chiara Frugoni

The Church's Point of View

IN GENESIS THE CURSE of bearing children is in-
flicted on Eve alone. The burden of carnal union
thus became woman's to bear: Eve's descendants
would be wives and mothers. In a miniature of the
Moûtier-Grandval Bible (circa 840), the story from
Creation to Fall is told in a sequence of images,
with Eve's negative role heavily underscored (fig.
1).[1] By contrast, the sweat on Adam's forehead as
he works the land can be interpreted as a sign of
joy: "And also that every man should eat and
drink, and enjoy the good of all his labor, it is the
gift of God" (Eccles. 3:13). Labor was one way to
open the closed doors of paradise.

Marriage, Saint Jerome stressed, is linked to
the human condition after the Fall. Virginity belonged to a heavenly sphere which only the first
progenitors were allowed to enjoy and to which
every Christian, in particular every Christian
woman, should aim to return. Eve, the active sinner, was compared and contrasted to the Virgin
Mary, who passively accepted becoming a vehicle
of redemption. As an anonymous rhyme dating
probably to the ninth century explained, the *Ave*
pronounced by the Angel of Annunciation, was a
palindrome of *Eva*.[2]

Mary, who gave birth while still a virgin, was
the only woman whose maternity could be praised

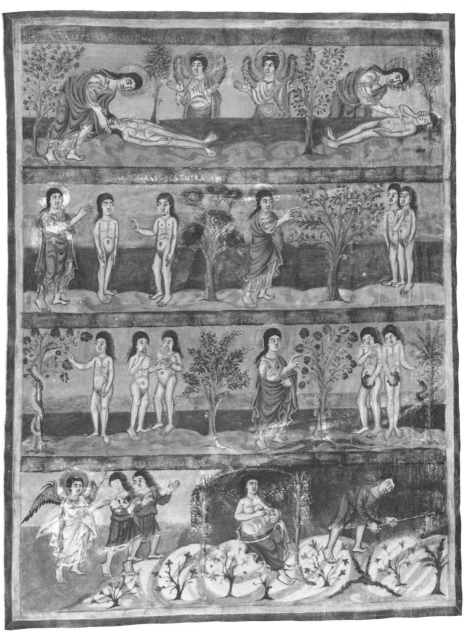

1. *The Story of Adam and Eve,* circa 840. London, British Library.

337

2. *Speculum virginum,* The
Three States, twelfth
century. Vatican City,
Biblioteca Apostolica
Vaticana.

precisely because her body had never experienced
matrimonial union. She was a role model for all
women, the model being one which placed no
value on a woman's body and its natural functions.
Of the three conditions into which the Church di-

vided humanity—married, widowed, or virgin— the last-named predictably enjoyed pride of place. The evangelical parable of the seed that, according to the good ground on which it fell, yielded one hundred, sixty, or thirty new plants (Matt. 13:4– 9) was applied by Saint Ambrose to virgins (one hundred times) and by Saint Jerome to all three conditions (the married state yielded least) in a comparison that had an extraordinary following.[3]

A twelfth-century poem, the *Speculum virginum,* analyzed this parable in minute detail, painting a picture filled with biblical and profane examples in which the three states are positioned in rising order of perfection.[4] In a miniature illustrating the poem in a twelfth-century manuscript (fig. 2), the three states are represented in little cameos formed of the inward-turning branches of a family tree whose roots rest on Adam and Eve, the prime example of *ordo coniugatorum.* The other married couples in the lower section of the tree are Noah, Abraham, and Isaac with their unnamed wives, and Zachariah with Elizabeth; the middle area is occupied by widows, the upper echelons by virgins. At the top of the tree is a bust of Christ. The rise to perfection suggested by the tree leads us, in Saint Jerome's words, "to free ourselves of the old man in us and come out new; then we shall be reborn in Christ, a virgin."[5]

The fact that the Western church wanted its clergy to remain celibate was translated into a negative view of marriage reinforced by Saint Paul's words (1 Cor. 7:6–9). Saint Augustine even had to reassure the faithful that marriage did not necessarily result in damnation.[6] But it was hard to find an influential model that offered a worthy alternative. Mary's parents, Anna and Joachim, were well beyond normal childbearing age, as were John the Baptist's parents, Elizabeth and Zachariah; neither set could act as a model for a couple illustrating the marriage tie. Their union was "transposed" visually into scenes representing symbolic union: a meeting at Porta Aurea, Mary greeting Elizabeth in her house. Their families were not generated according to the natural rhythms of human life, but as a result of an extraordinary, independent event late in life.

In classical antiquity, on the other hand, the wedding ritual was often depicted on sarcophaghi because it was considered an essential moment in one's life, together with scenes representing victory over an enemy, the winner's forgiveness, and sacrifice to the gods. These actions symbolized the four virtues required of a good Roman citizen: *concordia, virtus, clementia, pietas.* The imperial couple itself was depicted on coins with *dextrarum iunctio* (joined hands); the harmony they established in their private sphere guaranteed harmony in public life. The Church was uncomfortable in taking a similarly positive view of marriage. Consider how few married saints there are.

The Church was even more embarrassed when it came to the question of Joseph and Mary. Joseph was always portrayed as an old man; in Nativity scenes he was usually painted either asleep or with his back turned. In late antiquity, Alexander the Great's mythical birth from Olympia's union with the wizard-snake is shown by Philip's determinedly turning away from his wife; the scene appears on a floor-mosaic from around the fourth century A.D. preserved in Beirut's Baalbek Museum (fig. 3).[7] Joseph's position was not one of irreverence. It followed the ancient iconography of paternity disownment, discreetly allowing the Holy Spirit to illuminate the divine child.

Until the eleventh century representations of Joseph and Mary's wedding were extremely rare. In a miniature from a book of lessons of circa 1100 (fig. 4) we see a priest pulling Mary's hand as if to hasten her union with Joseph. Note that neither has a halo; they have acquired them in the scene that follows, the birth of Christ. Wedding

3. *The Birth of Alexander the Great,* mosaic, fourth century. Beirut, Baalbek Museum.

iconography in fact had such negative overtones that it just as easily served the purpose of portraying diabolical temptation, as a twelfth-century capital in Saint Madeleine's church at Vézelay shows (fig. 5). In place of the priest we see a devil; with an identical gesture he introduces a woman to Saint Benedict, encouraging an infernal "wedding." The monk's victory is portrayed by the sacred book he holds to his chest like a shield, though if we are to believe the words of Gregory the Great, it was not until Benedict had rolled in a bed of thorns that the scars on his soul were healed. The three figures are labeled: *Sanctus*

341

4. Mary's Wedding, circa
1100. Utrecht,
Aartbisschoppelijk
Museum.

5. The Temptation of
Saint Benedict, twelfth
century. Capital, Church of
Saint Madeleine, Vézelay.

Benedictus, diabolus, and again *diabolus.* A woman and a devil were perfectly interchangeable: figure and symbol, for the sculptor, were one and the same thing. As Gregory the Great said, "what is a wife if not the pleasure of the flesh?"[8]

A similar interpretation can be seen in an early twelfth-century capital (fig. 6) in a church in Civaux (Vienne), in which marriage is portrayed as a dangerous submission to temptation. The couple, locked in a desperate *dextrarum iunctio,* is approached by a siren—traditional symbol of lust and seduction—who causes the man to fall from

6. Sirens: Marriage, early twelfth century. Capital, Church of Saints Gervaise and Protaise, Civaux.

his boat into the rolling waves. The meaning is self-explanatory: a man who is obliged to marry because he is not strong enough to resist passion is on his way to perdition. A text once attributed to Saint Bernard compares a married woman to a siren.[9]

The picture I have sketched so far, with its bright, contrasting colors, requires some subtle shading before it is complete. The Church, by proclaiming marriage a sacrament at the beginning of the twelfth century, appropriated all rights to its regulation. This was the culmination of a century-

7. Hugo I of Vaudémont
and His Wife, after 1163.
Church of the Cordeliers,
Nancy.

old process aimed at spiritualizing the institution. The Church tried to forbid marriages forced upon the couple against their will, to reduce levels of consanguinity, and to sanction the indissolubility of the relationship. First and foremost, however, it tried to give the legal contract more dignity, accompanying it with special blessings so as to elevate it into a sacrament. (Nevertheless the idea that marriage was a "lesser evil," surpassed by the choice of chastity and virginity preferred by the Church, did not lose ground.)

A detailed study of the *Index of Christian Art* at Princeton University reveals that, although until the eleventh century there were only three miniatures depicting Joseph and Mary's wedding,[10] between the thirteenth and fourteenth centuries a proliferation of examples shows that the new sacrament had become the object of conscious and constant reflection. An echo of the reappraisal of marriage can be found in the wooden statue probably depicting Count Hugo I of Vaudémont and his wife, Anna, although the fact that it is a sculptured monument makes it quite exceptional for its time. Hugo left for the Crusades in 1147, returning a poor pilgrim many years later, and dying soon after, between 1161 and 1163. The funeral group (fig. 7) appears to portray the count's much anticipated meeting with his wife after a long separation. The count clutches a heavy walking stick, a highly visible cross on his robe bears witness to his journey to Jerusalem. His wife clutches him, one arm around his neck, the other resting on his chest in the iconographic tradition of Mary holding her son cut down from the cross. The embrace, in which his wife is the active partner, marks the end of a crusader's adventures. The religious and military exploits of an individual are finally unloaded and shared in a gesture expressing the strength, durability, and reciprocity of his relationship with his wife.

348

In the Devil's Company

A topos upon which I shall not dwell in much
detail is that of the devil who dresses up as a young
girl and—an essential part of a saint's biography—
appears unexpectedly to test the saint's virtue. I
shall mention only one example: a detailed fresco
in the *Tebaide* in Pisa's Monumental Cemetery
attributed to Buffalmacco in 1343 (fig. 8). The
Dominican Jacopo Passavanti tells the story.[11] One
day, the devil masqueraded as a female pilgrim
and managed to move a monk with her tears. It
was pitch black outside, and the night was full of
wild beasts. Once inside the monk's cell, she tried
seducing him, but the monk did not succumb because he saw through the disguise. The fresco
shows two salient moments in the tale. First the
monk's affectionate gesture, holding the beautiful
traveler's hand and gazing into her intense eyes
(though the black hooves reveal her true nature),
as he leads her into his cave, the mouth of which

8. Buffalmacco, Tebaide,
detail of *The Devil Dressed
as a Pilgrim,* circa 1343.
Pisa, Monumental
Cemetery.

is unwisely open. Then we have the scene of the devil's defeat. The hermit leans out from a rocky terrace which partly protects him—even the surroundings reflect the emotional transformation—and chases the false pilgrim away with his stick. All the while a hornless demon watches over the scene from on high, directly above the cave. An observer could not fail to be convinced that the demon was always at one's side, that the potential for sin could lurk behind even a gesture of charity, and that victory was certain only if one followed an ascetic life and avoided women altogether.

9. A Woman Possessed, detail of *St. Francis: Stories from His Life,* second half of the thirteenth century. Pisa, Museum of San Matteo (temporarily in the Church of San Francesco).

Another necessary part of a saint's biography was the act of exorcism. The numerical superiority of women possessed by the devil over possessed men can be explained by the well-known woman/devil correlation. This was so commonplace at the

time that the onlooker would have considered it perfectly natural for the devil to choose a member of the female sex as his favorite disguise. From a "woman's point of view," the long list of possessed women could be considered a symptom of the alienation and dissatisfaction women felt for the role assigned to them by society. The moment of possession by the devil marks a magical potential for liberation, with no outcome. A woman's excesses were readily attributed to the devil, with a happy ending assured by the gallant exorcist. In that moment, though, the woman was important. She became for a searing second the protagonist of an exceptional event, her forgotten life flashing into the limelight.

In a detail of the late-thirteenth-century painting *Saint Francis: Stories from His Life* (fig. 9), the powers of the saint's body are demonstrated by its healing an obsessed woman. The painter depicted her in chains, her inner battle written all over her face, but it would be captious to attribute the disheveled clothing that bared her breasts to the effort of fighting. Her long hair is enough to declare her unremitting threat to men; the little devil may have flown out of her body, but she will always be the daughter of Eve the temptress.

The Damned Woman at Home

The misogyny that inspired the composition of the huge *Universal Judgment* in the tympanum of the twelfth-century church of Saint Lazarus at Autun is evident from a simple numerical count: only two women are elected to heaven and four are condemned to hell.

Similarly, in the early-fourteenth-century *Inferno* fresco in Santa Maria Maggiore, Tuscania, near Viterbo (fig. 10), an oversized wolf's head with razor-sharp teeth engulfs only women as they are pitched down his insatiable throat by devils' forks. The painter fully exploited the space avail-

able to him in the pendentive of the triumphal arch by placing the monster's head vertically, thus increasing its fearsome aspect. The desperation of the women—their white veils define them as nuns—is heavily underscored as they tear at their cheeks in an obvious appeal to the emotions of the observer who contemplates them with horror as they are pronged and tortured by the ever-present forks. Nuns occupied the deepest recesses of hell because they had betrayed their chosen life-style; their punishment was proportionate to their transgression. These nuns had taken the irrevoca-

10. *The Throat of Hell,* detail, early fourteenth century. Fresco in the triumphal arch of the Church of Santa Maria Maggiore, Viterbo.

353

ble and extreme decision not to marry, thus setting themselves apart from other women. But they had failed to keep their vow and therefore had to be punished like rebel angels for having dragged the very model of a virtuous, ascetic life of renunciation into the dust. The fresco was aimed at church-goers, a mostly lay audience of men and women; the presence of nuns in the deepest darkest hell is witness to the pressure exerted on all recipients of the model. Men's misogyny was encouraged (even the holiest of women are deceitful and full of lies!), and women had to accept a negative image of their sex (not even the woman who repudiates marriage and embarks on the path of penitence is sure to get to heaven!).

An example of concern for women, expressed from a (very rare) woman's point of view, can be found in a detail of the *Universal Judgment* preserved in the Vatican Museum. The date is uncertain, possibly the second half of the eleventh century (fig. 11). The donor has been identified as the abbess of the Benedictine convent of Santa Maria in Campo Marzio in Rome. We can read *Constantia abatissa* together with *Do[(m)n]a Benedicta ancilla D(e)i* before the walls of Celestial Jerusalem, where the Virgin not by chance is surrounded by two saints. Dragged by the hair into hell by an angel is a figure labeled *q(ui) / patre / v(e)l / matre / maledi / xit;* already in the depths, pitched in by forks held by other angels, there are *periu / ros, homi / cidas, mulier / qui in [e] / clesia / loc(u)t(a), mere / trici, . . . sa / velata.*

Although the lengthy inscriptions that comment on various scenes on the panel are in correct Latin, some in Leonine verse, the language of the infernal scenes is less correct, closer to the vernacular. It seems to me that we can hear the commissioning voice in the abbess' concern for the destiny of fellow women, especially her nuns. The linguistic register is closer to the vernacular (conditioned by the impact with reality: the horrors portrayed

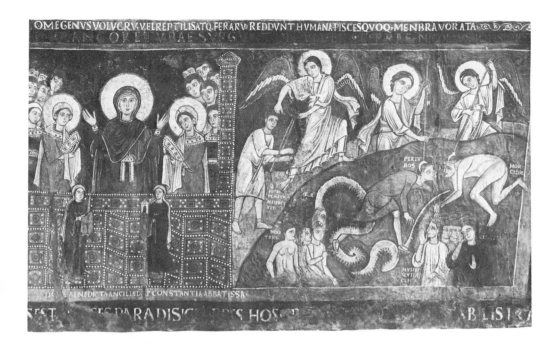

OME GENVS VOLVCRV: VEL REPTILIS ATQ. FERARV: REDDVNT HVMANA PISCESQVOQ: MEMBRA VOR ATA

11. Inferno, detail of Universal Judgment, table, second half of eleventh century. Vatican City, Pinacoteca Vaticana.

in the painting, mirroring a mistaken life, are experienced in the present by the onlooker). These women, who had opted for a chaste life of silent prayer, had to fear above all those vices which clashed with the virtues they were called upon to practice. This explains the emphasis placed on sins of speech, on the perverse and uncontrolled use of the tongue: woe betide the blasphemer; woe to the woman who breaks her vows or curses her parents; woe to the woman who talks in church (here the abbess' glance moves to her nuns assembled for liturgical functions).

Even from a compositional point of view this representation of hell is remarkable for the absolute visual domination of female components. At the top we have a perjurer and a murderer; at the bottom there two distinct groups identified by the inscriptions only as women. To the left a compact group of naked prostitutes is licked by flames, while one of them is being bitten by a snake: a prostitute who sells her body is the exact opposite

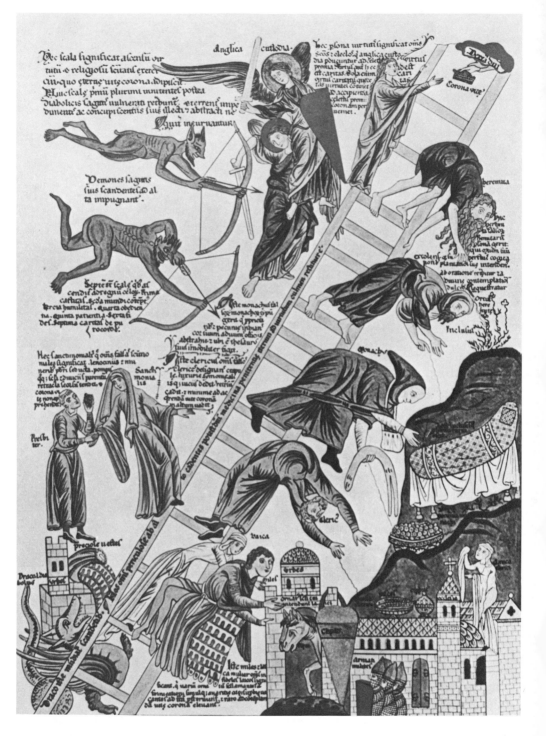

356

of a nun who has given it up entirely. To the right, next to the loquacious *mulier,* we see a young, darkly dressed woman with long hair, holding her hand to her head in an expression of pain (in the background a few men stare at her). The inscription has a few letters missing: . . . *sa / velata.* Saint Paul, in a passage of his first letter to the Corinthians in which he corroborates men's dominion over women (14:34–36), ordered women to hold their tongues during meetings: *turpe est enim mulieri loqui in ecclesia.* In the inscription near the garrulous woman there is an echo of this line. A few passages earlier (11:5–6) he proscribed that women should either wear a veil when they pray, or cut their hair: *nisi velatur mulier, tondeatur.* The painter, in order to stress the symbolism of the long-haired woman, must have remembered this passage, since it was so close to the other verse quoted, adapting it to his own purposes. The missing word could therefore be completed thus: *intonsa velata.* A nun had to cut her hair when she took her vows and keep her head covered. In this case the condemned woman who in her lifetime was not prepared to dispense with her locks (a temptation even for men who are attracted) displays her head of hair as an emblem of sinful vanity.

The Seductive Body

The *Ladder of Virtue* (fig. 12) is a miniature from Herrad of Hohenbourg's twelfth-century *Hortus deliciarum.*[12] It shows Christians, arranged according to life-style, desperately struggling to make their way up toward perfection. The married couple is the first to fall off.

In the lower part of the page material goods with a markedly seductive power are displayed: sumptuous clothes, a banquet table, precious objects, weapons, a beautiful city. At the foot of the ladder a dragon, jaws wide open, breathes threat-

12. Herrad of Hohenbourg, *Hortus deliciarum. The Ladder of Virtue,* twelfth century. Miniature from a drawing by A. de Bastard d'Estaing before the manuscript, then at the Strasbourg Municipal Library, was destroyed by fire.

eningly on those who undertake the ascent. The *laica* and the *miles* plummet almost instantly from the lowest rung. The caption reads: "this knight and his wife [*laica mulier*] represent all faithless lay people who, greedy, proud, and devoted to fornication, love the various delights of this world and are so attracted to earthly things that they rarely look up and contemplate the heavenly reward [*coronam vitae*]."

The next rung up spells doom for the cleric attracted by his girlfriend *(amica clerici)*, an elegant woman who calls to him from the city walls. The same fate is reserved for the nun attracted by a seductive priest's offers of gold and coins. The monk, recluse, and hermit, who in this order occupy the higher rungs of the ladder, begin to sway and lose their footing, attracted respectively by the power of wealth, the desire for a comfortable bed, and excessive attention dedicated to a kitchen garden. A young girl appears to be the only one deserving of the crown of eternal life held out by God. Alas, the figure turns out to be symbolic, a representation of the virtue of charity.

Not only do women occupy the lower rungs of the ladder, making them, Herrad suggests, more susceptible to the devil, they are themselves the incarnation of temptation. Out of six reasons for falling, three have something to do with the presence of women. The opportunity for committing a sin always seems to have the same matrix: weakness of the flesh. In the *Apocalypse* the most dangerous temptation is "obviously" that of female flesh offered by the "great prostitute," depicted in many miniatures astride a dragon.

In religious literature written by men, particularly monastic literature, women were stripped of humanity and deprived of psychological depth. They were no more and no less than a projection of men's—guilty—desires. The most obvious sign of this was the way in which the serpent in the scene of Adam and Eve's sin was often portrayed as having an attractive girl's head. The artist, aware of the classical tradition of the half-female, half-bird siren enchantresses who lured sailors into shipwrecks with their song, must have wanted to "explain" how a snake can whisper words of temptation. The convention was inherited and sustained in medieval Mystery Plays in which it was easier to put a human being on stage dressed up as a snake. (Surviving glosses establish that an ideal reptile should also have female breasts.)

One of the miniatures that preface an English psaltery (dated 1270–1280) depicts the Temptation and the Fall (fig. 13) in a single sequence.[13] The serpent is almost completely anthropomorphized, borrowing from women's fashion an attractive little bonnet with collar. The forbidden fruit is held out to Eve with an insinuating gesture; she hands it to her partner. A cycle of miniatures like this might have been used for educational purposes, for psalms were used to teach children Latin and help them learn to construct phrases with which to comment on the miniatures themselves. The danger in the female sex was thus learned along with the rudiments of language.

The fact that the serpent was given a woman's face indicates how sin was experienced and represented from a purely masculine point of view. But there is an inconsistency: Wouldn't Eve have been more attracted to the face of a handsome young man than to a young girl?

Because Eve did not know how to use the gift of language wisely, she was the first to answer the snake. This weakness was passed down to Eve's descendants who, encouraged by the devil, wasted idle chat, even in church, where every word should be dedicated to God. This seems to be the meaning of a stained-glass window in the Parish Church of Stanford (Northamptonshire), dating from around 1325–1340. In it a group of three women, the one

in the front ostentatiously holding an unused rosary, are surrounded in a sinister way by two rejoicing demons.[14]

Long hair was a traditional symbol of female seduction, an emblem of the danger women represented. Sirens always had long hair (mermaids were a medieval invention). So did Mary Magdalene at the foot of the cross, another medieval invention whose life comprises that of all the various Marys in the Gospel, in parts even that of Mary the Egyptian. Mary the Egyptian, a repentant courtesan who expiated her stormy past with penitence and solitude, naturally had long hair.[15] In the twelfth-century capital formerly in the cloisters at Saint Stephen's in Toulouse, one can see her metamorphosis. On the right hand side, whose detail is reproduced here (fig. 14), still dressed in

13. *The Temptation of Adam and Eve.* Cambridge, Saint John's College.

14. The Repentant Mary Magdalene, detail of capital, twelfth century. Toulouse, Toulouse Museum.

the sumptuous clothes of a sinner, she receives three coins from an unknown emissary of God with which to buy bread for her journey through the desert. On the left hand side she unties her long hair, which touches her feet as she paddles in the waters of the river Jordan, taking the first steps of her purification. The other side of the capital portrays her meeting with the Abbot Zozimus and the extraordinary burial for which a lion dug her grave.

According to the account of Domenico Cavalca, when Zozimus first saw the saint appear in the desert he did not even realize she was a woman. He was convinced she was "a great and holy father . . . a nude figure with black sun-dried skin and shoulder-length hair white as wool."[16] Her hair, now short and white, mistaken for a man's, no longer signified lust. In other versions of the story the saint's hair was long but only to conceal her female body like a sheepskin.

The message the Church handed down to its followers, feeding their fantasies and negatively influencing men's views of women and women's views of themselves, was that men were treated very differently from women. Men sinned when they misused their capabilities or ideas or when they were unable to control their impulses and sentiments. Nothing was required of women because their bodies led them inexorably toward transgression. *Women did not actively commit sins; they were a means of sinning offered men.*

The Face of Death

Eve allowed herself to be seduced by the devil and, through her, original sin, death, and eternal damnation came into the world. Eve's fatal weakness made her particularly vulnerable and guilty—she was the source of all evil! All women who succeeded her were the same, except for the Virgin

Mary. When, around 1340, Death was first represented as an abstract concept, symbol of the human condition overwhelming individual destinies (Death, not a dead person), the hybrid figure took on the aspect of a horrible old hag with clawed hands and feet and bat's wings (fig. 15). At Pisa's Monumental Cemetery she is portrayed flying over a group of corpses she has strewn along her path with her scythe. Features borrowed from the iconography of the devil, on the one hand, reveal her privileged relation with the underworld and its inhabitants. On the other hand, features showing the devastation of age symbolize the sinful desire to seduce that is frustrated by the onslaught of years. (The iconography of Death gradually took on the image of a skeleton with no specific gender.)

The attitude toward women was unambiguously expressed in a later fresco in the Parish Church of San Michele Arcangelo in Paganico (Siena), painted by Bartolo di Fredi. The landscape of hell is bleak, rocky, and thorny. A single sinner,

15. Buffalmacco, Death, detail of *The Triumph of Death*. Pisa, Monumental Cemetery.

16. Bartolo di Fredi, Hell,
Inferno, 1368.

seductively naked, her hands tied behind her back,
wanders toward the black mouth of a cave from
which a terrifying winged figure has just emerged
(fig. 16). This female figure's elongated body is
skeletal, her face diabolical; her hand holds a chain
that once must have reached the sinner's hands.
Her flaccid, wrinkled breasts and long white hair

17. Bartolo di Fredi,
Purgatory, 1368.
Frescoes on lower right
wall of the Church of San
Michele Arcangelo,
Paganico, Siena.

with bald patches underscore her repugnant femininity, further stressed by the gloss: "I'so mortal nimica d'ogni bene / serva del diaulo, donna dello 'nferno / madre di dolore in sempiterno (I am the mortal enemy of all that is good / servant of the devil, woman of hell, / mother of eternal pain)." Corporeal death, spiritual death, evil, and the devil combined to generate this monster that could be defined as the eternity of the torments of Hell.[17]

Of all the souls in the neighboring *Purgatory,* mostly women (fig. 17), who turn faithfully and imploringly toward the Madonna, one bare-breasted mother clutched by two children stands out. Her gesture is one of desperation as she indicates a cartouche, now empty. I think this is a quotation from a tale like the *Visio Alberici,* which placed in purgatory the souls of women who refused to breast-feed orphans.[18] In a fresco in the church of Santa Maria dei Ghirli, in Campione d'Italia, Lombardy, painted by Franco and Filippolo de Veris in 1400, there is a very vivid picture of a woman strangling her baby: infanticide. Baby-suffocation as a means of family planning was widely practiced at the time, though naturally unacceptable to the Church. We know this from textual sources, but the fresco bears further witness. In fact every condemned figure corresponds in an exemplary fashion to the types of sin most commonly committed. Women were vehicles of seduction for their mates; procreation, the only activity over which they were allowed relative jurisdiction, offered further opportunity for sin if women chose not to bring up their own offspring. It was hard for women to overcome or bypass the condition of being born female.

The Great Exception

At first it might seem that the faithful were offered the Virgin Mary's life as an alternative model. But Mary's body did not follow the rules of a human body, so the exception ended up confirming rather than disavowing traditional misogyny.[19] The Holy Virgin's life, apart from her Assumption into heaven, is celebrated in liturgy for events that are intimately connected with procreation, many of which represent a clear contrast to Eve's destiny. The Immaculate Conception established that Mary was the only human being without original sin. (This concept, however, was the subject of passionate debate throughout most of the Middle Ages.) The Annunciation and Visitation stressed the spiritual nature of the conception; the Birth of Christ emphasized her intact virginal state; the Purification in the Temple exemplified the Madonna's humility as she accepted the ritual although she was free of the impurity contracted by women in childbirth.[20] It would be superfluous to point out that since the Virgin was always represented as a devotional image together with her child, she lived in the hearts of her followers as a mother par excellence. The symbiosis between the two was total; her melancholy, resigned attitude was a portent of her son's cruel fate.[21] The message of the image, therefore, both denied and confirmed its contents: Mary was a model no woman could imitate.

Woman as Symbol

The eternal struggle between good and evil was formalized into a well-defined literary genre: the

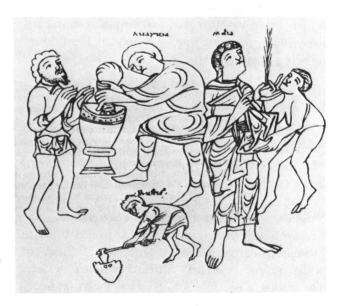

18. Ambrose Autperto, *The Battle between Vices and Virtues,* late eleventh century. Paris, Bibliothèque Nationale.
Avarice and Mercy.

battle between virtues and vices. On two pages of a late-eleventh-century manuscript illustrating Ambrose Autperto's *Battle between Vices and Virtues* corresponding vices and virtues were placed in contrasting pairs. On the first of these Avarice, the miser, is intent on emptying his bag of money into a container; his foot crushes a peasant *(rusticus)* doubled over to hoe the ground. A barefooted beggar in a short tunic tries to gain the attention of Avarice with a gesture of supplication, but the miser takes no notice. His glance is firmly directed toward his gold (fig. 18). His back toward the miser, Mercy has a palm leaf in his hand. He is about to rescue and dress a pauper who wears not even a rag. On the other page (fig. 19), Lust, a richly dressed, highly attractive woman, is crowned by a devil. Below her a two-headed monster grips her foot in a vise, shooting darts of fire at her from his open mouth. The woman's hands

369

are on her girdle, as if she is about to untie it; with her eyes she devours a man who lifts his tunic lewdly. Chastity also is turned away from Lust; she too holds a palm leaf in her hand. But her pedestal is the devil, utterly vanquished.

The fact that Avarice is represented by a man demonstrates that vices were not conditioned by the gender of the words denoting them.[22] In such abstractions the inertia usually generated by grammatical gender is usually replaced by the powerful everyday reality behind the symbol and the traditional link is broken. Avarice, as I have said, is a man. Charitability and chastity were virtues a woman could be proud of, but only a woman could represent Lust, the indefatigable temptress (of men of course). On the other hand, wherever activity and enterprise produced wealth and earning power, even if the objectives were sinful, men were the protagonists. While as a rule a characteristic feature was attributed to a vice, for the vice of Lust the body of a woman was enough. A woman's body was considered an allegory in itself.

A female image also was used to illustrate concepts or institutions: liberal arts, mechanical arts, geographical sites, cities, or, as above, vices and virtues. See, for example, a miniature dated about 850, illustrating Boethius' *De arithmetica*. Four veiled, similar-looking women are distinguished only by the instrument each holds. They represent respectively Music, Arithmetic, Geometry, and Astrology (fig. 20).

Two abstract female figures popular throughout the Middle Ages were *Ecclesia* and *Sinagoga,* the Jewish and Christian religions. As the centuries passed, their linked images underwent a transformation. The more the Church confirmed its resolute anti-Semitism, the more iconography moved away from images of two worlds brought closer together by the birth of Christ toward portrayals of a confrontation between the two religions marked by a crushing victory of Christianity and

20. The Quadrivium, in
Boethius, *De arithmetica*,
circa 850. Bamberg
Staatsbibliothek.

21. Atelier of Godefroy de Claire, 1155–1160, Synagogue, detail of a portable altar, Stavelot. Brussels, Musées Royaux d'Art et d'Histoire.

a humiliating defeat of Judaism. In a detail of the enameled champlevé portable altar at Stavelot (Belgium) produced by the atelier of Godefroy de Claire (1155–1160), Synagogue (fig. 21) is alone, without her rival. Her eyes are obstinately shut, because she refuses to recognize the Messiah. Recklessly she shows off evidence of Christ's crucifixion—the sponge, the spear, the crown of thorns. The implication is that she (or rather all the Jews of whom she was a symbol) was responsible for the death of the Redemptor and would bear the burden of guilt forever. In an early-twelfth-century miniature from Lambert of Saint Omer's *Liber Floridus*, Synagogue (fig. 22) appears in what then became the dominant image: defeat by the Church. The only thing missing is the blindfold. The Church, beside a huge baptismal font, goes up to Christ holding a banner and receives a crown from him. All the while she collects in a goblet the precious blood that trickles from his chest. On the opposite side we see Synagogue being pushed down by the Redemptor. Her crown is falling to the ground and her flagpole has broken into several pieces. The jaws of hell are ready to receive her. The inscriptions confirm: "Synagogue, in disavowing Christ the son of God, has rejected the prophets; distancing herself from God, she loses her crown, breaks her banner, and falls into the precipice of Hell."[23]

Even when a woman personified the Church, she did not always succeed in keeping up her positive connotations as a symbol. The legend of Pa-

22. Lambert of Saint Omer, Church and Synagogue, in *Liber Floridus,* miniature, early twelfth century. Gand, Bibliothèque van de Rijksuniversitet.

pess Joan circulated insistently in the thirteenth century. Supposedly she became pope in 855 by dressing as a man; her secret was disclosed only when she had birth contractions during a procession to the Lateran Basilica in Rome.[24]

Joan found her way onto a tarot card in a set commissioned by Francesco Sforza between 1451 and 1453 (fig. 23). Seated on a spacious throne with a mildly bemused expression, she holds a delicate cross and a closed book in her gloved hands. On her head a papal tiara partially covers her white veil; her wimple and tunic with its loose-fitting cloak of brown cloth and the knotted rope around her waist bring to mind a Franciscan habit. Papess Joan is not portrayed derisively. The portrait apparently was intended to serve as a memorial for a close female relative of Matteo Visconti's, Imperial Vicar at the beginning of the fourteenth century. This anonymous woman ended up at the stake suspected of heresy because she had taken on tasks only a pope was supposed to assume. The tarot card is a clue to the antipapist attitude of the Visconti-Sforza family. What is interesting in the story of Joan (originally a legend, but the way in which the legend was manipulated makes it real history) is the persistence of a twin obsession: first, the fear that a woman might dare exert male prerogatives—Joan was condemned for sacrilege; second, the fear of a woman's body as a vehicle for perverse seduction—Joan was unmasked by the fruit of her sin.

Women in Private and Daily Life

The Woman of the Couple

Until the late Middle Ages art was for the most part ecclesiastical. Images that have survived to our day are distorted because they reflect the Church's point of view. Even when a work of art was commissioned by a layperson, he or she in-

23. Bonifacio Bembo or Francesco Zavattari, Visconti-Sforza tarot cards, Papess Joan, 1451–1453. New York, Pierpont Morgan Library.

evitably had some relation to a religious institution, either as benefactor or founder. If a couple, the one who commissioned a portrait would have been the husband. Although a man might well have had other reasons to be remembered and might well order a solo portrait, a woman—if, that is, she belonged to the upper class—could only expect to be remembered in relation to that man. It is all the more unusual then to find Judith of Flanders, a countess and the commissioner of the work, in Mary Magdalene's place, embracing the foot of the cross. The portrait in question is in a mid-eleventh-century illuminated gospel donated by her to the Abbey of Weingarten (fig. 24). In this portrait, moreover, the Virgin Mary, following the iconography for the *Ecclesia* popular at the time, is represented on a par with Saint John, holding a book in her hand, traditionally a masculine attribute.[25]

Values such as strength, power, and feudal loyalty became all the more important at a time when violence, war, and outrage dominated life. In a marriage founded primarily on mutual interests (variable according to circumstance), a woman was the silent object of a gift or exchange between father and suitor. Even the wife of an emperor had no certain name. In a surviving copy of a Bible that Charles the Bald brought to Rome as a gift for Pope John VIII to commemorate the imperial election consecrated in Saint Peter's in 875, his portrait dominates the frontispiece. Sitting on a throne, surrounded by dignitaries, his wife, and a court lady (fig. 25), Charles is oversized in relation to the rest of the illustration (and proportions express a built-in value-system), demonstrating his power by being the only person seated, canopied by the cardinal virtues and winged angels. To the right is his diminutive wife without a crown, standing as a sign of respect. Clearly she shared neither his rank nor his throne. Her arms, raised in a gesture of acclamation, and therefore of subjuga-

24. *Crucifixion,* from the Gospels of the Countess Judith of Flanders, mid-eleventh century. New York, Pierpont Morgan Library.

377

25. King Charles the Bald
on His Throne, in the
Bible of King Charles the
Bald, circa 875. Rome, San
Paolo outside the walls.

tion, places her alongside the crowd of onlookers. The veiled woman might be Hirmintrudis, but is more likely Richildis, whom Charles married a few months after Hirmintrudis' death in 870.[26] In the long dedicatory inscription of the manuscript, although several lines were addressed to Charles' consort in the hope that she would be blessed with numerous offspring, her name was not mentioned once. We must remember, however, that it was extraordinary enough in Carolingian art for a queen to be depicted at all.

The adoration and commemoration of an important son was sometimes an occasion for a couple to be portrayed together. This was the case for the parents of Egilbert, archbishop of Treves. In an evangelistary donated to the Egmont monastery between 940 and 970, Dirk II of Holland and his wife, Countess Hildegard, appear on the same page, in proud commemoration of their son. All three names are mentioned in the dedication folio (fig. 26), though Hildegard is clearly less impor-

26. Count Dirk II of Holland and His Wife, Hildegard, Donate a Manuscript to the Egmont Monastery, 940–970. Aia, Koninklijksbibliotheek.

tant. The couple stand side by side under the two great arches of the monastery chapel, holding the donated manuscript open toward the viewer. The center of the composition is the gift. The evangelistary, against the background of the richly decorated altar, which looks almost like a throne, takes the place of the sovereign. It is toward the book that the count and countess turn, like faithful acolytes. The awkwardness the artist felt in representing real people in a concrete gesture is shown by the abstract nature of the surface on which the feet of the two central figures rest—to all appearances troubled waters. The absence of angels, holy,

27. Werner and Irmengard Offer Their Evangelistary, miniature Saint Mihiel's evangelistary, circa 1040. Lille, Bibliothèque des Facultés Catholiques.

28. Donizone, Matilda, Hugo of Cluny, and King Henry IV, miniature in Donizone, *Vita Mathildis,* 1115. Vatican City, Biblioteca Apostolica Vaticana.

or even divine, characters, led the artist to introduce a completely unreal detail in order to transcend the historical presence of the couple and place the scene outside time.

Another miniature, circa 1040, illustrates the donation of a manuscript. The beneficiary of the gift is Christ himself, seated on his throne next to Saint Michael the Archangel whom the couple Werner and Irmengard face. The composition is a precise transposition of that of an emperor guarded by an armed dignitary as he receives his subjects. Irmengard's position (fig. 27), partly hidden behind her husband, well expresses her twofold subjugation both to her husband and to Christ. She joins her husband in the gesture of donation by timidly resting her hand on her husband's outstretched arm. It is Werner who holds the gift for all to see.

In the Middle Ages a woman had no face of her own, unless she refused to marry and pledged herself to the divine spouse, had been widowed, or had chosen a solitary life. A good example is Matilda of Canossa, follower of Gregory VII and go-between in the pope's quarrels with Henry IV; her *Life* was written by Donizone in 1115.[27] The illuminated manuscript (fig. 28) portrays her in a decisive moment of mediation. Wrapped in sumptuous fur, seated under a kind of pavilion, with a gesture of her hand the countess advises the king to talk to Abbot Hugo of Cluny. The outsized abbot, seated on a stately stool, crosier in hand, seems to direct the emperor toward Matilda. A diminutive Henry IV, on his knees between the two dominant figures, effectively portrays the imploring attitude described in the caption. Note the relative sizes of the three figures. The abbot is gigantic; his supremacy is indisputable, both for his spiritual powers and his rank. Matilda, because she is a woman, has the same stature as the disgraced king, though her reputation places her within the framework of an architectural composition. But notice the bench on which she is sitting: it is too big for her, and her feet, which dangle over the edge unable to touch the floor, further emphasize her minute proportions.

To Enchant and to Cure

The fear of a woman's exerting male prerogatives, together with the fear of a woman's seduction, were two aspects—though certainly not the only ones—of an obsession with witches. (It is no chance that more witches than sorcerers were burnt at the stake.) Saint Bernardino of Siena (1380–1444) was one of the great propagators of this obsession which flourished during the Middle Ages. He personally condemned a great number of hapless women to the flames and made it his vocation to reconstruct and circulate, through his sermons, many characteristic habits of witches. In Saint Bernardino's church in Triora (Imperia) a late-fifteenth-century fresco (fig. 29) shows a group of witches inside the infernal furnace. These condemned women being skewered by demons, labeled as *fatucerie* (sorceresses), wear on their heads miters with a black devil painted on them—the same devil whose help they had invoked with their sorcery, a symbol of their blind trust.

29. Witches, detail of the *Inferno,* late fifteenth century. Fresco to the right of the nave, Church of Saint Bernardino in Triora (Imperia).

30. *Salome the Midwife,* detail of *Nativity,* eighth century? Fresco in the Church of Santa Maria Foris Portas, Castelseprio.

In witches' biographies constant references were made to their sexual relations—which inevitably degenerated into orgies—with the devil. Another aspect persistently underscored was that of ugliness. Witches were by definition old hags, an expression of the masculine division between the desire for and the fear of female beauty. Other elements constantly reiterated were the witches' hatred of newborn babes (whom they reportedly murdered by drinking their blood) and their capacity for creating unguents. These last two factors can be attributed to the familiarity women had with midwifery and to widespread paramedical experience with many feminine diseases. Given the staggeringly high infant and puerperal mortality rates, it is easy to understand how grief shifted responsibility for death onto the person who had assisted the mother or baby.

In all scenes of the Nativity of Mary or Christ

there are always some women—and only women
—present at the birth. Their presence was so natural that an apocryphal gospel (Saint James' proto-
evangelium, chapters XIX–XX), found it necessary
to construct a little fable,[28] which does not appear
in the canonic gospels and which was later circulated both in medieval theater and in the Dominican Jacob of Voragine's *Legenda Aurea*. According to this, Salome the midwife insisted on
personally testing Mary's virginity; when she continued to deny plain evidence, her arm became
paralyzed. Only after she had repented of her
obstinacy did her arm return to normal. In frescoes
at Castelseprio (Varese), of uncertain date but
probably from the seventh or eighth century, Salome nonchalantly holds up her withered arm as
she attends to her duties (fig. 30).

Around 1372 an anonymous artist painted an
unusual image of Mary.[29] Mary can be imagined
as completely naked, though all we see is her upper
torso emerging from the sheets. (At the time people
slept in the nude, leaving their clothes in the other
room in their desperate struggle against fleas and
all manner of bugs.) The painter placed Mary's
long leather-soled hose and tidily folded dress at
the foot of the Virgin's bed, as if she had carefully
undressed in order to give birth. The Madonna
tenderly cares for the newborn Christ child, float-
ing in the tub next to the bed in his first bath.
Joseph determinedly faces the other way, in a deep
sleep, while the midwife, on a low stool, stoops
over to fill a jug—doubtless with hot water to help
wash the baby. Mary's virginal appearance is emphasized by her girlish looks and long unveiled
hair. In contrast, the midwife's mature appearance
and the wimple covering her head and neck show
her to be a married woman with the experience of
age.

Accusations about mixing magic potions and
casting spells were caused by the knowledge, often
jealously guarded and passed down from mother

to daughter, of herbs and their medicinal properties. Women, closed up in the house and involved with the problems of bringing up children and taking care of the family, were "functionally" obliged to know about potions and remedies. The persecution of witches also had a great deal to do with the resentment of the erudite, masculine world of medicine against its popular feminine rival. A miniature from the *Epitre d'Othéa,* written by Christine de Pisan (circa 1361–1431), in which both Aesculapius and the sorceress Circe appear (fig. 31), illustrates this attitude very well. Aesculapius, considered at the time a great man of science and the father of surgery, is portrayed as a fifteenth-century doctor holding a patient's urine sample up to the light in a traditional examination required by his profession. Circe, cursed enchantress of Ulysses' companions who were held in her beauty's thrall, is depicted as an old woman in rags threading toads—the ingredients of her magic potions—onto a long stick in order to place them into two containers. The author and the illuminator compared and contrasted official and empirical medicine. The former was represented, not by chance, by a learned exponent of the male sex; the latter by a humble-looking female.

In an extraordinary miniature taken from Jean Bondol's *Histoire ancienne jusqu'à Cesar* of 1375,[30] we see three women involved in a birth by cesarean section (fig. 32). A female surgeon and two assistants are extracting a boy with long blond hair from the mother's womb. The scene is amazingly calm, almost serene; the only sign of the mother's suffering are her long fingers gripping the sheets. This image was clearly idealized; the operation only took place when the mother was already a corpse.

Canonization trials also provide some information about the talent many nuns had for handling surgical instruments. Her own convent sisters were responsible for opening up the heart of Clare of Montefalco (1268–1308) to find the cross and other signs of Christ's Passion that their mother superior had always sworn she bore in her breast.

I should like to insert a brief parenthesis here on the relations and mutual influences that flowed between visions and images, wellsprings for interior meditation and part of the daily experience of mysticism. Mystical exaltation was fueled by visions, basically composed of images, which in their turn provided the expressions with which to describe otherwise indescribable experiences. Image

31. Aesculapius and Circe, miniature in Christine de Pisan, *Epitre d'Othéa*, early fifteenth century. Paris, Bibliothèque Nationale.

32. A Woman Performing
a Cesarean Section, detail
of a miniature in Jean
Bondol, *Histoire ancienne
jusqu'à Cesar,* 1375.
Spikkestad, Martin
Schøgen Collection.

33. Meister Bertram, *Mary Knitting*, detail of *Buxtehuder Altar*, circa 1400. Hamburg, Hamburger Kunsthalle.

389

and description made up a language, a linguistic vehicle common to the "biography" of a mystic—that is, the way of life proposed as a model of perfection by the writer—and its readership. On the one hand, iconographic revisions regularly found their way into descriptions of visions; for example, nails on the cross become three rather than four following the parallel evolution of the crucifix-image. On the other, mystic visions often formed the core of new iconographies, such as the image of the Holy Crib which to this day is represented as Saint Bridget first saw it in a vision.

It was the vital role of images in the mystical experience of cloistered nuns that led Saint Clare's sisters to believe that the metaphor used by the holy woman might have had a material reality in her heart.[31] In the contradictory account given by witnesses of the exhausting operation (abandoned and taken up again several times), Clare's heart was reported to have brought forth all the objects heretofore only imagined, though Tommaso of Foligno courageously and passionately denied it. Like a little two-doored cupboard, her heart revealed on one side the cross, three nails, a spear, a sponge, and a rod; on the other, a column, a five-tailed whip, and the crown of thorns. The immediate reaction to the news was an explosive proliferation of miracles, together with throngs of pilgrims.[32]

Most available images of active women, other than nuns or widows, portray them as being engaged in some kind of domestic activity. Even the Madonna served as a good example to women when she was portrayed knitting (fig. 33). Housewifely virtues were also given a public dimension when the development of cities encouraged flourishing commerce; a merchant's wife was often expected to run the family business and keep up sales while her husband was away. An example of these organizational skills can be seen in the intense, daily correspondence between Margherita Datini and her husband, Francesco (1335–1410). The fer-

vor that animated Italian cities toward the end of
the thirteenth century was reflected in the proliferation and specialization of occupations and in
the absolute novelty of women's newly acquired
"right to appear" in images. A woman's presence
was registered, even if her family or religious institution did not belong to the upper class. She did
not even have to be a saint. A miniature in the

34. A Woman Selling Fish,
in *Tacuinum sanitatis*,
1385, Vienna,
Osterreichische
Nationalbibliothek.

391

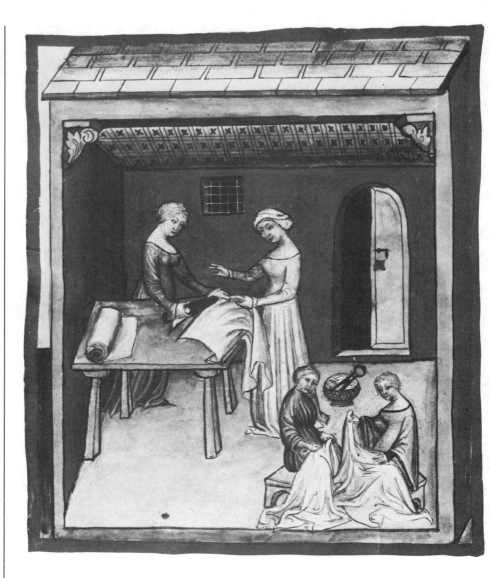

35. Women Cutting and
Sewing Clothes, in
Tacuinum sanitatis,
fourteenth century, Vienna,
Österreichische
Nationalbibliothek.

Tacuinum sanitatis of 1385 shows a woman selling fish (fig. 34), or bread. A miniature from another fourteenth-century *Tacuinum* portrays women as apprentice seamstresses sewing clothes alongside male colleagues in a tailor's workshop (fig. 35). There are countless examples of images of anonymous women nursing the sick in a hospital or hospice, making beds, or helping invalids eat.

Agricultural scenes, usually the most conservative, show some innovations when transposed onto the pulsing life of a thirteenth-century city. Women made their first appearance as *uxor* (wife) in the cycle of months on Perugia's Fontana Maggiore (1278), sculpted by Nicola and Giovanni Pisano (fig. 36). The complex program of bas-reliefs around this fountain attempted to express the social utility of labor in the interaction between city and country. A peasant was not required to remember Adam's trials and tribulations, and a peasant woman did not have to pay for Eve's sin; this is why she was free to help her husband in the fields. Wiligelmo, in the first decades of the twelfth century, audaciously anticipated this idea in his

36. Nicola and Giovanni Pisano, May: A Knight and His Wife Hunting with a Falcon, 1278. Relief on the Fontana Maggiore in Perugia.

sculptured facade of Modena Cathedral (fig. 37). In this rare representation Christ's redemption is shown to be already at work on Adam and Eve as they bend down together to hoe the hard ground, implicitly freeing women from their punishment (to give birth and take care of their offspring).[33]

If a woman's knowledge or competence in a male sphere of activity had nothing to do with the reassuring model of convent life or with domestic and family affairs, it had an ambiguous value. The group of women making music in *The Triumph of Death* in Pisa's Monumental Cemetery (fig. 15) could easily have been interpreted as a symbol of a futile occupation, a typical female pretext for sin and perdition. "Death" in fact is portrayed as being in the act of cutting their music short with her scythe. The group of maidens singing and dancing in Ambrogio Lorenzetti's *Buon Governo* fresco (1338–1340) in Siena's Palazzo Pubblico also served an allegorical function.[34] The profession of wandering minstrel, dancer, or musician was anathema for women in the Middle Ages.

37. Wiligelmo, Adam and Eve at Work, early twelfth century. Relief on the facade of the Duomo, Modena.

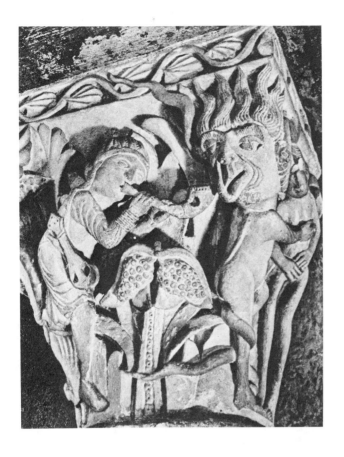

38. Minstrel, Devil, and
Woman, twelfth century.
Capital, Church of Saint
Madeleine, Vézelay.

Salome's beguiling dances that succeeded in ob-
taining John the Baptist's head from a recalcitrant
Herod were too close for comfort. In a twelfth-
century capital in the church of Thines (Ardèche),
a long-haired acrobat's show is accompanied by a
winged devil on a stringed instrument. A thirteenth-century manuscript comments: "just as a
hunter holds with a string or with a net a trained
bird that sings and flaps its wings as if it were free,
so the devil leads a minstrel-maiden who knows
all the songs to dance so she can drag other girls
into the circle."[35] On one side of a twelfth-century
capital in Vézelay's church of Saint Madeleine we
can see a juggler and a woman; on the other side
(fig. 38), the same minstrel with a rebeck around

his neck plays a flute. A devil with flaming hair has come between the musician and his girlfriend, who wrings her hands in desperation. The demon holds the girl as though she herself were a musical instrument: inasmuch as she represents the sin of lust, she is the instrument of the malignant spell that has struck both devil and minstrel.

Women and Literacy

A miniature (1470) from the fourth volume of Jean du Ries's *L'Histoire scolastique* allows us an opportunity to spy into a Flemish house (fig. 39). An old man lies asleep on his sickbed, a wooden divan-bench. A maid, holding a large pewter bowl, steps toward the mistress of the house, ready to receive the potion she has prepared. The lady sits on a low stool at the hearth, her skirts lifted to let the warmth in. A copper cauldron hanging from a rod and chain is surrounded by lively, flickering flames. The mistress is concentrating on ladling some kind of medicinal unguent spoon by spoon into a pot (of the same shape used by Circe) by the fire, balancing on her lap with her other hand a book of recipes whose instructions she is clearly following. Since the miniaturist no doubt wanted to portray the sick man's wife, the woman in this illustration is almost definitely a laywoman, of a certain class, but nevertheless a laywoman able to understand the written word.

Women's ability to read was probably more widespread than is generally believed.[36] A series of miniatures with the traditional theme of motherhood show women acting as their children's "first teachers." A fifteenth-century painting (fig. 40) conserved in Santa Maria's church at Capraia di Sillico near Lucca, attributed with a margin of doubt to Pietro da Talada,[37] portrays the Virgin looking up from the missal she is holding open at the *Magnificat* (the words with which Mary ac-

39. Woman Preparing a Recipe, Book in Hand, miniature in Jean du Ries, *Quart volume de l'Histoire scolastique,* 1470. London, British Library.

397

40. Maestro di Borsigliana
(Pietro da Talada?),
Madonna and Child,
fifteenth century. Church
of Santa Maria, Pieve
Fosciana, Lucca.

cepted her divine motherhood) in order to observe
the child Jesus seated on her lap. The young boy
is gripping a cutting-board-shaped chalk palette in
one hand on which the letters of the alphabet can
be clearly read. A series of syllables are formed by
combining each letter with a vowel sound. This
detail is very revealing in that it gives an idea of a

precise teaching method. The child was evidently learning to read from the board, using his finger so as not to lose his place.

In another panel with scenes from the life of the Virgin (circa 1335), Mary is the student (fig. 41). Quite grown up, she is portrayed learning to read from a psaltery resting on a high lectern. Her mother, Saint Anne, stands behind her, pointing to the lines Mary was supposed to read out loud, verses 10–11 of Psalm 45—an invitation to accept divine will. Mary, learning to read, learns her own

41. Saint Anne Teaches the Virgin Mary to Read, detail of *Panel with Scenes from the Life of the Virgin,* circa 1335. Paris, Musée National des Thermes et de l'Hotel de Cluny.

destiny. The written word in this case amplifies the image by calling to mind the voice of the Angel of the Annunciation. On the psaltery we can read, *Audi, filia, et vide, et inclina aurem tuam, / [et obliviscere populum tuum et domum patris tui] et concupiscet rex decorem tuum / [quoniam ipse est Dominus Deus tuus]* (Hearken, O daughter, and consider, and incline thine ear; [forget also thine own people, and thy father's house;] So shall the King greatly desire thy beauty: [for he is thy Lord; and worship thou him]).

The Family Scriptorium

Painstaking research leafing through dusty payment receipts and contracts has revealed the extraordinary fact that a university city with a flourishing book market, such as thirteenth- and fourteenth-century Bologna, employed many female miniaturists and calligraphers, who, it seems, worked with their husbands and fathers (from whom they had learned the trade).[38] Here are a few. The name of Donatella *miniatrix,* wife of a miniaturist, is mentioned in a contract for the sale of a house in 1271. In 1271–1272 the calligrapher Montanaria, wife of Onesto, received a contract from the Florentine book commissioner Bencivenne. In 1275 a father, Rodolfo del fu Gandolfo, committed his daughter Antonia to the activity of copying. And in 1279 Allegra, wife of Ivano, promised a Carmelite she would copy out an entire Bible. Other memorable examples, again in Bologna, are the calligraphers Flandina di Tebaldino, active in 1268, and Uliana de Benvenuto da Faenza, who signed a contract in 1289. In 1329 the couple Branca and Anastasio appeared under the gloss *qui faciunt artem scribendi.*

Family collaboration was by no means restricted to Italy. In thirteenth-century Cologne there are traces of a widow Tula, professional *rubeatrix* (copier of rubrics), and in the fourteenth century of a certain Hilda or Hilla, wife of Johann the miniaturist, who was a painter. Paris provides other examples. At the end of the thirteenth century a female painter worked with her husband, Richard de Verdun, at the school of miniaturists founded by Father Maitre Honoré. Two other women illuminators were Thomasse, who in 1292 lived in rue du Foin, and Bourgot who lived with her miniaturist father, Jean le Noir, in rue Troussevache in a house given to them by the king around 1358.[39]

A more complete record of the miniaturist Claricia is afforded by the psaltery from about 1200 that she signed with her name and a self-portrait (fig. 42). Her slender, maidenly figure, her long, loose hair, and her elegant wide-sleeved dress

42. Claricia the Miniaturist, psaltery, circa 1200; the initial Q of Psalm 51 (52). Baltimore, Walters Gallery.

401

43. A Woman Painting a Fresco, in Giovanni Boccaccio, *Le livre des cleres et nobles femmes,* fifteenth century. Paris, Bibliothèque Nationale.

are attractively incorporated into the tail of the letter Q; her head leans gracefully to one side, allowing space for the discreetly positioned letters of her name, and her upheld arms support the intricately interwoven patterns of the initial.

Christine de Pisan, best-known of medieval secular women writers, author and copyist of a number of splendidly miniatured works, cannot be ignored. With her flourishing activity, even as a widow she managed to support herself and her large family. Her commissioners were none other than noble courtiers and members of royal households. Portraits of her copying or composing appear in many illuminated manuscripts.[40] Boccaccio's *De claris mulieribus,* written between 1360 and 1362, with its 104 biographies of famous women starting with Eve, offered ample ground for illustrating a wide range of female qualities.[41] This work, instantly translated into the vernacular in several countries, has come down to us in many richly illustrated manuscripts. Despite the misogyny that pervades the work (some women are

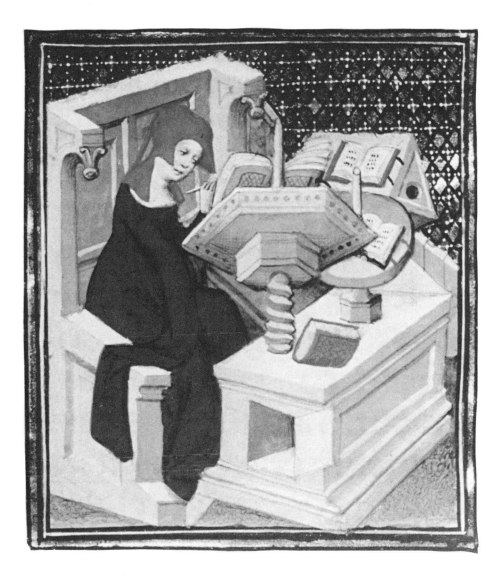

praised as exceptions that confirm the rule), readers at least were able to familiarize themselves with
a positive image of creative and active women.
Alongside the many traditional scenes, such as that
of a queen at her loom, surrounded by servants
weaving and spinning, we can admire a woman
expertly tracing a preliminary sketch for a fresco
(fig. 43); one copying and collating manuscripts

44. A Woman Copying a
Manuscript, in Giovanni
Boccaccio, *Le livre des
cleres et nobles femmes*,
fifteenth century. Paris,
Bibliothèque Nationale.

403

45. A Woman Sculpting, in Giovanni Boccaccio, *Le livre des cleres et nobles femmes,* fifteenth century. Paris, Bibliothèque Nationale.

46. A Woman Painting, with a Male Assistant, in Giovanni Boccaccio, *Le livre des cleres et nobles femmes,* fifteenth century. Paris, Bibliothèque Nationale.

(fig. 44); another adding the finishing chisel touches to the tombstone of a young maiden (fig. 45); and yet another painting an icon of the Madonna, while a (male!) assistant prepares her colors (fig. 46).

Were these last two images simply illustrations of the text or did they have some basis in reality? I think we can opt for the latter since the miniature of the *Tacuinum sanitatis* (fig. 35) representing a scene from daily life (by no means conditioned by an iconographic model) shows men and women working elbow to elbow. An enormous ceremonial

silver crucifix with crafted relief figures from early-twelfth-century Spain is further evidence of a woman's skill as goldsmith and sculptress. Sancia Guidosalvi in fact scattered letters proclaiming herself as author and dedicating her art to the glory of the Redemptor all along the cross in a delicate spiraling design which holds one spellbound.[42]

The Wives of Christ

A Room of One's Own

In hagiographic literature the topos of virgin spouses or wives who tried to live chastely despite their husband's determined opposition was very common. The king of the Franks, Clothaire (497–561), having exterminated her family in the massacre of Thuringia, obliged Radegund to marry him. Her answer was to spend her nights in prayer, abandoning the bridal chamber until such a time as she was able to flee from her husband and triumphantly found a convent (fig. 47). This was the beginning of her public life as a saint devoted to the poor, to the humblest tasks, and to miracles. Venantius Fortunatus told the story of her life in a biography modeled on that of Saint Martin whose influence spread far and wide for centuries to come.[43]

The only place a woman was allowed to have "a room of her own," in Virginia Woolf's words, was in a convent. In all likelihood, she would have been committed to the order at a tender age, still needing attention, games, and maternal affection, as a fresco portraying the very young Clare of Montefalco (fig. 48) shows. According to Saint Clare's own account of her life, the Virgin Mary used to give her permission to play with the Infant Jesus to help alleviate her distress at being forcibly separated from her family. Within the walls that insulated her from the rest of humanity and, more important, protected her from men, a nun was able

47. Radegund Kneeling in the Chapel; at the Table, in spite of Herself, with Her Husband; and Abandoning Him in order to Pray, end of the eleventh century. Poitiers, Bibliothèque Municipale.

408

to compete with the outside world in cultural terms if she devoted her life to meditation and prayer—which meant reading, writing, and studying. A fifteenth-century miniature (fig. 49) from the Henry VI Psaltery shows two rows of Poor Clares rigidly set out in the choir stalls, psalters in their hands as they sing and pray.

It is not surprising that the vast majority of women with strong personalities were nuns. After Radegund—inspiration, friend, and commissioner of Venantius Fortunatus—we might also consider the early-tenth-century Hrotswitha, chronicler and historian of her times as well as expert on Terence's works, who wrote *Primordia Coenobi*

48. *The Young Saint Clare with the Child Jesus,* 1333. Fresco, Chapel of Santa Croce, Church of Santa Chiara, Montefalco, Umbria.

49. Nuns in the Choir Stalls, Henry VI's psaltery, fifteenth century. London, British Library Board.

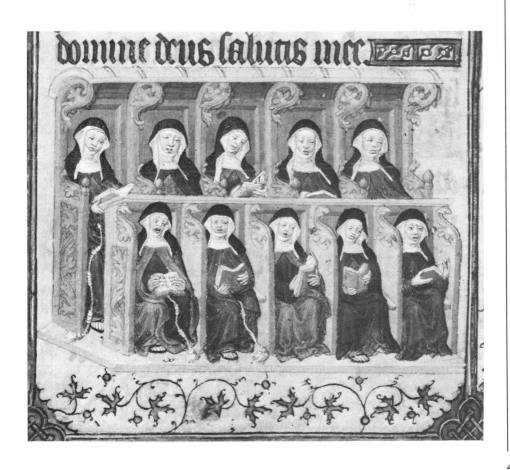

Gandershemensis and *Carmen de gestis Oddonis.* The twelfth-century (died 1195) Alsatian abbess of Hohenburg, Herrad, was the author of the renowned *Hortus deliciarum.* This work was a kind of religious encyclopedia dedicated to her fellow nuns (who almost certainly took part in its transcription and illustration) in which text, miniatures, and captions formed an inseparable whole. Like Clare of Montefalco, the great Hildegard of Bingen (1098–1179) was pledged to the Benedictine community at the early age of eight. In addition to works of religious instruction, she wrote books on the natural sciences, a medical tract, an autobiography, and a number of letters, fragments of which have survived to this day. Many manuscripts of her most famous work, *Liber scivias (sci vias lucis,* know the ways of the light), were decorated with intricately ornamented miniatures. One of the many miniatures in another richly illustrated work of hers, the *Revelations,* shows Hildegard, pen in hand, looking upward for heavenly inspiration and translating into words the vision of God creating first the universe and then the earth, already filled with cities and churches.[44]

In the convent a nun could commission works independently; as such, she acquired the right to be portrayed as the leading person, a role unlike that of a wife, who had to be the supporting actress to her husband, the commissioner. In an early-eleventh-century evangelistary *Hitda abatissa* was depicted with the same proportions as *Sancta Vualburga,* the holy founder of her convent to whom Hitda holds out the manuscript, sharing an almost entirely empty scenario with her dedicatee (fig. 50). This was also true of another contemporary miniature in which the Abbess Ute of Niedermünster, commissioner and donor, had herself portrayed kneeling before the Virgin Mary (fig. 51). A nun could even become dedicatee of a work. A miniature from about 800 (fig. 52) shows Isidore of Seville in the act of giving his book, *Contra*

50. The Abbess Offers a Book to Saint Walburg, miniature in Abbess Hitda's evangelistary, early eleventh century. Darmstadt, Hessische-und Hochschul-Bibliothek.

411

51. The Abbess Ute of
Niedermünster, Donor of
the Manuscript, miniature
in Ratisbon evangelistary,
early eleventh century.
Munich, Staatsbibliothek.

52. Isidore Gives a Book
to Sister Florentine,
miniature in Isidore of
Seville, *Contra Judaeos,*
circa 800. Paris,
Bibliothèque Nationale.

Judaeos, to Sister Florentine. The dedication is full
of affection: *Soror mea Florentina accipe codicem
quem tibi composui feliciter, amen* (my sister, Florentine, please accept this work that I composed
for you in the most amiable spirit; I wish you
happiness, amen). In the presence of a male, however, words were clearly not enough to invert the
tradition that obliged a nun to play the role of
humble donor. It is Isidore who is seated on a high
bench; he holds out the manuscript to Florentine,
noticeably smaller than he and almost on her knees
in front of him.

When one thinks of an illuminated manuscript,

the almost automatic association is that of a male copyist in the silence of his monastery. It is time to make room for another mental image: that of generations and generations of nuns, silently transcribing, collating, miniating, composing. A description in the biography of Ida von Leuwen, a thirteenth-century copyist, could well be applied to these women: "at all times were all her faculties engaged in writing, carefully copying books for the Church, correcting a fairly large manuscript of weekday lessons for matins; her name has been placed on numerous other manuscripts copied most diligently."[45] A few names out of this anonymous multitude have survived.[46]

53. Self-Portrait of Sister Guda, *Homilia super Evangilia,* second half of the twelfth century. Frankfurt, Stadt-und-Universitätsbibliothek.

The unusual designs and bright colors of the miniatures in a 975 manuscript that illustrate Beato di Liebana's Apocalypse result from the creative energy of a woman: the tenth-century illuminator Ende, in all likelihood a nun. Most of the text was copied by the monk Emeterius, but Ende adamantly signed her part: *Ende pintrix et Dei a(d)iutrix* (Ende, painter and servant of God). The subject of the book—the end of the world—haunted the tenth century. Obviously it fired the artist's racy imagination, for her pages teem with terrifying dragons and demons, scenes of catastrophe, and stylized, composed angels and saints. Brilliant colors against uneventful backgrounds and bizarre juxtapositions make this codex, which can still be admired in the archives of the Gerona cathedral, a masterpiece quoted in nearly every manual of art history.

A late-twelfth-century homiliary (collection of sermons) from a monastery in the middle Rhine region contains a veiled woman encapsulated within an initial letter D for Dominus (fig. 53). Its caption reads: *Guda, peccatrix mulier, scripsit et pinxit hunc librum* (Guda, sinful woman, wrote and illustrated this book). One hand grips the curved belly of the letter, the other is raised in the gesture of a witness who confirms the truth of the statement.[47] As modern observers, we can appreciate the significance of those long fingers, which, following a traditional convention, are held out with such confidence as a reminder of the lengthy task undertaken. This illumination is one of the oldest signed self-portraits, certainly the oldest of a woman artist.[48]

A Time to Think

A fourteenth-century painting portraying the life of the blessed Humility (died 1310) gives a good idea of day-to-day life in a convent, with its cadences of reading, learned lectures, and writing.

54. Humility Reads in the Refectory.

The saint, abbess and founder of the Vallumbrosian sisters, is portrayed reading instructional works aloud from the pulpit to her nuns in the refectory (fig. 54), and teaching two nuns who, crouched on the floor, conscientiously write down every word (fig. 55). Significantly, in these scenes

416

55. Humility Teaches the Nuns.
Pietro Lorenzetti, *Storie della Beata Umilta,* fourteenth century. Florence, Uffizi.

and at the center of the painting, where Humility is shown standing over her much smaller commissioner, she holds a book in her hands. In previous centuries this was a privilege accorded only to men.

Catherine of Siena (1347–1380), a Dominican tertiary who was an interlocutor of Pope Gregory

417

XI, was awarded nothing less than the triple halo and crown.[49] In addition to being a virgin and a martyr, for her uncomplaining suffering and vanquished temptations, she was also a "preacher," annulling Saint Paul's prohibition against women speaking in public. Her two biographers, Raimondo of Capua and Tommaso di Antonio of Siena (better known as the "Caffarini"), stressed in particular the authenticity of Saint Catherine's prophetic mission together with the elevated level of her doctrine. Analogies were drawn between her and Saint John, who preached glad tidings and wrote everything down in the Gospel.

This same award—the halo of doctors and preachers—was extended on a textual level to another saint with the same name, Catherine of Alexandria, whose cult reached the West after the Crusades had established new contacts overseas. One characteristic that portraits never failed to highlight was that of the holy queen's dialectic talents: her capacity to enlighten and convince the unbelieving pagan philosophers with whom she had occasion to converse. We see her, self-assured, book in hand, and emphasizing with a warning finger, sustain an argument alone against the king and a cluster of philosophers who wave books as evidence to dispute her—all in vain. The scene appears on a fifteenth-century fresco by Pizzocorno at the Abbey of Sant'Alberto, in Butrio near Pavia (fig. 56).

Catherine of Siena's initial approach to religious commitment was to become a sister mantellata, in the third order of the Dominicans, an order whose strong point had been converting heretics. She had ample room for using her special talents, which were well suited to the vocation of the order. The circulation of portraits of Saint Catherine helped spread her ideas, which were accepted despite the fact that she was a woman. The other Catherine became her corollary. Battling successfully against erudite pagan philosophers, she re-

56. Pizzocorno, *Catherine of Alexandria Preaches*, fresco, fifteenth century. Abbey of Sant'Alberto, Butrio.

420

inforced in the collective imagination the idea of a woman who was actively knowledgeable and able to stand up and defend her ideas rather than bending over backward with humility and obedience.

The Patron Saint

The birth of the Italian city-states led, among other things, to the development of a religious sensibility tied to the city.[50] This brought new saints to the altars, giving them greater power and influence over city affairs (when and if the faithful could identify them as fellow citizens). A great number of saints of both genders were canonized during this period.[51] An authentic canonization process was not always required; often they were proclaimed saints by local devotees. Sometimes these were local saints or laywomen, whose cult was limited to the city but whose presence reassured the populace as much as the bare city walls once had done. Among these were Saint Bona (died 1208) of Pisa[52] and Saint Fina (died 1253) of San Gimignano.[53] Such figures became—and this is an absolute novelty—a symbol of the city's conscience.

In a canvas by Nicolò Gerini, painted in 1402 and housed in the Civic Museum of San Gimignano, Saint Fina appears at the center of the composition, overlooking a scale model of her city. Around the edge scenes from her life demonstrate how the saint's destiny is and always has been intricately linked with that of the city of which she is patron. They show too how the previous patron, Gimignano, a bishop but an outsider, was less worthy of the honor. This painting is by no means an isolated example.

In a badly damaged fresco, painted sometime between 1360 and 1370 by a follower of Tommaso da Modena,[54] in the church of Saint Catherine of Alexandria in Treviso, the church of

57. Follower of Tommaso da Modena, *Saint Catherine with a Model of Her City*, fresco, 1360–1370, Church of Saint Catherine, Treviso.

Mary's Servants, the saint is portrayed holding the city (fig. 57). The gloss issuing from her mouth is: *haec est civitas mea Tarvisina pro quam Deum meum rogo* (This is my city of Treviso on which I invoke God's blessing). Flourishing city life can be deduced from the shields, towers, and banners; from the city's flag, which flutters in the breeze at the topmost point of an unfinished church; from the resounding bell which chimes out the rhythm of people's work, prayers, and the city's decisions. A crowd of citizens look beseechingly from the city walls. No longer simply commissioners of a devotional image based on the theme of the city's patron saint, they have become part of the painting, fixing forever their trust and their request for protection. The painting expresses a new concept of the city: a deep-seated link between men and stones, between the active presence of the city's inhabitants and the buildings that comprise their city, and, last but not least, between the city's faithful and the saint whose job it is to protect them.

With all these female figures rising to the surface, we can detect a gradual change in the condition of women. In the new "age of merchants," women played a more active role and participated more in the pulsation of everyday life. This is why Catherine, invoking God so self-assuredly, claims Treviso as her own.

After so many centuries in the Middle Ages when the path was barred to them, women began to recognize, not only in heaven but also on earth, "how to go to the city" (Eccles. 10:15).

TRANSLATED FROM THE ITALIAN
BY CLARISSA BOTSFORD

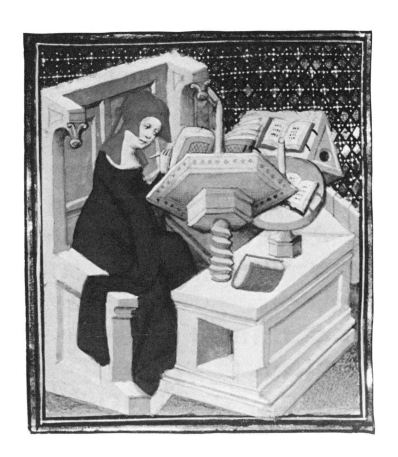

four

Women's Words

Daring to Speak

The voices of women were stifled, imprisoned by an ethic that treated sins of the tongue as gluttony and as harbingers of worse, of lust and pride. Women who presumed to speak out publicly only compounded the sin. Their words were open to condemnation on two counts. In the thirteenth century, perhaps because women had begun to find their voice, these denunciations became harsher than ever.

By the end of the Middle Ages women may well have discovered many new forms of expression. This was perhaps the area in which they made the greatest progress. A few were able to command attention, as Christine de Pisan did, by virtue of their learning and their courageous defiance of hostility, suspicion, and derision. Others usurped the right to speak in order to recount experiences they knew to be unique, experiences of mystical transport and union. They dared to speak out and to write of their experiences only after their senses and minds had been overwhelmed and their traditional notions of hierarchy had been overturned.

While educated women such as Christine and the fifteenth-century humanists, who battled fiercely in the narrow arena of letters,[1] knew who their audience was and how to reach it, the mystics did not. What words could capture the ineffable? Many of these women did not know how to write, at any rate not the language of the clergy. They had to rely on scribes, some of whom looked on them admiringly while others remained skeptical, some of whom hewed closely to what these female mystics actually said while others sought ingenuously to improve their style, to impart, preferably in good Latin, their troublesome message to other souls bent on the absolute. Who knows whether these women gave any thought to their audience when they began to write? Saying what they had to say in public was revolutionary enough. Listen to their voices. In few other eras have so many women dared to go beyond the limits of femininity in order to give it a voice.

C. K.-Z.

12

Literary and Mystical Voices

Danielle Régnier-Bohler

To resurrect the words of women from the silence of the sources—that is our project. The first human words were spoken by a woman, in the Garden of Eden; woman is at the origin, the inception, of language. A woman was the first to enter into relations with another human being; only the dialogue between Adam and God, that fundamental contractual exchange, preceded Eve's relation with Adam. Eve, Dante said in *De vulgari eloquentia,* was the institutor of language.[1] By partaking of the bitter fruit she also inaugurated man's misfortune. Her very name epitomizes the wailing of the countless babies who, as a result of her actions, would be born not in Eden but in the world.

Between woman and language there is a crucial bond: Eve means *life,* but Eve is above all a symbol of humankind's misfortune. Male babies, it was thought, cried *a,* whereas girl babies cried *e:* "Omnes dicunt e vel a / Quotquot nascuntur ab Eva" (All born of Eve say either *e* or *a*).[2] Thus the division between the sexes was inaugurated by these first cries, associated with the name "Eva," and woman introduced a caesura into time. Medieval theologians believed that Adam had proved weak in the face of Eve's words, weaker than Job. Women were henceforth enjoined to silence.

But there was much ambivalence; the texts contradict themselves at every turn. Even words contradict themselves. Certain striking images, with great force for the modern reader, emerge from this link between women and language. Sometimes the connection is benevolent. Ida of Bologna's first miracle endows a young girl, born deaf and dumb, with a social identity as well as powers of speech. Huddled in her clothes, the child is born into the world of language; her first words are *Mater, mater*.[3] In Jean Le Marchant's *Miracles of Our Lady of Chartres* the Virgin works a symbolic miracle: a loquacious child whose tongue has been cut out has his powers of speech restored, but not his tongue, the organ of speech, for which he must wait a while longer. Contrast this with the story of the unfortunate Philomena in a work attributed to Chrétien de Troyes (and based on Ovid). Philomena's tongue is cut out, not as punishment for overusing it but in order to prevent her from disclosing the fact that she is the victim of an incestuous rape. Deprived of speech, she invents another language, a language of gesture. With pieces of thread she tells the story of her misfortune and exile.

We know what language means and what part it plays in social compacts and rituals, communal practices, and dealings with the sacred. To explore the domain of language in a period for which no oral evidence is available is not easy. The only words of women we know are the words attributed to them, words largely filtered through the screen of male discourse. We take it on faith that creatures of flesh and blood spoke these words, expressed themselves, moaned and wailed, wrote and spoke. But even when women are granted their voice, that voice comes to us only through writing. Women's speech must be rescued from this paradox, whose consequences are inescapable.

When women's words, which are a kind of skin between self and others, are represented in texts, it is often their power to do evil that is singled out. For her daughters, for the countless ramifications of future generations, Eve became the model of an arduous relation to language. The dialogue concerning the apple, the first human speech, led to the expulsion from Eden and set humankind on the path of history. Women with voices, speaking for their sisters, would atone for this imprudent dialogue.

Thus humanity moved toward censorship, toward control of

language. But the constraints imposed on men pertained almost exclusively to their social being, whereas men used their language to control that of women in many different ways. Women's voices were disturbing, a troubling cacophony. The fear of female language was linked to the fear of female flesh and desire. Having sinned through speech—or so men claimed—woman had made her own destiny: her guilt was fabricated by the fearful words of men. Woman was sinful before the fact because she usurped language from man and with it invaded public and domestic space. She was dangerous too because of her charismatic and prophetic powers of speech, which reflected, from the thirteenth century on, female claims to a new relation with the sacred. From the intensity of certain inflections it is clear that in the realm of spirituality, a female discourse was in the process of finding its voice.

Misogyny did not always take the form of the strict moral injunctions we have encountered in preceding chapters. The author of one *Mirouer aux dames* (Mirror for Ladies) criticizes women for their aberrant dress, and especially for dressing up in men's clothes.[4] But the woman in this text is argumentative and draws on the "precedent" of such meritorious biblical women as Esther and Judith. Her male interlocutor is unconvinced, however: "What followed was language devoid of reason, and if there was reason in it, it was disorderly and incapable of adapting to the circumstances."[5] The biblical examples are cut down to size. Correcting women meant exposing them to righteous language while refuting their claims.

Women exercised their linguistic powers in a variety of ways, rich, subtle, and vehement; they spoke and they wrote. Men wrote about what women said, and women wrote to demand the right to speak. But it is difficult to say what the "reality" of the situation was, because the weight of the literary code stands in the way. Did a *trobairitz* (female troubadour) speak in her own name as a woman? Where was her individuality expressed? In marks on the manuscript over which the reader dreamily lingers? The words of medieval women are still waiting to be explored. If we recognize the existence of certain female troubadours, if we concede the existence of a Marie de France, if we follow the unmistakable but too little known traces of a Christine de Pisan, we enter the world of the literary woman and, more broadly, of female spirituality. For historians of literature, the language of women may well inspire exploration of a form of imagination that would have interested Gaston Bachelard in his quest for "the very root of the power to imagine" and Georges Poulet in his search for the signs of "interior time."

What we are looking for as we read the theologians and the moralists, the romance writers and the mystics, is the female voice. That voice was trained by a cultural code. Even as assertive a writer as Christine de Pisan, who dared to say in public "I, Christine," was a product of that code. What we hear may be nothing more than the lines spoken by literary "actresses" in a theater of language.

Yet the voice is crucial, for it is a fundamental aspect of the projection of self into the world of others. It is what an anthropologist would call a "total act," an act that is read, heard, or witnessed in the context of an established syntax of action. Words can fall on the ear as softly as a caress or with the force of a blow. The individual's narcissistic shell is partly verbal, a "skin of words."[6]

I propose to take a thematic approach, which is a way of asking questions more than of penetrating the opacity of the texts. The themes to be considered fall into two groups. One has to do with certain contradictions in language, with the endless "cackle" of women, the disorder it is supposed to engender, and the dangers of possession. The other involves the "good word" of Mary and the saints (who wield a powerful language, a rival of the language of men), as well as a more profane language, that of female myth, which presides over the invention of the world in the *City of Ladies.* The language of women is difficult to control because woman by nature exceeds her limits; she is a river that floods without fertilizing. But this unstanchable, lunatic female speech is countered by the solemnity of Christine's diction. Following Boccaccio's *De claris mulieribus,* she employs the metaphor of a utopian city to display the virtues of women of the past, from the Bible and myth. The invention of the world is work for women's hands and voices.

Thus, no matter whether we are dealing with the fearful prescriptions of moralists and preachers or with the audacious style of a woman of letters, woman by her very nature brings us face to face with what sociolinguists today consider to be a fundamental truth: language is an instrument of domination and judgment. The sexes are joined in battle over a common fief: linguistic expression.

Every damnable excess is crystallized in language. Female language duplicates male language; it reinforces itself with a rhetoric of abusive gestures; it transcends all boundaries, escapes all control. Worse even than the narcissistic deceptions of outward appearance, language is all the more pernicious in men's eyes because it emerges unpredictably out of silence. In the theater there is fanfare, but language comes unheralded. Malleable, it invades all spheres. Women use language to work evil magic, to deny male virility, to reveal the secrets of sex. The visual at least states openly that it is capable of fascinating, of paralyzing the gaze. But language enchants by infiltrating consciousness; it spreads, leaving almost imperceptible traces, nothing to which one can point. Hence it is less susceptible to ridicule.

Recall the myth of Echo: for speaking too much she is condemned to repeat the words of others. "Her voice is not her own, and the only person with whom she wishes to communicate is Narcissus, of whom she is enamored. But Narcissus, who loves only himself, does not speak to her. Both are condemned to silent infrasubjectivity."[7] Interpreted in this way, the myth is a myth of despair. Echo, reduced to parrotlike speech, encounters Narcissus, who sees only himself. Medieval woman is confronted with the inanity of her speech. She is the victim of a narcissistic censorship, imposed by a male counterpart obsessed with the danger of reproduction or in the grip of a diabolical fever that prevents him from seeing anyone but himself and therefore from recognizing the Other. But exactly what was being censored?

Another myth goes even further, a myth that deals with the expression of identity. This time a man is subjected to punishment, but the sex of the victim is unimportant. Actaeon, having surprised Artemis in her bath, is turned into a stag in order to prevent him from glimpsing the goddess in the nude. Like Narcissus, he catches sight of his new appearance in the water. "He moaned: that was the extent of his language" (Ovid, *Metamorphoses*). Henceforth he is not permitted to state his identity. An aphasia that renders identity inaccessible: that is what male discourse wants to inflict on woman. Her speech is limited to such a degree that her being is maimed.

The story of Griselda is emblematic. Woman is shown as mute, exalted, tested. The impotence of language is a heavy sentence. For what sin were women condemned? For the sin of their mother in Eden? Fictional texts, which may in some cases seem frivolous or parodic, have the merit of introducing a fantastic perspective, which can be valuable. What linguistic imagination finds its expression here?[8] Language, as Luce Irigaray says, "is never neuter,"[9] and even if the medieval corpus does not often allow an exhaustive examination of the contexts of voice, the questions raised by a linguistic approach attuned to the unconscious may provide some answers or at least hypotheses. The sexual dimension of the production of discourse—the sexualization of modes of communication—emerges with striking clarity. How do we measure its consequences for medieval culture, where the female voice (written as well as spoken) made itself heard persistently but prudently, yet where the language of men long remained the norm and that of women was taken to be defective or deviant?[10] The Beguines were considered to be deviants, and some of them paid with their lives; Marguerite Porete was burned at the stake. Moralists never relented in their criticism of defective female language in one form or another. The *fabliaux* rivaled one another in repeating these critiques in tales of marriage, female treachery, and women bent on revealing the secrets of sex.

Women spoke not only to one another but sometimes to themselves. In the moment prior to suicide, language could even be turned against the self. In fiction the destiny of internal speech was to be externalized. The tragic voice of women made itself heard in literature. But the crucial point is that it is women as a group who speak; often women's relation to language is magical. The language of women found expression in the gynaeceum as the language of solidarity and of the claim to power. In narrative literature we have bold fictions in which the image of woman is far from passive. The war in the *Quinze joyes de mariage* (Fifteen Joys of Marriage) is a victory for woman's language.

Woman facilitated access to language. Repository of the mother tongue, she opened the way to the universality of language, whether at the satanic boundaries of the Sibyl's cave or in those strange corrosions of linguistic barriers that we witness in connection with female sainthood. But the language of women also had its place in the world of letters. There were a few secular women of letters, like Christine de Pisan, but most cultivated women belonged to the world of religion: nuns, Beguines, anchoresses. Female mystics asserted the incompatibility of their language with that of men in a topos of modesty, yet they insistently proclaimed their inalienable right to invent a different tongue, one that enlisted the body as sensory support in the creation of a "total" language whose syntax incorporated shouts, tears, and silence as well as words.

The Statements of Women?

Women spoke in private as well as in public. They were forbidden to give legal testimony, it seems, because the only case in which their word could be trusted—according to Philippe de Beaumanoir's *Coutumes du Beauvaisis* (Customs of the Beauvais Region)—was when they were called upon to testify which of twins was born first. Given the anxiety of the ecclesiastical authorities at the desire of women to speak out in public, to proclaim the holy word without intermediary, the linguistic vigor that one finds in spiritual and mystical texts by women is astonishing. There are few if any areas in which women did not express their desire to speak.

Captive Voices

How can silenced voices be made to speak? The documentation is vast, and we must attend carefully to every murmur in lyrical poetry, to every expression of submission, and to the context in which each voice emerges. Thanks to their diversity, texts by women are irreplaceable evidence of the way in which women talked about themselves and above all of their mystical mission, in which the role of language was admittedly crucial. Literate women, generally prolix, sometimes had urgent things to say, but so did illiterate women, who were unable to avail themselves of writing despite the divine pressure to give voice to their spirituality. Of course it is difficult, as Peter Dronke points out, to find firsthand evidence.[11] Still, a vast range of sources is available, and our task is to listen beyond the manuscript for the sound of the authentic voice, the "voice as object."[12]

Were women captives of masculine language? In the second half of the ninth century Notker the Stutterer said that heaven's ladder could be climbed easily by virgins, married women, widows, prostitutes, and all women doing battle with the Devil. After surmounting trials of various sorts, they could attain the highest heaven and take the hand of the king, who would bestow on them the golden laurel of victory.[13] But at the court of Henry II Plantagenet, Walter of Châtillon rued the day a daughter was born to him yet observed that she would be the "future mainstay" of his "grumpy old age" and would take far better care of him than a son would.[14] Clearly there was a good deal of partiality in the representation of the Other. Women were too often described, and in fact defamed, in the language of men, in those "diverse words" whose validity Christine de Pisan questioned in her *Epistre au dieu d'Amours* (Epistle to the God of Love). It was a cruel society, in which language had the power to foist a hideous image on the female sex. In Chaucer the Wife of Bath is virulent in her denunciation of the power of the written word to fashion an image of the Other:

> By God, if wommen hadde writen stories,
> As clerkes han withinne hir oratories,
> They wolde han writen of men more wikkednesse
> Than all the mark of Adam may redresse.[15]

To judge by the scant literary evidence that has survived—a few female troubadours, a late-thirteenth-century writer of lays, and the more self-confident writers of the early humanist period such as Christine de Pisan and various Italian women of letters who asked nothing more than to be allowed the right to speak— it was not easy for women to express themselves. If the mystics soon aroused suspicions of abuse and heresy, fictional works, with their obvious lack of gravity, indicated that women frequently trespassed on a domain men regarded as their private preserve.

That such protected domains existed should not surprise us. Even today certain literary territories are reserved for women: the personal advice column in the daily newspaper, romance writing, and certain kinds of "female fiction," for example.[16] Medieval society made similar distinctions, but the territory assigned to women was on the whole less "personal" and "feminine" than it is today. It was an important undertaking for medieval women to occupy this territory, an enterprise accompanied by a sense of illicitness, of impudence, that grew out of the disabilities of the sex and the resulting timidity of women. Where and how did literate women hide? Did they conceal their difference from men, as women would continue to do for a long time to come? *Insignis femina, virilis femina* (remarkable woman, virile woman), Chancellor Jean Gerson said of Christine. We shall see how Christine attempted to change her sex in writing before embarking on a perilous adventure that required a man's strength.

In language, however, women did insist on their difference. To the clerics who interrogated her, the lay mystic Margery Kempe dared respond in a language all her own, insisting that what she said came to her from outside herself and that it was not only legitimate but reasonable. Two and a half centuries earlier Hildegard of Bingen had claimed that the "winds of God" passed through her. Women who gave themselves to the divine word assumed a mediating role that was hardly passive. Frequently as a precaution they turned to confessors and spiritual guides who not only kept a watchful eye on what they said but were sometimes moved by it to venture into the unexplored terrain of "total" emotional investment discovered by their charges.

Fictional Language?

In the *Vida* (Life) of Azalais de Pourcairagues we read: "E la domna si sabia trobar, e fez de lui mantas bonas cansos" (And the lady knew she was a troubadour and composed many good chansons).[17] In literature, however, access to the written word was shrouded in doubt. The prologues to the *Lais* and *Fables,* which announce the writer's intention to compile an anthology, speak of a woman, Marie de France, devoted to the art of writing, but there is no information about her identity.[18] The two prologues are concerned with the writer's activity. She gives her name, remarks on her relation to tradition, and speaks of her relation to the person to whom the works in progress are dedicated. The fear of praise she mentions may have been a topos, but it may also reflect an insistence on being allowed to write. "Without learning,"[19] she proposes to construct a work out of Breton folk tales. The importance of this inaugural declaration is clear. Marie wrote in a society where female patrons played an important cultural role, and this unknown woman's voice announces the beginning of a major body of work.

In the realm of lyrical poetry the female troubadours wore many masks. They were responsible for perhaps 1 percent of troubadour poetry, and nearly all their work is shrouded in mystery. The *Vidas,* biographical works written in the middle or late thirteenth century, after the composition of the poems, in five cases feature poets with female names; four other female names are mentioned in lives of male troubadours. The biographers attempted to explain the poems by fleshing out the people who wrote them. Their works were attempts to create reality out of mere names, but there is much doubt about the reality of the time they pretend to narrate, and the works contain very little actual information.

Azalais de Pourcairagues was "noble and educated." La Castelloza, who was from Auvergne, wrote chansons about her friend, as did the countess of Die, who was in love with Raimbaut of Orange. Maria de Ventadour is portrayed in a rhetorical dispute. A *"mise en abîme"* of the act of writing, narrativized lyric is economical. The writers are *eiseignada*, educated, and *fort maïstra*, highly skilled. Women are at least capable of "discovering," inventing, composing. But it is not easy to find traces of feminine expression. The female troubadours were interested in love poetry and in the poetry of debate, but, significantly, the emotional force of their work is not particularly great. It is hard to penetrate the masks, although certain readers have detected a more "uniform" tone in the work of the male troubadours and a more fragmentary approach in the work of their female counterparts. Statements are feminized by grammatical markers, which are the only signs of an attribution of sex to the "I" of the poems.[20] "Il ne me plairait pas d'être appelée Dame Bernarde par Bernard et Dame Arnaude par Arnaud" (I would not like to be called Lady Bernarde by Bernard or Lady Arnaude by Arnaud): the refusal to take the name of the male partner is eloquent but enigmatic. We have no choice but to consider the femininity of the *trobairitz* in terms of a "sexualization accomplished by poetic language."[21] Was this language of women therefore a fiction, created by an author whose identity and sex remain hidden? The female troubadours have even less of an individual identity than Marie or Christine. Is it therefore legitimate even to speak of a literature of women in the Middle Ages? Pierre Bec points out that what we take to be a woman's writing may be a text written by a man and ascribed to a woman or a text written by a woman but based on male models.[22] The works of the female troubadours would then have to be seen as "countertexts." The verse of the countess of Die, for example, falls well within the masculine code, but at the same time it lies outside that code because the author is a woman. And Bieiris of Romans' poem to another woman, the only Lesbian poem in the

Occitanian lyric repertoire, also appears to be a kind of protest, a seditious or satirical poem. In these countertexts the traditional "I" of the troubadours is supplanted by the lady—the absent figure made present.

Where is the authentic female voice to be found? What about those chansons whose protagonists are women, the so-called *chansons de toile* (weaving songs) that portray the woes of the woman in love, or the chansons from Germany, Galicia, and Portugal that sing of unhappy marriage? All the Galician-Portuguese love songs were written by men.[23] Hence the *cansos* of the *trobairitz* may be an Occitanian variant, women's songs composed by men, anonymous works that stood out from their courtly counterparts by virtue of their tone and anonymous authorship.[24]

Insignis Femina, Virilis Femina

Christine de Pisan stands out as the towering figure in the history of French literature from 1395 to 1405. Her problem was how to create a new and singular voice in the very heart of the codified literary tradition. It was not difficult for scholars to demonstrate that she must have been well educated, because her knowledge took the form of mastery of the traditional genres. It is much more difficult, however, to prove that she was a woman. She was the first woman to assert her identity as an author, to make solemn declaration of her entry into "the field of letters."[25]

"I, a woman, dare . . ." And Christine did in fact dare to assert herself as an author. That she was able to do so is a tribute to her remarkable self-confidence as a woman and as a writer, as a poet who found "a new place from which to write, the place of women."[26] She was also remarkable for her self-awareness as a writer. In *Avision Christine*, Dame Opinion tells Christine that some people say that her works "de sentement de femme venir ne pourroyent," that is, they could not possibly be the fruit of a female sensibility. Although Christine was interested in the business of making books and supervised the work of the copyists and illustrators, she was above all interested in the process by which she herself became a writer.

The death of her husband, which left her a widow with three children to support, weighed heavily on her, yet Christine was able to shuttle back and forth between managing her life and writing as she worked to perfect what she called "le stile a moy naturel," her natural style. She made her many voices heard in a variety of contexts, from philosophy to politics to religion, to say nothing of the lyrical tradition, from which she drew heavily while introducing her own subtle refinements. It was thanks to this poetic work that she entered into the well-known dispute over the *Roman de la Rose* (Romance of the Rose) that erupted around the turn of the fifteenth century.

She was careful about how she presented herself and used her learning. To Pierre Col she wrote that she loved "the study and the solitary life."[27] In the *Mutacion de Fortune, Avision Christine,* and the *Livre de la cité des dames* she shows herself to have been aware of the exclusion from knowledge that defined the status of women, a status whose limits she hoped to transcend: "Let no one accuse me of unreason, of arrogance or presumption, for daring, I, a woman, to challenge and answer back to so subtle an author, or for diminishing the praise due his work, when he, one man on his own, has dared to slander and reproach the entire female sex without exception."[28] These words conclude her letter to the provost of Lille. Jean de Meung, the author of the second part of the *Roman de la Rose,* was the chief target of accusation in the famous "quarrel," which Christine entered by seeking the support of another woman, Isabeau of Bavaria, against the many people who took Jean's part. On Candlemas eve 1401 she wrote that, despite her awareness of the weakness of her position, she felt herself "impelled by the truth . . . My limited intelligence wished, and wishes, to find employment here and in my other writings in battle against all who are hostile to and ready to indict it. I humbly beg Your Majesty to have faith in my just reasons and to allow me to say more, if I can, although I cannot express my thoughts in language as clever as some others."[29]

Her femininity had become a cause to champion. Let us not criticize the redundancy with which she expressed this crystallization of consciousness. Her ideal government was one that made a place for women in society. The *Livre des trois vertus* (Book of Three Virtues) is devoted to her sisters. Christine saw herself as a teacher whose mission was to defend her fragile sex. She was truly the first feminist in French letters.

Christine's message to women was part of her personal history, of what she called "my transmutation." One of the paradoxes of this pioneer feminist was her inevitable belief that, even as she championed the rights of women, she must "become a man."[30] In order to make herself heard, to validate her writing, Christine subjected herself to a regime of spiritual improvement which she describes in the *Livre du chemin de long estude* (Book of the Long Road of Study) as well as in the opening pages of the *Cité des dames:* "reclusive, dull, dejected, lonely, and tired." This state of depression and melancholia helped her gain access to knowledge and developed her appetite for a new self, one that would enable her to take her place among men of wisdom and learning. The woman who would become a legitimate writer had to forge for herself a man's heart. *Insignis femina, virilis femina:* this remarkable and virile woman wore no mask. She certainly was not being humble when she discussed her own name in the *Mutacion de Fortune:* the name Christine was in effect "the name of the most perfect man who ever existed" with the letters "ine" added in suffix.[31]

Christine's interest in her own name is connected with a peculiar transmutation. Matrilinear filiation is claimed, but the poetess posits "her identity through intervening males: first the intellectual heritage of the father, then the lineage of the husband."[32] As a result of this allegorical "narrativity," she becomes a conflux of heritages. Her father wanted a son, her mother ("who, without power, wanted a female like herself far more" than her husband wanted a son) hoped for a daughter. But this mother, though female, is tireless, immortal, and powerful: Nature herself. And Nature agrees that Christine should have her father's features and manner.[33] Later, Christine loses the captain of her vessel in a shipwreck (an allusion to her private life) and tells how she was "transmuted from a woman into a man" (line 1164). Fortune assumes the role of mother, recreating Christine. She awakens and finds herself transformed, her body strengthened and her voice deepened like a man's. Her psychology too is changed. Relieved of fear at last, she is now able to command the ship herself.

"And so I became a veritable man, that is the truth, capable of commanding ships. Fortune taught me how."[34] Christine, whose imagination has been shaped by a tradition of dream tales, must first undergo a change of sex. Perhaps this was a maneuver of prudence. But in creating the utopian city that only women can govern, Christine invokes the language and example of women.

In the *Chemin de long estude* the Sibyls play an important role. Christine addresses her inquiries to the Sibyl of Cumae, "lover of knowledge," in particular that of "the secret of God." After learning what she can from the Sibyls and from allegories of Nature, Justice, and Righteousness in *Cité des dames,* Christine is ready to play the role of a messenger to other women.

"In the Field of Letters"

Christine apparently found the *Lamentations de Mathéolus* depressing reading: "Alas! My God! Why didst thou not make me a man, so that I might serve thee with my predilections, never make mistakes, and be blessed with that great perfection that males claim for themselves?"[35] She encounters three ladies. The first, Dame Reason, who extols the mirror she holds as an instrument of understanding, is a prophet of things to come. The meetings with Righteousness and Justice come later, after this experience of inheritance through language. The city is in effect a realm of words: "Let us go to the field of letters, the rich and fertile land in which the city of women will be founded, a land of abundant fruits and gentle rivers where good things spring from the earth in plenty." The land of Canaan? It is land, in any case, to be worked by questioning: words are spades, the pen is a trowel.

Christine's concern is this: "My lady, among the weapons with which men reproach us is a Latin proverb: 'God created women to cry, to talk, and to weave.'" Chaucer's ferocious Wife of Bath countered that it was rather to deceive, talk, and weave. But Reason responds: "God did well to give them such a vocation, for many women have been saved by tears, distaffs, and words." None other than a woman announced the good news of Christ's resurrection. The woman of Canaan was quite right to talk so much, to shout at Christ and vex him, for he apparently "took pleasure in listening to the flood of words that came from the mouth of this woman, who endlessly pursued her questioning." The words of women thus redounded to the glory of God.

In the *Cité des dames* women hold high positions in the judicial system and the warriors are women of letters. Zenobia, the queen of Palmyra, accomplished in battle, devotes herself to study during her hours of leisure. She knows Latin and Greek and is writing an elegant summary of contemporary history in both languages. This "mirror of the prince" thus shows us another Christine.

If the language of women was sometimes a source of courage, it could also be quite crude. When Theodoric, commanding the army of Constantinople, showed a cowardly reluctance to fight, his mother resorted to extreme measures. Lifting the front of her dress, she said: "So, son, you want to run away. Then return to the womb from which you came."[36] The honor of the victory thus belongs to a woman who knew how to get her way, and who also understood the sterile oedipal desire to return to the womb.

Could women acquire learning? Christine asked Reason if God allowed women to have "keen intelligence and deep knowledge. Are their minds capable of it?" According to men, the intellectual capacity of women was strictly limited. But as Christine demonstrated, some women had lively, penetrating minds. And women were not just capable of learning the works of others; they could create their own. They could be philosophers and foretell the future. They could master both the subject matter and the style. Carmentis was celebrated for her role in the origination of language. She promulgated laws and possessed the gift of prophecy. She invented an original alphabet, which became the Latin alphabet, and both coined words and laid the foundations of grammar. Minerva invented the Greek letters called "characters," but she was also interested in the distaff and the art of weaving wool. Various kinds of knowledge from agriculture to weaving were essential to the acquisition of culture and the foundation of cities. Creative women helped define and assign the tasks essential to the formation of societies.

Eloquence was the quality admired in public speech. Its ingredients included memory, stylistic mastery, and charismatic power: "What is more, her manner of speaking, her expression, and her style were so beautiful, so agreeable, and so just that with her eloquence she could persuade anyone to do her bidding."[37] These words were spoken of Sempronia the Roman, who worked useful magic. As for the wise words of the Sibyl, the ability to predict the future and explain dreams created a kind of "consorority" of prophetesses: "Our Lord often revealed his secrets to the world through women."

Piling these portraits one on top of another, as a mason might build a wall, Christine built the memory of her sex. Dipping her mortar in ink, she made time the property of her sisters past and present. When Philip II, duke of Burgundy, wanted an official historian to write the history of his brother Charles V, he turned to Christine. The "virile woman" interviewed the duke, read the chronicles, and questioned people at court. In the *Livre des fais et bonnes meurs du sage Roy Charles V* (Deeds and Good Manners of the Wise King Charles V) she examined all aspects of the sovereign's perfection: the economy, martial exploits, culture, piety. But later she wrote the *Livre du corps de policie* (On the Body of Policy), which concerns women, as well as the *Cité des dames*.[38] Did she write as a "virile woman" in the hope of gaining a recognized status for women?

Christine's writing is a singular mixture of social concern and personal adventure, a mixture perceptible in her style, which is saturated in tradition yet highly innovative. It is a style to which female readers are particularly sensitive. Of course in reading her we must always be careful to respect the polemical context in which she wrote, and we must keep in mind the many screens that stand between her outlook and our own. In the end, however, one question remains: Why did she subject herself to such a strange "transmutation" of her sex, when she says that it was because she was a woman that she was able to conceive the admirable utopia in which she so fervently wished to believe?

Women and Letters

"Teach women neither letters nor writing."[39] It was no small feat for a woman to acquire the means of self-expression. One first had to gain access to the writing of others in order to imagine writing oneself. While not all moralists were as categorical as Philippe of Novare, it was considered dangerous to teach women to read and write. Literacy in women would for a long time to come arouse men's fears of both female impudence and their own impotence.

Evidence of women's self-expression is not easy to find in literature. It was in the realm of spirituality that truly individualized women writers first appeared: Hildegard of Bingen in the twelfth century, Beatrice of Nazareth, Hadewijch, Mechthild of Magdeburg, Marguerite d'Oingt, and others in the thirteenth and fourteenth centuries. These women were well aware of their writing abilities. Many wrote in the vernacular. Beatrice's *Seven Degrees of Love,* Hadewijch's *Letters,* Mechthild of Magdeburg's astonishingly complex *Streaming Light of the Deity,* and Marguerite Porete's admirable *Mirror of Simple and Devastated Souls* show that their authors aimed beyond literature. Of course their literary culture is remarkable, to say nothing of the theoretical baggage they carry with them. But these were women embarked on a spiritual quest. Touched by grace, they were spreading God's truth, and some sought to help others through teaching. They had a powerful intuition of the efficacy of the text, of literature, of language.

The literature produced by nuns seems less individualized. The convents produced countless lives of saints, of which numerous south-German examples have survived. Some recount the life of a single individual; others are compilations of brief biographies of a group of individuals that attempt to characterize the spiritual life of a particular convent. Although less personal perhaps than the works of the mystics, the lives prove that these Dominican nuns had read and absorbed the writings of their sisters.[40] The authors of these texts exhibit a keen awareness of having been chosen by the grace of God. They were women who felt privileged and therefore empowered to speak out and write.

The earliest personal writings by women were clearly the work of women of letters whose social and economic status was well-defined. The sources are fragmentary, but the works of the best-known figures, such as Eloise and Hildegard, allow us to enter into the more private parts of the self and to learn something about their inner development. It was not an easy thing to speak out, especially if one dared, as Hildegard did, to venture into theology and the history of science. Professions of humility were common. Hildegard wrote Bernard of Clairvaux that without the instruction of the Holy Spirit she would be unable to write. "Paupercula mulier et indocta"—this "poor, uneducated woman" disowned any literary skill and professed to know little Latin. Accomplished as she was, she seems to have been less confident of her linguistic skills than many men. But "within my soul I am learned," she claimed, and her abundant correspondence reflects her efforts to keep abreast of the intellectual ferment of her time. She wrote to the great of this world: Eleanor of Aquitaine, the countess of the Palatinate, and many others, including popes, emperors, and bishops. Theologians questioned her on points of doctrine, and her account of her visions was an ambitious undertaking that took in the origins of the world, the structure within which man found his place, and representations of the other world. In addition to her more theological concerns, Hildegard reflected on the condition of women.

Even earlier, in the second half of the eighth century, another woman, Hugeburc, took it upon herself to write a life of Saint

Willibald and later a life of Saint Wynnebald. We know how she began: Willibald himself dictated an account of his travels to her. She thus became conscious of a task, a mission.[41] There is other scattered evidence of women's thoughts and feelings. Dhuoda revealed something of a secret life in the handbook of moral and religious advice she prepared for her son. Attentive to the passage of time, she included dates of various events. Her work has a remarkable introspective character.[42] According to Peter Dronke, women's writing was more spontaneous than men's and exhibited greater curiosity about the inner life.

Female writers often began their texts with professions of humility, and even if Curtius was right that this was a topos, it is clear that the act of writing was an audacious thing for a woman to attempt.[43] For Hrotswitha, metrical verse was difficult for women and required divine assistance. When asked to write an official history, she told Gerberga, the abbess of Gandersheim, of her difficulties in writing and compared herself to a traveler attempting to negotiate a snowy pass without a guide. Her work—arduous for a woman—familiarized her with the panorama of glorious events.[44] Elsewhere she reveals that, doubtful of her knowledge and ability, she wrote in secret. She worked furtively and sometimes destroyed what she had written. Although Hildegard, who lived much later, was recognized by the great men of her time, she too confessed her acute awareness of the fragility of women, though she was also quick to assert confidence in her intellectual capabilities.

Many female writers, from Hrotswitha to Hildegard and Christine Ebner in the fourteenth century, say they were encouraged to write by the people around them, hence aware of writing to reach an audience.[45] The abbess of Rupertsberg may have referred to herself as a "paupercula mulier et indocta," but Mechthild of Magdeburg sent her book to all the men of the Church as a message: "Dis buch das sende ich nun ze botten allen geistlichen luten" (I send this book to all spiritual people). What we are witnessing is the birth of a consciousness on the part of women that they had something to say, and with it a fear of not being up to the task. But the works of women of letters were in many cases avidly read. So were the professions of humility a mere commonplace, or do they reflect genuine feelings of inferiority? The voices of nuns and Beguines can help answer this question.

A good deal of doubt remains about certain kinds of female writing. As we have seen, the voice of the female troubadours fell somewhere between the aristocratic register of their male counterparts and the more popular register of weaving songs and other female chansons.[46] But spiritual literature allows us to read women speaking in the vulgar tongue of their spiritual experiences. The literature of the convents is interesting for another reason. The major thirteenth-century works seem to have been produced in considerable independence: Beatrice, Hadewijch, and Marguerite Porete possessed extensive theological and literary knowledge. By contrast, the aims of convent writers were humbler. The *Lives* they wrote tell us a great deal about the communities they lived in. Although the "female mystics," as they are commonly called, wrote for a variety of reasons, all discovered writing as a means of expressing their spiritual progress.[47]

There is moreover a mystery about this writing, shaped to be sure by literary conventions but conventions freely used and often accompanied by protestations of a lack of cultivation on the writer's part. These women thought of themselves as chosen visionaries, authors singled out by God to write, but at the same time they liked to profess their unsuitability to the task. Mechthild said she lacked culture. Christine Ebner, who was surprised to discover that God spoke to her more readily than to priests, learned to think of her election as part of the divine plan. God chose certain women to reveal his power to the world, a privilege for which the reward was ecstasy.

It is an oversimplification to suggest that there was a sexual division of labor in the writing of spiritual texts, according to which men produced works of theology and pastoral manuals, while women recounted visions and wrote *Lives*. Women such as Beatrice of Nazareth wrote treatises on the love of God, and men such as Friedrich Sunder wrote *Lives*. But according to Ursula Peters, this tells us less about actual religious life than about the forms of spirituality that monks and nuns ascribed to the elect, whether chaplains or women.[48]

Contemporaries seem to have been particularly struck by one innovation. In the mid-thirteenth century Lamprecht of Regensburg voiced his astonishment at an "art" that had originated among women, among nuns and Beguines. Jan van Leewen addressed Hadewijch as "mistress," and Marguerite Porete was called "Beguine clergeresse" in recognition of her literary and religious learning. From studies of spiritual vocabulary and mystical metaphor scholars have concluded that such mystics as Meister Eckhart and Ruusbrook could not have written as they did had it not been for the women who preceded them. Specifically, German mysticism, and especially Meister Eckhart, drew heavily on the female mystics of the Netherlands, through whom accounts of the spiritual experience of the less cultivated, and primarily of women, found their way into theology. The Beguines found new ways to express the ineffable union with God: ecstatic descriptions, stories of visions, descriptions of the nakedness of the soul. They invented a novel diction, a comprehensive language that made room for the body in the spiritual vocabulary.

Accounts of visions were common in literature from the twelfth century on, and journeys to the other world were not an exclusive province of women. But the best-known visionaries wrote in the thirteenth century, inventing new images and elaborating vast, complex structures. From Hildegard to Marguerite d'Oingt, from the anchoress Julian of Norwich to her contemporary Margery Kempe, an avid reader of this literature of travel, women discovered a wide range of new styles.

In some cases we are able to follow the diffusion of their manuscripts and witness the success of those works that were quickly translated and widely read, such as Marguerite Porete's *Mirror of Simple and Devastated Souls,* but with other authors it is sometimes difficult to identify what kind of writing drew the widest readership. Christine Ebner is a case in point. The life and revelations of the Dominican nun Engelthal can be found in three texts of three different types. The first is an account of visions in the third person, including personal details of the mystical life keyed to the liturgical year, professions of admiration for a woman she considered exemplary, Mechthild, and information about her ties to Heinrich of Nördlingen. The second, apparently written in collaboration with the nun, is about the signs of Engelthal's extraordinary destiny, including apparitions of the Virgin and Christ. Here there is less concern with strict dating, and the accent is on the nun's religious childhood and dreams. The mystical expression at times involves use of the first-person pronoun. We learn that *gnaden und wunder,* graces and miracles, were recorded daily, much as the day's events might appear in a newspaper.[49] The third text, which develops certain themes from the second, is a biography of the saint Christine Ebner. The importance of the relation between the visionary and the person responsible for writing down her visions became a central theme of this spiritual literature. This is particularly interesting in the *Life of Saint Douceline,* a biography written, as was common in regions where the *langue d'oc* was spoken, by one of her sisters.

Significantly, mystics and nuns wrote in the vulgar tongue, be it German, French, Flemish, or Italian. Doing so not only allowed their work to be read more widely but also made possible a direct, unmediated relation with the Holy Ghost. But it also aroused suspicions about what some of these women, especially the Beguines, were up to.

From what environments did these writing women emerge? Some, like Hrotswitha and Hildegard, came from highly intellectual backgrounds. Others most likely came from circles imbued with the culture of the courts. Some of these women protested their lack of learning, but they did so in order to underscore what a privilege it was for "illiterates" such as themselves to live such intense spiritual lives. Contemporaries were astonished to see these women engage with the thorniest theological issues. According to Lamprecht of Regensburg, their quest for God seemed to take a form different from anything men were capable of. Much work remains to be done before we can say that there were indeed different routes to God for men and women. In any case, the female mystics encouraged preaching both inside and outside the convent. Margery Kempe reacted with great emotion to the sermons she heard. These women read and circulated the literature of piety, from which they derived encouragement to write. They felt called upon to impart knowledge of their spiritual progress to their sisters and to the men with whom they associated. Here, notwithstanding the cautions of Ursula Peters, it is tempting to see individuals turning inward and discovering ways to describe their own experiences.

One important point should be kept in mind, even though it may disappoint those in search of an authentic representation of women's feelings. Most of these texts were written after a meeting with a confessor, who urged that some spiritual event be recorded in writing. This cooperation between men and women marked an important step in the development of a capacity for self-analysis and self-expression. The confessors, as outside advisers, vouched for the authenticity of their disciples' words helping women skirt the danger they would have courted had they acted too independently. Ursula Peters among others has raised the question of whether this important relationship, essential to any authorized spiritual discourse, was a true stimulus or a source of literary mystification. At any rate, the *mulier religiosa,* ignorant by nature and therefore capable of the highest intuitions, profited from the spiritual companionship of the confessor.

Woman's relation to writing was complex. Women were long excluded from a university education, whether sacred or profane. They had no institutional training other than that occasionally provided by their convent. Beatrice of Nazareth, for example, completed her *trivium* and did all of her *quadrivium* in the convent setting. Cloistered women did translations, and many twelfth-century convents gained prestige by producing manuscripts.[50] Correspondence with well-known men attested to an ability to write in Latin; Hildegard is a shining example. Quite a few "semicloistered" women appear to have been educated.[51] For a long time, however, it would remain difficult for women to overcome their own sense of ineptitude, particularly in lay circles in the later Middle Ages where access to a literary education seems to have been easier. What was the reality of the situation? In a letter to Bianca Maria Visconti, Costanza Varana asked: "Quid igitur indocta, rudis, inexpertaque puella faciam?" (What shall I do in my ignorance and incompetence?). In Italy women did in fact find a place among the humanists. But they were women born to prominent families, members of an elite.[52] These young women of letters were keenly aware of the choice they faced: marriage meant an interruption of their studies, whereas refraining from marriage meant renouncing the world. In this period of flourishing knowledge and of opportunities for women to seek an education, we find women paradoxically suspicious of their own motives. Some spoke out in public. Isotta Nogarola defended Eve against the charge that she was responsible for the Fall of man by arguing that women are weak by nature. Other women sometimes made fun of young women of letters. Their sexual identity was not easy to assume. Christine, as we have seen, wrote of the benefits she reaped by her transformation into a man, and earlier Boccaccio, dedicating his work to Andrea Acciaiuoli, asserted that she owed her talents to a nature not too different from a man's.

Words in Action

Women were silent because the right to speak had to be granted by authority. Their silence reflects submission. In fiction we read how merciless marriage strategies condemned women to silence or at most to futile complaints that would not be heard outside their own rooms—unless a "miracle" intervened. The young woman in Marie de France's *Lai de Yonec* is "mismarried": "Cruel is my fate! says she. Here I am, imprisoned in a dungeon from which death is the only escape."[53] No sooner has this lament been uttered than she sees through the tiny window the shadow of a huge bird, a man-bird, come from the other world to father her child, Yonec. The heroine of the *Lai de Guigemar* is also a woman condemned to a life incommunicado. Her only recourse is to talk to the paintings, until one day a miraculous ship arrives to break the silence. These imprisoned women's laments are born of silence, and their words, forever unanswered, movingly evoke the reality of incarceration.

"In Great Silence, with Head Bowed"

Man, the overseer of his conjugal order, was a witness to restrained sorrow.[54] What women said never affected him, not even the entreaties of young girls pursued by incestuous fathers. The lamentations of Joïe, the lovely Manekine who mutilated herself rather than marry her father, were met with a silence that lasted for years—silence as to the father's sin as well as to her own identity. All one could do in a bad situation was implore God; rebellion was never permissible. Beautiful Helaine of Constantinople also fled her father's arms. She too was condemned to silence, or at any rate failed to make herself heard, until finally, at the end of her journeys, she, like Joïe, miraculously found her husband and father in Rome.

Prisoners of incestuous desire hid behind masks of silence. They relinquished their identities and resorted to nonverbal language to indicate their refusal to submit. The texts are extraordinarily reluctant to talk about such things, even where rape was involved. In *La fille du comte de Ponthieu* (The Count of Ponthieu's Daughter) a young woman is raped by five robbers while her husband is forced to watch. When she proves infertile, her outraged father casts her into the sea, but she is transported to another world where she learns a new language, Saracen, and ultimately regains the ability to bear children. Perhaps the story was some sort of initiation myth.[55]

Silence is also paramount in the strange stories of the "wager cycle," which belonged to an established tradition. Gaston Paris has identified many stories of this type, in which a man wagers that he can seduce a woman. The woman is reduced to silent waiting.[56] The seducer offers proof of success, and the woman is obliged to produce proof of the contrary, but her words of refusal or denial cannot be heard. In *Guillaume de Dole* an object proves that the man is lying. The woman uses false words, a tissue of lies, to bring out the truth: "If she had studied law for five whole years without letup, I do not think she could have presented her accusation or her case more clearly. No doubt about it."[57] Knowing full well that a woman's words will be ignored if not shrewdly presented, Lienor proves to be an excellent advocate, laying out the material evidence and distributing gifts before proceeding with her argument.

Silent women, forced to wander the world, must renounce their identity. Joïe becomes simply the Manekine. Helaine, daughter of the king of Constantinople, becomes a beautiful woman without a name. In many narratives a young woman vilified for illicit sexual relations refrains from protest and says nothing but flees with her child. The patience of women is infinite.

That patience was echoed through the centuries in oral tales such as the account of Griselda's lengthy ordeal. The heroine suffers humiliation after humiliation, a formula whose success influenced much subsequent literature (including many titles in the popular Blue Library, pamphlets sold by hawkers to the common folk). She loses her two children (ostensibly put to death) and is cast out by her husband. She acquiesces in these injustices in virtual silence and even agrees to make the bed for her husband's new wife—none other than her own daughter, whom she had believed dead. Her submissiveness, her silence, are put to the test. Griselda's symbolic silence attains almost hagiographic proportions. Ultimately she drowns.

Did these obvious male fantasies have a cathartic effect on male and female readers alike? Petrarch tells us that audiences were enchanted, and he himself translated the story of saintly Griselda and the virtues of silence. "There are people," he says,

"capable of doing things that seem impossible to vulgar eyes."
Griselda is exemplary: she "has no will of her own." Later Philippe
de Mézières translated Petrarch back into French in the *Livre de
la vertu du sacrement du mariage* (Book of the Virtue of the
Sacrament of Marriage). Griselda's tragic story found further
echoes in the work of the Chevalier de La Tour Landry, Thomas
de Saluces, *Le Ménagier de Paris,* Olivier de La Marche, and
others.[58] Surprisingly, submissiveness seems to have made Griselda
eloquent: "I left my father's house naked, and naked I shall return,
except that I think it unworthy and improper for this womb, which
bore children you fathered, to appear naked before the people. If
you would be so good as to consent, therefore, I ask you now, in
return for the virginity I brought to your palace but will not take
away with me, to order that I be left with one nightdress with
which to cover the belly of the woman who was once your wife."[59]
Griselda agrees to leave her husband's house "decently and in
shame, in great silence, with head bowed." She returns to her
father's cottage with a crying, wailing entourage.

Women were sold as commodities. Discourse about prostitution was masculine. Men speculated about the "ideal" prostitute,
about the relation between women and pleasure, about women
who worked in order to survive, and about "lustful" women,
women in love with their pleasure.[60] The pleasures of the flesh and
free love were serious matters to devout Catholics, as the controversy over the *Roman de la Rose* shows. But the victims have voices
in the texts, and the famous controversy took place against a
background of social practices described by other women. Their
testimony resurrects sexual behavior in the form of narrative. We
learn details of violent acts, of the infliction of pain, of the mis-
treatment of women in the street by groups of men. Now and then
we glimpse the ways in which women's complaints were hushed
up. We intuit the lapse of time between the act and the complaint:
the rape, the discovery of blood, the hand clapped over a mouth
to stifle a cry. By acting together, however, women were able to
bring charges in public. The authorities might ask questions. Why
did the victim not speak out between the time of the original
assault and the second act of violence? Why did she not complain
the morning after? Two neighbor women reported the attack to
the rapist's wife; "before that the woman did not dare to speak."
Rapes were sometimes repeated, as is clear from one complaint
filed by Marguerite Guillaume on Ascension Day 1449: "She who

is speaking hastily took up her distaff and went to the street, where she met several women: Perenot Viaulot, Favier's wife; Mme Chapelier; Mme Pageot; and Mme Corduier. In tears, she told them what had happened to her, and when they saw her, they went to see Pageot and tell her father; before that she had dared not speak."[61] Similarly, the count of Ponthieu's daughter, overcome by shame, hesitates to reveal the truth.

"Quite humble in conversation," Griselda is blessed with considerable eloquence. She quiets "the debates and discords of nobles with gentle and mature words," according to one anonymous fifteenth-century translation. Submissive, skilled at preserving order, she is included among the celebrated women in the *Cité des dames.* It is no small irony that Christine, drawing on Philippe de Mézières, praised Griselda and saw her as an exemplary woman.

The *Roman de silence,* written by Heldris of Cornwall in the thirteenth century, is a story of inheritance in a kingdom whose king has abolished cognatic succession in order to avoid controversies arising out of female claims. The birth of a daughter therefore confronts Eufamie and Cador with a serious problem. In order to allow their daughter to inherit Cornwall, they give her an ambiguous name and disguise her as a boy. "Let us name the child Silence, after Saint Patience, for silence dispels all worry. May Jesus Christ by his power grant us the power to hide her and keep the story quiet according to his will. I can think of nothing better. He will be named Silenscius. And if by chance someone discovers his true nature, we will change the -us to -a, and the name will be Silencia. If we remove the -us, we will restore her natural being, for the -us is imposed against nature, but the other is in accordance with nature."[62]

The name conceals the absence of a male line. Howard Bloch has analyzed the complex symbolism of the narrative. Nature is associated with the true name, with sexual difference, and with the rule of primogeniture. By contrast, artifice and dissimulation are linked to the violation of grammatical proprieties, sexual inversion, and illegitimate inheritance.[63] The child, Silence, is torn between his/her desire "to behave as women do," as they are required to do by nature, and the need to do otherwise: "Silencius! Who am I, then? I bear the name Silencius, I know, so am I other than I was. But there is one thing I know well, by faith, and that is that I am not a different person. Therefore I am Silencius, it seems, or I am no one."[64]

But Noreture puts an end to this confusion and Silence realizes that it is better to be a man than a woman.[65] Later, however, she goes off with jugglers, learns their trade, surpasses them in skill, acquires a public voice, and manages to seize the elusive Merlin in the forest, something only a woman can do. She thus reveals that she is in fact Silencia and, having acquired a woman's identity, marries the king of England. In the context of medieval literature the association of power with the acquisition of both a sexual identity and a name was particularly rich in symbolism.

Bad Language

Many allegorical figures, both good and bad, were women, as were the novel creatures of thirteenth-century poetry, born of the devil and given as brides in perverse wedding ceremonies: "Simony, Hypocrisy, Rapine, Usury, Fraud, Sacrilege, False Service, Pride, and Lechery." Allegory illustrated vice in the most vivid way, but it was also a distancing device. Sometimes the speech of women exceeded the bounds of propriety and became "bad language." There was no shortage of injunctions, however, about what constituted temperate speech: "Women should not wildly abandon themselves to harmful speech or wicked acts. For if they speak evil, they will be answered either with truth or falsehood, and the result will be life-long embarrassment or shame."[66] There could be no clearer indication of the fact that speech was a symbolic skin, an interface between the individual and the community. And speech led to more speech. The texts are prolix, evidence not only of narrative skill but of the importance of language in governing the world.

Women in fact enjoyed extravagant powers. They were gluttons for words, their own as well as those of others. They avidly took in what other people knew. Like hunters always on the alert, they lay in wait. Their strategy was shrewd. They seduced others with honeyed words, coaxed from hiding their secrets. Against such wiles, man's armor was fragile, his secrets vulnerable. Diabolically possessed by the desire to know all, to hoard all, woman proved incapable of coping with the knowledge she gained; she spent it unwisely, divulged it publicly. Uncontrollable gossip is still, according to sociologists, a "racial trait," a peculiarity of the "race" of women.[67] The drunk can keep no secrets, but the woman who drinks is particularly vulnerable: "Any man who tells his secrets to his wife makes her his sovereign. Unless he is drunk or has lost his senses, no man of mother born should reveal anything to a woman if he does not wish to hear it repeated by others," Genius says to Nature in one allegorical romance.[68]

A woman would risk her life for the pleasure of divulging a secret. A man seduced by a woman confides in her more readily than he would in a priest. And once a secret is out, it can never be called back. Samson confided all his secrets in Delilah. Countless misfortunes can be traced to the revelation of secrets. The Chevalier de La Tour Landry tells his daughters: "You should hide your lords' counsel and not tell anyone about it."[69] This attitude tells us a great deal about the impact of public language. Accordingly, husbands tested their wives by imparting false confidences to see if their secrets would be kept.

Group Language

Women spent a great deal of time together, and during that time they talked. Spinning and embroidering were activities conducive to conversation. It was a time for young beauties to confide in their mothers or governesses the names of the men they loved. It is significant that the women engaged in these everyday activities were confined, according to the literary code, within a well-defined space, often a room beside running water.[70] Clever authors portrayed women sewing and embroidering while singing about other women doing the same things. In the Occitanian romance *Flamenca*, scenes of this kind, at times animated and malicious, show how a young wife could fool a jealous husband and plan a meeting with her lover.

The *Gospels of the Distaff,* a unique work that used new forms to epitomize a long tradition, showed "wise and prudent matrons" gathering in the period between Christmas and Candlemas. One by one each presides over an evening's reading, and the ritual is observed with a discerning eye: "One of us would begin her reading and chapters in the presence of all who had gathered there so as to preserve the memory forever after."[71] The only man allowed to attend these vigils is ordered to write down the "gospels," much as the four evangelists recorded the life of Christ. There was a hierarchy, since one woman presides over each session, but the exchange is democratic, since each in turn contributes maxims and comments on what had been said. The audience grew with each passing day. There was an implicit connection with magic: three of the oldest women know something of the occult arts such as fortune-telling. One of them is familiar with the works of heretics, "from whose learning she had acquired a great deal." Their secrets are intended for other women, for the women of future generations. "From generation to generation [this knowledge] will be preserved and augmented," according to the "conclusions of the third day."

The male secretary says something that reveals the deep division between women as a group and the men excluded from their gatherings. He denies, first of all, that there is anything to what they say: "What they said seemed to me utterly without reason or good effect." But as they continue their idle chatter, he attempts to express his disapproval in a more graphic way: "Apparently they were not about to quiet down, so I placed myself in such a way that they could see me in the hope that my eyes would make them ashamed of their words, which were as chaotic as the end of a battle without victory or glory."[72]

Clearly the words women spoke in these vigils were distorted when they were written down. The writer advises his readers not to "look to anything written in this text for any fruit or substance of truth or useful application." The text is thus a parody of superstitious belief. It rejects things it takes to be equally peculiar: women, oral discourse, rural life, the irrational. In fact the word "gloss" took on an ironic meaning in the late Middle Ages: it was used sometimes to refer to the idle chatter of women.[73]

It was widely believed that women had the ability to interpret obscure signs of the powers that influenced men's lives. The husband who does not heed his wife's wise advice is compared to a perjurer who contradicts the truth (Monday, chapter 2 of the *Gospels of the Distaff*). If salt is placed on the head of a sleeping pregnant woman, she will reveal the sex of her unborn child by uttering its name (chapter 7). Naturally the salt has to be deposited by another woman. And a gloss to chapter 13 suggests that if a newborn child is given baked apple to eat before it sucks from its mother's breast, it will grow up to be not only frugal but also "more courteous in deed and word" toward women. One of the older women responds to this by saying that "when a child is born, if the small intestine [the umbilical cord?] is placed on its head, it will enjoy a long life with sweet breath, a fine voice, and gracious eloquence." Presumably these desirable consequences are the result of contact between the umbilical cord and the head, which is the seat of language. Oratorical talent was the mark of a mature and accomplished individual.[74] The umbilical cord was a source of social virtues because it symbolized the link with the mother, the original source of life. The immortality supposedly conferred by the wearing of a talisman was also a consequence of the maternal bond. The twelfth chapter of the *Gospels of the Distaff* claims that a man who wears "in battle a small bit of skin from his mother's belly" cannot be wounded, but this statement is followed by a derisive gloss. This compilation of female powers ends with what Berthe de Corne says is a "marvelous secret that few men know and that I would be greatly displeased if they did know" (Saturday, chapter 19).

The Bitter Division

Nature complains that she is the butt of too many insults: "I am a woman, I cannot hold my tongue, I want to reveal everything at once."[75] Man violates the rules of nature by sowing disorder: "I repent of having made man. But by the death that God suffered, he who received the kiss of Judas and was struck by Longis' sword, of him shall I give an accounting before God, who entrusted him to me when he made him in his own image, because he causes me so much torment . . . And so his vices will be laid bare, and I shall tell the whole truth."[76] Man is denounced as a slave to all the vices: he is a liar, a fraud, a traitor, a braggart. Women thus answered the normative male discourse that condemned them and their abuses. In Jean de Meung's philosophical poem Nature occupies a preeminent place.

The bitter division between the sexes was dramatized in many different ways. In de Meung's poem women as a group are portrayed, in the speech of the man who has married badly, as witches involved in diabolical practices: "All of you are, were, or will be whores by action or intention."[77] Here the target is the female sex as a whole, and especially relations between women. The stepmother who trades on her daughter's charms is branded a procuress and witch: "Like mother, like daughter, said the husband to his wife. You spoke to each other. Your two hearts are made of the same wood."

The power of women as a group is illustrated by the fifteen parodic tales collected in *Quinze joyes de mariage* (Fifteen Joys of

Marriage). Here the female protagonist flanked by accomplices is all-powerful. Her husband is caught in a trap. A tacit understanding grows among the women as they talk and weave. The husband is lonely and silent. The members of the household are assigned to immutable roles. Deprived of speech, the husband lives a nightmarish existence. Language, here the province of women, is the driving force in the war between the sexes that rages in this world turned upside down.[78]

Women who speak are usually portrayed as deviants. Language, according to La Tour Landry, is always a source of "deception," of fraud. His children are "fine linguists and well spoken," and this raises the problem of how to distinguish the truth underneath the falsehood. All language is a trap. But women are more likely than men to violate the code regulating the use of language in society. "Do not speak loquaciously: the person who talks too much does not always say wise things. Before speaking, moreover, one must listen carefully, and if you wait a while, you will answer better, more to the point. For the proverb says that a person who listens without really paying attention is like one who goes hunting and comes back empty-handed."[79]

Men were obsessed with the idea of excessive talk. Perhaps the interminable chatter of women was a consequence of Eve's "poor listening," which made her incapable of resisting the Devil's "sweet veiled words," words that were actually "deceitful and venomous." La Tour Landry suggests that "false language" may turn the world on its head and substitute day for night (chapter 62). The question of untruthful language was therefore an issue of social ethics, for it threatened the validity of the social contract. In one particularly cruel example of this women do not bear the full responsibility. A mother whose son has been killed in battle is deceived by "flattery" and false words to believe that he might still be alive. The power of such lies is like the power of spellbinders to transform reality for a short time, to "make a lump of coal look like a beautiful thing." Behind the fear of women's chatter was a more general fear of deception, which we find in many areas of medieval culture.

The Language of Death

In the *Roman de la Rose* the very name Malebouche (Evil Mouth) evokes the sins of language. Malebouche is the "son of a dispu-

457

tatious old woman," and he spreads the poison of his mother's sharp and bitter tongue. Various other allegorical figures represent proper uses of language: a meritorious knight, whose renown is reported in many tales, is taken by the hand and led about by Generosity; Frankness ensures nobility of language; Courtesy, polite and reasonable in assertion and response, mocks no one and makes everybody happy. By contrast, Malebouche embodies the dreadful power of language.

Women, as all men know, are a source of nothing but shame and trouble, and their tongues can be lethal. In *Le vilain de Bailleul* (The Peasant of Bailleul) a wife tries to convince her husband that he no longer exists: "My friend, death is taking you. It has so changed your heart and laid you low that nothing is left but your shadow, and soon that too will be gone . . . You are dead."[80]

Many husbands were forced to confront the sad fact of their impotence. But language was most effective in the bond between mother and daughter. The mother's role in shaping her daughter's individuality can be seen clearly in *Ecureuil* (Squirrel). A mother advises her daughter to be careful about what she says and never to mention a man's "thing," the "fishing pole that swings between their legs."[81] But women also know the true names of things, so the mother teaches her daughter that the "thing" is a "penis." The conversation is rich in symbolism: to name a thing is almost to commit a sin, but it is also an adult and creative act. When the taboo is violated, the daughter laughs: "May God give me a penis too so that I can name it." Man thus has the right to bestow names, but women, prone to excess, must submit to prohibitions on their use of words. This, as we shall see, had consequences for the language of sexuality.

From mother to daughter the women in the fabliau *La dame écouillé* (The Castrated Lady) dispose of what men propose. They are the embodiment of contradiction. The father warns his son-in-law that his wife will have all the power. The mother, concerned with preserving a matrilinear filiation, tells the young bride: "Model yourself after your mother, who always contradicts your father. He never says anything that she doesn't contradict, and she never follows his orders."[82] Having made up her mind not to betray the female "lineage," the young woman tells her husband about her mother's advice. Female pride receives a deserved lesson. If the male clan is less eloquent than the female, the husband can at any rate denounce disorder. On the wrong body testicles become "millstones" that give rise to "pride and stupidity."[83] The terrified wife looks on while a bizarre surgical operation is performed on her mother and testicles are extracted from her kidneys. This anatomical abnormality is responsible for her presumptuous appropriation of the language of authority.

Women are bound together as a group by language, but in life's great dance macabre there is another, more tragic bond among them, illustrated by the well-known topos of the suffering old woman. The *Mirouer des dames et damoyselles et de tout le sexe féminin* (Mirror of Ladies and Damsels and the Whole Female Sex) is a sort of *vanitas,* a lament of the ravages of time. In the fifteenth century Jean Castel dramatized the discourse of death. His heroine is a woman who dies young and who warns her sisters of the transience of beauty, power, nobility, and honor and the coming of poverty and sadness: "Look here, ladies and damsels, look here and see my face. Alas! If you are beautiful, think how death effaces all beauty."[84] In death equality is regained and all differences vanish.

Naming Sex

Genesis tells us that Eve was the first human being to initiate a dialogue with another. Adam enjoyed the privilege of being the first to name creatures and things. Eve merely arranged the use of what Adam instituted through language. Dante tells us how she answered the serpent: "We eat the fruit of the trees in the Garden, but God commanded us not to eat or touch the fruit of the tree in the center of the Garden, lest we die."[85] But the seductive serpent overcame her reluctance. The dialogue between Eve and the serpent, Dante says, strayed beyond the bounds of "reason"; it was damnable and "bestial." Adam, moreover, may have given names to things in his own mind only: it was not necessary to speak the names out loud. But woman did speak aloud when she designated, and asserted linguistic power over, sexual things.

There are times when language cannot be obscure, other times when there is significance to its failure to be direct. If the language of sexuality is ambiguous, it is because it needs a mask, because it expresses the ambiguity of its object. A well-known passage of the *Roman de la Rose* concerns naming. A lover reproaches Reason—an eloquent woman well equipped for argument—for naming the sexual organs rather than employing elegant circumlocution, which he thinks a lady might have found more fitting: "I do not consider you courteous, moreover, because a moment ago you spoke the word 'testicle,' which is hardly to be commended in the mouth of a courteous young lady."[86] Even wet nurses, noted for their bawdy language, were more careful than that. Reason responds: "I commit no sin in calling by their name, without further gloss, noble things that my father in paradise made with his own hands, along with all the other instruments that serve as pillars and props to human nature, without which man would soon perish. Deliberately and with no reluctance whatsoever, God invested testicles and penises with a marvelous intention, with the force of generation whereby the living species are maintained by natural renewal, that is, by birth, aging, death, and rebirth."[87] God, the lover angrily retorts, never created words offensive to the ear, whereupon Reason answers: "The tongue must be restrained. At the beginning of the *Almagest*, in fact, Ptolemy puts it quite well. Wise is the man, he says, who seeks to restrain his tongue, except when speaking with God."[88] God created things, not words, even if "things" were named when language originated. But to Reason he gave the power to coin names for common use: "He made me the gift of language, which is a most precious possession."[89]

Reason perceptively notes that if testicles had been called "relics," the lover would have found the word incongruous: "'Testicles' is a fine name. I like it as it is. Prick and penis too. No one has ever seen finer. I make up words, and I am certain that I have done nothing base. And God who knows and is wise is satisfied with what I have done. How, by the body of Saint Omer, would I dare not give proper names to my father's works?"[90] Reason considers the terms of sexuality "correct and proper," and if the women of France do not utter the incriminated word, habit is to blame. Reason thus affirms that the art of language is to give things their proper names, yet she also insists on the arbitrariness of all signs.

What women said among themselves and about their relations with men is often revealing. The *fabliaux* attest to the profusion of sexual terms. Linguistic taboos in general are closely intertwined with sexual taboos.[91] Casually uttering forbidden words, laughing over them, and punning on them helped bind women together as a group. At times this ribald talk amounted to something like a rite of initiation.

In *Ecureuil* a young woman talking with her mother laughingly exclaims that she wishes she were a man so that she might "name the thing that has no name . . . that must not be named either in public or in private."[92] Did the taboo extend to fantasy? In any case it was easily transgressed, as the mother's reply makes clear: "Though it is forbidden, and though the prohibition is reasonable and just, I tell you plainly that the thing is called a penis." The use of the term was subject to male censure, but girls learned about sex from their mothers, and their instruction began with words.

In contrast to this young woman's happy discovery we have the case of another young damsel, much given to euphemism, who cannot hear the word "fuck without a feeling of disgust." She cannot tolerate the words "prick or balls" either and prefers to hear nothing of what men say or do.[93] Yet she is a master of the art of metaphor and keen to be initiated into the secrets of sexuality, provided that the common words for things are avoided, as if the sin lay primarily in the naming. Was talk about sex reserved for men? In this story sex becomes legitimate as long as it is confined to the idyllic setting of a springtime escapade. Rural images replace the crude designation of the organs of pleasure: the female organ becomes a "meadow" or a "fountain," the male organ a "colt," and the colt is pleased when it finds grass and water to its heart's content.

Taboo words correspond to taboo objects. Metaphors and circumlocutions might distort the nature of the act. A man is the guilty party in one *fabliau*.[94] Delighted that he and his wife have such excellent sexual rapport, a young man decides that the sexual act should be designated by a mutually understood code. From now on, he tells his wife, she should ask for "oats for Morel." This euphemism, requested by the husband, allows the wife to pursue her pleasure without restraint. Encouraged to ask for oats for Morel "unhesitatingly every week and every day and every hour that might please her," the woman turns perverse and overwhelms her husband with her insatiable desire. Yet initially she had wanted no part of this verbal deception: "I'd rather have my throat cut than to say anything so shameful or learn to call it so."

Such delicate reluctance to use language was rare, however. A far greater number of texts reveal a troubling loquacity. Naming was conceived as a kind of appropriation. An aggressive component is already perceptible in the *Quatre souhaits de saint Martin* (Saint Martin's Four Wishes):

461

> I ask in God's name
> That you be loaded with penises,
> That from your eyes to your feet
> All your face and arms and flanks
> Be covered with cocks.
> May they never go soft or hang limp,
> and may each one have its balls.
> May all those cocks be stiff,
> and may you look like a man with horns.[95]

And there was equality between the sexes; the husband in turn hopes that his wife will be covered with "cunts down to her feet." There was a lively tradition of mocking the organs of the other sex, and the rawness of the language speaks for itself. In *Le souhait insensé* (The Senseless Wish) Jean Bodel has a woman dream of a cargo of penises and testicles, a hyperbole of female desire.[96] Sexual appetites are forthrightly expressed in Gautier Le Leu's minor masterpiece, *La veuve* (The Widow).[97] The widow of the title complains of her late husband: "My lap was wedded to his ass and nothing else, and he slept that way all night, so that I got no pleasure." Here the narrator takes on the role of naming: "Bothered and vexed by her gluttonous Goliath and consumed by ardor, she would snare a man in one of her nets. Once she held him in her coils, he might well regret it if he didn't know his way around the rings of the vagina. He had to be energetic and rapid, to screw and push and get some ass into it." When the man fails to perform up to expectations, he is rewarded with insults: impotent, eunuch, limp rag. The victim groans: "Your Goliath opens its mouth too often. I can't satisfy it, and your demands are killing me." Later he says: "You've got a gluttonous mouth that wants too much suck. Baucent's disgusted: I've just pulled him out of there in a wretched state and all dried up."[98] A woman's vagina, in other words, is a voracious mouth, a gullet of proportions as gigantic as Goliath.

The Wife of Bath's need to dominate is more ominous:

> In wyfhode I wol use myn instrument
> As frely as my Maker hath it sent.
> If I be daungerous, God yeve me sorwe!
> Myn housbond shal it have bothe eve morwe,
> Whan that him list com forth and paye his dette.
> An housbonde I wol have, I nil nat lette,

Which shal be bothe my dettour and my thral,
And have his tribulacioun withal
Upon his flessh, whyl that I am his wife.
I have the power duringe al my lyf
Upon his propre body, and noght he.[99]

Although the Wife of Bath also considers the procreative purpose
of the sexual organs, her prologue gives a remarkable account of
the war between the sexes. Violence takes on a symbolic ampli-
tude: men must be denied the advantages of learning. It was of
course impossible for a cleric to say anything good about any
woman less holy than a canonized saint, and having fought over
a book with a man of the cloth, the Wife makes him burn it,
thereby regaining her "mastery."[100]

Saying the Unsayable

Far from the bitterness hidden beneath the burlesque facades of
these bawdy texts, in the very different realm of spirituality women
shared an acute awareness of both the power of their speech and
the inability of *logos* to capture their inner experience. The language of the clergy was inadequate; words were too weak. Under
pressure language turned fluid, and, in an apparent regression, the
cry that preceded articulate language compensated for the poverty
of words. What began as a response to the inadequacy of language
became an implicit call for a language of enthusiasm, in which
words took fire, sentences knew no limits, sounds were uttered in
response to the dictates of God, and sobs expressed what disciplined discourse could not.

In the Middle Ages the mother tongue, the vernacular, was in
large part the language of the illiterate. Latin was a male bastion.[101]
In northern Europe the vulgar tongue became the language of
inward experience at an early date. Hadewijch and Beatrice of
Nazareth spoke Dutch; Mechthild, German; Marguerite Porete,
French.[102] Certain Italian saints, for whom reading and writing
were even further out of reach, nevertheless asserted their claim
to the spoken word. It is striking to observe how often mysticism
moved across linguistic boundaries, though it would be unwise to
suggest that women were somehow able to undo the damage done
at Babel, where, as Dante recalled in *De vulgari eloquentia*, the
vulgar tongues were born. The multiplicity of languages was an

impediment to women who wanted above all to make themselves understood.

Consider Margery who, after traveling across Europe, met, in Saint John of Lateran, a German-born priest who knew no English. The priest implored God, and Margery prayed that he be granted the grace "to understand her language and what she, with the grace of God, wished to say to him." After thirteen days "he understood what she said to him in English, and she understood what he said. Yet he did not understand English when spoken by others, even if they used the same words. The words had to be uttered by her."[103] Later Margery was accused of confessing to a priest who did not understand her tongue and therefore could not hear her avowal of sin. In chapter 40 she is put to the test. An English priest who has come to Rome to see her is conversing in his own language over dinner. The German priest, who does not understand unless the others speak Latin, remains silent. Then Margery quotes a passage from the Bible to him in English: "The others asked her confessor if he understood what she had said, and he immediately repeated it, word for word, but in Latin since he spoke no English and understood it only in this creature's mouth and never when it came from another person. Amazed, they were obliged to bow to the evidence."[104]

To digress for a moment to a text of a very different sort, the queen sibyl in Antoine de La Salle's cavern governs a satanic realm in which there are no boundaries between languages, where the denial of Babel is tantamount to a denial of God's authority. She receives the foolhardy knight and bestows upon him the power to speak all languages, the final stage of his initiation into the underworld. At first he understands nothing, then he can understand but not speak, and finally he can speak any language.

To return to our mystics, their attitude toward language spoke of a reverence for creation. Their dreams were compounded of something close to the primal language, to the wailing of a child or the tongue of Eden. Hildegard imagined Adam speaking German; for others it was Flemish. To be sure, the bold and beautiful style of Hildegard's enigmatic twelfth-century *lingua ignota* cannot be compared with the primitive language—little more than an inarticulate cry—employed by later mystics whose spiritual ambitions made do without the usual intellectual tools. Their spiritual development required a different kind of language, which did not always have to be learned. It was an emotional dialect, well adapted to vigorous self-expression, to spontaneity and immediacy. Marguerite d'Oingt's *Pagina meditationum* is full of interjections in dialect ("Ha las! quam grant damajo!"). Paul Zumthor points out the importance of the vocal context of medieval literature. The "unlettered" part of the self, he says, "had less mastery over words, and mastered fewer words, but it was closer to them and more subject to their power. Perhaps that is why salvation was best ensured by allowing the *illetrure* in oneself to triumph, as the Gospels themselves suggested."[105] "Divine words are things the earth cannot comprehend. For all that is found here below there are plenty of words in Flemish, but for what I want to say there is no Flemish and there are no words. Yet I know the language as well as any human can. For this, I repeat, there is no language, and no expression I know will do."[106] This moving avowal of incapacity expresses the profusion of God, who here addresses his creature directly, without intermediary. Yet the same women who spoke in these urgent tones often said—it was an unavoidable topos—that they knew far less about these matters than the priests whose judgment they awaited.

Female mystics, inwardly divided, often expressed themselves in convoluted ways. Marguerite d'Oingt, for example, spoke of a great favor that the Lord had done "not long ago for a person of [her] acquaintance."[107] Note the distancing. The "person" then applies herself to the study of the Bible; she feels as if Christ is present and holding the book in his hand. She had previously only imagined the black, white, and red letters of the book from outside, but when the book opens she beholds not letters and words but a wondrous sight: "The inside of the book was like a beautiful mirror, and there were only two pages. I shall tell you only a little of what she saw in the book, because I have not the intelligence to conceive it or the tongue to express it."[108]

In her letters Marguerite tells in very simple terms how "the woman who wrote these things down was rapt in Our Lord one night to the point where it seemed to her that she saw all these things." The transition from vision to written text—a text that never really refers to the word itself—was unsettling, and Marguerite d'Oingt lacked the linguistic gifts that allowed some others to traverse the distance more easily. She never dropped her mask.

At the age of sixty-five Hildegard spoke about the early days of her work: "Uneducated as I was, poor, infirm, afflicted with a host of ills, with trembling hand." Often, however, she was less modest and more confident.[109] The fragility she reveals here was compensated by astonishing vigor and apparent pride in her having been chosen. In the prologue to the *Book of Divine Works* she receives an imperious commandment: "Poor soul, child of so many miseries! You have been burnt by so many cruel physical ills! Yet here you are, traversed again by the flood from the depths of God's mysteries. For the benefit of mankind, do not relinquish your pen! Write down what your inner eye has seen and your inner ear has heard. Let men discover knowledge of their Creator, let them consent at last to worship him in dignity and to honor him. Write this text . . . You are not the creator of this vision, nor did any other person imagine it. I am the one who decided all things before the beginning of the world."[110]

This lavish inauguration of the language of revelation probably has no equal in women's spiritual literature. Yet many other mystics seem to have had an acute sense of the self behind the voice, an awareness of a mission to speak, of an authorization granted to women. They aspired to speak not the language of men but a language that was at once less and more. A woman's body made her a docile receptacle as well as uniquely fertile ground in which the Spirit could "reside." Her book, Hildegard says, "is not the fruit of any doctrine of human science but, in accordance with her desire and by a miracle, the fruit of this naive and uneducated woman. Let no man be so bold as to add anything to this text or to eliminate any passage who does not himself wish to be eliminated from the book of life and all earthly beatitude."[111] Unless, Hildegard adds, it is to correct a letter or sentence she unwittingly included while under the inspiration of the Holy Spirit! No one could have been more prudent yet at the same time more convinced of the glory of her election.

A Language of Fire

In the *Streaming Light of the Deity* Mechthild of Magdeburg says:

> I have been warned about this book,
> And this is what I was told:
> That if I did not bury it,
> it would be fed to the flames![112]

Hers, in other words, is an incendiary book threatened with burning. But God tells the dismayed author that no one can burn the truth and that language is the voice of the living Spirit.

A New Spirituality

At the beginning of the *Life of Marie d'Oignies* Jacques de Vitry describes to Fulk, bishop of Toulouse, a number of women subject to various physical and psychic manifestations of spirituality.[113] Rutebeuf may have sneered in his *Sayings of the Beguines,* but he was obliged to admit that what these women said now mattered, indeed was important enough to draw fire. The words of the Beguines were taken as prophecy and their tears as marks of devotion. Their sleep was a sign of ecstasy, and their dreams were visions. "But also, if she lies, do not believe any of it."[114] These concise remarks thus focus attention on a series of manifestations of the self: language, emotion, ecstatic piety, revelatory dreams. What we see is the emergence of a new linguistic order composed of words, laughter, tears, sleep, and dreams. The enthusiastic embrace of asceticism by women proved problematic, more so even than the feminist sympathies of Christine de Pisan. Christine entered the male world and fought her battles there. What happened in the world of female spirituality in the second half of the twelfth century was even more astonishing: women emerged out of nowhere and broke their silence. Groups of Beguines organized in the Netherlands and devoted themselves to work and prayer. The phenomenon spread from the banks of the Rhine to Italy; along the way it evolved into a variety of forms. Franciscans preached deliberately to the laity, including many women, in an atmosphere of exaltation and even frenzy. This now became the chief theater in which women found a voice.[115]

The change was slow, and it was associated with the new importance of asceticism and mysticism, "which, from the end of the thirteenth century on, became important criteria for the evaluation of sanctity."[116] The most astonishing examples we have of women's use of language stem from this shift, which is attested by biographies of female saints. Women began to make themselves heard on a regular basis because the new spirituality addressed itself to those willing to break the bond of marriage and family. But it also warned against the temptations of a life apart. Women sought proximity to God and mystical union in the midst of others.

467

A new language came into being, a language in which the body spoke as well as the voice. Indeed, the body became, as André Vauchez aptly states, "a primary instrument of communication." It became a language unto itself, with a new syntax that fused words and emotions. The saint who meditated in silence became a thing of the past.[117]

Preaching to heretics, Jacques de Vitry used Marie d'Oignies as an example of orthodox piety. Esclarmonde, the sister of the count of Foy, was a woman who went too far. She joined the Catharist heretics, presided over heretical meetings, and attempted to speak out in a public controversy, whereupon she was sent back to her distaff by a Cistercian monk. "It does not become you," he said, "to speak to a colloquium of this sort."[118] When concern began to mount about the activities of the Beguines in the diocese of Liège, Jacques de Vitry pointed to Marie d'Oignies as a model of the union with God, of ascetic and mystical sainthood, and granted her new powers: the gifts of healing and prophecy and also the gift of tears, a form of self-expression that some women developed to a remarkable degree.

"Sein selbst und aller Dinge frei, / Ohn Mittel sehen, was Gott sei" (Be free of oneself and all things, / See what God is without intermediary). The Franciscan Lamprecht of Regensburg attempted to characterize the spiritual existence of early-thirteenth-century Bavarian and Flemish Beguines in these terms in *Die Tochter Sione*. Hadewijch's seventh letter is quite clear about the nature of this speculative mysticism, this attempt to approach God without mediation and in the nakedness of one's soul. Protected by silence, the heart of the soul remains free, an open space in the center of one's being beyond all language or conceptualization. This made union with God possible: "Finding myself welcomed and illuminated in Unity, I understood this Essence and knew it more clearly than one can know anything knowable in this world by means of words, reasons, or visions."[119] Mysticism, then, transcended the power of reason, the potentiality of language, and the clarity of vision. Out of it came a new language, made possible by the body and sustained by the emotions.

The Language of the Body

Phenomena pertaining to the body are common in the literature: raptures, miraculous transports, instantaneous cures of horrifying diseases, resuscitations from near death. Catherine of Siena reported: "Scissoque corde, ut dixi, anima mea fuit ab hac carne soluta" (My heart, as I said, split open, and my soul was liberated from this flesh).[120] Women attended to themselves with new intensity, so it is hardly surprising that they detected pathologies. They also had ecstatic visions, almost initiatory experiences, of the space and time of revelation. They found ways to express the feelings of their senses more vividly than ever before, though drawing on a long tradition.[121]

A dream vision recounted in one of Marguerite d'Oingt's letters mentions the senses explicitly: "Before she said her prayers and left this place, he who is full of sweetness and pity wanted to comfort her and draw her spirit to him, and so it seemed to her that she was in a vast wasteland where there was nothing but a mountain, and at the foot of this mountain was a marvelous tree. On this tree were five branches, all dry and drooping. On the leaves of the first branch the word *visu* was written, on the second, *auditu,* on the third, *gustu,* on the fourth, *odoratu,* and on the fifth, *tactu.*"[122] Above the top of the tree was a round cover, like the top of a barrel, which protected the tree from the sun and dew. As the saint watched, a torrent of water poured down the mountain and toppled the tree. The treetop planted itself in the ground, the drooping branches turned heavenward, the dry leaves unshriveled, and the tree rose again toward the sky.

Spiritual expression relied heavily on the senses. The spiritual state was one of insatiable hunger, ready to devour the bitter along with the sweet in its search for intoxication, a metaphor for plenitude. Marguerite Porete said she was drunk on something she had never drunk and never would drink. Although the thirst of the senses could never be slaked, the spiritual quest brought release from the tension of desire, which was associated with an aesthetic of the sacred.

The body was a full participant in the spiritual experience. Prior to ecstasy it passed through states of languor and inebriation, and the exhaustion that followed was the most expressive symbol of the vision's power.[123] After feeling "rapt in Our Lord," Marguerite d'Oingt did not eat, drink, or sleep.[124] Her body fell into a state of such weakness that she was believed dead. When she recovered, she had the idea of writing down what Christ had said: the therapy of language brought healing. In *Showings* Julian of Norwich also described physical illness as an aspect of spiritual life: its symptoms included a deathlike torpor, paralysis, fixed stare, obscured vision, and aphasia, all described in precise physiological terms.

A language of the body evolved, and with it some haunting metaphors. Sometimes hearing was the dominant sense, sometimes sight. The wealth of sensory perceptions expressed infinite pleasure or ineffable suffering. Complex visions were common. Sight comes not only from the body's eyes but also, Margery Kempe says, from the soul's eyes. Visions can happen anywhere: in the bedroom, in the fields, in town, even in darkness. Mystics attended to all sorts of signs. A sound of wind might have been cause for alarm, but an "inner voice" comforts the mystic and tells her that the sound is of the Holy Spirit. At once the wailing of the wind turns into the cooing of a dove and later into the song of a robin. Visions were recounted with remarkable vividness and variety. Beatrice of Nazareth, a more learned as well as a more impassioned and spirited writer than Margery, described the seven forms of love. The senses, ennobled into instruments of the spirit, played an important role. Beatrice yields to the storm within her soul. Amid overwhelming noise and "delightful excess," her heart seems to break and her soul yearns for "fruition" in intimate union with God. Beatrice's language takes fire, as sentence tumbles over sentence:

> At times love throws off all restraint, it surges forth with such power and sets the heart beating so fast and furious that it feels wounded through and through, and those wounds are constantly reopened, each day more searing and painful than the last. The veins seem to open, the blood to run out, the marrow to wither. Bones crack, the chest explodes, the throat is parched. One's face and limbs burn inwardly with the sovereign rage of love. Sometimes it is as though an arrow were passing through the heart and into the throat, causing loss of consciousness; at other times it is like a fire that consumes everything in its vicinity. Such is the violence to which the soul is subjected, such is the effect on it of unrestrained and pitiless love, which wants and devours all things.[125]

The body becomes a theater of violence. Elsewhere, in the sixth of the seven degrees of love, the soul is compared, in a very feminine simile, to a "neat, well-kept" house, attesting to a rather different spiritual aesthetic, to the quietude of ultimate fulfillment.

470

Catherine of Siena's biographer, Raymond of Capua, makes abundant use of this language of the body. His descriptions abound in images of emptiness and exhaustion. Catherine relied heavily on odor and sight: she saw and smelled the beauty and ugliness, the fragrance and stench, of people's souls. Like other mystics, she fortified her self-expression with tears. Her heightened sensory powers helped lift her body from earth: "Often her body rose from the earth with her spirit, making it possible to perceive the splendor of the virtue that drew her spirit upward."[126]

At times Catherine renounced the life of the senses and fell into a state close to death, signifying her absence from the world. Speaking of later mystics, Michel de Certeau said that they "climbed the ladder of perceptions."[127] This ladder, this attentiveness to the language of the senses, was a good deal more than a metaphor. Mechthild of Magdeburg and Mechthild of Hackebon, for example, insisted on the connection between vision and taste. Taste was important because it energized the body caught in the grip of desire. This emphasis on the senses and on the energy that invigorated both body and soul was characteristic of women's spirituality in this period.

The semantics of mystical language made meaning out of cries, tears, screams. Mystics varied in their attitudes toward culture and language; therefore they handled this new syntax in different ways. To be sure words were important for demonstration, teaching, and explanation, but they were interwoven with intervals of silence, with what Barthes called the "interstices of language." Punctuated by sobs, expression was reduced to inarticulate cries, as if these women were searching, in a state of divinely induced agitation, for a primal language in response not to repression but to a need for creation. When Christians heard the shouts of Clara in Rimini and of Margery Kempe in Lynn and Rome, they were embarrassed yet somehow sensed that this seemingly chaotic language actually originated in some distant place.

Clara of Rimini, condemned to sin with her tongue, abandoned herself to an extreme language of frenzied screams. She wanted to "circumcise her mouth," to pluck out the tongue that got her into so much trouble.[128] Margery Kempe, an itinerant laywoman, became deeply involved in the invention of the new language of cries and sobs. Against a background of Lollardy and with Christ's passion always in mind, she cried "abundantly and violently," often so violently that monks, priests, and laymen all were critical

471

of her behavior. She and those around her worried a great deal about her crying. Was it feigned, or was it a gift from God?

Tears were remarkably effective: Margery Kempe's tormented the Devil and forced him to relinquish a great many souls. Her journey to the Holy Land was filled with tears. Her sobbing, her falling to the ground waving "her arms and screaming as if her heart were about to burst," made Christ's Passion real. She discovered screaming in Jerusalem, where it became part of her spiritual life. In a mounting crescendo she resorted to screams at first once a month, then once a week, then daily, and finally as many as fourteen times a day, depending on how often she was visited by God. Some took her to be an epileptic. Her screaming was a sign of elevated contemplation; when she tried to restrain it, she turned white as a sheet. The irresistible scream became an increasingly common form of spiritual expression, an extreme form of communication that some observers have rather facilely linked to hysteria. Some women fell into convulsive fits on viewing the scene of the passion or a crucifix or icon. But this language of screams, shouts, and sobs was willed by God, and Margery could neither initiate nor end it.

Margery Kempe cried for her own sins, and sometimes she also cried an extra hour for the souls in purgatory, another for the poor, and still another for Jews, Saracens, and heretics. Her tears became an instrument of intercession. When she asked Christ why he made her scream so loudly that other people asked what was wrong, Christ answered: "Sometimes I send heavy rains and violent storms, sometimes small showers. And I do the same with you when it pleases me to speak in your soul. As a token of my love for you, I sometimes send you sweet and gentle tears. Other times, as a token of my desire that you understand my mother's pain, I send you shouts and screams so that the grace I bestow on you will frighten people and inspire them with greater compassion for all that she suffered on my behalf."[129]

When Margery could not interpret a revelation, she sank into melancholy, and when she dictated the second part of her *Life* she cried so much that the priest (the second to work on her biography) also succumbed to fits of sobbing. He cried so much that his tears dampened his vestments and priestly accoutrements, and without the deep empathy that resulted from this experience he never would have believed what Margery revealed to him: here is proof that belief now depended on a language that transcended mere words.

Communal Scrutiny

Margery's emotional expressiveness was validated by the divine presence within her, but it was also subject to the scrutiny of others. Her confessor asked what she planned to do next. The Lollards, isolated from new forms of lay spirituality developed on the Continent, were calling for laypeople to be allowed greater access to the Bible in English, and Margery, who felt an urgent need to talk of God in her own tongue, began repeating words compulsively.

In some ways Margery was obviously seeking humiliation. She dressed strangely and courted sarcasm. But she also hoped, by emulating women such as Bridget of Sweden and Dorothy of Montau, to bring about a religious awakening.[130] Conscious of her mission, she embarked on numerous journeys. In Britain she sought out the anchoress Julian of Norwich, with whom she engaged in edifying conversations that went on for days. "On Christ's orders," she told Julian of the grace that had been bestowed on her and spoke of her meditations. "To demonstrate that she was not deluded, she made many other astonishing revelations to this anchoress, who was able to offer expert advice."[131]

Some of the men in whom Margery confided her soul's secrets received her warmly, but others put her to the test. In such cases she abandoned her extreme language and answered "difficult" questions, winning unstinting admiration for responding "so quickly and intelligently." Yet it was emotion, not rationality, that swayed her audiences. Many eminent personages wished to hear her. According to his biographer, the archbishop of Canterbury listened to her talk until nightfall because "her conversation evinced such love of God that those who listened to her often shed copious tears."

But questions were raised. It was possible to preach in a calm and disciplined manner, but conversing with the Virgin or the saints inspired "mimicry and shocking gestures accompanied by loud sobs and abundant tears." Margery was examined and found to be afflicted with an evil spirit. Already people were asking the great question: Where does madness come from? Women as a group played an important role in the response to Margery's behavior. They were virtually alone in understanding her more extreme behavior, behavior that perhaps expressed what they wanted to say themselves: "Sympathetic to her pain, these good women, struck by her tears and screams, only loved her all the more, and since they did not understand her language, they begged her by signs to go home with them. In a way they insisted, for they were that eager to comfort her following her spiritual ordeal."[132]

The therapeutic value of language is evident in the case of Marguerite d'Oingt. After receiving certain revelations, the Carthusian nun seems close to death. Thinking that if these "things" were written down, "since Our Lord placed them in her heart, her heart would be relieved, she began to write all that is in the book, and in the order in which she held it in her heart. And no sooner had she put the words in the book than it left her heart. And when she had written everything, she was completely cured. I firmly believe that if she had not written it down, she would have died or gone mad, for she had not slept or eaten for seven days."[133] Margery too, after receiving instruction from the Virgin, is embarrassed to speak to anyone other than her confessor, who, in his wisdom, urges her to tell him everything she felt: "she did so by virtue of obedience."

Women's words were often eloquent on various states of psychological depression: uncommunicativeness, melancholy, apathy. Hildegard wrote of her past suffering and described the exaltation she felt prior to experiencing a vision as well as her alternating sense of physical weakness and strength. She had great empathy, based on her own experience, for physical suffering and was acutely aware of the fragility of women, but she also exulted in their physical stamina and intellectual capacities: "O feminea forma, quam gloriosa es!" Later mystics, however, thought of themselves as a kind of vehicle for suffering, and their broken voices and lacerated bodies reflected the stress under which they labored.

Food for the Soul

Hadewijch spoke of "eating, savoring, seeing inwardly." In a masterful study Caroline Walker Bynum showed that one of the most original aspects of women's discourse was to take food—and the close connection between women and eating—not only as a term of comparison or a metaphor but as an important element of women's spirituality.[134]

Fasting and its opposite, the extreme hunger or desire for the Eucharist, made it possible to abolish the self in identification with the body of Christ. Earlier centuries had produced an extensive body of literature on dietary asceticism and eucharistic devotion. Food was a more central religious theme for women than for men, although preachers do not appear to have associated religious dietary practices specifically with women. Although men like Saint Francis have their place in this history of "oral" piety, others such as Ruusbrook and Tauler did not use food metaphors in speaking of union with God or relations with others. Nor did they use the act of absorbing food as a metaphor for identification with Christ's suffering or of mystical union or of the redemption of souls.

Tasting God in the host afforded women the most intimate possible experience of the annihilation of self in *fruitio*, or mystical union. This form of nourishment is the key to any feminine anthropology. The vocabulary of taste, eating, hunger, and satiety is vast, and it was easily linked to the vocabulary of heat, light, and sound.

In particular, the act of devouring food gave rise to an astonishing variety of metaphors involving bread and blood as symbols of relations with other people, with God, or with his creatures. Much of the imagery had a strong erotic component, as in this passage from Hadewijch: "This bond joins those who love in such a way that one penetrates the other completely in the pain or repose or wrath of love and eats his flesh and drinks his blood. The heart of each devours the heart of the other, the spirit assails the spirit and invades it completely, as we were shown by the One who is love itself, who made Himself our bread and nourishment and changed all human thoughts. He taught us that the most intimate union of love consists in eating, savoring, seeing inwardly. He eats us, and we believe we eat Him, as no doubt we do."[135]

Hunger and satiety are linked: love is filling when it comes, but it leaves the soul empty and in tears when it goes. Love's onslaught leaves a new hunger in its wake, a hunger so great, Hadewijch says, that it devours eternally the new gifts it brings.[136] For Beatrice of Nazareth the folly of love was an almost pathological condition, and drinking was her very physical image for union with the tortured body of Christ. The works of Catherine of Siena abound in metaphors that involve eating and drinking, bread and blood, feverish fasting and hunger for the eucharist. She was fond of extreme images: eating decomposed flesh without vomiting; sucking milk from Christ's breast. Catherine of Genoa, Mechthild of Magdeburg, and Angela of Foligno went in for similar symbols. While each woman retains her uniqueness, all drew on the same model of spirituality. Angela is fond of concrete details; she shivers because the host has "a meaty taste." The Carthusian nun from Lyons who wrote the *Life* of Beatrice d'Ornacieux reports that when Beatrice received the body of Christ, she felt that a piece "as big as a lentil" remained in her mouth, and when she could not swallow it, she began to cry: "The host she had had in her mouth began to grow until it filled her mouth completely. Feeling her mouth so full was most unsettling, and she raised her hand to pull the thing out. But she felt that someone was pulling it back in, and that it tasted of flesh and blood. No one would dare describe the terror she felt."[137] Such language is reminiscent of the poetry that Barthes saw as "full of holes and full of light, full of absence and of overnourishing signs."

Talk of Love

"Then the soul said . . ." So wrote Marguerite Porete in the *Miroir des âmes simples et anéanties*. The new style produced some singular formulations. Logic was discarded in favor of a vocal din. Seen with worldly eyes, this language may have seemed chaotic, but it came from God; God breathed it into his creatures. This new language, embodied in sometimes highly elaborate literary works, revealed the variety of the writers' temperaments, cultural heritages, and backgrounds. Often highly individualized, the amorous dialect of mysticism was sufficient unto itself. Each writer had her own themes, her verbal rituals, her obsessions, which others sometimes copied.

Spiritual progress came through a lover's discourse rich and complex enough to provide remarkably fertile ground for a literary criticism fortified by linguistics, psychoanalysis, and the cultural history. The constellation of images, the conjunction of opposites, the silence in the face of the ineffable—all these strained the power of words. Because the mystic was filled with "pressurized" language, she is an ideal specimen for studying the linguistic manifestations of the unconscious.

Heinrich de Nördlingen said that Margaret Ebner wrote "the most marvelous German" he ever read, that she wrote more movingly about love than any other German writer. Her use of familiar literary forms to write about very personal misfortunes attests not only to a wide knowledge of literature but also to an awareness of self and a freedom achieved through writing. Margaret was keenly attuned to the inner life, the seat of spiritual progress as well as the source of literary expression.

Mechthild of Magdeburg's *Streaming Light of the Deity,* written in the sixth decade of the thirteenth century, consists of a series of poems interspersed with prose recounting a dialogue between God and the Soul. The *Seven Kinds of Love,* Beatrice of Nazareth's shortest work, is a treatise on love that can be read against the background of her life. The recounting of visions required a new language, and the teller of the tale had to make choices. Beatrice appealed to the senses, to touch, hearing, and taste. Hadewijch was astonishingly well-read in both profane and theological literature. She is rightly counted as one of the greatest Dutch poets, and her lyrics show her to have been a master of courtly verse as well as a verbal virtuoso. At times her wordplay is somewhat precious, as when she says in the thirteenth poem of the *Mengeldichten* that love "is without rhyme or reason, and that is its poetry" or that "doubt in love is certain" or that "to be weakened by love is our strength." One might search the works of the troubadours in vain for more striking antitheses. And Peter Dronke points out that the beauty of Marguerite Porete's *Miroir* comes from its dramatization of internal forces, from the quality of its dialogues, and from an alternation of prose with rhyme that attests to a sure sense of the possibilities inherent in language.

The literature of love was not just well constructed; it also expressed the fervor and frenzy of desire and longing. Beatrice of Nazareth blends pain and joy. Dutch mystics used the word *orewoet* to refer to the frenzy in the depths of the soul *(ur-woet?),* "a violent desire of nature touched at its root, a frenzy of love that nothing finite can appease."[138] The word gave rise to a series of images encompassing all the possible states of desire, as in the nineteenth of the *Mengeldichten* with its many similes for love: chain, light, coal, fire, due, spring, hell—the last of these reminiscent of Angela of Foligno's audacious metaphors.[139]

The soul described itself as naked, naked in its desire, naked in its expectations. The language of love relied on the magic of words to express the inability to express. Hadewijch's twentieth letter propounds a veritable parable of amorous fusion: "The nature from which true love proceeds has twelve hours, during which we watch love first emerge and then disappear. When love disappears in this way, it takes home what it gathered in the course of its journey: the searching spirit, the hungry heart, the loving soul. Love throws these things into the abyss of its powerful nature, from which it is born and on which it feeds. And so it is that the unnamed hours return into unknown nature. Love thus returns home and revels in its nature over, under, and around itself."[140]

Beyond the verbal exuberance and cultivated inventiveness of the metaphor, this passage is intended as a kind of degree zero of language, a first stage of enunciation. "If one wants to know from within, beyond all intelligence," one must abandon "the tempests of reason, the forms of images."[141] Without wanting to renounce language, the mystic thus advances toward a nakedness of language. She seeks not to "understand" but to "know" the ineffable. She sets aside her claim to rationality and leaps into a fertile unknown:

In the intimacy of the One, these souls are pure and inwardly naked
Without images, without figures,
As if liberated from time, uncreated,
Freed from their limits in silent latitude.

—*Mengeldichten* 17

Language admits its incapacity: "Here I stop," the mystic says, "henceforth incapable of locating the end or the beginning or any point of reference that can justify words."[142] What better way of indicating both the limitation and the power of words than to emphasize at once the irrepressible need and the troubling inability to say what one feels? Marguerite Porete later would pose the same paradox in a somewhat different form: the impossibility, no matter how exuberant the writing, of expressing God. And Julian of Norwich in one of her visions states that the truest language is utterly inarticulate. What Christ revealed to her, she says, was in the form of "spoken words but without voice or movement of the lips."

Inner Time

"To desire, to wander, to wait indefinitely / for this spring, which is Love itself."[143] This image, which might also be used of profane love, here conveys a sense of the passage of time in the spiritual journey. Paradoxically, spiritual language is extroverted—it wants to express and be understood—yet it must describe the most extreme introversion, proclaim what lurks in the innermost self, where consciousness dissolves in ecstasy. It is when the soul is stripped bare and totally naked that the spirit passes most effectively through it ("perfuses" it, Hildegard would say). The secret event could be expressed in many different ways. One was the great cosmic vision, in the shadow of which Hildegard repeatedly asserted her fragility as a woman and yet her power to tell what she saw. Beatrice and Hadewijch described visions associated with liturgical events. Hadewijch says that all her senses turned inward. She then became rapt "in spirit," this turning inward preceding the vision itself and the message it contained. Next she says she was carried "far away from myself and all I had seen of Him, beyond all concepts, all knowledge, all intelligence except the conscious sense of being united with Him, of experiencing ecstasy in Him." Afterward she returned to ordinary life.[144] The literature of female spirituality is indispensable for understanding the history of subjectivity. In these works the subject—a personage that contemporary literary criticism finds fascinating and enigmatic, if at times an impediment to interpretation—is king, even if it is a subject perfused and agitated by God, visited by grace.

The spiritual literature also attests to a mutation of consciousness parallel to what we saw in romantic fiction and personalized poetry.[145] The soul visited by God chooses one of several possible forms of "narrativity." The "creature" may see herself in some "other place" in space and time. She may speak in the first person. Or she may, as in the *Miroir des âmes simples et anéanties*, turn herself into an allegorical theater.

In describing the early stages of progress along the arduous path to union with God, Hildegard, Hadewijch, Mechthild, and other mystics often provide deliberately skimpy autobiographical details. These are located in the past, not only because they concern the first steps of a spiritual journey but also because they attest to an astonishing identification with the time of the Redemption, an identification that gives a very particular structure to the *Lives* of, for example, Margery Kempe, Clara of Rimini, and Angela of Foligno.

It would be interesting to have a typology of these accounts of mystical experience. Some are narrated in the first person, while others are third-person accounts of the life of one of God's "creatures," a style that connotes an extreme distancing of the author's self. The third person appears to reduce the individual component, but in some cases it can actually result in a "thicker" description of the self, as when Marguerite Porete combines the story of her "soul" with a variety of first-person narratives, allowing her to play freely with time and its discontinuities. By contrast, Julian of Norwich and Margery Kempe bring the past stunningly back to life, and their rapid, breathless narration of an emotional present, of their reliving of the Passion, was perhaps a way of returning to a "primordial" time, a time that negates the passage of time and conveys the soul's fusion with the godhead.

Writing involves a conscious awareness of inner, subjective time. Proust's genius lay in working his way through the tattered fabric of memory. But, as Brian Stock has shown, the eleventh century anticipated him in its way of intertwining texts and consciousness of self.[146] Mystics were intensely interested in their personal histories, in the confession of the past and the reconstruction of lived experience. Paradoxically, their device for achieving these ends was in many cases a vision seemingly imposed from outside but in reality involving an exploration of inner time.

No one has yet developed a comprehensive analytic scheme for understanding the rich literature of visions.[147] The links in the chain of private time are easier to discern, however. Consider, for example, Hadewijch's eleventh letter: "Since the age of six, I have been so extraordinarily favored by love's compulsion that I would have died within two years had God not granted me strength different from that possessed by most human beings and had He not recreated my nature in the image of His own."[148] Later she gives the precise year and day (Ascension Day), the precise moment when Jesus appeared at the altar and she felt herself received and illuminated in the One. The "mysterious hours" mentioned in the twentieth letter are of course a parable, but it is no accident that the actors in this parable are "nameless" hours, chosen to illustrate the transcendent nature of the experience.

Michel Zink, looking for evidence of subjectivity in medieval literature, mentions Eloise's strikingly intense and immodest response to Abelard's letters, a response compounded of intoxication, bewilderment, introspection, and self-accusation.[149] Equally revealing is the following passage from Hadewijch's twenty-fifth letter, addressed to two women, a letter that is far more than just an ardent woman-to-woman confession: "And you, who can obtain more from me than anyone else in the world except Sarah, I embrace you, Emma and yourself, with the same affection. But both of you are too little concerned with the love that possesses me, whose clutch and violence I experience with such dread. Neither my heart nor my soul nor my senses have an hour's rest, day or night. This flame never ceases to burn in the marrow of my being."[150] To this confession Hadewijch adds, almost as an afterthought: "The other day . . . I heard a sermon in which Saint Augustine was mentioned. And at the moment I heard it I was so inflamed within that it seemed to me that the whole earth and all it contains would be consumed in that fire." She concludes with these impassioned words: "Love is all." Her message thus ends on a note of raw emotion, which contrasts with the refined and precious rhetoric found in the beginning of the letter (part of which may be lost).

There were many other ways of expressing inner time. Margery Kempe and Julian of Norwich carefully noted the details of spiritual events, at times splitting the self in order to bring out the transition from eye to mind, from vision to understanding: "I saw three heavens, and I thought: I see three heavens."[151] Margery, who shunned all authority, insisted on the right to speak. She did not want to preach or teach, only to speak of God: "The Gospel gives me the right to speak of God," to recount the pity she felt when the crucified Christ appeared to her in all his suffering and real blood flowed from his body. At the sight of an icon Clara of Rimini too fell into a fit of convulsions; images had hallucinatory powers.[152] Julian, one of the timeless witnesses of Christ's Passion, tended to see single images, whereas Bridget of Sweden and Margery saw sequences.

If the pleasure of love often expressed itself as pain, there was nevertheless momentary jubilation. This might well have affinities with Proust's exaltation and sensual fulfillment at the recovery of memory, but in the case of the mystics it involved a more intimate sense of oneness with the revealed time of eternity. One source of the power of mystical language was that the resurrection of the past made vision flesh.

Even Marguerite d'Oingt, simple as her language is, found subtle ways to express time. In the *Speculum,* a relatively brief piece, she talks about herself in the third person ("une persona que jo cognoisso"), and the phrase "not long ago," the negation of a lapse of time, is a litotes. In fact the purpose of mystical language was to indicate an exceptional relation to time, to express inexpressible joy and aesthetic emotion. Marguerite Porete's multiplicity of first persons expresses a frenetic sense of time, a time outside rationality, a time of intolerable exile and desire for mystical union.

The language and haunting metaphors of pleasure provided a way of losing oneself in language while denying all capacity to use words. It was a sensual enterprise in which the soul, open to penetration, sought to make itself naked. The feminization of language resulted in the invention of a new vocabulary that expressed the Absent through the extreme presence of the word. Humbly the mystics confessed that no language of love, no matter how determined to overcome the barriers of language, could fully express the joy of the mystical union with God. Courtly culture provided images and turns of phrase for expressing an emotion that no language could ever capture. Mystics therefore dreamed of discovering a more immediately comprehensible primal language; in so doing they developed a language of gestures, of inarticulate screams and cries. As Michel de Certeau remarked of the mystics of a later age, their project was to establish a place from which they could speak without anyone's authorization: "Turning endlessly around the production site, the in-finite and uncertain place of the 'I,' mystical language, redundant and vehement, laid it down that the only thing that mattered was the source of the inspired statement, the present act."[153] A challenge to the institutionalized discourse of the Church, this insistence on immediacy was a provocation.

The author herself thus became the focus of interest. Verbal pleasure brought to mind physical pleasure, as in Bachelard's poetics or Barthes's criticism. One was overwhelmed by words, by their echoes and eddies. The suffocating excess of mystical language overcame the inexpressiveness of words. The most intimate of confessions became a roar that echoed through time. To give a name to all this is impossible. As Hadewijch says in the fourth "unnamed hour," it is in the absence of names that "Love causes the soul to savor its most secret judgments, deeper and darker than the abyss."[154]

TRANSLATED AND ADAPTED FROM THE FRENCH BY
ARTHUR GOLDHAMMER

Affidavits and Confessions

Georges Duby

IN THE MEDIEVAL WEST, women talked. They talked a great deal. Men felt that they talked too much, and "chatter" was among the foremost of the faults of women denounced by preachers. Yet voluble as women were, very little of what they said has survived. Up to the end of the thirteenth century there is virtually total silence. True, some texts from earlier periods purport to be by women. But there are good reasons to attribute most of them to men. And the few women who did write tried to write as men did, perhaps even copying a tirade that some ancient author had placed in the mouth of one of his heroines.

To catch the sound of an authentic female voice, one not masculinized by the straitjacket of rhetoric or travestied by plagiarism, we must look to the scribbled notes of the scribes whose business it was to record testimony and confessions. These scribes almost always wrote in Latin, placing yet another screen between us and the actual voices of women. We must translate as we read and attempt to imagine the words actually spoken. Still, this is one of the few places where we can catch the unadorned sound of the female voice. But such evidence does not become available until quite late, until after powerful men began to surround themselves with scribes and after the courts, in their search for the truth, began to require written evidence and to examine the consciences of witnesses.

Of the various manuscript sources that preserve such statements, I have chosen one of the oldest and richest, a transcript compiled in 1326 on orders of Jacques Fournier, who later became Pope Benedict XII.[1]

In that year Fournier left the episcopal see of Mirepoix to become bishop of Pamiers. For nine years he had rigorously discharged the duties of his office, ferreting out deviants—people accused of casting spells or subscribing to the Catharist heresy—wherever they might be found in his diocese. Catharism, which had flared up again only a short while before, had once more subsided. The Dominicans and Franciscans had all but eliminated it from the lowlands. But in the mountain villages and high pastures it still flourished. In 1320, while investigating a woman accused of being a witch, Fournier had accidentally stumbled on another woman, Beatrice, who not only appeared to be mixed up in witchcraft herself but who also had made some suspicious remarks about Christ's body. After being interrogated by the bishop, the frightened woman fled, but she was tracked down and captured. Her confession led to a thorough investigation of the village of Montaillou. Men and women—the latter in particularly large numbers—were called before the bishop. Intelligent, curious, and keenly attuned to the slightest sign of wickedness, Fournier pressed the witnesses with his questions and ordered the clerk to prepare a very complete record of the confessions he elicited. The transcript is quite long. Here I give only brief excerpts from the testimony of two women. To be sure, these women were not speaking freely, but what they were coerced to say reflected their most private thoughts. Both were widows. One, Grazida, was a peasant of around twenty-two. The other, a noblewoman and the wife of a knight, was much older: she was none other than Beatrice, the woman with whom the scandal had originated. Under her maiden name, Béatrice de Planissolles, she has since become famous: the Occitanian philosopher René Nelli made her the protagonist of an operatic libretto, and, in 1975, the historian Emmanuel Le Roy Ladurie published an excellent, and widely read, ethnographic study of the village of Montaillou.

Let us begin with the testimony of Grazida, who was interrogated on August 19, 1320:

> Around seven years ago the curé [Pierre Clergue, the priest of Montaillou] came to the home of my mother, who was away in the fields for the harvest, and asked me to allow him to have carnal knowledge of me. I agreed. At the time I was a virgin of, I think, fourteen or fifteen. He deflowered me in the barn, where there was a pile of straw.

He used no violence. From then until the following January he knew me often, always in my mother's house, and with her knowledge and consent. It usually happened during the day.

Then, in January, the curé officiated at my marriage to Pierre Lizier, my late husband, and during the remaining four years of my husband's life the priest, with my husband's consent, frequently had carnal knowledge of me. When my husband asked me if the priest had had relations with me, I answered yes, and my husband told me to stay away from other men, except for this priest. Nevertheless, the priest never had relations with me when my husband was home, only when he was away . . .

— If you had known that your mother was the curé's first cousin, in fact by bastardy, would you have consented to be known by him?
— No. But because it pleased me as well as the curé when we had carnal knowledge of each other, I did not think I was committing a sin with him.
— When this priest had knowledge of you, either before you had a husband or during your marriage, did you believe you were committing a sin?
— Because at that time it pleased me and the curé too to have mutual knowledge of each other, I did not think so, and it did not seem to me that it was a sin. But because now it does not please me to be known by this priest, if it were to happen I would think it was a sin.
— If such a union had been forbidden by your husband, would you have thought you were committing a sin if you had subsequently copulated with this priest?
— Assuming that my husband had forbidden me to do it, which he did not, I would not have thought I was committing a sin if, despite his prohibition, I had copulated with this priest, since it pleased both me and the priest . . .
— Do you believe that people who behave properly and lead a holy life will go to heaven after death and that sinners will go to hell, and do you believe that hell and heaven exist?
— I do not know. I have heard that there is a heaven, and I believe it. I have heard that there is a hell, but I neither believe it nor deny it. I believe that there is a heaven

because it is a good thing, according to what I have heard, but I neither believe in nor deny hell, because it is a bad thing.

— Do you believe that carnal union is not a sin when it pleases the man and the woman?

— I do not believe that it is a sin.

— How long have you held this belief?

— Since this priest first had knowledge of me.

— Who taught you this error?

— No one. Myself.

— Have you taught it to anyone?

— No, no one has questioned me about it.

Beatrice's interrogation lasted two weeks, from August 13 to August 25, 1320. She reluctantly owned up to her many love affairs. Jacques Fournier forced her to talk about her lovers because some of them had taught her a little more about the heresy than she had learned from her father. We learn that noble women were no better protected than peasants from men's assaults or their own desires. When she was still a young bride, perhaps fifteen years old and already pregnant, she was living in the château of Montaillou, which at that time was in the safekeeping of her first husband. Raymond Roussel, the steward of the estate, begged her to go with him to Lombardy to join what he called the "good Christians," that is, the Catharist Perfecti:

This Raymond spoke to me of heretical things frequently and in many places and urged me to go off with him. Finally, one night, after we had dined together, he secretly entered my bedroom and hid under my bed. After straightening the house, I went to bed. The servants were resting or sleeping. I too fell asleep. Raymond came out from under the bed and, wearing a nightshirt, crept into bed with me, and began to act as though he wanted to sleep carnally with me. I said, "What is this?" He told me to keep quiet. I answered, "What do you mean, peasant, telling me to keep quiet?" I began to shout and called my maids, who were sleeping with me in the same room, telling them that there was a man in bed with me. Hearing that, Raymond left the bed and the room. The next day he told me that he had been wrong to hide in my room. I answered: "Now everything is clear. When you asked me to go with you to the good Christians, you were just saying that so you could have me and have carnal knowledge of me. If I weren't afraid that my husband would think I had done something dishonorable with you, I would have you locked up in the tower immediately."

Beatrice's ferocity soon abated, however.

> While my husband was still alive [she testified on August 10], one day Raymond Clergue, known as Pathau, the natural son of Guillaume Clergue, the brother of Pons Clergue who was the father of Pierre Clergue, now curé of Montaillou, took me by force in the castle and had carnal knowledge of me. And when my husband Béranger de Roquefort died a year later, this Raymond claimed me publicly.
>
> Although the aforementioned curé, Raymond's first cousin, knew that Raymond had relations with me, he asked me to allow him to have knowledge of me. I asked him how he could demand such a thing, knowing that his cousin was having carnal knowledge of me and would soon find out. The curé told me that there was nothing to worry or be embarrassed about. "I know how things stand, but I can be more useful to you and give you more than that bastard." He also told me that both of them, he, the curé, and Raymond, could claim me together. I told him that I would never allow such a thing as long as I lived, because there would be dissension between them because of me and each would vilify me on account of the other. From the time the priest first had carnal knowledge of me, I had no further carnal relations with Raymond, although from time to time he tried. Because of that there was, between Raymond and the priest, a concealed hatred, which I knew about.

Pierre Clergue had attacked her for the first time during Lent, when

> I went to the church of Montaillou to confess my sins. While I was there, I went to the curé, who was hearing confessions behind the altar of Saint Mary. When I knelt in front of him, he kissed me and said there was no woman in the world he loved as much as me. Dumbfounded, I left without confessing. Later, around the time of Easter, he came to see me several times and asked me to allow him to have carnal knowledge of me. Once, when he asked me this in my home, I told him

487

that I would rather be known by four men than by one priest, because I had heard that a woman who had been known carnally by a priest was not permitted to see the face of God. He answered that I was foolish and ignorant, because it was a great sin for a woman to be known by her husband or any other man and that the sin was the same no matter who the man was, husband or priest. According to him, it was even a greater sin with the husband because the wife believed she was not committing a sin with her husband but was committing one with other men.

One night in early July, Beatrice finally gave in at her home near the castle, where the priest subsequently called on her two or three times a week, not abstaining even during the most solemn holy occasions. The affair lasted for a year and a half, until Beatrice left Montaillou for Prades:

> Pierre Clergue [she confessed on August 22] came to see me there. He told me that he would send Jean, his novice, whose family name I do not know, to fetch me and asked me to come sleep with him the following night. Which I agreed to do. Early that night I was at home waiting for the novice. He came, and because the night was dark I followed him to Saint Peter's Church in Prades, which we entered. There we found Pierre Clergue, who had had a bed set up in the church. I said, "How can we do such a thing in the church of Saint Peter?" He answered: "O que gran dampnage y ora seint Peire?" [dialect meaning perhaps: What great damnation can it cause Saint Peter?] We then got into bed and slept together in the church. That night, in that church, he had carnal knowledge of me. Before dawn he led me out of the church himself and accompanied me to the door of the house I was living in.

Shortly thereafter, on August 15, 1301, Beatrice married her second husband, a man from the lowlands. At the next harvest the curé of Montaillou, pretending to be from Limoux, came to see her.

> He came into my house and told me that my sister Gentille, who lives in Limoux, sent her greetings, and I received him. We both went down to the cellar of the house, and there he had carnal knowledge of me, while Sibille, my servant, Arnaud Teisseyre's daughter, stood at the cellar door. The night before

she had brought, on behalf of the curé, a *bliaud* from Barcelona with red and yellow silk lace. She had told me that he would be coming the next day, so that nobody else would come, and that if anyone did come they would never suspect that the curé and I were committing a sin. That is why this servant stood in the middle of the open cellar door while I was copulating with the priest.

Widowed for a second time some five years prior to her interrogation, Beatrice's affections now turned to Barthélemy, the priest of the parish in which she was then living and her youngest daughter's teacher. From June until Pentecost she enjoyed sexual relations with him, always during the daytime when she was home alone. Later they went together to the Catalonian side of the Pyrenees, in the county of Pailars. In that region priests lived openly with their concubines, to whom they bound themselves with contracts drawn up by a notary, as for a marriage. This arrangement lasted a year. When Beatrice, terrified by Jacques Fournier's preliminary interrogation, sought to escape the inquisition, she tried in her panic to rejoin this former lover.

Certain strange objects were found in the baggage she took with her. The inquisitors were in no doubt about what they were: witch's equipment. Beatrice explained:

The umbilical cords came from my daughters' male babies, and I kept them because a Jewess, now baptized, told me that if I carried them and found myself in court, I could not lose. That is why I took my grandchildren's cords and kept them. Since then I have not been in court and have not had an opportunity to test their effectiveness.

The bloodstained sheets are stained with the menstrual blood of my daughter Philippa. The baptized Jewess told me that if I kept the first blood that came out of my daughter and if I gave that menstrual blood to her husband or any other man to drink, that man would never care for another woman. So when my daughter Philippa, a long time ago now, had her first period, I looked her in the face. It was blue, and I asked her what was wrong. She told me that she had lost blood through the vulva. Recalling what the baptized Jew had told me, I cut off a piece of my daughter Philippa's nightshirt, which was stained with this blood, and as it seemed to me that there was not enough of it, I gave my daughter another piece of very fine linen so that, when she got her period, she could dip this cloth in the blood and wet it. She did so. I dried these fabrics with the intention, after she married, of removing some of the menstrual blood from the cloth and giving it to her husband to drink. Philippa was engaged this year, and I planned to give such a drink to her betrothed. But I decided it would be better to wait until after he had had carnal knowledge of Philippa. She could give it to him herself. When I was arrested, the marriage had not yet been consummated, and there had been no wedding night, so I had not given the husband anything to drink.

When I put these pieces of cloth in my purse along with the grains of incense, I did not intend to use them in any curse. This is how it happened. The incense was not intended for any evil purpose. But this year my daughter had a headache. I was told that incense mixed with other things could cure this ailment. The grains of incense that were found on me in that bag were left over. I had no intention of doing anything else with them.

The mirror, the sheathed knife, and the piece of linen—I was not keeping them or carrying them with me to cast any spell or pronounce any curse.

The seed wrapped in muslin is the seed of the plant known as ground-ivy. This year a pilgrim gave me some and told me that it was good for falling sickness [epilepsy]. Since my grandson, the son of my daughter Condors, this year had a spell of falling sickness, I wanted to use this seed. But my daughter told me that she had taken her son to Saint Paul's Church, where he had been cured of the disease, and that she did not wish to treat her son for it in any way. So I did not use the seed.

— Have you cast any other evil spells? Have you taught them? Did you teach them to anyone?
— No. But sometimes I felt that the priest Barthélemy had cast a spell over me, because I loved him too passionately and always wanted to be with him, even though, after the first time I had carnal knowledge of him, my periods stopped. I asked him about it. He always denied it.

Both women abjured heresy, were absolved, and, on March 3, 1321, appeared before the inquisitor for heretical deviancy for the kingdom of France. On March 8, they were sentenced to "the wall," that is, life imprisonment. But on July 4, 1322, both had their sentences commuted. Set free, they were required as long as they lived to wear yellow crosses on their clothing, a sign to the public to beware and not to come too near these once-tainted bodies.

Translated from the French by Arthur Goldhammer

Notes

Bibliography

Contributors

Illustration Credits

Index

Notes

Including Women
CHRISTIANE KLAPISCH-ZUBER

1. Christine de Pisan, *La cité des dames*, trans. Eric Hicks and Thérèse Moreau (Paris: Stock-Moyen Age, 1986), pp. 37–38.

2. The expression is from Joan Kelly, "The Social Relation of the Sexes. Methodological Implications of Women's History," *Signs: Journal of Women in Culture and Society* 1(4)1976:810; reprinted in Joan Kelly, *Women, History, and Theory. The Essays of Joan Kelly* (Chicago: University of Chicago Press, 1984), p. 2.

3. A good example of recent French work in this vein is Régine Pernoud, *La femme au temps des cathédrales* (Paris: Stock, 1980), an outgrowth of many works devoted to exceptional women.

4. Such an overview was attempted in a colloquium held in 1976 in Poitiers. The proceedings, which contain a useful bibliography and some interesting working hypotheses, were published under the title *La femme dans les civilisations des Xe–XIIIe siècles* (Poitiers, 1977).

5. Kelly, "The Social Relation of the Sexes," p. 4.

6. See Sherry B. Ortner and Harriet Whitehead, eds., *Sexual Meanings: The Cultural Construction of Gender and Sexuality* (Cambridge: Cambridge University Press, 1981).

7. Gayle Rubin, "The Traffic in Women," in R. Reiter Rapp, ed., *Toward an Anthropology of Women* (New York: Monthly Review Press, 1976), pp. 159, 179.

8. C. P. MacCormack and M. Strathern, eds., *Nature, Culture, and Gender* (Cambridge: Cambridge University Press, 1980).

9. Among the earliest American collections, see Susan Mosher Stuard, ed., *Women in Medieval Society* (Philadelphia: University of Pennsylvania Press, 1976); R. Bridenthal and C. Koonz, *Becoming Visible. Women in European History*, rev. ed. (Boston: Houghton Mifflin, 1988), which extends well beyond the Middle Ages; Derek Baker, ed., *Medieval Women* (Oxford: Blackwell, 1978), which is concerned primarily with female rulers and religious women. More recently Stuard has published a new collection on the

historiography of women in England, Italy, France, the United States, and Germany: *Women in Medieval History and Historiography* (Philadelphia: University of Pennsylvania Press, 1987). See also Julius Kirshner and Suzanne F. Wemple, *Women of the Medieval World* (Oxford: Blackwell, 1985). Other collections on more specific topics are cited in the notes.

10. E. E. Power, *Medieval People* (Methuen, 1924), has two chapters on women. See also E. E. Power, *Medieval English Nunneries* (Cambridge, 1922). Eileen Power's posthumous *Medieval Women*, ed. M. M. Postan (1975), collects essays and lectures written before World War II, which had been intended as groundwork for a book Power did not live to write.

11. Yvonne Knibiehler, "Chronologie et histoire des femmes," in Michelle Perrot, ed., *Une histoire des femmes est-elle possible?* (Paris-Marseilles: Rivages, 1984), pp. 50–57.

12. Joan Kelly Gadol, "Did Women Have a Renaissance?" in Bridenthal and Koonz, *Becoming Visible*, pp. 137–164; reprinted in Kelly, *Women, History, and Theory*, pp. 19–50. Joann McNamara and Suzanne F. Wemple raise the problem in "The Power of Women through the Family in Medieval Europe, 500–1100," *Feminist Studies*, 1973, reprinted in Mary Hartman and Lois W. Banner, eds., *Clio's Consciousness Raised: New Perspectives on the History of Women* (New York: Harper-Row, 1974), pp. 103–118, and in Mary Erler and Maryanne Kowaleski, eds., *Women and Power in the Middle Ages* (Athens-London: University of Georgia Press, 1988), pp. 83–101; see also, by the same authors, "Sanctity and Power: The Dual Pursuit of Medieval Women," in Bridenthal and Koonz, *Becoming Visible*, pp. 90–118.

13. See Judith C. Brown, "A Woman's Place Was in the Home: Women's Work in Renaissance Tuscany," in Margaret W. Ferguson, Maureen Quilligan, and Nancy J. Vickers, eds., *Rewriting the Renaissance. The Discourses of Sexual Difference in Early Modern Europe* (Chicago: University of Chicago Press, 1986), pp. 206–226.

14. Erler and Kowaleski, eds., *Women and Power*, pp. 1–13.

Enforcing Order

C. K.-Z.

1. "Buon cavallo e mal cavallo vuole sprone; buona donna e mala donna vuol signore, e tale bastone." Paolo da Certaldo, *Libro di buoni costumi*, no. 209, in V. Branca, ed., *Mercanti scrittori* (Milan: Rusconi, 1986), p. 43.

2. On the consequences of this private/public dichotomy, see Jean B. Elshtain, *Public Man, Private Woman: Women in Social and Political Thought* (Princeton: Princeton University Press, 1981); Gianna Pomata, "La storia delle donne: Una questione di confine," in *Gli strumenti della ricerca*, vol. 2 (Florence: La Nuova Italia, 1983).

3. See S. B. Ortner, "Is Female to Male as Nature Is to Culture?" in M. Z. Rosaldo and I. Lamphere, eds., *Woman, Culture, and Society* (Stanford: Stanford University Press, 1974); and the critique of Eleanor Burke Leacock and J. Nash, "Ideologies of Sex: Archetypes and Stereotypes," in

Eleanor Burke Leacock, ed., *Myths of Male Dominance* (New York-London: Monthly Review Press, 1981); see also C. MacCormack and M. Strathern, eds., *Nature, Culture and Gender* (Cambridge: Cambridge University Press, 1980).

Chapter 1. The Clerical Gaze
JACQUES DALARUN

For convenience, even when better editions exist, references to patristic and medieval sources are generally given to Jacques Paul Migne, ed., *Patrologia Latina*, 221 vols. (Paris, 1844–1864); cited hereafter as *PL*.

1. Marie-Thérèse d'Alverny, "Comment les théologiens et les philosophes voient la femme," *Cahiers de civilisation médiévale* 20(1977):105.
2. René Metz, "Le statut de la femme en droit canonique médiéval," in *La Femme*, a special issue of *Recueils de la société Jean Bodin* 12(1962):59–82.
3. Raoul Manselli, "La Chiesa e il francescanesimo femminile," in *Movimento religioso femminile e francescanesimo nel secolo XIII* (Assisi, 1980), p. 242.
4. Geoffroy of Vendôme, *PL* 157, col. 168.
5. Genesis 2:20.
6. Roberto Zapperi, *L'homme enceint. L'homme, la femme et le pouvoir* (Paris, 1983), pp. 19–25.
7. Genesis 3:16–20.
8. Ambrose of Milan, *PL* 14, col. 303.
9. Tertullian, *PL* 1, col. 1305.
10. Odo of Cluny, *PL* 133, col. 556.
11. Yves of Chartres, *PL* 162, col. 279.
12. Geoffroy of Vendôme, *PL* 157, col. 126.
13. John 18:17.
14. Maxim of Turin, *PL* 57, col. 350.
15. Marbode of Rennes, *PL* 171, col. 1486.
16. Augustine, quoted by Jean Delumeau, *La peur en Occident (XIVe–XVIIIe siècle)* (Paris, 1978), p. 306.
17. Guy Devailly, "Un évêque et un prédicateur errant au XIIe siècle: Marbode de Rennes et Robert d'Arbrissel," *Mémoires de la société d'histoire et d'archéologie de Bretagne* 57(1980):163–170.
18. Rosario Leotta, ed., *Marbodi liber decem capitulorum* (Rome, 1984).
19. Marbode of Rennes, *PL* 171, cols. 1698–1699.
20. Hildebert of Lavardin, *PL* 171, col. 1428.
21. *I P* III, 7.
22. Isidore of Seville, *PL* 82, col. 417.
23. Roger of Caen, *PL* 158, col. 697.
24. Peter Damian, *PL* 145, col. 410.
25. Isidore of Seville, *PL* 82, col. 275.

26. Jerome, *PL* 22, col. 408.

27. Augustine, *PL* 38, col. 1108.

28. Anselm of Canterbury, *PL* 158, cols. 406–407.

29. See Henri Barré, *Prières anciennes de l'Occident à la Mère du Sauveur des origines à saint Anselme* (Paris, 1963), p. 75.

30. Geoffroy of Vendôme, *PL* 157, cols. 234–235.

31. Matthew 1:25.

32. Luke 1:34.

33. Gregory the Great, *PL* 76, col. 1197.

34. Hincmar of Rheims, *PL* 125, col. 694.

35. Ezra 44:2.

36. Rupert of Deutz, *PL* 167, col. 1493.

37. Geoffroy of Vendôme, *PL* 157, cols. 249–250.

38. Hildebert of Lavardin, *PL* 171, col. 813.

39. Geoffroy of Vendôme, *PL* 157, cols. 265–267.

40. *Sancti Ephraem Syri Hymni et Sermones,* ed. Thomas Lamy, Malines, II, 1886, p. 264.

41. Peter Chrysologus, *PL* 52, col. 576.

42. Hildebert of Lavardin, *PL* 171, cols. 193–194.

43. Ibid., col. 959.

44. Georges Duby, *Le chevalier, la femme et le prêtre. Le mariage dans la France féodale* (Paris, 1981), pp. 142–147, 192–193.

45. Marbode of Rennes, *PL* 171, col. 1700.

46. Hildebert of Lavardin, *PL* 171, col. 967.

47. Jean-Yves Tilliette, "Les modèles de sainteté du IXe au XIe siècle d'après le témoignage des récits hagiographiques en vers métriques," in *Santi e demoni nell'alto Medioevo, Atti della 36a Settimana di studi sull'alto Medioevo (Spoleto, 1988)* (Spoleto, 1989), pp. 381–406.

48. Peter Damian, *PL* 145, cols. 599–601.

49. Geneviève Hasenohr, "La vie quotidienne de la femme vue par l'Eglise: l'enseignement des 'Journées chrétiennes' de la fin du Moyen Age," in *Frau und spätmittelalterlicher Alltag* (Vienna, 1986).

50. Pierre Toubert, "La théorie du mariage chez les moralistes carolingiens," in *Il matrimonio nella società altomedievale* (Spoleto, 1977), pp. 259–260.

51. Patrick Corbet, *Les saints ottoniens. Sainteté dynastique, sainteté royale et sainteté féminine autour de l'an mil* (Sigmaringen, 1986).

52. François Dolbeau, "Vie latine de sainte Anne, composée au XIe siècle par Etienne, abbé de Saint-Urbain," *Analecta bollandiana* 105(1987):42–43, 52–57.

53. Duby, *La femme,* pp. 147–150.

54. Jane Tibbetts Schulenburg, "Sexism and the Celestial Gynaeceum, from 500 to 1200," *Journal of Medieval History* 4(1978):122.

55. Gottfried Koch, *Frauenfrage und Ketzertum im Mittelalter* (Berlin, 1962).

56. Hildebert of Lavardin, *PL* 171, col. 149.

57. Peter the Venerable, *PL* 189, col. 214.

58. Marbode of Rennes (?), *PL* 171, col. 1599.

59. Luke 7:38.

60. Victor Saxer, under "Maria Maddalena, santa," in *Bibliotheca sanctorum*, vol. 8 (Rome, 1967), col. 1089.

61. Dominique Iogna-Prat, "'Bienheureuse polysémie.' La Madeleine du 'Sermo in veneratione sanctae Mariae Magdalenae' attribué à Odon de Cluny (Xe s.)," in Eve Duperray, ed., *Marie Madeleine dans la mystique, les arts et les lettres* (Paris, 1989), pp. 21, 29.

62. Peter of Cella, *PL* 202, col. 837.

63. Geoffroy of Vendôme, *PL* 157, cols. 270–272.

64. Odo of Cluny (?), *PL* 133, col. 721.

65. Geoffroy of Vendôme, *PL* 157, col. 274.

66. Ibid.

67. Origen, *Patrologia graeca* 12, col. 158.

68. Ambrose of Milan, *PL* 14, col. 279.

69. Geoffroy of Vendôme, *PL* 157, cols. 231–234.

70. Jerome, *PL* 22, col. 398.

71. Marbode of Rennes (?), *PL* 171, cols. 1631–1632.

72. Genesis 1:27.

73. 1 Corinthians 11:7.

74. Jacques Dalarun, *Robert d'Arbrissel, fondateur de Fontevraud* (Paris, 1986), pp. 80–91, 101–113.

75. Jacques Le Goff, *La naissance du Purgatoire* (Paris, 1981).

76. Jean Leclercq, "Un témoin de l'antiféminisme au Moyen Age," *Revue bénédictine* 80(1970):304–305.

77. Jean Leclercq, "Saint Bernard et la dévotion médiévale envers Marie," *Revue d'ascétique et de mystique* 30(1954):368.

78. Thomas Aquinas, *Summa theologica* I, Q92.

79. Gilbert of Tournai, *Collectio de scandalis Ecclesiae*, ed. Autbert Stroick, in *Archivum franciscanum historicum* 24(1931):61–62.

80. Thomas Aquinas, *Summa theologica* II-II, Q 177, a 2.

81. Gratian, *Decretum* I, D XXIII, c 29, and II, C XXXIII, Q 5, c 12–19.

82. 1 Timothy 2:12.

83. Victor Saxer, *Le culte de Marie Madeleine en Occident des origines à la fin du Moyen Age* (Auxerre-Paris, 1959), I, 183–255.

84. Daniel Russo, "Entre le Christ et Marie: la Madeleine dans l'art italien des XIIIe–XIVe siècles," in Duperray, ed., *Marie Madeleine dans la mystique*, pp. 33–47.

85. Schulenburg, "Sexism," pp. 127, 131.

86. Rudolph Bell, *Holy Anorexia* (Chicago-London, 1985), p. 146.

87. Giunta Bevagnati, *Vita b. Margaritae de Cortona, Acta sanctorum* (Paris, 1865), p. 317.

Chapter 2. The Nature of Woman
CLAUDE THOMASSET

1. Mirko D. Grmek, *Les maladies à l'aube de la civilisation occidentale* (Paris: Payot, 1983), pp. 227ff.

2. Avicenna, *Canon*, trans. Gerard of Cremona (Milan: P. de Lavagnia, 1473), book 3, fen. 20, tr. I, c. I. The English translations here are based on French translations taken from Danielle Jacquart and Claude Thomasset, *Sexualité et savoir médical au Moyen Age* (Paris: Presses Universitaires de France, 1985).

3. Oswei Temkin, *Galenism: Rise and Decline of a Medical Philosophy* (Ithaca, N.Y.: Cornell University Press, 1973).

4. Claude Thomasset, ed., *Placides et Timéo ou Li Secrés as philosophes* (Paris-Geneva: Droz, 1980), p. 117, para. 259.

5. On medieval anatomy, see George Washington Corner, *Anatomical Texts of the Earlier Middle Ages,* Carnegie Institution of Washington, Publication no. 364 (Washington, D.C.: National Publishing Company, 1927). See also Franz Redeker, "Die 'Anatomia Magistri Nicolai Physici' und ihr Verhältnis zur 'Anatomia Cophonis' und 'Ricardi,'" dissertation, University of Leipzig, 1917, pp. 67–86.

6. William of Conches, *Dialogus de Substantiis* (Strasbourg: J. Rihelius, 1567), p. 253.

7. Published in *Spurii Libri Galeno ascripti* (Venice: Giunta, 1597), fol. 59 recto–60 verso; translated into Italian by V. Passalacqua, "Microtegni seu de spermate," *Traduzione e commento* (Rome: Institute for the History of Medicine of the University of Rome, 1958).

8. On sex and gynecology in Hildegard of Bingen, see Joan Cadden, "It Takes All Kinds: Sexuality and Gender Differences in Hildegard of Bingen's *Book of compound medicine,*" in *Tradition* (1984):149–174.

9. Thomas de Cantimpré, *Liber de natura rerum I,* ed. H. Boese (Berlin-New York: W. de Gruyter, 1973), p. 72.

10. M. A. Hewson, *Giles of Rome and the Medieval Theory of Conception* (London: Athlone, 1975), pp. 21ff.

11. The expression occurs frequently in Giles of Rome's *De formatione corporis humani* and in Thomas Aquinas' *Summa Theologica I,* XCII, I arg. 1.

12. René Descartes, *La description du corps humain et de toutes ses fonctions,* in Charles Adam and Paul Tannery, eds., *Oeuvres de Descartes* (Paris: Vrin, 1974), XI, 253.

13. Georges Duby, *Mâle Moyen Age: De l'amour et autres essais* (Paris: Flammarion, 1988), p. 42.

14. *Trotulae de Mulierum Passionibus ante, in et post Partum* (Strasbourg: J. Schott, 1654). Trotula de Ruggerio, *Sulle malattie delle donne,* ed. Pina Cavallo Boggi, trans. Matilde Nubié and Adriana Tocco (Turin: La Rosa, 1979).

15. Description of the manuscript in G. Beaujouan, "Manuscrits médi-

caux du Moyen Age conservés en Espagne," *Mélanges de la Casa de Velazquez* 8(1972):173.

16. P. F. Dembovski, ed., *Ami et Amile-Chanson de geste* (Paris: Champion, 1987).

Chapter 3. The Protected Woman
CARLA CASAGRANDE

1. Alan of Lille, *Summa de arte praedicatoria,* in J.-P. Migne, *Patrologia Latina* 210, pp. 111–195; James of Vitry, *Sermones vulgares,* Ms. Paris B.N. Lat. 17509; Gilbert of Tournai, *Sermones ad omnes status,* ed. Johannem de Vingle (Lyons, 1511).

2. Vincent of Beauvais, *De eruditione filiorum nobilium,* ed. Arpad Steiner (Cambridge, Mass.: The Medieval Academy of America, 1938); William Peraldo, *De eruditione principum,* in Saint Thomae Aquinatis, *Opera Omnia* (Parma 1865), XVI, 390–476.

3. John of Wales, *Communiloquium* (Georgium de Arrivabenis Mantuanus, Venetiis 1496); fols. 1r–166v; Jacob of Voragine, *Sermones de tempore,* ed. Simonem de Luere (Venice, 1497); *Chronica civitatis Ianuensis,* ed. Giovanni Monteleone (Rome, 1941).

4. Philip of Novara, *Les quattres âges de l'homme,* ed. Marcel de Fréville (Paris, 1888).

5. Louis IX of France, *Lettre à sa fille Ysabelle,* in *Vie de saint Louis par le confesseur de la reine Marguerite, Recueil des Historiens des Gaules et de la France,* ed. Daunon and Naudet (Paris, 1840), XX, 82–83; Durandus of Champagne, *Speculum dominarum,* Ms. Paris B.N. Lat. 6784.

6. Giles of Rome, *De regimine principum libri III,* ed. Bartholomaeum Zancttum (Rome, 1607).

7. Humbertus de Romanis, *Liber de eruditione praedicatorum,* in *Maxima Bibliotheca Veterum Patrum et antiquorum Scriptorum,* ed. Anissonios (Lyons, 1677), XXV, 424–567.

8. Francesco of Barberino, *Reggimento e costumi di donna,* ed. Giuseppe Edoardo Sansone (Turin: Loescher-Chiantore, 1957), p. 9.

9. William Peraldo, *Summa de virtutibus et vitiis,* ed. Paganinium de Paganinis (Venice, 1487), fol. 207r.

10. James of Vitry, *Ad viduas et continentes,* Sermon I, fol. 142v; Peraldo, *Summa,* fol. 207v.

11. Francesco of Barberino, *Reggimento,* p. 10.

12. Giles of Rome, *De regimine,* pp. 340–347.

13. Philip of Novara, *Les quatres âges,* p. 16.

14. Humbertus de Romanis, *Ad mulieres malas corpore sive meretrices,* p. 506.

15. Francesco of Barberino, *Reggimento,* p. 20.

16. Ibid., pp. 200–203.

17. Humbertus de Romanis, *Ad mulieres nobiles,* p. 504.

18. Louis IX, *Lettre à sa fille Ysabelle,* p. 83.

19. Durandus of Champagne, *Speculum dominarum,* fol. 15rv.

20. Francesco of Barberino, *Reggimento,* p. 15.

21. Thomas Aquinas, *Summa Theologica,* II-II, q. 151, a. 1, 1.

22. Christine de Pisan, *La cité des dames,* trans. Eric Hicks and Thérèse Moreau (Paris: Stock-Moyen Age, 1986), pp. 275–278; *Le trésor de la cité des dames (Le livre des trois vertus),* ed. Denis Janot (Paris, 1536).

23. *Le ménagier de Paris,* ed. Jérôme Pichon, 2 vols. (Paris: Techener, 1846); Giovanni Dominici, *Regola del governo di cura familiare,* ed. Piero Bargellini (Florence: Fiorentina, 1927); *Le livre du Chevalier de la Tour Landry pour l'enseignement de ses filles,* ed. Anatole de Montaiglon (Paris: P. Iannet, 1854); Simone Fidati da Cascia, *Regola ovvero dottrina a una sua figliuola spirituale,* in Nicola Mattioli, *Il beato Simone Fidati da Cascia. I suoi scritti editi ed inediti* (Rome: Tip. del Campidoglio, 1898), II, 223–241.

24. Francisco Ximenez, *Lo libre de les dones,* ed. F. Naccarato, 2 vols. (Barcelona: Curial, 1981).

25. Girolamo of Siena, "Il soccorso dei poveri," in *Scrittori di religione del Trecento. Testi originali,* ed. Giuseppe De Luca (Turin: Einaudi, 1977), II, 277–328.

26. Bernardino of Siena, *Le prediche volgari inedite. Firenze 1424–1425. Siena 1427,* ed. Dionisio Pacetti (Siena: Cantagalli, 1935); *Le prediche volgari,* ed. Ciro Cannarozzi, 5 vols. (Florence: Fiorentina, 1934–1940); *Quadragesimale de christiana religione,* in *Opera Omnia,* vols. I–II (Ad Claras Aquas, 1950); *Quadragesimale de Evangelio aeterno,* vols. III–V (1956); *Sermones imperfecti,* vol. VIII (1963), pp. 1–160; *Prediche volgari sul Campo di Siena 1427,* ed. Carlo Delcorno, 2 vols. (Milan: Rusconi, 1989).

27. Antonino of Florence, *Opera a buon vivere,* ed. Francesco Palermo (Florence, 1866).

28. Giovanni Certosino, *Decor puellarum,* for Nicolaum Jenson (Venice, 1461); *Gloria mulierum, ovvero Ordine delle donne maritate,* for Nicolaum Jenson (Venice, 1471).

29. Dionysius the Carthusian, *De laudabili vita coniugatorum,* in *Opera Omnia,* XXXVIII (Tournai, 1909), pp. 55–117; *De laudabili vita viduarum,* pp. 119–142; *De laudabili vita virginum,* pp. 157–178.

30. Giles of Rome, *De regimine,* p. 342.

31. William Peraldo, *Summa,* fol. 298r.

32. Ibid., fol. 210vb.

33. Philip of Novara, *Les quatres âges,* p. 18; Francesco of Barberino, *Reggimento,* pp. 12–13.

34. James of Vitry, *Ad virgines. Sermo I,* fol. 146v.

35. Francesco of Barberino, *Reggimento,* p. 95.

36. Conrad of Megenberg, *Yconomica,* ed. Sabine Krüger, in Monumenta Germaniae Historica, *Staatsschriften des späteren Mittelalters,* III, 5 (Stuttgart: A. Hiersemann, 1973–1984), pp. 112–113.

37. Durandus of Champagne, *Speculum dominarum,* fols. 37r–38r.

38. Andrea Cappellano, *De amore,* ed. E. Trojel (Munich: Eidos, 1964), p. 346.

39. Francisco Ximenez, *Lo libro de les dones*, I, 20.

40. Giles of Rome, *De regimine*, p. 272.

41. Francesco of Barberino, *Reggimento*, pp. 59, 62, 88.

42. Jacob of Voragine, *Chronica*, p. 191; Augustine, *Sermo IX: De decem cordis*, in *Sermones ad populum*, PL 38, 84.

43. Kari Elisabeth Børresen, *Subordination et équivalence. Nature et rôle de la femme d'après Augustin et Thomas d'Aquin* (Oslo, 1968).

44. Jacob of Voragine, *Quinta feria quintae hebd. Sermo II*, in *Sermones Quadrigesimales*, for Simonem de Luere (Venice, 1497), fol. 55rb–55va.

45. James of Vitry, *Ad virgines. Sermo I*, fol. 146rb; Gilbert of Tournai, *Ad virgines et puellas. Sermo II*, fol. 147vb.

46. Bernardino of Siena, *Sermo XLVI. Feria V post dom. de Passione. De multitudine malorum quae ex vanitatibus subsequuntur*, in *Quadragesimale de Christiana Religione*, II, 77.

47. Giles of Rome, *De regimine*, pp. 270–271.

48. James of Vitry, *Ad moniales grisias, cistercenses, albas*, fols. 53vb–55vb; Gilbert of Tournai, *Ad virgines et puellas. Sermo IV*, fols. 150vb-153ra.

49. Francesco of Barberino, *Reggimento*, pp. 13, 27, 213.

50. Giles of Rome, *De regimine*, pp. 278–281.

51. Gilbert of Tournai, *Ad virgines et puellas. Sermo V*, fol. 153va.

52. Francesco of Barberino, *Reggimento*, p. 27.

53. Antonino of Florence, *Opera a buon vivere*, p. 164.

54. Girolamo of Siena, *Il soccorso dei poveri*, p. 312.

55. Philip of Novara, *Les quatres âges*, p. 16.

56. Francesco of Barberino, *Reggimento*, p. 17.

57. Giles of Rome, *De regimine*, pp. 271–272.

58. Durandus of Champagne, *Speculum dominarum*, fol. 15v.

59. Christine de Pisan, *La cité des dames*, pp. 59–60.

60. Giles of Rome, *De regimine*, p. 272.

61. Ibid., pp. 283–286.

62. Philip of Novara, *Les quatres âges*, p. 16.

63. Paolo of Certaldo, *Libro di buoni costumi*, ed. Alfredo Schiaffini (Florence: Le Monnier, 1945), p. 126.

64. Vincent of Beauvais, *De eruditione*, pp. 176–177; William Peraldo, *De eruditione*, pp. 457–458; Francesco of Barberino, *Reggimento*, pp. 15, 17–19, 39, 148–149; Giles of Rome, *De regimine*, pp. 344–345.

65. Giovanni Dominici, *Regola*, pp. 11–12; Francisco Ximenez, *Lo libre de les dones*, I, 91–92; Giovanni Certosino, *Decor puellarum*, V, 9.

66. Vincent of Beauvais, *De eruditione*, p. 176.

Chapter 4. The Good Wife
SILVANA VECCHIO

1. Robert of Sorbonne, *De matrimonio*, in Jean Barthélemy Hauréau, *Notices et extraits de quelques manuscrits latines de la Bibliothèque nationale* (Paris: Klincksieck, 1890), I, 200.

2. Many of the texts cited in this chapter are the same as those in the previous chapter; references are to the same editions. For Gilbert of Tournai's *Sermones: Ad coniugatas* (all of which use the model of Sara), the edition cited previously contains only the third sermon, fols. 140va–142rb. The other two sermons are taken from the Ms. Milano Ambr. F. 57 supp., fols. 171rb-174ra. Jacob of Voragine, *Dom. II post fest. Trin. Sermo II* in *Sermones de tempore,* fols. 78v-79r; William Peraldo, *De eruditione,* pp. 463–464; Vincent of Beauvais, *De eruditione,* pp. 197–206; Paulinus the Minorite (died 1344), *Trattato de regimine rectoris,* ed. Adolfo Mussafia (Vienna-Florence: Tendler-Vieusseux, 1868), pp. 73–74.

3. Durandus of Champagne, *Speculum dominarum,* fols. 132r, 180v.

4. Georges Duby, *Le chevalier, la femme et le prêtre: le mariage dans la France féodale* (Paris: Hachette, 1982).

5. Philippe Delhaye, "Le dossier anti-matrimonial de l'*Adversus Jovinianum* et son influence sur quelques écrits latins du XIIe siècle," *Medieval Studies* 13(1951):65–86.

6. Francisco Ximenez, *Lo libre de los dones,* I, 117–144; Dionysius the Carthusian, *De laudab. vita coniug.,* p. 70; Cherubino of Spoleto, *Regola della vita matrimoniale* (Bologna: Romagnoli, 1888), pp. 28–32.

7. Gilbert of Tournai, *Ad coniugatas. Sermo I,* fols. 171v–172r.

8. Jacob of Voragine, *Dom. II post fest. Trin. Sermo II,* fol. 78v.

9. Nicolas Oresme, *Le livre de Yconomique d'Aristote,* ed. Albert Douglas Menut, in *Transactions of the American Philosophical Society* 47(1957):844.

10. Humbertus de Romanis, *In solemnibus conviviis nuptiarum,* pp. 539–540.

11. Albert of Saxony, *Expositio librorum Economicorum,* ed. Vicente Beltran de Heredia, in *La Sciencia Tomista* 46(1932):327–328.

12. Christine de Pisan, *Le trésor,* fols. 15r-17r.

13. Gilbert of Tournai, *Ad coniugatas. Sermo II,* fols. 173va–174vb.

14. William Peraldo, *Summa de virtutibus et vitiis,* fols. 70va–71rb.

15. Jacob of Voragine, *Chronica,* pp. 195–198.

16. Gilbert of Tournai, *Ad coniugatas. Sermo II,* fol. 174rb.

17. Albertus Magnus, *Super Ethica,* ed. Wilhelmus Kubel, in *Opera Omnia* (Münster: Aschendorff, 1987), XIV, 638; Thomas Aquinas, *Sententia libri Ethicorum,* in *Opera Omnia iussu Leonis XIII edita* (Rome: S. Sabina, 1969), XLVII, 489.

18. John Buridanus, *Quaestiones in decem libros Ethicorum Aristotelis ad Nicomachum* (Oxford: H. Cripps, 1637), p. 762.

19. Christine de Pisan, *Le trésor,* fols. 26v–27r.

20. Christine de Pisan, *Le ménagier,* I, 96–168.

21. James of Vitry, *Ad coniugatos. Sermo II,* fol. 137vb.

22. Gilbert of Tournai, *De decem praeceptis Decalogi. Sermo II,* fol. 220va-b.

23. Jacob of Voragine, *Dom. XX post fest. Trin. Sermo II,* fol. 123vb.

24. Giles of Rome, *De regimine,* pp. 248–249.

25. Thomas Aquinas, *Summa contra Gentiles*, III, 123; Albert of Saxony, *Expositio librorum economicorum*, p. 323; Nicolas Oresme, *Le livre de Yconomique*, p. 837; John Buridanus, *Quaestiones in octo libros Politicorum Arostotelis* (Oxford, 1640), p. 85.

26. Thomas of Chobham, *Summa confessorum*, ed. Frank Broomfield (Paris: Louvain, 1968), p. 375.

27. Pierre Dubois, *De recuperatione terre sancte*, ed. Charles-Victor Langlois (Paris: A. Picard, 1891), pp. 50–52.

28. James of Vitry, *Ad coniugatos. Sermo I*, fol. 135rb; Robert of Sorbonne, *De matrimonio*, pp. 199–200; William Peraldo, *De eruditione*, p. 443.

29. Bonaventure of Bagnoregio, *Commentaria in IV libros Sententiarum*, in *Opera Omnia* (Ad Claras Aquas, 1892–1902), II, 432; Conrad of Megenberg, *Yconomica*, pp. 32–34.

30. Jacob of Voragine, *Dom. I post oct. Epiph. Sermo I*, fol. 15v.

31. Francesco of Barberino, *Reggimento*, pp. 101–102.

32. Christine de Pisan, *Le ménagier*, pp. 185–186.

33. Christine de Pisan, *Le trésor*, fols. 27r, 101r, 118v, 130v.

34. William Peraldo, *De eruditione*, p. 444.

35. John Bromyard, *Summa praedicantium*, apud Dominicum Nicolinium (Venice, 1586), II, 15va.

36. Paolo of Certaldo, *Libro di buoni costumi*, p. 91.

37. Jacob of Voragine, *Chronica*, p. 188.

38. Giles of Rome, *De regimine*, pp. 256–257.

39. Gilbert of Tournai, *Ad coniugatas. Sermo II*, fol. 174ra.

40. Jacob of Voragine, *Dom. I post oct. Epiph. Sermo III*, fol. 16vb.

41. Nicholas of Gorran, *In omnes divi Pauli Epistolas elucidatio*, ed. J. Keerbergium (Antwerp, 1617), p. 525.

42. Bonaventure, *Comm. in Sent.*, IV, 678.

43. Gilbert of Tournai, *De sacramento matrimonii. Sermo*, fol. 217r; John Bromyard, *Summa praedicantium*, II, 15v; Francesco of Barberino, *Reggimento*, p. 109.

44. Durandus of Champagne, *Speculum dominarum*, fols. 11v–12r.

45. Francesco of Barberino, *Reggimento*, pp. 225, 227, 230.

46. Conrad of Megenberg, *Yconomica*, pp. 73–78.

47. Jacob of Voragine, *Chronica*, pp. 205–206.

48. Thomas Aquinas, *Sent. libri Ethicorum*, p. 469.

49. Albertus Magnus, *Super Ethica*, p. 665; Thomas Aquinas, *Summa Theologica*, II, II, q.26, a.10; John Buridanus, *Quaestiones in libros Ethicorum*, pp. 757–760.

50. Jacob of Voragine, *Dom. XVI post fest. Trin. Sermo III*, fol. 114r.

51. Jacob of Voragine, *Dom. infra oct. Epiph. Sermo I*, fol. 12vb; Gilbert of Tournai, *Ad coniugatas. Sermo III*, fol. 140va-b.

52. Philip of Novara, *Les quatres âges*, p. 20.

53. Gilbert of Tournai, *Ad adolescentes. Sermo I*, fol. 178v.

54. Francesco of Barberino, *Reggimento*, p. 133.

55. Thomas Aquinas, *Expositio in omnes S. Pauli Epistolas,* in *Opera Omnia* (Parma: Fiaccadori, 1862), XIII, 201.

56. Christine de Pisan, *Le trésor,* fols. 30r–32r, 100v, 120rv, 128v.

57. Gilbert of Tournai, *Ad coniugatas. Sermo III,* fol. 141vb.

58. Tolomeo of Lucca (died 1326–7), *De regimine principum ad regem Cypri,* in *S. Thomae de Aquino, Opera Omnia* (Parma: Fiaccadori, 1864), XVI, 275.

59. Nicolas Oresme, *Le livre de Yconomique,* p. 827.

60. Gilbert of Tournai, *Ad coniugatas. Sermo III,* fol. 142r.

61. Ibid., fol. 142ra-b.

62. William Peraldo, *De eruditione,* p. 464; Vincent of Beauvais, *De eruditione,* pp. 203–206.

63. Jacob of Voragine, *Dom. II post fest. Trin. Sermo II,* fol. 78vb.

64. Philip J. Jones, "Florentine Families and Florentine Diaries in the Fourteenth Century," in Evelyn M. Jamison, ed., *Studies in Italian Medieval History* (Rome, 1956), pp. 183–205; Fulvio Pezzarossa, "La memorialistica fiorentina tra Medioevo e Rinascimento. Rassegna di studi e testi," in *Lettere Italiane* (1979), pp. 96–138.

65. Francesco Barbaro. *De re uxoria liber,* ed. Attilio Gnesotto, in *Atti e memorie della R. Accademia di Sc. Lett. e Arti in Padova,* n.s., 32 (1915–16):6–105; Giovanni Campano, *De dignitate matrimonii,* in *Opera Omnia* (Rome, 1495; repr. Hain: Meisenheim, 1969); Matteo Palmieri, *Vita civile,* ed. Gino Belloni (Florence: Sansoni, 1982); Leon Battista Alberti, *I libri della famiglia,* ed. Ruggiero Romano and Alberto Tenenti (Turin: Einaudi, 1969); Antonio Ivani, *Del governo della famiglia civile* (Genoa, 1872).

66. Bernardino of Siena, *Serm. imperf, Sermo XIII. De matrimonio regulato inordinato et separato,* p. 59; Cherubino of Spoleto, *Regole,* pp. 18–22; Dionysius the Carthusian, *De laudab. vita coniug.,* p. 70.

67. Dominici, *Regola,* pp. 70–72.

68. Genevieve Hasenohr, "La vie quotidienne de la femme vue par l'église: l'enseignement des journées chrétiennes de la fin du Moyen Age," in *Frau und spätmittelalterlicher Alltag,* Intern. Kongress, Kresm an der Donau (October 1984), in "Sitzungberichte österr. Akad. der Wissenschaften, Philos.-Hist. Klasse," 473 Band (Vienna, 1986), pp. 38–77.

69. Antonino of Florence, *Opera a buon vivere,* p. 189.

70. Certosino, *Gloria mulierum,* chap. 3.

71. Dominici, *Regola,* pp. 35–48, 50–64.

72. André Vauchez, *Les laïcs au Moyen Age. Pratiques et expériences religueses* (Paris: Cerf, 1987), pp. 189–224.

73. Certosino, *Gloria mulierum,* chap. 3.

74. Bernardino of Siena, *Le prediche volgari,* ed. D. Pacetti (Siena, 1935), pp. 63–66, 80.

75. Dominici, *Regola,* pp. 101–116.

76. Maffeo Vegio, *De educatione liberorum et eorum claris moribus,* ed. Maria Wallburg Fanning (Washington: Catholic University of America, 1933), pp. 12–17, 48–50, 126–127.

77. Joan Kelly Gadol, "Did Women Have a Renaissance?," in Renate Bridental and Claudia Koonz, eds., *Becoming Visible: Women in European History* (Boston: Houghton Mifflin, 1977). Also in Joan Kelly, *Women, History and Theory. The Essays of Joan Kelly* (Chicago-London: University of Chicago Press, 1984), pp. 19–59.

78. David Herlihy, "Did Women Have a Renaissance? A Reconsideration," *Medievalia et Humanistica*, n.s. 16(1985):1–22.

Chapter 5. Regulating Women's Fashion
DIANE OWEN HUGHES

1. M. de Grenaille, *La mode ou charactère de la religion, de la vie, de la conversation, de la solitude, des compliments, des habits et du style du temps* (Paris: Nicolas Gasse, 1642); quoted by Louise Godard de Donville, *Signification de la mode sous Louis XIII* (Aix-en-Provence: Edisud, 1978), p. 144.

2. Ordericus Vitalis, *Historiae Ecclesiasticae*, ed. Auguste Le Prevost, 5 vols. (Paris, 1840–1855), III, 323.

3. Quoted by Ruth Matilda Anderson, *Hispanic Costume, 1480–1530* (New York: Hispanic Society of America, 1979), p. 143.

4. Two verses by Giovanni Fiorentino describe such extravagantly ornate costumes, with their "peasant cloaks and French-style coats." These "white as ermine paragons of German fashion" wear "visored helmets and capes like those of knights," with belts in the English style. See *Il Pecorone*, in G. Carducci, *Cantilene e ballate* (Pisa, 1871), bk. VII, p. 196.

5. Paris Archives Nationales, KK8, fol. 26v; quoted in Stella Mary Newton, *Fashion in the Age of the Black Prince* (Woodbridge, Suffolk: Boydell, 1980), p. 31.

6. Cesare Vecellio, *De gli habiti antichi, et moderni di diverse parti del mondo* (Venice, 1590), p. 140v.

7. Ibid., p. 100.

8. Florence, Archivio di Stato, Deliberazioni dei Signori a Collegi, Ordinaria Autorità, 42, fols. 5v–6r.

9. G. Buchheit, *Der Totentanz, seine Entwicklung und Entstehung* (Leipzig, 1926), p. 203.

10. Joseph Swetnam, *The Arraignment of Lewd, Idle, Froward and Unconstant Women: Or the Vanitie of Them, Choose You Whether* (London, 1615), p. 30.

11. John Rylands Library, Ms. Lat. 367, fol. 256.

12. Quoted from British Library, Ms. Harl. 4894, fol. 176b, by G. R. Owst, *Literature and Pulpit in Medieval England*, 2nd ed. (Oxford: Blackwell, 1961), p. 404.

13. *De Cultu Feminarum*, ed. Marie Turcan (Paris: Cerf, 1971), pp. 44–46.

14. *Le prediche volgari*, ed. Ciro Canarozzi, 5 vols. (Pistoia, 1934–1958), I, 244.

15. The Wife of Bath's Prologue, ll. 337–347.

16. San Bernardini *Opera Omnia* (Florence, 1950), II, 56.

17. Venice, Archivio di Stato, Maggior Consiglio, Ursa, fol. 81v.

18. Quoted by Anderson, *Hispanic Costume,* p. 209.

19. Quoted by L. T. Belgrano, *Della vita privata dei Genovesi,* 2nd ed. (Genoa, 1875), p. 270.

20. *Le blason de basquines et vertugalles* (Lyons, 1563), n.p.

21. Quoted by Michel Zink, "Les Destinaires des recueils de sermons en langue vulgaire au XIIe et au XIIIe siècle," in *La piété populaire au Moyen Age* (Paris: Bibliothèque Nationale, 1977), p. 70.

22. Ludovico Frati, ed., *La vita privata in Bologna dal secolo XIII al XVII,* 2nd ed. (Bologna, 1928), pp. 251–262.

23. *Laurae Ceretae Epistolae,* ed. J. F. Tomasini (Padua, 1640), pp. 70–71.

The Hidden Power of Women

C. K.-Z.

1. John Hajnal, "European Marriage Patterns in Perspective," in D. V. Glass and D. E. C. Eversley, eds., *Population in History* (London: Arnold, 1965), pp. 101–143.

2. Diane O. Hughes, "From Brideprice to Dowry in Mediterranean Europe," *Journal of Family History* 3(1978):263–296; R. Smith, "The People of Tuscany and Their Families in the Fifteenth Century: Medieval or Mediterranean?" *Journal of Family History* 6(1981):107–128, esp. 115–116.

3. David Herlihy, *Medieval Households* (Cambridge, Mass.: Harvard University Press, 1985), p. 67.

4. B. Guérard, ed., *Polyptyque de l'abbé Irminon* (Paris, 1844); A. Longnon, ed., *Polyptyque de l'abbaye de Saint-Germain des Prés* (Paris, 1886–1895); Herlihy, *Medieval Households,* p. 67; J.-P. Devroey, "Les premiers polyptyques rémois, VIIe–IXe siècles," in A. Verhulst, ed., *Le grand domaine aux époques mérovingienne et carolingienne* (Ghent, 1985), Belgisch Centrum voor lanedlijke Geschiedenis, Publication 81, pp. 112–124.

5. Monique Zerner-Chardavoine, "Enfants et jeunes au IXe siècle. La démographie du polyptyque de Marseille, 813–814," *Provence historique* 126(1981):335–384, esp. 359.

6. Richard M. Smith, "Hypothèses sur la nuptialité en Angleterre aux XIIIe–XIVe siècles," *Annales E.S.C.* 38(1)1981:107–136, esp. 116, and Smith, "The People of Tuscany."

7. David Herlihy and Christiane Klapisch-Zuber, *Les Toscans et leurs familles. Une étude du catasto florentin de 1427* (Paris: Presses de la Fondation Nationale des Sciences Politiques, 1978).

8. See Josiah C. Russell, "Late Medieval Population Patterns," *Speculum* 20(1945):163, discussed in Smith, "The People of Tuscany."

9. Richard Ring, "Early Medieval Peasant Households in Central Italy," *Journal of Family History* 2(1977):2–25; J.-P. Devroey, "Les méthodes d'analyse démographique des polyptyques du haut Moyen Age," in M.-A. Arnould et al., eds., *Histoire et méthode, Acta historica Bruxellensia* 4(1981):71–88.

10. E. R. Coleman, "L'infanticide dans le haut Moyen Age," *Annales E.S.C.* 29(1974):315–335.

11. Herlihy, *Medieval Households,* pp. 63–68; Monique Zerner, "La population de Villeneuve-Saint-Georges et de Nogent-sur-Marne au IXe siècle d'après le polyptyque de Saint-Germain-des-Prés," *Annales de la Faculté des lettres et sciences humaines de Nice* 37(1979):17–24; Robert H. Bautier, "Haut Moyen Age," in Jacques Dupâquier, ed., *Histoire de la population française* (Paris: Presses Universitaires de France, 1988), pp. 186, 202.

12. As has been done for later periods by Gérard Delille, "Un problème de démographie historique: hommes et femmes devant la mort," *Mélanges de l'Ecole française de Rome* 86(1974):419–443.

Chapter 6. Women from the Fifth to the Tenth Century
Suzanne Fonay Wemple

The following abbreviations have been used:
AS *Acta Sanctorum*
CCL *Corpus christianorum. Series latina*
CSEL *Corpus scriptorum ecclesiasticorum latinorum*
Mansi Mansi, *Sacrarum Conciliorum nova et amplissima Collectio*
MGH Capit. *Monumenta Germaniae historica, Capitularia*
MGH Epist. *Monumenta Germaniae historica, Epistolae*
MGH Form. *Monumenta Germaniae historica, Formulae*
MGH Leges *Monumenta Germaniae historica, Leges*
MGH Legum Sectio *Monumenta Germaniae historica, Legum Sectio*
MGH Script. rer. mer. *Monumenta Germaniae historica,*
  Scriptores rerum merowingcarum
PL J. P. Migne, *Patrologia latina*

1. Tacitus, *Germania,* 18–20, in *On Britain and Germany,* trans. H. Mattingly (Harmondsworth, 1960), pp. 115–120.

2. P. F. Girard, "Le manuel de mariage," in *Manuel élémentaire de droit romain,* 8th ed. (Paris, 1929), pp. 162–174.

3. *The Theodosian Code,* ed. Th. Mommsen (Berlin, 1905), I, 3.4.5–15.1.

4. *Acts of the Apostles,* 1:14; 5:14; 7:3; 9:2.36, 39; 12:12; 16:14–15; 17:4, 12.

5. 1 Cor. 14:34; 1 Tim. 2:8–14.

6. Ambrosiaster, *Comm. ad Corinthios Primam,* 7.11, CSEL, 81/2, 74–75.

7. Caesarius of Arles, *Sermones,* 32:4, 42, 43, ed. G. Morin, CCL, 103.1 (Turnhout, 1933), I, 141–142, 184–194.

8. Gregory the Great, *Registrum epistularum,* about female monasteries throughout the two volumes, *MGH Epist.,* 2 vols. (Berlin, 1957). On menstruating or expectant women, see II, 331–339.

9. *Historica ecclesiastica gentis Anglorum,* 1, 27, *Venerabilis Baedae* . . . , ed. C. Plummer (Oxford, 1966), I, 48–62.

509

10. Gregory of Tours, *The History of the Franks*, 8.21, *MGH Script. rer. mer.*, 1, 339; and O. Doppelfeld, "Das Fränkische Frauengrab unter dem Chor des kölner Domes," *Germania*, 38(1960):89–103.

11. *Lex Alam.*, 49, *MGH Leges*, I, 5/1, 108.

12. *Pactus legis Sal.*, 24.8–9, *MGH Legum Sectio*, I, 4/1.92; Lex. Rib., 12–13. *MGH Legum Sectio*, I, 3/2, 78–79.

13. Thomas A. Walker, *A History of the Law of Nations* (Cambridge, 1899), I, 65.

14. *Leges Burg.*, 12, 1–2, *MGH Legum Sectio*, I, 2/1.

15. Defensor Logiacensi monachus, *Scintillarum liber*, 13.9, *CCL*, 117, 1.

16. *History of the Lombards*, 6, 1 (Philadelphia: University of Pennsylvania, 1974), p. 250.

17. *Vita s. Balthildis*, 4, *MGH Script. rer. mer.*, 2, 485–486.

18. *Leges Burg.*, 100, *MGH Legum Sectio*, I, 2/1, 113.

19. *Lex Rom. Burg.*, 37. 2, *MGH Legum Sectio*, I, 2/1, 113.

20. P. D. King, *Law and Society in the Visigothic Kingdom* (Cambridge, 1972), p. 229.

21. For example, Anstrud was twelve at the time of her engagement, *Vita Anstrudis*, 2, *MGH Script. rer. mer.* 6, 67. On the age of the boys, see Eugen Ewig, "Studien zur merowingischen Dynastie," *Frühmittelalterliche Studien* 8(1974):17–24.

22. *Leges Burg.*, 52.1–4, *MGH Legum Sectio*, I, 2/1, 85–86.

23. *Pactus legis Sal.*, 65a, *MGH Legum Sectio*, I, 4/1, 234; *Lex Bai.*, 8.15, *MGH Legum Sectio*, I, 5/2, 359–360; *Lex Alam.*, 52 (53), *MGH Legum Sectio*, I, 5/1, 110.

24. Gregory of Tours, *History of the Franks*, 3.27, *MGH Script. rer. mer.*, 1, 163.

25. *Leges Langobardorum, Edictus Rotharii*, 178, *MGH Leges*, 4, 41–42.

26. Fortunatus, *De vita sanctae Radegundis*, 2, *MGH Script. rer. mer.*, 2, 365.

27. Gregory of Tours, *History of the Franks*, 10.5, *MGH Script. rer. mer.*, 1, 413.

28. Ibid., 4.3, *MGH Script. rer. mer.*, 1, 147.

29. Hucbald, *Vita sanctae Rictrudis*, 1.11, *AS 12 Maii*, 3, 83.

30. *Lex Rib.*, 16.14–18, *MGH Legum Sectio*, I, 3/2, 112; *Leges Burg.*, 35.1–2, *MGH Legum Sectio*, I, 2/1, 69.

31. *Pactus legis Sal.*, 13.11, *MGH Legum Sectio*, I, 4/1, 62–63; *Leges Burg.*, 36, *MGH Legum Sectio*, I, 2/1, 69; *Leges Vis.*, 3.5.1, 2.5, *MGH Legum Sectio*, I, 1, 159–161, 163–164.

32. Gregory of Tours, *History of the Franks*, 4.3, 9, 26, 28, *MGH Script. rer. mer.*, 1, 143, 147, 161–163; Fredegar, *Chron.*, 4.53, 58–60, *MGH Script. rer. mer.*, 2, 147, 150–151; *Liber hist. franc.*, 31, *MGH Script. rer. mer.*, 2, 292.

33. *Leges Vis.*, 3.4.9, 6.2, *MGH Legum Sectio*, I, 150, 168; *Lex Rom. Vis.*, 2.21.1, ed. Conrat, 132.

34. *Lex Rom. Burg.*, 21.1, *MGH Legum Sectio*, I, 2/1, 143; *Pactus Alam.*, 34.3, *MGH Legum Sectio*, I, 5/1, 33.

35. *Lex Rom. Vis.*, C.3.16.1, ed. Conrat 117; *Lex Rom. Burg.*, 21.2, *MGH Legum Sectio*, I, 2/1, 143–144.

36. *Leges Burg.*, 34.2–4, *MGH Legum Sectio*, I, 2/1, 68; *Leges Vis.*, 3.6.1, *MGH Legum Sectio*, I, 1, 166; *Lex Bai.*, 8.1, 13, *MGH Legum Sectio*, I, 5/1, 34; Gregory of Tours, *History of the Franks*, 6.36, 8.19, *MGH Script. rer. mer.*, 1, 276, 338; Fredegar, *Chron.*, 4.60, *MGH Script. rer. mer.*, 2, 151.

37. *Leges Burg.*, 34.1, *MGH Legum Sectio*, I, 2/1, 68.

38. *Lex Rom. Vis.*, C.3.16.1, ed. Conrat 117; *Lex Rom. Burg.*, 21.3, *MGH Legum Sectio*, I, 2/1, 144.

39. *Leges Vis.*, 3.5.4, *MGH Legum Sectio*, I, 1, 163.

40. *Liber historiae Francorum*, 35, *MGH Script. rer. mer.*, 2, 302, 304.

41. *Conc. Aurelianense*, 11, *CCL*, 148A, 100.

42. *Leges Langobardorum*, Edictus Rotharii, 189, 196, *MGH Leges*, 4, 45, 47–48.

43. *Leges Burg.*, 66.1–3, 69.1–2, 86.2, *MGH Legum Sectio*, I, 2/1, 94–95, 108; *Leges Vis.*, 3.1.6, *MGH Legum Sectio*, I, 1, 130; *Pactus legis Salicae*, 101.2, *MGH Legum Sectio*, I, 4/1, 256–257; *Lex Alam.*, 54.1–2, *MGH Legum Sectio*, I, 5/1, 112–113; *Lex Bai.*, 15.8, *MGH Legum Sectio*, I, 5/2, 427.

44. Saint Leander, *De Institutione Virginum et contemptu mundi ad Florentinam sororem liber*, ed. Lucas Holstenius, *Codex Regularum monasticarum et canonicarum* (Graz, 1957), I, 408.

45. Louis-Maurice-André Cornuey, *Le régime de la "dos" aux époques mérovingienne et carolingienne* (Algiers, 1929).

46. *Leges Vis.*, 4.2.1, *MGH Legum Sectio*, I, 1, 74; *Lex Thur.*, 26–30, *MGH Leges*, 5, 123–126; *Lex Saxonum*, 41, 44, 46–47, *MGH Leges*, 5, 71–74; *Pactus legis Salicae*, 59.6, *MGH Legum Sectio*, I, 4/1, 223.

47. Gregory of Tours, *History of the Franks*, 4.28, 6.45, *MGH Script. rer. mer.*, 1, 164, 284–285.

48. *Conc. Aurelianense* (541), 24, *CCL* 148A, 138.

49. *Leges Burg.*, 30.1–2, *MGH Legum Sectio*, I, 2/1, 66.

50. *Pactus legis Salicae*, 104.10–11, *MGH Legum Sectio*, I, 4/1, 261.

51. *Lex Rib.*, 61.11, *MGH Legum Sectio*, I, 3/2, 112.

52. *Marc Form.*, 2.29, *MGH Form.*, 93–97.

53. *III Conc. Tol.*, 14, Mansi, 9, 985.

54. *Gesta Dagoberti*, 6, 30, *MGH Script. rer. mer.*, 2, 400.

55. Jean Juster, *La condition légale des juifs sous les rois Visigoths* (Paris, 1911), p. 24; from *Etudes d'histoire juridique*, p. 298.

56. *Pippini regis Capit.* (754–755), 1; *Decr. Comp.* (757), 1–4, 13, 17–18; *Conc. Vernense* (755), 15; *MGH Capit.*, 1, 31, 36–39.

57. *Codex Carolinus*, 45, *MGH Epist.* 3, Mer. et kar. aevie 1, 561–562; L. Oelsner, *Jahrbücher des fränkischen Reiches unter König Pippin* (Leipzig, 1871), pp. 495–496.

58. *Liber hist. franc.*, 49, *MGH Script. rer. mer.*, 2, 324; and Eduard

Hlawitschka, "Die Vorfahren Karls des Grossen," in *Karl der Grosse,* vol. 1, ed. H. Beumann (Düsseldorf, 1965), nn. 16–18, 31–33, and the table.

59. *Marc. Form.,* 2.30, reiterated in *Form. Senon.,* 47; *Form. Turon.,* 19; *Sal. Merk.,* 18; *MGH Form.,* 94, 206, 248.

60. *Conc. Vernense* (755), 15, *MGH Capit.,* 1, 36.

61. *Admonitio generalis* (789), 43, *MGH Capit.,* 1, 56; *Conc. Foroiuliense,* 10, *MGH Conc.,* 2, 192; *Capit. missorum* (802), 22, *MGH Capit.,* 1, 103.

62. K. F. Werner, "Die Nachkommen Karl des Grossen," in *Karl der Grosse,* vol. 4, ed. W. Braunfels (Dusseldorf, 1967), p. 444, n. 8.

63. *Vita Hludowici,* 32.2, 37.2, 44.1–2, 52.1–2, 61.3, 62.1, 63.2; *MGH Script.,* 2, 624–647; *Annales regni francorum* (819), *MGH Script. rer. germ. in usum schol.,* 150; Nithard, *Historiarum,* 2, 3, 4, *MGH Script.,* 651–652; Paschasius Radbertus, *Vitae Walae,* 2.9, 21, *MGH Script.,* 2, 553–554, Agobard of Lyons, *Libri duo pro filiis et contra Judith uxorem Ludovici Pii, MGH Script.,* 15, 274–279.

64. Hincmar of Rheims, *De divortio Lotharii et Tetbergae,* 4, 21, *PL,* 125, 649A–B, 734A–B.

65. Ibid., 659A–675B.

66. Hadrian II, *Relatio de Theutbergae receptione scripta* (865), *MGH Capit.,* 2, 468–469; Nicholas I, *Epistolae,* 3, 5–6, 10–11, 16, 18–26, 29–32, 35–39, 42, 44–49, 51–53, *MGH Epist.,* 6, Kar. aevi, 4, 268–351.

67. *Conc. Duziancense* (874), Mansi, 17A, 282–288; *Conc. Colon.* (877), 6, Mansi, 18, 48; *Conc. Mog.* (888), 18, Mansi, 18, 69; *Conc. Met.* (888), 11, Mansi, 18, 80–81.

68. *Capitularis de villis,* 16, *MGH Capit.,* 1, 84.

69. Hincmar of Rheims, *De ordine palatii,* 22, *MGH Capit.,* 2, 525.

70. Dhuoda, *Manuel pour mon fils/Dhuoda; introduction, texte critique, notes,* ed. Pierre Riché, Sources chrétiennes 225 (Paris, 1975), pp. 350–352.

71. *Vita s. Liutbergae,* 1–7, *MGH Script.,* 4, 158–160.

72. Werner, *Die Nachkommen Karls der Grossen,* IV, 403–483.

73. J. Vives, T. M. Martinez, and G. M. Diez, eds., *Concilios Visigothicos e Hispano-romanos* (Madrid, 1963), pp. 4, 9.

74. Boniface, *Die Briefe,* 128, ed. Tangl, pp. 265–266.

75. *Capit. de disc. palatii,* 3 *MGH Legum Sectio,* II, I, 298.

76. Jonas of Orléans, *De Institutio laicali, PL,* 106–171.

77. Liudprand of Cremona, *Antapodosis,* 2, 48; *PL,* 136, 828A.

78. *Hrotsvithae Opera,* ed. Paul de Winterfeld (Berlin, 1902), Gongolfus, 543, p. 50; Abraham, 4.4, p. 153; Pafnutius, 1.23, p. 167, 10.2, p. 177, 11.2, p. 178; Dulcitius, 12.3, p. 133.

79. Elke Krüger, "Aspects of Family and Marriage in Frankish Penitential Books," unpublished paper, Twenty-second International Congress on Medieval Studies, May 7, 1987, Western Michigan University, Kalamazoo.

80. *Capitulare de villis,* 16, *MGH Capit.,* 1, 84.

81. Eileen Power, *Medieval People,* rev. ed. (London-New York, 1966), pp. 18–38.

82. K. J. Leyser enumerates several similar cases in *Rule and Conflict in an Early Medieval Society* (London, 1979), p. 52.

83. *Gesta Ottonis*, 139–155, *Hrotsvithea Opera, MGH Scriptores rerum germanicarum*, pp. 206–207.

84. Sabine Reiter, "The Position of Women and Their Families during the Tenth Century," unpublished paper, Twenty-second International Congress on Medieval Studies, May 7, 1987, Western Michigan University, Kalamazoo.

85. Liudprand of Cremona, *Antapodosis*, 4, 13, *PL*, 136, 864A–B.

86. *Vita Mathildis reginae posterior*, 11, *MGH Scriptores*, 4, 291.

87. Liudprand, *Antapodosis*, 2.48, *PL*, 827D–828C.

88. Ibid., 3, 44–45, *PL*, 136.852D–854C.

89. Rather of Verona, *Praeloquiorum libri sex*, II. tit. II, 3, III, 4–6, IV, 11, 18, *PL*, 136, 191A–B, 191C–D, 194B, 197D, 198D, 202D, 286B.

90. Liudprand, *Antapodosis*, 3.7, 3.46, 4.11, 5.32; *PL*, 136, 840A, 854C, 863B–C, 892A–D.

91. Gerbert of Aurillac, *The Letters*, 100, trans. Harriet Pratt Lattin (New York, 1961), p. 135.

92. *Vita Bernwardi Episcopi Hildesheimensis auctore Thaugmaro*, 2, *MGH Scriptores*, 4, 759.

93. Gregory of Tours, *History of the Franks*, 2.43, *MGH Script. rer. mer.*, 1, 394.

94. Angelica Baitelli, *Annali istorici dell'edificazione, erezione e dotazione del serenessimo monastero di S. Salvatore e S. Gulia di Brescia* (Brescia, 1794), p. 44. The almost contemporary Frankish account has Desiderius proceed with his wife to France, *Annales Alamann. Nazar.; Annales Laurissense Min.*, 7; *Annales Lobienses*, 744; in *MGH Scriptores*, 1, 40, 118; 2, 195.

95. *Historiam ecclesiasticam gentis Anglorum*, 4, 19, in *Venerabilis Baedae Historiam . . .*, I, 243.

96. Fortunatus, *De vita sanctae Radegundis*, 1.12, *MGH Script. rer. mer.*, 2.368. Gregory of Tours, *Liber vitae patrum*, 19.1; *MGH Script. rer. mer.*, 1, 737.

97. *Vita s. Sigolenae, AS 24 Iunii*, 5, 630–637.

98. *Vita Bertilae*, 1, *MGH Script. rer. mer.*, 6.101.

99. *Vita ss. Herlindis et Renildae*, 3, 6, *AS 22 Martii*, 3, 384–385; Agius, *Agii Vita et obitus Hathumodae*, 3, *MGH Script.*, 4, 167.

100. *Vita Sadalbergae*, 12; *MGH Script. rer. mer.*, 5, 56.

101. On Rome, see Gregory the Great, *Registrum Epistularum*, 2.10; 3.17; 6.12, new ed. P. Ewald and L. Hartmann, *MGH Epistolae*, 1, 108–109, 175–176, 390–391; and 9.137; 13.2 in vol. 2, 135–136, 367.

102. Ibid., 4, 9, *MGH Epistolae*, 1, 241.

103. Caesarius of Arles, *Regula sanctarum, virginium*, ed. Dom G. Morin, Florilegium patristicum 34 (Bonn, 1933), pp. 33–52.

104. Gregory of Tours, *History of the Franks*, 9.32, *MGH Script. rer. mer.*, 1, 378; *De virtutibus s. Martini*, 1.17, *MGH Script. rer. mer.*, 1, 598; *Liber vitae patrum*, 9.2, *MGH Script. rer. mer.*, 1, 703.

105. Gregory the Great, *Registrum Epistularum*, 3.58 in *MGH Epistolae*, 1, 217–218, and 9.54, 11.207 in *MGH Epistolae*, 2, 79, 195–196.

106. Ibid., 14.14, *MGH Epistolae*, 2, 433–434.

107. Ibid., 9.233, *MGH Epistolae*, 2, 228–229.

108. Ibid., 9.114, *MGH Epistolae*, 2, 119–120.

109. Ibid., 1.23, *MGH Epistolae*, 1, 27.

110. On Sardinia, see note 102 above, and 4.101, *MGH Epistolae*, 1, 243.

111. On Sicily, see ibid., 1.42, 2.78, 9.164, *MGH Epistolae*, 1.68, 134; 2, 163–164.

112. For instance, see Florentius, *Vita s. Rusticulae*, 3, *MGH Script. rer. mer.*, 4, 341.

113. *Conc. Latunense* (673–675), 12–13, CCL, 148A, 316.

114. *Leges Langobardorum, Liuprandi Leges*, 30.I, *MGH Leges*, 4, 122–123.

115. *Conc. Turonense*, 21 (20), CCL, 148A, 187; and René Metz, "La consecration des vierges en Gaule des origines à l'apparition des livres liturgiques," *Revue de droit canonique* 6(1956):321–339.

116. Waldabert, *Regula cuiusdam patris ad virgines*, 12, PL, 88, 1064.

117. Mary Bateson, *Origin and Early History of Double Monasteries*, Royal Historical Society Transactions, n.s. 13 (London, 1889).

118. Bede, *Historia ecclesiastica gentis Anglorum*, 3.8, *Venerabilis Baedae*, 1, 142.

119. Ibid., 3.24–25, 4.23, 4.258, 5.24, *Venerabilis Baedae*, 1, 179, 183, 252–258, 355.

120. On Saints Mary and Peter, see P. Cottineau, *Répertoire topo-bibliographique des abbayes et prieurés*, I, 343; on Saints Stephen and Cesario, see I. Schuster, *La Basilica e il monastero S. Paolo fuori le mura* (Turin, 1934), pp. 12–13.

121. *Conc. Germ.* (742), 6, *MGH Conc.*, 2, 4.

122. *Conc. Vernense*, 6, *MGH Cap.*, 1, 34. Eugen Ewig, "Beobachtungen zur Entwicklung der fränkischen Reichskirche unter Chrodegang von Metz," *Frühmittelalterliche Studien* 2(1928):67–77. *Conc. Cabil.*, 43–56, *MGH Conc.*, 2, 284–285.

123. *Inst. sanct.*, 23, 26–28, *MGH Conc.*, 2, 454, 455–456.

124. Rather of Verona, *Praeloquiorum*, 9.18, PL, 136C–D.

125. Atto of Vercelli, *Capitulare*, 11–12, 81, PL, 134, 30C, 31A, 44A.

126. *Conc. Vernense* (755), 6, *MGH Capit.*, 1, 34; *Duplex legationis edictum* (789), 19, *MGH Capit.*, 1, 63.

127. *Conc. Foroiulense*, 12, *MGH Conc.*, 2, 194.

128. *Conc. Risp. Fris. Salis.* (800), 12, *MGH Conc.*, 2, 194; *Conc. Aquis.* (816), 130, *MGH Conc.*, 2, 405; *Conc. Foroiuliense* (796–797), 12, *MGH Conc.*, 2, 194; *Conc. Cab.* (813), 60, *MGH Conc.*, 2, 285; *Conc. Par.* (820), 46, *MGH Conc.*, 2, 640.

129. *Capit. miss. spec.* (ca 802), 35, *MGH Capit.*, 2, 180.

130. *Capit. eccl. ad Salz data* (803), 7, *MGH Capit.*, 1, 119.

131. *Inst. sanct.*, 18, MGH *Conc.*, 2.455.

132. *Admonition generalis* (789), 76, MGH *Capit.*, 1, 60; repeated verbatim in *Ansegesi capit.*, 1.71, MGH *Capit.*, 1, 404; *Conc. Paris* (829), 45, MGH *Conc.*, 2, 639.

133. *Conc. Risp. Fris. Salis.*, 22, MGH *Conc.*, 22, MGH *Conc.*, 2, 210; *Conc. Mog.* (847), 16, MGH *Capit.*, 2, 180.

134. *Vita Anstrudis*, 28, 37, MGH *Script. rer. mer.*, 6, 75, 77.

135. *Vita S. Austrobertae*, 10, AS, 10 Feb.; 2.421.

136. Jean Guérout, "Le monastère à l'époque carolingienne," in *L'Abbaye royale Notre-Dame de Jouarre*, ed. Y. Chaussy et al. (Paris, 1961), I, 75–78.

137. Joseph Semmler, "Corvey und Herford in der benediktinischen Reformsbewegung des 9. Jahrhunderts," in *Frühmittelalterliche Studien* 4 (1970), pp. 289–319, is of the first opinion, and Hans Goetting, *Das Bistum Hildesheim*, 2 vols. (Neue Folge 7. Die Bistümer der Kirchenprovince Mainz), (Berlin-New York, 1973), of the second.

138. Albert Hauck, *Kirchengeschichte Deutschlands*, 3rd and 4th eds. (Leipzig, 1920), pt. 3, pp. 1011–1040.

139. For example, see *Vita Liudgeri*, 6, MGH *Scriptores*, 2, 406.

140. K. J. Leyser, *Rule and Conflict in an Early Medieval Society: Ottonian Saxony* (London, 1979), pp. 4–73.

141. *Annales Quedlinburgenses*, MGH *Script. rer. mer.*, 3, 75.

142. Fortunatus, *De vita s. Radegundis*, 12, MGH *Script. rer. mer.*, 2, 368.

143. *Conc. Epaon.* (517), 21; CCL, 148A, 29; *Conc. Aurel.* (533), 27–28; CCL, 148A, 124.

144. *Syn. Dioc. Autiss* (561–605), 36–37, 42, CCL, 148A, 269–270.

145. *Urkunderbuch zur Geschichte der jetzt die preussischen Regierungsberzirke Coblenz und Trier bindenden Mittelrheinischen Territorien*, ed. H. Beyer (Koblenz, 1860), I, 6. For the last three, see Marie-Joseph Aubert, *Des femmes diacres*, Le point théologique 47 (Paris, 1986), p. 136.

146. Wilhelm Levinson, "Sigolena," *Neues Archiv* 35(1910):219–231. This opinion was refuted by Jean Verdon, *Annales du Midi* 88(1976):122.

147. *Conc. Worm.* (868), 73, Mansi, 15, 882.

148. F. Maasen, "Glossen des canonischen Rechts aus dem karolingischen Zeitalter," *Akademie der Wissenschaften, Wien, phil.-hist. Klasse, Sitzungsberichte* 84(1876):174.

149. *Epistola*, 8, PL, 134, 114–115.

150. The Council of Orléans in 538 began this legislation, CCL, 148A, 114–115. Later councils were even stricter.

151. "Poenitentiale Burgundiense," 19, in H. J. Schmitz, ed., *Die Bussbücher und das kanonischen Bussverfahren* (Düsseldorf, 1898; repr. Graz, 1958), II, 321.

152. Boniface, *Die Briefe*, 50–51, ed. Tangl, pp. 82–88.

153. *Karoli Magni Capitulare generale*, 5, MGH *Legum*, 1, 33.

154. It begins with the legislation of the *Conc. Germ.* (742), 7, *MGH Conc.*, 2, 4, and ends with *Conc. Mog.* (888), 19, Mansi, 18, 69.

155. Atto of Vercelli, *Epistola*, 9, *PL*, 134, 118B; and *Capitulare*, 36, ibid. 36B–C.

156. Marcelle Thiebaux, *The Writings of Medieval Women* (New York, 1987), pp. 15–23, 63–64.

157. *Manuel pour mon fils/Dhuoda.*

158. Caesarius, *Regula sanctarum virginium*, 7, ed. Dom G. Morin, *Florilegium patristicum* 34 (Bonn, 1933), p. 7.

159. Fortunatus, *Opera poetica*, 8.1, *MGH Auct. ant.*, 4/1,1.

160. *Vita s. Geretrudis*, A6, *MGH Script. rer. mer.*, 2, 460.

161. Boniface, *Die Briefe*, 35, ed. Tangl, p. 60.

162. *Cap. eccl. ad Salz data* (803–804), 7, *MGH Capit.*, 1, 119.

163. *Recueil des chartes de l'Abbaye de Saint-Benoit-sur-Loire (876)* (Paris, 1900), I, 25.

164. *San Salvatore di Brescia* (1978), I, 81–117; G. Arnaldi, "Da Beregario agli Ottoni," in *Storia di Brescia*, 5 vols. (Brescia, 1963–1964), I, 485–517.

165. N. Tommasia, "Libri di monasteri e di chiese nell'Italia meridionale," in C. G. Mor, ed., *Studi sulla storia giuridicale dell'Italia meridionale* (Bari, 1957), pp. 331–349.

166. M. Camera, *Memorie storico-diplomatiche dell'antica citta ducato di Amalfi* (Naples, 1876), I, 151–152.

167. B. Bischoff, "Die Kölner Nonnenhandschriften und das Skriptorium von Chelles," in *Mittelalterliche Studien* (Stuttgart, 1966), I, 16–34.

168. *De vita s. Radegundis Liber II*, ed. B. Krusch, *MGH Script. rer. mer.*, 2, 377–395.

169. Thiebaux, *Writings of Medieval Women*, pp. 25–42.

170. *Vita Aldegundis abbatissae Malbodiensis*, ed. W. Levison. *MGH Script. rer. mer.*, 6, 79–90.

171. See Suzanne Fonay Wemple, "Female Spirituality and Mysticism in Frankish Monasticism," "Peaceweavers," in L. T. Shank and J. A. Nichols, eds., *Medieval Religious Women* (Kalamazoo, Mich., 1987), II, 39–53.

172. She has identified herself with a cryptograph in the introduction of her manuscript, Munich, MS Clm 1086.

173. Alcuin, *Epist.*, 15, 84, 88, 154, 195–196, 213–214, 216, 228, *MGH Epist.*, 4, *Kar. aevi*, 2, 40–42, 127–133, 249, 322–325, 354–360, 371–372.

174. *Hrotsvithae Opera*, ed. P. de Winterfeld (Berlin, 1902).

175. *San Salvatore di Brescia*, I, 178–179.

176. *Vita ss. Herlindis et Renildae*, 4–5, *AS*, 22 Martii 3; 384–385.

Chapter 7. The Feudal Order
PAULETTE L'HERMITE-LECLERCQ

1. Robert Fossier, *Le Moyen Age*, vol. 2: *L'éveil de l'Europe* (Paris: Armand Colin, 1982), pp. 321–324.

2. R. Bucaille, "L'ostéologie humaine du bas Moyen Age. Paléontologie ou anthropologie culturelle?" in *Hommage à G. Chevrier et A. Geslan* (Paris-Strasbourg: Centre d'Archéologie médiévale de Strasbourg, 1975), pp. 11–17.

3. Jacques Le Goff, *La civilisation de l'Occident médiéval* (Paris: Arthaud, 1972), p. 354.

4. Michel Mollat, *Les pauvres au Moyen Age. Etude sociale* (Paris: Hachette, 1978), p. 154.

5. Adam of Eynsham, *Magna Vita Sancti Hugonis,* ed. Decima L. Douie and David Hugh Farmer, 2 vols. (Edinburgh-London: Thomas Nelson, 1961–1962), vol. 2, chap. 5.

6. Robert Delort, *La vie au Moyen Age* (Paris: Seuil, 1982), p. 105; Robert Fossier, *Enfance de l'Europe* (Paris: Presses Universitaires de France, 1982), II, 930; David Herlihy, *Medieval Households* (Cambridge, Mass.: Harvard University Press, 1985).

7. *AA.SS,* XIII januarii, pp. 145–169.

8. Charles H. Talbot, ed., *The Life of Cristina of Markyate* (Oxford: Oxford University Press, 1959), 2nd ed. (Oxford: Clarendon, 1987), p. 204.

9. *Il matrimonio nella società altomedievale; Settimana di studio* (Spoleto, 1977), 2 vols.; Duby, *Le chevalier.*

10. Diane Owen Hughes, "Urban Growth and Family Structures in Medieval Genoa," *Past and Present* 66(1975):3–28.

11. Fossier, *Enfance,* I, 590.

12. Jean Leclercq, *Le mariage vu par les moines au XIIe siècle* (Paris: Cerf, 1983), p. 65.

13. Alexander C. Murray, *Reasons and Society in the Middle Ages* (Oxford: Clarendon, 1978).

14. Herlihy, *Medieval Households.*

15. Duby, *Le chevalier,* p. 141.

16. Richard H. Helmholz, *Marriage Litigation in Medieval England* (Cambridge: Cambridge University Press, 1974).

17. Juliette M. Turlan, "Recherches sur le mariage dans la pratique coutumière, XIIe–XVIe siècles," *Revue d'histoire du droit français et étranger* 35(1957):477–528.

18. See note 8.

19. Walter Holtzmann and Eric W. Kemp, eds., *Papal Decretals relating to the Diocese of Lincoln,* Lincoln Records Society Publication (Lincoln: The Society, 1954), p. 60.

20. John T. Noonan, "Marital Affection in the Canonists," in *Studia Gratiana* XII, Collectanea Stephan Kuttner, II, 481–509.

21. Adam of Eynsham, *Magna Vita Sancti Hugonis,* II, 31.

22. William Dugdale, *Monasticon Anglicanum* (London) 4(1830):vii.

23. Giles Constable, "Aelred of Rievaulx and the Nun of Watton," in Derek Baker, ed., *Medieval Women* (Oxford: Blackwell, 1978), p. 222.

24. Ibid., pp. 205–226.

25. Mary MacLaughlin, "Peter Abelard and the Dignity of Women," in

517

Pierre Abélard, Pierre le Vénérable (Paris: Centre National de Recherche Scientifique, 1975), pp. 287–334, 336.

26. See Chapter 11 by Chiara Frugoni.

27. Joseph S. Brewer, ed., *Giraldi Cambrensis Opera*, Gemma ecclesiastica (London, 1852), II, 250.

28. Pierre Toubert, "La théorie du mariage chez les moralistes carolingiens," in *Il matrimonio*, pp. 233–285.

29. Georges Duby, *Les trois ordres ou l'imaginaire du féodalisme* (Paris: Gallimard, 1978).

30. Marie-Thérèse Lorcin, *Société et cadre de vie en France, en Angleterre et Bourgogne* (Paris: S.E.D.E.S., 1985), p. 220.

31. Roberta Frank, "Marriage in Twelfth and Thirteenth Century Iceland," *Viator* 4(1973):174–184; Jenny M. Jochens, "En Islande médiévale: à la recherche de la famille nucléaire," *Annales E.S.C.* 40(1)1985:95–112.

32. Pierre Toubert, "Les status communaux et l'histoire des campagnes lombardes au XIVe siècle," in *Mélanges d'archéologie et d'histoire*, 1960, pp. 468ff.

33. Pierre Bonnassie, *La Catalogne du milieu du Xe siècle à la fin du XIe siècle*, 2 vols. (Toulouse: Le Mirail, 1975–1976).

34. Hughes, "Urban Growth."

35. Pierre Grimal, ed., *Histoire mondiale de la femme*, vol. 2: *L'Occident des Celtes à la Renaissance* (Paris: Nouvelle Librairie de France, 1966), pp. 154–171.

36. Fossier, *Enfance*, I, 571.

37. Leah Lydia Otis, *Prostitution in Medieval Society* (Chicago: University of Chicago Press, 1985), p. 17.

38. Joseph Strange, ed., *Caesarii Hestergbacensis Monachi Dialogus Miraculorum*, 2 vols. (Cologne, 1850–1857), I, 94–95.

39. Mary Erler and Maryanne Kowaleski, eds., *Women and Power in the Middle Ages* (Athens: University of Georgia Press, 1988), pp. 1–17.

40. Patrick Corbet, *Les saints ottoniens. Sainteté dynastique, sainteté royale et sainteté féminine autour de l'an mil* (Sigmaringen: Jan Thorbecke Verlag, 1986), pp. 81ff.

41. *Histoire mondiale de la femme*, pp. 57–58.

42. "Guillaume VIII de Montpellier, Marie et Pierre d'Aragon," in *Congrès de la Fédération historique du Languedoc-Roussillon, 15–18 mai 1980* (Montpellier, 1982), pp. 25–45.

43. Ibid.

44. *AA SS*, IV, junii, p. 65.

45. Arlette Farge and Christiane Klapisch-Zuber, eds., *Madame ou mademoiselle? Itinéraires de la solitude féminine (XVIIe–XXe siècles)* (Paris: Montalba, 1984), p. 7.

46. Matthäus Bernards, ed., *Speculum Virginum*, Behihefte zum Archiv für Kulturgeschichte 16 (Cologne: Graz, 1965).

47. Micheline de Fontette, *Les religieuses à l'âge classique du droit canon* (Paris: Vrin, 1967).

48. Paulette L'Hermite-Leclercq, "Les pouvoirs de la supérieure," paper read to the colloquium of the C.E.R.C.O.R. on *Les religieuses dans le cloître et dans le monde* (proceedings to come), Poitiers, 29 September–2 October 1988.

49. Paulette L'Hermite-Leclercq, "La femme à la festrelle du reclusoir," paper read to the colloquium on *Les femmes au Moyen Age,* University of Lille III, Maubeuge, 6–9 October 1988, published by the city of Maubeuge in 1990.

50. Otto Pacht, Charles R. Dodwell, and Francis Wormald, eds., *The St. Albans Psalter* (London, 1961), plates 13, 33, 72.

51. Adam of Eynsham, *Magna Vita Sancti Hugonis,* p. 117.

52. Corbet, *Les saints ottoniens,* pp. 261–268.

53. Donald Weinstein and R. M. Bell, *Saints and Society: The Two Worlds of Western Christendom, 1000–1700* (Chicago, 1982).

Chapter 8. The Courtly Model
GEORGES DUBY

1. J. H. Mundy, "Le mariage et les femmes à Toulouse au temps des Cathares," *Annales E.S.C.,* 1987.

2. Usama, *Des enseignements de la vie. Souvenirs d'un gentilhomme syrien au temps des croisades,* trans. A. Miquel (Paris, 1983).

3. J.-C. Huchet, *L'amour dit courtois. La "Fin'amors" chez les premiers troubadours* (Toulouse, 1987); H. Rey-Flaud, *La névrose courtoise* (Paris, 1983).

4. C. Marchello-Nizia, "Amour courtois, société masculine et figures de pouvoir," *Annales E.S.C.,* 1981.

5. A. Karnein, *"De Amore" in volksprachlicher Litteratur. Untersuchungen zur Andreas Capellanus Recepzion in Mettelalter und Renaissance* (Heidelberg, 1985).

6. R. Schnell, *Andreas Capellanus. Zur Recepzion des römischen und kanonischen Rechts in "De Amore"* (Munich, 1982).

7. Danielle Jacquart and Claude Thomasset, *Sexualité et savoir médical au Moyen Age* (Paris, 1983).

8. D. Rocher, "Le débat autour du mariage chez les clercs et les écrivains 'mondains' à la fin du XIIe et au début du XIIIe siècle," *Cahiers d'études germaniques,* 1987.

Chapter 9. Life in the Late Middle Ages
CLAUDIA OPITZ

1. Georges Duby, *Le chevalier, la femme et le prêtre: Le mariage dans la France féodale* (Paris: Hachette, 1981).

2. For more on the legal status of women in the various countries and regions of Europe, see *La femme,* Recueils de la Société Jean Bodin 12/2 (1962).

519

3. Thomas Kuehn, "*Cum consensu munduali:* Legal Guardianship of Women in Quattrocento Florence," *Viator* 13(1982):309–333, and "Women, Marriage, and *patria potestas* in Late Medieval Florence," *Revue d'histoire du droit* 49(1981):127–147.

4. Marianne Weber, *Ehefrau und Mutter in der Rechtsentwicklung* (Tübingen: Mohr, 1907), and Edith Ennen, *Frauen im Mittelalter* (Munich: Beck, 1986), pp. 134ff.

5. The population began to increase again from the middle of the fifteenth century, however, a development that reduced the value of female labor and contributed to changes in women's legal status (in central and northern Europe); see Ruggiero Romano and Alberto Tenenti, *Die Grundlegung der modernen Welt,* Fischer Weltgeschichte 12 (Frankfurt am Main: Fischer Taschenbuch, 1967), pp. 9–26.

6. Ennen, *Frauen im Mittelalter;* Christiane Klapisch-Zuber, "La fécondité des florentines (XIV–XVIe siècles)," *Annales de démographie historique* (1988):41–57.

7. See, for example, Karl Bücher, *Die Frauenfrage im Mittelalter* (Tübingen: H. Laupp'sche Buchhandlung, 1882).

8. Romano and Tenenti, *Die Grundlegung der modernen Welt;* Heide Wunder, "Frauen in der Gesellschaft Mitteleuropas im späten Mittelalter und in der frühen Neuzeit (15.–18. Jahrhundert)," in Helfried Valentinitsch, ed., *Hexen und Zauberer: Die grosse Verfolgung—ein europäisches Phänomen in der Steiermark* (Graz-Vienna: Leykam, 1987), pp. 123–154.

9. Romano and Tenenti, *Die Grundlegung der modernen Welt,* pp. 9ff.

10. This appears not to apply to Mediterranean regions, however; see David Herlihy and Christiane Klapisch-Zuber, *Les toscans et leurs familles: Une étude du "Catasto" florentin de 1427* (Paris: Fondation nationale des sciences politiques, 1978).

11. For more on the situation of domestic servants in Mediterranean regions, see R. M. Smith, "The People of Tuscany and Their Families in the Fifteenth Century: Medieval or Mediterranean?" *Journal of Family History* 6(1981):102–128; for central Europe, see David Nicholas, *The Domestic Life of a Medieval City: Women, Children, and the Family in Fourteenth-Century Ghent* (Lincoln: University of Nebraska Press, 1985); for England, see R. M. Smith, "Kin and Neighbors in a 13th Century Suffolk Community," *Journal of Family History* 4(1979):219–256.

12. Georges Duby expresses this idea most clearly in *Medieval Marriage: Two Models from Twelfth-Century France* (Baltimore: Johns Hopkins University Press, 1978).

13. John T. Noonan, Jr., "Power to Choose," *Viator* 4(1973):419ff.

14. David Nicholas discusses such cases in Flanders and Brabant, which were particularly well-developed areas economically in *The Domestic Life of a Medieval City.*

15. "De b. Agnete de Bohemia virgine Ord. S. Clarae Pragae vita," *Acta Sanctorum,* March I, 502–532; "De b. Elisabetha seu Isabella virgine regia fundatrice monasterii Longi Campi vita gallice scripta per Agnetem

de Harcourt abbaissam Longi Campi," *Acta Sanctorum*, August VI, 787–808.

16. The circumstances of girls' education among the aristocracy as described by Paulette L'Hermite-Leclerq for the high Middle Ages are also valid for the later part of the epoch; see Chapter 7, "The Feudal Order." The education of girls in other social classes was also affected by religious and practical notions, as Silvana Vecchio shows in Chapter 4, "The Good Wife."

17. Claudia Opitz, *Frauenalltag im Mittelalter: Biographien des 13. und 14. Jahrhunderts* (Weinheim: Beltz, 1985); Klapisch-Zuber, "La fécondité des florentines."

18. Petra Kellermann-Haaf, *Frau und Politik im Mittelalter: Untersuchungen zur politischen Rolle der Frau in den höfischen Romanen des 12., 13. und 14. Jahrhunderts* (Göppingen: Kümmerle, 1986).

19. "De b. Elisabetha," *Acta Sanctorum*.

20. "De s. Clara virgine, prima s. Francisci discipula vita auctore anonymo coaevo," *Acta Sanctorum*, August II, 739–768.

21. J. M. Turlan, "Recherches sur le mariage dans la pratique coutumière (XIIe–XVIe siècles)," *Revue historique de droit français et étranger*, 2nd ser. 17(1957):477–528.

22. "De s. Hedwige vidua, ducissa Sileasiae vita auctore anonymo subaequali," *Acta Sanctorum*, October VIII, 198–270.

23. See Jean-Philippe Lévy, "L'Officialité de Paris et les questions familiales à la fin du XIVe siècle," *Etudes de droit canonique dédiées à Gabriel LeBras* (Paris: Sirey, 1965) II, 1265–1294.

24. Women who murdered or plotted to murder their husbands and mothers who killed their newborn infants represent the main categories among the few recorded cases of violent crime committed by females during the late Middle Ages; see Barbara A. Hanawalt, "The Female Felon in Fourteenth-Century England," in Susan M. Stuard, ed., *Women in Medieval Society* (Philadelphia: University of Pennsylvania Press, 1976), pp. 125–140.

25. See Jacques Rossiaud, *La prostituzione nel medioevo* (Rome: Laterza, 1984); Ernst Schubert, "Gauner, Dirnen und Gelichter in deutschen Städten des Mittelalters," in Cord Meckseper and Elisabeth Schraut, eds., *Mentalität und Alltag im Spätmittelalter* (Göttingen: Vandenhoek und Ruprecht, 1985), pp. 97–128; and Richard Trexler, "La prostitution florentine au XVe siècle: Patronage et clientèles," *Annales. Economie, Société, Civilisation* 6(1981):983–1015.

26. Emmanuel Le Roy Ladurie, *Montaillou: The Promised Land of Error*, trans. Barbara Bray (New York: Braziller, 1978), p. 154.

27. Ibid., p. 161.

28. For two cases involving infidelity by both partners, see Lévy, "L'Officialité de Paris."

29. Walter Nigg, ed., *Die heilige Elisabeth von Thüringen* (Düsseldorf, 1963).

30. See Opitz, *Frauenalltag im Mittelalter*, pp. 126ff., and Kellermann-Haaf, *Frau und Politik im Mittelalter*.

31. For more on this couple, see André Vauchez, "Elzéar et Delphine ou le mariage virginal" *Les laïcs au moyen âge* and "Deux laïcs en quête de perfection: Elzéar de Sabran (+ 1323) et Delphine de Puimichel (+ 1360)," (Paris: Cerf, 1987), pp. 211–224, 83–92.

32. Theodor Knochenhauer, *Geschichte Thüringens zur Zeit des ersten Landgrafenhauses* (Gotha: Perthes, 1871; rpt. Aalen, 1969), pp. 304ff.

33. See Opitz, *Frauenalltag im Mittelalter,* p. 273, note 645.

34. See Chapter 4.

35. "Vita sanctae Salomeae reginae halicensis auctore Stanislao Franciscano," *Monumenta Poloniae Historica,* o.s. (Kraków, 1864–1872), IV, 776–796.

36. See Nicholas, *Domestic Life of a Medieval City;* his sources make no mention of spouses' relative ages, however.

37. Erika Uitz, "Zur Darstellung der Stadtbürgerin, ihrer Rolle in Ehe, Familie und Öffentlichkeit in der Chronistik und in den Rechtsquellen der spätmittelalterlichen deutschen Stadt," *Jahrbuch für die Geschichte des Feudalismus* 7(1983):130ff.

38. For class differences in behavior and family structure in Italy, see Diane O. Hughes, "Domestic Ideals and Social Behavior: Evidence from Medieval Genoa," in Charles E. Rosenberg, ed., *The Family in History* (Philadelphia: University of Pennsylvania Press, 1975), pp. 115–143.

39. For information on the division of Europe into various cultural regions, see Kathleen Casey, "The Cheshire Cat: Reconstructing the Experience of Medieval Women," in Berenice A. Carroll, ed., *Liberating Women's History* (Urbana-Chicago: University of Illinois Press, 1976), pp. 224–249.

40. Chistiane Klapisch-Zuber, "Parents de sang, parents de lait: La mise en nourrice à Florence (1300–1500)," *Annales de démographie historique* 19(1983):33–64; Leah L. Otis, "Municipal Wet Nurses in Fifteenth-Century Montpellier," in Barbara A. Hanawalt, ed., *Women and Work in Pre-industrial Europe* (Bloomington: Indiana University Press, 1986), pp. 83ff.

41. Shulamith Shahar, *The Fourth Estate: A History of Women in the Middle Ages,* trans. Chaya Galai (London-New York: Methuen, 1984).

42. Philippe Ariès, *Centuries of Childhood: A Social History of Family Life,* trans. Robert Baldick (New York: Knopf, 1962).

43. Question 92, Article 1: "Should woman have been made in the original creation of things?" *Summa Theologica* 13 (New York-London: Blackfriars, 1964), pp. 35–36.

44. André Vauchez, *La sainteté en occident aux derniers siècles du moyen âge,* rev. ed. (Rome: Ecole français de Rome, 1981), and "Un nouvel idéal au XIIIe siècle: La chasteté conjugale," in Vauchez, *Les laïcs au moyen âge,* pp. 203–209. See also Chapter 1 by Jacques Dalarun, "The Clerical Gaze." Gaze."

45. Z. Lazzeri, ed., "Il prozesso di Cannonizzazione di S. Chiara d'Assisi," *Archivum Franciscanum Historicum* 13(1920):439–493.

46. "Vita sanctae Salomeae," *Monumenta Poloniae Historica,* IV, 776–779.

47. Cited according to Heidi Dienst, "Dominus vir: Von der Herzogin-Markgräfin Agnes und anderen Frauen des Hochmittelalters," in Autorinnengruppe der Universität Wien, eds., *Das ewige Klischee* (Vienna: Böhlau, 1981), p. 23.

48. J. C. Russell, "Die Bevölkerung Europas 500–1500," in Carlo M. Cipolla and Knut Borcharts, eds., *Bevölkerungsgeschichte Europas* (Munich: Piper, 1969), pp. 9ff. On variations in family size in northern Italy caused by the practice of wet-nursing, see Hughes, "Domestic Ideals," pp. 115–143, and Klapisch-Zuber, "La fécondité des florentines."

49. Barbara A. Hanawalt, "Childrearing among the Lower Classes of Late Medieval England," *Journal of Interdisciplinary History* 8(1977–1978):1–22.

50. J. Farknoi, ed., "Kanonisationsprozeß der sel. Margarethe," *Monumenta Romana Episcopatus Vesprimiensis* 1 (Budapest, 1896).

51. "Leben der hl. Agnes von Montepulciano," *Acta Sanctorum*, April II, 791–817.

52. "De beata Ivetta, sive Jutta, vidua reclusa Hui in Gelgio vita auctore Hugone Floreffiensi," *Acta Sanctorum*, January I, 83–887.

53. Nigg, ed., *Die heilige Elisabeth von Thüringen*.

54. "De b. Angela di Fulginio vita auctore Arnaldo," *Acta Sanctorum*, January I, 186–234.

55. "De s. Humilitate abbatissa Ord. Vallombrosani Florentiae," *Acta Sanctorum*, May V, 203–222.

56. "De b. Margarita Poenitente tertii ord. s. Francisci vita ex mss. auctore f. Junctâ Bevagnate," *Acta Sanctorum*, February III, 298–357.

57. Le Roy Ladurie, *Montaillou*, pp. 172–173.

58. See the section "Von Kinderwunsch und Kindsmord: Mutterschaft und Mütterlichkeit vom 13. bis zum 15. Jahrhundert," in Claudia Opitz, *Evatöchter und Bräute Christi: Weiblicher Lebenszusammenhang und Frauenkultur im Mittelalter* (Weinheim: Deutscher Studienverlag, 1990).

59. "De s. Clara virgine," *Acta Sanctorum*, August II, 739–768.

60. "Vita sanctae Salomeae," *Monumenta Poloniae Historica*.

61. Cited according to Annik Porteau-Bitker, "Criminalité et délinquance féminines dans le droit pénal des XIIIe et XIVe siècles," *Revue historique de droit français et étranger*, 4th ser. 58(1980):27.

62. Yvonne B. Brissaud, "L'Infanticide à la fin du moyen âge: Ses motivations psychologiques et sa repression," *Revue historique de droit français et étranger*, 4th ser. 50(1972):229–256.

63. Cited according to Klaus Arnold, *Kind und Gesellschaft in Mittelalter und Renaissance* (Paderborn: Schöningh, 1980), p. 47.

64. Ibid.

65. John Boswell, *The Kindness of Strangers: The Abandonment of Children in Western Europe from Late Antiquity to the Renaissance* (New York: Pantheon, 1988).

66. David Herlihy, "Medieval Children," in Bede Karl Lackner and Ken-

neth Roy Philp, eds., *Essays on Medieval Civilization* (Austin: University of Texas Press, 1978), pp. 109–141.

67. This specialization unfortunately has led to a concentration of studies on conditions in central and western Europe; much less is known about women's working conditions in Mediterranean regions. My remarks reflect this state of scholarship.

68. Wunder, "Frauen in der Gesellschaft Mitteleuropas," pp. 123–154.

69. See Barbara A. Hanawalt, "Peasant Women's Contribution to the Home Economy in Late Medieval England," in Hanawalt, ed., *Women and Work*, pp. 3–19; and Judith M. Bennett, "The Village Ale-Wife: Women and Brewing in Fourteenth-Century England," ibid., pp. 20–36.

70. Cited according to Heide Dienst, "Rollenaspekte von Männern und Frauen im Mittelalter in zeitgenössischer Theorie und Praxis," in Claudia Opitz, ed., *Wieblichkeit oder Feminismus? Beiträge zur interdisziplinären Frauentagung Konstanz 1982* (Weingarten: Drumlin, 1984), pp. 137–157.

71. Cited according to Hermann Pleij, "Arbeitsteilung in der Ehe: Literatur und soziale Wirklichkeit im Spätmittelalter," in Maria E. Müller, ed., *Eheglück und Liebesjoch: Bilder von Liebe, Ehe und Familie in der Literatur des 15. und 16. Jahrhunderts* (Weinheim: Beltz, 1988), pp. 105–124.

72. Wunder, "Frauen in der Gesellschaft Mitteleuropas," pp. 123–154.

73. On the situation of servant girls, see R. M. Smith, "Kin and Neighbors in a Suffolk Community," pp. 219–256, and Christina Vanja, "Frauen im Dorf: Ihre Stellung unter besonderer Berücksichtigung landgräflich-hessischer Quellen des späten Mittelalters," *Zeitschrift für Agrargeschichte und Agrarsoziologie* 34(1986):147–159.

74. Erika Uitz, *Die Frau in der mittelalterlichen Stadt* (Stuttgart: Abend-Verlag, 1988), p. 41. Mary R. Beard cites examples from Italy in her chapter on "The Force of Woman in Medieval Economic and Social Life," in *Women as a Force in History* (New York: Collier, 1946), pp. 216–269.

75. Uitz, *Die Frau in der mittelalterlichen Stadt*, p. 65.

76. Ibid.

77. Ibid. Beard cites examples from England, in *Women as a Force in History*, pp. 223ff.

78. Uitz, *Die Frau in der mittelalterlichen Stadt*.

79. On the exceptional conditions in Cologne, see Margarethe M. Wensky, *Die Stellung der Frau in der stadkölnischen Wirtschaft im Spätmittelalter* (Cologne-Vienna, 1980).

80. See the introduction in Hanawalt, ed., *Women and Work*, pp. vii-xviii.

81. Léonce Reypens, S.J., ed., *Vita Beatricis: De autobiografie van de s. Beatrjis van Tienen, ord. cist. 1200 bis 1268* (Antwerp, 1964); J. Henriquez, ed., "Vita beatae Idae de Nivella sanctimonialis in monasterio de Remeya," *Quinque prudentes virgines* (Antwerp, 1630), pp. 199–297.

82. The examples cited here and in the following passage are taken from Uitz, *Die Frau in der mittelalterlichen Stadt*.

83. Beard, *Women as a Force in History*, pp. 246ff.

84. Barbara Kroemer, "Von Kauffrauen, Beamtinnen, Ärztinnen: Erwerbstätige Frauen in deutschen mittelalterlichen Städten," *Frauen in der Geschichte* 2(1982).

85. Uitz, *Die Frau in der mittelalterlichen Stadt,* pp. 97ff.

86. Ibid., p. 68.

87. Ibid., pp. 68–69, and Régine Pernoud, *La femme au temps des cathédrales* (Paris: Stock, 1980), pp. 202ff.

88. For more on academic medicine's concern with the theory of gynecology and obstetrics, see Chapter 2 by Claude Thomasset, "The Nature of Women."

89. A. Delva, *Vrowengeneeskunde in Vlandern tijdens de late middeluewen met mitgave van het Brugse Liber Trotula,* Vlaamse Historische Studies 2 (Bruges: Genootschap voor Geschiedenis, 1983).

90. See Georg Burckhard, *Die deutschen Hebammenordnungen von ihren ersten Anfängen* (Leipzig, 1914); Merry E. Wiesner, "Early Modern Midwifery: A Case Study," in Hanawalt, ed., *Women and Work,* pp. 94–114; and for a general survey, Paul Diepgen, *Frau und Frauenheilkunde in der Kultur des Mittelalters* (Stuttgart: Thieme, 1963).

91. For information on the women's guilds of Cologne, see Wensky, *Die Stellung der Frau;* for those in Paris, see Uitz, *Die Frau in der mittelalterlichen Stadt,* pp. 50–51. Kathleen Casey describes conditions in England in "Women in Norman and Plantagenet England," in Barbara Kanner, ed., *The Women of England: From Anglo-Saxon Times to the Present* (Hamden, Conn.: Archon, 1979), pp. 83–112. Much research on this topic remains to be done, however.

92. Uitz, *Die Frau in der mittelalterlichen Stadt,* pp. 54ff.

93. Christina Vanja, "Bergarbeiterinnen: Zur Geschichte der Frauenarbeit im Bergbau, Hütten- und Salinenwesen seit dem späten Mittelalter, Teil I: Mittelalter und frühe Neuzeit," *Der Anschnitt* 39(1987):2–15.

94. These figures are cited from Uitz, *Die Frau in der mittelalterlichen Stadt,* p. 65.

95. Cited according to Anke Wolf-Graaf, *Die verborgene Geschichte der Frauenarbeit* (Weinheim: Beltz, 1983), p. 82.

96. Barbara Händler-Lachmann, "Die Berufstätigkeit der Frau in den deutschen Städten des Spätmittelalters und der beginnenden Neuzeit," *Hessisches Jahrbuch für Landesgeschichte* 30(1980):131–175.

97. Ibid.

98. See Merry E. Wiesner, *Working Women in Renaissance Germany* (New Brunswick, N.J.: Rutgers University Press, 1986).

99. Wolf-Graaf, *Die verborgene Geschichte der Frauenarbeit,* pp. 72–82.

100. See Wunder, "Frauen in der Gesellschaft Mitteleuropas," pp. 138ff.

101. See the introduction to Hanawalt, *Women and Work,* pp. xiff.

102. Wolf-Graaf, *Die verborgene Geschichte der Frauenarbeit,* p. 82.

103. Russell, "Die Bevölkerung Europas 500–1500," pp. 9ff.

104. Albert Huyskens, ed., *Der sog. "libellus de dictis quattuor ancillarum s. Elisabethae confectus"* (Kempten-Munich, 1911).

105. On the differences between men's and women's wages, see Casey, "The Cheshire Cat," pp. 230–231.

106. Hanawalt, "The Female Felon," pp. 125–140; also Isabelle Chabot, "Poverty and Widows in Later Medieval Florence," *Continuity and Change* 3(1988):201–311.

107. "Ad mulieres pauperes in villulis," in Carla Casagrande, ed., *Prediche alle donne del secolo XIII* (Milan: Bompiani, 1978).

108. On the development and significance of prostitution in medieval cities, see Leah Otis, *Prostitution in Medieval Society* (Chicago: University of Chicago Press, 1985), esp. part I, and the works mentioned in note 25.

109. See Schubert, "Gauner, Dirnen und Gelichter," pp. 97–128. For more on the cult of Mary Magdalene, see Chapter 1 in this book.

110. "Vita b. Idiliae, viduae Leodiensis, libri duo priores," *Analecta Bollandiana* 13(1894):197–248.

111. Jean-Luc Dufresne, "Les comportements amoureux d'après les registres de l'officialité de Cérisy (XIV–XVe siècle), *Bulletin philologique et historique du comité des travaux historiques et scientifiques 1973* (1976):131–156.

112. Marie-Thérèse Lorcin, "Retraite des veuves et filles au couvent: Quelques aspects de la condition féminine à la fin du moyen âge," *Annales de démographie historique* 11(1975):187–201.

113. G. K. Schmelzeisen demonstrates this for urban women of central Europe in *Die Rechtsstellung der Frau in der deutschen Stadtwirtschaft* (Stuttgart: Kohlhammer, 1935); for rural conditions, see Lutz K. Berkner, "Inheritance, Land Tenure, and Peasant Family Structure: A German Regional Comparison," in Jack Goody et al., eds., *Family and Inheritance* (Cambridge: Cambridge University Press, 1976), pp. 71–95.

114. "De s. Aemiliana sive Humiliana vidua tertii ordinis s. Francisci vita auctore coaevo," *Acta Sanctorum*, May IV, 385–417.

115. Walter Heinemeyer, "Die Landgräfin Elisabeth von Thüringen," in Heinemeyer et al., eds., *Die heilige Elisabeth in Hessen* (exhibition catalogue; Marburg, 1983), pp. 29–56.

116. For information on this point in Mediterranean regions, see Thomas Kuehn, "Women, Marriage, and *patria potestas*," *Revue d'histoire du droit* 49(1981):127–147; Christiane Klapisch-Zuber, "La 'mère cruelle': Maternité, veuvage et dot dans le Florence des XIVe–XVe siècles," *Annales. Economie, Société, Civilisation* 3(1983):1097–1109; and Diane O. Hughes, "Brideprice and Dowry in Mediterranean Europe," *Journal of Family History* 3(1978):263–296.

117. Strasbourg, Archives municipales, Statutes of 1477, vol. 18, fol. 144.

118. Herbert Grundmann, *Religiöse Bewegungen im Mittelalter* (Darmstadt: Wiss. Buchgesellschaft, 1970).

119. Barbara Degler-Spengler, "Die religiöse Frauenbewegung des Mittelalters," *Rottenburger Jahrbuch für Kirchengeschichte* (1984), pp. 75–88.

120. Bücher, *Die Frauenfrage im Mittelalter*.

121. For information on the development and significance of the Beguines (including some heretical variants), see Ernest William McDonnell, *The Beguines and Beghards in Medieval Culture with Special Reference to the Belgian Scene* (New Brunswick, N.J.: 1954).

122. See Grundmann, *Religiöse Bewegungen im Mittelalter*, esp. chap. 7. The fact that this religious women's movement was not restricted to central Europe is demonstrated by studies such as John Martin's "Out of the Shadow: Heretical and Catholic Women in Renaissance Venice," *Journal of Family History* 10(1985):21–33, and Caroline Bynum's *Holy Feast and Holy Fast: The Religious Significance of Food to Medieval Women* (Berkeley: University of California Press, 1987), esp. chap. 1.

123. Cited according to Ursula Peters, "Frauenmystik im 14. Jahrhundert: Die Offenbarungen der Christine Ebner," in Opitz, ed., *Weiblichkeit oder Feminismus?*, pp. 213–227.

124. Kaspar Elm, "Ketzer oder fromme Frauen? Das Beginentum im europäischen Mittelalter," *Journal für Geschichte* 2(1980):42–46.

125. For information on the women mystics named, see Peter Dinzelbacher and Dieter R. Bauer, eds., *Frauenmystik im Mittelalter* (Filderstadt bei Stuttgart: Schwabenverlag, 1985), and John A. Nichols and Lilian T. Shank, eds., *Peace Weavers: Medieval Religious Women 2* (Kalamazoo, Mich.: Cistercian Publications, 1984).

126. Cited according to Peters, "Frauenmystik im 14. Jahrhundert."

127. Vauchez, *Les laïcs au moyen âge*, pp. 239–244.

128. Vauchez, *La sainteté en occident;* Donald Weinstein and Randolph M. Bell, *Saints and Society: The Two Worlds of Western Christendom* (Chicago: University of Chicago Press, 1982).

129. Martha C. Howell, *Women, Production, and Patriarchy in Late Medieval Cities* (Chicago: University of Chicago Press, 1986).

130. Vauchez, *Les laïcs au moyen âge*, pp. 265–276.

131. Christine de Pisan, *The Book of the City of Ladies*, trans. Earl J. Richards (New York: Persea Books, ca. 1982).

132. See Joan K. Kelly, "Early Feminist Theory and the 'Querelle des femmes' 1400–1789," *Signs* 8(1982):4–22.

Chapter 10. *The World of Women*

FRANÇOISE PIPONNIER

1. Michel Parisse, *Les nonnes au Moyen Age* (Le Puy: Christine Bonneton, 1983).

2. See, for example, Henri Dubois, *Les foires de Chalon et le commerce dans la vallée de la Saône* (Paris: Presses de la Sorbonne, 1976), pp. 146–147.

3. Michel Balard, "La femme esclave à Gênes (XIIIe–XVe siècles)," paper read to the colloquium on *Les femmes au Moyen Age,* University of Lille III, Maubeuge, 6–9 October 1988, published by the city of Maubeuge in 1990.

4. Perrine Mane, *Calendriers et techniques agricoles (France-Italie, XIIe–XIIIe siècles)* (Paris: Le Sycomore, 1983).

5. Private communication from Perrine Mane.

6. Richard Bucaille and Françoise Piponnier, "La belle ou la bête? Remarques sur l'apparence corporelle de la paysannerie médiévale," *Ethnologie française* 6(3–4)1976:227–232.

7. Françoise Piponnier, "Une maison paysanne au XIVe siècle: le mobilier," *Rotterdam Papers II* (Rotterdam, 1975), pp. 151–170.

8. Emmanuel Le Roy Ladurie, *Montaillou village occitan de 1294 à 1324* (Paris: Gallimard, 1973), p. 159.

9. Pierre Riché, *La vie quotidienne dans l'Empire carolingien* (Paris: Hachette, 1973), pp. 195–196.

10. Catalogue of the exhibition "Un village au temps de Charlemagne," Rémy Guadagnin, curator, Musée National des Arts et Traditions Populaires, Paris (Paris: Réunion des Musées Nationaux, 1988), pp. 278–283.

11. G. De Poerce, *La draperie médiévale en Flandre et en Artois,* 3 vols. (Ghent: De Tempel, 1951), vol. 1: *La Technique.*

12. Florence Edler De Roover, "Andrea Banchi Florentine Silk Manufacturer and Merchant in the Fifteenth Century," *Studies in Mediaeval and Renaissance History* 3(1960).

13. Renée and Michel Colardelle, "L'habitat médiéval immergé de Collétière à Charavines (Isère)," *Archéologie médiévale* 10(196):167–269.

14. Departmental archives of Côte-d'Or, B 2082, inventory of château d'Aisey (1380).

15. Quoted by Parisse, *Les nonnes,* p. 57.

16. For example, Gabrielle Demians d'Archimbaud, *Les fouilles de Rougiers* (Paris: Centre National de Recherche Scientifique, 1980), pp. 460–465.

17. Charles V. Langlois, *La société française au XIIIe siècle d'après dix romans d'aventure* (Paris: Hachette, 1904), p. 9.

18. Irena Turnau, "The Diffusion of Knitting in Medieval Europe," in *Cloth and Clothing in Medieval Europe* (London: Heinemann, 1983), pp. 368–389.

19. Catalogue of the exhibition "Costume Coutume" at the Grand Palais in Paris, Jean Cuisenier, curator (Paris: Réunion des Musées nationaux, 1987), p. 58: knitted wool bonnet found at Saint-Denis.

20. Françoise Piponnier, "Les ateliers des artisans dijonnais du textile d'après les inventaires mobiliers (XIVe–XVe siècles)," *Autour de l'habitat textile* (Tourcoing: Archives Municipales, 1987), pp. 1–9.

21. Danièle Alexandre-Bidon and Monique Closson, *L'enfant à l'ombre des cathédrales* (Lyons: Presses Universitaires de Lyon, 1985), pp. 158–161.

22. P. Demolon, *Le village mérovingien de Brebières (VIe–VIIe siècles)* (Arras, 1972), p. 134.

23. Le Roy Ladurie, *Montaillou,* p. 288.

24. Marie-Thérèse Lorcin, "Le feu apprivoisé, l'homme, la femme et le feu dans les fabliaux," *Revue historique* 268(543)1982:3–15.

25. Jean-Marie Pesez, "Le foyer de la maison paysanne (XIe–XVe siècle)," *Archéologie médiévale* 16(1986):65–92.

26. Françoise Piponnier, "Equipement et techniques culinaires en Bourgogne au XIVe siècle," *Bulletin philologique et historique du comité des travaux historiques et scientifiques, Année 1971* (Paris, 1977), pp. 57–80.

27. Françoise Desportes, *Le pain au Moyen Age* (Paris: Olivier Orban, 1987), pp. 121–143.

28. Quoted in Parisse, *Les nonnes*, pp. 140–141.

29. Le Roy Ladurie, *Montaillou*, p. 373.

30. Geneviève Bresc-Bautier, "Pour compléter les données de l'archéologie: le rôle du bois dans la maison sicilienne," *Atti del colloquiuo internazionale di archeologia medievale (Palermo-Erice 1974)* (Palermo: University of Palermo, 1976), pp. 435–464.

31. Günter P. Fehring, "Der Beitrag der Archäologie zum Leben in der Stadt des späten Mittelalters," in *Das Leben in der Stadt des Spätenmittelalters, Internationaler Kongress, Krems 1976* (Vienna: Oesterreichische Akademie der Wissenschaften, 1977), fig. 23.

32. Françoise Piponnier, "Les métaux et leurs emplois d'après les inventaires mobiliers (Bourgogne, XIVe–XVe siècles)," paper read to *Diciottesima Settimana di Studio (Prato 1986)*, to come.

33. J. Pichon, ed., *Le ménagier de Paris*, 2 vols. (Paris, 1846).

34. Le Roy Ladurie, *Montaillou*, pp. 203–204.

35. Langlois, *La société française*, p. 119.

36. Danièle Alexandre-Bidon and Françoise Piponnier, "Gestes et objets de la toilette aux XIVe et XVe siècles," in *Les soins de beauté, Moyen Age, début des Temps modernes* (Nice: Faculté des Lettres et Sciences Humaines, 1987), pp. 211–244.

37. Le Roy Ladurie, *Montaillou*, p. 72.

38. Maurice Beresford and John G. Hurst, *Deserted Medieval Villages* (London: Lutterworth, 1971); Gabrielle Démians d'Archimbaud, "L'habitation médiévale en Provence médiévale," in *La construction au Moyen Age, histoire et archéologie* (Paris: Les Belles Lettres, 1973), pp. 59–110; Jean-Marie Pesez, "L'habitation paysanne en Bourgogne médiévale," ibid., pp. 219–233; Jean Chapelot and Robert Fossier, *Le village et la maison au Moyen Age* (Paris: Hachette, 1980).

39. Quoted in Gabriel Fournier, *Le château dans la France médiévale* (Paris: Aubier, 1978), p. 290.

40. Jean-Marie Pesez, ed., *Brucato, histoire et archéologie d'un habitat médiéval en Sicile* (Rome: Ecole Française de Rome, 1985).

41. Jean-Marie Pesez, "Une maison villageoise au XIVe siècle: les structures," *Rotterdam Papers II* (Rotterdam, 1975), pp. 139–149; Françoise Piponner, "Une maison villageoise," ibid., pp. 151–170.

42. Le Roy Ladurie, *Montaillou*, p. 383.

43. Jean-Marie Pesez, "Obscure et enfumée, la maison paysanne au Moyen Age," *Fasciculi Archaeologiae Historicae* 2(1987):79–83.

44. Le Roy Ladurie, *Montaillou*, p. 383.

Chapter 11. The Imagined Woman

CHIARA FRUGONI

1. Jean Hubert, Jean Porcher, W. F. Volbach, *L'impero carolingio* (Milan: Feltrinelli, 1968), p. 135.

2. Victor Y. Haines, "The Iconography of the Felix Culpa," *Florilegium* 1(1979):151-158, 174.

3. Ambrose of Milan, *De virginibus,* I, chap. 9,60, in Jacques Paul Migne, *Patrologia Latina,* 221 vols. (Paris, 1844-1864), 16, col. 216 (cited hereafter as *PL*); Jerome, *Commentarium in Evangelium Matthaei,* l. II, chap. 13, in *PL* 26, col. 92.

4. See Chapter 7 by Paulette L'Hermite-Leclercq, "The Feudal Order."

5. *Adversus Jovinianum,* l. I, *PL* 23, col. 246.

6. On the practice of sexual abstinence, developed in Christian circles from the fifth century onward, see Peter Brown, *The Body and Society. Men, Women and Sexual Renunciation in Early Christianity* (New York: Columbia University Press, 1988).

7. D. J. A. Ross, "Olympias and the Serpent," *Journal of the Warburg and Courtauld Institutes* 26(1963):1-21, tab. Iab.

8. *Homiliae in Evang.,* l. II, XXVI, 5, *PL* 76, col. 1269.

9. *Liber de modo bene vivendi, PL* 184, col. 1285 (which appears to have been written by the Saint).

10. Apart from the previously cited Utrecht manuscript, the other two appear respectively in the *Evangelistary of Ottone III,* fol. 28r, Munich Staatsbibliothek, Ms. Clm. 4453, Cin 58, and in the drawing attached to the gospels at the Cathedral of Saint Omer, Ms. 154: fol. 1, both reproduced in Chiara Frugoni, "L'iconografia del matrimonio e della coppia nel Medioevo," in *Il matrimonio nella società Altomedievale* (Spoleto, 1977), pp. 901-963, figs. 28, 29, 31.

11. Jacopo Passavanti, *Specchio di vera penitenza,* ed. F. L. Polidori (Florence: Monnier, 1863), "Trattato della superbia," chap. 5, pp. 209-211.

12. In the recent edition of the work the abbess is called, more precisely, of Hohenbourg (rather than, as formerly, of Landsberg). Herrad of Hohenbourg, *Hortus deliciarum,* ed. Rosalie Green (London-Leiden: Warburg Institute-Brill, 1979), II, 352.

13. Reproduction in Jonathan Alexander and Paul Binski, eds., *Age of Chivalry, Art in Plantagenet England, 1200-1400* (London: Weidenfeld and Nicolson, 1987), p. 353.

14. Ibid., p. 446.

15. For the various versions of Mary Magdalene's biography (especially the legend according to which Lazarus' sister landed in France) see Chapter 1, by Jacques Dalarun, "The Clerical Gaze."

16. Domenico Cavalca, *Le vite de' santi Padri* (Milan: Istituto Editoriale Italiano, n.d.), I, 173, "Vita di Santa Maria Egiziaca."

17. Chiara Frugoni, "La morte propria, la morte degli altri," in Jean

Delumeau, ed., *Storia vissuto del popolo cristiano* (Turin: SEI, 1985), pp. 349–365, esp. 357–365.

18. *Visio Alberici*, ed. M. Inguanez, in *Miscellanea Cassinese* 9(1932): 83–103. For the various versions of the *Visio* by Alberico of Settefrati (a monk at Montecassino Abbey at the beginning of the eleventh century) see *Dizionario biografico degli italiani* (Rome: Treccani, 1960), under Anselmo Lentini's entry, "Alberico di Montecassino."

19. Marina Warner, *Alone of All Her Sex. The Myth and the Cult of the Virgin Mary* (London: Weidenfeld and Nicolson, 1976), pp. 60ff.

20. Jean-Louis Flandrin, *Un temps pour embrasser* (Paris: Seuil, 1983).

21. This iconography is constant even after the Middle Ages: see Gigetta Dalli Regoli, *La preveggenza della Vergine. Struttura, stile, iconografia nelle Madonne del Cinquecento* (Pisa: Pacini, 1984).

22. On the subject of the representation of vices see Adolfo Katzenellenbogen, *Allegories of the Virtues and Vices in Mediaeval Art, from Early Christian Times to the Thirteenth Century* (London: Warburg Institute, 1939; Liechtenstein: Kraus Reprint Nendeln, 1977).

23. Bernhard Blumenkranz, *Le Juif médieval au miroir de l'art chrétien*, Etudes Augustiniennes (Paris: Etudes Augustiniennes, 1966), esp. pp. 53ff., 57ff., 61ff., 112ff. Lambert de St. Omer, *Liber floridus*, ed. A. Derolez (Gand, 1968).

24. Alain Boureau, *La papesse Jeanne* (Paris: Aubier, 1988).

25. Frugoni, "L'iconografia del matrimonio," pp. 957ff.

26. On this complicated question, see Viviana Jemolo and Mirella Morelli, eds., *La Bibbia di S. Paolo Fuori le Mura* (Rome: De Luca, 1981), p. 11.

27. For the episode in question, see *Vita Mathildis a Donizone Presbytero*, l. II, ll. 8off., in L. A. Muratori, *Rerum italicarum scriptores* 2, bk. V, pt. 2.

28. *I Vangeli apocrifi*, ed. Marcello Craveri (Turin: Einaudi, 1969), pp. 21–22.

29. Sybille Harksen, *La femme au Moyen Age* (Leipzig: Volker Kuster, 1974), fig. p. 94; Sylvie Laurent, *Naître au Moyen Age* (Paris: Léopard d'Or, 1989).

30. Sally Fox, *The Medieval Woman, an Illuminated Book of Days* (Boston: Little, Brown, 1985), figure for the month of July.

31. Chiara Frugoni, "Le mistiche, le visioni e l'iconografia: rapporti ed influssi," *Atti del convegno su "La mistica femminile nel Trecento" Todi 1982* (Todi, 1983), pp. 5–45. On Clare of Montefalco in particular, see Chiara Frugoni, "Domine, in conspectu tuo omne desiderium meum: Visioni e immagini in Chiara da Montefalco," in Claudio Leonardi and Enrico Menesto, eds., *Chiara da Montefalco ed il suo tempo* (Florence: Nuova Italia, 1985), pp. 154–174.

32. Enrico Menestò, *Il processo di canonizzazione di Chiara da Montefalco* (Florence: Nuova Italia, 1985), p. 85 (fols. 33v–34r).

33. Chiara Frugoni, "Le lastre veterotestamentarie e il programma della facciata," in E. Castelnuovo, V. Fumagalli, A. Peroni, and S. Settis, eds.,

Lanfranco e Wiligelmo. Il Duomo di Modena (Modena, 1989), pp. 422–452, esp. 428; *Il Duomo di Modena. Atlante Fotografico* (Modena, 1989), pp. 144–151.

34. Chiara Frugoni, *Una lontana città* (Turin: Einaudi, 1983), pp. 173ff.

35. Paris: Bibliothèque Nationale, Ms. lat. 16515, fol. 204; Chiara Frugoni, "La rappresentazione dei giullari nelle chiese fino al XII secolo," *Il contributo dei giullari alla drammaturgia italiana delle origini* (Rome: Bulzoni, 1978), pp. 113–134, fig. 18.

36. See the story of the woman who, having read a book about the miracles of Saint Francis, rested the book on her diseased breast, which was promptly cured. The miracle is told by Tommaso da Celano, "Tractatus de miraculis B. Francisci," in *Analecta franciscana*, vol. X (Florence: Ad Claras Aquas, 1941), chap. 18, n. 193, pp. 328–329.

37. Gigetta Dalli Regoli, *Il maestro di Borsigliana. Un pittore del '400 in Alta Val di Serchio* (Lucca: Pacini Fazzi, 1987). A series of examples of this kind have been collected in Danièle Alexandre-Bidon, "La lettre volée, à lire à l'enfant au Moyen Age," in *Annales, E.S.C.* 4(July–August 1989):953–992.

38. Francesco Filippini, Guido Zucchini, *Miniatori e pittori a Bologna: documenti dei secoli XIII e XIV* (Florence: Sansoni, 1947).

39. Claudia Opitz and Elizabeth Schraut, "Frauen und Kunst im Mittelalter," in *Frauenkunstgeschichte . . .* (Giessen, 1984), pp. 33–52.

40. For a bibliography of the poetess and an analysis of her works, in particular the *Epistre,* two articles by Eliana Carrara are forthcoming in *Quaderni Medioevali* and in *Prospettiva.*

41. For this work, see Natalino Sapegno's acute observations in "Il Trecento," *Storia letteraria d'Italia* (Milan: Vallardi, 1966), pp. 358ff.

42. Conserved in The Metropolitan Museum of Art, New York. See the catalogue, *Europe in the Middle Ages* (New York: Metropolitan Museum, 1987), p. 53 and fig. 44.

43. For the various biographies dedicated through the centuries to Radegund, see Chapter 1 by Jacques Dalarun.

44. *Hildegardis Revelationes,* Lucca, Biblioteca Governativa, fol. 143r. For more about Hildegarde, see Maria Teresa Beonio Fumagalli Brocchieri, "Ildegarda, la profetessa," in Ferruccio Bertini, Franco Cardini, Maria Teresa Beonio Fumagalli Brocchieri, and Claudio Leonardi, *Medioevo al femminile* (Rome-Bari: Laterza, 1989), pp. 144–169. (The same volume contains two chapters that refer to Radegund and Hrotswitha.)

45. *De Ida Lewensi virgine,* in *Acta Sanctorum,* XIII, 113.

46. Some information can be gleaned from the following: Elizabeth Schraut and Claudia Opitz, *Frauen und Kunst im Mittelalter,* exhibition catalogue (Braunschweig, 1983); Opitz and Schraut, "Frauen und Kunst"; Claudia Opitz, ed., *Weiblichkeit oder Feminismus* (Weingarten: Drumlin, 1984).

47. Harksen, *La femme au Moyen Age,* p. 46.

48. I shall not discuss here the famous Bayeux tapestry (second half of the twelfth century), also known, in the French tradition though without docu-

mented evidence, as the "tapestry of Queen Matilde" (wife of William the Conqueror, whose gestures are shown on the tapestry). The problem as to who actually conceived and produced this extensively written and illustrated account has long been debated. See C. H. Gibbs-Smith, *The Bayeux Tapestry* (London, 1975), p. 5.

49. Antonio Volpato, "Il tema agiografico della triplice aureola nei secoli XIII–XV," in Sofia Boesch Gajano and Lucia Sebastiani, eds., *Culto dei santi, istituzioni e classi sociali in età preindustriale* (Roma-L'Aquila: Japadre, 1984), pp. 509–526.

50. André Vauchez, *Les Laïcs au Moyen Age. Pratiques et expériences religieuses* (Paris: Cerf, 1978), pp. 169–188, in chapter "Patronage des saints et religion civique dans l'Italie communale."

51. Jane Tibbets-Schulenburg, "Sexism and the Celestial Gynecaeum, from 500 to 1200," *Journal of Medieval History* 4(1978):117–133.

52. Chiara Frugoni, "Santa Bona, pellegrina per desiderio," *Gli universi del fantastico* (Florence: Vallecchi, 1988), pp. 259–272.

53. Chiara Frugoni, "La città e le sante novelline," in Acts of the Conference, *Athens and Rome, Florence and Venice. City-States in Classical Antiquity and Medieval Italy.* Brown University, Providence, Rhode Island (May 1989).

54. *Tommaso da Modena,* catalogue edited by Luigi Menegazzi (Treviso, 1979), figs. pp. 74, 165.

Daring to Speak
C. K.-Z.

1. M. I. King, "Thwarted Ambitions. Six Learned Women of the Italian Renaissance," *Soundings* 59(1976):280–304; P. H. Labalme, ed., *Beyond Their Sex: Learned Women of the European Past* (New York: New York University Press, 1980); M. I. King, *Venetian Humanism in an Age of Patrician Dominance* (Princeton: Princeton University Press, 1986).

Chapter 12. Literary and Mystical Voices
DANIELLE RÉGNIER-BOHLER

1. Dante Alighieri, *De vulgari eloquentia*, I, IV, 1.

2. Marie-Thérèse d'Alverny, "Comment les théologiens et les philosophes voient la femme," quoting Peter Comestor, *Historia scolastica*, in *La femme dans les civilisations des Xe–XIIe siècles* (Poitiers, 1977), pp. 112–113.

3. Georges Duby, *Mâle Moyen Age* (Paris: Flammarion, 1988), p. 57.

4. *Le mirouer aux dames, poème inédit du XVe siècle,* ed. A. Piaget (Paris-Neuchâtel, 1908), l. 500ff.

5. Ibid., l. 757ff.

6. Didier Anzieu, *Le moi-peau* (Paris: Dunod, 1985), p. 227.

7. Marina Mizzau, "Silence à deux voix," *Langages* 85(1987):45.

8. Anne-Marie Houdebine, "Sur les traces de l'imaginaire linguistique," in V. Aebischer and C. Forel, eds., *Parlers masculins, parlers féminins* (Paris,

1983), pp. 105–139; "Les femmes et la langue," *Tel quel* (1977):84–95; "La différence sexuelle et la langue," *Langage et société* 7(1979):3–30.

9. Luce Irigaray, *Parler n'est jamais neutre* (Paris: Minuit, 1985).

10. Verena Aebischer, introduction to Aebischer and Forel, eds., *Parlers masculins, parlers féminins*, p. 9; Irigaray, *Parler n'est jamais neutre*, pp. 281ff.

11. Peter Dronke, *Women Writers of the Middle Ages. A Critical Study of Texts from Perpetua to Marguerite Porete* (Cambridge: Cambridge University Press, 1984).

12. Paul Zumthor, "Litteratus/illiteratus. Remarques sur le contexte vocal de l'écriture médiévale," *Romania* 106(1985):1–18.

13. Pascale Bourgain, *Poésie lyrique latine du Moyen Age* (Paris: Union Générale de l'Edition, 1989), p. 53.

14. Ibid., p. 121.

15. Chaucer, *Canterbury Tales*, The Wife of Bath's Tale, ll. 692–697.

16. Béatrice Slama, "De la littérature féminine à l'écrire femme," *Littérature* 44(December 1981):51.

17. "And the lady was a great poetess and wrote very beautiful love poems about Guy the Battler." Margarita Egan, ed., *Les vies des troubadours* (Paris: Union Générale de l'Edition, 1985), pp. 52–53.

18. Marie-Louise Ollier, "Les lais de Marie de France ou le recueil comme forme," in M. Picone, G. Di Stefano, and P. Stewart, eds., *La nouvelle Genèse, codification et rayonnement d'un genre médiéval* (Montreal: Platon, 1983), pp. 64–78.

19. Ibid., p. 67.

20. Jean-Charles Huchet, "Noms de femme et écriture féminine au Moyen Age," *Poétique* 48(1981):407–430; "Les femmes troubadours ou la voix critique," *Littérature* 51(1983):58–90.

21. Huchet, "Les femmes troubadours," p. 84.

22. Pierre Bec, ed., *Burlesque et obscénité chez les troubadours. Le contre-texte au Moyen Age* (Paris: Stock, 1984), p. 193.

23. Henri Deluy, ed., *Troubadours galégo-portugais. Une anthologie* (Paris: P.O.L., 1987).

24. Bec, ed., *Burlesque et obscénité*, pp. 18–19.

25. Kevin Brownlee, "Discourses of the Self: Christine de Pizan and the *Rose*," *Romanic Review* 79(1988):199–221.

26. Jacqueline Cerchiglini, "L'étrangère," *Revue des langues romaines* 92(2)1988:240.

27. Eric Hicks, *Le débat sur le Roman de la rose* (Paris: Champion, 1977).

28. Ibid., p. 22.

29. Ibid., p. 6.

30. Cerchiglini, "L'étrangère," p. 241.

31. Christine de Pisan, *Le livre de la mutacion de Fortune,* ed. S. Solente (Paris: Picard, 1959–1966), ll. 374ff.

32. Eric Hicks, "Femme-auteur et auteur-femme: Christine de Pizan et

la question féministe," in *La femme et l'art au Moyen Age,* exhibition catalogue (Lausanne, 1984), p. 69.

33. Marie-Thérèse Lorcin, "Mère nature et le devoir social. La mère et l'enfant dans l'oeuvre de Christine de Pizan," *Revue historique,* to come.

34. Christine de Pisan, *Le livre de la mutacion de Fortune,* ll. 1391–1394.

35. Christine de Pisan, *La cité des dames,* trans. Thérèse Moreau and Eric Hicks (Paris: Stock-Moyen Age, 1986), p. 37.

36. Ibid., pp. 48, 58, 60, and 87.

37. Ibid., p. 114.

38. Nathalie Z. Davis, "Gender and Genre: Women as Historical Writers, 1480–1820," in P. H. Labalme, ed., *Beyond Their Sex. Learned Women of the European Past* (New York: New York University Press, 1984), pp. 157–160.

39. "Women should not be taught to read or write." Philippe de Novare, *Les quatre âges d'homme,* ed. Marcel de Fréville (Paris: SATF, 1888), p. 16.

40. Ursula Peters, "Frauenliteratur im Mittelalter? Ueber legungen zur Trobairitzpoesie, zur Frauenmystik und zur eministischen Literaturbetrachtung," *Germanisch-romanische Monatschrift* 69(1988):35–56; "Frauenmystik im 14 Jht. Die 'Offenbarungen' der Christine Ebner," in Claudia Opitz, ed., *Weiblichkeit oder Feminismus* (Weingarten, 1984), pp. 213–227.

41. Andreas Bauch, *Einleitung. Das Leben des Hl. Willibald* (Eichstätt, 1962), pp. 13–15.

42. Dronke, *Medieval Writers,* pp. 36ff.

43. Ernst R. Curtius, *La littérature européenne et le Moyen Age latin* (Paris: Presses Universitaires de France, 1956), chap. 5, pp. 103ff.

44. Dronke, *Women Writers,* p. 76.

45. See G. Epiney-Burgard and E. Zum Brunn, eds., *Femmes troubadours de Dieu* (Brepols, 1988).

46. Peters, "Frauenliteratur."

47. Claudia Opitz, "'. . . zu schreiben von gutten und selgen schwestren uebung.' Frauenmystik und geistliche Literatur in südwestdeutschen Frauenklöstern des Spätmittelalters," in Elisabeth Reuz, ed., *Die Frauenfeder* (Weingarten, 1986), pp. 75–104.

48. Peters, "Frauenmystik," pp. 216ff.

49. Ibid., p. 220.

50. Joan M. Ferrante, "The Education of Women in the Middle Ages in Theory, Fact and Fantasy," in Labalme, ed., *Beyond Their Sex,* pp. 9ff.

51. Michel Lauwers, "Paroles de femmes, sainteté féminine. L'Eglise du XIIIe siècle face aux béguines," in G. Braive and J.-M. Cauchies, eds., *La critique historique à l'épreuve. Liber discipulorum Jacques Paquet* (Brussels, 1989), pp. 108ff.

52. Margaret L. King, "Booklined Cells: Women and Humanism in the Early Italian Renaissance," in Labalme, ed., *Beyond Their Sex,* pp. 66ff.

53. Philippe de Mézières, "Histoire de Grisélidis," in Elie Golenistcheff-

Koutouzoff, *L'histoire de Grisélidis en France au XIVe et au XVe siècle* (Paris: Droz, 1933).

54. The words quoted in the subheading to this section are from "Lai de Yonec," ll. 68–70, in Marie de France, *Lais,* trans. Pierre Jonin (Paris: Champion, 1982), p. 89.

55. Marie-Françoise Notz, "Esthétique de la violence et cruauté de la prose dans 'La fille du comte de Ponthieu,'" *Eidolon* 22(1982):51–68.

56. Robert L. Krueger, "Double Jeopardy: The Appropriation of Woman in Four Old French Romances of the *Cycle de la Gageure,*" in S. Fisher and J. E. Halley, eds., *Seeking the Women in Late Medieval and Renaissance Writings: Essays in Feminist Contextual Criticism* (Knoxville: University of Tennessee Press, 1989), pp. 21–50.

57. F. Lecoy, ed., *Guillaum de Dole ou le Roman de la rose,* ll. 4768–4773, trans. J. Dufournet, J. Kooijman, R. Ménage, and C. Tronc (Paris: Champion, 1979; 2nd ed., 1988), p. 96.

58. Goleinstcheff-Koutouzoff, *L'histoire de Grisélidis en France.*

59. Philippe de Mézières, "Histoire de Grisélidis," ibid., p. 174.

60. Jacques Rossiaud, *La prostitution médiévale* (Paris: Flammarion, 1988), p. 165.

61. Ibid., p. 204.

62. Heldris of Cornwall, *The Romance of Silence,* ed. Lewis Thrope (Cambridge, 1972), ll. 2067–2082.

63. Howard Bloch, *Etymologie et généalogie. Une anthropologie littéraire du Moyen Age français* (Paris: Seuil, 1989), p. 263.

64. Heldris of Cornwall, *The Romance of Silence,* ll. 2532–2538.

65. Ibid., ll. 2637–2638.

66. Philippe de Novare, *Les quatre âges d'homme,* p. 14.

67. Verena Aebischer, "Bavardages, sens commun et linguistique," in Aebischer and Forel, eds., *Parlers masculins, parlers féminins,* p. 173.

68. Jean de Meung, *Roman de la rose,* ed. Daniel Poirion (Paris: Garnier-Flammarion, 1974), ll. 16347–16352; trans. A. Lanly, book 2, vol. 3, p. 151.

69. Anatole de Montaiglon, *Le livre du Chevalier de La Tour Landry pour l'enseignement de ses filles* (Paris: P. Jannet, 1854), p. 259.

70. Ibid., p. 116.

71. Madelein Jeay, ed., *Les Evangiles des quenouilles* (Montreal: Presses de l'Université de Montréal, 1985).

72. Ibid., p. 116.

73. Ibid., pp. 10–11.

74. Madeleine Jeay, "Savoir faire. Une analyse des croyances des *Evangiles des quenouilles,*" in *Le moyen français* 10(1982):232.

75. Poirion, ed., *Roman de la rose,* l. 19213; trans., book 2, vol. 4, p. 103.

76. Ibid., ll. 19209–19217; trans., book 2, vol. 4, pp. 102–103.

77. Ibid., ll. 9155–9156; trans., book 2, vol. 2, p. 36.

78. Danielle Régnier-Bohler, "Femme/faute/fantasme," *La condición de*

la mujer en la Edad Media (Madrid: Universidad Complutense, 1986), pp. 475–499.

79. Le livre du Chevalier de La Tour Landry, pp. 27–28.

80. "Le vilain de Bailleul," in A. de Montaiglon, ed., Recueil général et complet des fabliaux des XIIe et XIVe siècles (Paris: 1872–1890), IV, 213–214; trans. in Contes à rire du Nord de la France (La Ferté-Milon: Corps 9 Editions, 1987), p. 21.

81. Montaiglon, ed., Recueil, V, 50; trans. in Nora Scott, ed., Fabliaux des XIIIe et XIVe siècles. Contes pour rire? (Paris: Union Générale de l'Edition, 1977), p. 167.

82. Montaiglon, ed., Recueil, vol. 6, p. 103; trans. Fabliaux, p. 197.

83. Ibid., vol. 6, p. 114; trans. Fabliaux, p. 203.

84. G. A. Brunelli, "Jean Castel et le Mirouer des dames et damoyselles et de tout le sexe féminin," Le Moyen Age 62(1956):93–117.

85. Dante, "De vulgari eloquentia."

86. Poirion, ed., Roman de la rose, ll. 6928–6931; trans., book 2, vol. I, p. 113.

87. Ibid., ll. 6956–6972; trans., book 2, vol. I, pp. 117–118.

88. Ibid., ll. 7037–7043; trans., book 2, vol. I, pp. 117–118.

89. Ibid., ll. 7095–7096; trans., book I, vol. I, p. 120.

90. Ibid., ll. 7116–7125; trans., book 2, vol. I, p. 121.

91. Nancy Huston, Dire et interdire. Eléments de jurologie (Paris: Payot, 1980), p. 121.

92. Montaiglon, ed., Recueil, V, 103; trans. Fabliaux, p. 168.

93. "De la pucele qui abevra le poulain," in Montaiglon, ed., Recueil, IV, 199; trans. Fabliaux, pp. 172ff.

94. Montaiglon, ed., Recueil, I, 318ff.; trans. Fabliaux, pp. 176ff.

95. Montaiglon, ed., Recueil, V, 204; trans. Fabliaux, p. 60.

96. "Li sohaiz desvez," in Jean Bodel, Fabliaux, ed. P. Nardin (Paris: Nizet, 1965), p. 45; trans. Contes à rire du nord de la France, pp. 31–34.

97. C. H. Livingston, Le jongleur Gautier Le Leu. Etudes sur les fabliaux (Cambridge, Mass.: Harvard University Press, 1951); trans. in Contes à rire, p. 61.

98. Ibid., trans. p. 179.

99. Chaucer, The Canterbury Tales, prologue to the Wife of Bath, ll. 149–159.

100. "And whan that I hadde geten unto me / By maistrie al the soveraynetee." Ibid., ll. 817–818.

101. Jacques Dalarun, "Hors des sentiers battus. Saintes femmes d'Italie aux XIIIe–XIVe siècles," to come.

102. Lauwers, "Paroles de femmes," pp. 103–108.

103. Louis Magdinier, trans., Le livre de Margery Kempe. Une aventurière de la foi au Moyen Age (Paris: Cerf, 1989), p. 125.

104. Ibid., pp. 146–147.

105. Zumthor, "Litteratus/illiteratus," p. 6.

106. Hadewijch, *Lettres spirituelles,* trans. Fr. J.B. M.P. (Geneva: Claude Martingay, 1972), letter XVII, p. 143.

107. A. Duraffour, P. Gardette, and P. Durdilly, eds., *Les oeuvres de Marguerite d'Oingt* (Paris: Les Belles Lettres, 1965), p. 91.

108. Ibid., "Speculum," p. 95.

109. Marie-Christine Pouchelle, "Le corps féminin et ses paradoxes: l'imaginaire de l'intériorité dans les écrits médicaux et religieux (XIIe–XIVe siècles)," in *La condición de la mujer,* pp. 315–331.

110. Hildegard of Bingen, *Livre des oeuvres divines,* trans. B. Gorceix (Paris: Albin Michel, 1982), pp. 3–4.

111. Ibid., p. 216.

112. Quoted by Margot Schmidt, "Elemente der Schau bei Mechtild von Magdeburg und Mechtild von Hackeborn. Zur Bedeutung der geistlichen Sinne," in *Frauenmystik im Mittelalter,* p. 147. Excerpts from *La lumière ruisselante de la Déité* are translated in *Femmes troubadours de Dieu,* p. 84.

113. "Aliquas etiam vidisti mulieres tam speciali et mirabili in Deum amoris affectione bili in Deum amoris affectione resolutas, ut prae desiderio languerent, nec a lecto per multos annos nisi surgere possent," Jacques de Vitry goes on to say. See André Vauchez, "Prosélytisme et action antihérétique en milieu féminin au XIIIe siècle: la 'Vie de Marie d'Oignies' (1213) par Jacques de Vitry," in Jean Marx, ed., *Propagande et contre-propagande religieuses. Problèmes d'histoire du christianisme* (Brussels: Editions de l'Université, 1987), pp. 95–110.

114. Rubebeuf, *Oeuvres complètes,* ed. Michel Zink (Paris: Bordas, 1989), I, 239.

115. André Vauchez, "L'idéal de sainteté dans le mouvement féminin franciscain aux XIIIe et XIVe siècles," in *Movimento relgioso femminile e francescanesimo nel secolo XIII. Atti del VIIe Convegno della Società internazionale di studi francescani, Assisi, 11–13 ott. 1979* (Assisi, 1980), pp. 317–337; Anna Benvenuti Papi, "Penitenza e santità femminile in ambiente cateriniano e bernardiniano," in *Atti del simposio internazionale cateriniano bernardiniano (1980)* (Siena: Accademia Senese degli Intronati, 1982), pp. 865–875.

116. Vauchez, "L'idéal de sainteté," p. 326.

117. Vauchez, "Prosélytisme."

118. Ibid., p. 100.

119. Hadewijch, *Lettres spirituelles,* letter XVII, p. 142.

120. Raymond of Capua, "Vita," quoted by Odile Redon, "Catherine corps et âme," in *La représentation du corps dans la culture italienne. Actes du Colloque d'Aix-en-Provence, 1982* (Aix-en-Provence: Publications de l'Université de Provence, 1983), pp. 77–86 (quotation on p. 83).

121. Schmidt, "Elemente der Schau."

122. *Les oeuvres de Marguerite d'Oingt,* pp. 145–146.

123. Dalarun, "Hors des sentiers battus."

124. *Les oeuvres de Marguerite d'Oingt,* p. 142.

125. Beatrice of Nazareth, *Sept degrés d'amour,* trans. Fr. J.B. M.P. (Geneva: Claude Martingay, 1972), "fifth degree of love," p. 240.

126. "Saepe corpus ejus cum spiritu elevabatur a terra, ut quanta esset virtus spiritum attrahens cerneretur," *Legenda Maior,* quoted by Redon, "Catherine corps et âme," p. 85.

127. Michel de Certeau, *La fable mystique. XVIe–XVII siècles* (Paris: Gallimard, 1982), p. 15.

128. Dalarun, "Hors des sentiers battus."

129. *Le livre de Margery Kempe,* p. 265.

130. Ibid., p. viii.

131. Ibid., p. 68.

132. Ibid., pp. 148–149.

133. *Oeuvres de Marguerite d'Oingt,* p. 143.

134. Caroline W. Bynum, *Holy Feast and Holy Fast. The Religious Significance of Food to Medieval Women* (Berkeley: University of California Press, 1987), esp. chap. 5.

135. Hadewijch of Antwerp, *Ecrits mystiques des béguines traduits du moyen néerlandais, Mengeldichten,* 16, trans. J.-B. F. (Paris: Seuil, 1954), p. 124.

136. Ibid., *Strophische Gedichten,* XXXIII, p. 109.

137. "Vie de sainte Béatrice d'Ornacieux," in *Les oeuvres de Marguerite d'Oingt,* pp. 122–123.

138. See note 135 by the translator of these poems, p. 102.

139. Dalarun, "Hors des sentiers battus."

140. Hadewijch, *Lettres spirituelles,* letter XX, p. 158.

141. Hadewijch, *Mengeldichten,* XVII, trans. in *Femmes troubadours de Dieu,* p. 166.

142. Hadewijch, *Lettres spirituelles,* letter XX, p. 158.

143. Hadewijch of Antwerp, *Strophische Gedichten,* XXXI, p. 105.

144. Translated in *Femmes troubadours de Dieu,* p. 105.

145. Michel Zink, *La subjectivité littéraire* (Paris: Presses Universitaires de France, 1985).

146. Brian Stock, "Writing and Internal Time-Consciousness: Othloh of St. Emmeram," in *Le nombre du temps. En hommage à P. Zumthor* (Paris: Champion, 1988), pp. 163–271.

147. Peter Dinzelbacher, *Vision und Visionsliteratur im Mittelalter* (Stuttgart: Anton Hiersemann, 1981).

148. Hadewijch, *Lettres spirituelles,* letter XI, p. 110.

149. Zink, *La subjectivité littéraire,* p. 244.

150. Hadewijch, *Lettres spirituelles,* letter XXV, p. 195.

151. Quoted by Roland Maisonneuve, *L'univers visionnaire de Julian of Norwich* (Paris: Les Deux Rives, 1987), p. 50.

152. Dalarun, "Hors des sentiers battus."

153. De Certeau, *La fable mystique,* pp. 244ff.

154. Hadewijch, *Lettres spirituelles,* letter XX, p. 159.

Affidavits and Confessions
GEORGES DUBY

1. *Le registre d'inquisition de Jacques Fournier, évêque de Pamiers (1318–1325)*, 3 vols. (Toulouse, 1965), and *Le registre d'inquisition de Jacques Fournier* (Paris-The Hague-New York, 1978), 3 vols.

Bibliography

Aebischer, Verena. *Les femmes et le langage: Représentations sociales d'une différence*. Paris: P.U.F., 1985.

Agrimi, Jole, and Chiara Crisciani. "Immagini e ruoli della *vetula* tra sapere medico e antropologia religiosa (secoli XIII e XV)." In *Poteri carismatici e informali della chiesa e della società medievali*. Palermo: Sellerio, 1992, pp. 212–248.

Albistur, Maïté, and Daniel Armogathe. *Histoire du féminisme français du Moyen Age à nos jours*. Paris: Ed. des Femmes, 1977.

Alexandre-Bidon, Danièle, and Monique Closson. *L'enfant à l'ombre des cathédrales*. Lyons: P.U.L. / Ed. du C.N.R.S., 1985.

——— and Françoise Piponnier. "Gestes et objets de la toilette aux XIVe et XVe siècles." In *Les soins de beauté: Moyen Age, début des Temps modernes*. Nice: Faculté des Lettres et Sciences Humaines, 1987. Pp. 211–244.

Allen, Prudence. *The Concept of Woman: The Aristotelian Revolution, 750 B.C.–A.D. 1250*. Montreal: Eden Press, 1985.

Alverny, Marie-Thérèse d'. "Comment les théologiens et les philosophes voient la femme." In *La femme dans la civilisation des Xe–XIIIe siècles*. "Cahiers de civilisation médiévale," 20. Poitiers, 1977. Pp. 105–129.

Ariès, Philippe, and Georges Duby, eds. *Revelations of the Medieval World*. Vol. II of *A History of Private Life*. Cambridge, Mass.: Harvard University Press, 1988.

Atkinson, Clarissa W. "Precious Balsam in a Fragile Glass: The Ideology of Virginity in the Later Middle Ages." *Journal of Family History* 8 (1983): 131–143.

Baker, Derek, ed. *Medieval Women*. Oxford: Basil Blackwell, 1978.

Baldwin, Frances Elizabeth. *Sumptuary Legislation and Personal Regulation in England*. Baltimore: Johns Hopkins University Press, 1926.

Barchewitz, J. *Von der Wirtschaftstätigkeit der Frau in der vorgeschichtlichen Zeit bis zur Entfaltung der Stadtwirtschaft*. Breslau, 1937.

Barkai, Ron. "A Medieval Hebrew Treatise on Obstetrics." *Medical History* 33 (1988): 96–119.

Batany, Jean. *Approches du Roman de la rose*. Collection "Etudes," 363, Série bleue. Paris: Bordas, 1973.

——— "Les *Estats* au féminin: Un problème de vocabulaire social du XIIe au XVe siècle." *Annales de la Faculté des Lettres et Sciences Humaines de Nice* 48 (1984): 51–59.

Baur, Veronika. *Kleiderordnung in Bayern vom 14. bis zum 19. Jahrhundert.* Munich: R. Wolfe, 1975.

Bell, Rudolph M. *Holy Anorexia*. Chicago: University of Chicago Press, 1985.

Benton, John F. "Women's Problems and the Professionalization of Medicine in the Middle Ages." *Bulletin of the History of Medicine* 59 (1985): 30–53.

Benvenuti Papi, Anna. "'Velut in sepulchro': Cellane e recluse nella tradizione agiografica italiana." In Sofia Boesch Gajano and Lucia Sebastiani, eds., *Culto dei santi, istituzioni e classi sociali in età preindustriale*. Rome: Japadre, 1985. Pp. 365–455.

Berman, Constance H., Charles W. Connell, and Judith Rice Rothschild. *The Worlds of Medieval Women: Creativity, Influence, Imagination*. Morgantown: West Virginia University Press, 1985.

Bernis, Carmen. *Trajes y modas en la España de los Reyes Catolicos*. 2 vols. Madrid: Istituto Diego Velasquez del Consejo Superior de Investigaciones Cientificas, 1979.

Bertini, Ferruccio, Franco Cardini, Maria-Teresa Beonio-Brocchieri, and Claudio Leonardi. *Medievo al femminile*. Bari: Laterza, 1989.

Bibliotheca Sanctorum. 12 vols. Rome: Pontificia Università Lateranense, 1963–1969.

Bistort, G. *Il Magistrato alle pompe nella repubblica di Venezia: Studio storico*. Venice: La Società, 1912.

Bloch, Howard R. "Medieval Misogyny: Woman as Riot." *Representations* 20 (1987): 1–24.

——— *The Scandal of the Fabliaux*. Chicago: University of Chicago Press, 1986.

Blumenkranz, Bernard. *Le Juif médiéval au miroir de l'art chrétien*. Paris: Etudes Augustiniennes, 1966.

Bornstein, Diane. *The Lady in the Tower: Medieval Courtesy Literature for Women*. Hamden, Conn.: Archon, for Shoe String Press, 1983.

Børrensen, Kari Elisabeth. *Anthropologie médiévale et théologie mariale*. Oslo: Universitetsforlaget, 1971.

——— *Subordination et équivalence: Nature et rôle de la femme d'après Augustin et Thomas d'Aquin*. Oslo and Paris: Universitetsforlaget and Maison Mame, 1968.

Boschinger, Danielle, and André Crépin, eds. *Amour, mariage et transgressions au Moyen Age*. Proceedings of a colloquium held March 1983 at the University of Picardie, Centre d'Etudes Médiévales. Kümmerle: Goppingen, 1984.

Boswell, John. *Christianity, Social Tolerance and Homosexuality*. Chicago: University of Chicago Press, 1980.

Boucher, François. *Twenty-Thousand Years of Fashion*. New York: Harry Abrams, 1967.

Bridenthal, R., and C. Koonz, eds. *Becoming Visible: Women in European History*. Boston: Houghton Mifflin, 1977; new ed., 1987.

Brodmeier, Beate. *Die Frau im Handwerk in historischer und moderner Sicht*. Forschungsberichte aus dem Handwerk 9. Münster, 1963.

Brody, Saul N. *The Disease of the Soul: Leprosy in Medieval Literature*. Ithaca, N.Y.: Cornell University Press, 1974.

Brooke, Christopher. *The Medieval Idea of Marriage*. Oxford: Oxford University Press, 1989.

Brucato, histoire et archéologie d'un habitat médiéval en Sicile. Ed. J. M. Pesez. 2 vols. Rome: Ecole Française de Rome, 1984.

Brundage, James A. *Law, Sex, and Christian Society in Medieval Europe*. Chicago: University of Chicago Press, 1987.

———— "Sumptuary Laws and Prostitution in Late Medieval Italy." *Journal of Medieval History* 13 (1987): 343–355.

Bucaille, Richard, and Françoise Piponnier. "La belle ou la bête? Remarques sur l'apparence corporelle de la paysannerie médiévale." *Ethnologie française* 6, nos. 3–4 (1976): 227–232.

Bugge, John. *"Virginitas": An Essay on the History of a Medieval Ideal*. The Hague: M. Nijhoff, 1975.

Bullough, Vern L. "Medieval Medical and Scientific Views on Women." *Viator* 4 (1973): 485–501.

———— and James A. Brundage. *Sexual Practices and the Medieval Church*. New York: Prometheus Books, 1982.

Burguière, A., C. Klapisch-Zuber, M. Segalen, and F. Zonabend, eds. *Mondes lointains, mondes anciens*. Vol. 1 of *Histoire de la famille*. Paris: A. Colin.

Bynum, Caroline Walker. *Holy Feast and Holy Fast: The Religious Significance of Food to Medieval Women*. Berkeley: University of California Press, 1987.

———— *Jesus as Mother: Studies in the Spirituality of the High Middle Ages*. Los Angeles: University of California Press, 1982.

Cadden, Joan. "Medieval Scientific and Medical Views of Sexuality: Questions of Propriety." *Medievalia et Humanistica*, n.s. 14 (1986): 157–171.

Caroll, B. A., ed. *Liberating Women's History*. Urbana: University of Illinois Press, 1976.

Casagrande, Carla. *Prediche delle donne del secolo XIII*. Milan: Bompiani, 1978.

Chapelot, Jean, and Robert Fossier. *Le village et la maison au Moyen Age*. Paris: Hachette, 1980.

Charles, Lindsey, and Lorna Duffin, eds. *Women and Work in Pre-Industrial England*. London: Croom Helm, 1985.

Corbet, Patrick. *Les saints ottoniens: Sainteté dynastique, sainteté royale et sainteté féminine autour de l'an mil*. "Beilhefte der Francia," 15. Sigmaringen: Thorbecke, 1986.

543

Curtius, Ernst R. *La littérature européenne et le Moyen Age latin.* 2 vols. Paris: Agora, 1986.

Dalarun, Jacques. *Robert d'Arbrissel, fondateur de Fontevraud.* Paris: Albin Michel, 1986.

D'Alverny, Marie-Thérèse. "Comment les théologiens et les philosophes voient la femme." *Actes du colloque: La femme dans les civilisations des Xe–XIIIe siècles.* Poitiers, 1976. Also in *Cahiers de civilisation médiévale* 20 (1977): 105–128.

D'Ancona, Paolo. *Le vesti delle donne fiorentine nel sec. XIV.* Perugia, 1906.

Dauphin, Cécile, et al. "Culture et pouvoir des femmes: Essai d'historiographie." *Annales, E.S.C.* 41 (1986): 271–293.

D'Avray, David. "The Gospel of the Marriage Feast of Cana and Marriage Preaching in France." In K. Walsh and S. Wood, eds., *The Bible in the Medieval World: Essays in Memory of Beryl Smalley.* Oxford: Basil Blackwell, 1985. Pp. 207–224.

—— and L. M. Tauche. "Marriage Sermons in *ad status* Collections of the Central Middle Ages." *Archives d'histoire doctrinale et littéraire du Moyen Age* 47 (1980): 71–119.

Delort, Robert. *La vie au Moyen Age.* Paris: Seuil, 1982.

De Maio, Romeo. *Donna e Rinascimento.* Milan: Mondadori, 1987.

De Matteis, Maria Consiglia. *Idee sulla donna nel Medioevo: Fonti e aspetti giuridici, antropologici, religiosi, sociali e letterari della condizione femminile.* Bologna: Pàtron, 1981.

Demians D'Archimbaud, Gabrielle. *Les fouilles de Rougiers (Var): Contribution à l'étude de l'habitat rural médiéval en pays méditerranéen.* Paris: Ed. du C.N.R.S., 1981.

Desportes, Françoise. *Le pain au Moyen Age.* Paris: Olivier Orban, 1987.

Devailly, Guy. "Un évêque et un prédicateur errant au XIIe siècle: Marbode de Rennes et Robert d'Arbrissel." *Mémoires de la Société d'Histoire et d'Archéologie de Bretagne* 57 (1980): 163–170.

Diepgen, Paul. *Frau und Frauenheilkunde in der Kultur des Mittelalters.* Stuttgart: Georg Thieme, 1963.

Dinzelbacher, Peter, ed. *Vision und Visionliteratur im Mittelalter.* Stuttgart: A. Hiersemann, 1981.

—— and Dieter R. Bauer, eds. *Frauenmystik im Mittelalter.* Stuttgart: Schwabenverlag, 1985.

—— eds. *Religiöse Frauenbewegung und mystische Frömmigkeit im Mittelalter.* Cologne: Böhlau, 1988.

Dragonetti, Roger. *Le gai savoir dans la rhétorique courtoise.* Paris: Seuil, 1982.

Dronke, Peter. *Women Writers of the Middle Ages: A Critical Study of Texts from Perpetua to Marguerite Porete.* Cambridge: Cambridge University Press, 1984.

Duby, Georges. *Le chevalier, la femme et le prêtre: Le mariage dans la France féodale.* Paris: Hachette, 1981.

———— *Mâle Moyen Age: De l'amour et autres essais.* Paris: Flammarion, 1988.

———— *Medieval Marriage: Two Models from Twelfth-Century France.* Baltimore: Johns Hopkins University Press, 1978.

———— *Les trois ordres ou l'imaginaire du féodalisme.* Paris: Gallimard, 1978.

Dulac, Liliane. "Inspiration mystique et savoir politique: Les conseils aux veuves chez Francesco da Barberino et chez Christine de Pisan." In *Mélanges à la mémoire de Franco Simone,* vol. 1. Geneva: Slatkine, 1980. Pp. 113–141.

Duperray, Eve, ed. *Marie Madeleine dans la mystique, les arts et les lettres: Actes du colloque international, Avignon, 20–22 juillet 1988.* Paris: Beauchesne, 1989.

Eisenbart, Liselotte Constanze. *Kleiderordnungen der deutschen Städte zwischen 1350 und 1700.* Göttingen: Musterschmidt, 1962.

Elshtain, Jean Bethke. *Public Man, Private Woman: Women in Social and Political Thought.* Princeton: Princeton University Press, 1981.

Ennen, Edith. *The Medieval Woman.* Oxford: Basil Blackwell, 1989.

Epiney-Burgard, and E. Zum Brunn, eds. and trans. *Femmes troubadours de Dieu.* Collection "Trémoines de notre histoire." Brepols, 1988.

Erickson, Carolly, and Kathleen Casey. "Women in the Middle Ages: A Working Bibliography." *Medieval Studies* 37 (1975): 340–359.

Erler, M., and M. Kowaleski, eds. *Women and Power in the Middle Ages.* Athens, Ga.: University of Georgia Press, 1988.

Farmer, Sharon. "Persuasive Voices: Clerical Images of Medieval Wives." *Speculum* 61 (1986): 517–543.

Fehring, Günter P. "Der Beitrag der Archäologie zum Leben in der Stadt des späten Mittelalters." In *Das Leben in der Stadt des Spätmittelalters: International Kongress, Krems, sept. 1976.* Vienna: Österreichische Akademie der Wissenschaften, 1977.

La Femme. "Recueils de la Société Jean Bodin pour l'histoire comparative des institutions," 12, 2. Brussels: Librairie Encyclopédique, 1962.

La Femme et l'art au Moyen Age: Catalogue de l'exposition de Lausanne, 1984. Presented by E. Schraut and Claudia Opitz, with d'A. Rapetti, W. Lenschen, and E. Hicks. Lausanne, 1984.

La Femme dans les civilisations des Xe–XIIIe siècles: Actes du Colloque tenu à Poitiers les 23–25 septembre 1976. Poitiers: Centre d'Etudes Supérieures de Civilisation Médiévale, 1977.

Ferguson, Margaret W., Maureen Quilligan, and Nancy J. Vickers, eds. *Rewriting the Renaissance: The Discourses of Sexual Difference in Early Modern Europe.* Chicago: University of Chicago Press, 1986.

Ferrante, Joan M. "The Education of Women in the Middle Ages in Theory, Fact, and Fantasy." In Patricia H. Labalme, ed., *Beyond Their Sex: Learned Women of the European Past.* New York: New York University Press, 1980.

———— *Woman as Image in Medieval Literature from the Twelfth Century to Dante.* New York: Columbia University Press, 1975.

Flandrin, Jean-Louis. *Le sexe et l'Occident: Evolution des attitudes et des comportements*. Paris: Seuil, 1981.

———— *Un temps pour embrasser: Aux origines de la morale sexuelle occidentale (VIe–XIe siècles)*. Paris: Seuil, 1983.

Fonquerne, Yves-René, and Alfonso Esteban, eds. *La condición de la mujer en la Edad Media: Actas del coloquio celebrado en la Casa de Velasquez del 5 al 7 nov. de 1984*. Madrid: Universidad Complutense, 1986.

Fontette, Micheline Potenay de. *Les religieuses à l'âge classique du droit canon*. Paris: Vrin, 1967.

Fossier, Robert. *Enfance de l'Europe*. Collection "Nouvelle Clio." 2 vols. Paris: P.U.F., 1982.

Fox, John Howard. *Robert de Blois, son oeuvre didactique et narrative: Etude linguistique et littéraire*. Followed by *L'enseignement des princes* and *Le chastoiement des dames*. Paris: Nizet, 1948.

Frau und Spätmittelalterlicher Alltag: Internationaler Kongress. "Veröffentlichungen des Instituts für Mittelalterliche Realienkunde Österreichs," 9. Vienna: Verlag der Österreichischen Akademie der Wissenschaften, 1986.

Frugoni, Chiara. "L'iconographia del matrimonio e della coppia nel Medioevo." In *Il matrimonio nella società altomedievale: Settimane di studio del Centro Italiano di Studi sull'Alto Medioevo 24* (1976). 2 vols. Spoleto, 1977.

———— "L'iconographie de la femme au cours des Xe–XIIe siècles." In *La femme dans la civilisation des Xe–XIIIe siècle*. Proceedings of a colloquium held at Poitiers, Sept. 1976. In "Cahiers de civilisation medievale," 20. Poitiers: Centre d'Etudes Supérieures de Civilisation Médiévale, 1977. Pp. 177–188.

———— *Una lontana città: Sentimenti e immagini nel Medioevo*. Turin: Einaudi, 1983.

———— "Le mistiche, le visioni e l'iconografia: Rapporti ed influssi." In *La mistica femminile del Trecento: Atti del convegno di Todi, 1982*. Todi, 1983.

Garin, Eugenio. *L'educazione umanistica in Italia*. Bari: Laterza, 1949.

Gaudemet, Jean. *Le mariage en Occident: Les moeurs et le droit*. Paris: Cerf, 1987.

Gold, Penny Schine. *The Lady and the Virgin: Image, Attitude, and Experience in Twelfth-Century France*. Chicago: University of Chicago Press, 1985.

Goody, Jack. *The Development of the Family and Marriage in Europe*. Cambridge: Cambridge University Press, 1983.

Greer, Germaine. *The Obstacle Race: The Fortunes of Women Painters and Their Work*. New York: Farrar, Straus and Giroux, 1979.

Grimal, Pierre, ed. *Histoire mondiale de la femme*. Paris: Nouvelle Librairie de France, 1966.

Grundmann, Herbert. *Religiöse Bewegungen im Mittelalter*. Rev. ed. Hildesheim: G. Olms, 1961.

Hanawalt, Barbara A. *Crime and Conflict in English Communities, 1300–1348*. Cambridge, Mass.: Harvard University Press, 1979.

Harksen, Sibylle. *Die Frau im Mittelalter.* Leipzig: Aufbau-Verlag, 1974.

Hasenohr, Geneviève. "La vie quotidienne de la femme vue par l'Eglise: L'enseignement des 'Journées chrétiennes' de la fin du Moyen Age." In *Frau und Spätmittelalterlicher Alltag.* Vienna, 1986. Pp. 19–101.

Heaney, Seamus. *The Development of the Sacramentality of Marriage from Anselm of Laon to Thomas Aquinas.* Washington, D.C.: Catholic University of America Press, 1963.

Helmholz, Richard H. *Marriage Litigation in Medieval England.* Cambridge: Cambridge University Press, 1974.

Hentch, Alice Adèle. *De la littérature didactique du Moyen Age s'adressant spécialement aux femmes.* Cahors: Imprimerie Coueslaut, 1903.

Herald, Jacqueline. *Renaissance Dress in Italy, 1400–1500.* London: Bell and Hyman, 1981.

Herlihy, David. *Medieval Households.* Cambridge, Mass.: Harvard University Press, 1985.

——— *Women in Medieval Society.* "Smith History Lectures," 14. Houston, 1971.

——— and Christiane Klapisch-Zuber. *Les Toscans et leurs familles: Une étude du "catasto" florentin de 1427.* Paris: Presses de la Fondation Nationale des Sciences Politiques, 1978.

Herrade of Hoehenbourg. *Hortus Deliciarum.* Ed. R. Green. 2 vols. London: Warburg Institute, 1979.

Hewson, M. Anthony. *Giles of Rome and the Medieval Theory of Conception.* London: Athlone Press, 1975.

Hicks, Eric, ed. and trans. *Le débat sur le Roman de la rose: Christine de Pizan, Jean Gerson, Jean de Montreuil, Gontier et Pierre Col.* Collection "Bibliothèque du XVe siècle." Paris: Champion, 1977.

Howell, Martha C. *Women, Production, and Patriarchy in Late Medieval Cities.* Chicago: University of Chicago Press, 1986.

Huchet, Jean-Charles. *L'amour dit courtois: La "Fin amors" chez les premiers troubadours.* Toulouse: Privat, 1987.

Hughes, Diane Owen. "Distinguishing Signs: Ear-Rings, Jews and Franciscan Rhetoric in the Italian Renaissance City." *Past and Present* 112 (1986): 3–59.

——— "Sumptuary Law and Social Relations in Renaissance Italy." In John Bossy, ed., *Disputes and Settlements: Law and Human Relations in the West.* Cambridge: Cambridge University Press, 1983. Pp. 69–99.

Hughes, Muriel J. *Women Healers in Medieval Life and Literature.* New York: King's Crown Press, 1943.

Index of Christian Art. Princeton, N.J.: Princeton University Library.

Irigaray, Luce. *Ethique de la difference sexuelle.* Paris: Minuit, 1984.

Jacquart, Danielle, and Claude Thomasset. "Albert le Grand et les problèmes de la sexualité." *History and Philosophy of the Life Sciences* 3 (1981): 73–93.

——— *Sexuality and Medicine in the Middle Ages.* Princeton, N.J.: Princeton University Press, 1988.

547

Juster, Jean. *La condition légale des Juifs sous les rois Visigoths*. Paris: Geuthner, 1911.

Kaftal, George. *Iconography of the Saints in Central and South Italian Painting*. Florence: Le Lettere, 1986.

―――― *Iconography of the Saints in the Paintings of Northeast Italy*. Florence: Sansoni, 1978.

―――― *Iconography of the Saints in Tuscan Painting*. Florence: Sansoni, 1978.

―――― with F. Bisogni. *Iconography of the Saints in the Paintings of Northwest Italy*. Florence: Le Lettere, 1985.

Kantorowicz, Hermann, with N. Denholm-Young. "*De Ornatu Mulierum:* A Consilium of Antonius de Rosellis with an Introduction on Fifteenth-Century Sumptuary Legislation." In *Rechtshistorische Schriften*. Karlsruhe: C. M. Miller. Pp. 315–376.

Karnein, A. *"De Amore" in volkprachlicher Literatur: Untersuchungen zur Andreas Capellanus Rezeption in Mittelalter und Renaissance*. Heidelberg: C. Winter, 1985.

Katzenellenbogen, Adolf. *Allegories of the Virtues and Vices in Medieval Art, from Early Christian Times to the Thirteenth Century*. London: Warburg Institute, 1939. New ed., Liechtenstein: Kraus Reprints Nendeln, 1977.

Kelly, Joan. *Women, History, and Theory*. Chicago: University of Chicago Press, 1984.

Kelso, Ruth. *Doctrine for the Lady of the Renaissance*. Urbana: University of Illinois Press, 1956.

Kerbrat-Orecchioni, Catherine. *L'énonciation de la subjectivité dans le langage*. Paris: A. Colin, 1980.

―――― *L'Implicite*. Paris: A. Colin, 1986.

Ketsch, Peter. *Frauen im Mittelalter*. Ed. A. Kuhn. 2 vols. Düsseldorf: Schwann-Bagel, 1984.

King, Margaret L. *La donna nel Rinascimento*. Bari: Laterza, 1991.

King, P. D. *Law and Society in the Visigothic Kingdom*. Cambridge: Cambridge University Press, 1972. Pp. 222–250.

Kirschbaum, E., ed. *Lexikon der christlichen Ikonographie*. 8 vols. Freiburg: Herder, 1968–1976.

Kirshner, J., and Suzanne F. Wemple, eds. *Women of the Medieval World: Essays in Honor of John H. Mundy*. Oxford: Basil Blackwell, 1985.

Klapisch-Zuber, Christiane. *La famiglia e le donne nel Rinascimento e Firenze*. Bari: Laterza, 1988.

―――― *Women, Family, and Ritual in Renaissance Italy*. Tr. Lydia Cochrane. Chicago: University of Chicago Press, 1985.

Knibiehler, Yvonne, and Catherine Fouquet. *L'histoire des mères du Moyen Age à nos jours*. Paris: Montalba, 1980.

Koch, Gottfried. *Frauenfrage und Ketzertum im Mittelalter. Die Frauenbewegung im Rahmen des Katharismus und des Waldensertums und ihre sozialen Wurzeln (12.–14. Jahrhunderte)*. Berlin: Akademie Verlag, 1962.

Koehler, Théodore. "Marie (Vierge), III: Du Moyen Age aux Temps modernes." In *Dictionnaire de spiritualité, ascétique et mystique, doctrine et histoire,* vol. 1. Beauchesne, 1980.

Kraemer, Pierre. *Le luxe et les lois somptuaires au Moyen Age.* Paris: E. Sagot, 1920.

Kusche, Brigit. "Zur 'Secreta mulierum' Forschung." *Janus* 62 (1975): 103–123.

Labalme, Patricia H., ed. *Beyond Their Sex: Learned Women of the European Past.* New York: New York University Press, 1984.

——— "Venetian Women on Women: Three Early Modern Feminists." *Archivio veneto,* ser. V, 116 (1981): 81–109.

Lambertini, Roberto. "Per una storia dell'*economica* tra alto e basso Medioevo." *Cheiron* 4 (1985): 45–74.

Langlois, Charles V. *La société française au XIIIe siècle d'après dix romans d'aventure.* Paris: Hachette, 1904.

Laurent, Sylvie. *Naître au Moyen Age: De la conception à la naissance—la grossesse et l'accouchement (XIIe–XVe siècles).* Paris: Le Léopard d'Or, 1989.

Lawn, Brian. *The Prose Salernitan Questions.* Oxford: Oxford University Press, 1979.

Le Bras, Gabriel. "La doctrine du mariage chez les théologiens et les canonistes depuis l'an mil." In *Dictionnaire de théologie catholique* 9, 2.

Leclercq, Dom Jean. *Le mariage vu par les moines au XIIe siècle.* Paris: Cerf, 1983.

——— "Saint Bernard et la dévotion médiévale envers Marie." *Revue d'ascétique et de mystique* 30 (1954): 361–375.

Lefevre, Yves. "La femme du Moyen Age en France, dans la vie littéraire et spirituelle." In Pierre Grimal, ed., *Histoire mondiale de la femme,* vol. 2. Paris: Nouvelle Librairie de France, 1966. Pp. 79–134.

Le Goff, Jacques. *La civilisation de l'Occident médiéval.* Paris: Arthaud, 1972.

——— *La naissance du Purgatoire.* Paris: Gallimard, 1981.

Lenzi, Maria Ludovica. *Donne e madonne: L'educazione femminile nel primo Rinascimento italiano.* Turin: Loescher, 1982.

Le Roy Ladurie, Emmanuel. *Montaillou: The Promised Land of Error.* Tr. Barbara Bray. New York: Braziller, 1978.

Lesky, Erna. "Die Zeugungs- und Vererbungslehre der Antike und ihre Nachwirkungen." *Abhandlungen der Akademie der Wissenschaften und der Literatur in Mainz* 19 (1950).

Levi Pisetsky, Rosita. "La couleur dans l'habillement italien." In *Actes du premier Congrès international d'histoire du costume.* Venice, 1952, and Milan, 1955.

——— *Storia del costume in Italia.* 5 vols. Milan: Fondazione Treccani degli Alfieri, 1964–1969.

Leyser, K. J. *Rule and Conflict in an Early Medieval Society: Ottonian Saxony.* London: Edward Arnold, 1979.

L'Hermite-Leclercq, Paulette. *Le monachisme dans la société de son temps: Le monastère de La Celle (XIe–début du XVIe siècle)*. Paris: Cujas, 1989.

———— "La réclusion volontaire au Moyen Age: Une institution spécifiquement féminine." In Yves-René Fonquerne and Alfonso Esteban, eds., *La Condición de la mujer en la Edad Media: Actas del coloquio celebrado en la Casa de Velasquez del 5 al 7 nov. de 1984*. Madrid: Universidad Complutense, 1986.

Loeffler, Josef. *Die Störungen des geschlechtlichen Vermögens in der Literatur der autoritativen Theologie des Mittelalters: Ein Beitrag zur Geschichte der Impotenz und der medizinischen Sachverständigenbeweises in kanonischen Impotenzprozess*. Wiesbaden: F. Steiner, 1958.

Lorcin, Marie-Thérèse. *Façons de sentir et de penser: Les fabliaux français*. Paris: Champion, 1979.

———— "Le feu apprivoisé: L'homme, la femme et le feu dans les fabliaux." *Revue historique* 268, no. 1 (1982): 3–15.

Lucas, Angela M. *Women in the Middle Ages: Religion, Marriage and Letters*. Brighton: Harvester Press, 1983.

Lugli, Vittorio. *I trattatisti della famiglia nel Quattrocento*. Bologna: Formiggini, 1909.

MacCormack, S. C., and M. Strathern, eds. *Nature, Culture and Gender*. Cambridge: Cambridge University Press, 1980.

MacLean, Ian. *The Renaissance Notion of Women: A Study in the Fortunes of Scholasticism and Medical Science in European Intellectual Life*. London: Cambridge University Press, 1980.

Male, Emile. *L'art religieux de la fin du Moyen Age en France: Etude sur l'iconographie du Moyen Age et sur ses sources d'inspiration*. Paris: A. Colin, 1908; 5th ed., 1949.

Manselli, Raoul. "La chiesa e il francescanesimo femminile." In *Movimento religioso femminile e francescanesimo nel secolo XIII: Atti del VII Convegno internazionale, Assisi, 11–13 ottobre 1979*. Assisi, 1980. Pp. 239–261.

Marchello-Nizia, Christiane. "Amour courtois, société masculine et figures de pouvoir." *Annales, E.S.C.* 36, no. 6 (1981): 969–982.

Il matrimonio nella società altomedievale: 24a settimana di studio sulla società del alto Medioevo, Spoleto, 22–28 aprile 1976. 2 vols. Spoleto: Centro Italiano di Studi sull'Alto Medioevo, 1977.

Metz, René. *La femme et l'enfant dans le droit canonique médiéval*. London: Variorum Reprints, 1985.

———— "Le statut de la femme en droit canonique médiéval." In *La Femme*. "Recueils de la Société Jean Bodin pour l'histoire comparative des institutions," 12, 2. Brussels: Librairie Encyclopédique, 1962.

Molmenti, Pompeo. *La storia di Venezia nella vita dalle origini alla caduta della Repubblica*. 3 vols. 4th ed. Bergamo: Istituto Italiano d'Arti Grafiche, 1905–1908.

Monson, D. A. "Andreas Capellanus and the Problem of Irony." *Spectrum* (July 1988).

Morewedge, Rosemarie Thee. *The Role of Woman in the Middle Ages.* Albany: State University of New York Press, 1975.

Mundy, John Hine. "Le mariage et les femmes à Toulouse au temps des Cathares." *Annales, E.S.C.* 42, no. 1 (1987): 117–134.

Murray, Alexander C. *Reason and Society in the Middle Ages.* Oxford: Clarendon Press, 1978.

Nelli, René. *L'érotique des troubadours.* Toulouse: Privat, 1963; new ed., 2 vols., Paris: Union Générale d'Editions, Collection 10/18, 1974.

Nemesius d'Emese. *De natura hominis.*

Nicholas, David. *The Domestic Life of a Medieval City: Women, Children, and the Family in Fourteenth-Century Ghent.* Lincoln: University of Nebraska Press, 1985.

Nichols, John, and Lillian Thomas Shank, eds. *Distant Echoes: Medieval Religious Women.* Vol. 1. Kalamazoo: Cistercian Publications, 1984.

Noonan, John T. *Contraception: A History of Its Treatment by the Catholic Theologians and Canonists.* Cambridge, Mass.: Harvard University Press, 1966.

Opitz, Claudia. *Evatöchter und Bräute Christi: Weiblicher Lebenszusammenhang und Frauenkultur im späteren Mittelalter.* Weinheim: Deutscher Studienverlag, 1990.

——— *Frauenalltag im Mittelalter: Biographien des 13. und 14. Jahrhunderts.* Weinheim: Beltz, 1985.

——— ed. *Weiblichkeit oder Feminismus? Beiträge zur interdisciplinären Frauentagung (Konstanz, 1983).* Weingarten: Drumlin, 1984.

——— and Elizabeth Schraut. *Frauen und Kunst im Mittelalter.* Exhibition catalogue, Brauenschweig, 1983.

Ortner, S., and H. Whitehead, eds. *Sexual Meanings: The Cultural Construction of Gender and Sexuality.* Cambridge, Mass.: Harvard University Press, 1981.

Otis, Leah Lydia. *Prostitution in Medieval Society.* Chicago: University of Chicago Press, 1985.

Paris, Gaston. *Manuel d'ancien français: La littérature française au Moyen Age, XIe–XIVe siècles.* Paris: Hachette, 1888.

——— *La poésie du Moyen Age.* Paris: Hachette, 1913.

Parisse, Michel. *Les nonnes au Moyen Age.* Le Puy: Christine Bonneton, 1981.

Parmisano, Fabian. "Love and Marriage in the Middle Ages." *New Blackfriars* 50 (1969): 649–660.

Pereira, Michela. "L'educazione femminile alla fine del Medioevo: Considerazioni sul *De eruditione filiorum nobilium* di Vincenzo di Beauvais." In Egle Becchi, ed., *Per una storia del costume educativo (Età classica e Medio Evo).* "Quaderni della Fondazione Gian Giacomo Feltrinelli," 23. Torino, 1983.

——— *Né Eva né Maria: Condizione femminile e immagine della donna nel Medioevo.* Bologna: Zanichelli, 1981.

Pernoud, Régine. *La femme au temps des cathédrales.* Paris: Stock, 1980.

Perrot, Michelle, ed. *Une histoire des femmes est-elle possible?* Marseille: Rivages, 1984.

Pesez, Jean-Marie. "Le foyer de la maison paysanne (XIe–XVe siècles)." *Archéologie médiévale* 16 (1986): 65–92.

Piazza, Rosalba. *Adamo, Eva e il serpente.* Palermo: La Luna, 1988.

Pichon, Jérôme, ed. *Le ménagier de Paris.* 2 vols. Imprimerie de Crapelet, 1846.

Pilosu, Mario. *La donna, la lussuria e la chiesa nel Medioevo.* Genoa: ECIG, 1989.

Pinkaers, Servais. "Ce que le Moyen Age pensait du Mariage." *La vie spirituelle, ascétique et mystique* 82 (1967): 413–440.

Piponnier, Françoise. *Costume et vie sociale: La cour d'Ajour XIVe–XVe siècles.* Collection "Civilisations et sociétés," 21. The Hague: Mouton, 1970.

———— "Equipement et techniques culinaires en Bourgogne au XIVe siècle." *Bulletin philologique et historique du comité des travaux historiques et scientifiques, année 1971.* Paris, 1977. Pp. 57–80.

Planque, Michel. "Eve." In *Dictionnaire de spiritualité, ascétique et mystique, doctrine et histoire.* Vol 4. Paris: Beauchesne, 1961.

Platelle, H. "Le problème du scandale: Les nouvelles modes masculines aux XIe et XIIe siècles." *Revue belge* 53 (1975): 1071–1096.

Pomata, Gianna. "La storia delle donne: Una questione di confine." In *Il mondo contemporaneo*, vol. 10: *Gli strumenti della ricerca*, vol. 2. Florence: La Nuova Italia, 1983. Pp. 1434–1469.

Pouchelle, Marie-Christine. *Corps et chirurgie à l'apogée du Moyen Age: Savoir et imaginaire du corps chez Henri de Mondeville, chirurgien de Philippe le Bel.* Paris: Flammarion, 1983.

Power, Eileen. *Medieval Women.* Cambridge: Cambridge University Press, 1975.

Réau, Louis. *Iconographie de l'art chrétien.* 6 vols. Paris: P.U.F., 1955–1959.

Régnier-Bohler, Danielle. "Geste, parole et clôture: Les représentations du gynécée dans la littérature médiévale du XIIIe au XVe siècle." *Annales de la Faculté des lettres et sciences humaines de Nice* 48 (1984): 393–404.

Reiter, Rayna R., ed. *Toward an Anthropology of Women.* New York: Monthly Review Press, 1975.

Rey-Flaud, H. *La névrose courtoise.* Paris: Navarin, 1983.

Rocher, D. "Le débat autour du mariage chez les clercs et les écrivains 'mondains' à la fin du XIIe et au début du XIIIe siècle." *Cahiers d'études germaniques* (1987).

Rodnite-Lemay, Helen. "Anthonius Grainerius and Medieval Gynecology." In J. Kirshner and Suzanne F. Wemple, eds., *Women of the Medieval World: Essays in Honor of John H. Mundy.* Oxford: Basil Blackwell, 1985. Pp. 317–336.

Rosaldo, M. Z., and L. Lamphere, eds. *Women, Culture and Society.* Stanford: Stanford University Press, 1974.

Rossiaud, Jacques. *Medieval Prostitution.* Tr. Lydia Cochrane. New York: Basil Blackwell, 1988.

Roy, Bruno, ed. *L'erotisme au Moyen Age: Etudes présentées au troisième colloque de l'Institut d'Etudes Médiévales.* Montreal: Aurore, 1977.

Ruether, Rosemary R., ed. *Religion and Sexism: Images of Women in the Jewish and Christian Traditions.* New York: Simon and Schuster, 1974.

——— and Eleanor McLaughlin, eds. *Women of Spirit: Female Leadership in the Jewish and Christian Traditions.* New York: Simon and Schuster, 1979.

Russo, Daniel. "Entre le Christ et Marie: La Madeleine dans l'art italien des XIIIe–XVe siècles." In *Marie Madeleine dans la mystique.* Paris: Beauchesne, 1989. Pp. 33–47.

Saxer, Victor. *Le culte de Marie Madeleine en Occident des origines à la fin du Moyen Age.* 2 vols. Auxerre and Paris, 1959.

——— "Maria Maddalena, santa." In *Bibliotheca sanctorum,* vol. 8. Rome: Città Nuova, 1967.

Saxonhouse, Arlene W. *Women in the History of Political Thought: Ancient Greece to Machiavelli.* New York: Praeger, 1985.

Schiller, Gertrud. *Ikonographie der christlichen Kunst.* Guterslih: G. Mohn, 1980.

Schmelzeisen, Gustav K. *Die Rechtsstellung der Frau in der deutschen Stadtwirtschaft.* Stuttgart: Kohlhammer, 1935.

Shahar, Shulamith. *The Fourth Estate: A History of Women in the Middle Ages.* London: Methuen, 1983.

Sharpe, W. D. "Isidore of Seville: The Medical Writings." *Transactions of the American Philosophical Society,* n.s., 54, no. 2 (1964): 5–75.

Stuard, Susan M., ed. *Women in Medieval History and Historiography.* Philadelphia: University of Pennsylvania Press, 1987.

——— ed. *Women in Medieval Society.* Philadelphia: University of Pennsylvania Press, 1976.

Toubert, Pierre. "La théorie du mariage chez les moralistes carolingiens." In *Il matrimonio nella società altomedievale.* Spoleto, 1977. Pp. 233–282.

Turnau, Irena. "The Diffusion of Knitting in Medieval Europe." In *Cloth and Clothing in Medieval Europe.* London: Heinemann, 1983. Pp. 368–389.

Uitz, Erika. *Die Frau in der mittelalterlichen Stadt.* Stuttgart: Abendverlag, 1988.

Vauchez, André. *Les laïcs au Moyen Age.* Paris: Cerf, 1987.

——— *La sainteté en Occident aux derniers siècles du Moyen Age d'après les procès de canonisation et les documents hagiographiques.* Rome: Ecole Française de Rome, 1981.

Vaultier, Roger. *Le folklore pendant la guerre de Cent Ans d'après les lettres de rémission du Trésor des Chartes.* Paris: Librairie Guénégaud, 1965.

Vereecke, Louis. "Mariage et sexualité au declin du Moyen Age." *La vie spirituelle, ascétique et mystique* 57 (1961): 199–225.

Verga, Ettore. "Le legge suntuarie milanesi." *Archivo storico lombardo,* 3rd ser., 9 (1898).

Vetere, Benedetto, and Paolo Renzi, eds. *Profili di donne: Mito, immagine, realtà fra Medioevo ed età contemporanea.* Galatina: Congedo, 1986.

Vincent, John Martin. *Costume and Conduct in the Laws of Basel, Bern and Zurich, 1370–1800.* Baltimore: Johns Hopkins University Press, 1935.

Vincet-Casey, Mireille. "Péchés de femmes à la fin du Moyen Age." In Yves-René Fonquerne and Alfonso Esteban, eds., *La condición de la mujer en la Edad Media: Actas del Coloquio celebrado en la Casa de Velasquez del 5 al 7 novembre de 1984.* Madrid: Universidad Complutense, 1986. Pp. 501–517.

Wachendorf, Helmut. *Die wirtschaftliche Stellung der Frau in den deutschen Städten des späteren Mittelalters.* Osnabrück, 1934.

Warner, Marina. *Alone of All Her Sex: The Myth and the Cult of the Virgin Mary.* London: Weidenfeld and Nicolson, 1976.

Weinstein, Donald, and Rudolph M. Bell. *Saints and Society: The Two Worlds of Western Christendom, 1000–1700.* Chicago: University of Chicago Press, 1982.

Wemple, Suzanne Fonay. *Women in Frankish Society: Marriage and the Cloister, 500–900.* Philadelphia: University of Pennsylvania Press, 1981.

Wickersheimer, Ernest. *Anatomies de Mondino dei Luzzi et de Guido de Vigevano.* Geneva: Droz, 1926.

Wiesner, Merry E. *Working Women in Renaissance Germany.* New Brunswick, N.J.: Rutgers University Press, 1986.

Wilson, Katharina, ed. *Medieval Women Writers.* Atlanta: University of Georgia Press, 1984.

Wood, Charles T. "The Doctor's Dilemma: Sin, Salvation and the Menstrual Cycle in Medieval Thought." *Speculum* 56 (1981): 710–727.

Wunder, Heide. "Frauen in der Gesellschaft Mitteleuropas im späten Mittelalter und in der frühen Neuzeit (15–18 Jahrhundert)." In Helfried Valentinitsch and Ileane Schwarzkogler, eds., *Hexen und Zauberer: Die grosse Verfolgung—ein europäisches Phänomen in der Steiermark.* Graz: Leykam, 1987.

Zapperi, Roberto. *L'uomo incinto: La donna, l'uomo e il potere.* Rome, 1979.

Zentraleinrichtung zur Förderung von Frauenstudien und Frauenforschung an der Freien Universität Berlin. *Methoden in der Frauenforschung.* Berlin: Fischer, 1985.

Zink, Michel. *Les chansons de toile: Etude et traduction.* Paris: Champion, 1977.

——— *La pastourelle: Poésie et folklore au Moyen Age.* Collection "Études," 67, Littérature française. Paris: Bordas, 1972.

——— *La subjectivé littéraire: Autour du siècle de Saint Louis.* Paris: P.U.F., 1985.

Contributors

CARLA CASAGRANDE Research associate at the University of Pavia, where she teaches philosophy (value systems and rules of behavior in medieval civilization). She is the coauthor of *Prediche alle donne del secolo XIII* (1978), and *I Peccati della lingua. Disciplina ed etica della parola nella cultura medievale* (1987).

JACQUES DALARUN Director of medieval studies at the Ecole Française de Rome, where his research interests include medieval sainthood and religious and civic life in the diocese of Rimini. He is the author of *L'impossible sainteté; la vie retrouvée de Robert d'Arbrissel* (1985), and *Robert d'Arbrissel, fondateur de Fontevraud* (1986).

GEORGES DUBY A member of the Académie Française and the Institut, he has held the chair in the history of medieval societies at the Collège de France since 1970. His many works include: *L'An Mil* (1967); *Guerriers et paysans, essai sur la première croissance économique de l'Europe* (1973); *Les trois ordres ou l'imaginaire du féodalisme* (1978); *Le chevalier, la femme et le prêtre* (1981); *Guillaume de Maréchal ou le meilleur chevalier du monde* (1984). He is also coeditor of *Histoire de la France rurale* (1975); *Histoire de la France urbaine* (1980); and *Histoire de la vie privée (A History of Private Life* [1987–1991]).

CHIARA FRUGONI Professor of medieval history at the University of Rome II, where she teaches medieval cultural history and does research on the iconography of the ninth to the fourteenth centuries. She has published *Una lontana città, sentimenti ed immagini nel Medioevo* (1983), and *Francesco. Un'altra storia* (1988).

DIANE OWEN HUGHES Teaches at the University of Michigan and has published many articles on the history of social structures and families, particularly in Genoa. Her latest book, *The Death of Mourning*, is on sumptuary laws in Mediterranean cities in the Middle Ages.

CHRISTIANE KLAPISCH-ZUBER   Teaches the historical demography and anthropology of medieval Italy at the Ecoles des Hautes Etudes en Sciences Sociales. She is the author of works on subjects ranging from the history and sociology of art (*Les maîtres du marbre, Carrare, 1300–1600* [1969]) to the history of demographic structures (*Les Toscans et leurs familles,* in collaboration with David Herlihy [1978]) and family history (*La maison et le nom. Stratégies et rituels dans l'Italie de la Renaissance* [1990]).

PAULETTE L'HERMITE-LECLERCQ   Professor at the University of Paris I-Sorbonne, where she teaches religious history and the culture of the Christian West (twelfth and thirteenth centuries). She is the author of *Le monachisme féminin dans la société de son temps: le monastère de la Celle, XIe–début du XIVe siècle* (1989).

CLAUDIA OPITZ   Doctor of philosophy, specializing in the history of women from the late Middle Ages to the French Revolution. She is the author of *Frauenalltag im Mittelalter. Biographien des XIII–XIV Jahrhunderts* (1985) and *Evatöchter und Braüte Christi, Weiblicher Lebenszusammenhang und Frauenkultur im Mittelalter* (1990).

FRANÇOISE PIPONNIER   Archaeologist, director of studies at the Ecole des Hautes Etudes en Sciences Sociales, where she teaches a course on textiles, clothing, and urban and rural housing. She has contributed to many anthologies and is the author of *Costume et vie sociale. La cour d'Anjou (XIV–XVe siècle)* (1970).

DANIELLE RÉGNIER-BOHLER   Lecturer in medieval literature at the University of Paris III-New Sorbonne, she is primarily interested in anthropological approaches to symbolism. Her chapter, "Imagining the Self," appeared in *A History of Private Life,* volume II.

CLAUDE THOMASSET   Professor of medieval French at the University of Paris IV, he is also a specialist in the history of medicine and the author, in collaboration with Danielle Jacquart, of *Sexualité et savoir médical au Moyen Age* (1985).

SILVANA VECCHIO   Research associate in the history of medieval philosophy, she teaches a course on thirteenth-century ethics at the University of Pavia. She is the author of, among other works, *I Peccati della Lingua. Disciplina ed etica della parola nella cultura medievale* (1987).

SUZANNE FONAY WEMPLE   Teaches at Barnard College, Columbia University, where she specializes in the social history of women in the Middle Ages. She is the author of *Women in Frankish Society: Family and Cloister (500–900)* (1981).

Illustration Credits

1. Môutier-Grandvaal Bible, Ms. Add. 10546: fol. 25v. The British Library, London.
2. Ms. pal. lat. 565: fol. 71r. Biblioteca Apostolica Vaticana, Vatican City.
3. Baalbek Museum, Beirut. Photo by Frugoni.
4. Ms. 1053, *Lezionario:* fol. 7v. Aartbisschoppelijk Museum, Utrecht.
5. Church of St. Madeleine, Vézelay. Photo by Roger-Viollet.
6. Church of St. Gervaise and St. Protaise, Civaux. Photo by Combier.
7. Photo by Alinari.
8. Photo by Alinari.
9. Photo courtesy of Soprintendenza, Pisa.
10. Photo by Alinari.
11. Inv. N. 526. Pinacoteca Vaticana, Vatican City.
12. Bibliothèque municipale, Strasbourg. Photo by Frugoni.
13. Ms. K26 (231): fol. 4r. St. John's College, Cambridge.
14. Toulouse Museum, Toulouse. Photo by Yan.
15. Soprintendenza, Pisa; photo by Alinari.
16. Photo courtesy of Soprintendenza, Siena.
17. Photo courtesy of Soprintendenza, Siena.
18. Ms. 2077: fol. 170r. Bibliothèque Nationale, Paris.
19. Ms. 2077: fol. 173r. Bibliothèque Nationale, Paris.
20. Cod. II. J. IV. 12, Ms. Class. 5: fol. 9v. Staatsbibliothek, Bamberg.
21. Photo A.C.L., Brussels.
22. Ms. 92: fol. 253r. Bildarchiv Photo, Marburg.
23. The Pierpont Morgan Library, New York.
24. Ms. 709: fol. 1v. The Pierpont Morgan Library, New York.
25. Fol. 1r. San Paolo Outside the Walls, Rome.
26. Ms. 76 T 1: fol. 214v. Koninklijksbibliotheek, The Hague.
27. Fol. 253v. Bibliothèque Centrale, Lille.
28. Ms. Vat. Lat. 4922: fol. 49r. Biblioteca Apostolica Vaticana, Vatican City.
29. Church of Saint Bernardino in Tritora, Imperia. Photo by Frugoni.
30. Photo by Frugoni.
31. Ms. fr. 848: fol. 19v. Bibliothèque Nationale, Paris. Collection Martin Schagen, Spikkestad.
32. Vol. 2: fol. 199, detail. Martin Schøgen Collection, Spikkestad.
33. Hamburger Kunsthalle, Hamburg. Photo by Elke Walford.
34. Ms. s.n. 2644: fol. 82v. Österreichische Nationalbibliothek, Vienna.
35. Ms. s.n. 2644, fol. 105v. Österreichische Nationalbibliothek, Vienna.
36. The Fontana Maggiore, Perugia. Photo by Frugoni.
37. Photo by Alinari.
38. The Church of St. Madeleine, Vézelay. Photo by Roger-Viollet.
39. Ms. Royal 15 D 1: fol. 18. The British Library, London.

40. Photo courtesy of Soprintendenza, Pisa.
41. Photo Réunion des Musées nationaux, Paris.
42. Ms. W. 26: fol. 64. Walters Art Gallery, Baltimore.
43. Ms. fr. 599: fol. 53v. Bibliothèque Nationale, Paris.
44. Ms. fr. 598: fol. 43r. Bibliothèque Nationale, Paris.
45. Ms. fr. 599: fol. 58. Bibliothèque Nationale, Paris.
46. Ms. fr. 12420: fol. 86. Bibliothèque Nationale, Paris.
47. Ms. 250: fol. 24r. Bibliothèque Municipale, Poitiers.
48. Photo by Frugoni.

49. Ms. Cott Dom. A XVII: fol. 74v. The British Library, London.
50. Ms. 1640: fol. 6r. Hessische-und Hochschul-Bibliothek, Darmstadt.
51. Ms. lat. 13601: fol. 2r. Staatsbibliothek, Munich.
52. Ms. lat. 13396: fol. 1v. Bibliothèque Nationale, Paris.
53. Ms. lat. 13601: fol. 2r. Stadt-und-Universitätsbibliothek, Frankfurt.
54. Photo by Alinari.
55. Photo by Alinari.
56. Photo by Frugoni; courtesy of the Cassa di Risparmio delle Provincie Lombarde.
57. The Church of Santa Caterina, Treviso. Photo by Frugoni.

Index

References to illustrations are in bold-
face.

al-Abbas, Ali ibn: *Pantegni*, 45, 52, 54,
  62
Abduction, 171, 175, 188, 261, 275
Abelard, 38, 226, 253, 329, 480
Abortion, 122, 180, 289, 290
Acciaiuoli, Andrea, 448
Adalbero of Laon, 186
Adalbert of Ivrea, 185
Adalhad, 192
Adam, 21, 40, 336, 393, 427, 459, 464;
  and Eve, 19–20, 34, 89–90, 106, 111,
  144, 145, 226, 227, 427–428; images
  of, 337, 339, 359, 360, 394
Adam of Eynsham, 204, 206
Adam of Neville, 205–206, 209, 248
Adelaide, Queen, 29, 186, 200, 235
Adele of Blois, 30
Adelheid of Thermanskirchen, 307
*Admirable Magical Secrets of Albert the
  Great and the Small*, 65
Adultery, 196, 216, 237, 259, 278–279,
  291; and divorce, 176, 179, 181; and
  gender discrimination, 114–115, 228,
  276; punishments for, 171, 277, 279,
  291; in twelfth century, 203, 223
Aelred of Rievaulx, 239
Aesculapius, 386, 387
Agnes of Bohemia, 273
Agnes of Castille, 236, 237, 238
Agnes of Saleby, 204–207, 208, 209–
  210, 211–212, 231, 238
Agobard of Lyon, 179
Agriculture, 293–295, 324–325
Aidan (Bishop of Lindisfarland), 190

Alan of Lille, 72, 73, 79, 82
Alberic, 185
Alberich, Markgrave, 182
Alberti, Bartolomea degli, 128–129, 133
Alberti, Leon Battista: *I libri della fa-
  miglia*, 129
Albert of Saxony, 109, 114, 120
Albertus Magnus, 39, 45, 47, 48, 50,
  55, 57–58, 59, 63, 65; on conjugal
  friendship, 111; on maternal love, 123
Albizzi family, 140
Alcuin, 137
Aldegund of Maubeuge, 199
Aldhelm, Saint, 136
Alemania, Jacqueline Felicie de, 299
Alexander of Hales, 39
Alexander the Great, 66, 340, 341
Alexandre, Monique, 19
Alfanus of Salerno, 44
Alfonso of Aragon, 141
Alheyd of Bremen, 296
Amado, Claudie, 236
Amalasuntha, 197
Ambrose of Milan, 16, 20, 26, 28, 34,
  339
Ambrosiaster: *Commentary on the First
  Corinthians*, 172
Ame, Saint, 30
Ami et d'Amile (chanson de geste), 67
Anatomia magistri Nicolai physici, 51,
  53
Anatomy, 43, 45, 46; female, 43, 46–
  47, 51–58
"The Anatomy of a Sow," 52
Andreas of Regensburg, 294
Angela of Foligno, 475–476, 477, 479
Angevin period, 38

Anna of Vaudémont, 346, 347
Anne, Saint, 399
Annunciation, 92, 234, 368, 400
Ansa, Queen, 186
Anselm of Canterbury, 17, 23–24, 25, 30, 35, 38
Anti-Semitism, 232, 233, 370
Antonino of Florence, 95, 130, 132; *L'Opera a ben vivere*, 83, 129; *Regola di vita cristiana*, 83; *Summa theologica*, 129
Antonio, Tommaso di, 418
Apostles, 18, 106, 246
Aquinas, Thomas, 13, 29, 36, 39, 42, 54, 90, 114, 241; on chastity, 80; *Commentary on the Sententiae*, 46; on conjugal friendship, 111; on maternal love, 123; *Summa Theologica*, 46, 284; on women's love of clothing, 145; on women's speech, 40–41
Arabs, 44, 45, 217
Archeology, 321, 322, 323, 325, 326, 327; and arrangement of homes, 328–331; and medieval housing, 331–334
Aretino, 64
Arianism, 25, 178
Arienti, Sabadino degli, 154
Ariès, Philippe, 284
Aristotelians, 13, 14, 56, 61, 86, 87, 96, 101, 107, 114, 116; doctrine of marriage, 111; and fashion, 146; view of family, 121, 125, 126, 130. *See also* Aquinas, Thomas
Aristotle, 49, 66, 76, 94, 98; commentators of, 114; *De animalibus*, 45; *Economics*, 107, 108, 109, 119, 124, 125; *Ethica*, 89; on menstruation, 65; *Nicomachean Ethics*, 107; and physiology of women, 40, 46, 51, 54–55, 56, 58, 62; political theory of, 74, 78; *Politics*, 89, 101, 124; rediscovery of, 45, 103; and segregation of sexes, 3–4; and subjection of women, 14; on wives, 118, 125–126; on women as imperfect men, 57, 87
Arnaud de Villeneuve, 50
Arnaud of Bonneval, 36
Arnulf, Saint, 218–219
Arnulf II, 332
Art: ecclesiastical, 375–376; erotic, 62–64, 68; patronage of, 322; plastic, 321
Artists, female, 9

Asceticism, 23, 196, 467, 468, 475
Assisi, Saint Francis of, 41, 152, 274, 350, 475
Atalise, 28
Athelstan, King, 184
Atto of Vercelli, 195, 196; *Capitulary*, 190
Audoen (Dado), 187
Audofleda, 197
Augustine, Saint, 16, 23, 29, 33, 34, 36, 40, 42, 199, 481; on childbirth, 22; *Confessions*, 35; and custody of women, 89; on marriage, 223, 339; on virginity of Mary, 26; and woman's soul, 90
Augustines, 74, 83
Augustus: marriage laws of, 169
Autperto, Ambrosio: *The Battle of Vices and Virtues*, 368–369
Autti, 220, 222
Averroës, 45, 57
Avicenna: *Canon*, 45, 46, 47, 48, 50, 63, 66

Bachelard, Gaston, 430, 482
Badegisel (Bishop of Le Mans), 175
Baldwin of Jerusalem, 30
Balthild, Queen, 199
Barbaro, Francesco: *De re uxoria*, 129
Barbarossa, Frederick (Holy Roman Emperor), 286
Barre, Henri, 24, 25
Barthes, 471, 476, 482
Bartholomew the Englishman: *De proprietatibus rerum*, 46
Bateson, Mary: *The Origin and Early History of Double Monasteries*, 189
Battle of Muret, 238
Baudonivia, 29, 199
Baudri of Bourgueil, 28
Beatrice, 42. *See also* Dante
Beatrice (of Burgundy; wife of Frederick Barbarossa), 286
Beatrice of Nazareth, 314, 445, 448, 463, 470, 475, 479; *Seven Degrees of Love*, 442, 470, 477
Beaumanoir, Philippe de: *Coutumes du Beauvaisis*, 433
Beauvoir, Simone de, 207
Bec, Pierre, 436
Bede, the Venerable, 199; *History of the English Church and People*, 173

Beguines, 41, 42, 74, 76, 312–313, 432, 444, 445, 446, 447, 467, 468
Beier, Adrian, 303, 305
Bellemère, Gilles, 40
Belota, Johanna, 299
Benedict, Saint, 244, 341, 343
Benedictines, 17, 74, 190, 192, 229, 242, 309, 354, 410
Bentivoglio, Ginevra, 156
Berengar of Ivrea, 185
Berhtgyth, 192
Bernard, Saint, 239, 241, 345
Bernardino of Siena, 39, 83, 129, 130, 131, 132, 145, 146, 224; and witches, 382–383
Bernard IV (Count of Comminges), 236, 237
Bernard of Clairvaux, 25, 38, 42, 443
Bernard of Morlaix, 40
Bernard of Septimania, 179, 181, 197
Bernward of Hildesheim, 186
Béroul: Tristan, 67
Berthold of Regensburg, 307
Bertilla of Chelles, Saint, 187
Bessarion, Cardinal, 154
Bible, 26, 33, 102, 103, 112, 197, 241, 376; Book of Genesis in, 19, 35, 40, 46, 84, 106, 336, 459; and Church Fathers, 36–37; commentaries on, 16, 89; Gospel of John in, 21, 199, 418; marriage in, 339–340; Moûtier-Grandval, 336; study of, 465; translation of, 249, 473; on women, 13; women of, 31, 32, 92, 105, 429, 430, 440
Bieiris of Roman, 436
Bischoff, Bernhard, 199
Blason des basquines de vertugalles, Le, 150
Bloch, Howard, 452
Bloch, Marc, 27
Boccaccio, 2, 448; Decameron, 112; De claris mulieribus, 402, 430
Bodel, Jean: Le souhait insensé, 462
Bodo, 183
Boethius: De arithmetica, 370, 371
Boileau, Etienne: Livre des métiers, 232
Bona of Pisa, Saint, 421
Bona of Savoy, 156
Bonaventure, Saint, 39, 42, 116, 121–122
Bondol, Jean: Histoire ancienne jusqu'à Cesar, 386, 388

Boniface, Saint, 178, 179, 182, 190, 192, 196, 198
Bonnassie, Pierre, 231
Book of Gertrude, 24–25
Book of Ten Chapters (Marbode of Rennes), 22, 28
Bossuet, 208
Brides, 141, 164, 177, 184, 226, 273–274, 282
Bridget of Sweden, (Saint), 42, 315, 316, 390, 473, 481
Bromyard, John, 117, 122
Bruni, Leonardo, 130; De studiis et litteris, 133
Bruno, Saint, 241
Bruno the Schoolman, 29
Bücher, Karl, 164, 168
Buffalmacco, 349, 363; The Triumph of Death, 363, 394
Burckhardt, 156
Buridanus, John, 111, 114, 123
Bynum, Caroline Walker, 474

Caedmon, 190
Caesaria of Arles, 199
Caesarius, Saint (Bishop of Arles), 172, 188, 241; Regula sanctarum virginum, 197
Caesarius of Heisterbach, 233–234
Calligraphers, female, 400–401
Campano, Giovanni: De dignitate matrimonii, 129
Cana, miracle at, 106, 113
Capellanus, Andreas: Treatise on Love, 263–265
Capetian dynasty, 253, 262, 263, 264
Carl, Duke of Calabria, 299
Carmentis, 441
Carolingian period, 31, 161, 176, 178–183, 195, 201, 260; anthologies of, 24; art in, 378; clergy in, 196; marriage in, 200, 228, 245; monasteries in, 170, 188, 191, 193, 198; moralists of, 29, 260; population in, 163, 167
Carthusians, 18, 204, 217, 225, 242, 249, 474, 476
Casagrande, Carla, 3, 8, 70–104
Castel, Jean, 459
Catalonia, 231
Cathedrals, 16; building of, 24; schools of, 17
Catherine of Alexandria, 41, 418, 419, 420, 421–422

Catherine of Aragon, 138, 149
Catherine of Genoa, 135, 475
Catherine of Siena, 42, 135, 315, 316, 417–418, 469, 471, 475
Cavalca, Domenico, 362
Cecilia, Saint, 107, 116
Celestine III, Pope, 223
Celibacy, 7–8, 16, 18, 196, 214, 229, 259, 339
Cerchi, Umiliana dei, 152–153
Cereta, Laura, 155
Certeau, Michel de, 471, 482
Certosino, Giovanni: *Decor puellarum*, 83; *Gloria mulierum*, 83, 129, 131, 132, 133
Charity, 97–98, 358
Charlemagne, 137, 179, 186, 190, 191, 192, 196, 199, 235; *Capitulary to the Missi*, 179; *De Villis*, 181, 183
Charles the Bald, 179, 376, 378
Charles the Bold, 192
Charles II of Anjou, 280
Charles V, 441
Chastity, 28, 29–30, 79–80, 81–82, 83, 84, 88, 92, 96, 99, 102, 190, 370; conjugal, 113, 114, 115, 133, 172; of daughters, 124; and fashion, 94, 95, 146; in Germanic tribes, 171; of lower-class women, 177; vs. marriage, 347; vow of, 187, 225, 273, 313. *See also* Celibacy; Virginity
Chaucer, 146, 434, 440, 462–463
Cherubino of Spoleto, 107, 130, 131, 132; *Regola della vita matrimoniale*, 129
Childbirth, 22, 59, 121, 122, 167, 168, 292; aversion to, 22; and Caesarian section, 289, 300, 386, 388; fear of, 289; impurity of, 368; risks of, 228, 271, 281, 289–290
Childhood, 184, 210–213
Children: abandonment of, 291, 292; abuse of, 291; and the Church, 291; housing of, 332; orphan, 292, 367; rearing of, 284–285, 287–288, 291. *See also* Infanticide; Mothers: and children
Chilperic, King, 175, 177
Chlotar, 29
Chlothar II, 188
Chrétien de Troyes, 264
Christ: birth of, 16, 25–27, 340, 368, 370, 384–385; body of, 475, 476;

brides of, 30, 35, 222, 225, 240–241, 245, 249, 407–422; and the Church, 226, 275; conception of, 26, 46, 465; and concept of love, 223; images of, 322, 339, 373, 377, 381, 385, 398, 408, 481; and Mary Magdalene, 32, 33, 41, 98; resurrection of, 440; as son of God, 25; and submission of women, 89, 91; visions of, 469, 472, 480, 481; at wedding at Cana, 106; and woman's sin, 19, 21, 32, 33, 41, 88
Christianity, 25, 169, 229, 370; and family law, 170; and marriage, 178, 216; and morality, 44; and paganism, 21; reform movement of, 18; and women, 88, 172, 173, 192, 203
Christina of Markyate, 212, 220–224, 232, 233, 245–246, 247, 322
Christina of Stommeln, 238, 239
Christine de Pisan, 1–2, 83, 109, 112, 125, 267–268, 316–317, 425, 429, 437–442, 448; as author, 432, 435, 437–438; *Avision Christine*, 437, 438; *The City of Ladies (La cité des dames)*, 1, 2, 83, 98, 154, 317, 325–326, 430, 438, 439, 440, 452; as copyist, 402; *Epistre au dieu d'Amours*, 434; *Epitre d'Othéa*, 386, 387; feminism of, 467; *Livre des fais at bonnes meurs du sage Roy Charles V*, 441–442; *Livre des trois vertus*, 83, 117, 438; *Livre du chemin de long estude*, 439–440; *Livre du corps de policie*, 442; *Mutacion de Fortune*, 438, 439; style of, 442
Chrodegand of Metz, 190
Chrysostom, John, 20, 40, 120
Chuppa, 175
Church: attitude to marriage, 340; and care of infants, 291; challenges to, 482; cult of sainthood, 316; images of the, 372–373; and morality, 44, 203; and regulation of marriage, 162, 168, 221, 236, 247, 258, 265–266, 272, 273, 275, 345, 347; and regulation of sexuality, 60, 64, 68; strengthening of, 202; vs. secular world, 18; and women, 84, 88, 203, 210, 244
Church Fathers, 72, 92, 197; and marriage, 179, 223; view of women, 16, 19, 23, 36, 79, 172, 182
Circe, 386, 387, 397

Cistercians, 38, 217, 233, 239, 242, 286, 297, 309, 312, 468

Clara of Rimini, 471, 479, 481

Clare of Assisi, 274, 275, 285, 289, 314

Clare of Montefalco, 386–387, 390, 407, 408, 410

Claricia (miniaturist), 401–402

Classification of women, 73–84; young and old, 75–76, 82

Clement of Alexandria, 26, 136

Clergue, Pierre, 278, 289, 484–485, 487–488

Clergy: and conception of woman, 7, 10, 14, 15–42, 44, 103, 218, 248, 323, 325; and discipline of women, 42, 70, 72, 84, 100; and "good wives," 105–135; lascivious, 278, 484–489; and marriage, 214, 215, 339; vs. knights, 256–257, 265

Clothaire (King of Franks), 407

Clothing, 92–94, 119, 139–144. See also Fashion

Clotilda, 173, 186

Clovis, King, 29, 172, 173, 175, 186, 197

Cluniac order, 242

Cluny (monastery), 18, 29, 30, 242

Col, Pierre, 438

Coleman, Emily, 166

Columban, Saint, 189

Conception, 50–51, 55, 56, 57, 58, 64, 122

Concubines, 184, 196, 229

Conrad of Megenberg, 86, 116; Yconomica, 122

Conrad of Saxony, 39

Constantine, 169

Constantine the African, 45, 46, 47, 52, 56; On Coitus, 63

Constantinople, 4

Contraception, 122, 289

Convents, 30, 172, 180, 186, 222, 239, 241, 273, 305, 309, 311–312, 407; art in, 322, 410; daily life in, 415–417; men in, 188; and prostitutes, 307; writing in, 443, 448. See also Nuns

Corne, Berthe de, 456

Cosmetics, 92–93, 94, 119

Couette, Thomas, 146

Council of Auxerre, 195

Council of Chalcedonia, 25

Council of Chalon, 190

Council of Constance, 315

Council of Elvira, 182

Council of Epaon, 194

Council of Ephesus, 25

Council of Friuli, 191

Council of Mâcon, 34–35

Council of Orléans, 176, 194

Council of Trent, 274

Council of Verneuil, 179, 190, 191

Council of Worms, 195

Courtly love, 7, 9, 250–266, 314; and discipline of women, 262–263, 265; influence of, 168, 261–266, 278; literature of, 16, 63, 252–255, 263; and marriage, 258; model of, 250–252

Courts, feudal, 255–260, 261, 272

Creation and Fall, story of, 19–20, 90, 336, 359, 448

Cruce, Clara a, 315

Crusades, 18, 347, 456

Culture, 3, 71, 99; and anatomy, 51; clerical, 38; European, 178; knightly, 256, 262; and Nature, 14; traditional, 21; women's, 314

Curtius, 444

Custody of women, 87–91, 97, 98, 99, 101, 102, 103, 104, 115, 120; four elements of, 113; and home, 126. See also Modesty

Cynechilde, 192

Cyprian, 32

Czachmannın, 296

d'Abrissel, Robert, 21, 22

Dalarun, Jacques, 8, 15–42

d'Alverny, Marie-Thérèse, 16

Dame écouillé, La (The Castrated Lady), 458

Dante, 42, 254, 459; De vulgari eloquentia, 427, 463

d'Arbrissel, Robert, 36

Datini, Francesco, 390

Datini, Margherita, 390

Daughters, 166, 210–211, 213; fathers and, 224, 231, 241, 247, 303; and inheritance, 231, 452; and marriage, 215, 226, 272, 274, 275, 277; and mothers, 124, 458, 461

Death, 363, 366, 394

Decretum of Gratian, 221, 226

de' Luzzi, Mondino: Anatomia, 53

Demography, 5–6, 7, 9, 163, 165, 203, 207, 270–272

de Mondeville, Henri, 47, 48
de Romanis, Humbertus, 72, 74, 75, 76, 77, 78, 79, 108; on mothers, 124
Descartes, René, 58
Desert Fathers, 225, 244
De spermate, 45, 52
Deutsch, Nicholas Manuel, 143
Devailly, Guy, 22
Devil, 31, 316, 433; images of, 344, 348, 349–351, 358, 363, 366, 369–370, 383, 395, 397; and witches, 383, 384. *See also* Eve: and Devil
Dhuoda, 181, 444; *Liber Manualis*, 197
Dialogue of Placides and Timeo, 60, 61, 66
Die, Countess of, 436
Dionysius the Carthusian, 83, 107; *De laudabili vita coniugatorum*, 129, 130, 131
Dirk II of Holland, 379–380
Diseases, 64–68, 271, 292, 305; miraculous cures for, 468–469
Divorce, 172, 176, 179, 180–181, 200, 215, 218, 230
d'Oingt, Marguerite, 442, 446, 469, 474, 481; *Pagina meditationum*, 465; *Speculum*, 481
Dominicans, 39, 41, 57, 72, 74, 76, 77, 117, 128, 309, 312, 349, 385, 417; and conversion of heretics, 418, 484; and literature, 443; and preaching to women, 71, 73, 83, 121, 129
Dominici, Giovanni: *La regola del governo di cura familiare*, 83, 128–129, 131, 132, 133
Dom Leclercq, 217
Donizone, 381, 382
D'Ornacieux, Beatrice, 476
Dorothy of Montau, 473
Dowries, 141, 164, 219, 228, 231, 241, 244
Dragonetti, 257
Dress, female, 8, 429. *See also* Fashion
Dronke, Peter, 433, 444, 477
Dubois, Pierre, 116
Duby, Georges, 9, 10, 168, 203, 218–219, 238, 249, 250–266, 272, 277, 483–491
Duns Scotus, 39
Durandus of Champagne, 72, 74, 86, 97, 106, 122, 126; *Speculum dominarum*, 78, 79

Eadburga (abbess of Thanet), 198
Earcongota, 189
Ebner, Christine, 315, 444, 445, 446, 447
Ebner, Margarethe, 315, 476–477
Eckhard (Count of Autun and Macon), 198
Eckhart, Meister, 446
Ecurueil (Squirrel), 458, 461
Edith, Queen, 29, 184, 200
Education: of children, 123–125, 131, 133; in Germany, 298; in Paris, 298, 299; of wives, 119–120; of women, 73, 100, 197, 213, 263, 297, 304, 448; and women teachers, 298
Edwin, King of Northumbria, 189
Egfried, King, 186
Egilbert (Archbishop of Treves), 379
Eleanor of Aquitaine, 253, 262, 443
Elisabeth of Thuringia, 279, 280–281, 282, 288, 305, 310–311, 314
Elizabeth, Queen, 149
Elizabeth, Saint, of Hungary, 133
Emma (Queen of France), 186
Ende (painter), 415
Engelthal, 446
Ephraem, Saint, 26, 27
The Eremitic Life, 33, 35
Erler, M., 6
Ermengarde (Viscountess of Narbonne), 235–236
Ermentrud (abbess of Jouarre), 191
Ermentrud (Bodo's wife), 183
Eroticism, 58, 62–64, 143
Esclarmonde, 468
d'Este, Beatrice, 156, 158
d'Este, Isabella, 156, 157
Ethelberga of Northumbria, 173
Etheldreda, Queen, 186
Eucheria, 197
Eudoxia, 236, 238
Eugene III, 242
Euphrosine, Countess of Vendôme, 20
Europe, population of, 163, 167, 270–272, 292, 293
Eusebius, Saint (of Caesaria), 198
Eve, 8, 19–20, 21, 22, 27, 40, 90, 106, 111, 227, 367; biographies of, 402; curiosity of, 86; daughters of, 172, 428; and Devil, 37, 226, 362, 457; images of, 337, 339, 359, 360, 394; and language, 427, 428, 459; as temptress, 351; vs. Mary, 23–24, 29, 37, 367

Fallope, Gabriel, 47, 53–54
Family, 78, 84, 121–125; in eleventh
 and twelfth centuries, 228–229, 259;
 in fifteenth century, 128–135; and
 marriage, 272–284; nuclear, 108, 293;
 in tenth century, 183–186; and woman's work, 328, 331
Fara, Abbess, 189
Fashion, 136–158; and capitalism, 157–
 158; and chopines, 148–149, 150,
 155, 158; the color black in, 151,
 157; and corruption, 143–148; and
 empowerment of women, 157; and
 farthingales, 149–151, 158; renunciation of, 152–153; and sexuality, 143–
 144, 147–148; and social identity,
 139–142; and veils, 150–151, 158; in
 Venice, 155, 158
Fathers, 123, 124–125, 134, 230, 241,
 247, 251, 449–450
Femininity, 8, 19, 29, 34, 67, 426, 438
Feminism, 38, 438
Ferdinand, King of Spain, 147
Fidati, Simone, 83
Fille du comte de Ponthieu, La, 449
Fina of San Gimignano, Saint, 421
Flambard, Ranulph (Bishop of Durham),
 220
Foligno, Angela da, 288, 315
Fortunatus, Venantius, 197–198, 409;
 De vita sanctae Radegundis, 175, 187,
 194, 407
Fossier, Robert, 202, 231, 238
Fournier, Jacques (later Pope Benedict
 XII), 483–486
Francesca Romana, 153
Francesco of Barberino, 72, 74, 77, 79,
 86, 88, 95, 97, 101, 116, 122, 124;
 Reggimento e costumi di donna, 74,
 75, 76, 77, 78, 94
Franciscans, 72, 73, 74, 83, 129, 147,
 285, 312, 314, 375, 468, 484; and
 cult of Virgin Mary, 39; and Mary
 Magdalene, 41; preaching to women,
 71, 467
Francis I, 149, 156
Fredegar, 175
Fredegund, 176, 177
Fredi, Bartolo di, 363–364, 365, 366
Frugoni, Chiara, 9, 172, 322, 336–422
Fulbert of Chartres, 25, 31
Fulk (Bishop of Toulouse), 467
Fulk of Anjou, 137

Galen, 13; analogy of, 46–47; De usu
 partium, 45; De spermate, 52; medical theories of, 13, 44–45, 46–51, 54,
 55, 58, 60, 61, 65
Galetta, Rubaldus, 296
Gandersheim (monastery), 193, 199,
 200, 444
Gender, 5; and life expectancy, 271–
 272; use of term, 3
Gender difference, 3, 294, 335; and
 fashion, 138; and public vs. domestic
 sphere, 3–4
Gender relations, 3, 8, 257, 266, 316,
 322
Geoffroy of Vendôme, 17, 19, 20, 21,
 24, 25, 26, 27, 28, 31, 34, 35; "In
 Honor of the Blessed Mary Magda-
 lene" (sermon), 33; "On the Nativity
 of the Lord" (sermon), 26
Gerard of Cremona, 45
Gerberga, 193, 444
Gerini, Nicolò, 421
Germany, 136, 141, 166, 171, 173, 235,
 242, 245, 247; brothels in, 306; convents in, 192, 312; women in trade in,
 326. See also Law: German; Marriage: in Germanic tribes
Gerson, Jean, 435
Gertrude of Helfta, 243
Gertrud of Nivelles, 198
Gilbert (Bishop of Limerick), 229
Gilbert of Sempringham, 225, 239, 242
Gilbert of Tournai, 40, 72, 73, 79, 82,
 93, 94, 105, 107, 122; on fidelity in
 marriage, 113; on mothers, 124; on
 two types of love, 110; on women's
 work, 126, 127
Giles of Rome, 72, 74, 76, 78, 84–85,
 87, 97, 101; on choosing a wife, 117–
 118; on duties of husbands, 120; on
 female fashion, 14, 93–94; on "good"
 wives, 114; on marriage, 108, 111,
 114; "On the Formation of the Human Body in the Uterus," 56; on
 women's speech, 98
Gisla, 181
Godefroy de Claire, atelier of, 372
Godefroy of Bouillon, 30
Godelive, Saint, of Ghistelles, 28
Gospels of the Distaff, 454–456
Gosson, Stephen, 150
Grace of Saleby, 204–207, 208, 209,
 210, 211–212, 216, 248

Gratian, 36, 40
Gregorian reform, 18, 29, 42
Gregory of Nyssa, 26
Gregory of Tours: *The History of the Franks*, 174–175, 188
Gregory the Great, 26, 32, 34, 170, 172, 187, 188, 341, 344
Gregory VII, Pope, 18, 382
Gregory XI, Pope, 417–418
Griselda, 431, 450, 451, 452
Grundmann, Herbert, 313
Guda, Sister, 414, 415
Guibert of Nogent, 15, 27, 232, 239
Guidosalvi, Sancia, 407
Guilds, women in, 295, 297, 300–301, 302, 303, 304, 305, 306, 309, 313, 316, 317, 326
Guillaume of Poitiers. *See* William of Poitiers
Guillaume VIII (Lord of Montpellier), 236, 237–238
Gunhild, 30

Hadewijch, 314, 445, 463, 474, 475, 479; *Letters*, 442, 468, 477–478, 480–481, 482
Hadrian II, 180
Hajnal, 163
Hammer of Witches (Institoris and Sprenger), 40
Hanawalt, Barbara A., 287
Harold, King, 30
Hasenohr, Geneviève, 29, 131
Hathumoda, Saint, 187
Hauck, Albert, 192
Hedwig of Silesia, 275, 279
Heinrich of Nördlingen, 446
Helaine of Constantinople, 449, 450
Helaria, 194
Heldris of Cornwall: *Roman de silence*, 452
Hell, 363, 364, 373, 485–486. See also *Inferno* (fresco)
Héloïse, 203, 213, 243, 443, 480
Henry, Duke of Silesia, 275
Henry of Lausanne, 36
Henry Plantagenet, 253, 261–262
Henry I, 184, 221
Henry II, 193, 434
Henry IV, the Impotent, 150, 381, 382
Henry VI, 409
Heresy, 30, 71, 195, 237, 313, 314, 375, 455, 490–491; Catharist, 204,

236, 239, 328, 468, 484, 486; Waldensian, 204
Herlihy, David, 135, 163–164, 203
Herlinda, 187, 200
Hermaphrodite, 61, 67
Hermits, female, 239, 244, 245–246
Herod, 111
Herrad of Hohenbourg: *Hortus deliciarum*, 243, 356, 357–358, 410
Hierarchy, 71, 77, 89, 208, 242, 272, 425; of convents, 243; and costume, 139, 142, 147, 151, 153, 154, 155, 156, 157; of court, 264; household, 164, 454; of the sexes, 14, 266; social, 81, 83, 168, 247, 251, 260, 263, 324
Hilda (abbess of Whitby), 189–190
Hildebald of Cologne, 199
Hildebert of Lavardin, 17, 20, 21, 22, 24, 26, 28, 29, 30, 35; "Against the Jews" (sermon), 27; "On Mutual Consent" (sermon), 28
Hildegard, Countess, 379–380
Hildegard of Bingen, 56, 208, 212, 239, 243, 286, 315, 435, 442, 443, 444, 446, 447, 448, 464, 465–466, 479; on conception, 56, 59; *Liber scivias*, 410; *Revelations*, 410; visions of, 56, 474; on women's sexual pleasure, 61
Hincmar of Rheims, 26, 180, 181
Hippocrates, 48, 49, 53, 55, 59
History: of art, 322; demographic, 162–168; economic, 4, 5; feminist, 167; legal, 4; Marxist, 204; medieval, 3–4, 5, 6; micro-, 8–9; Occitanian, 253; social, 4, 5; and theology, 17; and written records, 6, 9
History of the Lombards, 173
History of Women, Volume I, 3
Hitda, Abbess, 410, 411
Holy Roman Empire, 235
Home: as symbol of stability, 126–127
Homosexuality, 63, 148, 257
Hostiensis, 219
Houses, 331–334
Howell, Martha, 316
Hoy, Jutta von, 288
Hrotswitha, 24, 31–32, 199–200, 444, 447; *The Conversion of the Harlot Thais*, 182; *The Fall and Conversion of Mary*, 182; *Gesta Ottonis*, 200, 410; *Gongolf*, 200; *Primordia Coenobii Gandeshemensis*, 200, 409–410

Huchet, Jean-Charles, 257
Hugeberc, 199, 443–444
Hugh, King of Italy, 182, 184, 185
Hughes, Diane Owen, 8, 136–158
Hugh of Fouilloy, 40
Hugh of Lincoln, 204–212 passim, 216, 217, 219, 223, 225, 227, 236–237, 241, 246
Hugh of Saint-Victor, 38
Hugo of Cluny, 381, 382
Hugo I of Vaudémont, 346
Humiliana, 310, 311
Humiliatae, 74
Humility (nun), 415, 416, 417
Husbands, 14, 22, 98, 99, 102, 109, 457; duties of, 118–121, 218; impotence of, 458; middle-class, 282–283; and paternity, 114; protection of, 308–309; shortage of, 164; and *sine manu* marriage, 172, 174; and wives, 70, 96, 103, 109–117, 130–133, 142, 186, 187, 224, 227, 249, 251, 272, 282, 294, 295, 454

Ianuarius (Bishop of Sardinia), 188
Iceland, women of, 229–230
Iconography, 39, 41, 321, 322, 329; of death, 363; of labor, 324; wedding, 340–341. *See also* Images
Ida of Bologna, 428
Ida of Nivelles, 297–298
Ide, Countess of Boulogne, 30
Images: of agricultural scenes, 393; female, 370, 391–393; and visions, 387, 390; of women baking bread, 329; of women cooking, 396; of women copyists, 403; of women hunting, 393; of women knitting, 327–328, 389; of women painting, 402, 405; of women sculpting, 404, 407; of women selling fish, 391, 392; of women sewing, 327, 392, 454
Immaculate Conception, 25, 39, 367–368. *See also* Virgin Mary
Incarnation, 38, 88
Incest, 127, 178, 180, 195, 214, 215
Index of Christian Art, 347
India, 55, 304
Infanticide, 122, 166–167, 192, 196, 207, 290–292, 300, 367
Inferno (fresco), 351, 352, 353
Innocent III, Pope, 236, 238, 243, 307; *De Contemptu Mundi,* 122

Inquisition, 314, 315, 329
Institoris, Henry, 40, 42
Institutio Sanctimonialium, 190
Iogna-Prat, Dominique, 33
Irigaray, Luce, 432
Irmengard, 380–381
Irminon (abbot of Saint-Germain-des-Prés), 167
Isabeau of Bavaria, 438
Isabel, Queen of Navarre, 78, 79
Isabella, Queen of Spain, 147, 148
Isabelle, Princess, 273, 274
Isidore of Seville, 22, 36, 51, 65, 108, 178; *Contra Judaeos,* 410, 412, 413; *Etymologies,* 23, 43
Isolde, 224
Ivani, Antonio: *Del governo della famiglia civile,* 129

Jacme (son of Marie of Montpellier), 237, 238
Jacob of Voragine, 72, 73, 108; on conjugal love, 110–111; on custody of women, 89, 113; on duties of husbands, 120; *Legenda Aurea,* 385; on Mary Magdalene, 90; on mothers and children, 123, 124; on wives, 105, 116, 117–118, 128
Jacopone of Todi, 39
Jacquart, Danièle, 265
James: Protogospel of, 26, 385
James of Vitry, 72, 73, 75, 79, 82, 84, 93, 94, 113, 116
al-Jazzar, Ibn: *De coitu,* 45; *Viaticum,* 45
Jerome, Saint, 16, 23, 28, 29, 30, 35, 41, 111, 127, 199, 223, 339; *Adversus Jovianum,* 106, 117; *Anti-Helvidius,* 26; on marriage, 336; on Virgin Mary, 26
Jerome of Siena: *Soccorso dei poveri,* 83, 95
Jerusalem, 18, 347, 472
Jewelry, 92, 93, 94, 119, 140, 141, 153, 155, 173
Jews, 146, 157, 178, 216, 233–234, 269, 277, 299, 370, 372, 489
Joan, Papess, 373, 374–375
Joan of Arc, 315, 316
Joan of Navarre, 78
Job, 51, 428
John, King, 209
John of Gaddesden, 63, 64

John of Wales, 72, 73, 79, 120
John the Baptist, 19
John VIII, Pope, 376
John XII, Pope, 185
Joie the Manekine, 449, 450
Jonas of Orléans, 182
Joseph, 26, 214–215, 340, 347, 385
Juana de Portugal, 150
Judith of Bavaria, 179
Judith of Flanders, 376
Juette of Huy, 211, 232, 239
Julian of Norwich, 135, 446, 469–470, 473, 478, 480, 481
Justinian, 197; *Digest*, 171
Juvenal, 62; *Sixth Satire*, 22

Karnein, Alfred, 264
Kaysersberg, Geiler von, 292
Kelly, Joan, 2, 6, 135
Kempe, Margery, 135, 435, 446, 447, 470, 471–474, 479, 480, 481
Kent, King of, 189
Klapisch-Zuber, Christiane, 1–10, 13–14, 161–168, 321–322, 425
Knights, 254, 255–257, 258–264 passim, 314
Knights of Saint John of Jerusalem, 310
Koller, Druitgen, 296
Kowaleski, 6

Labor: agricultural, 324–325; division of, 208, 293, 294, 445; female, 77, 97, 126, 168, 171, 183, 189, 283
Lacan, Jacques, 257
The Ladder of Virtue (miniature), 356, 357–358
Ladurie, Le Roy: *Montaillou*, 484
La Françoise, Agace, 290
La Madeleine of Fontevraud, 36
La Marche, Olivier de, 451
Lambert of Ardres, 332
Lambert of Saint Omer: *Liber Floridus*, 372, 373
Lamentations de Mathéolus, 440
Lamprecht of Regensburg, 314, 445, 447; *Die Tochter Sione*, 468
Lancelot, 254, 260
Lancelot in Prose, 260
Language, 43, 253; bad, 453–454; of the body, 468–474; of clergy, 463, 464; control of, 428–431; of death, 457–459; false, 457; feminization of, 482; of fire, 466–482; and food, 474–

476; group, 454–456; and inner time, 478–482; of revelation, 466; of sexuality, 458, 460–463; spiritual, 478–482; vernacular, 447, 463; women and, 427–428, 429, 430–433, 440, 457, 460, 467. *See also* Mystics: language of
La Riquedonne, Jehane, 290
La Salle, Antoine de, 464
La Tour Landry, Chevalier de, 83, 124, 451, 454, 457
Law, 161; Burgundian, 174, 176, 177; canon, 17, 40, 99, 180, 197, 206, 216, 217, 221, 222, 223, 264, 269, 276, 285, 291; civil, 197, 229; common, 206; and *coûtumes*, 269; craft, 303; customary, 219; divorce, 176; ethnic, 269, 292; family, 170; feudal, 206; German, 161, 169–170, 173, 176–177, 269–270; inheritance, 171, 177, 311; Lombard, 175, 176, 188; marriage, 173; Ripuarian, 174, 177; Roman, 161, 164, 169–170, 173–174, 176, 223, 264, 269; Salic, 173, 174, 177; Saxon, 177; secular, 291, 292; and status of women, 268–270; sumptuary, 8, 137, 139, 140, 141, 142–143, 147, 153, 154, 155, 157–158; thirteenth-century, 270; Thuringian, 177; Visigothic, 174, 176, 177, 231
Leander, Saint, 177
Leclercq, Jean, 24, 38
Leewen, Jan van, 445
Le Goff, Jacques, 37, 203
Le Leu, Gautier: *La veuve*, 462
Le Mans, 17, 20, 33, 36
Le Marchant, Jean: *Miracles of Our Lady of Chartres*, 428
Leonor of Castile, 138
Leo the Great, 26
Leo III, Pope, 195
Leotta, Rosario, 22
Leprosy, 44, 66–68
Lesbians, 183, 436
Leuwen, Ida von, 414
Lévy, Jean-Philippe, 278
Leyser, K. J., 193
L'Hermite-Leclercq, Paulette, 8–9, 164, 202–249, 322
Liber historiae Francorum, 175, 176
Liber Trotula, 300
Lichtenstein, Ulrich von, 313

Liebana, Beato di, 415
Lioba (abbess), 192, 198
Literacy, 1, 76, 101, 249, 397, 442
Literature, 62; and confessors, 447–448;
of courtly love, 252–255; of escape,
254; humanistic, 130–132, 426; misogynistic, 22; of nuns, 443; pastoral,
72–73, 83, 86, 92, 96, 97, 102, 103,
105, 106, 110, 119, 123; pedagogical,
72–73, 83, 86, 92, 96, 97, 103; religious, 101, 130, 131, 132, 197, 198,
294, 358, 445, 447, 466; ribald (fabliaux), 62, 432, 460, 461; and role
of women, 71–72, 84, 255; romantic,
254–255; secular, 16; sexual intercourse in, 63, 64, 66, 131; vernacular,
253, 447; of women, 267–268, 429–
430, 436, 442–449; and written evidence, 483–491
Liudolf, Count, 193
Liudprand of Cremona, 182, 184, 185
Liutberga, 181
Liutgard, 179
Lollards, 471, 473
Lombard, Peter, 34, 224
Lombard period, 172, 194
Lorenzetti, Ambrogio: Buon Governo
(fresco), 394
Lothar II (King of Lotharingia), 180–
181
Louis of Thuringia, 277, 280–281, 282
Louis the Pious, 178, 179, 182, 192
Louis IX of France (Saint Louis), 72,
73–74, 78, 79, 124, 137, 273
Louis XIII, 136
Love: art of, 64; and beauty, 224–226;
conjugal, 38, 109–112, 118, 120,
123, 222–224, 258, 282; free, 451; of
God, 239; literature of, 476–478,
481; maternal, 123; physical vs. ra-
tional, 123; and sex of embryo, 59;
vocabulary of, 35, 476–478, 482. See
also Courtly love
Luke, 26, 33
Lull, Raymond: Tree of Knowledge, 61–
62

Magninus, 63
Maillé, Jeanne-Marie de, 315
Maitre Honoré, Father, 401
Malatesta, Battista, 133
Manselli, Raoul, 17, 19
Map, Walter, 40

Marbode of Rennes, 17, 21–22, 24, 25,
31, 35, 40; "On the Virtuous
Woman," 28; "On the Wicked
Woman," 22, 23. See also Book of
Ten Chapters
Marcabrou (troubadour), 261
Margaret of Cortona, 41, 288
Margaret of Ypres, 299
Marguerite of Provence, 137
Marie de France, 429, 435, 449
Marie of Montpellier, 236–239
Marinelli, Lucrezia: La Nobilità e l'Eccellenza delle Donne, 155, 156, 157
Marozia, 182, 185
Marriage, 4, 7, 8, 247; age at, 216–218,
228, 271, 272, 281, 287; among the
aristocracy, 279–282; and bride-price,
171, 174, 176, 177, 230; by capture
(Raubehe), 171, 175, 188, 275; and
childbearing, 62, 168, 173, 181, 182,
185, 187, 228, 284; and the Church,
213–220, 221, 275, 340; and conjugal rights, 112–115, 131, 227–228,
248; and equality, 110, 226–228,
272; ethics of, 8; and the Fall, 336;
and families, 108, 121–125; from female perspective, 273–275; feudal,
28, 258; and fidelity, 14, 112, 113–
115, 118, 127, 176, 223, 226, 228; in
Germanic tribes, 171, 180; in Iceland,
229–230; images of, 344–345, 376;
in late Middle Ages, 270; and liberty,
215–220; in medieval cities, 282–284;
monogamous, 18, 140–141, 172, 215,
272; by mutual consent (Friedelehe),
171, 175, 176, 177, 179, 215–216;
and patrilineal descent, 140; and patrilocality, 273; political function of,
108; and power, 273; and property,
231, 273, 285; by purchase (Kaufehe),
171; regulation of, 44, 60, 106, 161,
212; as sacrament, 28, 162, 214, 223,
272, 345, 347; and salvation, 110,
115–117, 121, 124, 132; and sexual
activity, 38, 61, 103, 112–113, 118,
133, 146, 215, 227, 248–249; sine
manu, 172, 173–174; of slaves, 216;
and social harmony, 108–109; three
steps of, 174; trauma of, 213; and
trousseaux, 140–141, 142, 145, 177
Martin, Saint, 153, 407, 461–462
Mary Magdalene, 8, 31–34, 35, 41, 90–
91, 98, 152; cult of, 14, 29, 36, 37,

Mary Magdalene (*continued*)
203, 307; images of, 246, 361, 376;
as model, 77
Mary of Bethany, 32
Mary of Magdala, 32
Mary the Egyptian, 35, 361–362
Massacre of Béziers, 237
Mathilda, Queen, 29, 184
Mathilda of Quedlinburg, 193
Matilda of Canossa, 381, 382
Matthew, 26, 172
Maximus of Turin, 21
Mechthild of Bremen, 295–296
Mechthild of Magdeburg, 442, 444,
445, 446, 463, 471, 475, 479;
Streaming Light of the Deity, 314,
442, 466, 477
Mechtild of Hackebon, 471
Medicine, 44–69; Arabic, 47, 51, 52,
53, 63; and dissections, 52, 53; and
globus hystericus, 48; herbal, 386;
and vapors, 47–48
Men: and art, 376; conception of
women, 7, 255, 323; and courtly love,
254–256, 264; and culture, 14, 267–
268; domination of, 90, 247, 251; education of, 213; and fashion, 137–
139, 147, 154, 155–156, 157; fear of
women, 62, 68, 257, 382, 442; as
guardians of women, 89, 324; in history, 72; images of, 370; and language, 429, 457; and sin, 362; two
classes of, 255–256; and women's
talk, 483. *See also* Husbands
Ménagier de Paris, 83, 112, 117, 120
Mendicant friars, 39, 71, 147–148, 242
Menstruation, 54–58, 172, 182; fears
of, 65, 66
Merovingian period, 173–178, 186–187
Metz, René, 17
Mézières, Philippe de, 451, 452
Michelet, Jules, 24
Midwives, 62, 65, 289, 290, 292, 298,
299, 384, 385
Miracles of Autroberta, 191
*Mirouer des dames et damoyselles et de
tout le sexe féminin,* 459
Mirror of Virgins, 28, 240–249
"Mirrors of Married Couples," 29
Misogyny, 17, 19, 22, 36, 44, 67, 137,
154, 165; of clergy, 16, 20, 23, 202;
and courtly love, 265; and fear of

women, 257, 429; in images of
women, 351, 354, 367, 402
Mithridates, 66
Modena, Tommaso da, 421
Modesty, 88, 95, 102, 114, 127, 128,
134, 177, 185, 212
Monasteries, 17, 18, 173, 181, 186–
194, 197, 212, 241, 305; artistic
works in, 200; books in, 198–199;
double, 189–190; in Germany, 192–
193, 194; in Ireland, 189, 198; in
Saxony, 192. *See also* Convents
Monasticism, 187, 188, 228, 242, 244
Monegund, Saint, 187
Monica (Augustine's mother), 134–135
Monks, 34, 40, 71, 72, 84, 189, 242,
243, 278, 349; celibacy of, 18; and
Mariology, 38; and oblation, 15, 217,
241; view of women, 20, 23, 206. *See
also* Clergy
Montaigne, 148
Montaillou, village of, 325, 329–330,
332, 334, 484
Morgengabe. See Marriage: and bride-
price
Moschion, 44, 47
Motherhood, 8, 248, 284–292
Mothers, 15–16, 30, 103, 121–125,
328; and breast-feeding, 134, 328;
and children, 14, 122, 123–125, 133–
135, 134, 287–289, 291, 456. *See
also* Daughters: and mothers
Muslims, 178, 202, 231, 257
Mystics, 30, 39, 42, 241, 245, 434, 467,
468; female, of Netherlands, 446;
German, 446; and images, 387; language of, 445, 447, 463, 464–465,
466, 467, 470, 471, 476, 481–482;
and personal history, 443, 480; and
preaching, 100; women, 313–317,
425, 432–433, 445, 447

Neckham, Alexander: *De naturis rerum,*
46
Nelli, René, 253, 484
Nemesius of Emesa: *De natura hominis,*
44, 55
Nicholas, Pope, 180
Nicholas of Gorran, 121
Nider, Jean: *Formicarius,* 40
Noblewomen, 234–239, 290. *See also*
Queens

Nogarola, Isotta, 448
Noonan, J. T., 223
Nördlingen, Heinrich de, 476
Notker the Stutterer, 433
Notre-Dame de Chelles (abbey), 32, 189, 199
Nuns, 24, 41, 58, 73, 74, 76, 82, 91–92, 103, 188, 225, 239, 313, 445; Anglo-Saxon, 136–137, 191, 192; cloistering of, 190–192, 196, 200, 240, 241, 324; and education, 101, 197–199, 211, 298; expanded population of, 312; in Iceland, 229; images of, 352–355, 409; recruitment of, 240; and religious supervision, 243; silence of, 100, 102; skills of, 200, 386–387; sobriety of, 96, 102; Vallumbrosian, 416. See also Convents

Observantines, 39, 145
Occitanian period, 253, 437, 454, 484
Oda, 193
Ode, Saint, 217
Odilia, Saint, 308
Odo of Cluny, 20, 34
Oflaterin, Cristina, 296
Opitz, Claudia, 9, 164, 167, 267–317, 326
Oresme, Nicolas, 108, 114, 126
Orgasm, 51, 63, 258
Origen, 34
Original sin, 39, 40, 80, 88, 90, 112, 214, 368; and female body, 8, 362
Orlamünde, Count of, 280
Ortulana, 289
Ostrogoths, 172, 187, 197
Ottonian period, 29, 188, 193, 245
Otto I, 184, 193, 200, 235, 242
Otto II, 184, 235
Otto III, 186
Ovid, 61, 253, 428; Metamorphoses, 431

Pact of the Salic Code, 173, 177
Painters, female, 401, 402
Palmieri, Matteo: Vita civile, 129
Paolinus the Minorite, 105
Paolo of Certaldo, 101, 118
Paphnutius, 35
Paris, Gaston, 255, 450
Paschasius Radbertus, 26, 29, 179
Passavanti, Jacopo, 349

Patriarchy, 13, 153, 276, 316
Paul, 32, 89, 99, 107, 116, 119, 218, 226, 227, 315, 339, 418; epistles of, 19, 199, 357
Peace of God movement, 232
Peasants, 230–231, 248, 259, 278; and artisans, 324; in Carolingian period, 183; households of, 334–335; revolts of, 270
Pedro, King of Aragon, 237, 238
Pelayo, Alvaro, 40
Pepin, King of Franks, 178–179
Pepin the Younger, 178
Peraldo, William, 72, 73, 78; on choosing a wife, 117, 118; on marriage, 108, 110, 111, 112, 116; on mothers, 124; on old women, 75; on women's behavior, 79, 82, 85, 101, 105, 127–128
Peter, Saint, 20–21, 22, 32, 198
Peter Chrysologus, 26, 27
Peter Damian, 23, 26, 29, 35, 36, 41
Peter of Abano, 47, 63
Peter of Cella, 33
Peters, Ursula, 445, 447, 448
Peter the Painter, 40
Peter the Venerable (abbot of Cluny), 31
Petrarch, 450–451
Petrucci, Battista, 153
Philip of Novara, 72, 73, 75, 76, 84, 97, 101, 111, 117, 124, 442
Philip the Fair, 78, 139
Philip II (Duke of Burgundy), 441
Philo, 34
Philomena, 428
Physicians, 49, 60, 61, 63, 66, 68; Arab, 45, 50; female, 299
Physiognomy, 52–53
Physiology of women: male views of, 8, 43–58, 68
Pietà, theme of, 39
Pilgrimages, 191, 192
Piponnier, Françoise, 9, 322, 323–335
Pisano, Giovanni, 393
Pisano, Nicola, 393
Pizzocorno, 418
Planissoles, Béatrice de, 278, 289, 484
Plato: Timaeus, 48
Pliny, 65
Plutarch, 218
Polygamy, 176, 215, 229
Polygyny, 175, 176

Popes, 18, 178, 274, 307. *See also* individual popes

Porète, Marguerite, 315, 432, 445, 463, 469, 478, 482; *Mirror of Simple and Devastated Souls,* 446, 476, 477, 479, 480; "Mirror of the Divine Soul," 314, 442

Poulet, Georges, 430

Pourcairagues, Azalais de, 435, 436

Power, Eileen, 4, 183

Power, 71, 99, 202, 249; economic, 279–280; of husbands, 275–276; and land, 184; of language, 458, 463, 478; occult, 161, 249; of women, 6, 7, 13, 161, 168, 185–186, 251, 252, 256, 260, 262, 264, 265, 266, 279, 456

Prayer, 102, 127, 135, 243, 244, 245, 286, 289

Pregnancy, 21–22, 46, 56, 57, 122, 150, 211, 225, 233–234, 271, 278, 289; confirmation of, 290; and husbands, 134

Priests. *See* Clergy

Procreation, 46, 61, 64, 90, 114, 121, 122, 223; of legitimate children, 115, 130, 284–292; and original sin, 214, 258, 367; as women's primary function, 13, 43, 66, 80

Procuresses, 62, 75, 176, 456

Prostitutes (*meretrices*), 22, 31, 33, 36, 41, 74, 77, 182, 232, 233, 433, 451; and costume, 147–148, 150, 155; images of, **355**, **357**, **358**; and lower-class women, 278; and marriage, 307; and poverty, 306–307; and priests, 196; sterility of, 52, 56, 60, 114, 149

Proust, Marcel, 480, 481

Ptolemy, 460

Purgatory, 37, **366**, 367

Puymichel, Countess Dauphine de, 277, 280, 285

Queens, 78–79, 81, 102, 140, 147, 173, 179; canonization of, 235; Carolingian, 181, 182; ideal image of, 97, 116–117; Merovingian, 181, 186; widowed, 186

Quinze joyes de mariage (Fifteen Joys of Marriage), 432, 456–457

Rabanus Maurus, 44

Rabastens, Widow, 315

Radegund, Saint, 29, 175, 187, 194, 195, 199, **406**, 409

Raimondo of Capua, 418

Rape, 56, 220, 222, 261, 308, 428, 449, 451–452

Rather, Bishop of Verona, 185, 190

Raymond of Capua, 471

Reccared, 178

Recluses. *See* Hermits, female

Reformation, 292, 316

Régnier-Bohler, Danielle, 10, 427–482

Remy (Bishop of Rheims), 194

Renaissance, 1, 39, 53, 136, 156, 157, 167; fashion boom of, 142, 149; for women, 6

René of Anjou, 139

Reproduction. *See* Procreation

Rey-Flaud, H., 257

Rhazes: *Liber ad Almansorem,* 45

Richard of Saint-Victor, 38

Ries, Jean du: *L'Histoire scolastique,* 397

Robert of Arbrissel, 233, 239, 242

Robert of Sorbonne, 105, 116, 137

Rocher, Daniel, 265

Roger of Caen, 23; "Ode on Contempt for the World," 22

Rojas, Fernando de: *Celestina,* 62

Roman de la Rose (Jean de Meung), 61, 137, 154, 263, 438, 451, 456, 457, 459

Roman Empire, 21, 136, 161, 232; decline of, 169; marriage in, 130, 340; position of women in, 171–173, 182

Romano, Francesca, 299

Romans, Humbert de, 306

Rome, 130, 136, 195, 197, 198

Rosanensis (Umiltà), 288

Roussel, Raymond, 486

Rudolf, King, 184

Rupert of Deutz, 26

Russo, Daniel, 41

Rutebeuf: *Sayings of the Beguines,* 467

Ruusbrook, 446, 475

Sabrano, Count Elzeario de, 280, 285

Sainte-Croix monastery, 29

Saint Francis: Stories from His Life, 350, 351

Saint-Germain-des-Prés, 165, 167

Saint-Maximin, 33, 41

Saints: canonization of, 421; and exorcism, 350–351; female, 35, 41, 249,

315, 407, 432, 467; lives of, 443;
women as, 323, 325
Saint-Victor of Marseilles, 165–166
Salaberga, Saint, 187
Salerno School, 45, 48, 49, 52, 53, 56
Salome, 395
Salome the Midwife, 384–385
Saluces, Thomas de, 451
Sand, George, 213
Sanuti, Nicolosa, 154, 155
Sarah: as model "good wife," 105–106,
121, 127, 130
Savigny, Vital de, 36
Saxer, Victor, 32, 33, 41
Schnell, Rüdiger, 264
Scotus, Michael, 45
Sempronia the Roman, 441
Sergius, Pope, 185
Sermons, 72–75, 82, 83, 84, 90, 96, 98,
113, 124, 128, 161, 172
Servants, 121, 126, 216, 230, 232, 271,
277, 287, 295, 306, 309, 332
Sex, 258, 292; and the city, 233; nam-
ing, 459–463; and pleasure, 47, 48,
56, 57, 58, 59, 60–61, 63, 64, 68, 80,
485–486
Sexes: battle of, 283–284, 456, 457,
463; separation of, 257
Sexuality, 3, 13, 38, 43, 56, 61–62, 67,
68, 79–80, 81, 119, 124, 132, 229;
clerical, 196; and costume, 143–144,
147, 151, 155; and education, 210–
211; language of, 458–459; limits of,
113, 127, 273; and marriage, 277–
279; and masturbation, 61, 63, 183;
and orgasm, 51, 63, 258; and procreation, 61, 113, 258; and sterility,
146
Sexual knowledge, 61–62
Sexual morality: and leprosy, 44
Sforza, Francesco, 375
Sforza, Ippolita, 141
Shahar, Shulamith, 284
Sigolena of Albi, Saint, 187, 195
Silence of women, 449–453
Simon of Montfort, 237, 238
Simon the Pharisee, 32, 33
Sin: of Eve, 144, 145, 154, 336; and
long hair, 361, 362; and sex, 485–
486, 488; types of, 367
Single women, 305–311; poverty of,
305–306, 308
Slaves, 177, 231, 232, 324

Sobriety, 95–96, 114, 128, 134
Socrates, 66, 218
Song of Songs, 26, 42, 253
Soranus of Ephesus: Gynaecia, 44
Sorcery, 123, 176, 382, 383
Spain, 170, 202, 230; Visigothic, 247
Speculum al foderi (Mirror of Making
Love), 64
Speculum virginum, 338, 339
Sprenger, John, 40, 42
Sterility, 52, 56, 60, 64–65, 114, 122,
149, 204, 207, 212, 275, 285–286
Stock, Brian, 480
Subinus (abbot), 199
Suger of Saint-Denis (abbot), 38, 208
Sunder, Friedrich, 445

Tacitus, 136, 164, 171, 176; Germania,
171, 173
Talada, Pietro da, 397
Tauberbischofsheim (monastery), 192,
198
Tauler, 475
Tecla (abbess), 192
Tempier, Etienne, 45
Terence, 200
Tertullian, 20, 136, 144–145, 154; De
Habitu Muliebri, 145
Thais, 35, 244
Theodora, 185, 197
Theodoric the Great, 197, 440–441
Theodosian Code, 172
Theodrada, 192
Theophano, 184, 186
Theophilus, 24, 31–32
Theuderata, 173
Theutberga, 180
Thietmar (Bishop of Merseburg), 184,
200
Third Council of Toledo, 178
Thomas, Saint, 57, 123, 124–125
Thomas of Cantimpré, 56
Thomas of Chobham: Summa Confesso-
rum, 115–116, 117
Thomas of Saleby, 204–206, 207, 209,
212
Thomasset, Claude, 8, 40, 43–69, 265
Tienen, Beatrijis van, 297
Tilliette, Jean-Yves, 29
Tiresias, 61
Todi, Jacopone da, 152
Tommaso of Foligno, 390
Tornabuoni, Dianora, 129, 132

Totila, 173
Toubert, Pierre, 29
Toulouse, Count of, 237, 238
Trotula, 54, 61, 62, 64
Troubadours, 252, 253, 254, 257, 259,
  264; female, 429, 434, 435, 436, 445
Troyes, Chrétien de, 428
Truce of God movement, 232

Ubertino of Casale, 39
Ulysses, 386
Universal Judgment (fresco), 351, 354,
  355
Unwan, 181
Urban II, Pope, 18
Ute, Abbess of Niedermünster, 410, **412**

Varana, Costanza, 448
Vauchez, André, 468
Vecchio, Silvana, 3, 8, 105–135
Vecellio, Cesare, 142
Vegio, Maffeo, 130, 134
Veils, 190, 195, 357. *See also* Fashion:
  and veils
Venantius Fortunatus, 29
Verdun, Richard de, 401
Vergerio, 130
Vézelay, 32–33, 41, 341, 395
Vidal, Peire, 254
Vilain de Baillew, Le, 458
Vincent of Beauvais, 72, 73, 75, 78,
  108, 111; on male sperm, 57; *Specu-
  lum Naturale,* 46; on women's behav-
  ior, 79, 82, 101, 105, 112, 127–128
Virgil, 200
Virgin Birth. *See* Christ: birth of
Virginity, 24–30, 39, 93, 115, 187, 190,
  212–213, 228, 229, 230, 234, 240;
  and the Fall, 336; and marriage, 113,
  133, 221–222, 347; restoration of,
  62; and salvation, 41, 245
Virgin Mary, 8, 17, 23, 28, 29, 33, 41,
  82, 88, 92, 226, 260; Assumption of,
  25, 39, 367; cult of, 4, 7, 16, 24, 38,
  203, 212, 234, 286; and the Devil,
  31–32; dogmas concerning, 25–27,
  362–363; iconography of, 39, 327–
  328, 367, 376, 384–385, **389**, 390,
  397–398, 399, 404, **408**, 410; marriage of, 214; miracles attributed to,
  25, 428; as model, 107, 133, 172,
  190, 212, 249, 261, 338, 367, 368; as
  mother, 25–27, 39, 368, 407; purification in the temple, 368; sanctification of, 39; as vehicle of redemption,
  34, 336, 338; vs. Eve, 23–24, 37; virginity of, 26–27, 385; at wedding at
  Cana, 106; wedding of, 342, 347
Virgins, 29, 73, 79–84, 96, 118, 172,
  188, 190, 212, 240, 245, 248, 339,
  433
Visconti, Bianca Maria, 448
Visconti, Matteo, 375
Visions, 387, 390, 446, 467, 470, 480
Vitalis, Orderic, 137
Vitry, Jacques de: *Life of Marie d'Oignies,* 467, 468
Vitus, Saint, 199

Wala, 192
Waldrada, 180
Walter of Châtillon, 434
Waltger, 192
Welf, Count, 179
Wemple, Suzanne Fonay, 8, 9, 161,
  169–201
Werner, 380–381
Werner, K. F., 182
Wido of Tuscany, 182, 185
Widows, 29, 30, 64, 73, 74, 75, 79–84,
  96, 118, 124, 339, 433, 484; and cos-
  tume, 151; as deaconesses, 194; free-
  dom of, 91, 185, 308–311, 324; and
  monasticism, 188; and power, 186;
  remarriage of, 281, 308–310; rights
  of, 170, 174, 274, 310, 311; status of,
  228, 277, 306, 308
Wiligelmo, 393, 394
William of Aquitaine, 253, 258, 261
William of Conches, 66; *Dragmaticon,*
  46, 52, 56, 59
William of Moerbeke, 45
William of Poitiers, 252, 253, 256, 257
William the Conqueror, 30
Willibald, Saint, 443–444
Witches, 173, 384, 456, 484, 489; and
  old women, 62, 75; persecution of,
  42, 69, 268, 316, 317, 382–383, 386.
  See also Sorcery
Wives, 14, 29, 63, 73, 74, 79–84, 96,
  103, 170, 183, 224, 248, 433; administering the house, 125–127; of arti-
  sans, 326; beating, 120–121; choosing, 117–118, 181; of classical world,
  130; devotion of, 105; early Christian,
  107, 172; "good," 104, 105–135,

173, 285; in late Middle Ages, 270, 276, 309, 326; middle-class, 282; obedience of, 105, 112, 121, 130, 131, 132, 176, 185, 226, 247, 275–276; of Old Testament, 107; of peasants, 230–231, 248, 283, 287; of priests, 194–196; and servants, 121, 126, 279, 280, 282. *See also* Husbands; Marriage

Wollerin, Cecilie, 302

Woman: chaste, 73; as gossip, 40–41, 98, 453–454; lustful, 73, 370, 451; nature of, 43–69; the protected, 70–104; as Queen of Heaven, 38; as redeemed sinner, 38; and shift to "women," 73, 81; as temptress, 38, 358, 370. *See also* Eve; Mary Magdalene; Virgin Mary

Women's movement, medieval, 311–312

Words of women, 98–102, 355, 357, 359, 425–482, 483. *See also* Language

Work, women's, 292–305, 328–331, 334–335; and crafts, 293, 300–303, 326; and expansion of urban centers, 293; in health care, 298–300; in rural areas, 294–295, 324–325; in trade, 295–297, 303–305, 326. *See also* Labor: female

Wynnebald, Saint, 444

Ximenes, Francisco, 83, 107

Yves of Chartres, 17, 20, 216–217, 218, 221, 240

Zacchaeus, 32

Zeno of Verona, 26

Zink, Michel, 480

Zumthor, Paul, 465